Strategic Survey 2004/5

An evaluation and forecast of world affairs

WITHDRAWN

Published by

Routledge
Taylor & Francis Group

for
The International Institute for Strategic Studies
ARUNDEL HOUSE, 13–15 ARUNDEL STREET, TEMPLE PLACE, LONDON WC2R 3DX

Strategic Survey
2004/5

published by

 **Routledge**
Taylor & Francis Group

for

The International Institute for Strategic Studies
ARUNDEL HOUSE, 13–15 ARUNDEL STREET, TEMPLE PLACE, LONDON WC2R 3DX

DIRECTOR *Dr John Chipman*
EDITOR *Jonathan Stevenson*

ASSISTANT EDITOR *Dr Jeffrey Mazo*
MAP EDITOR *James Hackett*
EDITORIAL *Dr Ayse Abdullah*
DESIGNER *Jesse Simon*
CARTOGRAPHER *Steven Bernard*

This publication has been prepared by the Director of the Institute and his Staff, who accept full responsibility for its contents, which describe and analyse events up to 21 April 2005. These do not, and indeed cannot, represent a consensus of views among the worldwide membership of the Institute as a whole.

First published May 2005

ABSTRACTED AND INDEXED by Research Base Online, PAIS.

COVER IMAGES AP/Wide World Photos
EXCEPT *Arafat's Funeral* AND *Orange Revolution* IMAGES AFP/Getty

PRINTED IN THE UK by Bell & Bain Ltd, Glasgow.

ISBN 0-415-37394-8
ISSN 0459-7230

Strategic Survey is published annually by Routledge Journals, an imprint of Taylor & Francis Group Ltd, 4 Park Square, Milton Park, Abingdon, Oxfordshire OX14 4RN, UK.

A subscription to the institution print edition, ISSN 0459-7230, includes free access for any number of concurrent users across a local area network to the online edition, ISSN 1476-4997.

Dollar rates apply to subscribers in all countries except the UK and the Republic of Ireland where the pound sterling price applies. All subscriptions are payable in advance and all rates include postage. Journals are sent by air to the USA, Canada, Mexico, India, Japan and Australasia. Subscriptions are entered on an annual basis, i.e. January to December. Payment may be made by sterling cheque, dollar cheque, international money order, National Giro, or credit card (Amex, Visa, Mastercard).

For more information, visit our website:
http://www.tandf.co.uk/journals

ORDERING INFORMATION
USA/Canada: Taylor & Francis Inc., Journals Department, 325 Chestnut Street, 8th Floor, Philadelphia, PA 19106, USA. UK/ Europe/Rest of World: Routledge Journals, Taylor & Francis Group Ltd, Rankine Road, Basingstoke, Hampshire RG24 8PR, UK.

Contents

Strategic Geography 2004/5

List of Maps

Strategic Survey Online

Members of the IISS can access *Strategic Survey* 2004/5 online via the members area of the website at **www.iiss.org**. For more information about subscriptions, visit **www.tandf.co.uk/journals**.

Perspectives

Though less consuming than in early 2004, state-building in Iraq continued to be the most resonant single issue in world affairs in early 2005. But if May 2004 was marked by widespread despair over burgeoning insurgency in Iraq with disquieting contributions from three quarters – Iraqi Sunni, Iraqi Shi'ite and foreign jihadist – the watchword for Iraq in May 2005 was guarded hope. As predicted, the minority Sunni population, which Saddam Hussein had favoured as he repressed the majority Shi'ites, largely boycotted the election, and religiously based Shi'ites under the leadership of Grand Ayatollah Ali al-Sistani held sway. But conservative estimates of voter turnout indicated a relatively healthy 58%, and in the election's aftermath Sunni politicians agreed to participate in the drafting of a new Iraqi constitution. In March 2005, the US military estimated that there were 12,000–20,000 hard-core insurgents in Iraq, which represented no change from the previous October. But while insurgency attacks on coalition forces numbered 40–50 per day in March 2005, they had diminished substantially and the Iraqi populace had grown increasingly intolerant of them. The Kurds – Iraq's largest minority – and Shi'ites made positive steps towards secular coalition government and a form of federalism that would accord the Kurds an acceptable degree of sub-sovereign autonomy.

US Middle East policy vindicated?

Better prospects for Iraq seemed to signal brighter portents in general for the foreign policy of US President George W. Bush. Even though Bush policy was bold, controversial and sometimes divisive, his aggressive global agenda of promoting freedom and democracy appeared increasingly effective. Within the United States, this element of Bush doctrine was not especially revolutionary or politically divisive. Propagating democracy – however imperfectly – was an element of containment and then rollback during the Cold War. Anthony Lake, Bill Clinton's first national security adviser, had argued in a 1994 *Foreign Affairs* article entitled 'Confronting Backlash States' that 'our policy must face the reality of recalcitrant and outlaw states that not only choose to remain outside the family [of nations] but also assault its basic values'. He went on to say that 'as the sole superpower, the United States has a special responsibility for developing a strategy to neutralize, contain and, through selective pressure, perhaps eventually transform these backlash states into constructive members of the international community'. Indeed, the eminent historian John Lewis Gaddis of Yale University argued that Bush's policy of exuberantly spreading democracy prompted by 11 September was consistent with American reactions to the other two transformative strategic events in US history: the War of 1812 and the Second World War.

Bush's 21 February 2005 speech at the Concert Noble in Brussels, by which he sought to advance transatlantic reconciliation after the traumatic rift that had occurred over the Iraq intervention, resonated with these themes. For example, he noted that 'in the long run, we cannot live in peace and safety if the Middle East continues to produce ideologies of murder, and terrorists who seek the deadliest weapons. Regimes that terrorize their own people will not hesitate to support terror abroad.' Then he enunciated the role of 'the alliance of Europe and America' as the 'main pillar' of global security: 'Our challenge is to encourage … progress by taking up the duties of great democracies. We must be on the side of democratic reformers, we must encourage democratic movements, and support democratic transitions in practical ways.' Perhaps Bush's most historically poignant message of continuity was his reference to the Second World War and its aftermath as the blueprint for 11 September and his own foreign-policy agenda. 'Our transatlantic alliance', he remarked, 'frustrated the plans of dictators, served the highest ideals of humanity, and set a violent century on a new and better course. And as time goes by, we must never forget our shared achievements.'

Doubts about Bush policy within the United States, then, were raised not as to principle but as to the feasibility of sound execution: whether Arab and Asian countries that had not experienced mature democratic governance would or could readily convert to it; whether the United States and its partners would apply democratic principles even-handedly. Furthermore, American and European 'realists' alike questioned whether the implicit idealism of Bush's foreign policy – to wit, his faith that all people supremely valued individual liberty and participatory representative government – was valid, and feared that such an entrepreneurially Western policy would prompt resisters to bandwagon against the West. In the Brussels speech, Bush acknowledged that although Western ideals must be 'firm' and 'clear', 'our expectations must be realistic'. Thus, he did not purport to impose stringent timetables for reform or politically over-ambitious outcomes on the governments of the Middle East/Gulf region with which the speech was principally concerned. Shortly after the Brussels speech, Bush also had warm meetings with French President Jacques Chirac and German Chancellor Gerhard Schröder in which past differences were candidly discussed with a clear eye towards minimising future ones. These also confirmed that Bush, while not contrite about his policies, had recognised that he had been too cavalier in dealing with European allies during his first term and was out to make amends.

War in Iraq, in any case, was a risky way to foster the change that Washington wanted, and whether it will yield a net gain remains to be seen. Signs, however, are looking up. Palestinian Authority President Yasser Arafat – deemed a terminally unacceptable partner for peace by both Bush and Israeli Prime Minister Ariel Sharon – died in November 2004, giving way to the more moderate Mahmoud Abbas (familiarly known as Abu Mazen). Sharon changed his world-view, rejecting the notion of a 'Greater Israel' encompassing all or most of historical Palestine, perhaps in part because Bush's willingness to shed American blood in the region and spend political capital for remaking the Middle East made him confident in the American commitment to promoting region-wide political reform. These developments made the prospect of a formal settlement of the Israeli–Palestinian conflict by 2009 a real possibility.

Syria remained a troublesome state whose strategic options had shrunk significantly since the US intervention in Iraq had deprived it of cheap oil and a ready market for its goods, further still when Arafat's death revived the Israeli–Palestinian peace process and weakened Syria's pretext for provoking Israel through terrorist sponsorship. It had continued to provide political support to Palestinian armed groups and assistance to Hizbullah (which in turn sporadically harassed the Israel Defense Forces and aided Palestinian terrorists), and refused to withdraw its 14,000 troops and pervasive intelligence presence from Lebanon. Syria's suspected involvement in the 14 February 2005 bombing death of former Lebanese Prime Minister Rafik Hariri – who had opposed Syria's continued occupation of Lebanon – may have indicated desperation to hang on to its one remaining strategic asset. Full American support for democratisation in the region and its military proximity helped condition a popular uprising against Syria in Lebanon on account of Hariri's murder, which in turn prompted pro-Syrian Prime Minister Omar Karami to resign. The Lebanese people reasoned that if the United States was willing to risk the lives of its soldiers for freedom and democracy, they could at least risk arrest. Even larger pro-Syrian demonstrations, engineered by the Syria- and Iran-backed Lebanese militant group Hizbullah, followed in Beirut, whereupon Karami was briefly reinstated. But the Syria/Lebanon crisis paid the strategic dividend of aligning France and key Arab states – including Saudi Arabia – with the United States in pressing Syria to withdraw. Saudi Arabia, relieved of the burden of US military deployments in-country and awakened to the indigenous jihadist terrorist threat, was slowly undertaking political reform. With Israel taking a more concilia tory stance and Iraq at least making a go of the democratic experiment, in February 2005 Egyptian President Hosni Mubarak authorised multiparty elections.

Unsurprisingly, the Gulf state that proved hardest to manage was Iran. As the clerical establishment consolidated power in the unduly influenced parliamentary elections in February 2004, and reformists appeared just as intent as conservatives on developing a nuclear capability against the wishes of the United States, Europe and the Arab world, hopes that internal upheaval would push Iran along a path of international political rehabilitation like the one Libya ultimately took dimmed. Neither coercive American pressure – ultimately backed by a decidedly remote threat of regime-changing US military force – nor European economic incentives appeared to modify Iran's duplicitous behaviour vis-à-vis the International Atomic Energy Agency (IAEA) with respect to its uranium enrichment programme. With the 'good cop, bad cop' routine thus frustrated, both Europe's and the United States' Iran policies seemed adrift by February 2005. In March, however, the United States changed gears and announced its support for the European approach of attempting to dissuade Iran from pursuing a nuclear-weapons capability primarily by way of economic inducements. It was likely to give this approach a chance to succeed until summer 2005, when the June Iranian elections might furnish changed circumstances that could inform a new policy. Whether later in the year a crisis could be averted would depend on whether the EU and the US could agree on an acceptable definition of Iran's 'cessation' of nuclear activities – assuming, of course, that Iran was willing to accept curtailment of it enrichment activities, to which it has been publicly wedded.

On balance, US policy in 2004–05 appeared fairly effective in emboldening regional actors in the Middle East and Gulf to rally against rogue states and implement gentle political reforms. But the inspirational effect of the Iraq intervention on transnational Islamist terrorism remained the proverbial elephant in the living room.

Net assessment: transnational Islamist terrorism

Al-Qaeda remained a dangerous terrorist organisation, though ever more dependent on local groups and subject to decentralising influences. While key aspects of the US approach to the 'global war on terror' appeared counter-productive, opportunities for diminishing al-Qaeda's appeal seemed marginally enhanced. The US-led invasion and occupation of Iraq intensified many Muslims' worries about America's global intentions and made them more easily seduced by Osama bin Laden's arguments. He was able to cast the Iraq war quite persuasively as confirmation of Washington's wish to dominate the Arab and larger Muslim world politically, economically and militarily; its intention to loot Islam of its natural resources, in particular oil; and its inexorable support for Israel's repression of Palestinian Muslims. This rhetorical power seemed only to have reinforced the al-Qaeda leadership's extreme and non-negotiable agenda, which calls for the debilitation of the United States as a superpower through apocalyptic terrorism, the overthrow of 'apostate' Arab regimes and the establishment of a global Islamic caliphate.

The fraught occupation of Iraq also drained military resources from other areas of terrorist-related political instability, such as Afghanistan, and executive attention from the security of the US homeland, which is still al-Qaeda's prime target. Al-

Qaeda's leadership may have taken comfort from the fact that the terrorist network has remained essentially dispersed while also managing to refocus operationally on Iraq and the Arab world, and from the political impact that Abu Musab al-Zarqawi, bin Laden's anointed protégé in Iraq, made with relatively few personnel through decapitations and car bombings. From al-Qaeda's point of view, Bush's Iraq policies have arguably produced a confluence of propitious circumstances: a strategically bogged-down America hated by much of the Islamic world and regarded warily even by its allies. After the Iraq war began, jihadist recruits appeared to increase. Nevertheless, as of late 2004, al-Qaeda presided only very loosely over an informal confederation of terrorist outfits. The global jihadist movement remained, both in fact and by nature, physically and ideologically in flux. Furthermore, while the goals of al-Qaeda's leadership were still maximalist, its constituent groups shared objectives and methods only in a general and not necessarily sustainable sense. Finally, US foreign policy was yielding better results than it had during the previous two years in Iraq and the Middle East. The network, then, was subject to both binding and dispersing influences.

Al-Qaeda's extant first-generation leadership retained immense iconic power due to its long experience, rhetorical talents, survival against the odds and, in bin Laden's case, personal charisma. These factors drew recruits and sustained militant morale; Zarqawi was a notable example. Groups like the Moroccan Islamic Combat Group (MICG), which committed the Madrid bombings, had residual ties to al-Qaeda insofar as they coalesced around, or at least drew on, alumni of al-Qaeda's Afghan training camps, thousands of whom remained in circulation. Having been indoctrinated by al-Qaeda itself, those alumni were presumptively loyal to its leadership and possessed at least some basic terrorist know-how. Such formative connections helped enable al-Qaeda to continue to influence the strategic direction of the global movement.

From the point at which the US-led intervention in Afghanistan ousted the Taliban and deprived al-Qaeda of a physical base and forced members of the group's hard core to disperse, a besieged, decimated and isolated al-Qaeda leadership had little operational control over increasingly far-flung assets. Law-enforcement and intelligence efforts – for example, the arrest of al-Qaeda–Jemaah Islamiah (JI) liaison Riduan Isamuddin ('Hambali') in August 2003 – also compromised connections between al-Qaeda and local affiliates. Thus, al-Qaeda affiliates (e.g., the MICG) appeared increasingly independent in operational terms. Eventually, ideological cracks could emerge from agendas and degrees of commitment among jihadists. JI's strategic objective of a regional caliphate in Southeast Asia is more limited than the al-Qaeda leadership's goals. It may make tactical sense for JI to cooperate with al-Qaeda now, but in the long term JI may be more amenable to political influence or deterrence-by-denial. An essentially ethno-nationalist affiliate like the Moro Islamic Liberation Front in the Philippines – which was near a peace deal with the

Philippine government in 2001 – may be amenable to cooptation sooner. Similarly, while European Muslims aggrieved by adverse circumstances in their host countries derive energy and political affirmation from al-Qaeda, their support for its maximalism could flag if conditions for Muslims in Europe improve.

Methodologically, al-Qaeda proxies have so far just used conventional terrorist devices robustly, while the al-Qaeda leadership is demonstrably interested in weapons of mass destruction (WMD). Should that leadership push to use WMD, fears some jihadists may have of Western retaliation could compromise the global terrorist confederation. On balance, al-Qaeda's transnational character reinforced a strong tendency to decentralise, while its messianic cast and present strategic circumstances promoted opportunism and expansion. These attributes yielded the benefits of geographical pervasiveness and self-perpetuation for the global movement in general, but dictated ambiguity as to composition and cut against the consolidation of the al-Qaeda leadership's operational control as well as ideological and even methodological uniformity. Re-establishing such control and uniformity would require re-centralisation, which would likely require a new physical base. But because that would furnish a discrete target highly vulnerable to Western military power, al-Qaeda had strong disincentives to taking such a step. Defensively, it remained better off in its present hard-to-detect 'virtual' form. That said, Iraq could serve as a valuable proving ground for 'blooding' foreign jihadists, and could conceivably form the basis of a second generation of capable al-Qaeda leaders (for instance, Zarqawi) and middle-management players.

Although the continued failure to kill or capture bin Laden or second-in-command Ayman al-Zawahiri deferred a major blow to the global jihad's recruiting power, the cooperative multinational law-enforcement and intelligence effort continued to improve over the course of late 2003 and 2004. This was in part because the internal jihadist threats to the Pakistani and Saudi Arabian regimes became more apparent, prompting them to awaken to local Islamist threats and intensify law-enforcement, intelligence and military measures to neutralise them. Yet 'hard' counter-terrorism measures could at best contain the problem. A better Western political accommodation with most of Islam – more a function of soft than hard power – was also required. The violent US occupation of Iraq and the pendency of the Israeli–Palestinian conflict have hindered efforts to strike such an accommodation. Furthermore, the United States' approach to counter-terrorism has leveraged hard rather than soft power, which has produced 'blowback' by increasing recruits. The global jihad has been able to focus on both Iraq and other areas, such as Saudi Arabia, Morocco, Europe (Spain) and its periphery (Turkey). Al-Qaeda's Saudi affiliate – known as the al-Qaeda Organisation in the Arabian Peninsula – is of particular concern.

On balance, however, Western – including American – appreciation for the importance of 'soft power' to the global counter-terrorism campaign seemed to be growing as of early 2005. Bin Laden's deep and general sense of cultural and religious humiliation did not drive all, or even most, of his followers. The Israeli–Palestinian conflict, US occupation of Iraq, American support for authoritarian Arab regimes and relative economic deprivation (more in Asia than in the Arab world) were more proximate spurs to jihadist recruitment and activity, and three of the four factors had been mitigated by early 2005. To be sure, the year 2005 appeared likely to be another troubled one in Iraq. Nevertheless, the robustness of the US commitment to stabilising Iraq and following through with elections in January, the determination of increasing numbers of Iraqis to rebuild their country, and the political opportunities for both Israel and the Palestinian Authority that Arafat's death opened up allowed for a more optimistic counter-terrorism outlook than did circumstances at the end of 2003.

Net assessment: non-proliferation

There were no resounding diplomatic achievements in 2004–05 comparable to Libya's abandonment of its WMD programme in 2003–04. In fact, the 'red lines' beyond which the United States and allied nuclear powers would not allow would-be nuclear powers to go – drawn by Cold War-era events like the Cuban Missile Crisis in 1962 and Israel's destruction of Iraq's Osirak nuclear reactor in 1981 – became more blurred. Consequently, the ongoing nuclear programmes of Iran and North Korea were more difficult to address. At times, the Bush administration implicitly but nonetheless plainly threatened military action against both Iran and North Korea if they refused to abandon their nuclear-weapons programmes. At other points, Washington suggested that diplomacy was the best, if not the only, option. Furthermore, notwithstanding widespread condemnation, India, Pakistan and presumptively Israel have all developed nuclear capabilities without adhering to the rules set forth by the Nuclear Non-Proliferation Treaty (NPT) and without facing commensurate diplomatic or economic punishment. These confusing signals appeared to leave sufficient wiggle-room for Tehran and Pyongyang to try to get away with as much as they can. Both have wilfully concealed enrichment and reprocessing programmes from international bodies, and behaved duplicitously in multilateral negotiations with major powers and the IAEA.

North Korea probably already has at least one or two nuclear bombs – indeed, it announced as much in February 2005 – while Iran is likely several years away. Both have successfully tested intermediate-range ballistic missiles. Even Bush administration hardliners have mused that, at least in the case of North Korea, drawing red lines would simply tempt the regime to step over them, producing even greater danger. Respected realists, however, challenge this position for fear that absent red lines, other nations aspiring to great-power status and/or facing existential strategic threats – Brazil, Egypt, Saudi Arabia, Syria or Taiwan – would feel uninhibited about developing nuclear weapons. Thus, Brent Scowcroft and Arnold Kanter argued back in 1994 – when the now-dead Agreed Framework was signed – that the United States should tell North Korea in no uncertain terms that if it proceeds to turn its spent fuel into bomb-grade plutonium, its reprocessing facilities will be bombed. Even though Pyongyang can threaten most of South Korea's population with artillery and certainly is not risk averse, they contended that it would not test Washington's will to start a full-scale war that the United States would inevitably win.

Ten years later, North Korea did what Scowcroft and Kanter said it should not be allowed to do: expelled IAEA inspectors and cranked up its plutonium reprocessing facility. Washington was bogged down in Iraq and drew no red line, instead favouring multilateral diplomacy involving China, South Korea, Russia and Japan. With respect to Iran, the United States and European powers were hopeful that a combination of carrots and sticks akin to the one that worked so well with Libya would induce forbearance. Unfortunately, this approach did not bear fruit in 2004–05. Moreover, having now involved so many other players so intimately in efforts to stop Iran's and North Korea's nuclear programmes, the United States would face a far more complicated and subtle diplomatic task in drawing red lines: there would now be much heavier pressure to establish standards not unilaterally but by consensus, which would be difficult to forge given the divergent interests of the powers involved.

By default, the best hope for discouraging Iran and North Korea from continuing their nuclear programmes and others from commencing them may be to revamp the NPT, which is up for review in May 2005. Doing so, however, will be a complex matter that will have to take the specific features of the Iranian and North Korean situations on board. For instance, strengthened treaty-based security assurances by the nuclear-weapon states not to attack a country in compliance with its obligations under the NPT – and to come to the assistance of an NPT party that was threatened or attacked with nuclear weapons – could be an essential component of reaching an agreement with Iran and North Korea. But any multilateral initiatives or instruments – including the NPT review conference, US ratification of the Comprehensive Test Ban Treaty, a fissile material cut-off treaty – pale in importance compared to the Iran crisis. If that crisis continues, and Iran develops a nuclear capability, treaties could perforce appear impotent and be deemed substantially irrelevant to the proliferation problem.

Regional challenges in Asia

On the periphery of the broader Middle East, state-building in Afghanistan proceeded apace, as President Hamid Karzai was convincingly re-elected in December 2004, as 10.3 million Afghans – double the UN's prediction – registered to vote. Several warlords were weakened and Afghan national forces appeared more robust, while American counter-insurgency forces (18,000 strong) reported significantly less contact with hostile militant holdouts from al-Qaeda and the Taliban, which American and Pakistani forces continued to pursue. The Afghan National Army embodied 13,700 troops at the end of 2004 and was set to double that strength by the end of 2005. Large-scale humanitarian crises, predicted in 2001, have been averted. However, security throughout the country remained tenuous. In Kabul, presumed to be the safest part of the country, a British aid worker was shot dead in March 2005. Furthermore, Afghanistan's role in international drug trafficking continued to grow, and the US government was only just getting up to speed on this problem in late 2004.

Pragmatic American tolerance for Pakistani President Pervez Musharraf's anti-democratic tendencies, and economic and military rewards – $3 billion in aid over five years, plus 'major non-NATO ally status' – for his counter-terrorism assistance helped keep a key partner in the global campaign against Islamist terrorism in power. But although Musharraf's continued resistance against Islamist extremism within Pakistan, and Islamabad's military and intelligence cooperation in hunting down al-Qaeda and Taliban holdouts region-wide were foremost strategic concerns, there were other potentially destabilising developments on the subcontinent. The Congress Party's victory over the ruling Bharatiya Janata Party enervated former Indian Prime Minister Atal Bihari Vajpayee's initiative to resolve the Kashmir problem. India's conventional arms build-up – including ballistic missile defences and airborne-early-warning aircraft – suggested that the new government in New Delhi was sceptical about medium-term prospects for a deal and threatened to upset the strategic balance achieved after the full-scale military confrontation between India and Pakistan over Kashmir in 2002–03, trigger a regional arms race, and in any case weaken nuclear deterrence. Intensified bilateral contacts on both conventional and nuclear confidence-building measures were salutary but not entirely reassuring.

Farther east, North Korea continued to prove recalcitrant with respect to its nuclear programme, proclaiming its nuclear-weapon capability publicly for the first time in February 2005 and insisting on bilateral talks with the United States while rejecting the existing six-party format. Yet Pyongyang's roguish behaviour had the effect of strengthening Japan's, South Korea's and China's relationships with the United States. The saliency of the North Korean threat encouraged Japan to continue its evolutionary movement towards a more extroverted defence orientation. And the threat made South Koreans increasingly dubious of a conciliatory approach to North Korea – which had been reflected in the 'sunshine policy' – bringing Seoul's thinking more in line with Washington's. China – while diplomatically helpful in hosting the Six-Party Talks, generally viewed as interested in merely controlling rather than stifling Pyongyang's nuclear ambitions – openly condemned Kim Jong Il's regime after its brazen announcement that it possessed the bomb. Taiwan's occasional hints at a lurch towards independence and China's strident threats that any such move would not be permitted, however, continued to complicate Sino–American relations and to pose the possibility of strategic confrontation. In March 2005, Beijing promulgated a law that authorised 'non-peaceful means' should Taiwan attempt formally to secede from the mainland. But although

Taiwanese President Chen Shui-bian called the law the biggest threat to regional security, it also specified that the use of force should be considered a last resort and endorsed peaceful reunification.

The biggest story in Southeast Asia in late 2004 and early 2005 was apolitical: a massive tsunami, or tidal wave, generated by an earthquake in the Indian Ocean off Indonesia devastated coastal habitats throughout the region on 26 December 2004, resulting in over 200,000 dead, billions of dollars worth of damage, and over a million displaced persons. Indonesia, Thailand and Sri Lanka were especially hard hit. While the natural disaster produced a momentary surge of international solidarity, the United States was criticised for not pledging more relief aid sooner than it did, though it initially committed $360m and Bush intended to increase aid to almost $1bn. The chaos that the tsunami visited also belied greater strategic order in Southeast Asia than had prevailed during the previous year. In terms of regional counter-terrorism coopation, Indonesia had been considered the weak link. But a relatively low-key, law-enforcement approach appeared to be bearing fruit, as large numbers of JI members were arrested and convicted. The United States, in turn, sought to bolster Indonesia's cooperative spirit by reviving military-to-military contacts suspended for several years over human-rights concerns. More broadly, regional actors – particularly Indonesia, Malaysia and Singapore – appeared, at the IISS's annual Asia Security Conference in Singapore in June 2004, to find common cause in strengthening maritime security against potential terrorist acts in the Malacca Strait, which is among the world's most vital oil chokepoints and commercial shipping lanes. US security relationships (both military and law enforcement) with the Philippines, Thailand and Singapore deepened; the former two were named US 'major non-NATO allies'. An evolving American policy of qualified engagement with Myanmar, as opposed to one of isolation, may improve the US image in the region, which has generally suffered over its Middle East policy. While political and economic competition between the United States and China for primary influence in Southeast Asia remained a looming engine of strategic change, the détente between the two countries deferred serious disruption.

Southern accents

Sub-Saharan Africa appeared to move farther away rather than closer to strategic centre stage. In previous years the strategic preoccupations of outside powers had caused it to be sidelined. In 2004–05, this may have had more to do with an evolved consensus that sub-Saharan Africa probably would not, after all, become a hotbed of jihadist activity. East Africa and the Horn of Africa – the ranking putative loci of radical Islam in the region – do present weak security forces and pre-existing terrorist infrastructure (Kenya), failed states and substantial Sunni Muslim populations (Somalia) and unreconstructed Islamist governments (Sudan) that might allow relative freedom of action to jihadist groups. At the same time, indigenous Muslims – while perfunctorily critical of US policies in the Middle East – do not appear to harbour the same visceral hatred of the West that makes, say, Arab, Southeast Asian and Pakistani Muslims such ready recruits for al-Qaeda. Thus, the United States and its Western counter-terrorism partners maintained preventive and institution-building counter-terrorist measures in the region – special operations forces in Djibouti and in the Arabian Sea, maritime and airborne surveillance, heightened maritime security operations in and around the Gulf of Guinea, train-and-equip programmes – but little more.

Some African conflicts moved closer to resolution, some farther away. The Democratic Republic of the Congo continued to build the apparatus of national government slowly and fitfully – albeit hindered by the intrigues of former overt combatants Rwanda and Uganda – while Côte d'Ivoire's fragile peace process unravelled. The UN and the Economic Community of West African States appeared to keep political rebuilding processes in Sierra Leone under control, but struggled to maintain a cease-fire between the transitional government and rebel forces in Liberia. Formal peace accords between Khartoum and the southern Sudanese rebels were signed in November 2004, ostensibly ending over 20 years of bloodshed, but whether international actors – in particular, the fledgling African Union – could end the Sudanese government's ethnic cleansing in Darfur remained uncertain. The involvement of the two most powerful sub-Saharan African states – South Africa and Nigeria – in regional diplomacy continued to be hopefully robust. But endemic poverty and disease (notably AIDS) in the region still appeared insuperable without the deeper involvement of developed nations. Wholesale increases in foreign aid, while occasionally mentioned in exhortations or as aspirations, still seemed unlikely to materialise. On 11 March 2005, UK Prime Minister Tony Blair launched the report of the Commission for Africa, which he chaired. The report was long on ambition, enshrining the intention of major powers to more decisively tackle poverty, governance, corruption, trade and arms-control issues in Africa. But it was short on substance and new ideas. Blair pledged that the UK would revamp its foreign policy to deal more effectively with these issues, and the report is to be used as a briefing paper for the G8 summit that the UK will host in Gleneagles, Scotland on 6–8 July 2005. It seemed unlikely, however, that the UK, let alone other major powers, could shift policy so radically as to make a serious difference in short order.

In South America, a political renaissance of sorts continued to unfold. With Argentina still reeling from economic collapse, under the leadership of President Luis Inacio da Silva – 'Lula' – Brazil set the tone for a new regional foreign policy and left-leaning political orthodoxy increasingly impervious to American influence, and manifested hankerings for great-power status. While maintaining sufficient economic credibility through policies less revolutionary than his political pedigree might have suggested, Lula appeared to cast Brazil as the continent's diplomatic arbiter – unafraid, for example, of maintaining full diplomatic contact with anti-American Venezuelan President Hugo Chávez and agreeing to sell fighter aircraft to him despite American misgivings. Implicitly reinforcing the freedom of South American states to keep their own counsel, it emerged that the threat of a build-up of Islamist terrorist support infra-structure in areas such as the 'Triple Frontier' where the borders of Argentina, Brazil and Paraguay meet had probably been exaggerated, and that more salient threats prevailed farther to the north, in Trinidad and Tobago, Panama and Mexico. But the United States continued to have significant military and law-enforcement involve-ment in Colombia's counter-insurgency against the Revolutionary Armed Forces of Colombia (FARC), and counter-narcotics efforts and related activities in neighbouring countries. While Peru and Ecuador remained manageable, internal unrest plagued Bolivia. As Chávez reconsolidated his power through a highly questionable election, kept bruiting his ideological affinities with Cuban leader Fidel Castro and flirting with intensified support for FARC, and built up Venezuela's military capabilities, he appeared to become an even more acute annoyance to the United States than he had been during the previous two years.

International diplomacy before and after the US election

Inevitably, international diplomacy was largely determined by American diplo-macy. And President George W. Bush's diplomacy during his first term was, to say the least, internationally divisive. Before 11 September, the United States' summary rejection of the Kyoto treaty on global climate change and refusal to recognise the International Criminal Court – though positions more gently held by the preceding Clinton administration – set European allies and partners on edge. The world united behind the United States after the terrorist attacks, and most capitals agreed that intervention in Afghanistan was a virtually obligatory act of self-defence. Yet Bush's spurning of NATO's offer of help as a full alliance in favour of a 'coalition of the willing' over which the United States would enjoy greater control scanned as further indication of the Bush administration's unilateralist leanings. Then transatlantic tensions neared their breaking point over American insistence on intervening in Iraq without specific UN sanction, and they were strained further when it appeared that politically skewed intelligence had badly over-estimated Iraq's WMD and, therefore, the threat that Saddam Hussein's regime posed. The broadly based global counter-terrorism coalition of nations formed in the wake of 11 September, having vital strategic interests in common, remained intact.

As November 2004 approached, however, many, if not most, members of that coalition considered Bush's foreign policy – especially the intervention in and occu-pation of Iraq and the broader corresponding doctrine of military pre-emption and prevention of threats – to have antagonised rather than discouraged transnational Islamist terrorists and made an international order already shaken by 11 September less stable. In all likelihood, most governments preferred to see Bush replaced by Senator John Kerry. Instead, Bush won a clear if narrow majority on 2 November 2004, and construed his victory as a mandate in support of his policies. His rhetoric was unapologetic, as was his retention of controversial Secretary of Defense Donald Rumsfeld. His nomination of National Security Advisor Condoleezza Rice to become secretary of state indicated an intention to maintain close control over foreign policy from the White House rather than ceding authority to the State Department. The 30 January Iraqi election proceeded more smoothly than expected, and led Bush to reinforce the righteousness of his Iraq policy. All of these indicators were likely to give US allies and partners and multilateral organisations considerable pause, for fear that they were in for four more years of the same unilateral swagger that had distinguished Bush's first term.

Yet there was also reason for hope. Under the pressure of stickier counter-insurgency problems than anticipated in Iraq, the Bush administration had chosen diplomatic paths vis-à-vis North Korea and Iran and closely coordinated its efforts with, respectively, Asian and European powers. He also seemed to recognise that his aggressive entrepreneurship with respect to democratic ideals – most starkly highlighted by the leaked details of the so-called Greater Middle East Initiative, which was disdained by Arab capitals – might not work smoothly in Middle East/Gulf region. As counter-terrorism cooperation with Saudi Arabia improved, and the Gulf states quietly enhanced their military relationships with the United States, the American hard-sell seemed to diminish. Bush also appeared to understand that an ongoing rift between the United States and Europe was in neither camp's interest, as he and Rice followed up his January 2005 inauguration with fence-mending tours of Europe. He talked tough to Russian President Vladimir Putin about his movement away from democratic reforms, but – especially after Putin's maladroit support of the ultimately ousted regime in Ukraine – Bush's criticisms were hardly controversial or diplomatically incendiary. By 2005, he had dropped – at least in public discourse – any notion that a strong European Union with its own military capability was an impediment to good transatlantic relations; appeared to understand that American attempts to dilute supranational European power could have the perverse consequence of strengthening it; was cognisant of the reality that European help was needed to win the peace, if not the war, in Iraq; and saw the political utility of European involvement in the Israeli–Palestinian conflict. In Asia, Bush policies had never seemed ill-considered or rash, and those policies – including an effective détente with China – appeared set to continue.

Notwithstanding some self-satisfaction about the transformative success of the Iraq intervention, there appeared to be an underlying realisation in the US administration that its effect on Islamist terrorism was at the very least questionable, and that Iraq's political viability – even if it materialised – would not constitute a catalytic 'demonstration effect' visiting liberal democracy on other Arab and Muslim countries. From an international standpoint, Bush's Middle East policy also benefited from strategic serendipity. Arafat's death enabled Sharon to re-engage with a new secular Palestinian leadership and allowed Washington to re-assert itself as an honest broker in the Israeli–Palestinian conflict in a principled way. This development, insofar as it could produce less bloodshed and eventually a formal settlement, stood to improve US standing in the Muslim world. Syria's excesses – its continued occupation of Lebanon, its likely involvement in the murder of Hariri, its continued support for Palestinian terrorist groups in spite of the revival of the peace process – made the United States' Syria policy look more sensible to the extent that France and Saudi Arabia joined the US in pressuring Syria to withdraw fully from Lebanon.

Residual anxieties over Europe's absorption in its social-democratic experiment and lack of appreciation of the indispensability of hard power will probably persist. The United States will almost certainly continue to be more ready to use military power than any other country. This tendency could again bring the United States into conflict with the balance of the international community over Iran, but the United Sttes is more apt to pursue diplomatic options. There will be other transatlantic differences, such as US opposition to Europe's lifting an arms embargo against China. The Bush administration also still has serious doubts about the efficacy of the United Nations – not least in light of its reluctance to take on responsibilities in Iraq – and has yet to indicate whether it will take on board the December 2004 report of the UN's High-Level Panel on Threats, Challenges and Change. Yet there are several aspects of the report that square with the administration's world-view: the emphasis on the transnational character of new threats and the consequent difficulty of 'going it alone'. And the very failure of the panel to agree on Security Council reform tends to preserve US primacy within the UN. Of course, the panel's refusal to expand the right of self-defence under Article 51 of the UN Charter – to encompass pre-emption or prevention, for instance – clashes with Bush policy. Bush's nomination of first-term Under Secretary of State for Arms Control and International Security John R. Bolton – a hardliner noted for his scepticism towards multilateralism and his pointed criticisms of the UN – in March 2005 to become US permanent representative to the UN did not augur especially well for US–UN relations, either.

Nevertheless, international diplomacy during Bush's second term is likely to be considerably less turbulent and polarising than it was in his first. Overall, Bush appeared to learn from the Iraq experience that even the United States could not do anything it wanted – certainly not without the help of its allies, partners and sometimes even multilateral institutions. At the same time, the Iraq effort looked more salvageable than it had since May 2003, the strategic environment in Middle East/Gulf region significantly improved and transnational terrorism continued, at least, to be contained. Having narrowly escaped foreign-policy disaster, this time around Bush has made it clear – in the Brussels speech in particular, and his conduct in general – that he will be more inclined to solicit true international consensus in support of major strategic action. He may not get the undying love of the family of nations, but he may well win the respect that has proved elusive. And broad respect for the head of the world's only superpower cannot help but produce a more stable international order.

Strategic Policy Issues

The US Military and the Limits of 'Transformation'

As intellectual fads go, the notion of force 'transformation' has had a remarkably good run. The concept has evolved from ideas that appeared in Soviet military writings of the mid-1980s, first as commentary on the emergence of the 'recon-naissance-strike complex' and later as speculation about a broader impending 'military technical revolution'. By the early 1990s these ideas had jumped to the US defence community where people began ruminating on 'revolutions in military affairs' (RMA). By the late 1990s, cottage industries had sprung up in many Western defence establishments around the idea that 'transformation' could make forces dramatically more effective in prosecuting military operations. These notions have gathered growing numbers of adherents.

The phenomenon may be, in part, a consequence of the end of the Cold War. The confrontation between the United States and its allies on one side and the Soviet Union on the other created opportunities for academics to dabble in military affairs, first in the areas of nuclear strategy and arms control, and later in such topics as 'non-offensive defence'. As these issues faded in importance, a void emerged that demanded to be filled. No real knowledge of military operations and no serious analysis were required to write and speak about the issue. Force transformation met these requirements perfectly. In order to discuss the merits of transformation, one need not make reference to actual or hypothetical military operations, or to understand what forces actually do. Likewise, systems or 'technologies' can be judged to be transformational (or not) without recourse to time-consuming approaches such as war games, simulations and calculations, or sometimes even to data.

Thus it is not entirely surprising that transformation has become a popular subject for certain elements of the intelligentsia. What is surprising, however, is the seriousness with which the topic is treated within the US Department of Defense (DoD) and other official defence establishments. A prominent theme of the defence review of 1997, presided over by former Secretary of Defense William Cohen, was the importance of exploiting the RMA. This meant that efforts would be made to accelerate investments in 'a common command, control, communications, computers, intelligence, surveillance, and reconnaissance (C⁴ISR) architecture', to quote the 1997 report of the Quadrennial Defense Review (QDR). Secretary Cohen's review also called for the development of 'visions of warfare for 2010 and beyond' by the combatant commanders and the services, investments in promising new technologies, and the conduct of 'practical experiments' by the military services 'to test new doctrines, tactics, training, and organizational structures'. But enthusiasm for force transformation did not reach full flower until the Bush administration of 2001. Candidate Bush had sharply criticised the Clinton administration during the presidential campaign of 2000 for, among other things, misusing US military power for 'nation building' and other activities supposedly peripheral to the national interest, for allowing readiness to erode, and for failing to prepare the forces adequately for emerging challenges. Bush called for 'skipping a generation' of costly new platforms as a means of increasing the resources available for systems and capabilities that would be truly transformational.

Secretary of Defense Donald Rumsfeld evidently warmed to the notion of transforming US military forces because this was the central, dominant theme of his first QDR, the report of which was published in September 2001. In it Rumsfeld declared that the objectives of US defence strategy could not be achieved without 'transformation of the US Armed Forces'. His definition of transformation was broad. It was said to have 'intellectual, social, and technological dimensions'. It was also stated that 'fundamental changes in the conceptualisation of war as well as in organizational culture and behaviour' were required to bring about transformation. He established four 'pillars' on which his approach to transformation would rest. These were:

- strengthening joint operations through standing joint task force headquarters, improved joint command and control, joint training, and an expanded joint force presence policy;
- experimenting with new approaches to warfare, operational concepts and capabilities, and organisation constructs;
- exploiting US intelligence advantages through multiple intelligence collection assets, global surveillance and reconnaissance, and enhanced exploitation and dissemination; and
- developing transformational capabilities through increased and wide-ranging science and technology, selective increases in procurements, and innovations in DoD processes.

Rumsfeld also announced the creation of an Office of Force Transformation that would report directly to him, and he directed the services to develop 'transformation roadmaps' that would report on their efforts to develop capabilities intended to meet six 'critical operational goals' laid out in the QDR. And in 2002, DoD's Joint Forces Command (JFCOM) was designated as the department's primary agent for coordinating the transformation of America's joint warfighting forces'. Whether the decision to anoint a joint command with authority to involve itself in deliberations about force modernisation ultimately will facilitate or complicate the efforts of the military departments to field innovative capabilities is, as yet, unclear.

By 2004, all of this management attention and activity had led to an impressive accretion of jargon to which people and institutions across the US defence community and, increasingly, in allied military establishments, have had to pay obeisance. Among these terms are 'decision superiority', 'predictive battlespace awareness', the 'joint synthetic battlespace', 'effects-based operations' (EBO) and, the Holy Grail at the end of the transformation superhighway, 'network centric warfare' (NCW).

Have the notion of force transformation and the activities it has spawned facilitated or accelerated the fielding of new and, above all, useful military capabilities? Proponents of transformation might argue that they have. The armed forces of the United States and several of its allied partners have fielded some important new military capabilities over the past eight years. Among these are:

- Unmanned aerial vehicles (UAVs) equipped with sensors and data links. These give forces the ability to monitor activities and search for targets over large areas in near-real time.
- Improved networks of computers, display systems and high-volume communication links that allow staffs to compile, sort, assess and share large amounts of information, facilitating collaborative planning and decision-making.
- Air-delivered weapons guided by the Global Positioning System (GPS). These weapons make it possible for aircraft to attack surface targets with great accuracy in all weather conditions.

More examples could be cited, but the point is that it is not at all clear that interest in transformation per se has actually promoted the development and adoption of these or other new capabilities. This is because transformation itself yields no insights as to either the operational need for a certain capability or the utility of one system or concept over another. In fact, an irony lies at the heart of the defence community's fixation on transformation. On one hand, systems and concepts developed in the recent past – including stealth aircraft, precision-guided munitions, standoff robotic weapons and advanced sensors – are highly useful and effective, allowing modern, well-trained military forces to perform important tasks at levels of effectiveness many times greater than forces equipped with previous generation gear. (For example, the 1940s-vintage B-17 would require 240 tonnes of bombs to achieve a 90% probability of destroying a bridge. Fighter-bombers dropping unguided bombs in the Vietnam era required roughly 200 tonnes. The advent of laser-guided bombs in 1972 reduced this to 12.5 tonnes, and the F-117 in *Operation Desert Storm* could achieve this level of effectiveness with just four tonnes.) This, in turn, has enabled those forces to accomplish missions that might otherwise have been regarded as infeasible. On the other hand, what seems to have escaped the notice of too many of today's defence practitioners and intellectuals is that the people responsible for these breakthroughs in military capability were entirely innocent of the notion of force transformation. It never occurred to them to ask themselves whether the technologies and concepts on which they were working would be 'transformational'.

The transforming threat

It is difficult to escape the impression that this sterile fixation on transformation among Western defence establishments has had a pernicious effect on defence planning. In particular, while people in the West have been debating the question of what constitutes an RMA and whether a particular widget is transformational, several of our adversaries have been busy fielding capabilities based on old and proven technologies and tactics that pose grave threats to our concepts for power projection and military operations. The image of Nero fiddling while Rome burns comes to mind. A cursory examination of three of the most obvious emerging threats will suffice.

Theatre ballistic missiles (TBMs). American and allied military forces have become accustomed to fighting wars in which their rear areas, which play host to such vital assets as airfields, seaports, logistics stocks, headquarters and reserve formations, are in sanctuary. US and allied air forces have achieved a level of proficiency such that their adversaries find it exceedingly difficult to mount more than token efforts at offensive air operations. Theatre ballistic missiles allow countries with modest levels of resources and technology at their disposal to leap over many components of a sophisticated air defence. They are becoming the poor man's air force. Theatre ballistic missiles provide a means to conduct attacks on targets hundreds of miles from the front, yet they do not require the extensive and expensive physical or human infrastructures needed to field a serious air force. Training and doctrine for their use is fairly straightforward and, as yet, no effective means has been devised to defend against large salvoes of such missiles. And it has proven devilishly hard to locate and attack their mobile launchers.

To date, enemy ballistic missiles have not made much of an impression on our expeditionary forces because they have been used sparingly and, most importantly, because the ones to which our forces have been exposed are inaccurate.

The *Scud* missile, which is the system most ubiquitously deployed among the forces of regional adversaries, is said to have a range of 300km for the *Scud* B and 550km for the *Scud* C, with a circular error probable of 700 metres. This has made the missiles useful primarily as terror weapons against very large targets, such as cities or major bivouac areas. This limitation on the missiles' effectiveness, however, looks about to change. The Chinese are said to have tested ballistic missiles, such as newer models of the CSS-6, with accuracies in the order or 50 metres or less. This level of accuracy is achieved by the incorporation of GPS guidance and control mechanisms that allow missile warheads to compensate for wind drift. If accuracies of this sort can be achieved affordably, the implications for military operations will be profound.

The ability to put 500kg of high explosive within 50m or so of a target means that specific points on military facilities can be destroyed: runways, taxiways, fuel-storage tanks and living quarters on airbases, for example; or supply ships at quayside, loading facilities and marshalling yards at ports. If aircraft cannot take off from (or land at) regional bases, or ships cannot safely offload cargoes at ports, it is not clear how US land-based forces will be able to deploy forward or to conduct large-scale operations. And if enemies are able to develop means for finding and locating large mobile platforms (such as surface ships), naval forces engaged in power projection ashore will also face new and formidable challenges.

Fission weapons. The threats posed by ballistic missiles become far more challenging if some of those missiles are mated with nuclear weapons. Obviously, the destructive power of these weapons makes their operational effects orders of magnitude greater than those of conventional weapons: whole target complexes can be devastated by a single weapon. But the more profound difference is one of kind: nuclear weapons can be used to intimidate societies and governments. By holding the lives of hundreds of thousands at risk, a regional aggressor might be able to coerce its neighbours into dropping out of US-led coalitions or denying outside forces access to bases that they would need to support military operations in the region.

Some might argue that the United States' overwhelming superiority in nuclear weapons would allow it to deter any rational regional actor from using his own weapons. But lessons from the Cold War cannot be applied in a facile manner to the situations we face today or will face in the future. The inherent asymmetry in the stakes involved in conflicts between the United States and its adversaries these days means that deterrence of nuclear use through the threat of massive damage in retaliation is likely to be problematic at best. Take North Korea as an example. If war returns to the Korean Peninsula it will likely be either due to an act of desperate aggression by the North or, more likely, an outgrowth of allied reactions to some other unacceptable action on the part of Pyongyang, such as the sale of fissile material to a third party. In either case, the only satisfactory outcome of the conflict from the standpoint of the United States and its allies would be the elimination of Kim Jong Il's regime. But how is it possible to deter an adversary from using all of the weapons available to him in a conflict when he knows that the consequence of defeat is his own death and that of his regime?

As if the problems of destruction of targets by blast effects were not daunting enough, nuclear weapons detonated at high altitudes also have inherent capabilities to disable electronic systems over a wide area. Although the exact effects of the electro-magnetic pulse (EMP) generated by nuclear weapons cannot be predicted with precision, it is known that nuclear weapons detonated at altitudes of 40km or more will produce high-voltage EMPs of short duration, the effects of which manifest themselves within line-of-sight of the burst. Depending on their frequency, these pulses couple to antennae and conducting lines and can disrupt or disable important components of computers, integrated circuits, electronic sensors and other systems. Infrastructure supporting power distribution and communication networks may be disrupted, as can unhardened avionics in aircraft. High-altitude nuclear explosions can also damage or destroy satellites. And radars used by TMD systems to locate targets and guide interceptors can be severely disrupted by EMP and ionisation effects in the atmosphere following a high-altitude nuclear explosion. Thus, an enemy armed with a handful of nuclear weapons can use one weapon as a precursor to ensure the arrival of subsequent weapons, even against targets that are well-protected by current-generation missile defences.

Simple thought experiments such as these make it clear that US and allied defence planners face grave challenges from the proliferation of two 1940s-era technologies. Some of the tools of what Peter Wilson of the RAND Corporation has called 'RMA II' (i.e., ballistic missiles derived from the German V-2 and fission weapons similar to those used on Hiroshima and Nagasaki) have the potential to negate many of the capabilities fielded in 'RMA IV' – that is, so-called silicon-enabled warfighting systems. There is little sense of urgency among them for workable near-term solutions to these challenges. Yet policymakers will be compelled to adjust their expectations regarding their ability to defend and advance national interests when they discover that these challenges have not been addressed.

Terrorism and insurgency. Of course, ballistic missiles and nuclear weapons are not the only types of weapons or threats that US forces are ill-prepared to deal with. As the Bush administration and the people of Iraq are learning daily, terrorists and insurgents with even a modicum of support from the local populace can severely disrupt the life of a nation, impose serious casualties on foreign and home-grown security forces, and thwart economic and political development efforts. The attacks of 11 September 2001 make clear that threats to our way of life posed by terrorist groups must be taken quite seriously. The nightmare scenario in which a terrorist group somehow acquires a nuclear weapon is only the most extreme manifestation of the threat. Al-Qaeda's extended gestation period in Sudan and Afghanistan shows that areas long regarded as strategically insignificant must now be foci of attention and often of activities aimed at preventing new threats from developing. The secular trend of the proliferation of ever-more destructive potential into the hands of marginal states, sub-national groups and even individuals means that governments and their military establishments will be compelled to keep pressure on terrorist and insurgent groups across an extremely wide area for many years to come.

What is to be done?

The argument here is not that the forces of the United States and its leading allies do not need new and different capabilities. They do. But making 'transformation' the conceptual centrepiece of efforts to bring forth these new capabilities has been, as it was bound to be, counterproductive. In fact, despite the often-expressed determination of leading voices within the defence establishments of the United States and selected allies to accelerate the modernisation and transformation of their forces, the real dynamism one observes today in the international security environment is with those who would threaten the dominant powers. For those who value peace and stability this is not good news. The question is how to proceed.

As with any sound Socratic endeavour, first the right questions have to be asked. The foundation of sound defence planning is identifying the operational problems of greatest potential consequence. As the preceding discussion suggests, this cannot be done by studying past RMAs or ruminating on the nature of transformation. It can be done by assessing the international environment and how trends therein might impinge on national objectives. That is, how might adversaries – states as well as non-state actors – choose to challenge US and allied interests, given the resources, capabilities and opportunities available to them. Of these sorts of challenges, which are most suitable to being addressed by the application of military power?

Once a sense of the sorts of operational challenges that might be faced is established, the next step is to develop scenarios that capture the essential elements of those challenges. For a number of reasons, the use of scenarios in force planning is currently somewhat out of fashion in the United States. There seem to be three reasons for this. First, there is dissatisfaction in the fidelity (or lack thereof) of analyses of scenarios that have been done within DoD in the past. Second, planners recognise that the future is obscure and that we cannot hope to be able to predict the location, timing or, perhaps, the nature of future conflicts. Finally, scenarios and the tools that had been used to assess them may have been discredited simply because previous administrations used them. DoD claims to have moved beyond 'scenario-based planning' to a more enlightened approach called 'capabilities-based planning'. This is said to allow planners to assess alternative forces without having to be tied to rigidly defined scenarios. But it has never been clear how to gain a sense of what sorts of capabilities are called for without specifying, at some level, what sorts of operations the forces are to be prepared to carry out and under what sorts of conditions.

Thus, none of these considerations is compelling. While one can point to many flaws in past analyses of hypothetical military campaigns, it is a mistake to throw out the baby (scenarios) with the bathwater (poor analytical tools, poorly used.) As to the argument that scenarios must be wrong because we cannot predict the future, this reflects a misunderstanding of the role of scenarios. They are not meant to be predictions of the future. Rather, they are, when well crafted, reifications of one's beliefs and expectations regarding the types of challenges (not necessarily the specific challenges) for which one must prepare. All responsible officials in our defence establishments have such beliefs and expectations. Indeed, it is impossible to evaluate proposals or make decisions without recourse to them. The process of defining scenarios simply makes these explicit.

Scenarios do not themselves point to the most important operational challenges to be addressed. They simply provide the context within which those challenges can be identified. Once a set of scenarios is specified, the best way to identify new challenges is to engage in war games built around the scenarios. Like scenarios, games have fallen out of favour in some circles, where they are viewed as quaint. In the 1970s and 1980s, the constant focus on defending Central Europe as the centre-piece of force planning for NATO nations led to the emergence of a sort of stylised depiction of the Soviet military threat. The enemy's options and actions could be, essentially, scripted. This, plus the advent of more powerful and user-friendly computers led to an almost exclusive emphasis on computer-based simulations as means of evaluating force and capabilities.

The theatre-level models used in DoD were never highly satisfactory for a number of reasons, but since the end of the Cold War their flaws and shortcomings have increasingly been seen as outweighing whatever advantages they might have. In brief, big computer models of war can be useful accounting tools – keeping track of myriad interactions among forces. But they are not well suited to addressing what have become the most important questions, which, increasingly, centre on issues of what might be termed strategic choice. That is, what courses of action is the enemy likely to choose, given his objectives, capabilities and perceptions of the target's options? Well-constructed games that give 'Red' (the adversary) free play can be unexcelled as sources of insights about future challenges. When Red Teams are staffed by experts who are well versed in the adversary's culture, government, military capabilities and doctrines, games help 'Blue' decision-makers get beyond the 'mirror-imaging' that so often bedevils operational and force planners. Games also permit players to experience the sorts of intra-alliance dynamics that can shape military strategy and operations.

Of course the 'garbage in/garbage out' problem that bedevils complex computer models can plague games as well. In addition to using qualified players, it is important that the referees used to adjudicate the outcome of each move in the game be well informed about the capabilities of the forces that are likely to interact and that they be incorruptible. And games should be done iteratively: what is learned in previous games can be applied to subsequent ones built around the same or similar scenarios. As experience is gained, high-fidelity simulations of key interactions (e.g., the effect of TBM attacks on airbases, or the likelihood of Blue ISR assets locating a significant portion of Red's mobile missile launchers) can be developed to improve adjudications. The output of these activities is a set of insights about operational needs. These can be used for the crucially important task of focusing concept and system development on the most salient problems. The endemic malady of defence policy and planning in the United States is attention deficit disorder. US forces must be prepared to conduct a very wide range of missions, from humanitarian relief operations to forcible intervention and large-scale theatre war. Shortfalls in capabilities can always be found in any mission area and voices will always be heard advocating efforts to fill them. The DoD routinely spends in the neighbourhood of $40 billion annually on research and development – a sum that exceeds the entire defence budget of most other nations. For the 2005 fiscal year, the DoD will devote a record $70bn to research and development. The key to making that investment productive is to ensure that resources, time and talent are not spread thinly across a diffuse set of initiatives (as is all too often the case), but rather that they are focused on developing the capabilities that will matter most. This is one of the principal responsibilities of the official civilian leaders of a defence establishment.

Following the 2001 QDR, Rumsfeld spelled out six 'critical operational goals' that were to guide DoD's transformation efforts. Those goals were:

- protecting critical bases of operations (US homeland, forces abroad, allies and friends) and defeating chemical, biological, radiological, nuclear and enhanced effects (CBRNE) weapons and their means of delivery;
- assuring information systems in the face of attack and conducting effective information operations;
- projecting and sustaining US forces in distant anti-access or area-denial environments and defeating anti-access and area-denial threats;
- denying enemies sanctuary by providing persistent surveillance, tracking and rapid engagements with high-volume precision strike, through a combination of complementary air and ground capabilities, against critical mobile and fixed targets at various ranges and in all weather and terrains;
- enhancing the capability and survivability of space systems and supporting infrastructure;
- leveraging information technology and innovative concepts to develop an interoperable, joint C⁴ISR architecture and capability that includes a tailorable joint operational picture.

Articulating these goals was a step in the right direction: they represent an attempt to get beyond exhortations simply to 'transform' and to point the services toward focusing on developing capabilities that address what were seen as the most important operational needs. Nevertheless, these goals are framed too broadly to have much effect. One way to assess the information content of a statement of guidance is to ask what activities it rules out. In the case of these six goals there is almost no programme or initiative, from the ill-fated *Crusader* artillery piece to the most arcane software development project, that cannot be justified as contributing to one or more of them. It is therefore unlikely that guidance of this sort will have the desired effect. What is needed is a finite set of clear statements of need for new capabilities. These statements should be framed at the operational level of war and should reflect the most urgent needs of future commanders. They should begin with an active verb and eschew jargon. And the statements should point to the outputs of military operations (i.e., capabilities to accomplish operational tasks), not the inputs (i.e., types of systems). The goal is not to be comprehensive but rather to compel focus. A list of ten priorities is too long. Three is too few. Here are some suitable examples:

- Provide a robust, wide-area defence against theatre ballistic missiles, including those armed with nuclear warheads.
- Find, identify, and locate small mobile targets, such as missile launchers, in complex terrain.
- Detect and track nuclear weapons and fissile material remotely.
- Rapidly neutralise integrated air defences that incorporate significant numbers of the most modern surface-to-air missile systems.

Note that whatever list is devised for focusing development efforts, its purpose is manifestly not to guide all of the activities of the department. Other guidance will be needed to direct components to, for example, train forces properly for 'non-traditional' missions, such as counter-insurgency, or to provide sufficient airlift, sealift, or communications bandwidth for joint operations. And very short-term efforts to support ongoing operations (for example, the development of new techniques for defeating improvised explosive devices) should be separate from the sorts of sustained development efforts to which the list above is relevant.

Of course, leading a horse to water does not guarantee that he will drink. Simply telling the military departments what capabilities they are to focus on developing will not ensure that they will do so. In fact, the services have powerful incentives to disregard such guidance because the 'reward' for success can be devastating cuts to other programmes. Thus, any new start must overcome massive resistance both within the service and beyond it because it is seen as competing with programmes already on the books. To illustrate the problem, suppose some research lab in the navy comes up with a concept for shooting down TBMs in boost phase by launching high-speed interceptor missiles from P-3s or other large aircraft. Naturally, such a missile would be expensive to develop and build. If the resources for it had to come out of the navy's overall budget, other programmes would have to be killed or deferred. And other fiefdoms within the navy (carriers, submarines and surface fleets, to name three) might feel that their prerogatives might be slighted by the emergence of this new capability on the P-3. Those who have something to lose from the adoption of the new programme might choose to suppress it, notwithstanding its relevance to the leadership's call for new capabilities. Hence, if the leadership of the department really wants to spur innovation, it will have to find means of overcoming this perverse incentive structure.

The most obvious way to do this is to announce that the services' budget shares are not immutable, that resources will be added to the budgets of those services that come forward with promising new concepts for providing the capabilities called for, and that those resources will be taken from the services that fail to come forward with such proposals. Obviously, however, some crockery (in the form of existing programmes and force structure) would need to be broken in order to free up resources on the scale required. Even more daunting is the fact that Congressional authorisation and appropriation committees would have to support any such initiatives to create more 'head room' for new programmes.

Addressing the most pressing future needs

From this perspective in mind, it is hardly surprising that the fit between the development plans of the United States' armed forces and the demands likely to be placed upon them in the coming 10–15 years is imperfect.

The army and Marine Corps. The United States Army has embarked on an ambitious and sweeping effort to develop new operational concepts and associated equipment. Under General Eric Shinseki, who served as chief of staff from 1999 until 2003, the army developed plans that, if realised, would result in a wholesale makeover of its fleet of combat vehicles. In brief, the plan was ultimately to equip every brigade in the army with new, lightweight armoured vehicles from the 'future combat system' (FCS) family of weapons. Based on radical new designs, the aspiration is for these vehicles to offer levels of survivability and lethality comparable to that of today's *Abrams* and *Bradley* armoured vehicles but to shed as much as 70% of the vehicles' weight. (The M-1 *Abrams* tank, mainstay of the army's armoured force today, weighs approximately 70 tonnes. It is hoped that the comparable FCS vehicle might weigh as little as 20 tonnes.) The timetable for developing and fielding this new class of vehicles is ambitious: the first unit of action is scheduled to be operational by early in the next decade.

Equally important, the army has sketched out a revised concept of operations to go with its new vehicles. The motivation behind a lighter family of vehicles is twofold. Firstly, the army wants its units to be more deployable than today's heavy forces. It is felt that if the armoured vehicles can be made light enough, units can be transported quickly to areas of operation by air. Secondly, lighter armoured forces could adopt more flexible tactics once deployed. During operations in Bosnia and Kosovo in the late 1990s, the army found that units equipped with heavily armoured vehicles were unable to operate in many areas because the vehicles we too large and too heavy for many of the bridges there. Lighter armoured forces could be more agile. In fact, some envisage the army's future forces operating deep within enemy territory in semi-autonomous units along non-contiguous lines of battle. Inserted into rear areas by medium-lift transport aircraft, these forces could pose threats to critical nodes, such as major headquarters, without having to fight through outer lines of defences. The army's *Stryker* brigades – units that are being equipped with medium-weight, wheeled armoured vehicles – are said to be developing and testing tactics that will be transferable to units eventually equipped with the FCS.

Since their unveiling, these daring new concepts have provoked considerable debate, not to say scepticism, among students of military operations within DoD and beyond it. Even the most ardent enthusiasts of the FCS concede that, new technologies in armour plating notwithstanding, smaller, lighter vehicles are not likely to provide the level of protection that the M-1 tank provides. They emphasise in response that army units in the future will have to rely on improved levels of situational awareness so as to be able to engage enemy ground forces before they come within range of FCS-equipped units. Accordingly, future army units are to be equipped with new systems for acquiring and sharing information about their environment. These include UAVs, networked communications and computer displays inside of each vehicle. The problem with this concept, of course, is that tactically astute ground forces have demonstrated repeatedly their ability to use dispersal, camouflage and complex terrain in order to evade detection by remote sensors. Air forces have learned this lesson repeatedly: without a competent friendly ground force in the field, it can be very difficult to compel the enemy ground force to do things (such as move and concentrate) that make them susceptible to observation and attack from the air. Most recently, during major combat operations in Iraq, US Army and Marine forces found that, despite the commitment of unprecedented numbers of airborne sensors to the joint operation, their primary means of finding enemy ground forces was 'movement to contact' – essentially, driving ahead into the unknown until people start shooting at you. (The US Third Infantry Division's efforts to secure terrain around the Iraqi city of Najaf in March 2003 vividly portrayed the problems associated with rooting out dispersed and dug-in ground forces.) The proliferation of technologies for destroying armoured vehicles, ranging from 'brand name' guided anti-tank projectiles to homemade 'improvised explosive devices' will make this problem more acute as small, dispersed units acquire greater killing power.

This realisation has led the army's leadership to abandon the notion of a 'one size fits all' army, in which the entire force is equipped with the same family of armoured vehicle. Even so, it remains far from clear whether it will be feasible in many instances to insert armoured forces of any weight deep into contested territory and to sustain them once they are in place. Even the crippled air defence available to the Iraqis in *Operation Iraqi Freedom* was sufficient to give pause to airmen considering flying large, slow aircraft over Iraqi-held territory early in the war. How would a fleet of transports be expected to evade or defeat the air defences of a more capable adversary in the future? And can future commanders be confident of being able to seize and hold one or more airfields in enemy territory where this force might be landed? Or will giant, four-engine vertical take-off and landing aircraft (think V-22 *Osprey* on steroids) be required? Finally, of course, irrespective of the technical feasibility of such a concept, one must question the wisdom of placing a brigade-sized force deep in enemy territory. This is the sort of situation that spelled disaster for the allied troops who were dropped onto 'a bridge too far' at Arnhem in the Second World War.

During the tenure of General Peter Schoomaker, General Shinseki's successor, large doses of reality have begun to moderate somewhat the army's expansive conceptions of its future. Although the service is continuing to invest several billion dollars annually in the development of FCS, serious thought is being given to retaining indefinitely some number of *Abrams* and *Bradley* armoured vehicles. Furthermore, the drubbing received by the army's *Apache* helicopters when they were sent on deep raids in Iraq seems to have cooled the ardour for aerial insertion tactics, at least in some quarters of the army. In the end, though, all of the Sturm und Drang surrounding the FCS threatens to obscure the real question facing the army (and, to an extent, the Marine Corps). That is, whether a substantial segment of the force should be organised, trained and equipped primarily for counter-insurgency, counter-terrorism and stability operations, rather than for large-scale manoeuvre warfare.

Few doubt that counter-insurgency, counter-terrorism and stability operations will form an important component of the 'demand function' for US and allied ground forces in the years to come. Irrespective of the course of events in Iraq, US forces will be called upon to provide training and advisory assistance to the security forces of friendly governments in many regions of the world. Al-Qaeda has shown that serious threats can breed in under-governed or poorly governed territories. Therefore, the United States and its allies will have to place greater emphasis on enhancing the effectiveness of security forces in those countries where the government is willing to work against radical Islamist groups within their borders. Special operations forces (SOF) have always specialised in providing this sort of training and assistance, and since the successful overthrow of the Taliban regime in Afghanistan, DoD has announced its intention to increase the size and improve the capabilities of its SOF units. But a greater level of effort than what even an enlarged

SOF can provide will be needed. Moreover, the army has found that even in major combat operations, such as *Operation Iraqi Freedom*, it needs very large numbers of people with the sorts of skills it has heretofore tended to concentrate in its reserve component forces. These include human intelligence collection, civil assistance, military policing and engineering functions. Restructuring its active component forces so that they can undertake stability operations on a prolonged basis without having to mobilise reserve and National Guard forces will be a challenge in itself.

Many army and Marine Corps officers have argued that well-trained infantry forces are perfectly capable of accomplishing these sorts of 'low-end' missions, but operations in Iraq since the commencement of *Operation Iraqi Freedom* have raised new doubts regarding that assertion. Time and again, the insufficiently discriminate use of firepower in Iraq has created more problems than it has solved. Resistance in Fallujah, for example, first spiked after more than one dozen Iraqis were killed by US Army forces firing into a group of demonstrators. And the abuses at Abu Ghraib prison were attributable at least in part to the fact that people untrained in guarding and interrogating prisoners were given that responsibility. In general, what is needed most for these sorts of missions is people who can operate confidently in foreign cultures, who can establish relationships of trust with others, and whose first instinct is to use tools of persuasion rather than force to advance objectives. Nineteen-year old rifle toters – essential as they are for certain tasks – will never constitute the optimal demographic category for providing these qualifications.

Some who concede this point will argue that land forces' ability to create specialised units for counter-insurgency and stability operations is constrained by the require-ment that US forces be able to fight successfully in two major combat operations (MCOs) at once. US defence strategy does call for this capability, but with the demise of Saddam Hussein's regime, arguably North Korea is the only remaining adversary against which the United States or its allies would plausibly have to commit large numbers of ground forces. Certainly US ground forces would play no major role in any conflict with China over Taiwan (save for providing defences against TBMs). And it is difficult to imagine any sane administration contemplating the introduc-tion of large formations of troops in Iran for purposes of forcible regime change. In short, adapting the army and the marines so that they can contribute more effectively to the nation's security has at least as much to do with changing those institutions' human capital as it does with developing and fielding a new generation of fighting vehicles. Perhaps the most important single thing that the secretary of defense could do to promote the evolution of the army and the marines towards a force that is better suited to meeting future needs would be to relieve them of the requirement to provide forces to more than one MCO at a time.

The navy. Like the army, the US Navy has promulgated an explicit concept of opera-tions intended both to describe how its forces (including those of the Marine Corps) will provide the capabilities needed for future joint operations and to guide the service in developing the systems needed to enable these capabilities. Its concept is called Sea Power 21 – an umbrella term that encompasses four component concepts: sea basing, sea strike, sea shield and FORCEnet. Together, these concepts cover all of the major functions performed by naval forces, from deploying and sustaining forces, to attacking enemy forces on land, sea and air, and extending protection from enemy attacks to the fleet and ashore.

The great advantage of navies as a means for power projection is their relative independence from land bases. Modern surface ships and submarines can operate for weeks at a time, ranging over thousands of miles, without having to stop at a land base. In the Pacific campaign of the Second World War, this quality proved vital to the conduct of offensive operations against Japanese forces. This same quality is prized today in theatres where access to land bases may be questionable due to uncertainty about the policies and decisions of local governments or because of growing threats to fixed facilities by long-range strike means – principally, theatre ballistic missiles. For example, in the opening days of *Operation Enduring Freedom*, as US forces sought to defeat the forces of the Taliban, aircraft carriers operating off of the coast of Pakistan played key roles in enabling air support to friendly ground forces. The great disadvantage of navies derives from the difficulties they have in generating large-scale forces for projection ashore. Even a mighty Nimitz-class aircraft carrier can launch and recover only around 100–150 sorties per day on a sustained basis – the equivalent of about 30 B-52 sorties. Again, *Operation Enduring Freedom* is instructive: once land-based fighters gained permission to deploy to bases around Afghanistan and long-range bombers and tankers got into the act, the navy's contribution to the air effort was largely overshadowed. Carrier-based aircraft also face inherent limits on their range, payload and endurance. To remedy this problem, the navy has relied heavily on large aerial refuelling aircraft operated by the air force. Ships, for a variety of reasons, also face limitations on the volume of communications traffic they can handle – a significant handicap in an era when masses of timely and accurate information are so crucial to effective military operations.

Fortunately for the navy (and the nation), modern technology and the nature of warfare are changing in ways that make mass less important than precision. Precision weapons allow each sortie or missile to do a great deal of damage to the intended target. Further, to a growing degree, the effectiveness of an attack or an operation turns more on the availability of precise, timely information about the enemy than on the ability to saturate enemy airspace with aircraft. This trend plays to the navy's comparative advantage. In evaluating the navy's plans for modernisation, the question to address is to what degree the service is capitalising on these trends. Without question, the navy has moved smartly to exploit the revolution in air-delivered weapons made possible by precision. The navy led the air force by many years in developing and fielding significant numbers of long-range, conventional cruise missiles. And after *Operation Desert Storm*, during which the navy largely stood by while air force fighter-bombers lobbed thousands of laser-guided bombs into Iraq, the navy quickly retrofitted its fighters with systems to allow them to deliver precision-guided weapons. The navy and the marines have made less progress in fielding systems to allow them to find, identify and locate targets. The venerable EP-3 aircraft represents the navy's primary contribution to the joint force's surveillance effort, a contribution that is supplemented by reconnaissance pods carried by some of its fighter aircraft. The navy has shown interest in developing and fielding a version of the air force's *Global Hawk* – a long-range, high-altitude UAV capable of collecting multiple forms of intelligence. But, presumably, this aircraft, like the EP-3, will be launched and recovered at land bases. The navy, in cooperation with the army, is also developing the Aerial Common Sensor. This will be a manned aircraft equipped to carry and employ a variety of sensors, including electro-optical, signals intelligence and radar-imaging devices.

In short, while the concept of power projection from the sea has great merit, forces operating at sea face inherent limitations and are dependent upon land-based and space-based assets for support. The navy, then, does not today offer the joint commander a complete package. Nor should it seek to. Rather, efforts should be made to formalise, facilitate and expand integration between the navy and the air force so that effective joint operations can be mounted even in situations where significant portions of each service's force 'package' is, for one reason or another, not available.

Finally, the navy looks set to field the nation's first effective wide-area defence system against TBMs. The system includes the *Aegis* radar, already deployed on many navy cruisers and destroyers, and the Standard Missile 3 (SM-3), outfitted with a new hit-to-kill kinetic warhead. The system was successfully flight tested in 2002 and is expected to become operational in 2005. It will be capable of intercepting TBMs outside the atmosphere, in some cases when they are still in the ascent phase. As the most promising near-term approach to defeating TBMs, it should be anticipated that this system would be in great demand to defend not only the fleet itself but also large areas on land. This demand may have important implications for the navy's ability to execute other operational tasks with its surface ships.

The air force. Since *Operation Desert Storm* in 1991, air power, and the US Air Force in particular has, in many ways, been the star of the show in joint operations. In that war, to the surprise of many, US and allied air forces were able to shatter the morale and will to fight of Iraq's best troops. The USAF dropped the lion's share of all of the air-delivered munitions in *Desert Storm* and a vast majority of the precision-guided munitions. Air power also showed that, in certain situations, it can have considerable coercive potential; air attacks, for instance, compelled the Serbs to accept NATO's terms for settling conflicts in Bosnia and Kosovo. And air patrols were the principal instruments by which the United States and the United Kingdom enforced compliance with sanctions on Saddam Hussein's Iraq between 1991 and 2003. Like *Operation Iraqi Freedom*, all of these situations have one common feature: an air force built to confront a first-class opponent had the good fortune of being asked to take on a second- (or third-) class one. The results were most gratifying for the United States and its partners. The USAF, like the air arms of the navy and Marine Corps, and air forces of key allies, is planning to modernise extensively its inventory of platforms, munitions and support systems. In spite of this, planners would be rash to be too complacent about how the USAF of the future will fare against adversaries more capable than those it has thus far confronted in the post-Cold War period.

The air force's modernisation plans reflect an institution that is striving to do a better job at what it is used to doing. This is not entirely inappropriate. Joint and combined forces will continue to need an air force that performs at a high level of effectiveness in achieving such objectives as transporting forces and critical supplies, defeating enemy air attacks, defeating enemy air defences in order to open up enemy airspace for surveillance and attack operations, damaging and destroying enemy ground forces, and shattering infrastructure targets, such as command and control nodes and logistics complexes. The air force's modernisation plan, if carried out as envisaged, would go far towards providing the requisite capabilities to achieve these objectives in major theatre wars, provided the force was able to deploy forward and sustain operations. Three worries arise, however. First, will forces be able to deploy to forward bases and to sustain operations in the face of threats from enemy ballistic missiles? As noted above, the United States and its allies are losing their monopoly on accurate, high-explosive weapons. These can wreak havoc on airbases, ports and concentrations of troops and logistics assets. The mere threat of attack on the cities and economic infrastructures of regional allies can raise doubts about their willingness to grant access to bases on their territories. This points directly to the second worry – that is, whether the air force will be prepared to mount an effective defence against ballistic missile attacks. The third concern involves challenges that fall outside of the realm of conventional combat operations – namely, counter-insurgency, counter-terrorism and stability operations.

These worries go to the very heart of the air force's overall concept for power projection. If forward operating bases are not viable, the air force will need more long-range platforms that can allow it to conduct surveillance and combat operations from afar. These aircraft would be called upon to dwell for extended periods in enemy airspace. Since large defence suppression packages might not available to accompany them, they would need to be fairly stealthy. Given the trend of distributing 'finders', 'deciders' and 'shooters' among different locations, it is not clear that these aircraft would need to be manned.

Wide-area boost-phase and mid-course defences against ballistic missiles would not only be useful for protecting forward military forces and facilities; they are also key to extending protection to the cities and economic infrastructure of allies. The air force has seriously pursued the concept of the airborne laser, but has encountered numerous obstacles in development; the airborne laser appears to be an idea whose time has not yet come. This suggests that the air force should be focusing efforts on developing a truly effective missile that can be launched from aircraft and engage TBMs in boost phase.

Finally, air forces have much to offer by way of supporting operations against terrorist groups abroad. The following types of assets will be in high demand:

- surveillance platforms, operators, and analysts;
- language-qualified personnel – commissioned offices as well as enlisted – to help train and advise host country forces, interact with others in-country, and analyse the intelligence 'take' from human and communications intelligence sources;
- security police and other force protection assets;
- combat search-and-rescue (for US and host-country personnel) as well as SOF insertion and extraction capabilities;
- humanitarian relief assets, including engineers, doctors and dentists, public-health specialists, tactical-airlift aircraft and crews;
- from time to time, assets to conduct precise attacks on terrorists or insurgents.

With the exception of strike platforms, all of these are what is known in the Pentagon as 'low-density' assets, meaning that the services tend to field fewer of them than are called for. This institutional aversion to funding what are traditionally regarded as 'support' functions (a trait that is not peculiar to the air force) will have to change if the service is to be as relevant to the needs of the nation as it can be. Of particular importance will be a long-term effort to develop the sorts of officers and NCOs needed for conducting sustained non-combat operations in foreign countries. In short, the air force should take the initiative to create a true foreign area officer programme and career path, along the lines of the army's programme of the same name.

Functional transformation

The disassociation of the notion of transformation from the successful development of useful military capabilities is, as Soviet writers used to say, 'no accident'. Most often, significant innovation in military capabilities results from sustained and focused efforts devoted to solving some specific operational problem. The creators of today's war-winning capabilities were focused on finding better means of interdicting follow-on armoured forces in Central Europe, dropping bridges, defeating radar-guided surface-to-air missiles, shooting down enemy aircraft and other critically important operational tasks. In the literature on transformation, one rarely encounters mention of prosaic tasks such as these. Rather, proponents tend to gravitate more or less directly to new types of systems (UAVs and 'information systems' are popular) or to inflated concepts such as 'networks' or 'self-synchronisation'. Divorced from an operational context and explicit concepts of employment, it is not possible to gain much insight regarding the potential need for or utility of such systems and concepts. Focusing on transformation as an end in itself distracts from the important work of determining what operational capabilities are most in need of improvement, and the primary way to identify these priorities is through the exploration of well-crafted scenarios and war games. Defence ministries can do the most to spur relevant innovation, but must direct development efforts so as to focus on a few well-chosen operational tasks and ensure that the incentive structure presented to military services is, at a minimum, not dysfunctional.

Nuclear Proliferation: Avoiding the 'Greatest Possible Danger'

For over four decades, the international community has worked to prevent the proliferation of nuclear weapons. These efforts have demonstrably curtailed the spread of nuclear arms. Yet, today, there is a growing belief that the nuclear non-proliferation regime has reached a tipping point, where in the absence of measures to repair and strengthen the regime it might unravel altogether. The near-emergence of new nuclear-weapon states in Northeast Asia and the Middle East, the proliferation of technology for the production of enriched uranium and plutonium, illicit nuclear supplier networks, and a lack of leadership by the nuclear-weapon states all point to a major crisis that, if not urgently addressed, could lead to a nuclear catastrophe. The foundation for building a more robust system for mitigating nuclear threats is an unprecedented degree of cooperation by the international community and leadership by key states – in particular, nuclear-weapon states under the Treaty on the Non-Proliferation of Nuclear Weapons (NPT). In addition, there must be action on an urgent set of priorities, including securing nuclear weapons and materials, a renewed commitment to nuclear non-proliferation and disarmament, addressing the risks of enriched uranium and plutonium for civil uses, resolving the North Korean and Iranian nuclear crises, and strengthened inspection and enforcement.

The existing nuclear non-proliferation regime

In February 1963, US Secretary of Defense Robert S. McNamara presented President John F. Kennedy with a secret study on the possible proliferation of nuclear weapons. McNamara forecast that within ten years, there could be eight additional nuclear powers, and that shortly thereafter, many more countries might go nuclear.

One month later, President Kennedy confessed to the American people during an evening news conference that he was personally 'haunted' by the feeling that by 1970, there might be ten nuclear powers instead of four, and by 1975, 15 or 20 – a chilling forecast he described as 'the greatest possible danger and hazard'.

Reflecting the president's dire assessment of the threat, the Kennedy administration moved quickly in the summer of 1963 to conclude the Limited Test Ban Treaty (LTBT) banning nuclear tests in the atmosphere, in outer space and under water. President Kennedy viewed this agreement as a mechanism to 'check the spiralling arms race in one of its most dangerous areas' and 'place the nuclear powers in a position to deal more effectively with one of the greatest hazards which man faces in 1963, the further spread of nuclear arms'. Over the past 42 years, two other international agreements have been added to the regime for limiting the spread of nuclear weapons around the globe. The first and most important – the NPT – entered into force on 5 March 1970; while Israel, India and Pakistan have yet to sign, it is truly a global accord, with 188 signatories. The NPT's three central provisions include:

- a commitment by the five original nuclear-weapon states – the United States, Russia, China, France and the United Kingdom – to pursue nuclear disarmament;
- a commitment by all other states not to receive, manufacture or acquire nuclear weapons; and
- the 'inalienable right' of all signatories to nuclear energy for peaceful purposes – 'in conformity with' the Treaty's ban on non-nuclear-weapon states receiving, manufacturing or acquiring nuclear arms.

To monitor and police the NPT regime, the International Atomic Energy Agency (IAEA) was tasked with the inspection of nuclear facilities worldwide under 'safeguards' agreements with NPT states designed to ensure the peaceful use of atomic energy. In addition to the IAEA, two 'suppliers groups' have been established to prevent the diversion of peaceful nuclear technology and equipment to weapons programmes.

Finally, a Comprehensive Test Ban Treaty (CTBT) banning all nuclear tests was concluded and opened for signature in 1996. The CTBT has now been ratified by 120 states, including 33 of the 44 required for entry into force – the exceptions being China, Colombia, Egypt, Indonesia, Iran, Israel, the United States and Vietnam (who have signed, but not ratified), and India, Pakistan and North Korea (who have not signed or ratified).

Today's nuclear landscape

In large part due to the measures adopted over the past four decades to stem the proliferation of nuclear weapons, the world that President Kennedy had feared in the early 1960s – a world with upwards of 20 nuclear-weapon states – has not materialised. Today, in addition to the five nuclear-weapon states recognised in the NPT, three nations – India, Pakistan and Israel – are known to have manufactured nuclear arms, while a fourth – North Korea – declared itself a nuclear power in February 2005 and is believed to have produced enough plutonium for a handful of nuclear bombs. Beyond this group of nine nations, the good news is that a number of states with the capability to manufacture nuclear weapons have not done so (or, in some cases, have inherited or developed nuclear arms, but then made a decision to terminate their nuclear-weapons programmes). More alarming, however, is a shorter list of countries – most prominently, Iran – that today are suspected of proceeding with programmes to manufacture nuclear arms. In addition to the threats posed by the proliferation of nuclear arms to nation states, a new nuclear threat has emerged since McNamara's 1963 assessment: the possible acquisition of a nuclear weapon by a non-state actor. Today, the most chilling possibility is the acquisition of a nuclear weapon by al-Qaeda or a similar terrorist group dedicated to inflicting mass civilian casualties and impervious to threats of retaliation.

Finally, the two leading nuclear-weapon states – the United States and Russia – today each deploy roughly 5,000 strategic nuclear warheads, many of which are ready to launch and capable of hitting their targets in minutes. The 2002 Treaty of Moscow would cut this number to 1,700–2,200 by the year 2012. While the Moscow Treaty levels would represent a substantial reduction in deployed strategic warheads for both countries (an 80% reduction from 1990 levels in the United States alone), it would still leave each nation with roughly the same number of deployed strategic nuclear warheads as the Soviet Union had when the NPT entered into force in 1970. Moreover, both countries appear committed to policies that many believe are at cross-purposes with their NPT obligations to pursue nuclear disarmament. The Bush administration wants to proceed with research on a new, low-yield nuclear weapon and earth-penetrating 'bunker busting' nuclear bomb, while Russia has increased the prominence of nuclear arms in its defence strategy and reportedly is working on new weapons and delivery systems. As for the other NPT nuclear-weapon states: the British have removed air-delivered nuclear bombs from service and reduced the number of nuclear warheads deployed at sea; France has dismantled its land-based nuclear missiles but continues to deploy both air- and sea-based nuclear arms; and China appears committed to modernisation of its nuclear forces.

The possible emergence of new nuclear-weapon states in North Korea and Iran, the threat of nuclear terrorism around the globe and the relaxed pace of nuclear disarmament strongly suggest the existing nuclear non-proliferation regime – with the NPT at its core – is eroding. Moreover, it is being replaced with an 'every man for himself' mentality that, if left unchecked, could spawn a new generation of nuclear-weapon states and increase the risk that the transnational Islamist terrorist network over which Osama bin Laden loosely presides becomes a nuclear power.

Reasons for the erosion of the NPT regime

A number of related factors are today contributing to the risk of new nuclear-weapon states emerging over the next decade, as well as enhancing the prospects that terrorists will gain access to nuclear material for a bomb or even an actual weapon.

Regional instability. The continuing military stand-off on the Korean Peninsula – where North Korea deploys a large and well-equipped conventional armed force across from South Korean and US forces along a narrow demilitarised zone – has undoubtedly contributed to the development of North Korea's nuclear capabilities. North Korea clearly views its nuclear weapons programme as a means to deter a US strike that could topple the North Korean regime, as well as a potential 'export' for earning hard currency. In addition, North Korea may also view its nuclear arms programme as an essential bargaining chip to extract military, economic and political concessions from the United States, South Korea and others. Whether there is any combination of military, economic or political incentives that – in the absence of a change in North Korean leadership – could lead to North Korea making a decision to abandon its nuclear weapons programme remains uncertain.

Similarly, in the Middle East/Persian Gulf, the roots of Iran's nuclear programme go back to the days of the Shah and lie deep in the soil of regional antagonism and Iran's ambition to be the dominant power in the region. Most recently, Iran's eight-year war with Iraq during the 1980s almost certainly spurred a decision by Tehran to accelerate the development of a nuclear weapons option. While the threat from Iraq has been reduced significantly with the removal of Saddam Hussein from power and the destruction of the Iraqi armed forces (at least as a force capable of threatening its neighbours), Iran still faces off against a number of regional rivals – including a nuclear-armed Israel – as well as at least a remote prospect of a resurgent Iraq. Moreover, Iran – like North Korea – may well see the acquisition of nuclear arms as the only sure way to deter a US military strike to remove the Iranian regime from power, making it all the more difficult for Iran to agree to forgo its nuclear-weapon-related activities.

Finally, in addition to 'deterrent/defensive' motivations for seeking nuclear arms, North Korea and Iran may also view nuclear weapons as enhancing their 'offensive' military capabilities: that is, the ability to respond 'asymmetrically' with nuclear weapons to any attempt by the United States to intervene in their regions gives both countries a freer hand to coerce their neighbours. This too may complicate efforts to get either nation to forgo nuclear arms.

'Holes' in the NPT regime. Both North Korea and Iran have used the provisions of the NPT – in particular, the right to nuclear energy for peaceful purposes – to advance their nuclear programmes. For both countries, the experience gained in the construction and operation of 'civilian' reactors provides a baseline of indigenous expertise

that is relevant to a weapons programme. Even more troubling is the insistence by non-nuclear-weapon states with nuclear power programmes – like Iran – on their 'right' under the NPT to indigenously produce and reprocess nuclear fuel for these reactors, as this process can easily produce enriched uranium and plutonium for nuclear bombs. The NPT does, after all, have gaping loopholes. It permits signatory nations that swear off nuclear weapons to develop nuclear power for peaceful purposes, which gives them partial control over their nuclear fuel cycles. They can build and run nuclear reactors, and they are allowed to produce enriched uranium to fuel the reactors, to store spent radioactive fuel from those reactors and to reprocess that fuel. With respect to fuel cycles, the only express obligations that the NPT imposes on signatories are to report the existence of the reactors and to allow the IAEA to inspect them. Thus, in a noted December 2003 editorial, Brent Scowcroft, William Perry, Ashton Carter and Arnold Kanter argued that the NPT should be amended to preclude the operation of such a 'closed fuel cycle', which yields fissile material. Under their plan, NPT nations seeking a nuclear-power capability would, subject to sanctions, agree not to manufacture, store or reprocess nuclear fuel, and to submit to IAEA inspections; those with such a capability would, also subject to sanctions, agree not to supply enrichment technology to nuclear aspirants and to ensure a reliable and reasonably priced supply of nuclear fuel and inexpensive retrieval of spent fuel. President Bush, in his 11 February 2004 speech at the National Defense University, largely adopted the supply-side recommendations as official US policy.

This problem goes well beyond North Korea and Iran. According to a recent UN report, today, almost 60 states currently operate or are constructing nuclear power or research reactors, and at least 40 possess the industrial and scientific infrastructure to enable them, if they chose, to build nuclear weapons at relatively short notice if the legal and normative constraints of the NPT regime no longer applied.

Illegal supplier networks. The recent exposure of Pakistani nuclear scientist A. Q. Khan's elaborate global network to smuggle equipment for the production of nuclear material for weapons to third countries (including Libya, Iran and North Korea), as well as designs for nuclear warheads to at least one country (Libya), underscores the 'globalisation' of the nuclear arms trade. Khan's network included suppliers and middlemen in a number of countries, including Britain, Germany, Spain Switzerland, Italy, Turkey, South Africa, the United Arab Emirates, China, Malaysia and Singapore. Even with Khan on the sidelines, the breadth and depth of the network strongly suggests there is a growing ability on the part of nuclear aspirants – whether states or terrorist groups – to secure nuclear-weapon-related infrastructure, material and designs. The globalisation of the nuclear arms trade is closely linked to and exacerbated by globalisation in communications, information, finance, travel and trade – a phenomenon that is likely to accelerate, not decline, in the coming years.

Lax leadership by the nuclear-weapon states. In the run-up to the 1995 NPT Review Conference, where the crucial issue of whether to extend the NPT was addressed, the five nuclear-weapon states made a serious effort to demonstrate they were fulfilling their commitment under Article VI of the NPT to 'pursue negotiations in good faith on effective measures relating to cessation of the nuclear arms race at an early date and to nuclear disarmament'. The centrepiece of this effort was a commitment by all five nuclear-weapon states to negotiate a CTBT in the Geneva Conference on Disarmament, combined with continued US and Russian efforts to further reduce their strategic nuclear arsenals under the Strategic Arms Reduction Talks (START).

Over the past decade, progress relating to Article VI of the NPT has been mixed. The CTBT has been signed by all five nuclear-weapon states; however, neither the United States or China has ratified, and the treaty has yet to enter into force. Complementing reductions in deployed strategic nuclear warheads, the United States and Russia have each made substantial reductions in their nuclear stockpiles since the end of the Cold War (the United States reports having eliminated more than 13,000 nuclear weapons since 1988); however, there are no current talks between the United States and Russia to proceed with nuclear reductions beyond the 2002 Moscow Treaty, and no apparent effort by the five NPT nuclear-weapon states to reinvigorate their commitment to pursue nuclear disarmament under Article VI of the NPT.

It is a debatable point whether actions by the nuclear-weapon states with respect to Article VI has a significant – or even marginal – impact on whether North Korea or Iran develop nuclear arms. Indeed, technical assistance provided by the nuclear-weapon states in the area of 'peaceful' nuclear research and energy – or overt assistance to nuclear-weapon programmes – has arguably been a much greater contributory factor to nuclear-arms development in North Korea, Iran and other nations. That said, leadership towards fulfilling their Article VI commitment can boost the credibility of the nuclear-weapon states and assist their efforts to get other responsible members of the international community to join in applying pressure on nations still seeking nuclear arms (just as efforts by the nuclear-weapon states to negotiate a CTBT helped achieve the indefinite and unconditional extension of the NPT in 1995).

Separately, each of these four factors would be cause for urgent action by the international community. Together, they point to a first-order crisis that, if not urgently addressed, could trigger a nuclear catastrophe.

New attitudes and approaches to nuclear non-proliferation

The 'rethinking' of the nuclear non-proliferation regime is already under way, with changes in national and international attitudes and approaches to prevent the proliferation of nuclear weapons increasingly in evidence. Most prominent is a change in attitude and approach by the United States. While the Bush administration supports the NPT and has made proposals to strengthen the treaty, it has downgraded multilateral arms control as a tool for combating proliferation. Most notably, the administration continues to oppose CTBT ratification, and has announced it will not support verification provisions as part of a fissile material cut-off treaty.

Consistent with the view that it is superior US military power and not international treaties or norms that is the crucial element in combating nuclear proliferation, the United States has elevated a controversial military doctrine – pre-emption – as the linchpin of its national security strategy, implemented a policy of regime change through a preventive war in Iraq and put great faith in its missile defence programmes. In general, this approach has found few proponents outside the United States. Indeed, many believe the threat of pre-emptive or preventive military strikes and a policy of regime change only encourages the development of weapons of mass destruction (WMD) in states that fear, and thus want to deter, a US attack.

Perhaps as a counter to the US approach, other nations are working to invigorate diplomacy as a tool for derailing the most pressing challenges to the non-proliferation regime. Britain, France and Germany have banded together to try to convince Tehran to give up its efforts to develop the industrial infrastructure to produce nuclear fuel; and China – as a key party (and host) of the US-sponsored Six-Party Talks – has taken a leading role in diplomatic efforts to denuclearise the Korean Peninsula. These diplomatic initiatives might receive a boost by recognition in the United States that its political and military options for conducting pre-emptive or preventive military strikes have been severely limited by the ongoing war in Iraq.

The United States has had more success in achieving international support for its Proliferation Security Initiative (PSI). Conceived as a programme to enlist the cooperation of other states in interdicting the trafficking of WMD and related materials, the PSI gained multilateral support with the passage of UN Security Council Resolution 1540 in April 2004. Passed under Chapter VII of the UN Charter (implying the possible use of enforcement measures by the Security Council to achieve compliance), Resolution 1540 details a series of steps that shall be taken by all states to preclude support to non-state actors seeking weapons of mass destruction. Complementary to the PSI, the resolution also calls upon all states to take cooperative action to prevent illicit nuclear trafficking.

In addition to these approaches by the United States, Europeans, China and the UN, a number of proposals have been put forward to strengthen the non-proliferation regime and the NPT. In December 2004, the UN Secretary-General's High-Level Panel on Threats, Challenges and Change concluded: 'We are approaching a point at which the erosion of the non-proliferation regime could become irreversible and result in a cascade or proliferation.'

The UN panel's recommendations for strengthening the non-proliferation regime include universal adherence to the Model Additional Protocol to the NPT requiring more stringent inspections to verify NPT compliance, providing incentives for states to forego the development of domestic uranium enrichment and reprocessing facilities, a voluntary time-bound moratorium on the construction of any such facilities, and the negotiation of a verifiable fissile material cut-off treaty that ends production of highly enriched uranium for non-weapon and weapon purposes. The UN panel's report also notes that lacklustre disarmament by the nuclear-weapon states weakens the diplomatic force of the non-proliferation regime and thus its ability to constrain proliferation. The report recommends several steps to restart disarmament, including reaffirming previous commitments by the NPT's nuclear-weapon states not to use nuclear weapons against non-nuclear-weapon states; practical measures to reduce the risk of accidental nuclear war, including a progressive schedule for 'de-alerting' strategic nuclear weapons, a pledge by the Security Council to take collective action in response to a nuclear attack or the threat of such an attack on a non-nuclear-weapon state, and support for the CTBT, regional nuclear disarmament talks and nuclear-weapon-free zones.

In addition, in February 2005, Mohamed ElBaradei, the director general of the IAEA, put forward 'seven steps to raise world security' in advance of the May 2005 NPT Review Conference, including most prominently a five-year hold on additional facilities for uranium enrichment and plutonium separation, with a guaranteed supply of nuclear fuel from countries that already have such facilities. The five-year hiatus would be used to develop better long-term options for managing the technologies. The other steps mentioned by ElBaradei – some of which are already under way with support from the nuclear-weapon states, the G8 and others – include the removal of highly enriched uranium from research reactors, mandatory adherence to the NPT Model Additional Protocol, swift and decisive action by the Security Council in the case of any country that withdraws from the NPT, support for UN Security Council Resolution 1540, accelerated implementation of the unequivocal commitment by the five NPT nuclear-weapon states to nuclear disarmament, and action to resolve existing security problems in the Middle East and the Korean Peninsula.

In short, there is no shortage of ideas for repairing and strengthening the non-proliferation regime. The question is: what are the most urgent priorities, and how best to get them accomplished?

Rethinking the NPT regime: cooperation, leadership and priorities

The NPT Review Conference – involving all signatories to the treaty – was scheduled to meet for one month in New York in May 2005. The conference was to review the operation of the treaty with a view to 'assuring' that the purposes and provisions of the treaty were being 'realized'. The NPT Review Conference is likely to serve as a focal point for re-examining all aspects of the nuclear non-proliferation regime. But while it is clear going in to the conference that the NPT and the regime it underpins are under unprecedented stress, there is no consensus as to what is required to effectively deal with the issue.

One way to think about the problem is to first identify 'core principles' that are a necessary prerequisite for repairing and strengthening the nuclear-non-proliferation regime, then – taking into account the reasons for the erosion of the regime as well as current attitudes and approaches to non-proliferation – devising a short list of equally urgent and reinforcing priorities for the international community. At the core of any strategy to repair and strengthen the nuclear-non-proliferation regime is not the assertion of unilateral rights, but the pursuit of cooperation. Cooperation in principle and practice between nuclear- and non-nuclear-weapon states is the essential foundation for effective global efforts to secure dangerous nuclear materials wherever they may be; eliminate the lingering nuclear threats from the Cold War, stop North Korea's nuclear weapons programme and forestall a nuclear-armed Iran.

Heading in to the NPT Review Conference, the outlook for global cooperation is more than uncertain. The five nuclear-weapon states appear at best uninterested in furthering their commitment to nuclear disarmament, and they are struggling to harmonise approaches for dealing with Iran and North Korea. On the other side of the ledger, non-nuclear-weapon states are resisting efforts to curb their right under the NPT to utilise nuclear energy for peaceful purposes. And the global effort to secure nuclear weapons and materials at their source to reduce the threat of nuclear terrorism – involving both nuclear- and non-nuclear-weapon states – is suffering from a lack of resources, bureaucratic impediments and a relaxed timetable for implementation.

Breaking the log-jam and establishing the principle of cooperation at the core of a revitalised nuclear-non-proliferation regime will require leadership, in particular from those nations currently designated by the treaty as nuclear-weapon states. For each of the equally urgent priorities discussed below, cooperation and leadership are the essential 'one–two punch' for reducing the risk of a nuclear catastrophe to as close to 'zero' as possible.

The first priority is to secure nuclear weapons and materials. The international community must act urgently to secure nuclear weapons and materials at their source. This is the most effective way to prevent nuclear proliferation and catastrophic terrorism, because acquiring nuclear material for a weapon, as opposed to making the weapon itself, remains the most difficult challenge for a terrorist group. There are two essential tasks in securing nuclear weapons and materials around the globe. Firstly, the job of securing nuclear weapons and materials in the nations of the former Soviet Union needs to be completed. Secondly, many countries outside the former Soviet Union have unguarded research reactors that are old, obsolete, inoperative or in need of repair. In some cases, stocks of spent fuel are still stored in dangerously insecure facilities, while in others spent fuel has been allowed to build up for years with few opportunities for disposal. A global approach is needed to secure all fissile and radiological materials to safeguard against illicit nuclear weapons programmes, trafficking and terrorism.

Current national and international programmes and commitments – including the Nunn–Lugar Threat Reduction programme, the G8 Global Partnership Against the Spread of Weapons and Materials of Mass Destruction, and the Global Threat Reduction Initiative – optimistically imposed a ten-year timetable to complete this task. With terrorists racing to acquire nuclear material and weapons, the timetable for getting this done should be halved from ten to five years, as recommended by the UN High-Level Panel. Delivering on this commitment will require resources; but it will also require focused leadership in key capitals to break through the political, military, bureaucratic and legal impediments to cooperation that continue to plague these efforts.

The second priority is a renewed commitment to nuclear non-proliferation and disarmament. Nuclear-weapon states – those recognised by the NPT and those currently outside the NPT regime – need to re-establish their leadership in both non-proliferation and disarmament. The United States, the world's leading nuclear power, has a unique role to play in catalysing a successful effort to reinvigorate the principle of cooperation and strengthen the nuclear non-proliferation and disarmament regime. For example, curtailing plans to proceed with research into new low-yield or bunker-busting nuclear arms, continuing support for a moratorium on nuclear testing, and engaging Senate leaders in a process to move forward with CTBT ratification are all actions the Bush administration could take to re-establish US leadership on non-proliferation and substantially strengthen the ability of the United States to get others to take the necessary steps to develop a more robust system for managing nuclear threats.

A renewed commitment to bring the CTBT into force by all five NPT nuclear-weapon states – which would underscore their commitment to constrain themselves, as well as help put in place a constraint on other nations that could benefit from testing – would also receive a boost from China, the other NPT nuclear-weapon state who has signed, but not ratified, the accord. Moreover, as recommended by the UN High-Level Panel report, nuclear-weapon states not party to the NPT – Israel, India and Pakistan – could also pledge a commitment to non-proliferation and disarmament and demonstrate that commitment by ratifying the CTBT, which is open to NPT and non-NPT states alike.

Beyond this, the United States and Russia could take positive steps to reduce the role of nuclear weapons in their national-security policies. Both countries could start by committing to a process to remove all US and Russian nuclear weapons from high-alert/quick-launch status. Today, there is no justification for – and real risks in – maintaining force postures optimised for striking with nuclear weapons within minutes. Moreover, such force postures undercut efforts to mobilise international support for convincing others to forgo nuclear arms. As an intermediate step, the United States and Russia could reduce the number of warheads on high-alert/quick-launch status from several thousand to several hundred prior to the next NPT Review Conference in 2010. During that time, they could also begin a dialogue with other nuclear-weapon states to de-emphasise globally the importance of nuclear weapons and gain mutual assurances that no state will deploy its nuclear arms on high-alert /quick-launch status. Finally, both the United States and Russia could commit to a process to make further reductions, beyond the Moscow Treaty, in their nuclear stockpiles, including tactical nuclear weapons.

By reducing their reliance on nuclear arms, the United States and Russia would enhance their credibility to rally the world to secure all weapons-grade nuclear materials, make necessary adjustments in current arrangements to provide nuclear fuel for peaceful purposes, and join in applying pressure on nations still seeking nuclear weapons.

The third priority is to address more decisively the security risks inherent in the civil uses of enriched uranium and plutonium. Clear steps should be taken to ensure that non-nuclear-weapon states cannot use the NPT to acquire nuclear material for weapons under the guise of developing an indigenous nuclear fuel cycle for nuclear power plants – a course that is clearly prohibited by the NPT as written. A five-year moratorium on additional facilities for uranium enrichment and plutonium separation is a reasonable start, and will allow time for developing a new regime for supplying nuclear fuel for civilian users under strict safeguards, including inspections. The new regime would be constructed around three principles. Firstly, it would ensure that states can continue to reap the benefits of the peaceful uses of atomic energy, including nuclear power, as specified under the NPT. Secondly, it would preclude non-nuclear-weapon states from producing their own nuclear material for weapons. Thirdly, if a state were to persist in this effort, other nations would unite in stopping them.

The fourth priority is to resolve the North Korean and Iranian nuclear crises. These (presumably diplomatic) achievements could substantially reinvigorate the NPT regime. Conversely, however, the absence of resolution – perhaps more than any other single factor – could portend the unravelling of the NPT. North Korea presents the most imminent prospect of crisis. In the four years prior to declaring itself a nuclear power, North Korea kicked IAEA inspectors out of the country and resumed the reprocessing of nuclear fuel into plutonium for weapons (a programme frozen since 1994). North Korea is also suspected of having an illegal programme to produce enriched uranium for weapons, and has reportedly sold uranium hexafluoride gas – a key ingredient for producing enriched uranium – to Libya. Thus, North Korea raises the dual risk of a growing nuclear-weapon inventory in the world's most isolated regime, and the possibility of nuclear terrorism through the sale or transfer of nuclear material or weapons.

The Bush administration has moved slowly to engage North Korea, and only with the cooperation of other states in the region, including South Korea, China, Russia and Japan. While multilateral diplomacy can play a crucial part in resolving the North Korean crisis, there may be no alternative to a more urgent approach – including bilateral diplomacy between the United States and North Korea – before the situation deteriorates further. If multilateral diplomacy is ineffective and bilateral diplomacy withheld, one possibility is to move forward with additional sanctions on North Korea. For this to work, China – North Korea's major trading partner – would have to agree to support coercive measures. While this seemed a distant possibility before North Korea's express February 2005 declaration of its nuclear status, Beijing's subsequent displeasure may indicate its increased inclination towards punitive measures against Pyongyang. That said, a policy to further isolate an already isolated regime may not be an effective method of pressuring North Korea to give up its nuclear programme. The other alternative is to hope the international community can successfully interdict any transfer of nuclear materials or arms, and that North Korea can be forever deterred – neither of which by itself is a firm basis for reinvigorating the nuclear non-proliferation regime.

The international community must also ensure Iran does not proceed with a nuclear-weapon programme. Unlike North Korea, Iran does not yet possess nuclear material or arms. Yet it is clear from missile and uranium-enrichment developments over the past few years that Iran has had a secret programme to – at a minimum – develop a nuclear-weapon option. The British, Germans and French have engaged Iran in a diplomatic process designed to halt the Iranian nuclear programme, and the United States has allowed these European countries to take the lead. What has been achieved so far is a temporary freeze of Iran's uranium-enrichment programme, pending discussions with the Europeans on a broader package of incentives. For this process to succeed, there needs to be movement on two fronts. Firstly, Iran must be consistently and convincingly reminded that the alternative to giving up its nuclear weapons option is not benign. A strategy of 'carrots only' is unlikely to lead to success – and the Europeans may need to take the lead in 'brandishing sticks' to convince Tehran that the international community is serious about halting Iran's nuclear programme. Secondly, the United States must at some point engage on the question of incentives for Iran. A European diplomatic lead may have been inevitable at the start of this process, given the state of relations between the United States and Iran. But at some point, for diplomacy to succeed, the process must involve the United States, Russia and possibly others.

In the case of both North Korea and Iran, it would help if the international community – starting with those nations engaged with North Korea in the Six-Party Talks, and the Europeans, the United States and Russia in the case of Iran – could agree on a set of criteria for 'halting' the North Korean and Iranian nuclear programmes. Conceptually, one extreme would be to achieve a verifiable freeze of each programme – similar to the approach with North Korea that led to the 1994 Agreed Framework. The other extreme is to achieve the complete dismantling and destruction of all nuclear-programme-related activity, as was the case recently in Libya. In the absence of an agreed set of criteria, it will be difficult to coordinate the necessary incentives – or sanctions – required to effectively engage North Korea and Iran. Success in halting both the North Korean and Iranian nuclear programmes may also hinge on the ability of the five nuclear-weapon states to address the regional security concerns of both states. In this context, strengthened security assurances by the nuclear-weapon states not to attack a country in compliance with its obligations under the NPT – and to come to the assistance of an NPT party that was threatened or attacked with nuclear weapons – could be an essential component of reaching an agreement with Iran and North Korea. More broadly, addressing regional security concerns – including the possibility of security assurances and the establishment of nuclear weapon-free zones – must be at the core of any long-term effort to create a climate whereby those nuclear-weapon states currently outside the NPT (Israel, India and Pakistan) can be brought in to the treaty as non-nuclear-weapon states.

A fifth priority is strengthened inspection and enforcement. As recommended by the UN High-Level Panel, the G8 and the IAEA director general, all state parties to the NPT should move expeditiously to ratify the Model Additional Protocol requiring more stringent inspection procedures, and the protocol should be recognised as the new standard for IAEA safeguards even in advance of development of a new regime for providing nuclear fuel for civilian users. In addition, procedures for reporting information regarding NPT compliance to the Security Council should be streamlined; and the Security Council should make clear its determination to hold accountable states that violate their NPT obligations or withdraw from the treaty.

Opportunities foregone?

In December 2004, the international community was rocked by the Asian tsunami disaster. The scope of this tragedy – over 200,000 lives lost and billions of dollars in damage – was magnified by the fact the world did not do everything it could to deploy a system in the Indian Ocean to warn of a potential tsunami. Instead, we were left asking the sad questions: what could we have done to prevent this tragedy? And why didn't we do it sooner? In the case of repairing and strengthening the nuclear non-proliferation regime, the international community cannot run the risk of having to ask the same questions – what could we have done, and why didn't we? – in the aftermath of a nuclear explosion. The nature of states' right to withdraw from the NPT – the necessary and sufficient conditions – need to be more closely scrutinised. Clearly a state must, at the very least, give three months' notice and claim national security exigency (that is, 'extraordinary events') under Article X(1) of the treaty; arguably, under a common-sense interpretation of the treaty, it should have to demonstrate pristine historical compliance with IAEA requirements.

The United States' implicit threat of military force against rogue states pursuing nuclear weapons is a necessary element to deter proliferation, but not a reliably sufficient one. Securing nuclear weapons and materials, diplomacy that directly engages proliferators and offers some alternatives to nuclear capability, and a renewed commitment to arms control (including the CTBT and separation moratoriums) would reduce the pressure on US military power to absorb the full burden of deterrence and provide for a safer and more civil world. It is far from too late to bring these factors to bear on international security. But in order for a more stable and sustainable solution to the problem of nuclear proliferation to materialise, the United States will have to devote greater energy to multilateral diplomatic solutions, and European capitals will have to recognise the need for more 'American-style' threats to stem the nuclear ambitions of certain states – in particular, Iran – while presenting positive incentives for compliance (such as security guarantees) with non-proliferation norms. Transatlantic convergence along these lines – with the necessary support from the broader international community – would mean greater unity in non-proliferation and in all likelihood greater success in avoiding the 'greatest possible danger'.

Terrorism and the Stalled Evolution of International Law

Major campaigns against terrorist groups have always involved a degree of tension with national and international legal norms. The 'war on terror' announced by the US administration in September 2001 is no exception. It has raised numerous politically sensitive issues about the relation between action and law; these issues revolve around three main questions, each of which has ramifications that go well beyond the 'war on terror' itself:

- Whether the circumstances in which it is permissible for states to take military action within another sovereign state – for example, because of what it might do in the future, or because it is suspected of assisting terrorists in any of a variety of ways – have expanded.
- Whether the treatment of prisoners and detainees suspected of involvement in terrorism is governed by the standards enunciated in the laws of war, in human rights law and in the basic laws of democratic states, or whether departures from those regimes are permissible.
- Whether the major international legal institutions – the International Court of Justice (ICJ) and the United Nations (including the Security Council and the secretary-general) – are equal to the task of responding to the serious challenges posed by international terrorism and the war against it.

All three questions proved particularly controversial in 2004. The determination of the circumstances in which it is lawful to resort to force continued to be overshadowed by the controversy over a single case with a very unusual legal rationale – the decision to use force in Iraq in March 2003. There was a question mark as to whether that decision could properly be seen as part of the 'war on terror' at all, and it was therefore an imperfect test case for the legitimacy of the use of force in response to terrorist threats. In the event, key parts of the formal legal and factual justification for the Iraq war – concerning Iraq's compliance with the disarmament regime imposed upon it – proved weak, and in September 2004, the UN secretary-general criticised the decision to use force in Iraq as illegal. The debate about the lawfulness of the use of force also had a more general aspect: consideration of the circumstances in which military action may be lawful in international law when it does not have explicit authority from the Security Council. The Advisory Opinion of the International Court of Justice in July 2004 on the subject of the Israeli security wall in the West Bank, in touching tangentially on this question, made a remarkable statement on the limits of the right of self-defence. Further, the UN High-Level Panel, which reported in December 2004, suggested that in an age of terrorism self-defence could be interpreted more broadly than before to encompass the concept of pre-emption.

The question about treatment of detainees was marked in 2004 by a stream of revelations about mismanagement, abuses and torture in prisons in Guantanamo Bay, Iraq and Afghanistan; by the publication of earlier US government documents outlining policy on treatment of detainees; by several official reports; and by landmark decisions of the US Supreme Court and the UK Law Lords that called into question the right of the US and UK governments to detain suspects indefinitely without a right of legal challenge, and urged the observance of international norms in the treatment and trial of detainees.

The performance of major international legal institutions was called into question by some high-profile actions by the UN Security Council, UN Secretary-General Kofi Annan, the International Court of Justice, and the International Committee of the Red Cross (ICRC) in the course of 2004. These suggested that international institutions, while having essential and distinctive roles in relation to the international campaign against terrorism, are not self-evidently doing a better job of rising to the challenges than are states.

All three of these questions are often addressed on the straightforward understanding that law is there to be implemented. In this view, states have solemnly agreed national and international legal standards. Departure from such standards offers terrorists a victory they do not deserve, by demonstrating that they have changed the nature of the international order. Yet such an understanding, however strongly held, and however excellent as a starting point, is not enough. The events of the 'war on terror' have confirmed that, even if their basic structure remains sound, existing law and institutions have certain weaknesses and need to adapt. If law is an important restraint on war, it is also true that war is a test of law: is the law practicable in today's circumstances, and can it remain relevant to the ever-changing phenomenon of war?

At the heart of these questions is the tension between law and power. This tension is age-old and enduring, but has now assumed new forms. In past eras, when there was a rough balance of power between the major states, the main actors often took the view that legal rules operated within the broad framework of balance, and indeed depended on that balance for their existence and effective operation, but maintaining the balance itself was a foundational matter that sometimes had to take precedence over the observance of legal rules. Thus, sometimes states, especially great powers, felt entitled to take military action not because an adversary power had committed an illegal act but because certain developments (that might in themselves be legal) threatened the existing balance of power and therefore demanded a response if the power balance was to be maintained. In the Cold War, the US quarantine of Cuba in 1962 and the Soviet-led invasion of Czechoslovakia in 1968 can be seen in this light. In this view, law may still be considered to be an important basis of international relations, but on certain issues it may sometimes have to give way to what is seen by one or another government as the more foundational and essential requirement to maintain the balance of power.

US preponderance and legal exceptionalism

In the post-Cold War era, the debate about the relation between law and power has taken a special form. The most obvious new feature is that the United States is far more explicit than before that it seeks to preserve not the balance of power in the traditional sense but rather the United States' preponderance of power – an express goal of the White House's National Security Strategy of the United States, promulgated in September 2002. This is an understandable goal for a country that has military capabilities far exceeding those of any other state, and that has traditionally seen itself (often in contrast to the view of others) as having a unique responsibility to assist the world in moving beyond a corrupt system of international disorder and power politics. A further special feature of US thinking at the beginning of the 'war on terror' is that the United States had come to believe that it could wage wars almost alone. One facile but prevalent interpretation of the wars since 1990 was that the United States might indeed be better off fighting without some of its foot-dragging allies. A possible corollary: if you do not need allies, then the need to operate within the existing shared international legal framework may be reduced.

By 2001 a reshaping of the international order, including the legal order, had been made more urgent by the twin problems of terrorism and proliferation of weapons of mass destruction (WMD). The possibility that these problems could become conjoined, leading to terrorist acquisition and use of nuclear weapons, is real enough, even if the fears that this was happening in Saddam Hussein's Iraq were shown to have been greatly exaggerated. In the Bush administration's view, existing international legal rules and institutions have proved inadequate in coping with these problems. For example, under existing international rules it may be technically legal for one of the few states that is not among the 188 parties to the Nuclear Non-Proliferation Treaty to develop its own nuclear weapons capacity. Yet in certain cases such a development could be seen, at least by some states, as posing a threat to international order and therefore broadly illegitimate. It is not surprising, therefore, that some members of the Bush administration have expressed a degree of scepticism about the adequacy of existing law and institutions.

International debate about the US role is complicated by the fact that there has been little US articulation of the ways the international legal order needs to be changed. The National Security Strategy of the United States was the boldest foray into this field, but did not contain clear proposals for change in the legal order, and never once mentioned the words 'intervention' or 'non-intervention'. Even so, it ran into heavy international criticism, principally because of its advocacy of pre-emptive military action against 'imminent threats'. But while there have been many indications of US dissatisfaction with particular legal provisions and institutions, there have been few detailed proposals for how the defects might be put right. The US is not alone in its recognition of the need for some modification of international rules and institutions to take account of new threats. Some other states have accepted this, albeit in less forthright language. The European Union, riven by its disagreements over Iraq, has issued a number of Delphic statements indicating that it does not wholly exclude the idea that in certain circumstances it can be justifiable to attack a state on what are essentially preventive grounds. It has basically adhered to the position outlined in its document *A Secure Europe in a Better World*, approved by the European Council on 12 December 2003:

> Our traditional concept of self-defence – up to and including the Cold War – was based on the threat of invasion. With the new threats, the first line of defence will often be abroad. The new threats are dynamic. The risks of proliferation grow over time; left alone, terrorist networks will become ever more dangerous. State failure and organised crime spread if they are neglected – as we have seen in West Africa. This implies that we should be ready to act before a crisis occurs. Conflict prevention and threat prevention cannot start too early.

Notwithstanding such partial declaratory concessions to the United States, there remained a chasm between US positions on international legal matters and those of close US allies, especially in Europe. In particular, Bulgaria, Hungary, Poland and other states in what US Secretary of Defense Donald Rumsfeld dubbed the 'new Europe' combined, like the UK, a pro-US position in strategic terms with acceptance of an array of legal agreements that the United States viewed with suspicion. These included the 1977 Additional Protocol I to the Geneva Conventions, the 1997 Kyoto Protocol, and the 1998 Statute of the International Criminal Court. They were implicitly asserting what the United States appeared at times to reject: that existing international legal norms and institutions were not necessarily inimical to the effective conduct of the 'war on terror'.

In general, US suggestions that the international order may need to be radically recast have been met with suspicion or even hostility on the part of many other powers and their populations. In the more critical views of American conduct, the United States is undermining an existing order without having anything else to put in its place. In a darker interpretation, it is using the 'war on terror' as a justification for the exercise of US dominance without real principle, as oppressive governments are supported when convenient, certain countries are invaded or threatened with invasion, collateral damage is too readily accepted, prisoners are held indefinitely without trial, and international institutions are sidestepped or used only when convenient.

In 2004 such international debate as there was about the place of international law and institutions in the 'war on terror' assumed the form, not so much of a general philosophical or policy debate, but rather of a series of incidents, scandals, proposals, decisions and reports, on which different states and institutions took different and often rival positions. If there is an evolution in this area, it is largely by common law processes in which certain policies and practices come to be viewed as acceptable, while others do not. The central questions in the debate involve when military action can be viewed as legal even if it does not have the specific authorisation of the UN Security Council, and how, in an age of terrorism and proliferation, states should interpret the meaning of self-defence as outlined in Article 51 of the UN Charter.

Controversy over the Iraq intervention

In Iraq, the United States and its partners sought to put behind them debates about the legality and wisdom of their use of force in March 2003, and to get on with the task of reconstruction. They had, at best, limited success. The Iraqi interim government was established on 1 June 2004; and the occupation's formal ending, outlined in UN Security Council Resolution 1546 of 8 June, took place on 28 June. These events brought neither sudden transformation of the situation in Iraq nor closure to the debate about the decision to intervene. Continuing reservations in many countries about the legality of the original intervention, coupled with concerns about the chronic and continuing insecurity within Iraq, made it difficult to broaden the base of the multinational force tasked with maintaining order in Iraq. In the Iraqi elections at the end of January 2005, the high level of participation (just under 60% of the electorate) provided hope of an eventual political settlement, but did not end international controversy over the intervention.

The debate about Iraq was politically important but did not lead to any breakthrough in terms of acceptance of new norms of legitimate intervention. Although they placed less public emphasis on it, the United States and Britain stuck to the formal legal justification of their action that they had made in their letter of 20 March 2003 to the president of the UN Security Council. This had asserted that there was continuing authority to use force on the basis of certain earlier UN Security Council resolutions and Iraq's failure to comply fully with them. The letter did not mention terrorism. Thus, notwithstanding a number of imprecise statements made by both supporters and opponents of the intervention, the formal claim was not that this was a pre-emptive war, nor that it was a case of self-defence under Article 51 of the UN Charter, nor that it was an anti-terrorist war, but rather that it was a military action to enforce Security Council resolutions and was based on authority contained in those resolutions.

Even if this legal justification of the coalition powers were to be widely accepted, the question would remain as to whether the circumstances prevailing in March 2003 were such as to justify so drastic a use of that authority as the invasion and occupation of Iraq. The coalition powers' claim that this was so depended crucially on the strength of assertions that Iraq had been defying the Security Council resolutions about disarmament. While Iraq's compliance had indeed been patchy, the coalition claim was weakened by the failure to find WMD – a failure that was acknowledged as conclusive by the Bush administration when on 12 January 2005 the White House press secretary said that there was no longer an active search for WMD in Iraq. Already on 3 October 2003 David Kay, the first head of the coalition-appointed Iraq Survey Group (ISG), had issued an interim report indicating that Iraq's WMD programmes were much less extensive, advanced and threatening than pre-invasion US National Intelligence Estimates had asserted. This was confirmed in the ISG's further report (the Duelfer Report) issued on 6 October 2004, which concluded that Iraq had no deployable WMD of any kind as of March 2003. However, it qualified this conclusion by stressing that Saddam Hussein's strategic aim had been to preserve Iraq's capability to reconstitute its weapons once sanctions were over. Further, by giving details of lucrative contracts to French companies and individuals, it offered little political or moral comfort to France, which had most strongly opposed the US military action. The overall effect of the ISG's findings was to strengthen the view that there had been a lack of professionalism and judiciousness in the decision-making process leading to the use of force in March 2003.

Concern on this point led to the establishment of independent enquiries in both the United States and Britain into the use made of intelligence in the run-up to the Iraq war. At the same time, in implicit recognition of the weakness of their main legal claim, the US and UK governments tended increasingly in 2004 to justify the invasion politically on the grounds that it had deposed an evil dictator. As mass graves were uncovered and evidence emerged of Saddam Hussein's killing fields, these justifications carried some conviction, but were not enough to disarm critics of the Iraq invasion. In response to a question about the legality of the Iraq war, UN Secretary-General Kofi Annan stated in a BBC interview on 15 September 2004: 'I have indicated it is not in conformity with the UN Charter. From our point of view and from the Charter point of view it was illegal.'

Annan's statement, and the context in which it was made, was problematic. Annan was responding to a question from an interviewer, and he did not give his reasoning. He showed no sign of understanding the formal legal justification made by the coalition. In particular, he did not indicate which of two legal viewpoints he intended to register: (1) disagreement with the whole idea that major states that are members of the Security Council could have had continuing authority to act based on earlier UN Security Council resolutions; or (2) accepting that there can in principle be such authority, rejection of the proposition that the action taken in March 2003 was justified by the circumstances at that time. Annan's statement reopened the chasm of suspicion and misunderstanding between the United States and the UN. This became worse when, at the end of October 2004, Annan sent a letter to the leaders of the United States, Britain and Iraq expressing concern at the prospect of a major offensive in Falluja: this was no slip of the tongue, and the recipients saw it as inappropriate interference.

The course of the debate in 2004 about the lawfulness of the intervention in Iraq in 2003 suggests that the coalition powers (principally the United States and Britain) made little progress internationally with the claim of 'continuing authority'. Washington and London had argued that a series of 17 UN Security Council resolutions passed since the First Gulf War – including Resolution 687 in April 1991, which conditioned the cease-fire on Saddam Hussein's dismantling his WMD, and culminating in November 2002 with Resolution 1441, which cited 'material breach' as grounds for the imposition of 'serious consequences' – had furnished sufficient grounds for the 2003 military intervention. This argument raised live, debatable and important legal issues, but neither side appeared intent on resolving them. Indeed, they were more concerned about changing the subject, and securing international support for democratic development in Iraq, than raking over an unsatisfactory debate about the lawfulness of their earlier action. However, their failure to carry conviction on this point, combined with confusion in the conduct of the occupation, reinforced the doubts of potential troop-contributors about supplying forces to assist reconstruction. In addition, continuing concerns about the lawfulness and wisdom of the Iraq intervention contributed to widespread international caution about the separate question of whether there should be any explicit extension of how 'self-defence' is interpreted.

The debate about 'self-defence'
The legal debate about the meaning of 'self-defence' in the changed conditions of the contemporary era revolved around the exact meaning to be attached to the key

words in Article 51 of the UN Charter: 'Nothing in the present Charter shall impair the inherent right of individual or collective self-defence if an armed attack occurs against a Member of the United Nations'. This is the only article in the charter that accepts the use of force by states acting independently. Interpreting this article, most, but by no means all, international lawyers take the view that it simply recognises a pre-existing right of self-defence, which continues in the UN era. This interpretation makes a difference when it comes to two primary questions. Firstly, can attacks by non-state bodies be encompassed in the idea of 'armed attack'? Secondly, must there be an actual armed attack before the right of self-defence comes into play, or can states act to forestall an impending attack?

The question of exactly which forms of action can be understood as being encompassed in the notion of 'armed attack' is notoriously difficult. Article 51 specifies neither that an armed attack has to be by a state, nor that it has to assume a conventional form. There is a strong case for recognising openly that a major terrorist attack, and/or a sustained terrorist campaign, can constitute an 'armed attack'. The UN Security Council confirmed this in September 2001. In the wake of the events of the previous day, Security Council Resolution 1368 of 12 September 2001 recognised 'the inherent right of individual or collective self-defence in accordance with the Charter'. This was a green light to the United States to act militarily in Afghanistan, and it seemed to bring an armed response to terrorist attacks firmly within the framework of the law of self-defence. However, the Security Council did not settle all aspects of the matter. The terrorist attacks of 11 September 2001 had been unusual in that there was already significant evidence of a degree of responsibility of a state (Afghanistan). This episode left open the question, explored further below, of what kind of response may be permissible in response to terrorist attacks by non-state groups in cases where there is no clear evidence connecting them to a state.

The debate about pre-emption and prevention continued, with an apparent increase of acceptance of the legitimacy of pre-emptive action. However, the propriety of military action to nip a future threat in the bud – preventive action – proved much more problematic. This latter approach, which was one part of the package of ideas set out in the National Security Strategy of the United States, did not make much headway for many of the same reasons that international bodies have been reluctant to enunciate a general right of states to intervene militarily on humanitarian grounds: whatever the strength of the argument in particular cases, to concede a general right of states to take military action to prevent future dangers in circumstances other than immediate and urgent self-defence could be to open the door to abuse.

So far, in any case, an attack by a state against a long-term and remote threat is not authorised in contemporary international law. There is a further problem in the entire debate about the legitimacy of military action of a preventive character. If Security Council approval cannot be obtained for it, is it right to see preventive military action as necessarily falling into the category of 'self-defence'? What if, for example, it is evident that a terrorist group in a particular territory is equipped with nuclear weapons, but it is unclear against whom the weapons might be used? In such a situation, there would be a threat to international peace and security, giving the UN Security Council an entitlement to take action. However, if the Security Council does not act (e.g., on account of the veto), and major states wish to do so, it could be artificial to force their action into the juridical framework of self-defence. Indeed, the notion that unilateral action without Security Council approval is illegal, while a one-nation veto of presumptively multilateral action endorsed by 14 other members of the Security Council is intuitively problematic. The UN is not a perfect sounding board for the illegality of use of force, as the Security Council denies legal authority to some countries due to their political nature – which colours its purported neutrality – and the unilateral effect of veto qualifies the purity of UN authority. This was one consideration in the Proliferation Security Initiative (PSI), discussed below.

Two international bodies – the International Court of Justice and the UN High-Level Panel – were critical of any unfettered right of states to take interventionist military action in response to terrorism. The ICJ's observations relating to Article 51 were particularly controversial. The court's July 2004 non-binding Advisory Opinion on the Legal Consequences of the Construction of a Wall in the Occupied Palestinian Territory, given in response to a request from the UN General Assembly, concerned the legitimacy of Israel's construction, in the name of security, of the wall and fence within the occupied West Bank. The ICJ concluded that it was 'not convinced that the specific course Israel has chosen for the wall was necessary to attain its security objectives'. The construction of the wall 'constitutes breaches by Israel of various of its obligations under the applicable international humanitarian law and human rights instruments' (para. 137). Although this conclusion was based primarily on the ICJ's interpretation of Israel's obligations under the law governing military occupations and also human-rights law, it was, in addition, integrally related to the Court's notably narrow interpretation of the right of self-defence – a right to which Israel had referred in defending the construction of the barrier. On self-defence, the ICJ addressed briefly two closely related questions: firstly, whether the phrase 'armed attack' in Article 51 encompassed attacks by non-state groups; and secondly, whether the phrase could encompass attacks emanating from Israeli-occupied territory rather than from a foreign state.

The ICJ's Advisory Opinion, after quoting from Article 51, stated: 'Article 51 of the Charter thus recognises the existence of an inherent right of self-defence in the case of armed attack by one State against another State' (para. 139). In context, this was misleading, as the UN Charter is not specific that armed attack has to be 'by one State'. The ICJ opinion continued:

The Court also notes that Israel exercises control in the Occupied Palestinian Territory and that, as Israel itself states, the threat which it regards as justifying the construction of the wall originates within, and not outside, that territory. The situation is thus different from that contemplated by Security Council resolutions 1368 (2001) and 1373 (2001) [both of which concerned the attacks on the World Trade Center], and therefore Israel could not in any event invoke those resolutions in support of its claim to be exercising a right of self-defence ... Consequently, the Court concludes that Article 51 of the Charter has no relevance in this case. (Para 139.)

The first widely noted problem with this Advisory Opinion is that it appears to restrict the concept of armed attack exclusively to states. This is hard to square with the language of the UN Charter. Some international lawyers have in the past asserted that acts of terrorism committed by private groups or organisations as such are not armed attacks in the meaning of Article 51 of the UN Charter. In this view, only if such acts of terrorism are large scale and attributable to a state can they be considered to be armed attack in the sense of Article 51. However, the logic of this view is hard to follow. It would appear to suggest that states do not have a right of self-defence against pirates, 'barbarians', or armed gangs if they have no known connection with a particular state. Yet such groups have for centuries posed threats to states, and the right of states to defend themselves against ongoing attacks by such groups has been widely accepted.

A second problem concerns the ICJ's conclusion that when an attack emanates from an occupied territory, and takes place on the territory of the occupying power, it cannot constitute 'armed attack' within the meaning of Article 51. It is true that suicide bombings with which Israel has been faced in recent years have originated in the West Bank and Gaza (though some reportedly had help from outside), and that these territories have a special status, with much or all of them under Israeli occupation. The attacks from these territories are therefore significantly different from the assault on the United States of 11 September, which had its origins in a foreign sovereign state. However, it is questionable to imply, as the ICJ did, that the right of self-defence is not a legitimate basis for action against an attack that originates in territory in which Israel is deemed to exercise control. In most circumstances, the existence of a right of self-defence by a state is accepted. For example, if an attack originates within a state, that state would in principle be seen as entitled in international law to take action against those launching such an attack– that is part of its prerogative as a sovereign state. Similarly, if an attack originates in the territory of another state, then the attacked state would in principle be seen to be within its rights in taking action against it. All this raises the question of whether the status of occupied territory is so special and unique that the right of the occupying power to self-defence is in some way significantly more restricted than the rights of governments in other situations. The question is particularly pertinent when the occupier's degree of control is limited – in this case by the fact that some areas of the Israeli-occupied territories were under the Palestinian National Authority.

The ICJ was not suggesting that Israel had no right to take defensive action:

> The fact remains that Israel has to face numerous indiscriminate and deadly acts of violence against its civilian population. It has the right, and indeed the duty, to respond in order to protect the life of its citizens. The measures taken are bound nonetheless to remain in conformity with applicable international law.

The implication was that any right of Israel to take action within the occupied West Bank (as distinct from along the 'green line') had to be based first and foremost not on the law of self-defence, but on considerations contained in international conventions relating to military occupations and also those relating to human rights. These were the basis of the criticism of the course chosen for the wall. Criticism of the wall thus was tied to a somewhat arbitrary and unconvincing curtailment of the right of self-defence. The ICJ, then, risked reinforcing American fears that the new International Criminal Court would render decisions ignorant of the issues involved or reflecting political rather than legal considerations. More credibly, Judge Thomas Buergenthal, in dissent, while critical of the wall, rejected the 'legally dubious conclusion that the right of legitimate or inherent self-defence is not applicable in the present case'.

A More Secure World, the report of the UN High-Level Panel on Threats, Challenges and Change, was issued on 2 December 2004. One of the many tasks undertaken by the panel was to address 'the circumstances in which effective collective security may require the backing of military force, starting with the rules of international law that must govern any decision to go to war if anarchy is not to prevail'. The foundations of the panel's thinking are indicated at the beginning of its discussion of legality: 'There is little evident international acceptance of the idea of security being best preserved by a balance of power, or by any single – even benignly motivated – superpower' (para. 186). In discussing the meaning of self-defence under Article 51 of the UN Charter, the panel explored the lawfulness of pre-emptive and preventive military action:

> A threatened State, according to long established international law, can take military action as long as the threatened attack is imminent, no other means would deflect it and the action is proportionate. The problem arises where the threat in question is not imminent but still claimed to be real: for example the acquisition, with allegedly hostile intent, of nuclear weapons-making capability.
>
> Can a state, without going to the Security Council, claim in these circumstances the right to act, in anticipatory self-defence, not just pre-emptively (against an

imminent or proximate threat) but preventively (against a non-imminent or non-proximate one)? Those who say 'yes' argue that the potential harm from some threats (e.g., terrorists armed with a nuclear weapon) is so great that one simply cannot risk waiting until they become imminent, and that less harm may be done (e.g., avoiding a nuclear exchange or radioactive fallout from a reactor destruction) by acting earlier.

The short answer is that if there are good arguments for preventive military action, with good evidence to support them, they should be put to the Security Council, which can authorise such action if it chooses to. If it does not so choose, there will be, by definition, time to pursue other strategies, including persuasion, negotiation, deterrence and containment – and to visit again the military option. For those impatient with such a response, the answer must be that, in a world full of perceived potential threats, the risk to the global order and the norm of non-intervention on which it continues to be based is simply too great for the legality of unilateral preventive action, as distinct from collectively endorsed action, to be accepted. Allowing one to so act is to allow all.

We do not favour the rewriting or reinterpretation of Article 51 (paras. *188–192*).

The panel went on to emphasise the central truth that the UN Security Council is already, as things stand, fully entitled to authorise military action on a pre-emptive or a preventive basis. It also supported the authority of the Security Council to exercise a 'responsibility to protect' by authorising military intervention to stop large-scale killings within states. However, since even the Security Council must pay heed to considerations of legitimacy, it explored five 'basic criteria of legitimacy' that the Security Council should always address before endorsing any use of force: seriousness of threat, proper purpose, last resort, proportional means and balance of consequences. Although these five criteria are not problem-free, they constitute a useful checklist.

So far as questions of legitimate use of force are concerned, the main weakness of the High-Level Panel Report is that it says little about what action may be permissible in cases (whether of self-defence, or responsibility to protect) on which the Security Council is unable to agree. The five criteria that it proposes are needed less by the Security Council (the main problem of which is to get agreement at all) than by states acting alone, in coalitions or in regional organisations. This lack of attention to the use of force by states acting without explicit Security Council authority is a reflection of the panel's belief that what the UN must aim to establish is a 'collective security system'. The panel uses this term in an interesting way, to refer to a UN-centred system of international security that addresses a notably wide range of threats. However, the panel's report did not explore the reasons why past attempts to create a complete collective security system have run into difficulties, nor did it indicate the political hazards involved in setting a notably high target for the UN.

The panel's report generally won the respect of governments. It made some progress on the historically difficult question of defining terrorism, and issued a strong plea for non-state uses of force to be subject to a clear normative framework. Its justified preoccupation with a wide range of threats, and with cooperative aspects of security, did not blind it to the continuing key role of states and of national self-defence. Its suggestion that Article 51 of the UN Charter should not be rewritten is certainly wise. The report contributes notably to the evolving interpretation of Article 51 by recognising the principle that pre-emptive action against imminent attack may in certain circumstances be lawful.

Proposals for safeguards in a broad conception of 'self-defence'

Is a broad conception of 'self-defence' coming to be accepted? There is no general agreement on a single new verbal formula. However, the ICJ Advisory Opinion notwithstanding, there is a strong body of opinion that the right of self-defence is broad enough to encompass two principles: firstly, the right of states to act pre-emptively, with the aim of eliminating the prospect of an imminent attack by disabling a threatening enemy; and secondly, the right of states to take action in response to international terrorism. The acceptance of these two principles is partly a recognition of enduring facts of life – that states and their citizens are inevitably attracted to the idea of reducing or eliminating the possibility of attacks once they are seen as inevitable, rather than waiting until they occur and then responding; and there are occasions, albeit rare, on which a military response to terrorism may be appropriate. However, there are risks in opening the door to military action by states in such circumstances. The risks may be especially serious in cases of pre-emption. 'Imminence' of attack has to mean intent, capacity, plans and active preparations to attack, but producing timely evidence of all this is likely to be difficult. Indeed, pre-emption is likely to depend on thoroughly subjective judgements about a presumed threat. Information from intelligence agencies may be inaccurate or tainted. Other states may be sceptical about the justifications made by a state engaging in pre-emptive action. Because of the high risk of abuse of any right of pre-emption (however qualified that right was), there would have to be a high standard of evidence. The evidence should be thoroughly tested by proper procedures within government and perhaps also more broadly. How all this could be achieved was far from clear: the failures in assessment and decision-making over Iraq cast a long shadow over the Bush administration's doctrine of pre-emption.

There are many similar difficulties in the position that major terrorist attacks, whether or not they are clearly linked to a particular state, may constitute 'armed attack' and may therefore, by implication, justify a military response. Most of the difficulties relate to the consequences that flow from such a position, as the following considerations suggest:

- It is not always possible to be sure whence an attack came, or which (if any) states bear responsibility for it.
- The exact nature of a state's responsibility for a terrorist attack may be complex and debatable. Is a state responsible when it tries, albeit ineffectually, to stop terrorist activities within its borders? Or when a small faction of the government has got out of hand and encourages activities of which the rest of the government disapproves?
- Even if a victim state is fairly sure which state is responsible for an attack, the evidence that can be presented in public at the time may be incomplete, and unconvincing to third parties. Although the United States quickly bombed Tripoli on a stated justification of self-defence in retaliation for Libya's perceived responsibility for the Berlin discotheque bombing in 1986, that responsibility was conclusively confirmed only in August 2004, when Libya agreed to pay compensation to victims.

The historical record of wars against alleged sources of terrorism is not strong. Cases that give grounds for doubt about any kind of blanket approval of military action in purported response to terrorist attacks include Serbia 1914, Lebanon 1982 and Iraq 2003. These considerations point to a simple conclusion: if 'armed attack' is accepted as encompassing certain types or patterns of terrorist attacks, then that should not be taken as an automatic licence to respond militarily. Prudential considerations have to be taken into account. Moreover, precisely because of the debatable character of the use of force in such cases, a multilateral response would be likely to command more legitimacy than a purely unilateral one. In these circumstances, it is not surprising that attempts to bring both pre-emption and responses to terrorist attack within the ambit of the law of self-defence have not proceeded very far beyond the point of identification of these as possible justifications of military action. There is not yet a definite advance acceptance of their general legitimacy.

Treatment of detainees

Of all the international legal issues raised in the 'war on terror', the most sensitive politically remains the treatment of detainees. Two theoretically distinct issues – the proper legal regime that should apply to detainees, and abuses in the actual treatment of detainees – have merged and contributed to the political disasters associated with the occupation of Iraq. How should detainees in the 'war on terror' be classified legally? Two essentially simple answers – often put forward in dogmatic form as universally applicable – have been particularly prevalent. The first is that such prisoners must be considered either as prisoners of war or as civilians, and in all respects must be treated in accord with the relevant 1949 Geneva Conventions. The second is that, because many of those suspected of involvement in terrorism do not meet the stated criteria for the status either of prisoner of war or civilian, the normal legal framework does not fit their case; and in particular, because what they have been involved in is criminal and obtaining intelligence from them is vital, a military detention regime may be justified in departing from the norms pursued in 'normal' wars.

Various international bodies including the International Committee of the Red Cross (ICRC) have inclined to the first view, the US administration to the second. If presented as general solutions, both approaches are flawed. As was officially recognised in Iraq, enemy soldiers taken in some aspects of the 'war on terror' must be treated as prisoners of war. However, the ICRC may have been wrong to deny, as it had done early in the 'war on terror', that there could be a category of 'unlawful combatant' or 'unprivileged belligerent', and it remained too reluctant to explore the possible need for a legal framework for a detention regime distinct in certain respects from those laid down for prisoners of war and civilians in the 1949 Geneva Conventions. For its part, the United States was wrong to apply the term 'unlawful combatant' indiscriminately, and with insufficient respect for clear compass points to govern the treatment of all detainees, regardless of how categorised. Such compass points could be found in existing law and practice. Firstly, they are contained in certain parts of human rights law, especially the 1984 Torture Convention. Secondly, they are in the 1977 Additional Protocol I, Article 75, on 'Fundamental Guarantees'. The United States has in the past stated that, despite its rejection of the protocol as a whole, it accepts this article as one of a number that are 'either legally binding as customary international law or unacceptable practice though not legally binding'. However, some Pentagon officials now appear to have played down this commitment, which has scarcely been mentioned in official statement, in the 'war on terror'. Thirdly, important compass points regarding the treatment of detainees who do not qualify as prisoners of war can be found in some state practices, including that of the UK in Northern Ireland. For the United States in particular, the apparent absence of such signposts resulted in muddled policy, a pattern of abuses within detention facilities, and public relations disasters outside.

The most extreme manifestations of these problems arose in the occupation of Iraq that began in April 2003. The circumstances were harsh. The whole international presence in Iraq, especially that of the occupying armed forces and administration, was under constant threat from suicide bombings and other forms of attack, the detention facilities being no exception. Of the many policies and practices of the coalition that aroused antagonism in the Iraqi population, prisoner abuse was perhaps the most serious. In theory, the United States accepted that prisoners taken in Iraq were to be treated in accord with the Geneva Conventions. Yet by the end of 2003 there were reports (some published at the time, some internal) of abuse and torture of prisoners. Already in January 2004 one consequence of these reports had been the establishment of a US Army investigation into the activities of the 800th Military Police Brigade in detention and internment operations in Iraq, specifically at Abu Ghraib prison. The investigation, conducted by Major-General Antonio Taguba, reported in May 2004. Taguba's findings were damning.

> In many centres, not limited to Abu Ghraib, there was a pattern of poor training, slack record keeping, inefficiency, cultural insensitivity and systematic cruelty. There was also a high rate of escapes. Criminal conduct involved Military Intelligence personnel as well as Military Police. Key units 'had received no training in detention/internee operations. I also find that very little instruction or training was provided to MP personnel on the applicable rules of the Geneva Convention Relative to the Treatment of Prisoners of War.' (Part One, Findings of Fact, para. 12)

Subsequently, formal charges were brought against some of the US military personnel directly involved in the abuse of detainees, on which basis convictions were obtained, but no senior officer was punished for having a role in these failures and crimes.

Concern about the conduct of coalition forces in Iraq was confirmed in other sources. April 2004 saw the publication of the first of many photographs showing sadistic treatment and sexual abuse of prisoners at Abu Ghraib prison in Baghdad, the existence of which had been known since January at certain levels in the Pentagon. A confidential ICRC report, completed in February 2004 and leaked to the Wall Street Journal the following May, contained disturbing accounts of how searches and arrests were carried out in Iraqi homes. It stated that no information was given to Iraqi citizens about which units were conducting the arrests, the causes of arrest, or the destination to which arrestees were being taken. Coalition military intelligence officers told the ICRC that between 70 and 90% of the persons deprived of their liberty in Iraq had been arrested by mistake. There was, the ICRC had reported, a general pattern of mistreatment of detainees, particularly in Baghdad, Basra, Ramadi and Tikrit.

The furore about the cruelty towards detainees and the professional incompetence of their captors led to assurances from the Bush administration that the illegal practices would cease. These assurances failed to stop repeated suggestions that the US maltreatment of detainees was not due only to local excesses and abuses, but rather reflected a policy that came from above, even from the administration itself. Accusations and press leaks on this point resulted in the establishment of numerous enquiries and the publication of earlier memoranda. On 22 June the Pentagon released the texts of nine key documents on the matter that had been drawn up in 2002–03. These showed a number of vacillations in Rumsfeld's approach to the use of harsh methods of interrogation. In addition, at about the same time, several memoranda from the Justice Department were leaked or released, advancing a wide variety of reasons for asserting that the provisions of international conventions, including the 1949 Geneva Convention on Prisoners of War, were not applicable to detainees taken in Afghanistan in particular or in the 'war on terror' more generally. The most notorious of these was a memorandum sent from the Justice Department to the White House on 1 August 2002, redefining torture in such a way as to allow a huge range of cruel and inhuman treatment to escape the definitional net of US and international legislation against torture, and stating that the president had total and unfettered discretion to ensure that prisoners were effectively interrogated, even to the point of authorising torture. This memorandum was withdrawn by the Justice Department in summer 2004, and was superseded on 30 December 2004 by a new text. Only one of these documents was signed by President Bush – a White House memorandum of 7 February 2002, which had rejected formal application of the Geneva Prisoners of War Convention to captured Taliban and al-Qaeda personnel, but had nonetheless stated that as a matter of policy they would be treated humanely. Although there was no unequivocal paper trail leading directly from the White House to Abu Ghraib, it is not difficult to see that an amateurish official legal debate in Washington, in which it had been incorrectly suggested that certain prisoners were 'not legally entitled' to humane treatment, and which had left many laws-of-war specialists in the Pentagon unhappy, had played at least some part in the shocking events in detention facilities used in the 'war on terror'.

The central problem was that the Bush administration had invented a new category – 'battlefield detainees' – which fell into neither the category of prisoners of war nor that of criminals – and then conveniently placed them outside of existing international norms. This point was reinforced by the publication on 24 August 2004 of the Final Report of the Independent Panel to Review Department of Defense Detention Operations, chaired by former Secretary of Defense James R. Schlesinger. It 'found the details of the current policy vague and lacking' and noted the absence of 'consistent guidance from higher levels'. It criticised 'the migration of interrogation techniques' from Guantanamo and Afghanistan to Iraq. It was concerned about the apparently casual classification of prisoners in Iraq as 'unlawful combatants' notwithstanding the fact that US policy in Iraq was supposed to be to apply the Geneva Conventions fully. It called for substantial reform in the Pentagon's policies, training and procedures. It also had some criticisms of the ICRC, saying that it had failed to recognise that there was a valid category of 'unprivileged belligerents' and to advance a legally sound and practical regime for them. It suggested that the ICRC was wrong to assume that terrorist suspects should not be subject to interrogation.

The furore in the United States about detainees continued. Indeed, the day after the Schlesinger report, two other major reports on Abu Ghraib were issued by the Pentagon. In December 2004 FBI memoranda and e-mails, obtained under a Freedom of Information Act request, were published, expressing concern about numerous abuses from 2002 onwards at Guantanamo, in Afghanistan and in Iraq. As a result, on 5 January 2005 the US Southern Command set up an investigation into allegations of prisoner abuse at Guantanamo. This brought to over ten the number of major official investigations into allegations of prisoner abuse in Iraq, Afghanistan and Guantanamo.

At the same time as a pattern of abuse was emerging from numerous official reports, courts both in the United States and in Britain reached decisions requiring that the status and treatment of prisoners taken in the 'war on terror' be brought within at least a rudimentary framework of law. On 28 June 2004, in the case of Hamdi v. Rumsfeld, the US Supreme Court ruled that the petitioner Yaser Esam Hamdi, a US citizen captured in Afghanistan and being held in the United States as an enemy combatant, should 'be given a meaningful opportunity to contest the factual basis for that detention before a neutral decisionmaker'. Another case decided on the same day, Rasul v. Bush, was of broader significance as it concerned non-US citizens. The Supreme Court, following a petition lodged on behalf of 12 Kuwaiti and two Australian detainees, decided that US courts 'have jurisdiction to consider challenges to the legality of the detention of foreign nationals captured abroad in connection with hostilities and incarcerated at Guantanamo Bay'. In response, the Pentagon set up combatant status review panels at Guantanamo, but after hearing more than 500 cases the panels recommended release for only two detainees.

The longstanding plan for military tribunals at Guantanamo to try detainees for offences also ran into trouble. On 8 November 2004, in Hamdan v. Rumsfeld, a US district judge in Washington DC ruled that they flouted the constitution and improperly ignored provisions of the Geneva Conventions. The military commission process was blocked pending consideration by higher courts. The sense of confusion and indirection was reinforced when, on 20 and 31 January 2005, in two separate cases in the same district court involving different groups of Guantanamo detainees, one US federal judge stated that although they could file petitions in his court, he could not issue a writ of habeas corpus; while in the second case, another judge in the same court ruled that the detainees had the right to challenge their status, and also the military tribunal procedures, which were ruled to be unconstitutional.

In the UK, the courts became involved in cases arising from the coalition role in Iraq and in the 'war on terror'. In addition to several court-martials of troops accused of abuses, the High Court ruled on 15 December 2004 that in certain circumstances British troops on foreign operations are bound by the Human Rights Act, which incorporates provisions of the European Convention on Human Rights. It accepted this position in respect of a case involving mistreatment (leading to death) of an individual who had been in custody in Iraq, and thus paved the way for certain allegations of wrongdoing by British soldiers to be independently investigated. It rejected five similar applications that related to combat situations, in which considerations of military necessity would loom larger. Then on 16 December, in a major blow to the government's anti-terror measures, the Appeal Judges of the House of Lords ruled that detaining foreign terrorist suspects without trial was a violation of human-rights laws. Concern was not limited to treatment of prisoners in the hands of the United States and Britain, but also extended to those prisoners handed over for detention and interrogation in states not necessarily bound by the same legal norms regarding treatment of detainees. This secret 'rendition' of detainees to third states, and the subsequent use of confessions obtained from them, was a disturbing aspect of the 'war on terror'.

Whether or not illegal ill-treatment extracted more useful information than could have been gained by time-proven, professional and legal interrogation techniques may be uncertain. The Schlesinger Report suggests that it may have done so in a few cases at Guantanamo, but equally it may have led to the drying up of other sources, especially in Iraq. In many cases the ill-treatment had little or no connection with inter-rogation; and where it did, there was the high risk of false confessions. The torture of detainees, irrespective of how they are classified or how operationally useful it may be, is a violation of the prohibition of torture in both international law and the domestic law of states. Such illegal practices made the achievement of any broad international coalition in Iraq even more difficult than it was already, and strengthened the cause of the insurgents. Another effect was to contribute to the process whereby the normal non-military courts in the United States and Britain began to assert the principle that certain basic norms of their countries' legal systems must apply even to actions taken by their armed forces overseas, and to foreign detainees.

International agreement on measures to combat terrorism

Since 2001 there has been some progress in securing international agreement on specific measures to combat terrorism, and also on the related problem of supply of certain weapons-related material to states of concern. Some of these measures centred on the UN. The UN Security Council partially recovered from its March 2003 nadir over Iraq, and helped in the maintenance of a significant degree of international consensus in addressing terrorism. The Council's Counter-Terrorism Committee (CTC), which had been established in the wake of 11 September, continued to monitor and assist implementation of the Council's main resolutions on terrorism, especially the comprehensive provisions of Resolution 1373 of 28 September 2001. In 2004 it established the Counter-Terrorism Executive Directorate (CTED), intended to assist the capacity-building of states, and to enable the UN 'to exercise leader-ship in the global campaign against terrorism'. Yet any verdict on the work of the CTC must take into account the evident slowing of momentum of states in certain key matters. The body needs to confront the question of whether there is, as to the status of battlefield detainees, a genuine vacuum in international law between pris-oner of war and criminal status, and if so to try to generate a consensus on filling it. Moreover, the way in which entities and individuals were added to the Security Council's terrorist list raised concerns. Operationally, as the High-Level Panel report ruefully noted, while in the three months after 11 September 2001 $112 million in alleged terrorist funds were frozen, only $24m were frozen in the two years that followed. The Organisation for Economic Cooperation and Development played as important a part as the UN in attempts to control money laundering.

The UN Security Council itself maintained a strong record of condemning terrorist acts. This record was marred by one extraordinary failure. On the day of the Madrid bombing, 11 March 2004, the Council passed a resolution in which it stated that it 'condemns in the strongest terms the bomb attacks in Madrid, Spain, perpetrated by the terrorist group ETA on 11 March 2004'. It was obvious at the time, and confirmed later, that a likely source of the bombing was an Islamic extremist group. There was no need to identify the perpetrators of the bombing in a resolution: the Security Council had not done this immediately after the 11 September attack, nor in numerous other resolutions on terrorist incidents. The fact that it did so on this occasion – at the insistence of the Spanish government, which promptly paid the price of electoral defeat for its imprudence – was a collective failure of major states to make proper and judicious use of international institutions.

The terrorist threat highlighted the importance of international initiatives to limit the spread of nuclear, biological and chemical weapons. The US-led PSI had its genesis in US frustration at the situation in December 2002 when a Spanish frigate, operating in connection with *Operation Enduring Freedom* in Afghanistan, intercepted the *So San*, a merchant vessel headed for Yemen carrying North Korean *Scud* missiles. Subsequently, after the US administration concluded that there was no strong basis in existing international law for confiscating the missiles, the ship was released. The United States subsequently launched the PSI, which is based on a non-binding 'Statement of Interdiction Principles' released on 4 September 2003, including measures for halting that transfer of nuclear, biological and chemical weapons and delivery systems to 'states and non-state actors of proliferation concern'. In essence, this regime encourages its participants to control certain goods, in a manner similar to the rights to control contraband claimed by belligerent states in numerous past wars – and indeed by the United States in the 1962 Cuban missile crisis. Current activities focus on actions within the territorial waters of participating states, although reference is sometimes made to actions in conformity with international law that might be taken on the high seas. Over 60 states are involved in various ways in this multilateral process, but certain key states, including China, remain outside. One concern of critics is that the United States might secure unwarranted power to act as a global policeman. Supporters of the process argue that the October 2003 interdiction of nuclear enrichment components under PSI aegis may have helped to tilt Libya towards its December 2003 decision to move out of isolation and into a more cooperative relation with the international community. This much-vaunted US initiative faces severe difficulties, especially in developing a robust legal basis for seizure of proliferation-related materials in international waters, in building up a system of pooled intelligence to enable a policing system to work, and in addressing transfers by air, which are the most obvious form of evasion of the proposed regime.

Law and institutions in the 'war on terror'

How have law and legal institutions performed in, and adapted to, the events of the 'war on terror'? And how well or badly have decision-makers crafted their policies in relation to them? The simple answer is that events have confirmed law's key role as a factor in policy-making: any version of 'realism' predicated on the belief that key legal provisions and institutions can be ignored is liable to run into serious trouble. What is more difficult to establish is the extent to which law and legal institutions have succeeded in pointing the way to effective action, or in moderating the activities of states and indeed their non-state adversaries.

The year ended with a strengthened sense that – whatever the pressures of the 'war on terror', of the need to control nuclear proliferation, and of demands for humanitarian intervention – no generally agreed paradigm was emerging to replace the foundational rule of the existing international legal order that individual states remain bound by the non-intervention norm. As a result, debate on the legitimacy of interventions with anti-terrorist or anti-proliferation purposes appears to be pursuing a path comparable to the debate of a few years earlier about humanitarian intervention. States seem to accept in principle some stretching of the concept of self-defence, especially in face of absolutely imminent attack, but they will not agree to a formula to define the circumstances in which intervention without Security Council authorisation is permissible. Rather, those intervening will have the burden of knowing that they may be accused of violating international norms against intervention. At times the world may accept interventionist acts where they are clearly well tailored to achieving an urgent and important objective, but an intervention that is poorly conceived or executed can expect harsh condemnation. The PSI appeared to be one modest but promising route for securing a modicum of agreement extending the range of circumstances in which force might legitimately be used.

Several UN-related international bodies demonstrated certain weaknesses when faced with issues related to the 'war on terror'. This was particularly the case as regards the pronouncement of international bodies on the law relating to the resort to force – the jus ad bellum. Here, the problem was not necessarily in the conclusions that were ultimately reached – the illegality of the wall in Israeli-occupied territories, or of the invasion of Iraq – but in serious omissions in the argument. There were weaknesses in what was said about the right of self-defence (and also about the law on occupations) in the ICJ's Advisory Opinion on the wall. These are likely to reinforce concerns that the ICJ is not as rigorous, and not as knowledgeable about security issues, as it should be. Similarly, the impact of Kofi Annan's remarks in September 2004 on the illegality of the US-led intervention in Iraq was reduced by his failure to demonstrate an understanding of the case for intervention than had been made by the United States and Britain. On the question of the legitimacy of resort to force by states, there were also some omissions in the generally well-considered report of the UN High-Level Panel. Concerned primarily with action in a Security Council framework, the panel said disappointingly little about the circumstances in which action outside a framework of Security Council authority (but sometimes in support of UN-proclaimed purposes) may be justified. Perhaps, in light of events in Iraq, 2004 was not a good year in which to address the topic of the legitimacy of interventions not mandated by the UN.

Some non-UN international bodies were exposed to criticism in the ongoing 'war on terror'. For example, the ICRC was at times faulted for excessive inflexibility in its interpretation of the law. While its work in the field has been impressive, and its insistence on the observance of basic norms justified, its legal pronouncements have arguably shown insufficient willingness to recognise the possible implications of the category of 'unprivileged belligerents'. The Schlesinger Report on US detention operations concluded that 'the ICRC, no less than the Defense Department, needs to adapt itself to the new realities of conflict'. Among the many criticisms it made of ICRC, it noted the way in which the ICRC pressed the United States to observe certain provisions of 1977 Geneva Protocol I despite the fact that the United States had declined to become a party precisely on the grounds that the protocol did not address adequately the problem of terrorism.

The well-known difficulties in applying the laws of war to terrorist and counter-terrorist activities remain. Most terrorists do not conform to the well-known requirements for the status of lawful belligerent, entitled to full prisoner-of-war status. Further, few states could accept application of the law if it meant that all terrorists were deemed to be legitimate belligerents on a par with the regular uniformed forces of a government. However, application of the law does not require acceptance of either of these doubtful propositions. Rather, it means recognition that, even in a war against ruthless terrorists, the observance of certain restraints may be legally obligatory and politically desirable – especially as regards treatment of detainees. The United States may or may not have been technically correct in its conclusion that many of those detained, at least outside Iraq, may not qualify for prisoner of war status. Irrespective of that issue, however, it has lost many opportunities to demonstrate that strong legal standards do apply to their treatment, and it has been unprofessional in its management of the prisoner regime. The result has been a continuous and damaging stream of adverse publicity, which has impacted on the question – in theory separate – of the legitimacy of the 'war on terror' itself. Confidence in these matters, once lost, is hard to regain.

There is a paradox at the heart of the 'war on terror' – a paradox that was already evident in the 1980s, at the time of the Iran–Contra scandal and the row over the US mining of Nicaraguan waters. The situation is one in which the same body of law applies, in theory, more or less equally to all states – but in which the United States sees itself as having exceptional responsibilities. This is a problem for the United States as well as for the rest of the world. The United States has affirmed its belief in unilateral action, yet it recognises that the war cannot be won without major multilateral support, including through the UN. It believes that in its long-term struggle against a ruthless adversary, it should not be excessively hampered by international law, yet it relies heavily on law for the wide range of measures that states are asked to take regarding such matters as terrorist money laundering. This paradox is linked to another: the international strategic situation is one which is neither war nor peace, so the application of a body of international law, much of which assumes a clear distinction between war and peace, is necessarily complex. While these paradoxes are not such as can be resolved by any simple formula, prudent policymaking can reduce them to manageable proportions.

There was some limited progress in 2004 and early 2005, both in debates on intervention and in the application of legal rules to the detention and interrogation of internees. In particular, the US government recognised, albeit belatedly and incompletely, the importance of operating within a framework of international institutions and law. However, the array of problems has not been handled with skill. There has been strategic, moral and legal muddle and lassitude. As a result, opportunities for consolidating the global campaign against terrorism have been missed. The coalition leaders have yet to absorb fully the pre-eminent lesson of the 'war on terror': that effective leadership of a complex and multi-faceted international campaign requires both a high level of professional competence and a demonstrable respect for the rules of domestic and international law.

If coalition leaders need to raise their performance, so too do international legal institutions. UN bodies, the ICJ and the ICRC would do well not to be inhibited by the prospect of controversy, and to confront burningly relevant issues such as the breadth and elasticity of the right of self-defence and the status of detainees who are not part of a state's armed forces. The fact that there have been such acute controversies over the legality of recent actions virtually guarantees that many governments will attach great weight to well-thought-out pronouncements of international bodies. Indeed, the legal controversies presented by current strategic circumstances hold out more, not less, hope for enhancing the authority of international law – provided international legal institutions, as well as governments, step up to the plate.

Challenges of US Intelligence Reform

And it follows, as the day the night, that if there is a serious, or perceived, intelligence failure there will be a cry for reform. The archetype for this truism was the reaction to the shock of the Japanese attack on Pearl Harbor on 7 December 1941. Although there had been enough 'signals in the noise' to have clearly indicated that an attack was on its way – even if pinpointing the target would have been very difficult – the mechanisms for assuring that the vital information was quickly assembled and disseminated were lacking. A compete overhaul of the national security apparatus, including the creation of the Central Intelligence Agency (CIA), was the necessary, and for many decades effective, answer. By the time the reconstruction was completed, the Second World War had ended; and the perceived enemy had shifted from the wartime Axis to the Soviet Union and its acolytes. With adjustments, such as the creation of the National Security Agency (NSA) for signals intelligence and the establishment of the recently renamed National Geospatial Intelligence Agency (NGA) for the analysis of imagery intelligence, the basic structure served reasonably well for some 50 years.

While the structure has been enduring, the intelligence community, and particularly the CIA, has come under attack on a number of occasions, either for what were perceived as failures to inform Congress of various covert actions, including efforts to assassinate Fidel Castro, or intelligence blunders, such as the failure to foresee the Soviet invasion of Czechoslovakia in 1968. A more recent effort at change came in 1995–96, when President Clinton set up a commission headed by former Secretary of Defense Les Aspin to review what was perceived to be an intelligence failure regarding the debacle in Somalia in 1993, when clan-based militiamen killed 18 American soldiers and dragged their bodies through the dusty streets in triumph –scenes that were played over and over on television throughout the world. Forced by the public and congressional outcry that followed to find the official responsible, Clinton had made Aspin, then defense secretary, the scapegoat. This did not assuage those who were demanding to know why the CIA had not been able to warn of the surprisingly powerful arms available to the Somali militia. Although he was not eager to set up a commission, Clinton decided that it would quiet the uproar.

Aspin was well suited for the task. A one-time member of the House of Representatives, he combined a keen intelligence (every biography notes that he was a summa cum laude Harvard graduate) with a long-standing interest in intelligence matters. But that created a problem. Many members of Congress feared that the disdain for the CIA that he had manifested while a member of one of the committees in the 1970s examining CIA missteps would lead him to take on the position recently espoused by Senator Daniel Moynihan: abolish the agency entirely. Leaders of the Senate, particularly Senator John Warner of Virginia, were initially against even the establishment of this commission, but decided that it could be turned to an examination of a far more serious aberration that had just come to light. Aldrich Ames, a senior CIA officer involved with intelligence efforts to penetrate the Soviet Union, had been uncovered as a Soviet (and then Russian) spy for more than ten years. Warner manoeuvred his way onto the commission as one of its ranking members. He had a dual mission in mind: to block any significant upheaval at the CIA while at the same time uncovering how Ames could have remained an unsuspected spy, feeding the Soviet and Russian intelligence operations with the names and modus operandi of US agents thus sent to certain death.

There was therefore serious dysfunction taking hold of the commission process. The president who had established the commission had only a minimal interest in intelligence matters and no ideas of his own about restructuring the community. He had acted primarily to quiet louder and louder demands that something be done. The commission was split between the chairman and his staff, who wanted to bring about significant change, and senators whose interest lay elsewhere and who were against such change. A further impediment was the unexpected death of Les Aspin from a cerebral haemorrhage; he was replaced by Harold Brown, another former defense secretary, who perhaps did not have the same drive to restructure the intelligence apparatus that had motivated Les Aspin. Given these built-in impediments the outcome was almost foreordained: the major change was a recommendation that the overall intelligence budget, without any details as to how it was allocated, be made public. This was accepted by all and in 1996 it was duly published.

The inevitable result of the terrorist attack on the Pentagon and the World Trade Center on 11 September 2001 was an almost unified view that there had been a massive intelligence failure and that something must be done about it. While it is true that none of the many US intelligence agencies pinpointed the exact date that the attack was to take place, the precise target of the attack, or the particular mechanism that the terrorists used, it is not fully accurate to see this as a simple intelligence failure. There had indeed been a failure, but it included administrators at many levels of the government, in many agencies, including the top-most leaders at the Department of Defense and the White House. They had failed to act on the many warnings that they had been given; even though these warnings were not exact they were sufficient to have made preventive action sensible. Instead, no action was taken. For example, the Federal Aviation Administration received over 100 warnings of possible terrorist attacks on the United States, including 52 which mentioned al-Qaeda or Osama bin Laden specifically, and many of which pinpointed the dangers of aircraft hijacking and possible bombings. It had done nothing to provide security for aircraft, nor had it even raised an alarm. Nevertheless, the overwhelming perception that this was purely an intelligence failure was what counted and it was strong enough among the populace and in the Congress to gradually override President Bush's initial reluctance to establish a commission to review what had gone wrong and what needed to be done to ensure that it would not happen again.

More than a year after the attack, the National Commission on Terrorist Attacks Upon The United States (henceforth the 9/11 Commission) was created. From its earliest days it was clear that this was going to be a different kind of commission than the many that had preceded it. The president first recommended Henry Kissinger as chairman, but in the face of widespread criticism that he was too politically tainted to give any perception of objectivity, Kissinger removed his own name from consideration. A number of other notable figures were approached, but turned down the post, before the president finally settled on Thomas Kean, president of Drew University and a former Republican governor of New Jersey, as chairman, supported by Lee Hamilton, for 34 years Democratic representative from Indiana and now director of the Woodrow Wilson International Center for Scholars, as vice-chairman. The bipartisan nature of the commission was continued by the choice of eight supporting members, four Republicans and four Democrats, all with government or legislative experience. Despite their varied political and career backgrounds all ten members were determined early in the proceedings to act in unison and to produce a report whose recommendations bore the stamp of the commission as a whole. There were no cross-purposes involved. The commission also was favoured with the wholehearted support of the Steering Committee of the Families of the Victims of 9/11, which automatically created a wellspring of sympathy from the public and thus assured a powerful impetus for change.

The 9/11 Commission proposes...

The salient missteps identified by the 9/11 Commission in the chain of events leading up to the attacks involved the inability of US agencies to act on time or in coordination with one another, and, especially, to communicate vital information to the NSC, which is responsible for coordinating and implementing American foreign and security policy. This kind of dysfunction stemmed essentially from statutory barriers separating foreign intelligence operations from domestic law-enforcement activity, the inefficiency of several agencies and, with respect to the Federal Bureau of Investigation (FBI), a law-enforcement culture attuned to investigating crimes but unsuited to preventing mass-casualty terrorism. The consequence was the NSC's inability to generate an accurate terrorist threat picture in summer 2001.

During the course of its 20 months of existence, the commission read 2.5m pages of documents, interviewed more than 1,200 individuals in ten countries, held 19 open hearings with 160 public witnesses, and concluded it all with a report published on 2 July 2004 that numbered over 500 pages. The report is a rich, exhaustive review of the background to the 9/11 attacks, an assessment of what took place, and an examination of the many bungles, on the part of the intelligence community and of various parts of the administration, that should not have happened. As Chairman Kean observed to the press, but the report does not, the attacks were eminently preventable. In the last two chapters, the commission sets forth a series of recommendations, both in suggested foreign policy directions and for restructuring the intelligence components of the national security apparatus. The latter fall essentially in five areas: establishing a National Counterterrorism Center; creating the post of national intelligence director; setting up a network-based information-sharing system; consolidating congressional oversight committees; and strengthening FBI and homeland intelligence structures.

National Counterterrorism Center (NCTC). The commission concluded that the existing counter-terrorism efforts suffered by having no one in charge of either intelligence analysis or useful actions that could flow from that analysis. The large number of units which had grown up in the government since 9/11 – including the Terrorist Threat Integration Center (TTIC), based at CIA headquarters; the CIA's own Counterterrorism Center; one in the Defense Intelligence Agency (DIA), another in the Department of Homeland Security (DHS); and one soon to be established at the Federal Bureau of Investigation (FBI) – failed to coordinate their activities, could not engage in joint planning, and sucked assets from the limited pool of experts in the field. The commission thus recommended the creation of the NCTC, built upon the structure of the TTIC, but unlike that body combining both joint operational planning and joint strategic intelligence functions. It would be staffed by personnel drawn from the various agencies. Its head would be appointed by the president, be the equivalent of the deputy head of a cabinet department, and report to the proposed National Intelligence Director.

National intelligence director (NID). Such a position was hardly a new idea. President Truman in 1946, when setting up the Central Intelligence Group, had created the position of director of central intelligence (DCI) to manage overall intelligence functions within the government. When the CIA was established under the National Security Act of 1947 the DCI was also given the position of director of the CIA. Every occupant of the position since then has tended to concentrate most of his effort on leading the CIA, at least partially because as DCI he was in theory responsible for the intelligence community's performance but did not have the statutory power to carry out that responsibility. He did not control the overall intelligence budget, he could not hire or fire any personnel outside of the CIA, he could not set standards for other agencies. He could make recommendations on all these matters, but the final decisions were taken within the individual agencies. Over the years, new technical intelligence functions had developed for signal and image intelligence. The national intelligence agencies established to deal with these targets, the National Security Agency (NSA), the National Reconnaissance Office (NRO) and the NGA had all migrated to the Department of Defense (DoD). When Congress appropriated the yearly budget for intelligence, which was hidden within the DoD budget to keep the amounts for intelligence secret, the money went to the DoD, which transferred CIA's money to its director, but disbursed the national agencies money itself. Thus the DoD had ended up controlling some 80% of the overall intelligence budget, making it impossible for the DCI to fulfil his responsibilities. The commission therefore recommended replacing the DCI with a national intelligence director with 'two main areas of responsibility: (1) to oversee national intelligence centers on specific subjects of interest across the US government and (2) to manage the national intelligence program and oversee the agencies that contribute to it'. To ensure that he would be in a position to do this the NID should have control of the budgets for each intelligence agency, and have a nominating and approval function with regard to the heads of national intelligence units. To emphasise his importance, the commission recommended that the NID be housed in the White House.

Information sharing. The 9/11 Commission was struck by the prevalence of what in intelligence jargon is called 'stovepiping': the bureaucratic phenomenon whereby each agency develops its own databases, and then shares them vertically according to the 'need to know' principle. The smoke only goes up the chimney. The commission recommended that a better balance between security and shared knowledge be found. Information should be shared horizontally, across new networks that overarch individual agencies. A model would be the decentralised network that spurs much of the information revolution. 'The president should lead a government-wide effort to bring the major national security institutions into the information revolution. He should coordinate the resolution of the legal, policy, and technical issues across agencies to create a "trusted information network".'

Strengthening congressional oversight. The commission's assessment of the current congressional oversight mechanism was typically blunt: it was 'dysfunctional'. There were too many committees of various stripes with a finger in the pot. None of them had overall authority for the budget or for oversight. Recognising that there was probably nothing more difficult in the US government structure than asking congressional committees to give up some aspect of their power, the commission nevertheless recommended that Congress form either a joint committee along the lines of the Joint Committee on Atomic Energy or set up a single committee in each house of Congress, combining authorising and appropriating authority. With regard to homeland security, the commission noted that leaders of the DHS appear before 88 committees and subcommittees of Congress. In the words of one expert witness, 'this is perhaps the single largest obstacle impeding the department's successful development'. Congress, said the commission, should create a single principal point of oversight and review for homeland security – a permanent standing committee in the House and one in the Senate with non-partisan staffs.

The FBI and homeland security. Although it expressed considerable misgivings with regard to past FBI failures in dealing with terrorists and terrorism in the United States, the commission noted that the agency had made a number of changes, which if continued, would solve many of its problems. In effect, then, its recommendation concerning the FBI was to make the changes permanent, to establish within the FBI 'a specialized and integrated national security workforce ... recruited, trained, rewarded and retained to ensure the development of an institutional culture imbued with a deep expertise in intelligence and national security'. Its recommendations for the DHS were, in effect, to do more, to do it quicker, and to do it better.

And Congress disposes...

President Bush may have hoped to be able to sidestep the wide-ranging recommendations of the 9/11 Commission by warmly welcoming them in public while quietly filing them away in private. This was the historical fate of most reports of this kind but this commission had different ideas. Its handling of the public relations aftermath of its report forced the president's hand. The commission had arranged to have its report published as an inexpensive paperback by W. W. Norton & Co.; then, instead of folding its tent and dispersing back to individual jobs, the commission reconstituted itself as a publicity body dedicated to pushing for the acceptance of its 42 recommendations. Key to its efforts was the support it received from the families of the victims of the 9/11 attack, support which proved crucial to its efforts. It also benefited by the fact that 2004 was an election year. The Democratic Party candidate, John Kerry, proclaimed that as one of his first acts in office, if elected, he would send to Congress a bill that incorporated all of the commission's recommendations. The Democratic Party, sensing public backing for this position, threw its weight behind immediate action as well. The pressure on the president, and the Republicans in control of both houses of Congress, ratcheted up swiftly. Bipartisan bills to reorganise the intelligence community along the lines recommended by the 9/11 Commission were presented to both Senate and the House. There was basic agreement on most questions, with only the vexing question of the amount of budgetary and personnel power to accompany the DNI's increasing responsibilities.

At first, Bush hedged his position suggesting that while establishing the office of a national intelligence director might be a valuable option, he did not think it was necessary to give that office control over the overall intelligence budget or over the selection of key personnel of other intelligence units. In the wake of the ensuing outcry of protest, the president retreated to a more comfortable position: he would leave the decision in the hands of Congress and be prepared to sign into law whatever the Congress in its wisdom would decide.

The burden of opposing the investment of the DNI with the complete authority recommended by the commission fell to the DoD and its supporters in the House of Representatives, particularly Secretary of Defense Donald Rumsfeld, Chairman of the Joint Chiefs of Staff Richard Meyers, and Chairman of the House Armed Services Committee Dennis Hunter of California. In testimony in congressional hearings, appearances on TV talk shows, and speeches around the country, Rumsfeld and Meyers vehemently opposed the loss of budget control by the Pentagon, arguing that it would adversely affect the ability of the armed forces to carry out their duties in time of war. The Senate nevertheless passed a bill that closely followed the advice of the commission. Hunter's adamant opposition to a similar outcome led to a House bill that created a Director of National Intelligence but did not provide him the control that would make him any more effective that the DCI had been in the past. The compromise position in the final reconciled bill on the question of the budget is, as would be expected, ambiguous: in place of the Senate version, which said the DNI would 'determine' the annual budget, he is now responsible for 'developing' a consolidated budget for the overall National Intelligence Program, and the bill 'permits' his 'participation' in formulating budgets for tactical and other intelligence. In another example of legislative legerdemain, the bill proclaims that nothing in it will abrogate the statutory authority of other heads of cabinet departments. Both CIA and the Secretary of Defense retain huge statutory authority over intelligence gathering and analysis. Whether they retain and can exercise this authority will be determined by the turf battles that are certain to arise in coming years and will depend heavily on how effectively the DNI fights his corner and what support he gets from the ultimate decider, the president.

The 9/11 Commission did not get everything it wanted, but the final bill tracks its recommendations for restructuring the intelligence community closely. Besides the question of the budget control there are a few key differences. To demonstrate the closeness that it wanted to see develop between the president and the DNI the commission had recommended that the DNI be housed in the White House; Congress, however, preferred to emphasise a degree of independence for the DNI and the bill explicitly forbids the DNI from occupying an office in the White House. Congress also did not do anything to reorganise its own competing committees and subcommittees. But the reforming architecture that the commission had envisioned for the intelligence community had survived remarkably well. The president signed the bill into law on 17 December 2004.

Cure or chimera?

When the president signed the bill into law he called it 'the most dramatic reform of our nation's intelligence capabilities since President Harry S. Truman signed the National Security Act of 1947'. This characterisation was essentially correct, but his subsequent remarks – noting that the bill ensured the integration of better intelligence – were open to doubt. In a couple of throw-away sentences, the 9/11 Commission report demonstrated that it recognised the limitations of what it was recommending: 'We recommend significant changes in the organisation of government. We know that the quality of the people is more important than the quality of the wiring diagram ... Good people can overcome bad structure. They should not have to.' What the authors of the report did not bother to note is that, just as obviously, bad people can make a hash of good structure.

Well before 9/11, there was a bureaucratic mechanism in place for gathering intelligence at the appropriate level in the form of the Counterterrorism and Security

Group (CSG), which had been enshrined by presidential directive as the government's counter-terrorism crisis-management nerve centre at the National Security Council (NSC). As chairman of the CSG, Deputy National Security Advisor Richard Clarke made breaking down inter-agency anxieties about sharing information a priority but had not been completely successful. The problem before 9/11, then, was not so much the absence of a top-level clearinghouse for pooling intelligence on terrorist threats from multiple agencies. Rather, the primary trouble was that key officials in the individual agencies themselves did not rate intelligence that turned out to be important as sufficiently probative to filter up to the NSC.

Giving full budgetary and supervisory authority to the NID is supposed to ameliorate this problem. But this overhaul, in its implicit rejection of the putative competitive dimension of intelligence judgements, could end up over-centralising the process of generating polished intelligence. The NID would have greater responsibility than the current DCI for the finished intelligence product that informs the NSC's coordination of foreign policy and, ultimately, the president's policy decisions. There is an understandable temptation to establish a single arbiter of what is important among several streams or categories of intelligence. But the statutory concentration of authority in one person could institutionalise the very capacity for politically skewing 'actionable' intelligence that many have accused former DCI George Tenet and other high-level officials of indulging with respect to the threats posed by Saddam Hussein's regime.

Shortly before the House version of the intelligence reform bill was introduced, Kissinger, with the support of a bipartisan group of former high-ranking officials, in testimony before the Senate Appropriations Committee cautioned Congress against taking 'irrevocable legislative action' prompted by a false sense of urgency that the election cycle might have created. Kissinger was generally concerned with creating another layer – in the form of the NID – between the president and existing intelligence institutions. His specific worries included:

- weakening the relationship between intelligence analysts and operations officers;
- potentially compromising democratic principles by institutionally melding domestic intelligence with foreign intelligence;
- suppressing competing views;
- blurring lines of authority between the NID and the NSC;
- the questionable advisability of folding tactical and operational military intelligence into a predominantly civilian multi-agency structure; and
- the inclination of the 9/11 Commission to ignore more incremental and less disruptive means of achieving reform through existing institutions, such as the DCI.

The White House raised similar objections to the Senate bill. Two of the most senior and influential senators on the Appropriations Committee – Chairman Ted Stevens, a Republican from Alaska, and ranking Democrat Robert Byrd of West Virginia – also counselled against quick pre-election action.

Thus, there remains considerable uncertainty and debate about whether the new structure is the right one to solve current intelligence problems. The commission had been concerned with the failures surrounding 9/11 and their recommendations had concentrated on creating better integration and sharing of information with regard to terrorist activities. In the years since 9/11, however, arguably more serious failures with regard to intelligence acquisition, analysis and its use had surfaced. The mistaken insistence on the existence of weapons of mass destruction (WMD) in Iraq, the inaccurate linking of Saddam Hussein with al-Qaeda and the 11 September attacks, and thus the need espoused by the Bush administration that this growing danger be removed led directly to the invasion of Iraq. If the intelligence had been more accurate, or even if it had raised more insistently the doubts that existed as to the accuracy of these positions, it is clear that the Senate would not have backed the administration's drive to war.

The leading members of the administration have consistently maintained that they merely accepted the views of the intelligence community, citing the now infamous National Intelligence Estimate (NIE) of 1 October 2002 as justification for their belief that Saddam Hussein possessed WMD. Although the CIA had expressed 'high confidence' that once US soldiers could range freely over Iraq they would quickly uncover stockpiles of chemical and biological weapons, facilities for the construction of atomic bombs and plans to develop more of both, more than a year's intensive searching turned up no WMD at all. The Senate Select Committee on Intelligence investigating this intelligence failure issued its first Report on the Intelligence Community's Prewar Intelligence Assessments on Iraq early in July 2004. The committee found that the CIA's assessment had exaggerated, stretched or misrepresented the evidence it was supposedly based on, and that some conflicting evidence was ignored. The errors all ran in one direction, in portraying Iraq, and its vicious ruler Saddam Hussein, as more dangerous than they really were. It should be no surprise that this is the direction that the key policymakers in the government thought the intelligence should be running. Not surprisingly, anonymous analysts and intelligence figures expressed strong feeling that they had felt under considerable pressure to provide evidence that would support a policy decision that had already been made. There is no clear evidence that this was the case, but critics point to the fact that Vice President Dick Cheney made a number of unprecedented visits to CIA's Langley headquarters, that Rumsfeld set up a new intelligence unit within the DoD under Douglas Feith, undersecretary of defense for policy, to ferret out information on Saddam and Iraq that other intelligence units were supposedly missing.

Much has been made of the so-called 'group-think' permeating the analytical areas of the intelligence community. Supposedly almost all analysts, working together, basing their thinking on similar fundamentals, could not see that what was going on around them differed from the accepted norm. In fact, there is considerable evidence, not least in the Senate committee report, that questions had been raised on all the basic points at issue. An oft-repeated claim was that the Iraqis were accumulating aluminium tubes that were intended for use in a centrifuge; the opinion expressed forcefully by the experts in the intelligence units of the Department of Energy and the Department of State that these tubes were wrong for centrifuge use, and that they resembled others Iraq had acquired for use in missiles, was dismissed and ignored by high-level members of the administration, including, on this issue particularly, then-National Security Advisor Condoleezza Rice. The weak evidence of some collusion between Saddam Hussein and al-Qaeda was shown to be wrong over and over again and was condemned outright by the 9/11 Commission. This did not stop Cheney from continuing to maintain that there was indeed such collusion, even after the president himself in 2004 had stated publicly that the evidence did not bear the weight of the accusation. There was indeed 'group-think' in the government in the run-up to the war again Saddam, but it could be found more easily and clearly within the high levels of the administration than in the lower levels of the intelligence community.

This record illustrates one of the enduring paradoxes of strategic intelligence. Intelligence analysis must take policy needs into consideration if it is to be relevant and useful. There is a very fine line, however, between being relevant and being overly supportive. There have been times when the head of intelligence and his analysts have tried to maintain a purely neutral attitude toward the existing policy; independent objectivity was the watchword. The result has inevitably been that their efforts and estimates were ignored by the president and his major foreign policy advisors. In such circumstances, the head of intelligence quickly went from being ignored to being replaced. Yet if the relationship between policy and intelligence becomes too close – if the leaders of the intelligence community, either because of ideological affinity or a failure to recognise when the line of engagement is being crossed, cross that line – the result will be falsified, dangerously inaccurate intelligence, however useful it may be in a political sense. The errors concerning WMD in Iraq, which produced an atmosphere buttressing inaccurate claims of the necessity to go to war, seem to have grown out of the latter trap. The characterisation of the Iraqi population as one panting to strew flowers in the path of American troops who would overthrow the vicious Saddam regime led to a failure to plan properly for the more probable reaction: a strewing of bombs in the path of American troops seen by many Iraqis as occupiers rather than liberators. No reorganisation, however drastic, will overcome this paradox. Only when the president and his advisors are prepared to allow intelligence occasionally to come up with bad news about their policies can there be both relevant and accurate appraisals.

When George Tenet resigned as DCI in July 2004 and was replaced by his experienced and respected Deputy Director John McLaughlin as acting director of the CIA, there was an opportunity to judge whether the president had recognised what had gone wrong and why. Many suggested that he hold off in naming a replacement until after the November 2004 presidential election; others stressed the necessity of finding someone non-political and with acknowledged independence. The president instead chose Porter Goss, Republican representative from Florida, who was then chairman of the House Permanent Select Committee on Intelligence. Though a former CIA operations officer, in his ten-year service on that committee Representative Goss had exuded a disdain for the CIA; he made it clear from the beginning of his tenure at the agency that he was under orders, with which he fully agreed, to take a massive broom, if not a meat-axe, to agency personnel and their methods of operation. He brought with him a number of Republican aides from Congress whom he placed in high positions in the agency. As one of his first acts, Goss issued a 'secret' memorandum, since leaked to the press, which laid out his rules of the road: 'We support the Administration in our work. As Agency employees we do not identify with, support or champion opposition to the Administration or its policies'. Deputy Director McLaughlin resigned. High-level resignations from both the Directorate of Operations and the Directorate of Intelligence, starting with the heads of both directorates, swiftly followed; and reports from former and current intelligence personnel circulated throughout Washington that Goss and his picked team were weeding out the 'dissenters'. Although the new director has not yet been tested, these are both disturbing indicators. It is vital that the intelligence that might lead the country into new military action be seen as untainted. It behoves Congress to scrutinise the intelligence upon which future military action might be based more closely than it had with regard to Iraq.

The need for such care was underscored by the publication, on 31 March 2005, of the report of the Commission on the Intelligence Capabilities of the US Regarding Weapons of Mass Destruction. This commission, under the joint leadership of Judge Lawrence Silberman, a Republican, and former Virginian Democratic Senator Charles Robb, had spent a year concentrating on the intelligence failures with regard to Iraq, and examining the intelligence efforts with regard to the nuclear programmes in Iran and Korea. Its conclusions about both were damning. On Iraq, it concluded, the intelligence community had been 'dead wrong', and with regard to nuclear threats it noted that 'across the board, the intelligence community knows disturbingly little about the nuclear programs of many of the world's most dangerous actors'. The commission made some 70 recommendations for change and reform of the intelligence community, many of them built upon the work of the 9/11 Commission. Even if all 70 were sound, it obviously would be many years before they could assure faultless intelligence. In the interim the intelligence which the administration cites to support its policies must be closely reviewed.

Reconstructing intelligence

With regard to the new intelligence structure, the second vital personnel test for the president was choosing the DNI. It took him two months to do so. He had not been dilatory; at least four strong candidates, including former CIA Director Robert Gates and former Senator Sam Nunn, had reportedly turned down an offer of the position. Their reasons had undoubtedly varied widely from age and family requirements to contentment with their present positions, but press reports centred on their reported reluctance to bear the heavy responsibilities of the position without concomitant strong budget and personnel control and an assurance of independence. In the end the president nominated Ambassador to Iraq John D. Negroponte as his choice for the DNI. Negroponte has been a stalwart civil servant for over 40 years, rising through State Department ranks to ambassadorial rank in a number of countries before leaving government service in 1997. President Bush convinced Negroponte to return as ambassador to the UN in early 2001; the Senate held up his confirmation for six months, however, because of discomfort over his role as ambassador in Honduras during the period when the United States was attempting to topple the government in neighbouring Nicaragua. Negroponte was accused by civil rights groups of overlooking, and perhaps overseeing, a CIA-backed death squad while also directing the secret arming of Contra rebels for attacks in Nicaragua. Negroponte's admirers dismiss these accusations and instead dwell on his brilliance and urbanity, noting that he carries out orders with quiet efficiency. They see him as a dedicated diplomat who does the bidding of whatever administration is in office – a quality friends see as loyalty and critics as amorality. When Negroponte moved from the UN to become ambassador to Iraq in June 2004, his confirmation hearings ran more smoothly. It seems probable that, despite continuing disquiet at his refusal to acknowledge the role he played in Honduras (in the face of overwhelming evidence to the contrary, he has said that 'to this day, I do not believe that death squads were operating in Honduras'), he will have little trouble gaining confirmation as DNI. If he does he will be trading a difficult and unpleasant job in Iraq, one he was reportedly very anxious to leave, for a daunting one in Washington.

The new DNI, in the first months at least, will be taking on three vital tasks. He will need immediately to begin filling in the structure of the Office of the DNI that Congress outlined, but left purposely vague so as to leave him flexibility. He must work out how he is to coordinate the work of CIA and DIA – a job complicated by the Pentagon's reported move to take over some of the CIA's human-intelligence collection, case-officer duties in foreign countries. The defense secretary is developing new units which are to be dispatched to collect human intelligence, using newly earned congressional authority to recruit foreign agents when it is helpful. There is a brewing conflict between the FBI and the CIA to adjudicate as well. The FBI wants to replace the CIA's role in recruiting US-based foreign officials to spy for the United States when they return to their homes. It is also trying to mimic the CIA's use of corporate contacts to gain information from overseas business travellers.

Second, the DNI must consider and advise on an overall budget for intelligence and how it is to be allocated among the 15 existing intelligence units. And in addition, as the president emphasised when he announced his nomination, he is to be the president's chief intelligence advisor, identifying threats to the nation and finding ways to thwart them. In this role, Bush announced, Negroponte would be 'my primary briefer' on a daily basis and would have regular access to the president. In effect, this erases the small distance that Congress tried to write into the position by ruling that the DNI could not occupy an office in the White House. Taken literally, the president's words assure that the DNI will be firmly in the policy loop. Whether this will help improve the quality of intelligence, or, as it has in the past, hinder it is as yet uncertain. What is certain is that no matter what structure is cemented into place the information that intelligence analysts receive will continue to be as ambiguous as ever. Good intelligence estimates will depend, as always, on good judgement, unfettered by preconceptions and ideological biases. Even under the best circumstances, however, surprise can never be ruled out. Unless this is recognised and acknowledged there will be no end to identifiable 'intelligence failures' and calls for new intelligence reform.

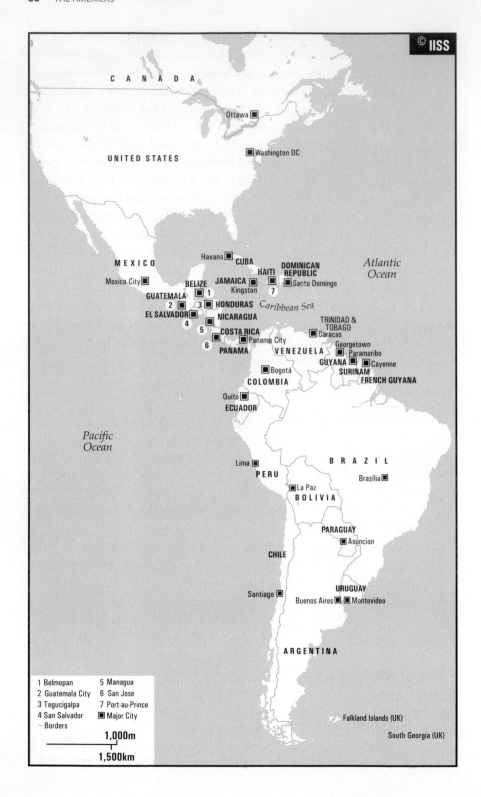

© IISS

C A N A D A

Ottawa ■

UNITED STATES

Washington DC ■

Atlantic Ocean

MEXICO

Havana ■ CUBA

DOMINICAN REPUBLIC

HAITI

Mexico City ■

BELIZE

JAMAICA ■

Santo Domingo ■

1

Kingston

7

GUATEMALA

2 ■ 3

HONDURAS

Caribbean Sea

EL SALVADOR

4

NICARAGUA

5

COSTA RICA

6

PANAMA

Panama City ■

TRINIDAD & TOBAGO

Caracas ■

Georgetown ■

VENEZUELA

Paramaribo ■

GUYANA ■

Cayenne ■

SURINAM

FRENCH GUYANA

Bogotá ■

COLOMBIA

Quito ■

ECUADOR

Pacific Ocean

B R A Z I L

Lima ■

PERU

Brasília ■

La Paz ■

BOLIVIA

PARAGUAY

Asuncion ■

CHILE

URUGUAY

Santiago ■

Buenos Aires ■ ■ Montevideo

A R G E N T I N A

Falkland Islands (UK)

South Georgia (UK)

1 Belmopan   5 Managua
2 Guatemala City   6 San Jose
3 Tegucigalpa   7 Port-au-Prince
4 San Salvador   ■ Major City
— Borders

1,000m

1,500km

The Americas

In his January 2005 State of the Union address, US President George W. Bush boldly declared that America's 'ultimate goal' was 'ending tyranny in our world'. This ambitious and idealistic proclamation took many of a more realist persuasion aback, and may have seemed too triumphal in light of the narrowness of Bush's victory over Senator John Kerry in the November 2004 presidential election and the president's rather low approval ratings. But it was consistent with the highly entrepreneurial foreign policy – which included the option of pre-emptive and preventive military intervention – that the United States brought to bear after 11 September 2001. Furthermore, although the 2004 election was perceived as one driven by foreign policy, Bush's main political battles during his second term were shaping up as domestic ones involving Social Security, taxes and judicial appointments. And in the context of developments in the Middle East and the Gulf – including unexpectedly successful Iraqi elections and the revival of the Israeli–Palestinian peace process after the death of Palestinian Authority President Yasser Arafat – optimism about the viability of US foreign policy seemed at least partially justified. In any case, subsequent European visits of Bush and US Secretary of State Condoleezza Rice suggested that the United States would listen harder to the concerns of allies and partners during Bush's second term than it did in his first, allaying fears that US policy would become more aggressive. Yet, from a hemispheric point of view, the United States was relatively inactive. While counter-insurgency and counter-narcotics operations in Colombia remained a major American military and political commitment, strategic preoccupations with proliferation and terrorism in other parts of the world continued to sideline pre-11 September priorities such as trade in the Western Hemisphere.

Andean security and stability did not enjoy a good year in 2004–05. Though it is unclear whether it was out of desperation or renewed strength, the Revolutionary

Armed Forces of Colombia (FARC) proved surprisingly resilient in the face of the best counter-insurgency efforts of the Colombian government and, in close financial and operational support, the United States. Populist Venezuelan President Hugo Chávez snatched victory from the jaws of defeat, re-consolidating power as an out-manoeuvred opposition faltered, and appeared to become more inclined to provoke neighbours like Colombia as well as the United States by way of troubling flirtations with the FARC and Cuba. Grassroots mobilisations – especially involving indig-enous Indian populations – spurred by the unwillingness or incapacity of central governments to effectively redistribute national wealth or otherwise improve the lot of the worst-off, threatened political stability in Bolivia, Ecuador and Peru. The respective 'wars' on terrorism and drugs also took a hit. In Bolivia, coca production rose to offset lower production in Colombia, and collusion between rural popula-tions, on one hand, and Peruvian terrorist movements and narco-traffickers, on the other, appeared to grow. In Peru – customarily among the most diligent enlis-tees in anti-drug and anti-terrorist efforts – coca growers gained popular sympathy against the government's failure to enrich the poor, which, along with coca transit revenues, helped revive the rurally based Shining Path guerrilla movement. While all five governments of the region demonstrated political dexterity in surviving various popular challenges, none, save arguably for Colombia, manifested the improvements in governance that would justify optimism about medium-term substantial advances in security and stability.

Outside the Andes, the most salient development in Latin America was the continuing emergence of Brazil as both a regional leader and a larger interna-tional presence. Brazilian President Luis Inacio da Silva's proactive foreign policy continued to promote South American assertiveness in foreign affairs. Overall, political movement to the left and away from the United States in Latin America was coming slowly and was subject to constraints. But it was unmistakably happening, which suggested that the United States would be prompted in the medium term to focus foreign policy more sharply on its own hemisphere.

The United States: Whose Nationalism?

That America has been scared since 11 September 2001 is generally accepted as the key to much of its recent politics, including the results of the 2004 elections. Yet there is a puzzle that such explanations do not quite solve. For it was precisely the voters in population centres of indisputably greater risk from mass-casualty terrorism – including, most obviously, the citizens of New York City – who overwhelmingly rejected the supposedly strong and reassuring leadership of President George W.

Bush. To suggest that these New Yorkers or Chicagoans or Angelinos are especially naive about the gravity of their danger or how best to face it is no more convincing than the idea that Republican voters in Biloxi, Mississippi or Butte, Montana suffer from paranoid fantasies of being targeted by terrorists. Something else is going on, at least as important as fear; it is a fervent nationalism that the felling of the Twin Towers aroused. The United States, by the standards of most other rich democracies, was a notably nationalistic country well before 11 September. Since those events, American nationalism has been both heightened and bifurcated along a fault line that has become familiar, persistent and worrying for US politics and society.

Bush won re-election by the smallest margin, in percentage popular-vote terms, of any incumbent president in US history. In electoral-vote terms, it was the narrowest re-election of any president except Woodrow Wilson. Yet the gains by his party in the Senate and House of Representatives reinforced the reality of one-party rule that the Republicans are enjoying for the first time since the Eisenhower administration. Again, these gains were not achieved anywhere al-Qaeda is partic-ularly likely to strike. Rather, the already thin ranks of Democratic Senators and Congressmen was further winnowed in what was – only a generation ago – the solidly Democratic South. This region can be considered the epicentre of American nationalism – something of a paradox since the spirit of southern patriotism was forged in an armed rebellion against national government. Although defeated on the battlefield in 1865, the rebellion continued for another century through various forms of sullen defiance until the concept of full democratic rights for the descend-ents of African slaves was finally imposed everywhere in the 1960s. It doesn't matter. The South wears its American nationalism on its sleeve, so ostentatiously that its regional dialects, evangelical Christianity, devotion to military service and tradition, and – it must be said – resistance to many aspects of modernity are often identified abroad and at home as the authentic American 'brand'.

The South is Bush's base. His increasingly right-wing Republican Party also holds on solidly to the thinly populated Rocky Mountain and adjacent prairie states but has lost its ability to compete in the urban Northeast and Pacific West. Bush essentially won his second term because he eeked out 60,000 more votes than John Kerry in Ohio and thus took four of the eight mixed urban-rural Midwestern states clustered around the Great Lakes and northern Mississippi River. In this light, it is worth remembering that Ronald Reagan won re-election in 1984 with the elec-toral votes of 49 out of 50 states. By this standard – indeed, by the standard of all presidential re-elections since Harry Truman's – the Republicans in 2004 did not present the profile of a national party. Their position would seem quite perilous – except for the fact that the Democrats' predicament was worse. On the eve of the election, John Kerry seemed to have the winning momentum, propelled by disil-lusionment with the Iraq war and an aroused centre-left's determination to reverse the Republicans' ambitious right-wing agenda. But if he was gong to lose the entire

South, the Democrats required the political equivalent of an inside straight across the rest of the battleground states. This would have been difficult in the best of circumstances and proved, on the day, impossible.

The Democrats: a party in search of a story

The character of nationalism in the American South has everything to do with the Democrats' continuing predicament, and not only because it is mathematically difficult to win the presidency without a few southern states. It is also because the distinctively Southern culture extends into parts of important Midwestern states, including Missouri and, notably, Ohio. Kerry tried to appeal to this culture by emphasising his early career as a federal prosecutor who 'sent people to jail for life' and with a publicised duck-hunting outing in Ohio. Unfortunately for Kerry, these pictures of him with a hunting rifle were juxtaposed in people's minds with a photograph from earlier in the campaign of Kerry in floral-printed swimming trunks, windsurfing off of Nantucket. The more serious part of the effort to speak the language of nationalism involved reminders of Kerry's war service in Vietnam, where he was wounded commanding US Navy Swift boats patrolling the Mekong Delta, earning a Silver Star for gallantry as well as a Purple Heart. The Democrats' nominating convention, held in Boston in late July, was the culminating setpiece of a long effort to emphasise this service. 'Send me', was the Vietnam-era refrain that former President Bill Clinton, in his early convention speech, attributed to Kerry, drawing the comparison with Bush's, Vice-President Dick Cheney's and (self-deprecatingly) Clinton's own successful efforts to avoid fighting in that war. On the convention's closing night, Kerry mounted a stage full of Vietnam veterans, saluted and proclaimed that he was 'reporting for duty'. Though the acceptance speech that followed was fine, this was a bit much, and some commentators found it patronising for Kerry to rely so much on mere biography in an attempt to overcome the Republicans' well-established political advantage on matters of national security.

The bigger problem was not that it was patronising, but that it was complicated. A clear majority of those Democratic Convention delegates who were old enough to have argued about Vietnam had opposed the war. There was nothing inherently disingenuous about those delegates' feeling lumps in their throats for a man who became famous as a leader of anti-war protesters, but had first fought honourably and bravely in that same war. But these highly nuanced feelings, and the Democrats' complex message about the current Iraq war, were no match for the certainties of the other side. Through the month of August Kerry's character was impugned through a series of advertisements – amplified in the echo chamber of cable television and Internet blogs – alleging that Kerry had besmirched his comrades by speaking of atrocities when he came home to protest, and then lied about his military service when he became a politician. The accusations against Kerry were baseless, while the atrocities in Vietnam were real. It didn't matter. The Republican Convention in late August featured a trophy Democrat, retiring Georgia Senator Zell Miller, railing against Kerry's '"yes-no-maybe" bowl of mush that can only encourage our enemy and confuse our friends'. Cheney, on the campaign trail, warned that voting for Kerry would increase the terrorist threat. Bush himself seized on Kerry's mildly subtle argument that the United States should try to pass a 'truth test' to persuade allies and other nations of the wisdom and justice of its cause when it went to war. In Bush's retelling, this amounted to America offering foreigners a 'veto' before it could defend itself.

Kerry and the Democrats also got tangled up in their position about the Iraq war. As the election campaign gathered momentum, the Sunni insurgency grew along with evidence of a botched occupation. In May 2004 had come the stunning pictures and story – revealed by CBS television and the investigative reporting of Seymour Hersh – of ritual humiliation and mistreatment of Iraqi prisoners by the American captors who had taken over Saddam Hussein's notorious Abu Ghraib prison. It emerged that many if not most of the prisoners there were innocent, swept up in the increasingly desperate sweeps by American forces who lacked the most basic intelligence about the sea of rage in which they now found themselves. Later it emerged that the 'interrogation techniques' at Abu Ghraib had 'migrated' – in the words of a commission appointed by the president – from the al-Qaeda holding pen at Guantanamo Bay, Cuba, and had been sanctioned (to a degree one could argue about) in legal analyses by the President's Counsel Alberto Gonzales. (Gonzales became Bush's attorney general in his second term.) It also emerged that – by the government's count as of March 2005 – at least 108 prisoners had died in US custody throughout the archipelago of extraterritorial prisons set up during the Afghanistan and Iraq wars. Secretary of State Colin Powell, himself a former general, had fiercely opposed this new jurisprudence of holding and handling terrorist suspects, as had many US military lawyers and other uniformed officers. The US Supreme Court in 2004 finally handed down some key rulings that, in the administration's sweeping assumption of the right to hold terrorist suspects indefinitely without trial, an impermissible line had been crossed.

A corresponding line had been crossed in Iraq where American soldiers, deployed and operating with the best of intentions, found themselves on the slippery slope of counter-insurgency, wherein the brutality of occupation – to an extent unavoidable in fighting unseen enemies and staving off of chaos – was the image that the insurgents hoped that the occupiers would present to Sunni civilians. What were Kerry and the Democrats to say about this? Although much of the Democratic rank-and-file may be viscerally anti-war, their party leadership is not. Even if the Iraq war was growing increasingly unpopular with the electorate, it was very much in Bush's political interest to present the war question as a starkly binary question: 'yes or no to the war' got translated in the reductionist media as 'hawkish or dovish against America's enemies'. The arguments the Democrats tried to put forward had little or nothing to do with the binary question. Kerry had voted in October 2002 in favour of a war-powers resolution to empower the president to face down Saddam in an act of coercive diplomacy to bring about his disarmament of weapons of mass destruction (WMD). Such coercive diplomacy entailed – if it had any strategic and moral force – the real possibility that war would result. But that did not answer the question of whether the war option was the wise one in the spring of 2003, with the UN Security Council opposed and the UN weapons inspectors on the ground starting to consider the possibility that Saddam might not be hiding any robust WMD programmes after all.

During the 2004 campaign to unseat President Bush, the Democrats were energised and united as never before in living memory. But the Democrats' foreign-policy dilemmas will beset them long after the memory of that intensity fades. Ironically, the shortest route to overcoming these dilemmas may require – as Richard Holbrooke and others have suggested – that President Bush's policies on Iraq turn into a success. This is not only because such success would return national focus to domestic issues – where Democrats are presumed to have the advantage – but because liberal internationalism, successful nation-building and the spread of democracy are the necessary ingredients of any successful Democratic foreign-policy vision. Some liberal analysts have called on the Democrats to set out a vision of 'nationalist liberalism' akin to the hawkish and anti-Communist liberalism of Franklin Roosevelt, Harry Truman, John F. Kennedy and Lyndon Johnson. The trick would be to articulate an American nationalist narrative that again tied liberal domestic values to the defence and even expansion of such values abroad. Of course, that is what Johnson was attempting when he combined landmark civil-rights legislation, the 'war on poverty' and the war in Vietnam. His failure in Vietnam debilitated the Democratic Party, damaged the prospects of nationalist liberalism and had baleful knock-on effects for domestic liberalism.

It will not be easy to resurrect. American voters appear to accord Republicans an automatic advantage on national security issues. Moreover, the Democrats as an opposition party do have an obligation to warn the nation about how its actions are perceived abroad. This obligation is in tension – if not directly at odds – with the imperatives of nationalist liberalism, which probably explains why Kerry said next to nothing during his campaign about the abuse of Iraqi prisoners in American custody. America seems well on its way to forgetting about Abu Ghraib. The rest of the world has not.

Republican narrowcast

If the Democratic vernacular of American nationalism seemed stilted, contradictory, hesitant and arguably inauthentic, Republican nationalism was strong, clear and narrow. Its clarity and muscularity probably won Bush re-election. But its narrowness makes a problematic base for either reconciling the world to America's exuberant power and readiness to use military force, or for governing at home. That Bush gave no quarter to self-doubt – regarding the repudiated basis for going to war in Iraq, the management of occupation and counter-insurgency afterwards or, indeed, whether a world leader should acquaint himself with outside views by reading newspapers – is the principal reason he seems unlikely ever to regain the commanding approval ratings of 90% that he enjoyed in the aftermath of the 11 September attacks. (In the months after the election, as in the months before, these ratings hovered near 50%.) Bush's outward confidence extended to an ambitious agenda for his second term, one that conceded nothing to the fact that one in two voters had chosen his opponent, and conceded nothing to the notion of putting ideological projects in abeyance for the sake of wartime unity. Indeed, Senate Republicans contemplated exploiting their majority to ban filibusters of judicial nominations to neutralise the Democrats' capacity to thwart the appointment of conservative judges – the so-called 'nuclear option'. More broadly, the president's chief political adviser, Karl Rove, is open in his ambition to achieve through this presidency a long-term realignment for a conservative governing majority, such as the Republicans enjoyed for three decades after the presidency of William McKinley at the turn of the twentieth century (this Republican run was interrupted once, for the presidency of Woodrow Wilson).

Confidence in such a realignment was probably bolstered by the fact that in the more closely divided Congress of Bush's first term, he had suffered no serious legislative defeat – suggesting that, whatever the polls said, political power and momentum were on the Republican side. He was, to be sure, unable to make his signature tax cuts permanent – they are set to expire between the end of 2005 and 2010 as a way to ameliorate (or hide) their long-term fiscal impact. But there is also no sign, even as federal deficits and debt balloon, that this or a foreseeable future Congress is going to let upper-income tax brackets return to their Clinton-era levels approaching 40%. So, in April 2005, it was undoubtedly dangerous to predict a major legislative defeat for the president. That said, there was no question but that, two months after his second inauguration, Bush's top domestic priority was in trouble.

The president was stuck in what looked like a losing battle over Social Security, America's universal public pensions programme. Bush claimed the programme was facing a crisis of bankruptcy some decades out, and he proposed (without laying out any specific plan) a system whereby younger workers could divert a portion of their payroll taxes to private pension accounts. Republicans argued that much of this money would be put into stocks, which – over the course of decades have a better record of growth than the government bonds that make up the Social Security trust fund. Democrats challenged the notion of a 'crisis' – although pension programmes the world over faced the demographic challenge of fewer children supporting more retirees, they argued that the US Social Security system had in fact been shored up considerably by a bipartisan reform package enacted under the Reagan administration. The measures required to further secure it were fairly obvious: raising the retirement age; increasing the income ceiling subject to payroll taxes; cutting some benefit. Yet even these reforms could wait, since long-term projections based on assumptions about demographics and the future growth of the economy were notoriously unreliable.

Moreover, there was a fundamental fallacy in the way Bush and his supporters were using these growth assumptions. The notion of future crisis depended on a relatively pessimistic projection of the growth of national income. Yet the notion that private accounts containing stocks would perform much better depended on considerably faster national-income growth. Bush's case also did not factor in the transition costs – conservatively estimated at a trillion dollars – of paying to support current retirees while much of Social Security's funding was being diverted to the new private accounts. Finally, the projected shortfall of the Social Security trust fund was in fact small compared to the overall budget shortfall tied to recent tax cuts, or the deficit for Medicare – old-age health care provision – that had been greatly exacerbated by prescriptions-drug benefit pushed through by the president and the Republican Congressional leadership in Bush's first term.

In the course of a nationwide tour to sell his vision, Bush in fact admitted that the introduction of private accounts would not 'solve' Social Security's funding problems. This concession served to confirm that the debate was about ideology rather than accounting. Conservative Republicans had opposed the introduction of social security from the time of its enactment as centrepiece of Franklin Roosevelt's 'New Deal'. Then it was seen, correctly, as socialist – though subsequent American and, indeed, Western European experience showed that elements of socialism do not inexorably lead to a socialist system. Now Social Security is seen as an obstacle to creating what Bush likes to call an 'ownership society' in which greater economic autonomy means enhanced economic and overall freedom. The Republicans consider increased personal risk to be a small price to pay for such freedom. In political terms, Rove and other Republican strategists envision the ownership society as machine to create more Republicans. The more people who have a stake in the stock market, Rove reasons, the more people who will be open to the party's doctrines of low taxes, less regulation and small government. Social Security, a massive – and massively popular – government programme to spread risk and, not incidentally, redistribute income, stands in the way.

The Democratic opponents of partial privatisation insist on maintaining Social Security's fundamental integrity as a programme of universal *insurance* against the unpredictable risks of living longer, suffering financial setback, not doing well in the stock market, or simply never making enough money to retire. They know that as the risk pool of any insurance programme starts to narrow, the individual premiums become costlier to the point of being unaffordable. (The premiums in this case are the payroll taxes, which are already highly regressive in their impact upon those who can least afford them.) The opponents also suspect that Rove's political reasoning is right on target. Social Security is politically sustainable precisely because it is a programme that benefits and reassures the middle class. As members of that middle class come to have a greater stake in the privatised system and a lower stake in Social Security, any promise to keep a residual retirement programme for the poor becomes politically shaky. Social Security would in essence become a welfare programme, and welfare programmes – by definition for the poor alone – are never popular, even if they are for the elderly poor.

As of April 2005, members of the American middle class were not enticed by the president's vision of ownership, freedom and risk. The more he toured the country to sell the vision, the less Americans – according to public opinion surveys – liked what they heard. The Democrats in Congress, although now a reduced minority, were in no mood to compromise, and their Republican colleagues were fearful of moving without bipartisan 'cover'. Senate Majority Leader Bill Frist intimated that passage of the new bill was unlikely in 2005, which meant carrying it into the even more unfavourable terrain of Congressional elections in 2006.

There were plenty of other issues to fight about. In March 2005, a 15-year tragedy concluded in a national farce. Terry Schiavo, a Florida woman, had lain unconscious in a 'persistent vegetative state' since the 1990, nourished through a feeding tube. Her husband, referring to general conversations in which he claimed that she expressed aversion to such measures, sought to have the tube removed so that she would die. Florida courts agreed that her prognosis was hopeless, and deferred to the husband as her legal guardian. Terri's parents and siblings opposed having the tube withdrawn. The case had already caused a tempest in Florida where the governor – President Bush's brother Jeb – had sought and failed to enact legislation to keep her alive. With the decision of Florida courts about to be implemented, the US Congress met in extraordinary session to pass an extraordinary bill giving federal courts jurisdiction over this – and only this – individual tragedy. Though it could have been sent to his ranch, President Bush made a show of flying back from Texas in the middle of the night to sign the legislation in Washington. The federal courts duly reviewed the case and concurred, all the way up to the Supreme Court, that Florida's judges had been correct in their interpretation of the law. The tube was removed and Terry Schiavo died.

This brief recitation cannot begin to convey the fierce emotions, television circus, rhetorical bashing of judges and – perhaps more creditably – religious and philosophical struggle that the case aroused. Bush, Frist and House Majority Leader Tom Delay were aligning themselves very publicly with an alliance of evangelical Protestants and conservative Catholics dedicated to the proposition that the protection of innocent human life was an absolute imperative – even if that human life consisted of a few fertilised cells or a woman whose brain was inert. In one of those coincidences of history, the campaign to save Terry Schiavo coincided with the death of Pope John Paul II, whose papacy had been dedicated to the same absolutism.

Americans in general were not convinced. Just as they generally favour abortion rights, an overwhelming majority believe that such difficult decisions about prolonging life and accepting death should have been left to the husband and the courts. Politically, the Republican stance looked as though it had backfired. But the vehemence of pro-life crusaders outside Terry Schiavo's deathbed could leave no one in doubt: this American struggle over the boundaries of life, the proper use of life science (and, not incidentally the intersection with sexual morality) is not going to subside anytime soon.

America facing the world

In his January 2005 State of the Union address, President Bush took the breath away from even some of his supporters when he declared that America's 'ultimate goal' was 'ending tyranny in our world'. His spokesmen – and even his father – immediately went out of their way to emphasise the operational limits of this declaration. As discussed in 'Perspectives', Bush himself then took a trip to Europe during which he tried to signal that the need to quarrel with allies had passed. The strongest substantive element in this was the agreement to back European Union diplomacy to stave off an Iranian nuclear programme with some modest American inducements.

European and American observers also studied the president's second-term appointments to judge whether the second administration would take a more moderate course. Evidence was mixed. The nomination of Gonzales as attorney general and retention of Donald Rumsfeld as secretary of defense made it clear that Bush intended no high-level accounting for the abuses at Abu Ghraib or missteps in the planning and management of Iraq's occupation. At the CIA and throughout the intelligence community there was anxiety about the focus on 'intelligence failure' regarding WMD. Intelligence failure there was, but the spies and analysts had reason to complain that a policy determination to dispose of Saddam Hussein was what really drove the war. The new CIA director, Porter Goss, installed several aides from his House Intelligence Committee who immediately clashed with high-level CIA veterans; the veterans resigned. On the other hand, the appointment of John Negroponte – a career diplomat who was most recently US ambassador to Iraq – to the new post of national intelligence director was generally welcomed by career intelligence officers.

At the head of the State Department, Colin Powell – who had resisted the war, denounced evasion of the Geneva Conventions, and generally enjoyed the warmest relations with allied governments – was not asked to stay. His successor, Condoleezza Rice, was moved from the position of Bush's national security adviser. She was so much a part the president's inner circle that she could immediately be said to conduct foreign policy with more authority, but could hardly be considered a harbinger of significant moderation. Yet she immediately appointed some top State Department officials – Robert Zoellick as deputy secretary of state, Nicholas Burns as under secretary of state for political affairs, Christopher Hill as assistant secretary of state for East Asia – who were considered moderates in the tradition of centrist foreign policies under Reagan, the elder Bush and Clinton.

Two Bush nominations in particular highlighted the uncertainties of a Bush second term. Bush nominated Deputy Defense Secretary Paul Wolfowitz to take over as president of the World Bank, and Under Secretary of State John Bolton to become US Ambassador to the UN. Viewed from abroad, both were identified with the most unpopular aspects of Bush foreign policy and labelled 'neo-conservatives'. But the label obscured more than it revealed. Wolfowitz is a genuine neo-conservative, which is to say a proponent of asserting *liberal* American values abroad, with force if necessary. He is justifiably associated with some of the Iraq war's grave mistakes, including a gross underestimation of the number of troops that would be required in the aftermath. But there is nothing either in his temperament or philosophy that would necessarily put him at odds with the generally accepted mission of the World Bank to alleviate human misery. Indeed, if there is a future Democratic administration, one could easily imagine Wolfowitz as a forceful and – most important – effective advocate of generous American development aid before a conservative Congress.

Bolton's philosophical profile is much starker. His harsh judgements of the United Nations were grounded in an absolutist rejection of any international organisations or agreements that could impinge on American sovereignty. His supporters have suggested that he could represent American interests in New York as forcefully as Daniel Patrick Moynihan in the 1970s. (Moynihan, wrote Russell Baker at the time, 'spoke English, an ancient tongue which, though long fallen into disuse, still has the power to sway men's minds, and upon arrival at the United Nations, he outraged all humanity by speaking it aloud.') But Moynihan was a proponent, not an antagonist, of international law. As Peter Beinart of *The New Republic* has observed, he was ambassador to the UN at a time when the values and principles of international order and decency were defied and defiled by a majority of UN states. This is not the case today.

One of the great challenges of American foreign policy under Bush is to recognise that, in the community of nations, America was until recently among friends – and could be again. Bush's nationalism is still ostensibly an unsettling element of international diplomacy. Yet the signals that the Bush administration sent early in his second term – a warmer embrace of European allies and partners, a degree of deference to Europe on Iran – suggests some understanding of this fact and a consequent willingness to temper nationalistic and unilateral instincts.

Retrogression in the Andes

Andean security and stability did not enjoy a good year in 2004–05. Though it is unclear whether out of desperation or renewed strength, the Revolutionary Armed Forces of Colombia (FARC) proved surprisingly resilient in the face of the best counter-insurgency efforts of the Colombian government and, in close financial and operational support, the United States. Populist Venezuelan President Hugo Chávez snatched victory from the jaws of defeat, re-consolidating power as an out-manoeuvred opposition faltered, and appeared to become more inclined to provoke neighbours like Colombia as well as the United States by way of troubling flirtations with the FARC and Cuba. Grassroots mobilisations – especially involving indig-enous Indian populations – spurred by the unwillingness or incapacity of central governments to effectively redistribute national wealth or otherwise improve the lot of the worst-off – threatened political stability in Bolivia, Ecuador and Peru. The respective 'wars' on terrorism and drugs also took a hit. In Bolivia, coca production rose to offset lower production in Colombia, and collusion between rural popula-tions, on the one hand, and Peruvian terrorist movements and narco-traffickers, on the other, appeared to grow. In Peru – customarily among the most diligent enlis-tees in anti-drug and anti-terrorist efforts – coca growers gained popular sympathy against the government's failure to enrich the poor, which, along with coca transit revenues, helped revive the rurally based Shining Path guerrilla movement. While all five governments of the region demonstrated political dexterity in surviving various popular challenges, none (save, arguably, for Colombia's) manifested the improvements in governance that would justify optimism about substantial medium-term advances in security and stability.

The FARC's revival and Colombia's challenges

Ending a two-year retreat into Colombia's dense southern jungles, the FARC opened 2005 with a vicious counter-offensive. Over 60 soldiers and a dozen civilians were killed in February alone, and over 1,000 Colombians were cut off from food and medical supplies as rebels encircled their towns. FARC guerrillas also bombed an oil pipeline and an electricity substation, and blockaded multiple highways as they stepped up their assault on the country's infrastructure. FARC second-in-command Raúl Reyes vowed that this was only the beginning of the onslaught to put an end to President Alvaro Uribe's 'democratic security' strategy, which aims to defeat or disarm the rebels in order to extend state authority throughout Colombian territory.

Attacks are likely to increase with the approach of the 2006 elections. The FARC will probably attempt to damage Uribe's re-election bid by discrediting his much-praised success against the rebels. Congress amended Colombia's constitution on 30 November 2004 to enable immediate presidential re-election, while limiting any president to a total of two terms. Uribe, maintaining an unprecedented 70–80%

approval rating throughout his term, is likely to win a second election as 64% support his re-election and there remains no other clear contender. Uribe would be the first Colombian president to serve consecutive terms since Simon Bolívar in the nineteenth century. Like Bolívar, Uribe holds the status of virtual saviour among many Colombians due his remarkable success in bringing the country back from the brink of state collapse. After past presidents' promises of peace and reconciliation in Colombia's 40-year war remained unfulfilled and the FARC shifted away from rural guerrilla warfare in favour of a brutal urban terrorist campaign, Uribe was the first in decades to be elected on pledges to take the fight to the rebels.

Embarking on the largest counter-insurgency offensive in the nation's history, Uribe launched the *Patriot Plan* in 2003 by deploying 15,000 troops to assault the FARC. The military offensive succeeded: the FARC's urban campaign ended as the rebels went into retreat, and by early 2004 the Colombian National Police established a presence in all 1,098 municipalities for the first time in the nation's history. Homicides have fallen by 25%, kidnappings by 45% and acts of terror by 37%. Over 10,000 members of illegal armed groups have died, deserted or disarmed, and 170 alleged drug traffickers have been extradited to the United States. Defence Minister Jorge Uribe declared that 'the tide has turned and there is an end in sight', yet he and others may have been overly optimistic.

The FARC has proved remarkably resilient, and its recent resurgence appears to confirm the fears of many that the guerrillas have merely been biding their time in retreat, waiting for the military offensive to run out of steam or become over-extended. The rebels' continued strength sheds light on the transitory nature of Uribe's territorial gains. Reluctant to engage in direct battle with the military, the rebel forces have until now retreated from territory without much resistance and sustaining few casualties. Yet investment in civilian institutions has failed to follow the extension of military control. Armed rebels have been able to easily resume operations once troops have been redeployed because no permanent state authority has been established to enforce the law. While the Colombian National Police are nominally present in each municipality, the US State Department estimates that up to 40% of national territory remains outside government control.

The Uribe administration pardoned 23 FARC rebels on 2 December 2004 in what appeared to be a conciliatory move. The extradition of rebel leader Simon Trinidad on 31 December, however, cut off hopes for hostage exchanges and guaranteed retaliation. The rebel pardons appeared, in retrospect, to have been aimed more at deflecting widespread criticism that Uribe favours the right-wing paramilitary groups notorious for their human-rights abuses. The rebel resurgence has tarnished not only Uribe's military successes, but also his efforts at paramilitary demobilisation. Uribe commenced talks with the paramilitary umbrella-organisation United Self-defence Forces of Colombia (AUC) on 1 July 2004 as AUC leaders negotiated from a 'concentration zone' located in the paramilitary stronghold of Córdoba.

Demobilisation has moved forward despite repeated violations of the AUC cease-fire, cases of fraudulent disarmament, and the continuation of drug-related and other illegal activity. Over 4,000 paramilitaries have disarmed since November 2003 and the remaining 12,000 are supposed to disarm by the close of 2005. However, disputes over prosecution for war crimes may derail the process.

While Congress debates legislation governing legal aspects of demobilisation, unconvinced international donors are suspending sorely needed funds for the estimated $170m task of reincorporating paramilitaries into civilian life. The demobilisation effort would, to be sure, leave AUC structures intact. At the same time, dismantling those structures poses a threat to Uribe's security efforts because the government lacks the money, manpower and institutional capacity to fill the law-enforcement vacuum. Uribe's administration is likely to face further difficulty as FARC retaliation increases their dependence on paramilitary cooperation.

Uribe's democratic security policy has come under relentless attack from human-rights groups who assert that his hard-line approach leads to abuses such as mass detentions and collusion between government, security forces and paramilitaries, and that his civilian-informant network and peasant-soldier programme blur the line between combatants and non-combatants. The president worsened his relationship with such groups when he launched a war of words with Amnesty International after its failure to condemn a 14 June 2004 massacre of peasants by the FARC. Uribe's anti-insurgent policies retain a 67% approval rating among Colombians. But whether Colombian communities are cohesive enough for civilian mobilisation to prove useful, as in the Peruvian highlands, or whether it will merely promote vigilante violence and outright treason, remains to be seen. The February 2005 detention of several peasant soldiers with FARC connections called into question the effectiveness of the president's peasant-soldier force.

In any event, consolidating and extending the gains Uribe has made in expanding state authority will continue to depend heavily on US aid, particularly as the FARC retains the strength to pose a serious threat to destabilisation. The $3.3bn spent by Washington on *Plan Colombia* since 2000 has failed to decrease the amount of cocaine flowing into the United States despite a 33% decrease in Colombian coca cultivation. However, since 2002 funds from US counter-narcotics programmes have been permitted to support Colombian counter-insurgency efforts, and these funds have been essential to the viability of Uribe's *Patriot Plan*. President George W. Bush considers *Plan Colombia* part of the 'war on terror' – in this case, narco-terrorism – and at his request in October 2004 Congress raised the ceiling for US troops in Colombia from 400 to 800 and the cap on American civilian contractors from 400 to 600. *Plan Colombia* is set to expire in September 2005, and while Washington has expressed its commitment to continued assistance, policymakers are aiming to shift emphasis from military to social aid. Uribe insists that military aid must be maintained, and considering that the Colombian military remains underfunded and understaffed while the FARC has gone on the offensive, there is concern that without increased funding security gains will be reversed. Nevertheless, lasting security cannot be achieved with a purely military solution, and expansion of state presence through social and development programmes aimed at attacking the roots of insurgency and coca cultivation will depend on international assistance to offset the Colombian state's institutional weakness.

President Uribe used the strong mandate with which he was elected to push through crucial macroeconomic reforms aimed at long-term liberalisation and trade promotion which, along with increased security, have helped turn Colombia's economy around. 2004 saw four straight quarters of growth for the first time since 1995, totalling 4%, and inflation hit a 30-year low of 6%. Labour-market liberalisation spurred the creation of 1.15m new jobs, decreasing unemployment from 20% in 2002 to 13% in 2004, and a recent World Bank report ranked Colombia as the second-most-improved country to do business with in 2005. Nevertheless, a severe social crisis remains, as 60% of the country's 44m people live in poverty. Less than 1% of Colombians own 60% of the land, and only 20% of arable land is utilised as 79% of the rural population lives in poverty.

Ironically, as social protest has increased along with security, the need for sacrifice is perceived as less pressing and Colombians begin to focus on needs other than physical safety. State oil workers staged a 37-day strike in April–May 2004, continuing in defiance of government orders to desist until a settlement was reached. On the heels of a three-week truckers' strike in September, the government faced a one-day national strike which included around 1.4m state workers and was accompanied by a protest march involving unions, students, indigenous groups and peasants in opposition to a pending free-trade agreement with the United States, Uribe's re-election efforts and proposed new tax regimes.

Despite economic growth, deregulation remains unpopular, 60% of Colombians disapprove of the way the administration is fighting unemployment, and 42% disapprove of its policies regarding quality and coverage of social services. Further economic reforms are necessary to equip the government with the long-term ability to address Colombia's social ills, yet such reforms remain unpopular. The president has been unsuccessful in reining in public finances, reforming the bankrupt social security system and increasing taxes to the level necessary to pay down public debt totalling 53% of GDP. Reforms were put on the back burner as Uribe courted Congress for the necessary votes to pass a re-election amendment. As elections approach, both president and Congress will likely be further disinclined to advocate unpopular reform.

Opponents of Uribe's re-election efforts have pointed to the dictatorial regimes of Alberto Fujimori in Peru and Hugo Chávez in Venezuela as evidence that reforming the constitution to allow for one's own re-election is inherently anti-democratic. Uribe is unlikely to mimic such authoritarian figures; nevertheless, his re-election efforts may damage his credibility as an independent, honest president due to prom-ises of key government posts and increased spending made to the Conservative Party to secure the amendment. Strong support among the Colombian electorate for a second Uribe term appears to reflect – in addition to the charismatic appeal of the president – the fear that without Uribe Colombia may not be capable of further progress and will slip back into chaos. Among Uribe's primary goals for a second term should be pushing through the reforms necessary to strengthen Colombian institutions to ensure that the government has both the financial and administrative capacity to pursue progress without his involvement.

Venezuela: Chávez's dubious resurrection

President Hugo Chávez's surprising consolidation of power in virtually all spheres of Venezuela's political life has presented an increasingly intense headache for Washington. Extra-hemispheric preoccupations have left less room for Latin America in US foreign policy than President George W. Bush would have preferred before the 11 September attacks, but Washington has at least been able over the last three years to advance its support for Colombia's counter-narcotics and counter-insurgency efforts. Chávez's virulent anti-Americanism, which has led him into dalliances with Colombia's FARC rebel group, as well as with Cuba, has thus been regarded in the dimmest light. In the wider context of Latin America's relatively gentle leftward political tilt, Washington views Chávez as a potential source and catalyst of more extreme reactions against the traditional hemispheric dominance of the United States.

Polls conducted in late 2003 suggested that 64% of Venezuelans would vote to remove Chávez in a recall referendum, while only 26% would vote to retain the president. Windfall oil revenues, however, led to unprecedented economic growth of 17.3% in 2004, largely fuelled by government spending. Chávez launched 11 'missions' to distribute oil wealth through a variety of social programmes, and from January to September 2004 alone he infused health and education programmes with $1.7bn. Chávez's support surged, allowing him to win the 15 August 2004 recall referendum with a comfortable 59% of the vote. As a consequence, Chávez will be able to serve out his six-year term, which ends in January 2007.

Some 70% of Venezuela's 14.2m-strong electorate turned out for the referendum, and independent audits conducted by the Organization of American States (OAS) and Atlanta-based Carter Center declared the process legitimate. Nevertheless, the opposition umbrella organisation Democratic Coordinator (CD) refused to concede and alleged fraud. The CD's rejection of the referendum result dealt a blow to the democratic process by allowing Chávez to paint the opposition as irrational, as well as by weakening the legitimacy of the Venezuelan electoral system in the eyes of the CD's staunchest supporters. To make matters worse, the opposition was slow to begin campaigning for the 31 October 2004 regional elections, as CD efforts instead focused on denouncing the referendum and debating whether to abstain from the upcoming elections in protest. Lacking primaries in many places, opposition votes were split. Meanwhile, Chávez had begun to publicise his endorsees as far back as 2003 and campaigned tirelessly for his roster of 'official' candidates, despite consti-tutional prohibitions on presidential campaigning. Opposition protests led to high voter abstention (ranging from 55% to 60%), further weakening anti-government candidates. Caracas's mayoral seat was taken over by a pro-government candidate as incumbent Alfredo Peña withdrew from the contest in protest, and government allies won 21 of the country's 23 governorships.

Chávez proclaimed in his referendum victory speech that 'the Venezuelan people have spoken, and the people's voice is the voice of God', and with this purportedly divine mandate pledged to deepen his Bolivarian Revolution. A key element of this commitment to social 'revolution' appears to be the consolidation of personal power over the Venezuelan state. Capitalising on the death of prosecutor Danilo Anderson (the country's first political assassination in 40 years), the administration launched its new penal code in November 2004, criminalising most forms of public protest. Rebuffing criticism from the OAS, among others, Chávez's Fifth Republic Movement (MVR) pushed through a new media law on 7 December. Dubbed the 'gag law' by its detractors, the new legislation restricts broadcasts of vulgarity or violence, words or images that 'cause anguish', and information or commentary which could defame officials or threaten national security. Aside from inhibiting criticism of the government, the regulations curtail coverage of events such as coup attempts, violent protest or natural disasters, and carry punishments ranging from fines to imprisonment. Another new law penalises any resident of Venezuela who receives anything of value from any country, group or foreign organisation that can be used 'to the detriment' – as determined by the judge – of the republic. It is now also a crime to insult the president even in the privacy of one's own home. Acting on laws passed in mid-2004 expanding the Supreme Court from 20 to 32 justices and reducing the votes necessary to replace justices from two-thirds of the legisla-ture to a simple majority, the National Assembly appointed 17 new justices on 13 December 2004, ensuring Chávez's control of the judiciary.

While he has reduced the opposition and suppressed internal dissent in the name of a 'revolution', the substance of Chávez's policies remains far from radical. The president's only structural reform centres upon rural land redistribution, which will benefit few, considering that 90% of Venezuelans live in urban areas and the government remains the largest rural landholder. While Chávez has launched numerous social initiatives, and the state-run oil company Petróleos de Venezuela has earmarked an unprecedented $3.7bn for social programmes in 2005, misman-agement and lack of institutional capacity have kept 70% of Venezuelans in poverty. Use of oil revenues to fund distributive policies instead of reinvestment will hurt the sector's long-term prospects and the country's future ability to address social ills, while current windfall gains and their use in electioneering discourage the structural reforms necessary to ensure future economic stability.

As Chávez's domestic opposition has weakened, he has increasingly focused his revolutionary rhetoric abroad, casting the United States as the impediment to social justice in Venezuela. Referring to Bush as the 'Emperor of Evil', Chávez has stridently condemned the US-led wars in both Afghanistan in 2001 and Iraq in 2003. He has frequently accused the United States of plotting his overthrow with Venezuelan expatriates, opposition extremists and Colombian paramilitaries. In May 2004, the government arrested 100 Colombian 'paramilitaries' who possessed one handgun among them. While some accused Chávez of staging the event to distract from the referendum, the president threatened to launch a 100-year war on Washington if it did not stop its so-called invasion. Among his allies, suspicions about US motives stem from its perceived role in an April 2002 coup attempt and its tacit support for the short-lived regime that took power for two days. In late February 2005, routine US Navy exercises off the coast of Venezuela triggered rumours in several cities of an 'imminent US invasion' and popular calls to 'prepare to fight'. National Assembly Deputy William Lara, a leader of the MVR, told reporters that the naval presence was 'part of a plan to intimidate and provoke by the US'. Chávez has also warned of US plots to assassinate him and began preparing the Venezuelan military 'to confront world imperialism', personally assuming control of the army reserves, doubling their number to over 100,000, and launching 'people's defence units' of 50–500 civilians – supposedly to guard Venezuela's sovereignty.

Washington, for its part, has criticised Chávez for flirting with providing support for the FARC and threatening a regional arms race. Venezuela has been negotiating to buy up to 24 multipurpose *Super Tucano* combat aircraft from Brazil, and has secured agreements to purchase at least a dozen attack helicopters from Brazil as well as 44 Mi-17 and Mi-35 helicopters and 100,000 AK-103 and AK-104 assault rifles from Russia. There have been reports that Venezuela might purchase MiG-29 fighters from Russia as well. Venezuela has also signed a deal with Spain to buy four corvettes, four patrol boats, ten C-295 military transport planes and two CN-235 maritime patrol aircraft. Caracas claims merely to be replacing old equipment, making up for US delays in supplying spare parts for Venezuela's F-16s, and ensuring that it can secure its border against the FARC. The United States, however, believes that the purchases increase the possibility of an arms race with Colombia and other Latin American nations.

This is not an idle fear. Most of Venezuela's neighbours reduced their military spending after the Cold War, so new investments, in response to a major increase by Venezuela, would constitute predictable balancing behaviour. Moreover, Venezuela's bilateral relations with Colombia – an American ally – are tenuous. Because of Colombia's close political and military relationship with the United States and a history of border disputes with Venezuela, the Venezuelan military doctrinally regards Colombia as a potential adversary. Frictions over Venezuela's suspected connections to the FARC have made boosted the prospect of direct military conflict. Chávez suspended diplomatic relations and trade with Colombia in January 2005 due to Colombia's use of bounty hunters who kidnapped FARC leader Rodrigo Granda in Caracas the previous December. (Washington openly and staunchly supported Bogotá in this matter.) Chávez used the opportunity to expound on the importance of protecting Venezuelan sovereignty, showing offence at accusations of harbouring terrorists despite evidence of Venezuelan assistance to the FARC. Official relations between Chávez and Colombian President Alvaro Uribe were restored by mid-February, but trouble could easily flare up again.

Washington also fears that the rifles being replaced will end up in the hands of the FARC. Although no hard evidence has been made public, there is some apparent justification for this worry: even if the National Guard (militarised police) is included, Venezuela's armed forces number only 82,000; furthermore, Venezuela is negotiating to buy a factory that makes small-arms ammunition, of which the FARC is in short supply. The United States has long disapproved of Chávez's relationship with the FARC and alliance with Cuba. US Assistant Secretary of State for Western Hemisphere Affairs Roger Noriega has stated that the United States will attempt to raise regional awareness about the destabilising actions of Chávez's administration.

Chávez, meanwhile, has stepped up his oil diplomacy in an attempt to guard against diplomatic isolation, making numerous regional pacts in addition to seeking agreements with Russia, Iran and China. Venezuela is the world's fifth-largest oil exporter and supplies about 15% of US oil imports. Chávez's interest in developing economic links with China is particularly keen. In December 2004, he and Chinese President Hu Jintao signed eight documents of cooperation in Beijing, and Chávez solicited Chinese investment in Venezuela's energy sector. Significantly, he cited the need to 'break with unilateralism' as the basis for his support for Chinese economic development. In an effort to reduce reliance on the United States, Chávez is looking to sell Venezuelan interests in eight US oil refineries. He has decreed that Venezuela stop selling oil to the United States if he is killed, and has hinted at diverting oil to China in any case. Chinese refineries currently lack the capacity to handle heavy Venezuelan crude, however, and officials promise that Venezuela will remain a reliable oil source for the United States as long as Washington refrains from acts of aggression.

Chávez's anti-American stance is likely to persist for the foreseeable future, as the domestic political value of having an external 'threat' to point to is considerable. Yet despite Chávez's provocative rhetoric towards Washington, he remains heavily dependent on US oil purchases to finance the social policies that are keeping afloat his chances for re-election, and to finance Venezuela's military build-up. While the replacement of the United States with China as a primary source of oil revenues may be a medium-term possibility, China's present inability to refine heavy Venezuelan crude means that US economic leverage as an oil importer appears to be in no immediate jeopardy.

US Secretary of State Condoleezza Rice has called Chávez a 'negative force' in Latin America. Since the inception of the Cold War, US policy in Latin America has aimed to preclude the emergence of a 'second Cuba' – an aspiration which Chávez, in both his friendship with Cuban leader Fidel Castro and his political rhetoric, has made no secret about harbouring. The Bush administration would like to isolate Chávez, but regional powers that are leaning increasingly towards the left of the political spectrum make this a difficult proposition. The most significant of those powers is Brazil. It has cast itself as a mediator between Caracas and Washington, and in February 2005 established a 'strategic alliance' with Venezuela by signing trade and investment accords. Diplomatically, Argentina, Chile, Mexico and Peru have tended to emulate Brazil's moderate approach. The regional consensus appears to be that Chávez has not yet conducted himself in ways that might legitimately merit application to Venezuela of the label 'rogue state', that his 'revolution' is not exportable because it is uniquely bankrolled by oil wealth, and that it is therefore safer to engage him than to risk pushing him towards belligerent authoritarianism.

Nevertheless, although Chávez's brand of populism superficially reinforces the leftward movement of regional powers such as Brazil, pragmatic leaders like Brazilian President Luis Inacio da Silva ('Lula') may be unlikely to align themselves too closely with him for fear of losing credibility with the United States. In addition, Chávez's antagonism towards the United States (and to a degree, Colombia) increases in proportion to the economic unhappiness of his domestic constituency, for which he requires both a distraction and a scapegoat. If oil revenues keep the post-referendum pro-Chávez national mood buoyant, effectively certifying his Bolivarian Revolution (however mistakenly), he may be less inclined to take risks on the foreign-policy front. With these constraining factors in mind, Washington is likely to apprehend Chávez not as a Gadhafi-style rogue in America's backyard – and a potential strategic problem – but rather as an acute annoyance.

Bolivia's ongoing crisis

Bolivian democracy continues to be in crisis. Presently, fractured government institutions are challenged by a number of powerful social protest movements. In October 2003, radical indigenous groups, coca growers, opponents of neo-liberal economic policies, and other disgruntled groups came together in opposition to government industrial policy and led to the toppling of President Gonzalo Sánchez de Lozada. As of early 2005, this combination of forces threatened his successor, President Carlos Mesa, with the same fate. Taking office in October 2003, Mesa, a political independent, has attempted to navigate the ethnic, political and regional divisions of Bolivia by appointing a largely apolitical cabinet and forming ad hoc alliances in Congress. While his separation from party politics has boosted his personal popularity – which, having dropped by one-third since he assumed office, still stood at a respectable 53% in early 2005 – the dearth of coherent pro- and anti-government blocs in Congress has impeded efficient legislation.

Upon taking office, Mesa immediately established a referendum on the natural gas industry as the centrepiece of his effort to repair the relationship between state and society. The 18 July 2004 referendum was nominally a success for the president, with 77% voting in at least some form to increase state involvement in the natural gas industry and raise export royalties for multinational corporations. Labour unions and indigenous groups failed to mobilise support to burn ballot boxes and shut down the country with roadblocks. The vague nature of the questions on the referendum, however, allowed for vastly different interpretations of the mandate provided, and a new hydrocarbons law has yet to be passed. In October 2004, the lower house of Congress rejected the executive branch's bill and instead approved draft legislation prepared by its Economic Development Committee, which is chaired by coca-grower leader Evo Morales's *Movimiento Al Socialismo* (MAS). The new bill abruptly raised royalties from 18 to 50% and, most controversially, applied the change to existing contracts.

Despite Mesa's pledge to protect current contracts, the international community threatened to cut off financial assistance, and the legal insecurity evaporated hopes of a long-term stand-by agreement with the International Monetary Fund (IMF). Still, many Bolivians remained unsatisfied because the bill fell short of full nationalisation of the industry. A May 2004 poll showed that 83% are in favour of nationalisation, but Mesa insists that this is impossible because in addition to a potential economic blockade and drop in foreign investment, Bolivia simply cannot afford the $4–6bn that would be required to compensate companies as well as the further $4bn necessary to develop the gas fields. Delay in approving a new hydrocarbons law has caused suspension of investments in exploration of new fields and development of natural gas reserves. Bolivia holds South America's second-largest natural-gas reserves, with 55 trillion cubic feet, of which only 5% will be required in the coming decades and 80% remains undeveloped. The Bolivian Chamber of Hydrocarbons has warned that the current uncertainty is jeopardising the $1.8bn in investment needed for development of proven reserves. Gas exportation is, according to most economic analysts, the only long-term solution to the country's budget deficit and feasible opportunity for growth and thus the key to addressing the country's social concerns.

Nevertheless, many remain suspicious after a long history of unfulfilled promises of export driven wealth, and in September 2004 MAS organised nationwide protests demanding 'renationalisation' of the hydrocarbons industry and annulment of the 76 existing contracts in the sector. The uncertainty of future tax revenues due to the legislative delay caused the Mesa government to reduce social spending in its 2005 budget proposal, perpetuating the vicious circle in which disaffected sectors impede the very measures necessary for their satisfaction.

President Mesa initially refused to approve any legislation until Congress passed his version of the hydrocarbons bill, but then backed away from his threat in order to garner more congressional support outside of MAS. In July 2004, however, frustrated with stalling in the congressional ratification process, Mesa filled 17 posts by decree. But the Constitutional Court ruled that Mesa had overstepped his authority and reprimanded Congress for the delay, demanding completion of the process within 60 days. In January 2005, Congress again went head-to-head with the president when it censured four of Mesa's ministers for their unpopular decision to raise fuel prices.

In addition to conflicts with the president, Congress has also experienced fissures from within. Indigenous leader Felipe Quispe resigned from his congressional seat in June 2004 in order to dedicate himself to the 'revolutionary struggle', saying he could not participate in a Congress which approved immunity for US soldiers and where members are 'compromised by corruption' or have been 'stained with indigenous blood'. MAS's congressional representation split in July over its then-conciliatory stance towards the Mesa administration, with both factions accusing the other of collusion with Washington. Congressman and former interim-president Jorge Quiroga Ramírez resigned as the leader of National Democratic Action (AND) in order to launch a new political movement ahead of the December municipal elections. Tapping into Bolivia's widespread disillusion with traditional party politics, Quiroga pledged to establish a movement 'beyond the boundaries' of political parties.

As Bolivia's government has fractured, the country has continued to be shaken by social protest movements. President Mesa appeared for some time to be making headway by appealing to what he claimed was Bolivia's 'silent majority'. A new middle-class movement emerged in response to Mesa's call to 'support democracy by not joining the strikes and marches', and in March and May 2004 anti-government mobilisations failed to garner significant support. Violent protest, however, has drowned out calls for moderate action. Demonstrations on 17 March 2004 turned violent for the first time since Sánchez de Lozada's ouster, as Bolivians marched in opposition to the government's economic policies and the proposed hydrocarbons law. On 30 March, a disgruntled former employee of the state mining corporation blew himself up on the premises of Congress in protest at losing his pension, killing two government workers and wounding ten. On 21 April 2004, ten leaders of the landless movement (MST) occupied and threatened to blow up the office of the National Institute for Agrarian Reform. The Mesa administration, in an attempt to avoid the repression of protesters that fuelled the opposition to Sánchez de Lozada, has responded with largely conciliatory measures. Pension arrangements were made with retired miners to avoid further public suicides, and a settlement was reached with MST after land seizures and bomb threats. Weeks of protests in January 2005 in El Alto prompted the administration to lower its fuel-price hike and annul a water-privatisation contract, but this time concessions did not immediately halt the opposition.

The Mesa administration also faces increased danger from terrorism. Authorities arrested 16 Islamic terror suspects on 2 December 2003. Later that month suspected terrorists from the National Liberation Army of Bolivia (ELN-B), a left-wing indigenous group backed by coca growers, were arrested, although some were released following Morales's threats to destabilise the government. Quispe denies the existence of indigenous rebel groups, yet authorities uncovered an armed rebel group near La Paz known as the 'Secret Indigenous Revolutionary Committee Juan Comse Apaza'. The group was formed in early 2004 and soon thereafter urged Bolivia's 56 indigenous nations to affiliate themselves with the Popular Liberation Army.

In April 2004 Special Prosecutor Rene Arzabe warned he had become convinced that terrorism in Bolivia exists and is on the rise, citing recent arms seizures and reports of connections between coca growers and foreign terrorist groups. Morales denounced the claims as part of a US plot to justify military intervention in Bolivia. In fact, Peruvian terrorist groups Revolutionary Movement Tupác Amarú (MRTA) and Sendero Luminoso (Shining Path) appear to be operating in Bolivia in collusion with Colombian narco-terrorists. Counter-terrorism analysts suspect the groups are planning to carve out 'liberated zones' around Cochabamba and Lake Titicaca, where arms transports were intercepted in June 2004.

Drug-enforcement efforts have been weakened by both Bolivia's continued political disarray and Morales' recent strength in government and ability to negotiate on behalf of coca growers, and the profits from the resultant rise in coca production may pad the coffers of terrorist groups operating within the country. In 2005, Bolivia is expected to overtake Peru as the world's second-largest coca producer. Most of the increase is occurring in the Yungas region, where production rose over 30% in 2003 and 18% in 2004 due to the incursion of coca growers displaced by eradication elsewhere in the country (the 'balloon effect'). Shifting away from the unpopular policy of forced eradication, the Bolivian government plans to spend $1bn over the next five years on generating alternative employment for coca growers as well as to compensate communities for voluntary destruction of coca crops. Such cooperation will be increasingly necessary as eradication efforts are increased in Yungas, where poor law-enforcement and intelligence infrastructure impedes surveillance.

As Mesa faced these various threats, rumours of coups involving the political opposition, the United States and others abounded. Simultaneously, in April 2004, the military high command ordered troops to nationwide barracks confinement in protests of a Constitutional Court ruling permitting civilian trials of officers after a military court acquitted them of charges related to the February and October 2003 mass mobilisations. Fearing the military would refuse to restore order, Congress passed a law granting US and Bolivian soldiers immunity in Bolivian courts. While the immediate crisis was dispelled, the country's constitutional, congressional and judicial institutions were weakened by their apparent malleability.

Amid the crisis on the national stage, Bolivia has suffered widespread conflict at the municipal level. On 15 June 2004, Benjamín Altamirano, a mayor of the Andean town of Ayo Ayo, was lynched due to corruption allegations. This reflected systemic problems. Ayo Ayo for a period had two mayors, each with their own municipal councils, making effective governance and distribution of resources impossible. Meanwhile, another municipality had seven deputy mayors, and another remained mayorless after the previous officeholder fled. The government's Ministry of People's Participation reported that 40 of the 314 municipal governments were in crisis. According to the Finance Ministry's Municipal Directorate, resources were frozen in close to 100 municipalities because vetting bodies refused to approve mayors' accounts or accounts had been invalidated. Over half the municipalities have no court of law or other institution with which to resolve local conflicts. Such conflicts, in turn, have helped fuel a rise in vigilante violence, which has been most common not where crime is highest but where there is little faith in civic institutions.

The disarray of Bolivia's municipal governments does not bode well for the results of the increasing trend toward regionalism. The traditional parties won less than 10% of the vote in the 5 December 2004 municipal elections. MAS won 20% of the vote – the same proportion as it won in the 2002 elections – but failed to win key strategic seats. The opening of elections to civic and indigenous movements created the potential for constructing effective channels for political representation and for handling of grievances within the democratic process. But the country could still fracture into strong regional powers with little cross-region cooperation, further weakening the central government and the cohesion of the Bolivian state. Bolivia remains plagued by centuries-old divisions between highland indigenous populations, constituting around 70% of the population, and the wealthier, lighter-skinned populations of the traditional ruling classes residing in the lowlands. The gas referendum, upcoming constituent assembly, and shift towards the left in the December municipal elections have fuelled separatist sentiments in the lowlands.

At the centre of the push for autonomy has been the city of Santa Cruz, which alone generates nearly one-third of the country's GDP, and whose 1.4m residents, called *cruceños*, feel Mesa's gas policy is jeopardising their hydrocarbon-based economy with protectionism. Despite their wealth in a country where the richest 20% live off of 54% of GDP and the poorest quintile only 4%, *cruceños* allege that the highlands have, since independence, demanded a disproportionate share of national income. As a challenge to the indigenous nations, some *cruceño* elites have formed the Movement for the Liberation of the Camba Nation, a group which proposes secession of the existing departments of Beni, Pando, Santa Cruz, Chuquisaca and Tarija – which account for two-thirds of the existing Bolivian state – and the formation of a new nation. While the secession movement remains on the fringe, its sentiments are gaining increasing support. A 29 October joint manifesto of the departments of

Santa Cruz, Tarija, and Beni threatened that these areas would become unilaterally autonomous unless a referendum was held on regional autonomy. A two-day strike demanding autonomy on 11–12 November caused the loss of $10.12m and provoked Mesa to announce he would hold a referendum on the issue in April 2005. Mesa's proposed referendum would include only the question 'Do you agree regional autonomy to be adopted in Bolivia?' and autonomy would be allowed only in regions whose citizens approved the referendum. If the aftermath of the gas referendum is any indication, however, the lack of detail in the question will surely provoke various interpretations of autonomy and increased conflict.

In any case, promises of a referendum did not pacify *cruceños*. In January 2005, the Pro-Santa Cruz Civic Committee announced its intention to unilaterally set up an autonomous government and hold a gubernatorial election. Mesa, scrambling to avert a constitutional crisis, immediately announced that Bolivia's nine departments would be permitted to elect their own governors on 12 June 2005. Two of Mesa's cabinet members resigned as Santa Cruz declared its autonomy, forcing the president to reshuffle his cabinet in early February in what he called the first step towards the 'refounding of the Republic'. In early March, however, nationwide protests that Mesa had made Bolivia 'ungovernable' arose. On 8 March, he tendered his resignation. Latin America analysts interpreted the move as a political gambit on Mesa's part to generate stronger and more cohesive political backing, and the Bolivian Congress did in fact unanimously reject his resignation in less than five minutes. But Mesa's victory appeared hollow. While most congressmen and citizens agreed that Mesa should stay in office, they differed widely on the substance of nearly all critical policy questions. Their rallying around Mesa probably did not mean Bolivia will be any more governable. In April 2005, he still seemed unlikely to be able to forge an investor-friendly hydrocarbons law or measures to alleviate the government's budget deficit. The government was more likely to pass a hydrocarbons law that significantly increased royalties and taxes and still avoided a reduction of fuel subsidies. Opposition groups would probably also hold Mesa to his promise to call regional elections to select new governors, on pain of further protests. The round rejection of his resignation, however, may have made him more apt to use force to break up protests.

President Mesa aims to forge a new 'social pact' via a constituent assembly and the drafting of a new constitution in 2005. While the latter has the potential to renew the relationship between government and society and provide democratic avenues of representation, the process alone is likely to raise fresh conflicts and protests and intensified regional demands that could institutionalise the geographical and cultural tensions in Bolivian society. It remains unclear whether the splintered Bolivian government has the strength to establish institutions capable of channelling social discontent, or whether social protest movements will wait for the political and economic measures necessary for the Bolivian state to address their needs.

Ecuador's dysfunction

President Lucio Gutiérrez was elected in 2002 with support from Ecuador's impoverished, mostly indigenous majority. The indigenous population became a part of a governing coalition for the first time in the country's history. The populist policies of Gutiérrez's electoral platform quickly evaporated, however, when he assumed the presidency and faced a budget deficit of 6% of GDP, debt payments consuming 42% of the budget, and one of the highest unemployment rates in the hemisphere. Gutiérrez's increasingly orthodox economic policies led the indigenous political party Pachakutik to end its partnership with the government in September 2003, forcing the president to form a short-lived alliance with the conservative Social Christian Party (PSC). After the dissolution of this alliance, Gutiérrez could rely only on the five seats his party held in the 100-member unicameral Congress. In the face of November 2004 impeachment efforts, however, Gutiérrez managed to piece together a coalition whose strongest pillars were exiled former president Abdala Bucaram's Ecuadorian Roldosist Party (PRE) and Alvaro Noboa's National Action Independent Renewal Party (PRIAN), both former Gutiérrez rivals. With this makeshift alliance Gutiérrez sought to tighten his political control as well as initiate a series of economic and political reforms.

While Gutiérrez's economic policies brought Ecuador international credibility following the country's 1999 default, they have also caused the president's popularity rating to sink from 60% to 10%. His administration has continuously teetered on the brink of collapse. In November 2003, five of the administration's cabinet members resigned as Gutiérrez faced pressure to step down due to allegations that his campaign was financed by drug money. Unemployment reached a three-year high of 12.1% in April 2004, and the government's unrelenting austerity measures provoked renewed protests. Gutiérrez was forced to remove welfare minister and confidant Patricio Acosta in May 2004 when he appeared on a US list of officials suspected of corruption. In June the government was dealt a severe blow when Finance Minister Mauricio Pozo became the third minister in a week to resign. Pozo was the architect of Ecuador's orthodox macroeconomic policy as well as chief mediator with the IMF, thus hailed by some for his fiscal austerity while demonised by the poor, who demanded expenditure increases. In mid-2004, the Gutiérrez administration faced renewed indigenous protests as well as burgeoning rumours of military unrest, making the president's ouster appear a real possibility.

Despite tireless campaigning, the president's party performed miserably in the 17 October 2004 local elections, winning only one of the 22 prefectures and reviving opposition calls for Gutiérrez's resignation. Gutiérrez's Patriotic Society Party of January 12 (PSP) barely garnered the 5% support necessary to retain its party registration. Immediately following the elections, Gutiérrez invited the legislative and judicial branches to enter into dialogue with the government but both declined, citing the president's lack of credibility. A month-long strike by over 40,000 state workers demanding wage increases commenced in October, and the dispute intensified as some began hunger strikes. As the PSP wielded little power and the executive was increasingly isolated, calls for impeachment increased. Opponents pushed for Gutiérrez's impeachment based upon allegations of misusing public funds for campaigning ahead of the October local elections. Those elections, however, changed the balance of political party power, unexpectedly aiding Gutiérrez in his effort to thwart impeachment. The Democratic Left (ID) and the PSC emerged strengthened, while the PRE and PRIAN both lost ground, increasing the incentive for them to bolster their waning power by allying with the government. Last-minute manoeuvrings caused the opposition to fall two votes short of the 51 needed to launch impeachment proceedings.

The political rewards the government appeared to have offered its newfound allies left Gutiérrez little running room as he attempted to appease the narrow business interests of the PRE and PRIAN. His immediate priority, however, was to consolidate power. In December 2004, Congress voted to remove 28 of the 31 Supreme Court of Justice (CSJ) justices during a session in which all but three opposition legislators stormed out in protest. Police then barred dismissed magistrates from returning, and thousands of judicial workers began indefinite strikes. Former Chief Justice Hugo Quintana denounced the move as 'illegal' and proclaimed that he and the other deposed justices would continue as a 'supreme court in exile'. The governing coalition initially justified the judicial firings based on a dubious interpretation of a transitory constitutional provision, arguing that the justices' terms had expired in January 2003. Gutiérrez later pledged that the dismissal would be made legal retroactively through a referendum on judicial reform. In another stab at retroactive legitimacy, the pro-government chief justice of the revamped CSJ, Ramiro Román, announced his intention to investigate allegations of corruption against the deposed opposition justices. More broadly, the governing coalition denounced the Ecuadorian courts as beholden to the PSC and asserted that 'sweeping political reform' – still pending as of April 2005 – was necessary in order to increase the judiciary's institutional independence. The sacking of the court prompted severe backlash from the Church, prominent media outlets, business groups and international agencies. Yet most Ecuadorians viewed the court as an instrument of the corrupt oligarchy, and polls showed 51% of the populace approved of the purge despite 45% disapproving of its method. The upshot of the purge, then, was simply to reinforce the broad lack of credibility of Ecuadorian rule of law.

The purge of the PSC-dominated Supreme Court increased suspicions that Gutiérrez is making way for the return of exiled former president Abdala Bucaram of the PRE, widely referred to as 'El Loco'. The PRE considers the return of its leader due reward for sparing Gutiérrez's presidency, and many speculate that this political debt fuelled the firing of opposition magistrates unlikely to dismiss Bucaram's pending corruption charges. Though the new justices did not assure his return, the former president ominously hailed Gutiérrez's sacking of the court as a 'Christmas present for the Ecuadorian people'. Further strengthening Bucaram and the PRE, the newly appointed chief justice of the CSJ resigned after only 35 days, making room for long-time Bucaram friend and PRE co-founder Guillermo Castro to assume control.

Ecuador's institutional disarray also placed at risk $7.5m in American military aid. In November the US Embassy announced the suspension of military aid to Ecuador due to its refusal to grant US soldiers International Criminal Court (ICC) immunity. In April 2005, Ecuador had yet to respond to the immunity request, referred to as 'Article 98', because President Gutiérrez insisted he could not act until Congress came to a decision. But the head of the commission on constitutional matters, Carlos Vallejo, asserted that the decision remained the executive branch's to make. The American military's presence at Manta military base had been highly unpopular due to fears of the country becoming involved in the war in Colombia, and it appeared that neither branch of government desired the political backlash accompanying responsibility for the ICC decision.

While Gutiérrez's nimble shifting of alliances helped his administration to step away from the brink of collapse, in large measure the president owes his survival to rises in the price of oil. High oil prices allowed Gutiérrez to stay within the good graces of international financial institutions while pledging increases in public-sector wages and pensions as he faced diminishing popularity and impending local elections. Ecuador's GDP grew by 6% in 2004, and inflation hit a 30-year low of 1.95%, down from 6.07% in 2003. Ecuador's 12-month stand-by agreement with the IMF expired in April 2004 with only $85m of $211m released and another $200m in associated lending withheld due to reform stagnation. In December 2004, however, the IMF praised the country's economic performance, which freed aid from both the IMF and the World Bank, allowing Ecuador to meet its financial requirements and re-enter the international capital market from which it had been excluded since its sovereign debt default in 1999. At the same time, high oil prices increased discontent with austerity measures, as Ecuadorians perceive windfall revenues despite the fact that above-budget oil income is largely needed to reduce debt and is funnelled into the Debt Reduction, Economic Recovery, Investment and Stabilization Fund (FEIREP). Of FEIREP assets, 70% is used to buy back debt, 20% to stabilise revenues and 10% for health and education. The IMF has warned, however, that structural reforms remain necessary, including opening of the oil and electricity sectors to private investment. State-owned Petroecuador's oil production sunk 3.5% to a ten-year low in 2004, following a 7.5% decline in 2003, though private companies have continued to increase output. The electricity sector's inefficient infrastructure keeps energy costs among the region's highest.

While political disorder has impeded crucial economic reforms, Gutiérrez's government appeared more secure in early 2005 than it had in 2004. Although the indigenous movement had a key role in ousting Bucaram in 1997 and President Jamil Mahuad in 2000, it has been disillusioned and in disarray since abandoning Gutiérrez. Indigenous groups continued anti-government actions, including nationwide strikes in June 2004 and marches in Quito during a congressional session in November. But Pachakutik repeatedly failed to muster support for uprisings. Pachakutik supported Gutiérrez's impeachment in Congress, yet declined any further alliance with the PSC. While future indigenous mobilisations remain a distinct possibility, the president in early 2005 did not appear to imminently face the formidable Bolivia-style uprisings that Ecuador has also experienced in the past.

In late January 2005, Gutiérrez submitted to Congress ten questions pertaining to the judiciary for inclusion in a referendum. The questions addressed whether an electoral college composed of civil society representatives should appoint magistrates, whether the number of CSJ justices should be decreased from 31 to 16, whether age and term limits should be implemented, and whether judges should be forbidden affiliation with any political party. Congress, however, remained cool towards judicial reform once it had gained control over the CSJ by way of the purge. In all likelihood, future reforms will merely rubber-stamp the purge, consolidate political party power, and further diminish the independence and legitimacy of the Ecuadorian judicial branch. Additional political reforms Gutiérrez wanted to include in the referendum were, likewise, self-serving. Proposals included removal of the vice-presidential candidate from the presidential ballot in favour of presidential control over the office. Vice-President Alfredo Palacio, who proclaimed the 'country is going to the devil' following the court purge, called for nationwide protests. Other reforms involve granting each presidency one opportunity to dissolve Congress at will, reduction of congressional deputies from 100 to 69, and the possibility of immediate presidential re-election. While Gutiérrez has stated his desire for a second term, Deputy Enrique Alaya Mora expressed the opinion of most in Congress when he stated that if Gutiérrez managed to finish his current term, 'he should thank God and all of the saints, and he should not even dream about re-election'.

Notwithstanding Gutiérrez's political agility, the Ecuadorian people remained largely impoverished and disillusioned with government. Gutiérrez won the title of 'most dislikeable' man of the year in 2004 with 28% of the vote, yet was closely tailed by PSC leader Leon Febres Cordero with 13.5%. A December 2004 report by the Berlin-based Transparency International designated Ecuador's political parties as having the highest level of perceived corruption in the world. Legislative gridlock, government scandal or a decline in oil revenues stood to transform widespread dissatisfaction into presidency-toppling mass mobilisations. The government's 'institutional majority' was likely to disintegrate with the approach of the 2006 presidential elections, if not before, as the PRE pushed for Bucaram's restoration, the PRIAN and Noboa sought to block the return of presidential competition, and both parties increasingly benefited from positioning themselves in opposition to the administration. Unfortunately, instead of consolidating Ecuador's recent economic successes, Gutiérrez's agenda threatened to further debilitate Ecuador's feeble democratic institutions. On 15 April, Gutierrez dissolved the Supreme Court to defuse mass protests over its failure to try Burcaram and Noboa on corruption charges. He declared a state of emergency in Quito, which permitted the curtailment to civil liberties to quell demonstrations. On 20 April, however, Congress voted Gutiérrez out of office on the grounds that his manipulation of the CSJ was unconstitutional. Palacio took over as president, and indicated that his government would use more of its budget for social spending, probably at the expense of debt service.

Peru: Toledo's twilight

Embattled Peruvian President Alejandro Toledo appeared set to hang onto the presidency through the end of his term in 2006 despite the weakness of his scandal-ridden administration. The approval rating of 60% with which Toledo assumed office in 2001 quickly eroded; it has hovered around 10% since mid-2003, hitting a nadir of 6% in June 2004, making Toledo the least-popular president in Latin America. Despite Toledo's utter lack of popular support, Peru's economy has been among the strongest in the region. It is the Toledo administration's failure to translate macroeconomic success into tangible gains for the majority that has left the populace disillusioned with a government and president they consider inept and corrupt.

After corruption and nepotism scandals led to several resignations, including that of Vice-President Raul Diez Canseco in January 2004, Toledo attempted to stave off calls for early elections in mid-February by revamping his cabinet for the fifth time in 30 months. Nevertheless, scandals continued to plague the administration, and by June the president had lost his sixth minister in as many months. Toledo, First Lady Eliane Karp and the president's sister-in-law all face allegations of having forged the signatures required to register Toledo's political party, Perú Posible (PP), for the 2000 elections. Though immune from prosecution while president, Toledo – ironically, the first South-American president to ratify his country's signature of the United Nations Convention Against Corruption – and Karp have been summoned to testify before a legislative committee. Toledo is accused by former presidential aide Cesar Almeyda – who is in prison awaiting his own corruption trial – of having accepted a $5m bribe to expedite a privatisation sale. Though Toledo urged an audit of his bank accounts during his third State of the Nation address, his credibility has been damaged by his attack on a unit of anti-corruption prosecutors, which he had formerly praised for their investigations of the indubitably corrupt administration of Alberto Fujimori.

In a blow to his own integrity as well as to the long-term prospects for justice in Peru, Toledo chose in December 2004 not to renew the contract of Chief Prosecutor Luis Vargas Valdivia. The removal of Vargas Valdivia may damage the progress of the roughly 1,500 investigations and 150 prosecutions in progress against the network of corruption established by Fujimori and his spymaster Vladimir Montesinos. Vargas Valdivia and the so-called Ad Hoc Prosecutors Unit have scored crucial convictions including those of Congressman Ernesto Gamara, Supreme Court Justice Alejandro Rodríguez, former Attorney General Blanca Nélida Colán, and former armed forces chief General José Villanueva. Some $174m sent abroad by corrupt officials has been repatriated. The prosecutors also persuaded Montesinos to break his self-imposed silence to plead guilty to charges of corruption and embezzlement. The unit, however, still faces some of its most important cases, such as those pertaining to allegations of arms trafficking to the FARC and unleashing death squads on MRTA and Shining Path militants. While the Truth and Reconciliation Commission has been considered among the most effective and earnest bodies of its kind, prosecution has been hindered by Peru's weak judicial institutions.

The justice system's sclerosis was brought to the forefront of national attention when the courtroom antics of Shining Path leader Abimael Gúzman and his co-defendants managed to bring their trial to a halt. Gúzman's conviction and life sentence by a military court were overturned in January 2003 when Peru's Supreme Court ruled the country's anti-terrorism laws unconstitutional. (Courts have since been preparing to retry over 2,000 inmates, and 212 have already been released.) During Gúzman's November 2004 retrial proceedings, he and his co-defendants shouted revolutionary slogans at the media, fuelling fears that the pulpit provided by the open civilian trials could fuel the rebirth of the Shining Path. The outbursts led to chaos as prosecutors and judges began blaming one another for the incident and cameras were ushered out of the courtroom. Toledo quickly tightened prison security and accused the courts of undercutting his efforts and having a 'trembling hand' when they barred monitoring of attorney–client conversations in prison. The executive's harsh criticism further undermined the already low credibility of the Peruvian judicial process.

Also driving Toledo's unpopularity is his failure to effectively distribute gains from the country's impressive macroeconomic growth. Real GDP growth was 4.4% in 2004 and is projected at 4.1% for 2005. Yet, under Toledo, the formal jobless rate has risen from 9.2% in 2001 to 11% in 2004, while the majority of government investment has been concentrated in capital-intensive projects. Toledo has faced large-scale protests, including Peru's first general strike since 1999. The regional demands of protestors have spurred the administration to devolve more political and economic power to regional governments, but this has merely 'decentralised' the crisis such that many Peruvians have decided to take matters into their own hands. Citizens have, for instance, erected over 1,000 gates blocking public streets in the capital city of Lima due to the inability of the city's underfunded police force to stem rising crime. Perhaps the most blatant example of such response occurred on 26 April 2004, when the indigenous residents of the city of Illave dragged their mayor from his home and beat him to death due to corruption allegations. The lynching of the Illave mayor sparked sympathetic protests across the country while independently miners struck and coca growers marched on Lima, marking the third national uprising of Toledo's term. Interior Minister Rospigliosi, who resigned after the 2002 Arequipa riots and was later reinstated, was censured by Congress and forced to resign in May 2004 following the unrest. Before the year's end, Indian populations rose up against six other town governments in the region and attacked the troops sent to reinforce local police, and three other Peruvian mayors died at the hands of similar waves of vigilante justice.

Retired Army Major Antauro Humala's ultra-nationalist 'Movimiento Ethnocacerista' calls for, among other things, state ownership of strategic industries, freedom to grow and sell coca, and the death penalty for corrupt officials. The movement appeals to Peru's Andean indigenous heritage and claims to have organised battalions of some 3,000 'reservists'. Despite a May 2004 judicial probe request by the Interior Ministry, the office of the attorney general failed to investigate Humala's movement. Nor did the national intelligence service follow up on reports that the movement was stockpiling arms. On 1 January 2005, Humala and some 150 armed followers seized the police station in the southern provincial city of Andahuaylas, taking 17 hostages and demanding Toledo's resignation. Toledo then declared a state of emergency and deployed 1,000 troops to the region. After four days, during which four policemen and two rebels were killed, Humala was arrested and the siege collapsed. Interior Minister Reategui resigned, denying allegations that he had received information about Humala's assault. Though most Peruvians reject Humala's violent methods, thousands in provincial cities marched in support of his movement. Support for such action may grow if the larger pattern of lawlessness and government ineffectuality continues unabated in Peru.

The government also faces a threat from the resurgent Shining Path rebel group. The group is less ideological than its previous far-left Maoist incarnation, and is increasingly linked to narco-trafficking. Shining Path currently gains much of its revenue from charging drug traffickers to move coca paste through the rebel-controlled territories of the Apurimac and Upper Huallaga valleys. Despite US pressure to boost eradication efforts, Lima continues to refrain from eradication in areas where Shining Path is active, and the bounty from coca-transit fees give the group the potential to wage war with vastly greater resources than it previously had at its command. In mid-September 2004, the government claimed drug traffickers had turned the departments of Ayacucho and Cuzco into a 'coca paradise' in which they operate with support from Shining Path. Nonetheless, the Toledo administration has softened its stance against coca growers due to continued protests calling for decriminalisation. In April 2004, Shining Path gave the government a 60-day deadline to meet its demands for a political solution, though the demands and impending consequences remained unspecified. A November 2004 government study warned of renewed terrorist activity in the high Andes and predicted Shining Path would attempt to penetrate universities, labour unions, law-enforcement agencies and other national institutions as it geared up for a resumption of armed conflict.

In order to adequately assess and combat the Shining Path threat, the government must speed up its restructuring and strengthening of intelligence services, which were disbanded and reconfigured to purge the corrupting influences of the previous administration. While Shining Path is certainly not the existential threat it once was, the group retains the possibility of winning the hearts and minds of impoverished Peruvians, particularly since it has foregone targeting civilians.

In an effort to boost his popularity, Toledo has undertaken more 'populist' economic policies. The president supported removing the state-owned PetroPeru from the privatisation process, refused to grant a five-year extension to Telefónica de Peru's main contracts, and approved a new royalty tax on the mining sector. While these policies aroused the concern of international investors and the local business sector, they failed to stem the flow of protests or popular calls for Toledo's resignation. In May 2004, the civil association Foro Democratic (Democratic Forum) launched their 'No lo Toledo' (a play on the president's name suggesting 'I don't tolerate') campaign, which demanded immediate elections due to the president's unpopularity and 'extreme incompetence'. Peru's principal newspaper, *El Comercio*, called for steps to be taken to avert the 'madness' of Toledo's overthrow. The president faced further humiliation in May when the country's three most powerful opposition leaders, former president Alan García, former presidential candidate Lourdes Flores and former interim president Valentín Paniagua, met to craft suggestions to improve 'governability' so that Toledo could retain the presidency.

Despite popular dissatisfaction with the president, Peru's major political actors have backed away from demanding his removal. On 3 June 2004, Congress voted to increase the number of votes necessary to remove the president from 61 to 80, indicating both the real possibility of 61 legislators voting against the president as well as the desire for him to finish his term for the sake of stability. As of March 2005, Toledo appeared likely to serve out the remainder of his term. In the meantime, the weakness of both his administration and the institutions of the Peruvian government more generally threaten to facilitate a slide into violence and chaos. Prospects for marked improvement in governance via the 2006 elections remain dim, as the former populist García and the exiled Fujimori remain top contenders for the presidency despite the disastrous consequences of their previous administrations. Unless Peru manages to strengthen the effectiveness of its democratic institutions, as well as translate macroeconomic growth into benefits for the majority of its populace, the country faces the danger that its citizens will increasingly, as in Illave, reject democratic channels of representation in favour of anti-systemic methods.

Looking ahead

Curiously enough, in the near future impediments to improving security and stability throughout the region could stem in considerable part from Colombia's relatively successful US-backed fight against civil war and narco-trafficking. The

FARC's persistence has helped gird remnants of Shining Path in Peru; the plight of poor Colombian farmers seeking to maximise revenues through coca production inspires their economic brethren in Bolivia, Ecuador and Peru; and the FARC's left-wing fascism allows Chávez to feel that he is not alone on the continent. Yet the destabilising elements in the four Andean countries other than Colombia also have indigenous roots. Chávez initially came to power on a wave of populism premised on the maldistribution of oil revenues. Inequitable distribution and corruption have fuelled social protests in the Andean 'southern crescent' of Bolivia, Ecuador and Peru – and, in Peru's case, the refusal of Shining Path to die. Chávez himself cued political radicals in Bolivia and Peru. Thus, even if Washington's focus on Colombia through heavy military and political support ameliorates its problems – still a medium-term proposition at best – other challenges in the region will not necessarily abate. In fact, the long regional reach of narco-traffickers in general, and the rise of coca production in Bolivia as it has diminished in Colombia (the 'balloon effect') in particular, indicates that security and stability improvements in Colombia could actually worsen disruptive conditions elsewhere. Indeed, it was successful US-backed drug eradication efforts in Bolivia and Peru in the late 1990s that created that effect in terms of coca cultivation – and produced windfall illicit profits – in Colombia.

Washington is already facing a challenge to the United States' traditionally preferred neo-liberal political–economic orthodoxy for Latin America from a left-leaning Brazil and, to a lesser extent, from Argentina. The pragmatism of Brazilian President da Silva ('Lula'), however, has provided Washington with a measure of reassurance, and perhaps allowed it to continue to focus regional concern narrowly on trade issues, on Colombia and on Venezuela as a potential rogue state. Neighbourhood actors such as Brazil, Argentina, Chile and Mexico have primarily economic interests (e.g., in Bolivian natural gas) in the Andes but limited political clout. The upshot of the Andean situation is that the United States may have to revisit its policies with respect to the 'southern crescent'. There is a risk that one, two or all three of these countries could step into any narco-trafficking breach left by a pacified Colombia, and internal political decadence in each leaves sparse hope for political or economic reforms that might produce intramural quiescence without outside help. The United States will have to work harder to re-engage these countries in order to influence economic reform and reconciliation between elites and deprived classes (especially, in Bolivia and Ecuador, indigenous peoples) sufficiently to ensure political stability and sustainable government commitments to security and anti-drug policies. Possible tools include more robust trade benefits and preferences, but deeper political as well as economic engagement will be required for substantial effect. With the US government still preoccupied by large and urgent strategic problems outside the western hemisphere, however, it appeared unlikely in April 2005 that any major rethink of Latin American policy was forthcoming.

Brazil: Regional Leadership and Beyond

The year 2004 saw a further consolidation of Brazil's emerging role as both a regional leader and, on selected global issues, a larger international presence. The aggressive and proactive foreign policy of Brazilian President Luis Inacio da Silva ('Lula') continued to push South American assertiveness in foreign affairs, relative independence from American influence, and left-leaning social democracy over the free-market capitalism that marked the post-Cold War political and economic emergence of the continent. At the same time, Lula continued to be cautious and avoided alienating Washington.

Trade – a vehicle for Brazilian leadership

A summit of South American presidents convened in Cuzco, Peru in December 2004 to launch a 'South American Community of Nations' showcased Brazil's regional leadership. Speaking at the event, held in Cuzco, capital of the old Incan empire, Lula commented that 'the integration dreamed of by 19th-century South American independence hero Simon Bolivar becomes reality in the years ahead'. The Cuzco Summit outlined an ambitious programme of continental integration. The two existing free-trade agreements – Mercosur, the customs union comprising Brazil, Argentina, Uruguay and Paraguay, and the Andean Community, made up of Venezuela, Colombia, Peru, Bolivia and Ecuador – will be merged over a 15-year period. Chile, Surinam and Guyana were also expected to sign the agreement, which will eventually end tariffs on currently extremely limited intra-regional trade. The agreement also provides for radical improvements in transport, energy connections and other infrastructure, so that countries such as Brazil and Argentina that have traditionally developed towards the Atlantic Ocean can conduct business more easily with their Pacific neighbours.

Government officials have already sorted more than 300 projects into 31 priorities, of which only ten items cost more than $100m. Funding would come from such multilateral institutions as the Inter-American Development Bank (IADB), the Andean Development Corporation and private sources. Brazil and its Mercosur partners have made significant trade concessions in the process of building support for the Andean Community. The deal offers Venezuela, Ecuador and Peru duty-free access to Brazil for 90% of their exports within two years. By contrast, Mercosur exporters will have to wait more than 10 years for the same benefits.

Sceptics will argue that this is merely another false start in achieving Bolivar's dream of a united South America. But this effort complements a number of trends in recent years. Following the creation of the North American Free Trade Area (NAFTA) in 1994, the highly competent Brazilian foreign ministry – known as Itamarati – began separating South America from North America. Central America, and especially Mexico, is viewed as within the United States' sphere of interest.

The deepening integration of the Mexican economy with its northern neighbours has confirmed that trend. The recent Central American Free Trade Agreement (CAFTA), awaiting approval by the US Congress, clearly places those countries – and the Dominican Republic – in the North American orbit.

Mercosur is another vehicle for Brazilian leadership in South America. While far from achieving its ambitious goals as a customs union, it has served as a very useful point of departure for asserting Brazil's *primus inter pares* position. The EU decided some years ago that it wanted to deal with the Mercosur, not with individual countries. That decision logically gave Brazil a major say in setting the agenda and moving the talks forward. The talks stalled in late 2004, but Brazil remains the principal interlocutor with Brussels, as efforts are underway to reinvigorate the negotiations. Brazil's lead in Mercosur is aided, of course, by the weak bargaining position of Argentina since the severe financial and political crises of 2000–01. While the government of President Nestor Kirchner has restored some faith in the political process internally, its pariah status in the international financial community limits the country's capacity to take a lead in setting the Mercosur agenda. Until Argentina's debt restructuring is completed, and discussions with the IMF are successfully terminated, Buenos Aires will remain a relatively weak player in Mercosur diplomacy.

Diplomatic platforms

In the late 1990s, then-president Fernando Henrique Cardoso of Brazil convened, in Brazil, the first summit of the presidents of South America. Symbolically, the message was clear – two Americas, one of which is led by the United States and, with somewhat more modesty, the other led by Brazil. The candidacy of Brazil – along with Japan, India and Germany – for a permanent seat on the UN Security Council confirms Brazil's claim to pre-eminence in South America. While Argentina also believes it has a stake in the race, it is obvious that Brazil has the support of the other Spanish-speaking states. Any pretence by Mexico to a seat is muted by its growing identification with North America and the United States.

Brazilian leadership in Haiti is another facet of the expanding diplomatic role in the hemisphere. At the biennial meeting of the defense ministers of the Americas, held in Quito, Ecuador, in November 2004, Brazil was singled out for praise by US Secretary of Defense Donald Rumsfeld for its leadership role in the peacekeeping mission in Haiti. The secretary said the Haiti mission was an example of beneficial security cooperation among Latin American countries. Brazil, Argentina and other countries in the region have provided the bulk of the troops serving with the 4,500-member UN force on the island. Rumsfeld and Brazilian Defence Minister (and Vice-President) Jose Alencar met to discuss future strategy in Haiti during the session.

In another effort to extend Brazil's diplomatic reach, Lula volunteered to mediate a now-resolved political dispute between Colombia and Venezuela over the return of a leader of the FARC from Venezuela. More telling, Lula and Venezuelan President Hugo Chávez met in Caracas in February 2005 and signed agreements establishing a strategic, economic and military alliance between the two nations. Venezuela is also negotiating to buy as many as 24 *Super Tucano* multi-purpose combat aircraft from the giant Brazilian aircraft manufacturer Empresa Brasileira de Aeronautica (Embraer). The deal would be worth approximately $170m.

The two countries also signed energy and mining accords that permit Brazil's oil and gas company, Petrobras, to develop offshore natural-gas projects and oil fields in Venezuela's lucrative Orinoco heavy-oil belt. Trade between the two governments doubled to $1.6bn in 2004 from the previous year and could reach $3bn in 2005 – a development that the anti-American Chávez celebrated as a sign of Latin American integration at the expense of the United States. In this connection, it worth noting that Chávez's 'revolution' is named for Simón Bolivar, from whom Lula also draws inspiration.

Touchy relations with the United States

The recent agreements with Brazil are of growing concern to Venezuela's neighbour, Colombia, and to the United States. Washington wants to prevent an arms race on the continent. Chavez raises concerns for the government in Bogotá by providing increasingly active support for the FARC guerrilla movement. The heightened anti-American rhetoric in Caracas has escalated in recent months. The Brazilian government is well aware of this situation but claims that state-to-state relations are normal and there are important affinities between Venezuela and Brazil. They share a long Amazon frontier. Questions of drugs and smuggling are of increased concern in both capitals. Brazil, from the time Chávez was elected, has sought to keep Venezuela in the South American framework. Thus President Lula's positive reference to Simón Bolivar's vision at the Cuzco Summit last year. How this will play out with Brazil's thus far reasonably agreeable relationship with the United States remains to be seen. *Plan Colombia*, the American aid and military support programme that aims to strengthen Colombia's armed forces, neutralise the FARC and substantially curtail the drug trade, remains the principal focus of Washington policy in the Andes. Any country viewed as sympathetic to Caracas runs the risk of being viewed with heightened suspicion by US policymakers. Brazil's more assertive diplomacy on the South American continent deliberately downplays that possibility. Itamarati's long-range strategy is to position Brazil as the pivot in continental diplomacy and politics – and the regional power that Washington should regard as key to its leverage.

Will Brazil's deepening commercial relationship with China and its more assertive regional and international diplomacy strain relations with Washington? While there were testy exchanges between the two countries following the collapse of the WTO ministerial talks in Cancun in 2003, relations and levels of cooperation are broadly viewed as positive. While Brazil retains diplomatic ties to Fidel Castro's

Cuba, as does the entire region, this has not emerged as a major issue in the bilateral relationship, and appears increasingly unlikely to do so as Castro ages and post-Cold-War Cuba evolves – though the development of a provocative and revolutionary link between Venezuela and Cuba could heighten US diplomatic pressure on Chávez's South American neighbours to keep him in line.

Efforts to link Lula to a new 'axis of populists' in the region have failed. It is clearly understood that the foreign policy of the Lula government is centrist. Indeed, in January 2005 on the way to the World Economic Forum in Davos, Switzerland, Lula stopped briefly in the southern city of Porto Alegre to speak at the World Social Forum – and was booed. More radical elements in his Workers Party (PT) resigned after his appearance, alleging that he and his closest collaborators have abandoned their early ideals and principles. Lula, for his part, has been steadfast in publicly defending the fiscal austerity position of the government and his staunch support of democratic politics.

Trade and global diplomacy

There are two significant trade negotiations under way in which Brazil plays a central role. The first is the Free Trade Area of the Americas (FTAA), for which Brazil co-chairs the final round of talks with the United States. The other is the World Trade Organization (WTO) 'Doha Round'. Both are moving far more slowly than originally imagined and Brazil's strategic position in both has become a contentious issue in Washington. Brazil's emergence in a leadership role in both rounds reflects a growing sense that the twenty-first century will see a new and important constellation of players in international trade, investment and finance. C. Fred Bergsten and his colleagues at the Institute of International Economics have termed this group the 'Large Emerging Market Economies', or LEMs, in a recent publication. There are 11 LEMs, and a core of five: Brazil, China, India, Russia and South Africa. (The others are Argentina, Indonesia, Korea, Mexico, Saudi Arabia and Turkey.) This classification reaffirms the emergence of Brazil as an increasingly significant player in issues extending beyond South America.

Launched in November 2001, the Doha Round has moved slowly. After a meeting marked by violence in Seattle in 1999, the impetus for new negotiations stalled. An effort was made to jump-start talks at a ministerial meeting in Cancun, Mexico in September 2003. There Brazil, joined by the other core states, plus many of the remaining 11, formed the 'Group of 20'. While the number of states involved fluctuates, the core states have remained firm in their determination to redefine the global trade agenda. The Cancun meeting ended with an acrimonious exchange over the unwillingness of the EU and the United States to change their current agricultural policies.

An effort was made in July 2004 in Geneva once again to move forward. New guidelines were negotiated for trade reforms in agriculture, industrial products and services. Another ministerial meeting is now scheduled for December 2005 in Hong Kong. Brazil, as well as the other core players, has made it clear that it expects reciprocity from the EU and the United States on a wide range of issues, including the elimination of export subsidies, a substantial reduction of domestic farm-support programmes, and implementation of tariff cuts. The G-20 formally and informally has made it clear that a 'level playing field' is now required for any progress on these issues.

The FTAA has its origins in a hemispheric summit in Miami in 2004. Because Congress denied President Bill Clinton 'fast track' negotiating authority, little progress has been made. President George W. Bush succeeded in getting a 'Trade Promotion Authority' (TPA) approved and negotiations restarted. The talks advanced only sluggishly during the first Bush administration – again over Brazil's insistence that the United States must revise its agricultural subsidies programme. A ministerial meeting was held in Miami in late 2003 to seek common ground. Brazil, the co-chair with the United States, would agree to nothing more than an 'FTAA-lite' in which countries could or could not agree to a series of liberalisation measures. The stumbling blocks for a deeper agreement remain market-access reforms, covering agriculture and others goods and services. The January 2005 completion target has come and gone and it is not clear when talks will resume or in what venue. Brazil has continued to insist that the FTAA goal remains within reach – if the United States is willing to introduce substantial policy changes. The United States has responded that Brazil and other states in the region need to be more open on issues such as intellectual-property rights. There appears to be little hope of substantive progress in 2005 with national elections scheduled in 2006 in Brazil.

Brazil has been able to capitalise on its LEM status to dominate the FTAA discussions and to play a central role in the Doha Round talks. Deftly building strategic coalitions in both sets of discussions, the Brazilian government has positioned itself as a mediator and as a defender of emerging economies position in talks that until very recently were highly asymmetrical.

The China card

One of the extraordinary developments of the early twenty-first century has been the emergence of China as a key player in world trade and investment. That country is now the world's third-largest trading economy, after the United States and Germany. It is now the sixth-largest economy in the world – and will overtake the United Kingdom and France within two years, if current trends continue. China has been the largest developing country recipient of foreign direct investment (FDI) for more than a decade. In 2003, China alone accounted for one-fifth of global trade expansion. In the western hemisphere, China is now the number-two trading partner of both Canada and Mexico, ahead of each in the other's market, despite the dynamics of NAFTA. And 2004 was the year in which the China card played in Brazil's favour. Trade between Brazil and China quadrupled between 1999 and 2003. In 2004, one-half of Brazil's global export growth and one-quarter of the country's targeted 3.5% GDP growth resulted from the China connection.

The China card trumped other players with the state visit of Chinese President Hu Jintao to South America in November 2004. The justification for the visit was the Asia–Pacific Cooperation Forum in Santiago, Chile. But the principal reason for the trip was to signal a new strategic alliance with the countries in the Southern Cone, principally Brazil. The Chinese president announced more than $30bn in new investments and signed long-term contracts that will guarantee China supplies of the vital materials it needs for its factories and for the foodstuffs to feed its people.

Hu Jintao's stay in Brazil – a five-day state visit – was preceded by an impressive state visit to China by Lula in May 2004. Nearly 500 business executives accompanied the Brazilian president. During the visit, the two countries signed 14 accords. In November, Chinese officials predicted that trade with Brazil could grow to $35bn by 2010. China is anxious to expand its purchase of a range of goods and commodities from Brazil, ranging from soybeans to iron ore for steel production. Little noticed, agriculture is now a $150bn-a-year business in Brazil, accounting for more than 40% of the country's exports and creating what Brazilians call the 'green anchor' of their economy. China – along with other Asian consumers – is expected to continue to drive the surplus produced by the agricultural and raw-material trading for the foreseeable future.

It appears that China has chosen Brazil as its strategic partner in the region. Lula stated during his May 2004 visit to China that Brazil wanted a partnership that integrates their economies and serves as a paradigm for South–South cooperation. There is talk of China – and South Korea – becoming members of the IADB. China and Brazil are two of the five core countries of the LEM grouping. They cooperate closely in the G-20, and China supports Brazil's candidacy for a seat on the UN Security Council. It is apparent that the Brazilian government views closer ties with China as a card to be played to offset American influence and trade dominance. The US government, to date, has apparently been unconcerned by, or perhaps not fully aware of, the potential implications of the arrival of China in South America. But while Brasilia has not suggested that China could soon replace the United States as Brazil's main customer and partner, the aim of its partnership with Beijing is clearly to force trade and other concessions from the United States and the rich industrialised countries.

The economic backdrop

Much of what Brazil is accomplishing regionally, and at the international level, is based on the perception that the country has finally moved towards sustained economic growth. Brazil grew at an estimated 5% in 2004. While growth in 2005 will be somewhat lower it will exceed 3%. Inflation in 2004 was below 8%, within the range prescribed by the National Monetary Council, and the downward trend is expected to continue. While debt obligations remain high, there appears to be little doubt that the necessary financing will be available.

Driving much of the economy is, as mentioned, the 'green anchor'. Already the world's biggest exporter of chickens, orange juice, sugar, coffee and tobacco, Brazil soon hopes to add soybeans to the list, depending on what happens in that volatile market in 2005. With a grass-fed herd of 175m cattle that is the world's largest, it passed the United States as the world's largest exporter of beef in 2003. Beef exports in 2004 are estimated at $2.5bn. The agricultural bonanza in 2004 will give Brazil a record trade surplus of $33.7bn. The expectations for 2005 are as, if not more, ambitious, given continued demand from Asia for South American products, generally, and Brazil specifically.

Finally, Brazil has easy access to the capital markets. Risk premiums are at the lowest they have been in recent years. FDI is strong and is predicted to remain so as most of the 'Fortune 500' companies have a significant stake in the internal economy. The country's relations with the international financial institutions are very positive and, if needed, 'backup' financing is available.

Limited potential

In early 2005, Lula was politically armed with high domestic popularity, national financial health and increasing international prestige. At the same time, the PT – which represents his principal constituency – was undergoing what Brazilian journalists described as an 'existential crisis' over its inability to balance satisfactorily its revolutionary roots with Lula's more pragmatic inclinations. This quandary limits Lula's freedom of action both domestically and internationally. In the October 2004 municipal elections, the party lost serious ground in its traditional urban strongholds of São Paulo and Porto Alegre. Within the party, Lula is seen as peremptory and authoritarian. Neither the revolutionary nor the pragmatic factions within the PT would readily disparage Lula's proven ability to elevate Brazil's stature and influence in international affairs. But disgruntled champions of the working class that Lula is perceived to have ill-served since his inauguration in January 2003 – either outside or inside the party – could well pressure the president to give basic philosophical matters closer to home greater priority and reduce his international extroversion.

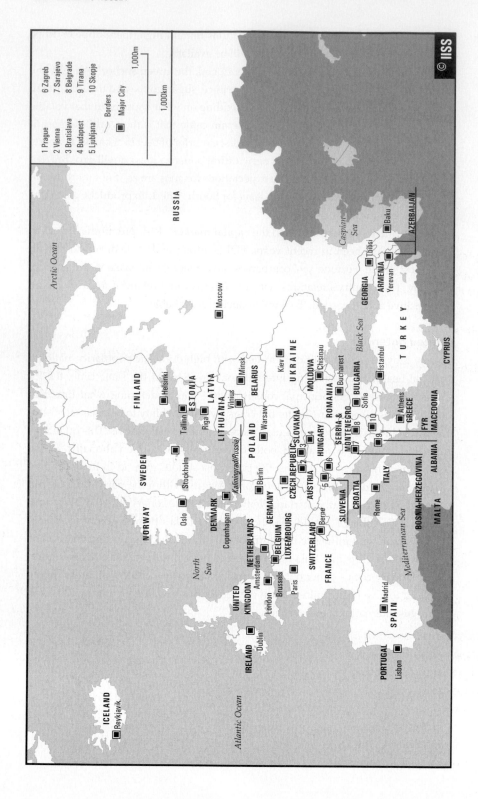

1 Prague
2 Vienna
3 Bratislava
4 Budapest
5 Ljubljana
6 Zagreb
7 Sarajevo
8 Belgrade
9 Tirana
10 Skopje

Borders
Major City

1,000m
1,000km

Europe / Russia

The Madrid bombings of 11 March 2004 highlighted a number of hard choices that European governments had to face if they were to secure their future in a more integrated world. It became clear that Europe could not be the model for multinational harmony that its leaders hoped it could be until it first demonstrated its own political cohesion and its own competence in protecting itself from external threats. The successful completion of EU enlargement and the negotiation of a new constitutional structure were the two chief political challenges, with the establishment of a coherent common foreign and security policy and improvement in economic performance and governance persistent subsidiary problems. Generating a collective counter-terrorism posture and a standing European military force with power-projection capabilities constituted the principal security challenges. As of April 2005, both endeavours seemed in some doubt. While enlargement was proceeding fitfully, it appeared that some key EU member states would reject the European Constitutional Treaty, which would make the once-dreaded prospect of a 'Europe à la carte' a distinct possibility. EU accomplishments in the security and defence arena were more palpable. The Madrid bombings prompted improvements in both the EU's counter-terrorism infrastructure and its performance. The European Defence Agency was created, EU–NATO relationships were institutionalised and NATO transferred operational control of security operations in Bosnia and Herzegovina to a European Union Force of 7,000. But the EU still had considerable difficulty projecting force abroad and had yet to define the parameters of its military mission.

In 2004–05, Russia continued to pull back from the West. There were several factors at work. The EU expanded to Russia's borders, increasing the latter's sense of geopolitical siege. Moscow's sensitivity manifested itself in its maladroit backing of pro-Russian incumbent Victor Yanukovich, who ultimately lost power in Ukraine under the pressure of the popular 'Orange Revolution'. But Russia's decreasing influence with former Soviet republics appeared real throughout Eurasia, as the people of both Georgia and Kyrgyzstan ousted authoritarian rulers who enjoyed Russia's support. Russian President Vladimir Putin both explicitly and implicitly recognised Russia's evolving weakness within its putative sphere of influence, but sought to strengthen his own power within Russia. Prompted by the tragic terrorist siege in Beslan, North Ossetia, in September 2004, in which over 300 people died, and rising terrorism within Russia, he adopted increasingly hard-line security policies at home. While Russia's policy on the separatist (and to an extent Islamist terrorist) conflict in Chechnya featured attempts to tame the larger Chechen population through political and material rewards, it remained unclear, pending October 2005 parliamentary elections, whether this effort would succeed. It was also uncertain how Putin would try to ensure that kindred political figures succeeded him when he stepped down in 2008, as required by law, though his political opponents did not appear well organised. While the Russian economy continued to rely on high oil prices, Putin's increasingly autocratic and illiberal inclinations – in particular, the state's seizure of Yukos, Russia's largest oil production company – prompted both the flight of Western capital and the criticisms of Western leaders, including US President George W. Bush.

In contrast to Russia, Turkey – in many ways the bridge between Asia and Europe, East and West – moved nominally closer to Europe, as Brussels finally, in December 2004, gave Ankara a fixed date for the beginning of accession negotiations. At the same time, Turkey's ruling Justice and Development Party (JDP)'s looming confrontation with the military over JDP attempts to compromise Kemalist secularism, questions about its appreciation of the requirements of EU membership, lingering discomfort over compromising on Turkish Cypriot sovereign rights, and economic problems cast doubts on its European vocation. Furthermore, cooler post-Iraq relations with the United States and Israel, closer links with Iran and Syria, anxieties about the resurgence of the Kurdish independence movement in Turkey cued by the political ascent of Iraqi Kurds, the JDP's islamist leanings, and a surge of insular Turkish nationalism made Turkey's strategic position less firmly aligned with the West than it had been before the Iraq war. Finally, despite its electoral success, the JDP's internal disarray (and a large number of resignations) betrayed a brittle and unsteady government. While its long-term aspirations to act as a strategic bridge and converge with Europe remained intact, for Turkey, as well as Europe and Russia, 2004–05 was marked by difficult adjustments and transitions rather than any particularly satisfying sense of arrival.

Europe: Soft Power, Hard Choices

The terrorist attacks in Madrid that took place on 11 March 2004 marked a turning point in the political development of the European continent. The changes that followed were not of the same magnitude as those experienced in the United States after the terrorist attacks of 11 September 2001; the Madrid bombings did not force Europeans to engage in a fundamental reconsideration of power and security. But the bombings did underscore a number of hard choices that European governments had to face if they were to secure their future in a more integrated world. Europe, it became clear, could not be a model for peaceful coexistence until it first put its own affairs in order. The successful completion of European Union (EU) enlargement and the negotiation of a new constitutional structure are only the two most obvious challenges to be faced. Improvement in underlying economic performance (and overlying economic governance) is important as well. Beyond such internal matters, Europe must prepare to protect its interests and project its influence with hard power as well as soft. It must secure its new borders in Eurasia, the Middle East and North Africa. And it must do all this without alienating or antagonising domestic public opinion. The speed and decisiveness with which the Spanish electorate turned against the centre-right incumbents in the March election that closely followed the bombings underscored the need to maintain political legitimacy. Perhaps even more than the threat of terrorism itself, this is a lesson that European politicians will not soon forget.

Deepening and widening

The Madrid tragedy broke the logjam in intergovernmental negotiations over the draft Treaty Establishing a Constitution for Europe (Constitutional Treaty). Almost as soon as it was clear that the Spanish Socialist Workers Party (PSOE) had triumphed over the centre-right Popular Party (PP) in the 14 March 2004 elections, incoming Prime Minister José Luís Rodríguez Zapatero made it known that he would seek to improve relations with France and Germany. In part, this declaration was a logical extension of Zapatero's pre-election commitment to withdraw Spanish troops from participation in military operations in Iraq. It also signalled that Zapatero would welcome a compromise proposal on the allocation of voting weights in the EU's Council of Ministers. Spanish withdrawal from Iraq (completed by 21 May) weakened the US-led coalition, albeit perhaps only symbolically. By contrast, the prospect of Spanish concessions gave strength to European constitution-building.

The intransigence of the preceding centre-right government of José Maria Aznar on the distribution of voting weights in the Council played an important role in bringing negotiation of the Constitutional Treaty to a halt at the 13 December 2003 meeting. Together with Leszek Miller's government in Poland, Aznar's government wanted to preserve the voting weights as allocated in the December 2000 Treaty of

Nice and which would come into force on 1 November 2004. These weights give Spain and Poland (with 27 votes each) almost as much influence in the Council as the four largest EU Member States (with 29 votes each). By contrast, the governments of Germany and France insisted on moving to a dual majority system that would count both the number of states and their relative shares of the total EU population. Such a dual majority voting system would strengthen the larger Member States at the expense of their middle-sized and smaller counterparts. Spain and Poland had the most to lose as a result.

Zapatero's willingness to concede to some form of dual majority voting left Miller isolated in his support for the Nice voting weights. Soon after Zapatero came to power, Miller indicated that he would give ground. Then, on 26 March, Miller announced his intention to resign as Poland's prime minister with effect from 2 May – one day after the EU's enlargement to include ten new Member States from Central and Eastern Europe and the Mediterranean. Meanwhile, the Irish presidency of the Council declared its intention to complete negotiation of the Constitutional Treaty in advance of the June 2004 Council summit. Progress thereafter was rapid, and the negotiations were completed in time for the June summit. The legal editing took place over the summer, and the document was signed by representatives of all 25 Member States on 29 October. Less than 12 months after the intergovernmental conference appeared to fail in Brussels, the Member States could begin ratification efforts.

The institutional changes brought about in the draft Constitutional Treaty are less sweeping that the term 'constitution' suggests. In legal fact, the document remains a 'treaty' and not a constitution. It is an agreement among states, not a social contract among peoples. It does succeed in bringing the existing European treaties (the Treaty on European Union and the Treaty Establishing the European Communities) within a common framework, yet it does little either to simplify or to shorten the combined text, which is still more than 250 pages long. While the Constitutional Treaty attempts to distinguish among EU, Member State and shared competencies, the distinctions remain difficult to discern with legal precision. The Constitutional Treaty nevertheless offers some improvements. As mentioned, it provides for qualified majority voting to take place on a dual majority basis – with 'majorities' requiring the support of 55% of the Member States representing 65% of the population. It creates a 'Union Minister for Foreign Affairs' who will combine powers from the Council and the European Commission in a single office responsible for the whole spectrum of foreign relations from security to trade. On 29 June, the Council of Ministers named Javier Solana the first 'Union Minister', while also announcing that he would remain for another five years as Secretary General of the Council and High Representative of the EU's Common Foreign and Security Policy. The Treaty also establishes the Council as a separate institution with a president who serves for two-and-one-half years rather than rotating among the Member

States every six months, and it incorporates the European 'Charter for Fundamental Rights' within the legal framework for the EU.

Such changes in the constitutional structure of the EU are marginal, yet important. With the expansion of the EU from 15 to 25 Member States on 1 May 2004, the range of challenges confronting the Union expanded considerably in terms of both issues and procedures. This is obvious with respect to the increasing number of Member States. But it is also relevant when looking at the dynamics at work within the accession countries. Just weeks before enlargement took place (on 6 April), the Lithuanian parliament voted to impeach President Rolandas Paksas for alleged links to organised crime. Poland's Prime Minister Miller resigned on 2 May, not only because he was forced to concede in European negotiations but, more importantly, because he lost control over his own Alliance of the Democratic Left (SLD). The problems are not limited to Central or Eastern Europe. With the failure of the referendum on 24 April, Cyprus remains divided in fact if not according to the principles upon which it was admitted to the EU. Moreover, relations between the Greek Cypriot government and Turkey continue to complicate European affairs. Hence it is not enough to strengthen EU procedures against the increase in membership; it is necessary to strengthen them in response to the potential for political instability within the new Member States as well.

Finally, the revisions made in the Constitutional Treaty are necessary to prepare the institutions for future enlargements. The June 2004 European Council 'recalled' that Bulgaria and Romania 'are part of the same inclusive and irreversible enlargement process' that 'saw ten new Member States join the Union on 1 May 2004'. In turn, the Council acknowledged that both countries remain on track to join the Union in 2007. If anything, these countries are somewhat more unstable politically than the preceding ten. In the 2001 Bulgarian parliamentary elections, a former Bulgarian monarch, Simeon II, was able to create a successful political movement within less than six weeks of the polling date. From that basis, he captured a bare majority of the seats in parliament. Soon thereafter, the internal discipline of his movement began to waver and his popularity with the voters fluctuated wildly. Simeon II must return to the polls in 2005 and is widely expected to lose. The situation in Romania is no more promising in terms of political stability. The centre-right presidential candidate, Traian Basescu, came from behind after the first round of voting in November 2004. In a second round of voting the following December, Basescu defeated his centre-left opponent, Adrian Nastase. This shift to the centre-right constitutes an important break with the recent past. During the transition period, Romanian politics was dominated by communist-successor groups. Nevertheless, it is still too early to tell whether Basescu's victory marks a lasting political stabilisation. Indeed, the Romanian electorate shows a troubling propensity toward extremism. In the first-round polling, the right-wing nationalist Vadim Tudor gained almost 13% of the vote. Subsequently, Tudor's approval ratings climbed to more than 20%. Such support may not seem striking when compared to that garnered by right-wing extremists in either Belgium or France. Still there is reason to believe that the Romanian case is qualitatively different. The country is ethnically more diverse, it is poorer and its political parties are more fragile. When Bulgaria and Romania join the European Union in 2007, the danger is that neither country will be stable enough domestically to participate as effective negotiating partners. Without a more robust set of European institutions, the decision-making process may become moribund as a result. The Madrid tragedy broke one such logjam, but it would be unrealistic to expect similar shocks to liberate European decision-making from others that might emerge.

Money and power

The completion of enlargement and the negotiation of the Constitutional Treaty were important events. Nevertheless, they failed to capture the popular imagination – at least in the 15 pre-existing Member States of the European Union (EU-15). The new Member States held major celebrations on enlargement day, as did the Irish EU Council presidency in Dublin. However, festivities elsewhere in the EU-15 were much more subdued. This lack of enthusiasm is unsurprising. During the months leading up to enlargement day, support for an expansion of the EU to ten new Member States started to decline. In a survey taken during February and March 2004, only 42% of respondents in the EU-15 favoured enlargement while 39% were against (with 19% still undecided). Among the larger countries, proponents of enlargement outnumbered opponents only in Italy. In France, Germany and the United Kingdom, public opinion skewed strongly against enlargement.

Lack of enthusiasm for the Constitutional Treaty was more uniform across the two parts of Europe, large and small, old and new. A *Flash Eurobarometer* published in July 2004 on the basis of fieldwork undertaken in June and July revealed that only 30% of the EU population felt well informed about the Constitutional Treaty. Meanwhile, knowledge about the contents of the Constitutional Treaty was relatively low and remained unchanged from previous surveys, despite the conclusion of negotiations among the Member States. Public information campaigns between the end of negotiations in June and the signing of the Treaty in October did little to dent these statistics. A reiteration of *Eurobarometer* polling across the enlarged European Union (EU-25) in early October revealed that 11% felt they knew something about the treaty's contents, 33% were aware of its existence, and 33% knew little or nothing at all.

The problem is not so much ignorance as preoccupation. Even if Europeans were aware of enlargement and constitutional reform, the focus of their concern lay elsewhere. The contrast with the United States is striking. In the US, 11 September recast American politics around security and the war on terror. The Madrid bombings had no such effect. Despite widespread outrage about the tragedy, the bombings failed to drive security issues – including terrorism – to the top of the popular political agenda. Instead, European electorates continued to focus on economic concerns, principally unemployment. When European voters went to elect a new European Parliament in June, 51% of respondents across the EU-25 felt that unemployment should be the major theme in campaigning, as compared to only 32% for terrorism, 30% for economic growth, 30% for crime and 29% for the future of pensions. The contrast between unemployment and terrorism is less sharp, at 47% and 35% respectively, when the sample is restricted to the EU-15, but it is much more pronounced in the new Member States, where unemployment is the major theme for 72% of respondents and terrorism is a distant fifth at only 17%. These concerns translated into abstentions at the polls. At just under 46%, participation rates in the June 2004 elections to European Parliament were the lowest since the introduction of direct elections in 1979. In Slovakia, turnout was a derisory 17%.

Such concern for economic issues can be explained by three factors: the weakness of European economic performance; the controversy surrounding the Stability and Growth Pact; and the failure of the Lisbon strategy to transform Europe into the world's most competitive and dynamic knowledge-based economy. Of the three, the weakness of macroeconomic performance is the most easily described. In 2003, real growth in GDP was only 0.5% in the EU-15 and 0.9% across the EU-25 as a whole – with unemployment averaging 8.9% of the labour force in the EU-15 and 9.1% in the EU-25. Growth accelerated moderately during the first half of 2004, but unemployment remained level. Such aggregates do obscure huge disparities in performance from one country to the next. A few of the smaller countries – the Baltic states, Ireland, Greece, Slovakia – grew at a much higher rate. However, even these countries continue to suffer from unemployment. The Baltic states and Greece have unemployment rates above the European average. Unemployment in Slovakia is more than 17%. And while Ireland's unemployment rate is much lower – 4.6% in 2003 – it is nevertheless increasing year on year and in spite of the country's relatively high growth rate.

The controversy over the stability and growth pact is a holdover from the events of 25 November 2003. At that time, the governments of France and Germany moved in the EU's Council of Economics and Finance Ministers (ECOFIN Council) to suspend the rules for fiscal performance required of all countries that participate in the euro. Both the French and German governments were running fiscal deficits in excess of 3% of GDP. Both also faced sanctions for having failed to rectify the situation. Nevertheless, neither government was willing to cut back on fiscal outlays in a manner that might trigger (or deepen) a domestic economic recession. Suspending the rules was the only way they could see to square the circle. The reactions of the smaller Member States and from the European institutions fuelled the controversy. The Dutch government decried the abuse of European procedures even though it too would be found in breach of the fiscal rules on 2

June 2004. The Commission filed a petition before the European Court of Justice (ECJ) on 27 January 2004 to annul the actions of the ECOFIN Council for abuse of procedure. The ECJ upheld the Commission's request for annulment, but maintained that control over the stability and growth pact remained within the power of the Member States.

The ECJ ruling added impetus to calls to reform the stability and growth pact in order to make the rules for fiscal behaviour more compatible with the promotion of economic growth. Nevertheless, the tension between small-country emphasis on strict adherence and large-country demands for fiscal flexibility remained acute. This division extended all the way down to public opinion, with 49% of respondents favouring strict interpretation of the rules and 43% accepting the need for greater flexibility. In autumn 2004 and winter 2005, successive Council presidencies struggled to find a formula for successful stability and growth pact reform. Ultimately the Luxembourg presidency settled on a fudge. At the March 2005 European Council Summit, the Member States agreed to retain strict rules for enforcing fiscal stability but also to enumerate ambiguous conditions under which the rules could be ignored.

The failure of the Lisbon strategy is another recurrent theme. The original goal of the Lisbon strategy as announced in March 2000 was to create the world's most competitive and dynamic knowledge-based economy. However, data indicating slow growth and high unemployment made it clear this was not in train. The Council therefore called for the appointment of a high-level group chaired by former Dutch prime minister Wim Kok to make recommendations as to how the Lisbon strategy could be improved. The findings in the Kok report, presented on 1 November 2004, were damning. According to Kok, the Lisbon strategy was overloaded with too many goals and targets. Member state activities were spread too thinly, priorities for action were unclear and progress was slow. Kok therefore argued that the Lisbon strategy should focus more narrowly on growth and employment. He conceded that the goal should be to maintain Europe's position as 'one of' the world's most competitive and dynamic knowledge-based economies, and insisted on prompt action to ensure the survival of the European social model. These findings informed the deliberations of the European Council in March 2005. As the Member States wrestled with the complicated problem of reforming the stability and growth pact, they had less difficulty accepting the need to re-consecrate their economic policies around the goal of promoting more growth and employment. The problem, however, is that the EU has little or no influence over the success of such efforts. Although the Lisbon strategy is announced at the European level, the real task of reforming inefficient market structures and over-burdened welfare states remains firmly within the ambit of national governments, and national reform efforts continue to encounter significant opposition – especially from labour unions.

Security and defence

The reaction of European political elites to the Madrid bombings was to pull together a number of ideas and projects that were already emerging both in the development of a European security and defence identity writ large and in the European approach to the 'war on terror' more narrowly. In March 2004, on the first day of the European Council summit – usually reserved for economic matters – the Council presidency issued a series of documents and declarations on combating terrorism. It invoked the solidarity clause set out in Article 42 of the draft Constitutional Treaty committing the Member States to 'mobilize all the instruments at their disposal, including military resources' to prevent further terrorist atrocities. It created a revised plan of action and set specific timetables to improve the flow of information among the Schengen countries and to strengthen border controls and travel document security. Most important, perhaps, the European Council created a counter-terrorism coordinator to operate within the Secretariat of the Council of Ministers. Javier Solana, secretary-general of the Council, appointed former Dutch deputy interior minister Gijs de Vries to fill the new counter-terrorism post. Subsequently, the development of EU counter-terrorism policy became a predominant theme in Council deliberations. At the June 2004 summit, the Council enumerated the achievements made in the previous three months – particularly with respect to information flow and border controls. It called for more active work to combat terrorist financing, to facilitate information exchange between intelligence agencies, and to enhance civil protection. It also underlined 'the importance of making use of the wide-ranging instruments of the European Union in the context of all factors which contribute to terrorism'. Finally, the Council announced its intention to review progress twice a year beginning December 2004.

Counter-terrorism was again a major theme at the Council summit held in November 2004. However, the main purpose of the summit was to reinforce the development of the EU as an area of freedom, security and justice. The 'Hague Programme' is a comprehensive initiative to embed the principle 'that when preserving national security, the Member States should take full account of the security of the Union as a whole'. As such, it embraces the full range of domestic security concerns from drugs and crime to citizenship, asylum and immigration. The programme draws inspiration from aspirations set out in the Constitutional Treaty, but the legal basis for action can also be found in the existing treaties. Within the overarching framework of the Hague Programme, the European Union has already made particular progress on terrorist financing, intelligence cooperation and border security. In November, the European Council called on the Council of Ministers to develop 'a long-term strategy to address the factors which contribute to radicalization and recruitment for terrorist activities'. On 22 November, the Council also adopted 'a conceptual framework on the European Security and Defence Policy (ESDP) dimension of the fight against terror'.

European action in the area of security and defence was not limited either to counter-terrorism or domestic notions of public safety. Both the EU and the Member States made progress in bringing the December 2003 European Security Strategy (ESS) to life. The ESS stresses the importance of developing a real capability for European force projection both within and outside the context of the Atlantic alliance. Given the ongoing tension in the transatlantic relationship, Europeans on all sides of the debate were eager to make progress with this agenda. Strengthened European capabilities would not only liberate European politicians from American tutelage, but they would also increase the potential for transatlantic cooperation in foreign and security policy. Notable progress was made in three areas: the creation of a European Defence Agency; the strengthening of relations between the EU and NATO; and the elaboration of new European battle groups for future force projection.

The European Defence Agency (EDA) was first proposed during the June 2003 European Council summit as the EU Member States considered an early draft of the European Security Strategy. The purpose of the EDA is fourfold: to improve member state capabilities; to facilitate armaments cooperation between Member States; to strengthen the competitiveness of European defence industries; and to foster new research and development. Institutionally, the EDA operates under the authority of the Council and is open to participation from all Member States. A joint action plan to create the EDA was agreed shortly before the June 2004 European Council, which welcomed the EDA's establishment. Javier Solana, as secretary-general of the Council, assumed responsibility as chair of the EDA steering board. On 30 July, Solana appointed Nick Witney, a former director general for international security policy from the UK Ministry of Defence, to be the EDA's first executive director. Thereafter, the agency's activities have remained predominantly organisational. The steering board met in September and November 2004 to review progress, agree budgets and outline strategies for growth and consolidation. The work programme for 2005 leads off with the priorities of ensuring that the agency is 'properly established', of making sure that it has 'the right relations with participating Member States' and that it has 'the right relations with other key stakeholders'. Should the EDA succeed, it will go a long way to supporting the more efficient use of European defence capabilities.

Strengthening relations between NATO and the EU was a necessary complement to the enlargement of both organisations. NATO expanded to 26 Member States in March 2004, taking in a number of countries about to join the EU and two countries, Bulgaria and Romania, which will not become EU members until 2007. While the expanded membership of both organisations presented a host of new challenges and opportunities, they remained constrained by an imperfect overlap in membership and by the disagreement between the United States and some of its European allies over the conduct of the war in Iraq. Hence while the EU and NATO had finally agreed on procedures for European use of NATO assets under the Berlin Plus framework in 2003, the use of this arrangement remained limited. The June 2004 NATO summit in Istanbul, however, was an important step toward institutional coopera-tion. To begin with, NATO leaders agreed to scale down alliance deployments in Bosnia and Herzegovina and to transfer operational control to a new European Union Force (EUFOR) that would operate under a UN mandate within the context of Berlin Plus. When it took up position in December 2004, this 7,000-strong force would be the largest-ever EU deployment. NATO leaders also agreed to participate in the training of Iraqi security forces, strengthened Euro-Atlantic cooperation in the Caucasus and Central Asia, and launched a new 'Istanbul Cooperation Initiative' for the Middle East. The summit was not the major breakthrough that some observers had hoped for, but it offered hope for progress nonetheless.

The US presidential elections and the ongoing violence in Iraq initially lowered expectations for a transatlantic rapprochement. The November 2004 European Council congratulated President Bush on his victory; however, it also issued a decla-ration on Iraq that not only failed to mention either the United States or the coalition forces but also emphasised that EU involvement could not take place inside Iraq until 'all security concerns' were 'appropriately addressed'. Nevertheless, progress continued on the institutional front. Soon after EUFOR took up its positions in Bosnia and Herzegovina, the European Council agreed detailed plans for the creation of permanent liaison facilities for the EU at Supreme Headquarters Allied Powers Europe and for NATO within the European Union Military Staff. During the early months of 2005, institutional accommodation between NATO and the EU prevailed over political unease or ill will. US Secretary of State Condoleezza Rice and President Bush came to Europe for their first official visits abroad during Bush's second term. Coming on the heels of fairly successful democratic elections in Iraq, these visits helped change the tone of the transatlantic relationship. More importantly, they provided an opportunity for the Bush administration to state clearly its support for the creation of a European security and defence identity and for European integra-tion more generally. President Bush made a point of going to Brussels. In a statement of the North Atlantic Council, the heads of state and government declared that 'a stronger EU will further contribute to our common security'.

The promise of European integration – and to an extent transatlantic relations – lies in the better use of European defence capabilities. The EDA goes part of the way toward making European security policy more efficient. Strengthened rela-tions between the EU and NATO go further still. Yet the EU has considerable difficulty projecting force abroad. The November 2004 decision to develop 13 small and readily deployable battle groups (each with about 1,500 personnel) provides one possible solution. While it does not answer demands for EU force creation, it has the virtue of furnishing relatively discrete units that can be assembled individu-ally. These units could be used for crisis management operations worldwide. The first such group is to be set up in 2005 and the rest are to be operational by 2007.

Friends and neighbours

Whatever the success of the European battle groups, NATO–EU relations or the EDA, Europeans will continue to emphasise the role of soft power rather than hard power. European-preferred security responsibilities are almost certain to be more regional than global in nature. And European soft power is more influential when exercised more closely to home. The best example of this is the process of European enlargement. During the aftermath of the 1999 Kosovo crisis, the Cologne European Council called on the European Commission to draw up plans to make the prospect of membership real to all candidate countries in Central and Eastern Europe. The results culminated in the vast enlargement on 1 May 2004. While concern may be warranted about the political stability of some of the new Member States, it is necessary also to recognise the intrinsically stabilising influence that the process of accession to EU membership provided. But as the EU has expanded to encompass almost the whole European continent, the opportunities to apply 'enlargement' as an instrument of security policy have become more restricted and the potential costs – both economic and political – have become higher. The EU officially recognises only a few countries as actual or potential candidates for membership. Bulgaria and Romania will join in 2007. The European Council agreed at its December 1999 summit in Helsinki to treat Turkey as a candidate like any other, and acknowledged at the Feira summit in June 2000 that all countries in the western Balkans are potential candidates for EU membership. In practice, however, only one of the western Balkan countries, Croatia, has been allowed to submit a formal application for membership.

Bulgaria and Romania remain firmly on track to join the EU in 2007. The situation for Turkey is more complicated. Turkey has long sought to join in the process of European integration. Time and again, however, the Member States have resisted Turkish applications. The arguments against Turkey's joining centre on the relative size and poverty of the country as well as its poor record on human rights. The decision taken at Helsinki did not ignore such concerns, but insisted that Turkey must adhere to the same criteria for membership as all other candidates. These include reference to the rule of law, respect for human rights and demonstration of the economic capacity to participate in the single European market. Since 1999, Turkey has made tremendous efforts at reform. It has brought the police under tighter control, abolished the death penalty and made headway in market liberalisation. The December 2003 European Council acknowledged this progress and called for the Commission to undertake a formal review of Turkey's application so that the December 2004 Council could announce a starting date for negotiations. The Council of Europe also recognised the extent of Turkish reforms and in March recommended that close monitoring of Turkey could be discontinued.

Despite such positive recognition, public opinion in much of the EU remained steadfastly opposed to Turkish accession. In October, French President Jacques Chirac attempted to allay popular concerns by promising to hold a referendum on Turkish membership at some point in the future, but this commitment only heightened concerns about the accession process. When the Commission finally released its report on Turkey, observers noted both its positive conclusion and its strong conditions. The subsequent Council decision struck a similar balance. Turkey would be allowed to begin negotiations on membership from 3 October 2005, but accession could not take place before 2014. Meanwhile Turkey would have to continue with reforms, and recognise the government of Cyprus. It could be subject to 'long transition periods', and in any case accept that 'these negotiations are an open-ended process, the outcome of which cannot be guaranteed beforehand'. Progress for Turkey since the December 2004 Council has been mixed. At the start of 2005, the introduction of a new Turkish lira (taking six zeros off the old lira) provided significant economic improvements. However, a police assault on a group of women's rights protestors in March was a setback, tarnishing Turkey's human-rights reputation. Negotiations are still set to begin on 3 October 2005, but public opinion is unlikely to become any more receptive to Turkish membership.

The situation for Croatia is at once straightforward and intractable. The June 2004 European Council accepted a Commission recommendation that Croatia be allowed to apply for EU membership. In turn it called for negotiations to begin early in 2005. The only strong condition it required is that Croatia cooperate with the International Criminal Tribunal for the former Yugoslavia (ICTY) and hand over 'the remaining indictee', the fugitive general Ante Gotovina. When the Council returned to this issue the following December, it clarified that negotiations could start on 17 March 2005 and it 'reiterated that the remaining indictee must be located and transferred to the Hague as soon as possible'. As the date for negotiations to start approached, however, the Croatian government claimed it could not find Gotovina in order to hand him over. On 16 March 2004, the European Council presidency decided to postpone negotiations until a resolution of this issue could be found.

The other countries in the western Balkans are unlikely to be ready for membership in the near future. The Former Yugoslav Republic of Macedonia is perhaps the closest, but still must struggle with the deep ethnic divisions in the country. The April 2004 presidential elections offered some reassurance that the voters were more interested in conventional economic matters than in ethnic conflict. The potential for a renewal of conflict remains a concern nonetheless. Certainly the ethnic violence witnessed across the border in Kosovo the previous March gave considerable cause for alarm. Over a two day period, ethnic Albanian Kosovars destroyed over 700 homes and 30 orthodox churches while at the same time displacing approximately 4,500 ethnic Serbs, Ashkali and Roma residents. This outburst of violence underscored both the need to maintain a strong NATO presence in the country and the difficulty of resolving the final status of Kosovo relative to the Republic of Serbia and Montenegro. Bosnia and Herzegovina also has difficulties. Soon after EUFOR assumed operational control in the country in December 2004, the high representative, Paddy Ashdown, had a major confrontation with the Bosnian Serb government. Ashdown accused them of failing to pursue Ratko Mladic and Radovan Karadzic, perhaps the two best known of the ICTY's outstanding indictees. When Ashdown sacked a group of police and security officers, he provoked the resignation of a number of Bosnian Serb officials and brought into crisis the functioning of the country's central government.

The readiness of the western Balkans for membership in the EU may not be the most important issue. As the European Council noted in June 1999, what matters most is that the prospect of membership is real for the countries concerned. In this sense, the problems in the western Balkans are nevertheless still best addressed within the context of eventual membership – leaving aside when that eventuality will come to pass. Signs in Bosnia advertising the transition from SFOR to EUFOR are subtitled 'from stabilisation to integration'. Even in the most troubled parts of the Balkans, this slogan rings true. This is not so for those countries outside the ambit of actual or potential membership. For them, European soft power is projected without the promise of membership attached. In March 2003, the European Commission proposed that the EU develop a new 'Neighbourhood Policy' to bring together many of the disparate instruments in use for the development of good relations with the remaining formerly Soviet republics of Belarus, Ukraine, Moldova and Russia, as well as the countries of the Caucasus, the Middle East and the South Mediterranean. In this way, the Commission could develop a common framework for encouraging reform, promoting development and structuring bilateral relations between the EU and the many diverse countries along its borders. The Commission further elaborated this new instrument in a communication published in July 2003, and came out with a full-blown strategy paper in May 2004 that was adopted by the European Council the following June.

The Neighbourhood Policy has been very successful in structuring relations between the EU and its bordering regions, particularly with those countries that never seriously entertained aspirations to full membership. However, it has been less effective in countries, like the Ukraine, that fear the Neighbourhood Policy is designed to keep them out. The controversy and aftermath of the 2004 presidential elections in the Ukraine illustrates the problems that this poses. When Victor Yanukovich defeated Victor Yushchenko in a poll held on 21 November, the EU refused to recognise the outcome. As popular protests mounted, the EU supported calls for a re-running of the contest. Moreover, the personal intervention of Polish President Aleksander Kwasniewski provided essential mediation between the opposition, the government and the courts. Ultimately, the Ukrainian Supreme Court annulled the first contest. On 8 December the Ukrainian Parliament called for fresh elections, and on 26 December, Victor Yushchenko achieved a decisive victory. Almost immediately, he began to pressure for Ukrainian membership in the EU, with strong Polish support. In a non-binding resolution, Members of the European Parliament voted 467 to 19 in favour of giving the Ukraine 'a clear

European perspective'. The European Commission is left with the awkward task of explaining why a democratic Ukraine can only expect to be a 'neighbour' and not a 'member state'. Nevertheless, the arguments against an early Ukrainian application are at least as strong as those against Turkish membership. With almost 50m people and a per capita income of only $4,155 (adjusted for purchasing power), the Ukraine is both very large and very poor. It has unstable political institutions and it is still in need of major market reforms. President Yushchenko believes that only the promise of membership can motivate Ukrainians to stay on the reform path. President Kwasniewski insists that Ukraine be given the chance to rejoin the European fold. Yet it is an open question whether the EU actually has the soft-power resources to underwrite a successful transition of the Ukraine from stabilisation into membership. Given Brussels' difficulty in negotiating a financial framework for the period 2007–13, there is considerable reason to believe that it does not.

Democracy and solidarity

The role of public opinion in this new European dispensation remains unclear. The relative importance of the EU in contrast to the various countries of Europe remains unclear as well. It is possible to review European political developments with the EU at the centre of the analysis, but that is no guarantee as to where the real power in Europe actually lies. The Spanish electorate has signalled the danger of losing legitimacy in the eyes of the voters. The Ukrainian electorate underscores the power of popular aspirations to democracy. In both instances, the focus is on domestic and not European politics. By contrast, the low turnout in European parliamentary elections suggests either frustration or disengagement. The EU is a focal point for analysts, but not for popular political support. The weakness of popular identification with Europe reveals itself in three areas: growing opposition to multi-cultural society, tense bargaining over European financial resources, and the difficulty of ratifying the European constitutional treaty through popular referendums.

The assassination of the Dutch filmmaker Theo van Gogh on 2 November 2004 by a man believed to be a Muslim radical – van Gogh had made a movie critical of the treatment of women in Islamic culture – triggered a powerful wave of anti-Islamic sentiment across the Netherlands. In the immediate aftermath, this sentiment was expressed in attacks on mosques and Islamic schools. Over the longer term, however, it centred on support for the right-wing politician Geert Wilders – a former Liberal who left his party to start a self-named list (GroepWilders) in the style of another recent Dutch populist, the late Pim Fortuyn. Wilders, like Fortuyn before him, hopes to tap into popular concerns about the threat of immigration to Dutch cultural identity. In making this appeal, Wilders achieved strong initial success. November polling data indicated that his self-styled list could capture up to 16% of the popular vote, or 24 seats out of 150 in the second chamber of the Dutch parliament. Although that support has died down, the potential for Dutch voters to mobilise around xenophobic platforms remains. The link between such anti-immigrant mobilisation and anti-European sentiment remains as well. Wilders is both a leading campaigner against ratification of the European constitution and an ardent supporter of regaining Dutch independence in Europe.

The rejection of multiculturalism is not limited to racism. It also extends to sincerely held beliefs within European countries. The initial failure to appoint the European Commission is a good example. The European Council announced the appointment of José Manuel Durão Barroso as president-designate of the European Commission at the same time it reappointed Javier Solana in late June 2004. Soon thereafter, Barroso began assembling his Commission team. Among the candidates on offer was the Italian philosopher and Christian Democratic politician Rocco Buttiglione. Barroso allocated Buttiglione the portfolio for 'Freedom and Security'. But during the confirmation hearings in the European Parliament it emerged that Buttiglione held very conservative Catholic beliefs about homosexuals and about the social role of women. More liberal members of the European Parliament objected strongly both to the candidate commissioner and to the portfolio which he had been allocated. Buttiglione expressed concern that he was being discriminated against on the basis of his religion. Ultimately, the Commission was reshuffled and Buttiglione agreed to be dropped.

At least part of the reason that politicians like Wilders achieve success in the Netherlands is that country's high level of net contributions to EU coffers. As a share of domestic product, the Dutch give more than any other Member State – including the UK. Such high net contributions make it easy for populist politicians to charge that the EU is a drain on national resources. In December 2003, the six largest net contributor countries wrote a letter to then European Commission president Romano Prodi arguing that the level of EU finances should be restricted to no more than 1% of gross national income (GNI). The Commission responded that a failure to fund the EU adequately would cut deeply into the resources available for essential EU projects like the Hague Programme, the EDA and the Neighbourhood Policy. The European Council accepted this argument at its December 2004 summit, and agreed 'to maintain the ceiling for the own resources [sic] at the current level of 1.24% of EU GNI'. Nevertheless, it failed to arrive a formula for distributing the burden. The British government insists on receiving its rebate, the Dutch government demands a reduction in its net contribution and the German government points to the costs it shoulders for the unification of Germany. Finding a compromise between these positions was not possible and negotiations over the financial framework at the March 2005 European Council summit offered no results.

Meanwhile, the EU Member States must move forward with the ratification of the constitutional treaty. The difficulty is twofold. Firstly, at least ten countries have chosen to consult the people through referendums. In at least three of those countries, the outcomes remain uncertain. The British public is the most Euro-sceptical and therefore the least likely to support ratification. However, the British referendum will also be the last held, and it will take place long after the 5 May 2005 parliamentary contest. Prime Minister Tony Blair is widely expected to win a third mandate and could therefore be in a good position to wage an aggressive pro-ratification campaign. Even then, he may not have to. The French referendum on the EU Constitutional Treaty is scheduled for 29 May 2005. Opinion polls taken in March and April show a strong lead for the opposition vote. If the motion fails to pass in France, it will likely be withdrawn in Britain. The same is true for the Netherlands, whose citizens will go to the polls in an increasingly Euro-sceptical environment. Although the Netherlands is a small country, it is also a founding member of both the EU and NATO. Its failure to win a popular endorsement of the Constitutional Treaty would be a significant blow to European integration. Certainly it would be more difficult to ignore than unfavourable results recorded in previous small-country referendums in Denmark (1992) and Ireland (2001).

Although the Spanish electorate overwhelmingly endorsed the European Constitutional Treaty with 77% support in a referendum held on 20 February 2005, and the Italian parliament added its endorsement the following April, it appeared that France and the Netherlands could well vote 'no'. Generally, it is clear that Europe has shifted farther away from getting its own collective house in order in terms of allocating acceptable financial burdens, imposing realistic economic constraints and using the prospect of EU membership equitably. If the constitution is voted down by France and the Netherlands at the end of May 2005, then Europe will be in for a period of navel-gazing that would be unprecedented even against the highly introverted standards that the EU has so frequently set. Enlargement would be at risk, but so would the idea of the EU as a semi-coherent political–economic entity. The concept of a Europe à la carte would then have to be seriously debated.

Putin's Dilemmas

The second half of 2004 and first half of 2005 witnessed a number of strategic developments in Eurasia that are likely to determine the future trends in an increasingly complex region. In Russia itself, the year was dominated by the tragic events in Beslan, North Ossetia, where on 1 September 2004 a group of terrorists captured a school, taking more than 1,300 people hostage. In the chaotic events that followed, over 335 people died. To many Russians, the Beslan tragedy became Russia's 11 September. It has had a profound impact on the North Caucasus region, and has led to major political changes throughout the Russian Federation. President Vladimir Putin moved to consolidate his power through controversial political reforms. Yet the concentration of power in the hands of the president and Russia's federal centre could weaken rather than strengthen the ability of the state to deal with future crises.

In the economic sphere Russia gained from high oil prices, but suffered from capital flight as a result of the government's effective seizure and dismantlement of Yukos, Russia's largest oil production company, and the indictment of Mikhail Khodorkovsky, its chief executive officer, for fraud and tax evasion. In foreign policy, Russia struggled to consolidate its influence in the face of revolutionary regime changes in neighbouring Ukraine and Kyrgyzstan, which prompted a further increase in American and European engagement in Eurasia. Russia welcomed the re-election of US President George W. Bush in November 2004, and his second term is likely to produce a stable but increasingly limited agenda in US–Russia relations. In Asia, Russia strengthened its economic ties with China and India, granting their companies stakes in Russia's energy sector. However, Russia's quest to become an Asian power remained constrained. Relations with traditional European partners such as Germany, France, Italy and Spain provided rare examples of Russian foreign-policy successes amid growing tensions between the EU and Russia over developments in Ukraine, the South Caucasus and Russia's relations with the Baltic states.

In Eurasia, the year brought a number of profound changes. The concept of the 'former Soviet space' became history as the region moved towards a new geostrategic reality. In May, the three Baltic states become members of the EU. EU enlargement and the November 2003 'Rose Revolution' in Georgia led to the expansion of ties between Europe and all three South Caucasus states. The war in Iraq and the 'Greater Middle East' project of the Bush administration provided the strategic rationale behind increasing US engagement in the Black Sea region, fostering closer political and security ties with Georgia, Armenia and Azerbaijan. In November 2004, the 'Orange Revolution' in Ukraine consolidated the country's orientation towards the EU and closer ties with NATO. The message of European integration dominated the 6 March parliamentary elections in Moldova, which borders Romania, an EU candidate country. An unexpected and chaotic ousting of Kyrgyzstan's President Askar Akayev in March 2005 amid allegations of election fraud is likely to have a major impact on other Central Asia states.

Just as in the early 1990s, popular revolutions raised new hopes about democratisation and improvement in economic well-being among millions of people in Eurasia. The new governments, which swept to power on waves of popular discontent with old regimes, will struggle to meet their expectations. Success depends on the capacity of new elites to deliver quick political and economic change, as well as on whether Russia, Europe and the United States find a pragmatic modus vivendi to reconcile their diverse interests in the region. There are growing concerns that government in countries which so far have managed to contain mass popular protests could take drastic measures to safeguard their regimes and resort to repression and violence. At the same time, if popular uprisings spread to other states in Eurasia, the region could be thrown into a period of instability with worrying consequences for neighbouring Europe and Asia. In Russia itself, the political succession process for President Putin, who is due to step down in 2008, represents a major concern. While revolutionary change of power is less likely in Russia with a strong centralised government and weak political opposition, there is little chance of a democratic transfer of power. In the meantime, nationalist political groups, who perceive the growing Western engagement in Eurasia as a threat and call for a tougher Russian policy towards its neighbours, are gaining popularity and political influence.

Putin's political challenges

After securing an easy, practically unchallenged re-election on 14 March 2004, in which he won more than 70% of the vote, Putin faces a number of formidable challenges during his second term in office. The first challenge relates to preparing the ground for political succession. It is likely to dominate many key political and economic decisions during the next four years. Under the 1993 Russian Constitution, Putin is due to step down in 2008 and his time to prepare the country and its political elite for the transition to a new leadership is shrinking. However, it appears increasingly difficult for Putin to ensure that succession will leave his allies in place to continue with his policies. In March 2005, the State Duma authorised the creation of the Public Chamber – in effect, a shadow parliament that will be composed entirely of Putin appointees, and empowered to propose constitutional changes. Some Russian political observers have construed this innovation as presaging a move by the Kremlin to amend the constitution to allow Putin to stay in office beyond 2008. The elite that has emerged under Putin's rule has incentives to keep him in office. These incentives relate primarily to their financial interests as new 'political clans' gain control through their appointment to the boards of the state-owned companies and through transfer of assets through new re-privatisation deals (as in the case of Yukos). However, members of the political elite who supported Putin not for financial but for specific political and ideological reasons are growing increasingly critical of what they perceive as his failure to reassert Russia's great power role in the face of its 'encirclement' by NATO and in the wake of revolutions in Eurasia.

Nevertheless, Putin himself still enjoys considerable popularity, and polls indicate that – notwithstanding Beslan and unpopular social reforms – the people generally approve of his strong hand. Yet Ukraine's 'Orange Revolution' (in which the Russian-backed incumbent prime minister ultimately had to relinquish his post) and a pensioners' revolt have inspired dissent and made Putin look vulnerable. Although Putin's political opposition remains divided both among liberal parties on the right, and among nationalist and communist movements on the left, the party in power, Unity, also remains nothing more than a bureaucratic coalition behind President Putin, lacking a clear platform or capacity to take independent positions on key domestic and foreign policies. It needs vast administrative resources within the central and regional bureaucracies to keep control beyond 2008. Therefore, consolidation of power and greater control over regional political elites are among Putin's highest priorities. However, consolidation of power does not improve its efficiency. On the contrary, it focuses all responsibility for policy failures on Putin and his government. Moreover, without an effective system of checks and balances, the government is increasingly unable to prevent and handle political, socio-economic and security crises within Russia, which are set to snowball in the next few years.

The second major challenge for the Russian leadership relates to security within Russia. In 2000, Putin was elected largely on the 'security and order' platform. However, since 2003, Russia has witnessed growing insecurity both on the level of individuals and the state as a whole. A growing number of terrorist attacks exposed flawed policies in Chechnya and the inability of Russia's security forces to prevent and manage major terrorist incidents. In the quantity and scale of terrorist attacks, 2004 was the record year in Russia's post-Soviet history. Over 600 people were killed by acts of terrorism. Radical elements among Chechen separatist fighters, who were disenfranchised from the political process in Chechnya, unleashed a major wave of terrorist attacks in summer 2004. On 21–22 June, they conducted a major attack against the Interior Ministry of Ingushetia, the region neighbouring Chechnya, killing over 90 police officials and others. On 24 August two airliners went down simultaneously as a result of bombs planted by Chechen terrorists, killing all 89 people on board. A week later a suicide bomber killed ten in Moscow. Finally, in September 2004, a group of terrorists captured a school in Beslan, a small town near Vladikavkaz, the capital of North Ossetia. The terrorists held more than 1,300 people hostage. Local security services and law enforcement structures failed to react quickly and efficiently. Publicly, the authorities deliberately understated the number of hostages in the school, provoking a strong reaction among local people. There was a great deal of confusion on the ground and security services did little to prepare for possible outcomes. Moreover, talks with the terrorists did not yield productive results. According to witnesses, many officials refused to enter into dialogue when contacted by the terrorists. On 3 September, an explosion in the school gymnasium where the hostages were being held provoked chaos in which over 335 hostages died, either killed by terrorists or falling victim to a fire-fight among terrorists, Russian security forces and the local armed population.

Speculation persists as to whether the explosion was an accidental detonation of terrorists' explosives, which were placed throughout the school, or whether it was carried out as part of a covert operation by the Russian security services to allow hostages to escape. The evidence suggests that no coordinated attempt to storm the school was carried out. Russian forces were poorly prepared, and over 30 died trying to save children escaping from the school and in the fire-fight with terrorists that lasted for over 12 hours after the first explosion. The entire day of fighting was broadcast live on Russian TV and internationally. Horrific pictures of chaos and dying children shocked people in Russia and across the world, and exposed the extreme nature of the terrorism which Russia faces.

The media broadcasts of Beslan exposed the inability of the Russian domestic security system to handle this growing terrorist threat. Beslan had a major impact on the Russian public, exacerbating doubts about the government's assurances that the Second Chechen War made Russians safer. However, as in any situation of national tragedy, people rallied around their leaders and awaited Putin's response. On 4 September, Putin addressed the nation, outlining major political reforms and the overhaul of the security system for the North Caucasus region, but signalling no change of policy in Chechnya. The political reforms increased presidential powers by introducing the de facto appointment of governors (who now have to be elected by local legislatures upon the presentation of a candidate by the president), a new proportional system for election in the parliament (which favoured the pro-presidential party already holding a majority in the State Duma) and establishing a Civic Chamber composed of representatives of civil-society organisations to provide some form of oversight, although its composition and powers remain unclear.

Many analysts believe that these reforms were in the making long before the tragedy in Beslan. They seem to focus more on addressing the challenge of succession, rather than strengthening the security system in order to address growing terrorist threats. Putin's reforms were widely criticised by Russian liberals and foreign critics as diverting Russia from its democratic path. The reforms have produced no real changes at the regional level. Between January and March 2005, after the law entered into force, Putin reappointed many previously elected governors, indicating that many regional leaders had accumulated enough power that Moscow might risk instability across the country in trying to remove them. Moreover, there is a severe shortage of administrative capacity in the current administration, which gives rise to powerful new professional leaders in the regions.

Following the tragedy in Beslan, some measures were implemented to address specific lessons identified by the government. Putin established a new 'Special Federal Commission for the North Caucasus' headed by Dmitry Kozak. A new crisis-management system was set up aimed at coordinating police, security and military forces' responses to potential terrorist threats. However, this system has yet to demonstrate improved results. Some regional security officials were dismissed, but no major changes were made at the top of Russia's security institutions, headed by Putin's close allies from his career in the Soviet KGB. Finally, in response to demands from relatives of the Beslan victims, a special parliamentary commission was set up, composed of representatives of the upper and lower chambers of parliament, to investigate events in Beslan. The commission is due to publish part of their report, but it is unlikely to reassure relatives who continue to demand a full report from regional and central authorities. The Russian government, and Putin himself, have invested considerable efforts to prevent possible revenge attacks against ethnic Ingush and Chechens, who were among the terrorists in Beslan. It seems that the threat of escalation in the Ossetian–Ingush conflict, dormant since 1992, has been contained and no major incidents of ethnic violence have taken place between the Ossetian and Ingush populations.

While Moscow moved to re-establish order in the North Caucasus, instances of crime, assassination and inter-ethnic tension spread throughout the region. In October 2004, in the Karachaevo–Cherkessian Republic, a relative of the governor allegedly ordered the deliberate assassination of his business partners, sparking protests against the regional administration. In January–March 2005, Russian forces conducted a number of special operations against alleged terrorist cells in Kabardino–Balkaria and Ingushetia. Dozens of police were assassinated in Daghestan, including the deputy minister of interior, Magomed Omarov, who was killed in a broad daylight in Makhachkala, the capital, on 2 February 2005.

Instability in the North Caucasus significantly increased in 2004–05, and it is likely to grow further. Developments in the region are bound to have a major impact on Russia's domestic security, and potentially on the security of Russia's neighbours in the South Caucasus. The Russian government, however, does not seem to have a clear strategy on how to stabilise the North Caucasus. The region is among the least economically developed in Russia. The seven republics of the North Caucasus – Daghestan, Chechnya, Ingushetia, North Ossetia, Kabardino–Balkaria, Karachaevo–Cherkessia and Adygea – are ethnically diverse and have a history of inter-ethnic conflict. While the Russian government heavily subsidises their regional budgets (in 2003, for example, 80.7% of the budget in Daghestan, 84.1% in Ingushetia and 100% in Chechnya), the republics fail to generate employment and economic growth due to high levels of corruption, lack of opportunities, inadequate education and plain administrative incompetence. The new Commission for the North Caucasus was set up to address the challenge of economic development, but it has been preoccupied with the rapidly proliferating security crisis across the region and managing political tensions among regional elites and an increasingly desperate and impoverished population.

To complicate matters, most of Russia's Muslim population resides in the North Caucasus. In recent years, it has witnessed growing Islamist extremism. This phenomenon stems primarily from economic and social upheaval, high unemployment among the young population, widespread criminal violence, endemic corruption among security and law enforcement bodies, widespread human-rights violations, growing nationalism and anti-Muslim sentiments across Russia inspired by the war in Chechnya, as well as revived interest in Islam after 70 years of Soviet repression, exploited by a new generation of foreign-educated preachers, who believe in extreme interpretations of Islam. To diminish these influences, political and economic solutions are required to promote fundamental changes in governance and spur development. As of April 2005, these solutions had not materialised. In December 2004, during his visit to Germany, Putin welcomed EU involvement in the economic development of the North Caucasus. Subsequently, the EU and UN have sent a number of missions to the North Caucasus to explore possibilities for strategic development assistance. However, poor security, European reservations about Russia's policy in Chechnya, lack of access and information on the ground, and an unclear mandate from the Russian government – which seems primarily interested in European financial assistance – constitute important constraints on any prospective European involvement in a regional development programme.

The unfinished conflict in Chechnya

The Beslan tragedy highlighted another major challenge for Putin: the continuing violence in Chechnya, which has had a devastating impact on the entire North Caucasus region for over a decade and accounts for much of the insecurity that plagues Russia. While the situation across the North Caucasus continued to deteriorate, the Russian government had yet to find a comprehensive settlement of the ongoing conflict in Chechnya. Unfortunately, there are few clear options for launching a comprehensive peace and national reconciliation process. Terrorist attacks in a Moscow theatre in October 2002 and in Beslan rule out any negotiations with the most notorious Chechen warlords, including Shamil Basaev, who has influence over separatist fighter groups, including control over the training of terrorists and suicide-bombers to conduct acts of terrorism across Russia. Moderate leaders are either indirectly implicated in terrorist acts or too weak to represent the fighting groups in any formal negotiations. It is clear, however, that without some negotiating framework it is hard to imagine any lasting settlement, an end to fighting or eventual disarmament. These steps represent the key preconditions for stability and security in Chechnya and the North Caucasus region as a whole.

Chechens themselves remain divided, both between and within pro-Moscow groups and separatists opposing Russian rule. As a result, fighting now often takes place not between the Russian forces and Chechen warlords, but among different Chechen groups themselves. Moscow-backed Chechen paramilitary groups are known to be involved in major human-rights violations targeting suspected fighters and their relatives as well as the civilian population. Many are active in organised criminal groups that now operate across the North Caucasus region and other parts of Russia. It may therefore be impossible to develop a comprehensive negotiation process that would engage moderate elements of the diverse Chechen groups and produce an agreement. Moscow, therefore, by default continues to impose the political process, rather than facilitating it.

After terrorists assassinated pro-Moscow Chechen President Akhmad Kadyrov during public celebrations on 9 May 2004, a new election was quickly carried out on 29 August. Alu Alkhanov, a former interior minister, became president amid allegations of major electoral fraud. OSCE did not observe the election, citing poor access and security concerns. Since the election of Alkhanov, a semblance of stability has emerged in Chechnya. Large-scale military operations against rebels have been confined to small mountainous regions in the south, and the numbers of military personnel and checkpoints have been reduced. However, rebel raids in Grozny in August 2004 demonstrated that Russian forces still do not fully control the territory of Chechnya even outside the traditional rebel areas. The rebels, who continue to enjoy popularity among some parts of the population and support among their family clans, are still capable of moving across the territory undetected. There are some signs of economic rehabilitation, particularly in Grozny and other larger towns. Those who lost their property during the conflict are being compensated: 300,000 rubles for lost housing and 50,000 rubles for lost property. By the beginning of 2005, 39,000 compensation claims were reported paid, with 130,000 applications pending. However, the availability of compensation led to widespread corruption, such that recipients were being forced to pay a significant percentage (sometimes over 50%) of their benefits as bribes to local officials and paramilitary groups.

In an attempt to promote a political settlement, the Russian government has drafted an agreement on divisions of power between Moscow and the Chechen Republic, offering the latter broad access to economic benefits from oil exploration in Chechnya, but anchoring Chechnya firmly within the Russian Federation without any prospect for a 'legitimate' succession. Russian military forces, in cooperation with Chechen police and paramilitary groups led by Deputy Prime Minister Ramzan Kadyrov, who oversees Chechen security structures, had some success in killing leaders of Chechen separatist fighters and terrorist groups. On 8 March 2005 they killed Aslan Maskhadov, the official leader of the Chechen separatists, who had been elected president of Chechnya in 1997, serving until the start of the Second Chechen War in August 1999. Maskhadov was considered the key moderate figure among leaders of the Chechen fighters, and many Western analysts had pinned their hopes on (ultimately unsuccessful) political negotiations between Maskhadov and the Kremlin. Russian authorities, however, considered Maskhadov a terrorist and alleged his involvement in preparing the Moscow theatre and Beslan sieges. After the Moscow theatre attack, Putin refused to acknowledge Maskhadov's legitimacy or enter into any talks with him, despite international pressure. In January 2005, Maskhadov announced a unilateral ceasefire, offering to enter into talks with Moscow. After his death, the leadership of Chechen separatist fighters is liable to be dominated by more radical elements. Maskhadov's successor as formal leader of the separatists, Abdul-Khalim Saidullaev, is known as a moderate but has little power over radicals like Basaev. If radicals have their way, terrorism is set to increase across Russia, potentially including some spectacular attacks against strategic infrastructure for which Russia is still poorly prepared. If terrorism proliferates, Putin's popularly is likely to decline.

Parliamentary elections in Chechnya tentatively set for October 2005 offer a real opportunity to begin constructing a more representative system of government and to provide a platform for reconciliation and political bargaining between and among different groups within Chechnya. If elected freely, without major fraud, the parliament will probably be empowered to undertake the meaningful supervision of political and economic policies in Chechnya. If, however, the parliamentary elections involve a level of fraud comparable to that alleged in recent elections, lasting stability would be unlikely.

Economic reforms

Another quandary for Putin's second term lies in the economic sphere. High oil prices provide a favourable environment for the government's economic policy. Budgetary revenues and gold reserves have been at an all-time high. A special stabilisation fund drawn from oil revenues now stands at $22.97bn. Salaries have been paid on time and there is growing wealth across all major economic centres in Russia. The Russian government has been paying off its debts and is maintaining relative macroeconomic stability, although inflation was at 11.7% in 2004. At the same time, high oil prices had a negative impact on long-term economic trends by removing incentives for structural economic reforms, which were part of Putin's economic programme in 2000. As a result, there are signs of stagnation in Russia's economic growth, which stood at 6.9% in 2004 (compared to 7.3% in 2003). Plans to double GDP by 2010 look increasingly unrealistic. Moreover, the oil economy has caused the gap between rich and poor in Russia to widen. Little investment has been made in small and medium-sized businesses, so that the middle class has grown very slowly, while the number of rich people has increased significantly. Finally, the Yukos affair provoked another upsurge in capital flight, which had been on the decline in 2003 before the arrest of Khodorkovsky in October of that year. Foreign direct investment did increase to over $9bn in 2004, mostly in the energy sector, and capital flight, on some estimates, abated slightly in 2004 from $15bn to $13.5bn. But there was little reason to be confident in continued net capital inflows.

The energy sector is increasingly viewed by Putin and his administration not only as an economic asset but also a strategic foreign policy instrument. In 2004 Russia produced 9.27m barrels/day (bbl/d) of oil and exported over 6.7m bbl/d. As a result, there is a strong effort to consolidate state control over the energy sector. In 2004, the Russian government announced plans for a merger between its monopoly state gas company Gazprom and state-owned oil company Rosneft, creating one of the largest energy companies in the world. Transneft, a state-owned company holding a virtual monopoly over the pipeline network from Russia, is known to be notoriously inefficient. There has been no talk about offering private companies rights to develop private pipelines for the export of oil. The shortage of pipeline capacity creates major bottlenecks for Russian exports. However, Transneft has now received a state contract to construct a strategic Asian pipeline network, which is set to bring Russian oil to Nakhodka in the Russian Far East. In Asia, China and Japan are competing for access to Russian oil exports. However, the economics of the Asian pipeline have not yet been completely worked out, and neither Japan nor China is prepared to finance the project without securing some stake in Russia's oil production.

In 2004–05, the Russian government moved to limit foreign investment in the Russian energy sector both directly and indirectly, by initiating tax probes into activities of such major energy joint ventures as TNK-BP. In February 2005, the Russian Energy Ministry announced that foreign companies will not be allowed to bid for particular exploration contracts in such areas as Sakhalin Island, where foreign companies hold a controlling share in the Sakhalin I and Sakhalin II production-sharing agreements. However, the Russian energy sector badly needs more foreign investment to begin exploration of new oil and gas deposits; otherwise, Russia could face a major economic crisis when its current deposits start to decline. The new deposits awaiting exploration lie in eastern Siberia, where costs of exploration are particularly high and thus foreign investment is critical. The Russian government sold stakes in its oil production to Indian and Chinese companies in its search to secure investment without political preconditions, since Indian and Chinese concerns are more likely to accept greater state interference than Western companies. However, their share in the Russian energy sector remains small.

Russian gas production is already falling, and Russia now depends on gas imports from Turkmenistan to fulfil its domestic and export commitments. Russian cooperation with Turkmenistan continues to be bumpy, as the Turkmen side halted all gas exports after January 2005, protesting the low prices that Russia offers for Turkmen exports. Ukraine and the South Caucasus states are seeking to gain access to Turkmen gas resources. Growing state control over the energy sector is likely not only to decrease its efficiency, but also to drive some consumers of Russia's oil and gas in Eastern Europe and the Commonwealth of Independent States to seek alternative suppliers to diminish their dependence on state-controlled Russian exports, which could potentially be used as political instruments.

While oil generated substantial revenues for the state budget and considerable private wealth for parts of Russia's economic and political elite, Putin started to implement major social reforms that removed benefits for pensioners and other categories of citizen. While the system of benefits had to be reformed, the replacement of in-kind benefits and subsidies with small cash payments caused significant social tensions among the most vulnerable parts of the Russian population. In January 2005, more than 40,000 people took to the streets across Russia protesting Putin's reforms and putting forward political demands. These seem to have taken the government by surprise. The benefits debacle highlighted the ineffectiveness of an over-centralised system of government in which all responsibility resides at the top, and leaders are furnished with incomplete information about situations in different regions. Moreover, regional officials who owe their loyalty to Moscow (as opposed to their electorates) are unlikely to represent the interests of their population vis-à-vis the federal centre, thus provoking more social tension. Putin was quick to blame regional leaders and government ministers for the poor implementation of reforms. Nevertheless, painful social reforms are set to continue, including the liberalisation of utilities whereby subsidies for gas and oil products would be reduced.

Political prospects

Protests over the monetisation of benefits played an important role not only as an indicator of social tension, but also as a signal for Putin's opposition that there is an internal capacity for popular protest within the so far politically passive Russian population. Opposition parties and movements inside Russia that are actively preparing for the 2008 elections are trying to capitalise on social problems. Liberal forces created 'Committee 2008' and a number of other coalitions campaigning on democratic platforms. However, these coalitions may not survive until the next elections and democratic forces remain deeply divided, often competing with each other. Democrats lack a clear leader who enjoys popularity in society at large, beyond the traditional supporters of liberal parties who received less than 5% of the vote in December 2004 parliamentary elections. In March 2005, one such political heavyweight, former prime minister Mikhail Kasyanov, declared his intention to lead a coalition of democratic forces in the next election. Kasyanov lost his job as prime minister in March 2004 after opposing the government's actions against Yukos.Kasyanov suggested that Russia needed its own Orange Revolution; however, his support among the population and his ability to consolidate and lead those who oppose the current government remain in doubt. Kasyanov's previous political alignment with Putin is viewed negatively by traditional liberal opposition parties such as Yabloko and parts of the Union of Right Forces. They are unlikely to unite around him in a coalition. (Less formidably, chess grandmaster Garry Kasparov, an outspoken human-rights activist and Kremlin critic, also declared his candidacy.) Other political leaders on the right, including Anatoly Chubais, Boris Nemtsov and Irina Khakamada, do not enjoy wide support among the Russian population, who see their legacy as economic crisis during President Boris Yeltsin's term in office.

As a result of these internal divisions, it was not liberals but nationalists who most energetically sought to gain politically from social protests. However, nationalist parties, such as Motherland – which won a surprisingly high proportion of the vote in the December 2004 parliamentary elections, prevailed in regional elections in the Sakhalin region in autumn 2004 and came second after the pro-Kremlin Unity Party in a number of other regional elections – subsequently lost much of its political clout. The party could, however, reconstitute its popular base on the wave of anti-Western hysteria in the Russian media prompted by revolutions in Ukraine and elsewhere.

Communists, who traditionally campaigned in support of social guarantees and pensioners' rights, failed to gain significant political capital from the social protests in January. Their popularity ratings have been consistently dropping since the fall of the Soviet Union, and they are unlikely to emerge as a credible challenger to the party in power by 2008. Given these systemic weaknesses in Russia's political system, combined with the strong vertical authority of the executive branch, it is hard to predict how the political succession process will develop up to 2008. There is no doubt that popular revolutions in neighbouring states, particularly Ukraine, are having a profound impact on Russia's domestic and foreign policies as well as on the Russian population and its political elite. But it remains unlikely that Georgian-style popular discontent against the current ruling elite could take hold in Russia due to Putin's overall (if diminishing) popularity, continuing economic growth and increased control by security and police forces over political movements across the country. In early 2005, the increasing visibility of Defence Minister Sergei Ivanov and parliamentary Speaker Boris Gryzlov – especially on television – led to speculation that Putin was grooming them as likely successors.

Eurasian developments and implications for Russian policy

A dramatic political change occurred in November 2003 in Georgia. Peaceful popular protests against the government's attempt to rig the election ousted President Eduard Shevardnadze and brought to power a new dynamic leader, Mikhail Saakashvili. Georgia's Rose Revolution (named for the roses carried by protesters) encouraged people in other former Soviet states to push for wholesale changes of elites in the political process. What took place in Ukraine a year later was arguably even more profound. The government of outgoing President Leonid Kuchma rigged the presidential election to bring to power his chosen successor, Prime Minister Victor Yanukovich. Yanukovich enjoyed the support of Putin, who twice visited Kiev during the pre-election period, expressing his support for the pro-government candidate. However, allegations of election fraud, later confirmed by the Supreme Court of Ukraine, sparked political protests. In sub-zero temperatures thousands of protestors took to the streets of Kiev and other cities in support of opposition candidate Victor Yushchenko, who campaigned on the platform of Ukraine's integration with Europe. Peaceful protests continued for almost a month until the election re-run on 26 December, in which Yushchenko won 51% of the vote against just over 44% for Yanukovich. Both elections demonstrated regional divisions within Ukraine, with western parts and the capital backing Yushchenko and the eastern part, which is closely linked to Russia, voting for Yanukovich. However, speculations about a potential split of the country did not prove valid. On 23 January, Yushchenko was sworn in as the president of Ukraine. He declared his commitment to seek unity within the country, implement sweeping democratic and economic reforms, and lead Ukraine into the EU.

The Ukrainian Orange Revolution (so-called because the colour orange was chosen to symbolise the opposition) has considerable strategic significance. Firstly, it shifted Ukraine's geostrategic orientation from de facto integration with Russia towards closer ties with the West. Ukraine's location in Europe and the size of its economy offers Ukraine a prospect, albeit remote, for integration with the EU if necessary reforms are carried out. A new coalition of Georgia and Ukraine now represents a powerful force in Eurasia, promoting closer ties with European institutions. They enjoy support among new EU member states – especially Poland and Lithuania, who together with EU foreign policy chief Javier Solana played a key role in brokering a political compromise between the two presidential candidates. The peaceful resolution of Ukraine's electoral dispute represents a major foreign policy success for the EU, which acted with one voice. It also highlighted the first major contribution from the new member states to the EU's foreign policy agenda.

Secondly, Ukraine's revolution had a major impact on Russian policy towards Eurasia and on Russia's relations with Europe. Despite Russia's political and financial backing of Yanukovich, Moscow was unable to influence the outcome of the elections. This was perceived by many in Russia as the first major political defeat in the former Soviet space, which signalled Moscow's weakening influence and poor understanding of dynamics in neighbouring states where it claims special interests. Moscow's policy fiasco in Ukraine received abundant commentary among Russian experts and the press – the predominant view being that the West orchestrated a change of regime in Ukraine in order to push Russia out of the CIS and weaken its influence. This Cold-War-generated zero-sum perception of Russia and the West's interests has been strengthened by the Orange Revolution, intensifying nationalism and resentment towards the West and prompting calls for a tougher and more proactive policy towards neighbours, which could provoke instability.

Thirdly, Russia's actions, in turn, have affected Europe's policy towards Russia. Many European states, particularly new EU member states, expressed concerns over Russia's interference in Ukraine's affairs leading up to and during the Orange Revolution. These concerns prompted calls for a reassessment of the EU's strategic partnership and closer integration with Russia. Mutual suspicions prompted yet another crisis in EU–Russian relations when the November 2004 EU–Russia summit ended in a failure to make any decisions, despite previous expectations that it should advance EU–Russia cooperation by reaching agreement on action plans for the so-called 'four common spaces'.

After the revolution, Putin and the new Ukrainian leadership moved to establish a commitment to friendly, pragmatic relations. Yushchenko travelled to Moscow a day after his inauguration to reaffirm his desire for good relations. In March, Putin visited Kiev to discuss the agenda for cooperation, including Ukraine's participation in the Single Economic Space (SES), which Russia set up in September 2003 with Belarus, Kazakhstan and Ukraine to promote economic integration. Seen as one of Russia's foreign-policy successes, the project is under threat if Ukraine leaves to pursue integration with the EU. Russia and Ukraine share important economic interests beyond the SES, with bilateral trade exceeding $17bn in 2004. Ukraine is the main transit country for the export of Russian oil and gas to Europe. Russian companies made large investments in Ukraine's economy, particularly in the industrial enterprises in the eastern part of the country, which supported Yanukovich. Finally, Russia and Ukraine have close cooperation between their defence industrial sectors, an inheritance from the Soviet period.

These interests virtually ensure that the two countries will try to find some common ground to secure economic benefits for both sides. But the Russian government remains concerned that the policies of the new Ukrainian leadership could be detrimental to Russia's strategic interests. In the economic sphere, Ukraine is likely to promote increased complementarity with EU norms. This is not compatible with Russia's Single Economic Space, which includes harmonisation of legislation with Russia. Also, those in the Russian business sector are worried that some privatisation deals concluded by Russian companies under the previous Ukrainian government could be reconsidered and Russian business could be replaced by increased investment from Europe and the United States. Also, Russia is keen that Ukraine's Odessa–Brody oil pipeline network transports Russian oil to Black Sea ports. Putin's government invested substantial effort to reach such an agreement with Kuchma. Under Kuchma, Ukraine and Russia established a joint consortium to operate Ukraine's pipeline network. The new Ukrainian government, however, might reconsider in light of its new foreign and economic policy priorities. The new government could return to the original idea of using the pipeline in the other direction, for transporting Caspian oil from the Black Sea terminal to Europe – an option supported by many Eastern European states, which seek ways to lessen their dependency on energy imports from Russia.

In the political and security spheres, Russia's concerns regarding the change of government in Kiev include the extension of an agreement with Ukraine on the leasing of naval infrastructure used by the Russian Black Sea Fleet in Crimea. Russian officials, particularly in the military, are concerned about expanding ties between Ukraine and NATO and the possibility of Ukraine's future membership in the alliance. Ukraine also plays a key role in the Black Sea region, where both the United States and NATO seek to increase their presence, as indicated at the NATO summit in Istanbul in June 2004. Russia wants to keep NATO out of the Black Sea, but after the last round of NATO enlargement it remains the only Black Sea state in opposition to NATO's greater role in the region. In autumn 2003, Russia and Ukraine clashed over a disputed border in the Sea of Azov. The crisis led to the deployment of the Ukrainian military to a disputed island in the Kerch Straits. The border has not yet been agreed, and new crises could emerge if Russia perceives its security interests in the Black Sea to be under threat. Finally, many analysts in Russia view closer strategic ties between Georgia and Ukraine, which are supported by new NATO and EU members, as a form of 'encirclement'. This perception, however, runs counter to Russia's own expanding ties with NATO, the EU and the United States. Nevertheless, there is a strong belief that the revitalisation of GUUAM (a political grouping to provide an alternative to the Russian-centric CIS, created in 1997 by Georgia, Ukraine, Azerbaijan and Moldova, and joined by Uzbekistan in 1999) on the basis of new strategic relations between Ukraine and Georgia could undermine the already weakened Russia-dominated CIS and exclude Russia from integration projects in Eurasia.

While Russia has few levers with which to pressure Ukraine to accommodate its interests, it is likely to continue an active policy to promote them directly with the new Ukrainian leadership. One approach would be a dialogue seeking to influence key European states, such as France and Germany, which play an important role with regard to Ukraine's integration prospects with the EU. The issue of Russia's relations with Ukraine were discussed at an informal meeting between Putin and the leaders of Germany, France and Spain on 18 March 2005. Putin has given reassurances that Russia will not interfere in Ukrainian internal affairs or apply pressure on its neighbours. However, concerns over Russia's policy towards Ukraine and other neighbours seeking closer ties with Europe are likely to persist, particularly among new EU members who actively support Ukraine's European integration.

In addition to economic and geopolitical outcomes from the soft revolutions in Georgia and Ukraine, there are also implications for security in Eurasia. The first includes the developing military relations of these and other Eurasian states with NATO, the United States and Europe. Georgia has concluded an agreement with the United States to extend a $64m train-and-equip programme. The new US Stability and Security Operations Program for sustaining cooperation with Georgia will run from April 2005 to April 2006 and will cost the United States another $65m. It will involve the training of an additional 2,000 Georgian military personnel by US instructors. The outcome of first train-and-equip programme was the improvement of Georgian military capabilities and the deployment of over 600 Georgian troops in Iraq. In contrast, in March 2005 President Yushchenko signed a decree authorising the withdrawal of Ukranian forces from Iraq. However, Ukraine is set to continue cooperation with NATO and its individual members to bring its post-Soviet military closer to NATO standards. The appointment of a new reform-minded defence minister, Anatoly Hrytsenko, is likely to further this goal. This would provide an opportunity for Ukraine to take part in future NATO operations or operations by 'coalitions of the willing'.

The Georgian and Ukrainian revolutions could also potentially affect 'frozen' conflicts in Eurasia. In Georgia, the new president declared as policy priorities restoration of Georgian territorial integrity and the resolution of long-running disputes with the breakaway republics of Abkhazia and South Ossetia. However, post-revolutionary euphoria and success in bringing the region of Adjara under Tbilisi's control provoked the escalation of conflict in South Ossetia in summer 2004. After a cease-fire that lasted more than a decade, the new outbreak of violence in the zone of conflict undermined trust between the parties. This has complicated the resolution process.

Despite the Georgian leadership's genuine intent to pursue a political settlement with its breakaway regions, it is unlikely that a political agreement will be reached in the near future. In South Ossetia, President Saakashvili's initiatives for peaceful resolution of the conflict, presented in Strasbourg in January 2005, offer a new window of opportunity. However, any political process should be preceded by a lengthy confidence-building process. So far there is little room for a compromise, as Tbilisi demands territorial integrity and Tskhinvali insists on independence. In Abkhazia, after several months of crisis over the disputed presidential election there, the new leader Sergei Bagapsh signalled his readiness to enter into dialogue with Tbilisi on economic cooperation and limited refugee and IDP return, but the Abkhazian leadership continues to rule out any compromises on the status of Abkhazia, which seeks recognition as an independent state.

The international community, including Russia, declared support for Georgia's territorial integrity but cautioned against hasty policies which could provoke a new outbreak of violence in the zone of conflict and beyond. The US and EU have been urging Georgia to adhere to its commitment to peaceful conflict resolution. However, political deadlock, aggressive rhetoric coming from the Georgian leadership, Russia's economic and military support for the separatist regimes, and a lack of progress on demilitarisation in the conflict zone all signal that a new military confrontation cannot be ruled out in the foreseeable future. This could have a devastating impact for the population of separatist regions, for Georgia's prospects for European integration and for stability and security in the South and North Caucasus. Conflict resolution is further complicated by the deterioration in Russia–Georgia relations. Following the Rose Revolution, Moscow moved to establish closer ties with both separatist regions, which are likely to strengthen further as Georgian government battles Russia over the withdrawal of its military bases from Georgia on the basis of its 1999 OSCE Istanbul commitments. Georgia also signalled its intention to explore possibilities to replace Russian peacekeeping troops which are stationed in Abkhazia and South Ossetia by international forces, potentially some form of a coalition of the willing comprising GUUAM states. Georgia also requested the EU and its member states to provide a replacement for OSCE border-monitoring mission on the Georgia–Russia border near Chechnya, which was pulled out after Russia vetoed extension of its mandate at the OSCE summit in December. While there is no consensus within the EU about deployment of its observers on Russia's border without the latter's approval, the EU, and particularly some of its new Member States, have been actively liaising with the Georgian government to find possible alternatives to the OSCE mission. This action in itself signals a growing EU role in the region and increasing attention to the Caucasus within ESDP following EU enlargement in May 2004.

The change of government in Ukraine created momentum for the resolution of another separatist conflict in the neighbouring republic of Moldova, which has struggled to bring its breakaway region of Transnistria, where many ethnic Ukrainians reside, under its control. Yushchenko signalled that Ukraine, which borders Transnistria, will make active efforts to resolve the conflict. The EU also signalled its interest in promoting settlement by appointing an EU special representative for Moldova, Adrian Jacobovits. After the change in Ukraine's policy, Russia remains the only external source of support for the Transnistrian leadership. Moscow continues to deploy troops in the region despite strong pressure from Moldova and the international community on Russia to fulfil its obligation to withdraw military bases from both Moldova and Georgia. The fact that Russia does not border Moldova, however, makes it increasingly difficult for Moscow to exercise control over the situation in Transnistria. If real progress is achieved on reintegrating Transnistria with Moldova under a special agreement on autonomy with international guarantees, it could have a major positive impact on the resolution of conflicts in the South Caucasus.

Another security implication of the revolutionary changes in Ukraine and Georgia relates to the possible spread of popular uprisings to other, less stable parts of Eurasia. In late March 2005, such a change of regime took place in the Central Asian Republic of Kyrgyzstan. Following alleged election fraud, which was confirmed by Organisation for Security and Cooperation in Europe (OSCE) observers, opposition forces initiated protests in the south of the country and gradually brought these to Bishkek, the capital, where a small group of young men took over government buildings and forced President Askar Akayev into exile. The unexpected ouster of the government prompted chaos, in which the capital was looted and a number of injuries were reported. Although the opposition managed to re-establish control, concerns remain about future tensions and clashes between pro-government and opposition forces. Unease has also arisen over possible inter-ethnic violence and the potential for radical Islamist forces to gain control in parts of the country. Moreover, deterioration of law and order could increase the flow of drugs from Afghanistan through Kyrgyzstan to Asia and Europe. While the new government managed to temporarily stabilise the situation, its long-term prospects offer grounds for concern.

Kyrgyzstan's strategic resonance stems from the fact that it hosts both Russian and American military bases that operate some coalition missions in Afghanistan. While the key international players – Russia, the United States, the EU and the OSCE – have largely worked together to bring order and prevent a long-term crisis in the country, their long-term interests remain different. This suggests that the balance among them is tenuous and presumptively susceptible to political instability. Indeed, the Russian government is deeply unsettled about the proliferation of 'popular revolutions' across neighbouring states, particularly those in Central Asia, and is therefore likely to encourage governments in these states to take more drastic measures to prevent popular protests. The EU and the United States, for their part, are concerned that events in Kyrgyzstan could provoke already authoritarian regimes in Central Asia to undertake further repressions and human-rights violations. These differences between Russia and Western perspectives could, on balance, prompt Central Asian governments to seek closer ties with Russia, which supports the preservation of the current regimes in power.

Similar trends might take root in other Eurasian states, such as Azerbaijan, where there is growing opposition to the leadership of Ilkham Aliev, who in 2003 took power from his father through a 'dynastic' succession legitimised by elections in which the OSCE found many irregularities. Counting on Russia's support in an event of public discontent, the Azerbaijani government has already distanced itself from its GUUAM partners, Ukraine and Georgia, who seek to revitalise the organisation. In Belarus, Europe's last authoritarian state, President Alexander Lukashenko is under increased pressure from the now-neighbouring EU and from the United States. US Secretary of State Condoleezza Rice, in February 2005, called Belarus one of the 'outposts of tyranny', signalling an increased US commitment to advance the values of democratisation and freedom in that country. Belarus has long sought some form of union with Russia, and is likely to move closer to Moscow in search of guarantees – if not of regime survival, then of the personal safety of its leader in case of sudden political change.

Moving beyond a tenuous status quo

The Beslan tragedy and subsequent political changes in Russia have highlighted growing challenges for Russia's leadership as it begins to prepare for transition in 2008. The Orange Revolution in Ukraine transformed the geopolitical landscape in Eastern Europe, the South Caucasus and Central Asia. These two events are likely to define Russia's political and security agenda in the region, which can no longer fit the definition of the 'former Soviet space'. However, a new term may never be found beyond the loose geographic definition of 'Eurasia'. This area now includes increasingly diverse sub-regions, sets of strategic partnerships, security alliances and economic interests. Russia's domestic challenges made it a less attractive source of integration for its neighbours. Many of the extant alliances between those neighbours and Moscow are premised on their regimes' desire to protect themselves against potentially revolutionary public discontent. Those alliances are to an extent offset by other governments that have united to help one another consolidate their 'independence' from potential Russian pressure.

A new modus vivendi should ideally be found for developing relations between Russia and its Western partners, modelled perhaps on how Russia and China managed to find a mutually acceptable model for cooperation in Central Asia. To this end, inspirational success stories of cooperation are badly needed. Hopeful possibilities include the resolution of the Transnistria conflict in Moldova and support for a stable political transition in Kyrgyzstan. The improvement of Georgian–Russian relations could also open new avenues for addressing security problems and promoting economic development in both the South and the North Caucasus. Finally, the development of closer cooperation in the Black Sea region, with Russia joining other regional states and European partners, could bring the entire region closer to the EU, in much the same way that Baltic Sea cooperation promoted regional cooperation regardless of whether regional states belong to the EU or NATO.

However unenlightened Russia's present approach to the region may be, without Moscow's constructive engagement, no lasting stability, security and economic prosperity can be envisioned in Eurasia. Such engagement, however, would itself be destabilising if pursued on the basis of geopolitical rivalry. The main lesson from the post-revolutionary period in Ukraine and recent events in Kyrgyzstan is that Russia could and should develop cooperation with other regional players, including Europe, the United States and their key institutions, in the interest of stability and development in what has become their 'common neighbourhood'. EU enlargement and the war on terrorism have provided a lasting strategic rationale for Western engagement in Eurasia. Russia has yet to formulate clear strategic interests in relations with neighbours on the basis of post-Cold War and post-11 September realities – that is, beyond historic legacies and fears of encirclement. Putin has substantial reasons to avoid geopolitical rivalry, which could produce instability along Russia's borders and make it difficult for his government to address pressing problems of terrorism and economic reform inside Russia. But regional provocations could force him to default to a Cold War mentality and react confrontationally. In his speech in Brussels on 21 February 2005, US President George W. Bush appeared to recognise the need for a degree of restraint vis-à-vis Moscow. He was unabashed in his belief that 'Russia's future lies within the family of Europe and the transatlantic community' as well as his view that 'the Russian government must renew a commitment to democracy and the of law'. Yet he also acknowledged that 'reform will not happen overnight'. It would be best if Russia's neighbours and major powers interpreted this message so as to refrain from opportunistic strategies that might play on tensions between Russia and the West, and instead found more conciliatory ways to promote common interests and common projects to more gently dismantle Cold-War legacies in Eurasia. Russia, for its part, could make improved cooperation, security and development in Eurasia (particularly the South Caucasus and Central Asia) a priority for its G8 presidency in 2006, which could become a vehicle for launching joint projects. That kind of initiative would be a salutary signal that Russia is prepared to share responsibility for regional stability with other G8 states, and thereby prompt improvement in EU–Russia relations as well as in Russia–US bilateral ties.

Turkey: Pyrrhic Victory In Brussels?

Hope, goes the Turkish saying, is the bread of the poor: however much is consumed, the supply can never be exhausted. In mid-December 2004, after years of riding a roller-coaster of hope and despair, the long-suffering Turkish people finally appeared to have something substantial to celebrate. A little over two years since its landslide election in November 2002, the governing Justice and Development Party (JDP) seemed not only united and stable but, suggested the opinion polls, more popular than ever. The economy had bounced back from a crippling recession in 2001 and was enjoying its third year of robust growth. Exports and prices on the Istanbul Stock Exchange had hit record highs, while interest and inflation rates had fallen to their lowest levels in a generation. Although disagreements over Washington's policy towards Iraq meant that relations with the US were cooler than they had been a few years earlier, there appeared no immediate cause for concern. The war in Iraq itself, though deeply unpopular in Turkey, had created a thriving cross-border trade and given a massive boost to the local economy in the impoverished southeast of the country. Most important of all, at its summit in Brussels on 17 December 2004, the EU had finally set 3 October 2005 for the beginning of full accession negotiations.

But throughout 2003 and 2004, nagging doubts had remained about the sustainability of the high level of economic growth, and about the long-term agenda of the JDP and its commitment to – or even understanding of – the demands of EU accession. More critically, the process of trying to secure a date from the EU had served as a catalytic and unifying force, providing the JDP with momentum, binding the party's disparate elements together and enabling it to postpone solutions to such potentially explosive issues as the role of religion in public life, over which the expectations of its constituency were incompatible with the strict interpretation of secularism espoused by the Turkish establishment – particularly the country's still-powerful military. By late March 2005, however, the energy expended on securing a set date from the EU appeared to have punctured the JDP's momentum, leaving it deflated, defensive and divided, unwilling or unable to formulate policy and apparently without a strategy for what to do next. Perhaps more worryingly, the confusion and loss of direction extended to the general public. As economic growth began to slow and with no realistic prospect of full EU membership for at least ten years, the Turkish people appeared increasingly introverted, retreating into improbable conspiracy theories and an insecure nationalism.

The EU date – an end or a beginning?

Since it took power in November 2002, the prospect of securing a date for the beginning of EU accession negotiations in December 2004 had dominated the JDP's foreign and domestic policy agenda. Although most of the party's nucleus had radical Islamist – and anti-Western – roots, the government not only continued but accelerated the process initiated by the previous government of harmonising Turkish legislation with the body of EU law known as the *acquis communautaire*. In the 18 months between December 2002 and May 2004, the JDP passed five packages of legal and constitutional reforms whose effects ranged from reducing the political influence of the Turkish military to easing restrictions on freedom of expression and cultural diversity. But implementation lagged far behind legislation. The tendency among most foreign observers and many Turkish liberals was to attribute this discrepancy to resistance from Turkey's instinctively conservative bureaucratic establishment. More sceptical commentators claimed that the JDP was either exploiting the EU process for its own ideological goals (e.g., using the EU insistence on civilian control of the armed forces to weaken the staunchly secularist Turkish military and ultimately facilitate the introduction of a secret Islamist agenda), or that it was imitating rather than internalising and simply did not understand that promulgating legislation was not an end in itself but needed to be rooted in Turkey's genuine acceptance of basic EU values. Nevertheless, at a summit in Brussels on 17–18 June 2004, the EU indicated that Turkey had done enough, if not for full membership, at least to be given a date for the opening of official accession negotiations at its next summit in Brussels on 16–17 December 2004.

Doubts about the JDP's understanding of the implications of EU membership were reinforced in September 2004. Turkish MPs had been recalled from their summer recess to pass a reform of the Penal Code before the European Commission published its annual progress report on Turkey's candidacy at the beginning of October. At the last moment, Prime Minister Recep Tayyip Erdogan attempted to add a clause criminalising adultery. When Gunther Verheugen, the European Commission's Commissioner for Enlargement, expressed concern about criminalising what was essentially a private matter, Erdogan angrily responded that the EU had no right to interfere in Turkey's internal affairs. Nevertheless, Erdogan withdrew the adultery clause when he realised that it could jeopardise Turkey's chance of receiving a positive Commission assessment. The new Penal Code was subsequently passed by parliament, effective 1 April 2005. When the Commission's progress report was published on 6 October 2004, it recommended that Turkey be given a date for the opening of accession negotiations at the EU summit in December.

The prospect of Turkey starting official accession negotiations – which to date have invariably resulted in the candidate country's being granted eventual membership – galvanised opponents of Turkish accession within the EU, particularly in France, Germany and Austria. But when EU leaders met in Brussels in December 2004, the issue of Cyprus once again proved the greatest obstacle. After years of at best half-hearted support for – and often outright opposition to – UN proposals to reunify the divided island, in early 2004 Ankara had suddenly performed an about-face and announced that it backed a resumption of negotiations based on a draft solution known as the Annan Plan, after UN Secretary-General Kofi Annan. Previous attempts to reach a settlement based on the Annan Plan had collapsed in March 2003 in the face of the intransigence of veteran Turkish Cypriot leader Rauf Denktash; and Turkey had declined to pressure Denktash to return to the negotiating table. Although the EU had agreed to grant full membership to the Republic of Cyprus on 1 May 2004, in practice the latter's internationally recognised government only administered the Greek Cypriot southern two-thirds of the island, while the north was run by the breakaway Turkish Republic of Northern Cyprus (TRNC), which only Turkey recognised. Ankara simply did not believe that the EU would ever admit the Republic of Cyprus as a member without a settlement to reunify the island. By late 2003, however, Turkey had finally begun to realise not only that the EU would admit the Republic of Cyprus but that Ankara's perceived refusal to support a settlement – as manifested in its backing for Denktash – could seriously damage its own prospects for accession.

In many ways, Ankara's reversal was a calculated gamble. Ever since the 1974 Turkish invasion of the island to prevent its unity with Greece, most Turks have seen the TRNC, and the continued presence of 35,000 Turkish troops in the north of the island, as a matter of national honour. Any Turkish government that agreed to a settlement would, regardless of its terms, face a severe domestic backlash. But by early 2004 the Turkish analysis – backed by intelligence reports – was that, even if the Turkish Cypriots accepted the Annan Plan, the Greek Cypriots would reject it. This would leave the Greek Cypriots, uncharacteristically, to face international opprobrium, removing an impediment to Turkey's hopes of accession and perhaps even eventually leading to international recognition of the TRNC – always Turkey's preferred outcome.

Initially, the gamble appeared to have paid off. After nearly two months of inconclusive UN-brokered negotiations, the Annan Plan was put to twin referenda in the two communities on the island on 24 April 2004. The Turkish Cypriots voted for acceptance by 64.9% to 35.1%, while the Greek Cypriots rejected the plan by 75.8% to 24.2%. One week later, on 1 May, the Republic of Cyprus officially became a member of the EU. Both EU officials and representatives of member states issued statements promising to reward the Turkish Cypriots by easing their international economic and political isolation. Turkish officials declared that they had done all that could be expected of them and that it was now up to the EU either to pressure the Greek Cypriots into accepting the Annan Plan or to allow the TRNC to function as a de facto independent state.

The first sign that Turkey had misjudged the situation came in October 2004. At a meeting in Istanbul on 14–16 June 2004, the Organisation of Islamic Conference (OIC) had acceded to a Turkish request to grant membership to the TRNC as the 'Turkish Cypriot State', the name assigned to it in the Annan Plan. However, a meeting between the foreign ministers of the OIC and the EU, originally scheduled for 4–5 October 2004, was cancelled over EU objections to the participation of the 'Turkish Cypriot State' on the grounds that it was not an internationally recognised entity. Worse was to follow. Turkey had extended its 1963 Association Agreement with the then-European Economic Community, which still formed the legal basis of its relations with the EU, to cover nine of the ten states which had joined on 1 May 2004. But it had refused to include the Republic of Cyprus, which it did not recognise diplomatically. Far from being, as Ankara had hoped, a mere formality, the December 2004 EU summit was overshadowed by Turkey's continuing refusal to recognise the Republic of Cyprus, and the Greek Cypriots threatening to use their veto to block Turkey receiving a date for the opening of accession negotiations. In the end, a compromise was reached, whereby the Greek Cypriots grudgingly withdrew this threat. Turkey, for its part, agreed to include the Republic of Cyprus in the Association Agreement before accession negotiations officially opened on 3 October 2005 after being assured that, as Ankara's relations with the EU were primarily economic (the two having been in a customs union since January 1996), extending the agreement would not amount to de jure political recognition. To make matters worse, in a sop to those member states whose governments were wary of domestic opposition to Turkish accession, the final summit declaration included a sentence which stated that the opening of negotiations was no guarantee of eventual membership – the first time any such caveat had been issued to a potential member.

In the weeks leading up to Brussels summit, the JDP had prepared banners, bunting and posters venerating Erdogan and showing the EU and Turkish flags intertwined. When Erdogan returned to Ankara on the morning of 18 December 2004, JDP supporters dutifully turned out to welcome him and his entourage on a procession through festooned streets. But beneath the trappings of triumph, there was a palpable sense of disappointment and disillusion. Opposition parties and nationalist media were already lambasting the JDP for allegedly selling out the Turkish Cypriots.

Even before the Brussels summit, few in Turkey had expected full membership to come before 2015 at the earliest. But liberals had hoped that the securing of a date for accession negotiations would serve as a springboard for further reform. Given the huge support for EU membership amongst the Turkish public, the JDP had expected the Brussels summit to enhance the party's prestige to such an extent as to make it unassailable at the next election, and guarantee a second strong parliamentary majority. But in the months following the December 2004 summit, the JDP appeared to lose direction. By late March 2005, not only had it failed to pass any more reforms or even name a chief negotiator to handle the preparations for the opening of accession talks, but Erdogan was still procrastinating on extending the Association Agreement to the Republic of Cyprus. The EU was also becoming increasingly frustrated by Turkey's use of its NATO membership to block the Republic of Cyprus from participating in any EU military action involving access to NATO capabilities, severely inhibiting the development of the EU's European Security and Defence Policy (ESDP). But it was not just Turkey's ties with the EU that were coming under strain. Turkey also appeared to be recoiling into a suspicious and defensive introversion that was exacerbating tensions in its already troubled relations with its other Western ally, the US.

From transatlantic allies to regional rivals?

In early 2004, Turkey's relations with the US appeared to have recovered from their nadir of mid-2003, when the Turkish parliament's failure on 1 March 2003 to approve the transit of 62,000 US troops to attack Iraq from the north had been compounded on 4 July 2003 by the US seizure of Turkish special forces in northern Iraq on suspicion of plotting to assassinate Iraqi Kurdish officials. Even though there was none of the emotional warmth which had characterised the months following the 11 September 2001 terrorist attacks on the US – when traditionally strong ties between the two countries' militaries had been boosted by Washington touting Turkey as a model for other Muslim states to follow – by the end of 2003 it had at least been possible to re-establish a working relationship. But the improvement proved relatively short-lived. Ironically, given that it had once promised to bring the two countries closer together, Washington's global war on terrorism – particularly the continuing instability in Iraq – became the main factor driving them apart.

Since it came to power, the JDP had taken a pragmatic approach to relations with the US – that is, it understood that it needed good relations with Washington more than it actually wanted them. But in private, most of the party's members remained almost viscerally anti-American and instinctively sympathetic to other Muslim countries in the region, and this attitude intensified whenever a Muslim country came under pressure from the US. By early 2004, Turkish relations with Israel, Washington's main ally in the region, had cooled to their lowest point in more than a decade. Even the Turkish military, which had been the primary driving force behind the rapprochement with Israel in the mid-1990s, had lost its enthusiasm for the relationship. It was infuriated by press and intelligence reports of increasingly close ties between Israel and the Iraqi Kurds – whom it feared would use the continuing turmoil in Iraq to establish an independent state, which in turn would serve as an inspiration for Turkey's still restless Kurdish minority – and exasperated by a string of problems in defence industry contracts awarded to Israeli firms. More insidiously, while leading members of the JDP were careful to pay public lip service to the merits of closer ties with Israel, in private most party members remained anti-Semitic. In general, the government pursued a policy of constructive neglect towards Israel while working to build closer ties with Turkey's Muslim neighbours.

Through 2004 and into 2005, these prejudices and perceptions of Turkish national interest converged and fed on each other. The main flashpoint remained northern Iraq, where Turkish fears of an independent Kurdish state were compounded by US reluctance to move against an estimated 5,000 militants of Kongra-Gel, the former Kurdistan Workers' Party (PKK), who were holed up in camps in the mountains along the border between Iraq and Turkey. Ankara's protests intensified following Kongra-Gel's announcement on 1 June 2004 that it was abandoning its five-year unilateral ceasefire and resuming its violent campaign for greater rights for Turkey's Kurdish minority. During the second half of the year, Kongra-Gel killed more than 50 Turkish civilians and members of the security forces – mostly in rural areas in southeast Turkey. although in August 2004 five people were killed in separate bomb explosions in Istanbul and the coastal resort of Antalya. The Turkish security forces put Kongra-Gel losses over the same period at 200–300 killed. Most of the Kongra-Gel militants involved in clashes seem to have been those who had gone into hiding in Turkey following the 1999 cease-fire. But Turkish intelligence reports claimed that they were being directed, and sometimes reinforced, from the camps in northern Iraq. Through 2004 and into 2005, Turkish officials raised the issue at virtually every meeting with their US counterparts but received no concrete assurance of imminent action. Privately, US officials freely admitted that the continuing insurgency in the rest of Iraq meant that the US did not have sufficient forces for any additional military operations.

Relations were further strained by Washington's reluctance to address what Turkey maintained were Iraqi Kurdish attempts to marginalise the Turkish-speaking Turkmen minority in northern Iraq and resettle Kurds in the oil-rich city of Kirkuk prior to declaring it the capital of an independent Kurdistan. Not only was the US unwilling to intervene, but by early 2005 it had also become clear that Ankara's hopes of using the Turkmen as a counter to the Iraqi Kurds had failed. Turkey had attempted to rally the Turkmen behind the Iraqi Turkmen Front (ITF), which it had provided with considerable financial and logistical support. But Ankara had consistently overestimated not only the influence of the ITF but the ethnic unity and even the size of the Iraqi Turkmen population. Unlike their co-linguists in Turkey, many of the Turkmen were Shi'ite rather than Sunni Muslims and identified more strongly with the Iraqi Shi'ites than the ITF. Although Turkey claimed that the Turkmen accounted for at least 10% of the Iraqi population, in the Iraqi elections of 30 January 2005 the ITF won just 1.1% of the total vote. In Kirkuk, which Ankara had long maintained was a predominantly Turkmen city, the ITF won only 18.4% of the vote.

Washington's failure to move against either Kongra-Gel or the Iraqi Kurds antagonised even the Turkish military, which has traditionally been the strongest advocate in Turkey of closer ties with the US. On 25 January 2005, Deputy Chief of Staff General Ilker Basbug warned that Turkey would not stand idly by if the Iraqi Kurds attempted to take control of Kirkuk or persecuted the Turkmens. On 14 March 2005, Land Forces Commander Yasar Buyukanit attacked the JDP government for both neglecting the Turkmen and failing to exert pressure on the US and the Iraqi authorities to prevent militants from the Kongra-Gel camps infiltrating into Turkey. But Turkey's options were limited. US officials had repeatedly warned that any cross-border military action would trigger a military response from US forces in Iraq. Nor could the JDP apply economic pressure. Cross-border trade with the Iraqi Kurds and the sale of provisions to US-led occupation forces had given a massive boost to the local economy in southeastern Turkey, whose underdevelopment continued both to fuel recruitment to Kongra-Gel and other violent leftist and Islamist groups, and also to exacerbate the social problems resulting from mass migration to Turkey's already overburdened metropolitan areas. Although more than 90 Turkish truck drivers were killed by Iraqi insurgents in the 18 months through March 2005, the levels of unemployment in southeastern Turkey meant that there was never any shortage of replacements.

The continuing turmoil in Iraq gave an added impetus to already growing anti-Americanism in Turkey. In an international BBC poll conducted in late 2004, only 1% of Turks said that they approved of US President George W. Bush's foreign policy, while 91% disapproved – the highest rate of any country. Although leading members of the JDP were usually careful to avoid criticising the US too harshly in public, occasionally they were unable to control themselves. On 27 November 2004 Mehmet Elkatmis, the head of the Parliamentary Human Rights Commission, accused the US of conducting a 'genocide' during its military operations against Iraqi insurgents in Falluja and described the Bush administration as being 'worse than Hitler'. In Washington, frustration at the continuing insurgency in Iraq – which several US commentators suggested was partly the result of the 1 March 2003 refusal to allow the opening of a second front against Saddam Hussein – and Ankara's reluctance to allow its airbase at Incirlik in southern Turkey to be used to resupply US forces in Iraq had been aggravated by the JDP's failure to curb public anti-Americanism. After the tsunami in Southeast Asia on 26 December 2004, the US Embassy in Ankara was forced to issue a public statement refuting reports in the pro-JDP *Yeni Safak* daily newspaper that the quake had been caused by a US underground explosion which was designed to kill Muslims. During February and March 2005 the Turkish bestseller lists were dominated by a thriller called *Metal Firtinasi* ('Metal Storm'), in which a clash between Turkish and US forces in northern Iraq triggered a war between the two countries.

Perhaps more alarming was the appearance near the top of the bestseller lists of Adolf Hitler's *Mein Kampf*, as public anger at Israeli policies towards the Palestinians descended into often blatant anti-Semitism. Following the Israeli 'targeted killing' of Hamas leader Sheikh Ahmed Yassin on 22 March 2004 and again in May 2004, after Israeli forces had razed the houses of the families of suspected militants in the Gaza town of Rafah, Erdogan publicly accused Israel of 'state terrorism'. He declined an Israeli invitation to visit the country and in June 2004 even briefly recalled Turkey's ambassador to Israel for consultations. In contrast, Turkey continued to strengthen its ties with both Syria and Iran. When he paid an official two-day visit to Tehran in July 2004, Erdogan defied US concerns about economic links with Iran by taking with him more than 130 businessmen, and publicly defended Iran's right to a nuclear power programme. In December 2004, Erdogan paid a two-day visit to Damascus, where he and Syrian President Bashar al-Assad signed a free-trade agreement between their countries. In March 2005, Turkish President Ahmet Necdet Sezer announced that he would be paying an official visit to Syria in April 2005 – the first ever by a serving Turkish head of state. In turn, Turkey was initially silent when the 14 February 2005 assassination of former Lebanese prime minister Rafik Hariri was followed by a chorus of international calls for Syria to withdraw from Lebanon. In an opinion poll conducted in late February 2005, 69.4% of Turks supported closer ties with Syria and 67.1% closer relations with Iran, while 59.5% had a negative view of the US and 38.9% saw it as an enemy of Turkey.

Domestic politics: honeymoon over

The period between the JDP's coming to power in November 2002 and the granting of a date for opening of EU accession negotiations in December 2004 was domestically one of the quietest and most stable periods in recent Turkish history. The JDP's electoral victory had coincided with – and was partly a product of – the discrediting and collapse of virtually every other major political party. Through 2003 and 2004, with around two thirds of the seats in the 550-seat unicameral parliament and in the absence of an effective opposition, the JDP's grip on power was unchallenged and, barring the emergence of a viable alternative, unchallengeable. After more than a decade of fractious, incompetent and corrupt coalition governments, most Turks – even many of those who harboured suspicions about the party's long-term agenda – were prepared to give the JDP a chance. Both they and the new government were aware that any domestic political turmoil could jeopardise not only Turkey's chances of receiving a date from the EU but also its recovery – based on an International Monetary Fund (IMF)-backed economic stabilisation programme – from the devastating recession of 2001. As a result, the JDP pursued polices that appeared superficially bold (e.g., the raft of democratic reforms) but were essentially cautious, driven by the expectations of the EU and the IMF rather than its own instincts. Confident that it would win a second five-year term in power, the government believed that it could afford to be patient. It therefore concentrated initially on issues for which there was a broad consensus, such as EU membership, and postponed confronting more controversial subjects, such as the role of religion in public life.

Although the JDP almost certainly has a less radical Islamist agenda than its detractors fear, there is also no doubt that most of its members favour a relaxation of aspects of the current interpretation of secularism in Turkey, including the restrictions on religious education and the ban on women wearing headscarves in state institutions. Others would like to see the regulation of social interaction more closely modelled on Islamic moral codes, if not full sharia law. Although the government did not add any anti-secularist laws to the statute book during 2004, Islamist reflexes occasionally surfaced in statements by its members and it twice had to withdraw legislation in the face of reactions.

In the local elections on 28 March 2004, the JDP won 41.7% of the national vote, up from 34.3% in the general elections of November 2002. Apparently emboldened by its success, the government announced a draft package of educational reforms – included easing restrictions on graduates of Islamic schools – on 4 May 2004. Although the Turkish General Staff (TGS) still sees itself as the ultimate guardian of the state ideology of Kemalism – named after the republic's founder Mustafa Kemal Ataturk (1881–1938) and based on the principles of territorial integrity and secularism – since his appointment in August 2002, Chief of Staff General Hilmi Ozkok had been anxious to minimise any public confrontation with the government, not least for fear of antagonising the EU. However, on 6 May 2004 the TGS published a statement describing the draft reforms as a threat to secularism and commenting that the TGS would remain as committed to the fundamental principles of the republic as it had ever been. In a country where the military has overthrown four governments in the last 45 years, such a statement could only be construed as a thinly veiled warning that there were limits to what degree of erosion to secularism the TGS would tolerate. The draft legislation was passed by parliament on 13 May 2004. Two weeks later, on 27 May 2004, President Sezer vetoed it on the grounds that it was incompatible with the constitutional principle of secularism. Under Turkish law, the president can only veto legislation once. But the JDP declined to resubmit the law to parliament. On 3 July 2004, Erdogan ruefully admitted that 'as a government we are not ready to pay the price'.

Many in the JDP had assumed that membership of the EU would not only reduce the political influence of the TGS but also under the guise of freedom of religion, allow Islam a more prominent role in public life in Turkey. However, dismay at the French decision to ban religious symbols – including the headscarf – in schools from 15 March 2004 was compounded in September 2004 when the decisive opposition to the criminalising of adultery in the new Turkish Penal Code came not from inside the country but from the EU. Even before the 17 December 2004 summit in Brussels, although they remained committed to the goal of receiving a date for the opening of accession negotiations, many in the JDP had already become disillusioned with the EU and were privately indifferent to the prospect of eventual membership. The difficulties over Cyprus in Brussels merely deepened their disenchantment. As a result, by end-March 2005 the granting of a date on 17 December 2004 appeared increasingly not so much a stage on a long journey as the end of a prolonged and artificial calm. Bereft of the momentum of the period leading up to the Brussels summit, the JDP lost vigour and direction.

At the same time, a host of issues that had been postponed or temporarily suppressed over the previous two years began to resurface. Not only were no further reforms passed, but impatience at Erdogan's increasingly authoritarian leadership style triggered a series of resignations. Even though there was no viable alternative party to which to defect, by 7 April 2005 11 MPs had resigned from the JDP in a little over three months, compared with just two in the previous two years. Erdogan responded by spending an increasing amount of time outside the country and lashing out at any criticism. For example, he sued one of the country's leading cartoonists for libel for a playful portrayal of Erdogan as a cat entangled in a ball of wool, and accused television stations who showed footage of police beating up peaceful protestors at a 6 March 2005 rally in Istanbul ahead of International Women's Day of being 'EU agents'. The siege mentality seemed infectious. In early March 2005, the Turkish Forestry Ministry announced that it was changing some Latin names describing fauna and flora in eastern Turkey as 'Armenian' or 'Kurdish' on the grounds that they were part of a Western plot to divide the country. Later that month, tens of thousands of Turks marched and hundreds of thousands more hung flags from their apartments and workplaces to protest what they saw as a conspiracy: the unsuccessful attempt of two boys – aged 12 and 14 – to set fire to a Turkish flag during a 21 March 2005 rally to mark the southwest Asian New Year festival of Newroz.

The same sense of uncertainty and loss of direction that had permeated domestic politics could also be seen in the economy. In December 2004, the JDP agreed to the terms of a new $10 billion standby agreement with the IMF to replace the previous agreement, which was due to expire in February 2005. But as of the beginning of April 2005, the agreement had still not been signed as the government continued to prevaricate over some of the conditions required by the IMF – most importantly, tightening tax collection and bank regulation, and reforming the country's ailing social security system. The IMF loan was important less for the actual cash inflows it would yield than for the confidence it would give to the international lending community to reduce the interest on Turkey's still considerable foreign debt. The delay in signing the agreement came amid increasing signs that the Turkish economy was cooling. In the first nine months of 2004, Turkey's Gross National Product (GNP) grew by an annual rate of 9.7%, up from 5.9% in 2003. Although the pace of growth was expected to slow during the final quarter of the year, during 2004 as a whole Turkish GNP grew by 9.9% in real terms. Within the year, however, the trend was downward. In the first quarter of 2004, Turkish GNP grew by an annual rate of 13.9%; by the final quarter of 2004, the annual rate of growth had slowed to 6.6%. Inflation seemed under control. From the year to end-March 2005, consumer prices rose by 7.9%, down from 11.8% one year earlier. The Turkish lira was stable, even overvalued. But despite the currency's strength, Turkish exports set a new record of $62.8bn in 2004, up 32.8% on the previous year.

Growth in 2003 and 2004 had been primarily driven by an increase in domestic demand as consumers took advantage of the fall in interest rates (due to domestic political stability) to make purchases postponed in the wake of the 2001 recession. During 2004, credit-card purchases increased by 79.1% in real terms while consumer loans grew by 133.3%. Yet real incomes increased by an average of only 1.3% during 2004, and actually contracted by an annual rate of 0.5% in the final quarter of the year. By March 2005, demand appeared to have peaked and, faced with a rapid rise in credit card defaults, the government announced plans to try to rein in consumer spending. The 2004 increase in consumer spending also fuelled a rapid rise in imports to $97.2bn, resulting in a record trade deficit of $34.4bn. More seriously, the current account deficit widened by 93.8% to $15.6bn, or around 5% of Turkish GNP. An adjustment in the exchange rate appeared inevitable. However, for Turkish textile producers, who account for approximately one-third of Turkey's total exports, the likelihood is that many of the gains of a cheaper Turkish lira will be wiped out by competition from China in their main markets – the US and the EU – following the lifting of all quotas from 1 January 2005.

Perhaps more worryingly for the JDP, even the boom years of 2003 and 2004 failed to create enough jobs. Official figures showed that the rate of unemployment fell from 10.5% at year-end 2003 to 10.3% at year-end 2004. But the total number of unemployed edged up by 5,000 during 2004 to 2.5 million as the total working age population grew by 994,000. Unemployment among those in the 15–24 age group, who account for 10.5% of the total workforce, stood at 19.7%, rising to 25.2% in urban areas, which in recent years have witnessed a dramatic increase in crime levels. An estimated 53% of the 21.8m Turks who had jobs were working in the unregistered black economy, up from 51.7% in 2003.

Drifting not sinking

In early April 2005, in its international relations, the JDP appeared to be paying the price for past errors and omissions in the first months of its administration. These included, in particular, its rejection of the Annan Plan while the international community still had time to apply pressure on the Greek Cypriots before the Republic of Cyprus acceded to the EU and the 1 March 2003 rejection of the US request to open a second front against Iraq. Given the nationalist paranoia that has developed in Turkey, the Cyprus problem is unlikely to be solved any time soon, and a relatively minor incident could spiral into a crisis. Yet Turkey's relations with the EU and the US are not irretrievably negative. Eventually, the government will have to extend the Ankara Agreement to include the Republic of Cyprus and hope that it could minimise the domestic damage by convincing as many Turks as possible that this did not amount to political recognition. EU accession negotiations are likely to start on 3 October 2005 or soon thereafter, though they could drag on for years with little perceptible progress.

In early April 2005, it seemed likely that Ankara would eventually agree to allow Washington to use the Incirlik airbase for logistical supplies to its forces in Iraq. Erdogan was also expected to attempt to repair some of the damage to transatlantic relations by holding talks with US officials during an informal visit to the US in late May or early June 2005. In March 2005, Erdogan's press office even announced that he would be paying an official visit to Israel on 1–3 May 2005, although it was quick to emphasise that he would be meeting both Israeli and Palestinian officials. But frictions between the US and Turkey over northern Iraq could at some stage produce a crisis. The Turkish military has been hatching plans to launch an operation to dismantle the Kongra-Gel camps; however, current projections are that such an operation would require 10,000–25,000 ground troops, backed by air support. Any Turkish action along these lines would probably prompt a US military response and would certainly outrage the EU. By Turkish standards, however, the Kurdish issue has already manifested a relatively long fuse. Although the Iraqi Kurds appear determined to gain full independence eventually, they seem to understand that any Kurdish state would not be internationally recognised unless the process of establishing a remade Iraqi state had been completely played out. In the near and perhaps medium term, they will probably be satisfied with de facto autonomy, towards which they are moving. Unless the Kurds do something rash – e.g., massacring Turkmen protesters – the Kurds' patience, American threats and the need to preserve the EU's good will would probably defer Turkish military action against the Kurds. In the meantime, provided the US does not use force against Syria or Iran, Turkey is likely to continue to strengthen its ties with both countries while its relations with Israel revert to arm's length.

As fraught as foreign policy may be for the JDP, domestic affairs pose even bigger problems for the party. In late March 2005, Turkey appeared to be experiencing a psychological, rather than an economic or political, crisis; however, under the combined pressure of deteriorating social conditions, the growth in irrational conspiracy theories and a rise in a frenzied nationalism, Turkey's potential vulnerability to both seemed to be increasing. At some point, the JDP will have to try to deliver on its supporters' expectations of a relaxation of the restrictions on religious education and the wearing of headscarves. Yet any attempt to amend the current interpretation of secularism would trigger a confrontation with the Turkish establishment, particularly the military. Although Erdogan has established an amicable working relationship with General Ozkok, the latter is due to step down as chief of staff in August 2006, and all of his potential successors are likely to be considerably more assertive.

In late March 2005, several of Erdogan's advisors privately admitted that they believed that popular support for the JDP had probably peaked in the March 2004 local elections and that they favoured holding early general elections in autumn 2005 before a viable alternative to the government had time to emerge. But there was no indication of whether or when Erdogan would make a decision. Indeed, after two years in which both political and economic momentum had been primarily driven by commitments to outside forces – namely the EU and the IMF – in the aftermath of the Brussels summit Erdogan and the rest of the JDP government appeared confused and disoriented. If they were not sinking, they were certainly drifting. In his public speeches, Erdogan continued to defend the JDP's record since it took power. But it was clear that the real test – both of Erdogan's own abilities and the party's long-term agenda – was yet to come.

Strategic Geography
2004/5

Legend

——————— subject country
international boundaries

———————— other international boundaries

.... province or state boundaries

ANBAR province or state

▣ capital cities

◉ state or province capital cities

• cities/ towns/ villages

✗ ✹ shooting(s)/ attack(s)/ incident(s)
and skirmishes

GLOSSARY AE: Ammunition ship (US) • AGF: Command ship (US) • AOOH: Survey ship with helicopter • AOE: Fast combat support ship • AORH: Replenishment oiler with helicopter • AORHM: Replenishment oiler with helicopter and GM • AORH/AS: Replenishment and repair ship • AO/T: Tanker with/without RAS capability • ARH: Forward repair ship • ATC: Air traffic control • CG: Cruiser (US) • CSF: Combined support force (US) • CSG: Carrier strike group • CVHG: Helicopter carrier with GM • CV/CVN: Aircraft carrier (US) • DDG: Destroyer with guided weapons • DDGHM: Destroyer with GM and helicopter • DDHM: Destroyer with helicopter • ESG: Expeditionary strike group • FFG: Frigate with guided weapons • FFGH: Frigate with GM and helicopter • FSGHM: Corvette with GM and helicopter • FFH: Frigate with helicopter • HSV: High speed vessel (US) • LCAC: Landing craft air cushion • LCC: Amphibious command ship (US) • LHA/LHD: Amphibious assault ship (USO) • LPA: Landing platform amphibious • LPD/LSD: Landing platform/ship dock • LST: Landing ship tank • MPS: Maritime prepositioning ship (US) • PSOH: Offshore patrol vessel with helicopter • T-AFS: Combat stores ship (US) • T-AGS: Oceanographic survey ship (US) • T-AH: Hospital ship (US) • T-AO: Fleet replenishment oiler (US) • T-AOE: Fast combat support ship (US)

GLOBAL TRENDS Maritime security initiatives

Much attention is now devoted to addressing threats to maritime security. The potentially devastating impact on national physical infrastructure and national and international economic activity that could result from sea-based terrorist activity (such as the attacks on the *USS Cole* and the *Limburg* tanker) has led to fresh measures that have bolstered moves to combat longstanding threats from piracy, other criminal and conflict-related insurgent actions.

Legend:
- ▦ PSI 'core group'
- ★ PSI exercise
- ☆ Proposed PSI exercise
- ● Ports participating in the CSI
- ○ Future CSI ports
- □ Possible CSI expansion ports

- ● Montreal ● Vancouver
- ● Halifax also participate in the CSI

Map labels:
3–7/10/05 ☆ PSI annual wargame
8–10/10/03 Air CPX SWEDEN
Liverpool
Felixstowe Bremerhaven Gothenburg June 2005 Ex *Bohemian Guard*
Tilbury UK NETH. Hamburg
Thamesport Rotterdam POLAND 19–21/4/04 Ex *Safe Borders*
Southampton Antwerp
23–24/6/04 Le Havre Zeebrugge GERMANY 31/3–1/4/04 Ex *Hawkeye*
Ex *Apse 04*
FRANCE
13–17/10/03 Genoa La Spezia 19–22/4/04 Ex *Clever Sentinel*
Ex *Sanso 03* Marseille Livorno
CANADA SPAIN ITALY Naples
8–15/4/05 PORTUGAL Barcelona GREECE TURKEY
Ex *Ninfa 05* Valencia Gioia Tauro Piraeus Izmir
June 2005
Algeciras Ex *Blue Action*
27/9–1/10/04 25–27/11/03 18–19/2/04
PSI gaming exercise Ex *Basilac 03* Ex *Air Brake 04*
UNITED STATES
Feb 2005
Ex *Air Net* at CENTCOM
8–18/11/04
Ex *Chokepoint 04*
Caribbean: 2
Colon Caribbean: 19
PANAMA West Africa: 9
Balboa
Pacific Ocean: 2 West Africa: 35
BRAZIL
Pacific Ocean: 5
Santos
Atlantic Ocean: 6
Buenos Aires SOUTH AFRICA
ARGENTINA

Initiatives:

• **Operation** *Active Endeavour*
After NATO's invocation of its Article 5 provision for collective defence in the wake of the terrorist attacks of 11 September 2001, NATO's Standing Naval Force Mediterranean (STANAVFORMED), which was on exercise at the time, has been redirected to provide a military presence in the eastern Mediterranean. NATO's standing naval forces, STANAVFORMED and its Atlantic counterpart, STANAVFORLANT, are rotated to enable prolonged operations in the region. Task Force Endeavour operates in the eastern Mediterranean, and another has operated, since 10 March 2003, in the Gibraltar Strait. On 16 March 2003, the operational area of responsibility was extended to the whole Mediterranean and 'since the start of the operation, 41,000 merchant vessels have been monitored (as of 17 March 2004)'.

• **Proliferation Security Initiative (PSI)**
Unveiled by President Bush in Krakow on 31 May 2003, the PSI is a multilateral strategy to 'prevent the flow of WMD, their delivery systems, and related materials on the ground, in the air and at sea to and from countries of proliferation concern'. As of November 2004, PSI members had conducted 13 exercises.

• **CTF-150 (and CJTF-HOA)**
Combined Task Force 150 (CTF-150) works with the US Fifth Fleet, headquartered in Bahrain, and within its AOR. CTF-150 is an international maritime patrol, presently led by Germany, operating in support of the US-led 'war on terror'.

• **Container Security Initiative (CSI)**
Announced in January 2002 and now operated by US Customs and Border Protection (CBP), the CSI is designed to identify and facilitate inspection of maritime containers vulnerable to terrorist infiltration at foreign ports before shipment to the US. According to CBP, 'almost half of incoming trade (by value) arrives in the US by sea containers. Nearly 9 million cargo containers arrive and are offloaded in US seaports each year'. CBP personnel are deployed to work with host nation personnel in targeting potential container threats. CSI is a reciprocal programme, and as such participating countries can also send customs officers to US ports to target containers inbound to their countries.

• **Regional Maritime Security Initiative**
This US initiative, focused on Southeast Asia, is aimed at combating 'piracy, maritime terrorism and sea-trafficking in people and narcotics' involving, according to Adm Thomas Fargo, former commander of US Pacific Command, 'not only closer intelligence-sharing with Southeast Asian states, but also deployment of US Marines and special forces on high-speed vessels to interdict maritime threats, particularly from terrorists'. Although both Indonesia and Malaysia 'asserted that security there [in the Malacca Strait] was the responsibility of the coastal states', Indonesia later agreed that extra-regional states had 'legitimate interests' in the Straits.

• **Malacca Straits Coordinated Patrol (MALSINDO)**
In June 2004, soon after the IISS *Shangri-La Dialogue* in Singapore, 'Indonesia proposed trilateral coordinated maritime patrols in the Malacca Strait, involving its own forces and those of Malaysia and Singapore'. The first patrol,

involving 17 ships, took place in late July 2004. Bilateral exercises aimed at reinforcing maritime security in the area have also recently taken place between Indonesia and Singapore, and Malaysia and Singapore.

• **Five Power Defence Arrangements (FPDA)**
These defence arrangements, entered into in 1971 by Australia, Malaysia, New Zealand, Singapore and the UK, commit these nations to consult in the event of an attack on Malaysia or Singapore. FPDA exercises were widened in 2004 to take into account non-conventional security threats, including maritime terrorism, while during the 2004 *Shangri-La Dialogue*, Australian Defence Minister Robert Hill floated the idea that the membership of the FPDA could be expanded to include other Southeast Asian states. From 10–25 September 2004, the FPDA Exercise *Bersama Lima 2004* included a maritime interdiction operation conducted against a simulated sea-borne target.

25–27/10/04
Ex *Team Samurai 04*

Japan runs bilateral anti-piracy exercises between its Coast Guard and regional states' security forces. In June 2004, the Asia Maritime Security Initiative 2004 (AMARSECTIVE 2004) was adopted after a meeting of the heads of Asian coast guard agencies in Tokyo. The aim of AMARSECTIVE 2004 is to demonstrate the coast guard agencies' 'resolve to expeditiously commit coordination and cooperation in strengthening measures to combat piracy and armed robbery against ships, and other unlawful acts at sea including maritime terrorism'.

11–7/1/04
Ex *Sea Saber*

15–18/8/05
Ex *Deep Sabre 05*

10–13/9/03
Ex *Pacific Protector*

10–14/10/05
UK-led maritime / ground interdiction exercise

Piracy incidents reported to the International Maritime Organisation worldwide

Acts of piracy allegedly committed January–Sept 2004

Acts of piracy allegedly attempted January–Sept 2004

*These are not precise locations

• **International Ship and Port Security (ISPS) Code**
The ISPS code entered force in July 2004, after initial agreement at a December 2002 conference to amend the 1974 Safety of Life at Sea Convention (SOLAS). According to the International Maritime Organisation, 'the code contains detailed security-related requirements for Governments, port authorities and shipping companies in a mandatory section … together with a series of guidelines about how to meet these requirements in a second, non-mandatory section'. 'The ISPS code is mandatory for the 148 contracting parties to SOLAS.' The level of threat for ports and ships must be assessed and communicated according to three levels: 1 (normal); 2 (medium); and 3 (high threat). Vessels will be required to have a Ship Security Plan, with the vessel always at level 1. Contracting governments' ports serving ships on international voyages have to be subject to a Port Facility Security Assessment, which will help to determine which facilites are required to, for instance, prepare a Port Facility Security Plan.

Amendments to SOLAS include: 'Ships, other than passenger ships and tankers, of 300 gross tonnage and upwards but less than 50,000 gross tonnage, will be required to fit Automatic Information Systems.' Meanwhile, ships' identification numbers must be permanently marked in a visible place either on the superstructure or hull. Ships must also be provided with a ship security alert system that, when activated, 'shall initiate and transmit a ship-to-shore alert … identifying the ship, its location and indicating that the security of the ship is under threat or it has been compromised'.

© IISS

GLOBAL TRENDS Addressing the spread of missiles and related technologies

The 2002 International Code of Conduct Against Ballistic Missile Proliferation (ICOC) calls on signatories to 'exercise maximum possible restraint in the development, testing and deployment of Ballistic Missiles capable of delivering weapons of mass destruction ...' and 'not to contribute to, support or assist any Ballistic Missile programme in countries which might be developing weapons of mass destruction ...'. Allied with the Proliferation Security Initiative (PSI), which exemplifies a more assertive stance, the ICOC should make it more difficult for states to transfer missiles and associated technologies. However, the ICOC lacks any provisions to ban or prohibit missile-related activities. Furthermore, as demonstrated by North Korea's sale of *Scud* missiles to Yemen in 2002, such transfers can still legally take place. Meanwhile, as noted by the Missile Technology Control Regime (MTCR), ballistic missiles are not the only possible means of delivering weapons of mass destruction: Unmanned Aerial Vehicles, cruise missiles and even kit aircraft must be considered potential delivery systems.

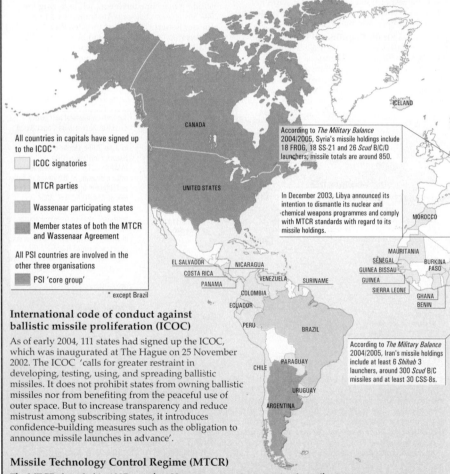

All countries in capitals have signed up to the ICOC*

- ICOC signatories
- MTCR parties
- Wassenaar participating states
- Member states of both the MTCR and Wassenaar Agreement

All PSI countries are involved in the other three organisations

- PSI 'core group'

* except Brazil

According to *The Military Balance* 2004/2005, Syria's missile holdings include 18 FROG, 18 SS-21 and 26 *Scud* B/C/D launchers; missile totals are around 850.

In December 2003, Libya announced its intention to dismantle its nuclear and chemical weapons programmes and comply with MTCR standards with regard to its missile holdings.

According to *The Military Balance* 2004/2005, Iran's missile holdings include at least 6 *Shihab* 3 launchers, around 300 *Scud* B/C missiles and at least 30 CSS-8s.

International code of conduct against ballistic missile proliferation (ICOC)

As of early 2004, 111 states had signed up the ICOC, which was inaugurated at The Hague on 25 November 2002. The ICOC 'calls for greater restraint in developing, testing, using, and spreading ballistic missiles. It does not prohibit states from owning ballistic missiles nor from benefiting from the peaceful use of outer space. But to increase transparency and reduce mistrust among subscribing states, it introduces confidence-building measures such as the obligation to announce missile launches in advance'.

Missile Technology Control Regime (MTCR)

The MTCR, founded in 1987, now has 33 partner countries committed to adhering to common export control guidelines (the MTCR guidelines), applied to an integral common list of controlled items (the MTCR Equipment, Software and Technology Annex). The objective of the MTCR is 'to restrict the proliferation of missiles, complete rocket systems, unmanned air vehicles, and related technology for those systems capable of carrying a 500 kilogram payload at least 300 kilometres, as well as systems intended for the delivery of weapons of mass destruction (WMD)'. Partner countries also 'recognize the importance of controlling the transfer of missile-related technology without disrupting legitimate trade…'.

Wassenaar Arrangement

Agreed in July 1996, the Wassenaar Arrangement is intended to 'promote transparency, exchange of views and information and greater responsibility in transfers of conventional arms and dual-use goods and technologies … '. Participating states use their national policies to control items and technologies noted on a list of dual use goods and technologies, as well as on a list of munitions. 'The Arrangement's specific information exchange requirements involve semi-annual notifications of arms transfers, currently covering seven categories derived from the UN Register of Conventional Arms.'

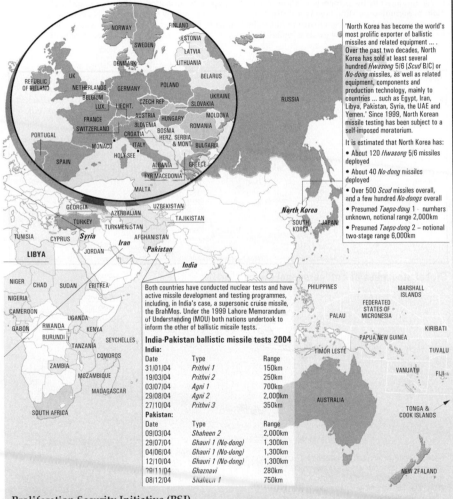

'North Korea has become the world's most prolific exporter of ballistic missiles and related equipment … . Over the past two decades, North Korea has sold at least several hundred *Hwasong* 5/6 (*Scud* B/C) or *No-dong* missiles, as well as related equipment, components and production technology, mainly to countries … such as Egypt, Iran, Libya, Pakistan, Syria, the UAE and Yemen.' Since 1999, North Korean missile testing has been subject to a self-imposed moratorium.

It is estimated that North Korea has:

• About 120 *Hwasong* 5/6 missiles deployed

• About 40 *No-dong* missiles deployed

• Over 500 *Scud* missiles overall, and a few hundred *No-dongs* overall

• Presumed *Taepo-dong* 1   numbers unknown, notional range 2,000km

• Presumed *Taepo-dong* 2 – notional two-stage range 6,000km

Both countries have conducted nuclear tests and have active missile development and testing programmes, including, in India's case, a supersonic cruise missile, the BrahMos. Under the 1999 Lahore Memorandum of Understanding (MOU) both nations undertook to inform the other of ballistic missile tests.

India-Pakistan ballistic missile tests 2004

India:

Date	Type	Range
31/01/04	*Prithvi 1*	150km
19/03/04	*Prithvi 2*	250km
03/07/04	*Agni 1*	700km
29/08/04	*Agni 2*	2,000km
27/10/04	*Prithvi 3*	350km

Pakistan:

Date	Type	Range
09/03/04	*Shaheen 2*	2,000km
29/07/04	*Ghauri 1 (No-dong)*	1,300km
04/06/04	*Ghauri 1 (No-dong)*	1,300km
12/10/04	*Ghauri 1 (No-dong)*	1,300km
29/11/04	*Ghaznavi*	280km
08/12/04	*Shaheen 1*	750km

Proliferation Security Initiative (PSI)

Unveiled by President Bush in Krakow on 31 May 2003, the PSI is a multilateral strategy to 'prevent the flow of WMD, their delivery systems, and related materials on the ground, in the air and at sea to and from countries of proliferation concern.' The US sees the PSI as an activity, not an organisation which, therefore, can build on existing non-proliferation agreements. As seen in last year's *Strategic Survey*, PSI members are committed to act according to a number of interdiction principles. As of November 2004, PSI members had conducted 13 exercises.

© IISS

GLOBAL TRENDS The world's landmine problem

Substantial progress has been made in addressing the problems posed to individuals and societies by the use of anti-personnel landmines, particularly since the 1997 Convention on the Prohibition of the Use, Stockpiling, Production, and Transfer of Anti-Personnel Mines and on their Destruction (the Ottawa Convention) entered into force in 1999. However, the fact remains that since 2003, the International Campaign to Ban Landmines (ICBL) has noted 16 cases of landmine use by states or non-state armed groups, with four more cases of alleged use.

The presence of landmines and unexploded ordnance leads to long-term costs in terms of the treatment and rehabilitation of victims, as well as the more direct impact of the injury to the individual. Furthermore, the recovery and economic reintegration of areas in some of the 63 mine-affected countries* is also hindered by the presence of landmines and unexploded ordnance. In December 2004, at the Nairobi Summit on a Mine Free World (the Convention's first review conference), UN Secretary General Kofi Annan noted that a legal instrument for dealing with the explosive remnants of war (as opposed to landmines specifically) now exists with 2003's Protocol V to the Convention on Certain Conventional Weapons.**

*Countries where some form of mine clearance is taking place, UN – November 2004

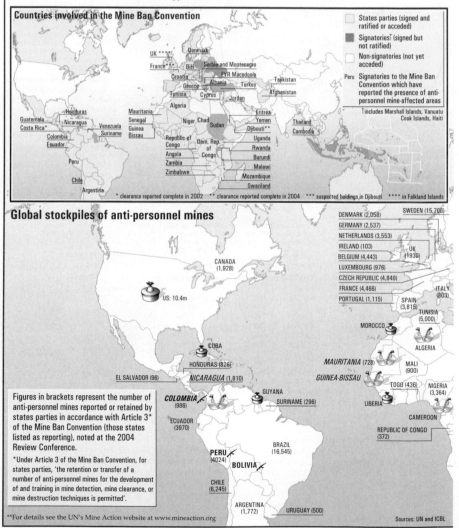

Countries involved in the Mine Ban Convention

☐ States parties (signed and ratified or acceded)
■ Signatories† (signed but not ratified)
☐ Non-signatories (not yet acceded)
Peru Signatories to the Mine Ban Convention which have reported the presence of anti-personnel mine-affected areas

†Includes Marshall Islands, Vanuatu Cook Islands, Haiti

UK **** Denmark
France *** BiH Serbia and Montenegro
Croatia FYR Macedonia
Greece Albania Turkey Tajikistan
Tunisia Cyprus Jordan Afghanistan
Algeria
Mauritania Niger Chad Eritrea
Guatemala Senegal Sudan Yemen Thailand
Honduras Guinea Djibouti** Cambodia
Nicaragua Venezuela Bissau Uganda
Costa Rica* Suriname Republic of Dem. Rep. Rwanda
Colombia Congo of Burundi
Ecuador Angola Congo Malawi
Peru Zambia Mozambique
Chile Zimbabwe Swaziland
Argentina

* clearance reported complete in 2002   ** clearance reported complete in 2004   *** suspected holdings in Djibouti   **** in Falkland Islands

Global stockpiles of anti-personnel mines

DENMARK (2,058)   SWEDEN (15,706)
GERMANY (2,537)
NETHERLANDS (3,553)
IRELAND (103)
BELGIUM (4,443)   UK (1930)
LUXEMBOURG (976)
CZECH REPUBLIC (4,849)
FRANCE (4,466)   ITALY (803)
PORTUGAL (1,115)   SPAIN (3,819)
TUNISIA (5,000)
MOROCCO
ALGERIA
MAURITANIA (728)   MALI (900)
GUINEA-BISSAU   TOGO (436)   NIGERIA (3,364)
LIBERIA
CAMEROON
REPUBLIC OF CONGO (372)

CANADA (1,928)

US: 10.4m

CUBA
HONDURAS (826)
EL SALVADOR (96)   NICARAGUA (1,810)
GUYANA
COLOMBIA (986)   SURINAME (296)
ECUADOR (3970)
GUYANA
BRAZIL (16,545)
PERU (4024)
BOLIVIA
CHILE (6,245)
ARGENTINA (1,772)   URUGUAY (500)

Figures in brackets represent the number of anti-personnel mines reported or retained by states parties in accordance with Article 3* of the Mine Ban Convention (those states listed as reporting), noted at the 2004 Review Conference.

*Under Article 3 of the Mine Ban Convention, for states parties, 'the retention or transfer of a number of anti-personnel mines for the development of and training in mine detection, mine clearance, or mine destruction techniques is permitted'.

**For details see the UN's Mine Action website at www.mineaction.org

Sources: UN and ICBL

Obligations in the Mine Ban Convention

• Never to use, develop, produce, stockpile or transfer anti-personnel landmines, or to assist any other party to conduct these activities

• To destroy all stockpiled anti-personnel landmines within four years of the Convention's entry into force

• To clear all laid landmines within ten years of the Convention's entry into force

• When it is within a signatory's means, to provide assistance to mine clearance, mine awareness, stockpile destruction, and victim assistance worlwide.

Source: UN

Between 1999–2004:

• 62 million stockpiled anti-personnel mines have been destroyed, including over 37 million by Mine Ban Treaty States Parties

• Over 1,100 square kilometres of land cleared since 1999, and three Convention member states – Costa Rica, Djibouti and Honduras – have completed their clearance obligations under the Convention

• Since 1997, over US$ 2.7 billion has been generated to fulfill the Convention's aims

• About 22.9 million people attended mine risk education sessions between 1999 and 2003

• There has been no publicly acknowledged, legal trade in anti-personnel mines

Source: ICBL, Nairobi Review Conference website

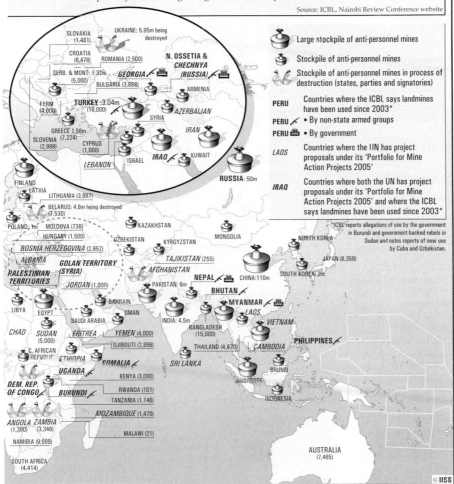

© IISS

MIDDLE EAST / GULF Iraq's year of elections

Iraq's first democratic elections, on 30 January 2005, took place in an atmosphere of high tension and real and threatened violence. Boycotts and fear of violence led to a low turnout in many Sunni areas, and the results for the Transitional National Assembly, which saw a landslide win for the United Iraqi Alliance – the formation of which was encouraged by the Shi'ite Grand Ayatollah Ali al-Sistani – overturned the historical rule by Iraq's Sunni minority. Overall turnout was placed at 58%. Negotiations over the formation of Iraq's first democratically elected government were close to resolution in early April, with Jalal Talabani appointed president (with Ghazi al-Yawar and Adel Abd al-Mahdi as his deputies) and Ibrahim Jaafari as prime minister. The Assembly's main task is to draft a constitution, on which the Iraqi people are slated to vote in a referendum on 15 October 2005.

What elections?
- 275-member Transitional National Assembly
- 18 governorate elections
- Kurdistan Regional Government election.

Governorate Council elections:
Party named won most votes

Nineva: • National Kurdistan Democratic List
• TOTAL VOTES: 0.14million

Dohuk: • Democratic Party of Kurdistan (PDK)
• TOTAL VOTES: 0.37m

Erbil: • List of Democratic Kurdistan Voters
• TOTAL VOTES: 0.63m

Ta'mim: • Kirkuk Brotherhood List
• TOTAL VOTES: 0.38m

Salahuddin: • List of the United Democratic Alliance in Salaheddin
• TOTAL VOTES: 0.12m

Anbar: • Iraqi Islamic Party
• TOTAL VOTES: 3,775

Babil: • Iraqi Faithful group
• TOTAL VOTES: 0.31m

Karbala: • SCIRI
• TOTAL VOTES: 0.20m

Qadisiya: • 'Martyr Mohammed Baqr al-Hakim' grouping
• TOTAL VOTES: 0.21m

Dhi-Qar: • Islamic Virtue Party
• TOTAL VOTES: 0.38m

Kurdistan Regional Assembly
(Number of seats in brackets)

Islamic Group of Kurdistan 0.08m (6)

Kurdistan Toilers Party 0.02m (1)

Democratic Patriotic Alliiance of Kurdistan 1.57m (104)

Suleimaniya: • Patriotic Union of Kurdistan (PUK)
• TOTAL VOTES: 0.71m

Diyala: • Coalition of Islamic Forces in Diyala
• TOTAL VOTES: 0.17m

Baghdad: • 'Tribe/family of Baghdad'
• TOTAL VOTES: 1.27m

Wasit: • Iraqi Select Party
• TOTAL VOTES: 0.25m

Maysan: • Dawa party
• TOTAL VOTES: 0.21m

Note: names are approximate translations

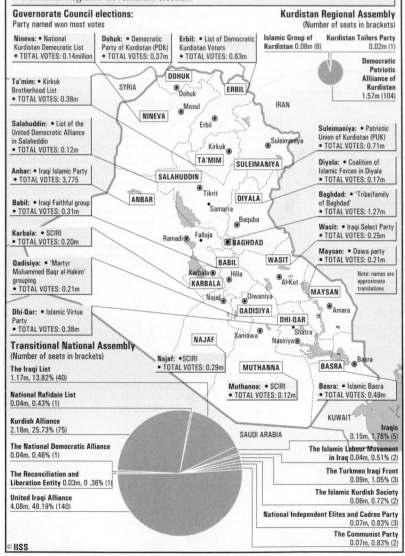

Transitional National Assembly
(Number of seats in brackets)

The Iraqi List
1.17m, 13.82% (40)

National Rafidain List
0.04m, 0.43% (1)

Kurdish Alliance
2.18m, 25.73% (75)

The National Democratic Alliance
0.04m, 0.46% (1)

The Reconciliation and Liberation Entity 0.03m, 0.36% (1)

United Iraqi Alliance
4.08m, 48.19% (140)

Najaf: • SCIRI
• TOTAL VOTES: 0.29m

Muthanna: • SCIRI
• TOTAL VOTES: 0.12m

Basra: • Islamic Basra
• TOTAL VOTES: 0.49m

Iraqis
0.15m, 1.78% (5)

The Islamic Labour Movement in Iraq 0.04m, 0.51% (2)

The Turkmen Iraqi Front
0.09m, 1.05% (3)

The Islamic Kurdish Society
0.06m, 0.72% (2)

National Independent Elites and Cadres Party
0.07m, 0.83% (3)

The Communist Party in Iraq 0.07m, 0.83% (2)

© IISS

MIDDLE EAST / GULF Iraq's continuing security problems

Although the transfer of sovereignty and elections may have taken place in Iraq, insurgent and terrorist attacks continue to occur. The number of American troops who have died in Iraq rose above 1,500 in 2005, while the number of Iraqis killed continues to rise to a level estimated to be thousands higher than Coalition losses. The Iraqi government may hope that, as more power is transferred into Iraqi hands, the attackers will lose much of their support and motivation, while the emergence of better trained and equipped domestic security forces will impose additional disincentives. The attackers, meanwhile, seem to be increasingly targeting Iraqis either in positions of responsibility (even at the relatively low level of hospital director) or who are working for, or wanting to work for, the Iraqi state. Data on the map below shows selected attacks from January–March 2005.

Figures quoted on this page are from media sources. As such they will be limited in detail, given the threats to the media generally in Iraq, which can restrict access. Many more 'low-level' attacks and incidents of intimidation will have taken place that are not listed on this map.

19 Mar: Policemen targeted
24 Feb: Police targeted
26 Jan: Incl. 3 police in 3 car bombs at Riyadh (nr Kirkuk)

20 Mar: Incl. police commander
10 Mar: Attack on funeral procession
27 Feb: Blast at Hammam Ali nr Mosul
7 Feb: Police targeted
26 Jan: Political offices
3 Jan: Police targeted

17 Jan: Attack on police station
3 Jan: Iraqi security personnel

22 Mar: Insurgents die in attack on training camp
24 Feb: Attack on police station
11 Jan: Police targeted
3 Jan: Iraqi soldiers

8 Mar: 20 suspected Iraqi security personnel found shot near al-Qaim

31 Mar
9 Feb: Police targeted
27 Jan
11 Jan
9 Jan: Deputy police chief of Samarra killed

7 March
3 Jan: Iraqi soldiers
2 Jan: Iraqi soldiers

23 Mar: Police targeted
29 Jan: Baghdad and Ramadi

15-17 Jan: Baghdad says 25 insurgents killed near Falluja

27 Jan

18 Feb

28 Feb: Applicants for security jobs
5 Jan: Police graduation

31 Mar: Incl. 2 soldiers in Tuz Khumartu (180km N of Baghdad)
28 Mar: Incl. 2 police targeted in Musayib (70 km S of Baghdad); snr policeman killed in Baghdad
8 Mar: Interior Ministry official
3 Mar: 2 car bombs (Interior Ministry targeted)
2 Mar: 2 car bombs kill Iraqi soldiers
19 Feb: 17 on bus; 2 Iraqi soldiers; 7 others
18 Feb: 19 die in attack
12 Feb: Hospital in Musayib (70km S of Baghdad)
11 Feb
10 Feb: 3 in car bomb; 20 truck drivers S of Baghdad
9 Feb: Senior civil servant
8 Feb: Army recruits
30 Jan
29 Jan: Raghdad and Ramadi
26 Jan: Political offices
24 Jan: Offices of Ayad Allawi's party
21 Jan: Including 7 in Yousfiya (20km S of Baghdad)
19 Jan: Including on police post and Australian embassy
11 Jan: Iraqis killed
10 Jan: Baghdad deputy police chief
4 Jan: Police; Governor of Baghdad
3 Jan: Allawi party offices

7 Mar: Series of attacks
19 Feb: Latifiya and Baquba
7 Feb: Police recruits
26 Jan: Political offices
17 Jan: Iraqi security forces
5 Jan: Police targeted
4 Jan: Iraqi Nat'l Guards killed

10 Feb: Police targeted
13 Jan: Sistani representative

12 Feb: Judge
9 Feb: Local politician and journalist

TURKEY

Mosul

Kirkuk

Baji

Tikrit

Al-Qaim

Samarra

Balad

Falluja

Baquba

Ramadi

BAGHDAD

Mahmudia

Iskandariya

Salman Pak

Hilla

IRAN

Basra

KUWAIT

SAUDI ARABIA

(5) Number of people killed in attack

 Suicide bomber

 Unspecified attack

 Car bomb attack

 Suicide car bomb attack

 Shooting

© IISS

MIDDLE EAST / GULF Iran's nuclear programmes

In February 2005, Iran reached agreement with Russia whereby Moscow would supply nuclear fuel to Iran's now-completed light water nuclear power reactor at Bushehr. As a safeguard, Iran has to return spent fuel to Russia. This deal was concluded amid much criticism of Iran's nuclear ambitions which are, according to the Bush administration and many European capitals, unnecessary given Iran's vast oil and (particularly) natural gas reserves. The EU and US both fear that Iran's nuclear programmes, with the country's haphazard history of accounting to the IAEA and pattern of concealment, as well as allegations of connection with A.Q. Khan's nuclear trading network and that Iran's facilities are not wholly compatible with its declared light water power reactor programme, could assist in any search by Tehran for a nuclear weapons capability. Washington and European capitals had been pursuing somewhat differing diplomatic courses, although recent indications are that the extent of Iran's nuclear progress, coupled with political pressures for action, could foster a more coherent plan of action.

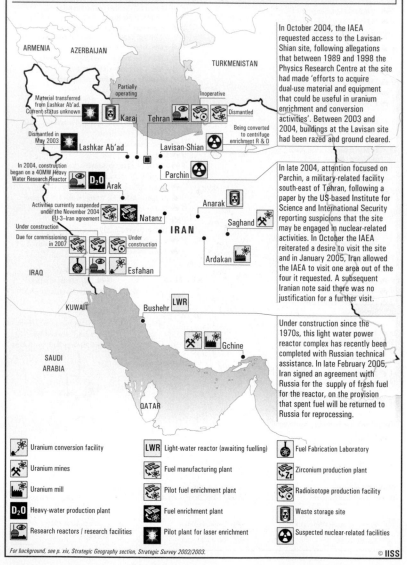

In October 2004, the IAEA requested access to the Lavisan-Shian site, following allegations that between 1989 and 1998 the Physics Research Centre at the site had made 'efforts to acquire dual-use material and equipment that could be useful in uranium enrichment and conversion activities'. Between 2003 and 2004, buildings at the Lavisan site had been razed and ground cleared.

In late 2004, attention focused on Parchin, a military-related facility south-east of Tehran, following a paper by the US-based Institute for Science and International Security reporting suspicions that the site may be engaged in nuclear-related activities. In October the IAEA reiterated a desire to visit the site and in January 2005, Iran allowed the IAEA to visit one area out of the four it requested. A subsequent Iranian note said there was no justification for a further visit.

Under construction since the 1970s, this light water power reactor complex has recently been completed with Russian technical assistance. In late February 2005, Iran signed an agreement with Russia for the supply of fresh fuel for the reactor, on the provision that spent fuel will be returned to Russia for reprocessing.

Map labels: ARMENIA, AZERBAIJAN, TURKMENISTAN, Material transferred from Lashkar Ab'ad. Current status unknown, Partially operating, Karaj, Tehran, Inoperative, Dismantled, Being converted to centrifuge enrichment R & D, Dismantled in May 2003, Lashkar Ab'ad, Lavisan-Shian, In 2004, construction began on a 40MW Heavy Water Research Reactor, D₂O Arak, Parchin, Anarak, Activities currently suspended under the November 2004 EU-3–Iran agreement, Natanz, Saghand, IRAN, Under construction, Due for commissioning in 2007, Under construction, Ardakan, IRAQ, Esfahan, KUWAIT, Bushehr, LWR, Gchine, SAUDI ARABIA, QATAR

Legend:
- Uranium conversion facility
- Uranium mines
- Uranium mill
- D₂O Heavy-water production plant
- Research reactors / research facilities
- LWR Light-water reactor (awaiting fuelling)
- Fuel manufacturing plant
- Pilot fuel enrichment plant
- Fuel enrichment plant
- Pilot plant for laser enrichment
- Fuel Fabrication Laboratory
- Zr Zirconium production plant
- Radioisotope production facility
- Waste storage site
- Suspected nuclear-related facilities

For background, see p. xiv, Strategic Geography section, Strategic Survey 2002/2003.

© IISS

EUROPE / RUSSIA Ukraine: the election of Yushchenko

The inauguration of Victor Yushchenko as President of Ukraine, on 23 January 2005, ended a period of political uncertainty in the country. The first round of the Presidential election, to succeed Leonid Kuchma, took place on 31 October. This election, with its narrow victory for then-candidate Yushchenko over his opponent Victor Yanukovich triggered a second round ballot on 21 November. Both elections were, however, criticised by an International Election Observation Mission, with a number of criticisms raised, including that there was 'abuse of state resources in favor of the Prime Minister … as well as an overwhelming media bias in his favor'. The Prime Minister at the time was Victor Yanukovich. Following domestic and international protests against the declared results of the repeat round of voting, the Ukrainian Supreme Court declared the result invalid on 3 December. Meanwhile, protests continued in parts of Ukraine, with many dispersing only after a parliamentary vote on 8 December that included steps designed to reform the Central Election Commission and to limit the possibility of electoral fraud. A second repeat round of voting on 26 December resulted in victory for Victor Yushchenko. This ballot was, according to Bruce George MP, President Emeritus of the OSCE Parliamentary Assembly and Special Coordinator of the short term [international] observers, 'substantially closer to meeting OSCE and other European standards'.

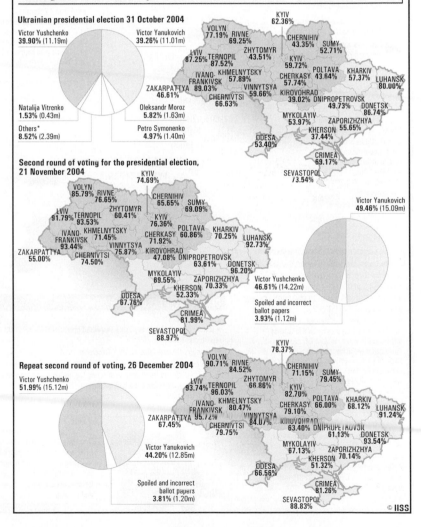

Ukrainian presidential election 31 October 2004

Victor Yushchenko
39.90% (11.19m)

Victor Yanukovich
39.26% (11.01m)

Natalija Vitrenko
1.53% (0.43m)

Oleksandr Moroz
5.82% (1.63m)

Others*
8.52% (2.39m)

Petro Symonenko
4.97% (1.40m)

KYIV 62.36%
VOLYN 77.19%
RIVNE 69.25%
CHERNIHIV 43.35%
SUMY 52.71%
ZHYTOMYR 43.51%
LVIV 87.25%
TERNOPIL 87.52%
KYIV 59.72%
POLTAVA 43.64%
KHARKIV 57.37%
LUHANSK 80.00%
IVANO-FRANKIVSK 89.03%
KHMELNYTSKY 57.89%
CHERKASY 57.74%
ZAKARPATTYA 46.61%
VINNYTSYA 59.66%
KIROVOHRAD 39.02%
DNIPROPETROVSK 49.73%
CHERNIVTSI 66.63%
DONETSK 86.74%
MYKOLAYIV 53.97%
ZAPORIZHZHYA 55.65%
KHERSON 37.44%
ODESA 53.40%
CRIMEA 69.17%
SEVASTOPOL 73.54%

Second round of voting for the presidential election, 21 November 2004

KYIV 74.69%
VOLYN 85.79%
RIVNE 76.65%
CHERNIHIV 65.65%
SUMY 69.09%
LVIV 91.79%
TERNOPIL 93.53%
ZHYTOMYR 60.41%
KYIV 76.36%
IVANO-FRANKIVSK 93.44%
KHMELNYTSKY 71.45%
CHERKASY 60.86%
POLTAVA 71.92%
KHARKIV 70.25%
LUHANSK 92.73%
ZAKARPATTYA 55.00%
VINNYTSYA 75.87%
CHERNIVTSI 74.50%
KIROVOHRAD 47.08%
DNIPROPETROVSK 63.61%
DONETSK 96.20%
MYKOLAYIV 69.55%
ZAPORIZHZHYA 70.33%
KHERSON 52.33%
ODESA 67.76%
CRIMEA 81.99%
SEVASTOPOL 88.97%

Victor Yanukovich
49.46% (15.09m)

Victor Yushchenko
46.61% (14.22m)

Spoiled and incorrect ballot papers
3.93% (1.12m)

Repeat second round of voting, 26 December 2004

Victor Yushchenko
51.99% (15.12m)

KYIV 78.37%
VOLYN 90.71%
RIVNE 84.52%
CHERNIHIV 71.15%
SUMY 79.45%
ZHYTOMYR 66.86%
LVIV 93.74%
TERNOPIL 96.03%
KYIV 82.70%
IVANO-FRANKIVSK 80.47%
KHMELNYTSKY
CHERKASY 66.00%
POLTAVA
KHARKIV 68.12%
LUHANSK 91.24%
ZAKARPATTYA 67.45%
VINNYTSYA 79.10%
CHERNIVTSI 79.75%
KIROVOHRAD 63.40%
DNIPROPETROVSK 61.13%
DONETSK 93.54%
MYKOLAYIV 67.13%
ZAPORIZHZHYA 70.14%
KHERSON 51.32%
ODESA 66.56%
CRIMEA 81.26%
SEVASTOPOL 88.83%

Victor Yanukovich
44.20% (12.85m)

Spoiled and incorrect ballot papers
3.81% (1.20m)

© IISS

EUROPE / RUSSIA The EU's political, military and security missions

On 2 December 2004, the European Union (EU) launched *Operation Althea* in Bosnia–Herzegovina (BiH), its most far-reaching military operation to date, when it took over from NATO's Stabilisation Force mission. Building on the process under development since 1992's first version of the Treaty on European Union (TEU), these moves have been spurred by events such as the Balkan wars of the 1990s and more recent terrorist attacks. The current TEU (amended at Amsterdam and Nice in 1997 and 2001, respectively), incorporates in its Article 17 the Western European Union's (WEU) 1992 'Petersberg Tasks'. This makes the EU responsible for the WEU's former crisis management operations: 'questions referred to in this article shall include humanitarian and rescue tasks, peacekeeping tasks and tasks of combat forces in crisis management, including peacemaking'.

Until initiatives in the late 1990s, however, Europe lacked the structures and capabilities required to realise even its more limited ambitions of the early part of that decade. The Kosovo conflict prompted what has been termed a 'rapid Europeanisation' of the 1998 St Malo agreement between Britain and

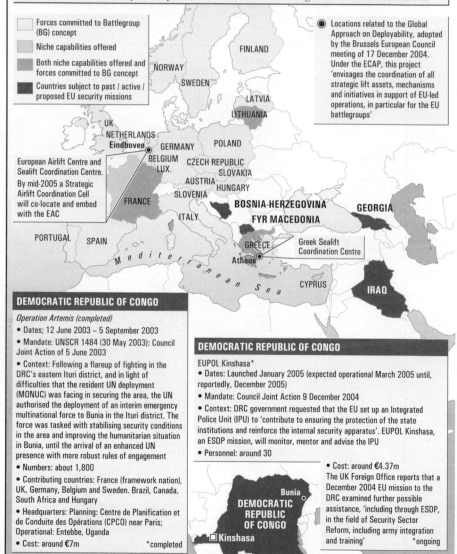

Forces committed to Battlegroup (BG) concept

Niche capabilities offered

Both niche capabilities offered and forces committed to BG concept

Countries subject to past / active / proposed EU security missions

Locations related to the Global Approach on Deployability, adopted by the Brussels European Council meeting of 17 December 2004. Under the ECAP, this project 'envisages the coordination of all strategic lift assets, mechanisms and initiatives in support of EU-led operations, in particular for the EU battlegroups'

European Airlift Centre and Sealift Coordination Centre. By mid-2005 a Strategic Airlift Coordination Cell will co-locate and embed with the EAC

Greek Sealift Coordination Centre

DEMOCRATIC REPUBLIC OF CONGO

Operation Artemis (completed)

● Dates; 12 June 2003 – 5 September 2003

● Mandate: UNSCR 1484 (30 May 2003): Council Joint Action of 5 June 2003

● Context: Following a flareup of fighting in the DRC's eastern Ituri district, and in light of difficulties that the resident UN deployment (MONUC) was facing in securing the area, the UN authorised the deployment of an interim emergency multinational force to Bunia in the Ituri district. The force was tasked with stabilising security conditions in the area and improving the humanitarian situation in Bunia, until the arrival of an enhanced UN presence with more robust rules of engagement

● Numbers: about 1,800

● Contributing countries: France (framework nation), UK, Germany, Belgium and Sweden. Brazil, Canada, South Africa and Hungary

● Headquarters: Planning: Centre de Planification et de Conduite des Opérations (CPCO) near Paris; Operational: Entebbe, Uganda

● Cost: around €7m   *completed

DEMOCRATIC REPUBLIC OF CONGO

EUPOL Kinshasa*

● Dates: Launched January 2005 (expected operational March 2005 until, reportedly, December 2005)

● Mandate: Council Joint Action 9 December 2004

● Context: DRC government requested that the EU set up an Integrated Police Unit (IPU) to 'contribute to ensuring the protection of the state institutions and reinforce the internal security apparatus'. EUPOL Kinshasa, an ESDP mission, will monitor, mentor and advise the IPU

● Personnel: around 30

● Cost: around €4.37m
The UK Foreign Office reports that a December 2004 EU mission to the DRC examined further possible assistance, 'including through ESDP, in the field of Security Sector Reform, including army integration and training'   *ongoing

France, which stated that if the Union was to be in a position to 'play a full role on the international stage' it 'must have the capacity for autonomous action, backed up by credible military forces…'. Following this, the European Council's June 1999 and December 1999 meetings in Cologne and Helsinki respectively established the following bodies, among other decisions:

- Political and Security Committee (PSC)
- European Union Satellite Centre
- European Union Military and Security Committee (EUMC)
- European Union Military Staff (EUMS)
- European Institute for Strategic Studies

According to Javier Solana, the EU's High Representative for the Common Foreign and Security Policy, 'the Union's security and defence policy is no longer a choice but a necessity', one given a framework in his December 2003 European Security Strategy (ESS). The ESS listed a number of perceived threats to Europe: terrorism; the proliferation of weapons of mass destruction; regional conflicts; state failure; and organised crime. Furthermore, it noted that although none of these threats was purely military and all required a mix of instruments, threats could grow over time, while 'conflict prevention and threat prevention cannot start too early' and 'preventive engagement can avoid more serious problems in the future'.

Realising the headline goal

The Helsinki summit also saw member states set out a headline goal of being able to deploy, by 2003, a Corps level body of 60,000 troops within 60 days, capable of sustaining themselves for one year. Moves towards achieving this objective led to the identification of capability shortfalls. The outcome was the 20 November 2000 Capabilities Commitment Conference where, although enough forces were pledged, shortfalls in the key areas of airlift and sealift, for example, were noted. The 19 November 2001 Capabilities Improvement Conference (CIC), which reduced the number of shortfalls to 40, saw the launch of a European Capabilities Action Plan (ECAP) to identify solutions. The EU is establishing a new 'Headline Goals 2010' plan. In parallel, it has set new targets for the creation of battlegroups and has established a European Defence Agency to focus on member states' defence capability development, research, acquisition and armaments.

GEORGIA

EU Rule of Law Mission to Georgia (EUJUST THEMIS)*
- Dates: 16 July 2004 – estimated one year duration
- Mandate: Council decision of 28 June 2004 following invitation from Georgian Prime Minister
- Context: 'The EU has been invited by the Georgian government to launch an EU Rule of Law mission to Georgia in the context of the European Security and Defence Policy … . The Mission will support the authorities in addressing urgent challenges in the criminal justice system, assisting the Georgian government in developing a coordinated approach to the reform process, in a way that fully complements current EU assistance and other international community activities and bilateral Member State initiatives in the Rule of Law area'
- Mission HQ: Tbilisi
- Personnel: 10 international, plus local staff   *ongoing

IRAQ

An exploratory EU mission visited Baghdad from 29-31 August 2004 to 'explore options for concrete EU engagement in the civilian crisis management areas of police, rule of law and civilian administration as well as elections'. In March 2005, 'the EU council adopted a Joint Action on the EU Integrated Rule of Law Mission for Iraq (EUJUST LEX) aimed at addressing the needs of Iraq's criminal justice system through training. Training will take place in the EU or the region and EUJUST LEX will maintain a liaison office in Baghdad. The mission will begin no later than July 2005, lasting an initial 12 months with a €10m budget

Battlegroups concept

The November 2004 Capabilities Commitment Conference saw a commitment to create 13 Battlegroups (BG) distinct from the headline goal capability. According to the UK Foreign Office, 'each will consist of around 1,500 troops, ready to deploy within 15 days of a crisis, primarily in support of the UN, and normally for a period of about 30 days'. Initial operating capacity is slated for 2005–06, when the EU should be able to run one BG formation; full capability should be reached in 2007. During a speech at the opening session of the Commission for Africa in October 2004, UK Prime Minister Tony Blair has said 'I want Africa to be the top priority for the … battle groups … . These battle groups would allow the European Union to respond to a crisis in Africa within 10 days … giving time for the AU [African Union] or UN to prepare a longer-term intervention'.

Working with NATO

Under the 'Berlin Plus' arrangements (from a NATO summit in 1996), mechanisms exist whereby the EU is able to 'borrow' assets from NATO in order to carry out regional crisis management missions. Possibilities would include: access to NATO operational planning; 'presumption of availability' to the EU of NATO capabilities and common assets; and NATO European Command options for EU-led operations. An EU cell is to be located at SHAPE, and a NATO liaison presence at the EUMS has been mooted.

© IISS

EUROPE / RUSSIA The EU's political, military and security missions

Bosnia and Herzegovina

Multinational Task Force Northwest (MNTF NW) Under UK command
• HQ: Banja Luka • Personnel: 2,000
• Participating countries: Austria, Bulgaria, Canada, Chile, Netherlands, New Zealand, Norway, Romania, Switzerland and UK.

Multinational Task Force North (MNTF N) Under Finnish command
• HQ: Tuzla • Personnel: 1,800
• Participating countries: Austria, Belgium, Czech Rep, Finland, Greece, Ireland, Latvia, Poland, Portugal, Slovenia, Sweden and Turkey.

Multinational Task Force Southeast (MNTF SE)
Under French command
• HQ: Mostar
• Personnel: 1,800
• Participating countries include Germany, Italy and Spain.

Theatre troops
• Personnel: 1,000
• Theatre troops are based at various locations in Bosnia and Herzegovina.

Operation Althea (Berlin Plus)

• Dates: 2 December 2004 – present (for an initial 12-month period)
• Mandate: UNSCR 1575 (22 November 2004); NATO Istanbul summit June 2004
• Replacing: NATO's *Operation Joint Forge* SFOR mission
• Context: EU sees the western Balkans' future as within the EU. 'It is within this wider context of European integration that a comprehensive policy for addressing BiH's security needs has to be situated'
• EU Operations HQ at SHAPE in Mons, Belgium
• Troop numbers: around 7,000
• Contributing nations: 22 EU member states and Albania, Argentina, Bulgaria, Canada, Chile, Morocco, New Zealand, Norway, Romania, Switzerland, Turkey
• Cost: Reference amount of €71.7m
• NATO retains a headquarters in Sarajevo

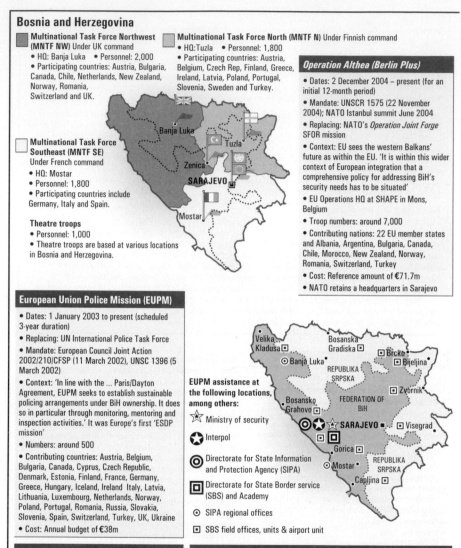

European Union Police Mission (EUPM)

• Dates: 1 January 2003 to present (scheduled 3-year duration)
• Replacing: UN International Police Task Force
• Mandate: European Council Joint Action 2002/210/CFSP (11 March 2002), UNSC 1396 (5 March 2002)
• Context: 'In line with the ... Paris/Dayton Agreement, EUPM seeks to establish sustainable policing arrangements under BiH ownership. It does so in particular through monitoring, mentoring and inspection activities.' It was Europe's first 'ESDP mission'
• Numbers: around 500
• Contributing countries: Austria, Belgium, Bulgaria, Canada, Cyprus, Czech Republic, Denmark, Estonia, Finland, France, Germany, Greece, Hungary, Iceland, Ireland Italy, Latvia, Lithuania, Luxembourg, Netherlands, Norway, Poland, Portugal, Romania, Russia, Slovakia, Slovenia, Spain, Switzerland, Turkey, UK, Ukraine
• Cost: Annual budget of €38m

EUPM assistance at the following locations, among others:
☆ Ministry of security
★ Interpol
◎ Directorate for State Information and Protection Agency (SIPA)
▯ Directorate for State Border service (SBS) and Academy
⊙ SIPA regional offices
▣ SBS field offices, units & airport unit

DEPLOYMENTS

'EUPM units are deployed in the field, as co-locators in BiH State-, Entities- and Brcko District-level police units, as well as advisors to the Ministry of Security (state level), to some State-level Police Organisations and to both Ministries of Interior (Federation and Republika Srpska)'

MAIN PROGRAMMES

• 'Crime Police' Programme
• Police Administration Programme
• State Border Service Programme (SBS)
• Police Training and Education System Programme
• State Information and Protection Agency Programme (SIPA)
• Internal Affairs Programme
• Public Order and Security Programme

European Gendarmerie Force

On 17 September 2004, defence ministers from France, Italy, Spain, Portugal and the Netherlands signed a Declaration of Intent concerning the establishment of a European Gendarmerie Force (EGF). A police force with military status, the EGF will be able to conduct general police missions, and (according to the declaration of intent) 'it is excellently suited to deployment during or immediately after a military operation for maintaining public order and safety. It should also be possible for the rapidly-deployable

The former Yugoslav Republic of Macedonia

Operation Concordia (Berlin Plus)	European Union Police Mission *(EUPOL Proxima II)* -see map below
• Dates: 31 March 2003 – 15 December 2003 • Mandate: Following request from President Trajkovski and UNSC 1371 • Replacing: NATO's *Operation Allied Harmony* • Replaced by EUPOL Proxima • Objective: 'at the explicit request of the FYROM government, to contribute further to a stable secure environment and to allow the implementation of the August 2001 Ohrid Framework Agreement' • Troop numbers: around 400 • Contributing nations: EU: Austria, Belgium, Finland, France, Germany, Greece, Italy, Luxembourg, the Netherlands, Portugal, Spain, Sweden, United Kingdom. Non-EU NATO: Czech Republic, Hungary, Iceland, Norway, Poland, Turkey Non-EU non-NATO: Bulgaria, Estonia, Latvia, Lithuania, Romania, Slovakia, Slovenia • EUFOR HQ in Skopje ; 3 regional HQs in Skopje, Tetovo, Kumanovo. 22 Light field liaison teams; 8 heavy field liaison teams; + support elements. • Cost: €6.2m	• Dates: 15 December 2003 to present (one year duration - renewable) • Replaced: EU's *Operation Concordia* military mission • Mandate: established by Council Joint Action 2003/681/CFSP • Context: The mission was established in line with the objectives of 2001's Ohrid Framework Agreement • Objective: 'EUPOL Proxima shall support ... through monitoring, mentoring and advising, as appropriate, the consolidation of law and order, including the fight against organised crime ... [and] the practical implementation of the comprehensive reform of the Ministry of Internal Affairs, including the police' • Mission: consolidation of law and order, including the fight against organised crime; implementation of the reform of the Ministry of Interior, including the police; transition towards and the creation of a border police; local policing and confidence building within the population; cooperation with neighbouring States in the field of policing • Numbers: Around 200 international staff • Contributing countries: Germany, France, Netherlands, Italy, Sweden, Spain, Greece, Finland, Turkey, UK, Denmark and Belgium, Hungary, Norway, Slovenia, Ukraine, Cyprus, Austria, Czech Republic, Poland, Switzerland, Ireland, Latvia and Lithuania, Luxembourg and Portugal, and local staff • Cost: €15 million for the first year, including set-up costs of €7.3 million, funded through the Community budget **Main programmes** • Uniformed Police Programme • Border Police Programme • Internal Control / Law Enforcement Monitoring Programme • Criminal Police Programme • UBK Programme (Ministry of State security and counterintelligence)

EUPOL Proxima II – future deployment of Proxima personnel in the field (as of December 2004)

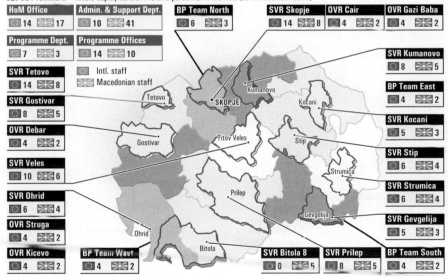

EGF to conduct operations in support of the fight against organised crime and the protection of participants in civil missions'. The EGF is intended for possible use by the UN, the OSCE and NATO as well as the EU.

• Possible numbers: 800 from 2005, with permanent HQ of 30–40. (Some sources note possible end-strength of 3,000.)

• HQ: Vicenza, Italy. • Nations involved: France, Italy, Spain, Portugal and the Netherlands.

© IISS

EUROPE / RUSSIA Chechnya: continuing troubles

The last year has been bleak for the inhabitants of the north Caucasus. Terrorist attacks, actions by federal forces and the rumoured war profiteering from the conflict in Chechnya were ongoing and continue to impact the wider region; a solution to the conflict seems distant. The killing of president Ahmad Kadyrov in May 2004 led to a new vote in October, which Alu Alkhanov won with 74% of the vote, though his key opponent was barred from taking part. A US State Department spokesman said that the 'presidential vote did not meet international standards for a democratic election'. Meanwhile, parliamentary elections are scheduled for late-2005.

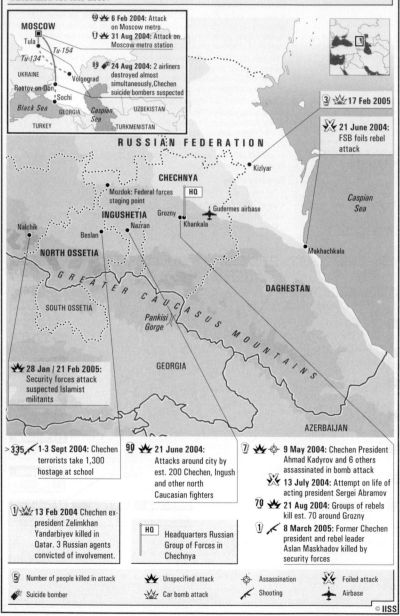

49 🗲 **6 Feb 2004:** Attack on Moscow metro

1J 🗲 **31 Aug 2004:** Attack on Moscow metro station

89 ✈ **24 Aug 2004:** 2 airliners destroyed almost simultaneously, Chechen suicide bombers suspected

3 🗲 **17 Feb 2005**

🗲 **21 June 2004:** FSB foils rebel attack

28 Jan / 21 Feb 2005: Security forces attack suspected Islamist militants

>335 🗲 **1-3 Sept 2004:** Chechen terrorists take 1,300 hostage at school

90 🗲 **21 June 2004:** Attacks around city by est. 200 Chechen, Ingush and other north Caucasian fighters

1 🗲 **13 Feb 2004** Chechen ex-president Zelimkhan Yandarbiyev killed in Qatar. 3 Russian agents convicted of involvement.

7 🗲 **9 May 2004:** Chechen President Ahmad Kadyrov and 6 others assassinated in bomb attack

🗲 **13 July 2004:** Attempt on life of acting president Sergei Abramov

70 🗲 **21 Aug 2004:** Groups of rebels kill est. 70 around Grozny

1 🗲 **8 March 2005:** Former Chechen president and rebel leader Aslan Maskhadov killed by security forces

🏳 **HQ** Headquarters Russian Group of Forces in Chechnya

5 Number of people killed in attack

🗲 Suicide bomber

🗲 Unspecified attack

🗲 Car bomb attack

⊕ Assassination

🗲 Shooting

🗲 Foiled attack

✈ Airbase

© IISS

The problem

According to a paper supplied to the Northern Dimension Environmental Partnership (NDEP) by the European Bank for Reconstruction and Development, Russia constructed 248 nuclear submarines between 1955–2001. The Contact Experts Group (CEG), established under the auspices of the IAEA, says that 90 of these were strategic vessels carrying ballistic missiles and the remainder were general purpose, carrying torpedoes and/or cruise missiles. Under the provisions of the START 1 and START 2 arms reduction treaties, as well as Russia's Government Resolution no. 548 of 28 May 1994, Moscow has been working to progressively reduce its nuclear submarine force.

Starting with the US-Russian Cooperative Threat Reduction (CTR) Program (which has in the main concentrated on the dismantlement and destruction of strategic armaments, including the dismantlement of ballistic missile submarines) the international community, and individual nations, have recognised the need to assist in this process. The 2002 G8 summit adopted the 'G8 Global Partnership Against the Spread of Weapons of Mass Destruction'. Some bilateral programmes assist in the dismantlement process, while some nations work through multinational programmes or fund dismantlement activities by third parties. Arms reduction concerns are not the only motivation: fears exist that unsecured radioactive sources could be transferred to potentially hostile actors, while the poor storage conditions in which many decommissioned boats and their reactors (and indeed the fuel itself) are kept in has led to concerns for the environment.

The CEG's October 2004 meeting heard that 195 nuclear submarines had been retired from the Russian navy by the beginning of 2004. 103 of these had been dismantled, and a further 18 were scheduled to be dismantled during 2004, including five with international funding. 83 submarines were awaiting dismantling, with 42 in the Pacific region. Moscow has set 2010 as the deadline for completing the dismantlement of those submarines presently retired.

Initiatives

- **Contact Experts Group**
A 'Contact Expert Group (CEG) for International Radwaste Projects in the Russian Federation' was established under the auspices of the IAEA in 1996 to promote and facilitate assistance, and improve coordination in order to help Russia deal with its legacy of nuclear waste and spent fuel.

- **G8 Global Partnership**
The 2002 G8 summit adopted the 'G8 Global Partnership Against the Spread of Weapons of Mass Destruction'. G8 participants pledged to raise up to $20billion to support the Global Partnership's priority concerns: the destruction of chemical weapons; the dismantlement of decommissioned nuclear submarines; the disposition of fissile materials; and the employment of former weapons scientists.

- **Multilateral Nuclear Environment Programme in the Russian Federation (MNEPR)**
Signed on 21 May 2003, MNEPR is designed to facilitate international cooperation over the safety of spent nuclear fuel, radioactive waste management and the decommissioning of nuclear submarines and icebreakers by developing a legal framework for such activities.

- **Northern Dimension Environmental Partnership (NDEP)**
The NDEP was developed during 2001 in response to calls to address environmental problems in north-west Russia, particularly those relating to water, wastewater, solid waste, energy efficiency and nuclear waste. Its Support Fund finances activities in two areas: nuclear safety; and more traditional non-nuclear environmental concerns, such as water, wastewater, solid waste and energy efficiency.

- **Arctic Military Environmental Co-operation (AMEC) Programme**
This partnership between the defence ministries of the US, Russia, Norway and the UK was established in 1996. (The UK joined in 2003.) AMEC is designed to 'solve environmental problems caused by military activities' in the Arctic region.

- **US Cooperative Threat Reduction Program (CTR)**
The CTR Program, established in 1992, is designed to prevent the proliferation of weapons of mass destruction (WMD) and related materials, technologies and expertise from the former Soviet Union. In 2003, the Pentagon allocated almost $290 million for CTR programmes in Russia, which are also managed by the Department of Energy and the State Department With regard to submarine programmes, the CTR Program is primarily concerned with the dismantlement of strategic missile submarines.

EUROPE / RUSSIA Russia's naval nuclear legacy

International involvement

• US

The US has pledged $10bn to the G8 Global Partnership – an amount divided between the three departments that implement CTR assistance. Besides decommissioning and dismantling Russian strategic missile submarines (SSBNs), the US also focuses its assistance on, for example, eliminating strategic delivery vehicles as well the employment of former scientists and border and environmental safety issues. The CTR Program's Annual Report to Congress for 2004 stated that as of end-2003, 27 SSBNs had been destroyed (including 3 during 2003) out of a baseline figure of 48. The target for 2007 was 35 destroyed SSBNs, and for 2012, 40. The US is involved in other initiatives, such as the AMEC and MNEPR.

• Germany

Out of a total Global Partnership amount of $1.5bn, Germany has pledged $300m to submarine dismantlement. In October 2003, Germany signed an agreement with Russia on the safe disposal of approximately 120 nuclear powered submarines from the Northern Fleet. The project has as its focus the construction of a land-based reactor compartment interim storage facility at Sayda Bay – building started in 2004. Dismantling was to take place at the Nerpa shipyard, which Berlin agreed to refurbish. Germany is also active through the NDEP, and indicated a willingness to provide €10m for five years to this partnership, from 2004.

• Canada

Ottawa has pledged C$1bn to the Global Partnership fund. Its first project announcement, in 2003, included monies for the NDEP, while its second, in 2004, included over C$100m for submarine dismantlement in northern Russia. The programme will involve the dismantlement of twelve boats over four years. A July 2004 'implementing arrangement' with the Zvezdocha shipyard for contributions (some C$24.4m) towards the dismantling of three *Victor* I and *Victor* III submarines should be completed by August 2005. In December 2004, agreement was reached on a second 'implementing arrangement' to transport six *Victor* and two *Echo*-class boats to Zvezdocha, fully dismantle three *Victor* boats and unload spent nuclear fuel (SNF) from one more *Victor* – to be completed between April 2005–June 2006.

Northern Fleet

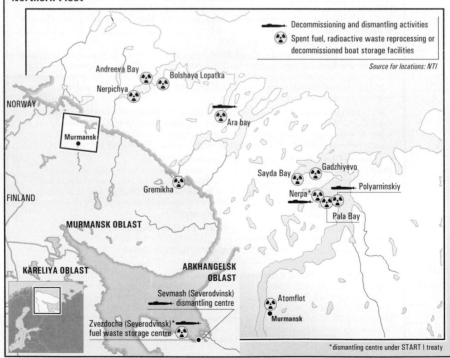

• **Norway**
Given its proximity to the bases of the Northern Fleet and related storage facilties, Oslo has long been interested in nuclear safety, decommissioning and storage issues. In 1995, a Plan of Action on nuclear safety issues was launched with Russia, and Norway has also been active through the AMEC programme. In 2003, Oslo financed the dismantling of two *Victor*-II general purpose nuclear-powered submarines at the Nerpa and Zvezdocha shipyards and in mid-2004, announced its intention to undertake 'more of the same'.

• **UK**
As of 2004, the UK was providing £36.5m per year to the Global Partnership, and the ten-year investment is expected to reach £750m. The UK has funded the dismantlement of two *Oscar* I submarines at the Sevmash and Zvezdocha shipyards, has assisted in the construction of a SNF storage facility at the Atomflot site in Murmansk, and has a number of projects 'to assist in the eventual safe and secure storage of some 20,000 SNF assemblies at a former Russian navy base – Andreeva Bay in NW Russia', among other initiatives. Furthermore, under the AMEC programme, the UK is working with the US and Norway to develop buoyancy and safe transportation technology for decommissioned submarines. The UK is also providing funding to the NDEP's 'nuclear window'.

• **Japan**
Japanese assistance is focused on Pacific Fleet submarines. With Russia it operates a project called 'Star of Hope' and in December 2004 announced the completion of its first project, the dismantling of a *Victor*-II boat. The G8 Consolidated Report of Global Partnership projects estimates that Japan allocates $100m for dismantlement programmes, out of a pledge of over $200m. On 13 January 2005, it was agreed that cooperation would start on the decommissioning of five more nuclear submarines. Japan intends that low-level waste will be treated in the Suzuran (Landysh) floating facility, with SNF eventually being transferred to the Mayak reprocessing plant in the Urals and reactor compartments stored afloat or on land. **Australia** pledged $10m towards the dismantling of Russian submarines, and plans to extend this assistance through existing Japanese–Russian arrangements.

• **Others**
The EU partly funds NDEP, as do Finland, France, the Netherlands and Sweden. Of course Russia funds dismantlement programmes for its own submarines.

Pacific Fleet

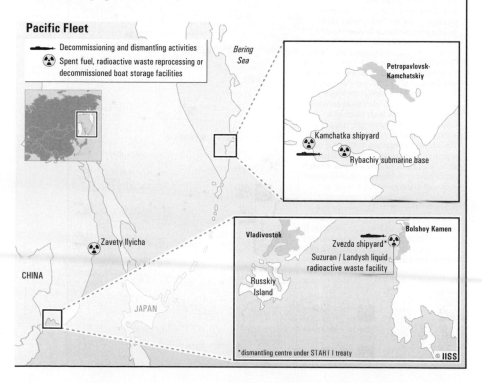

AMERICAS Brazil's high ambitions

Under the administration of President Luis Inácio da Silva, Brazil has taken an internationalist and forceful stance in its foreign policy. Brazil has led the UN presence in Haiti, since taking over from the Multinational Force initially deployed after the ouster of former president Jean-Bertrand Aristide and, in late 2004, joined with Germany, Japan and India to form the 'G4' calling for their presence, as permanent members, on the UN Security Council. However, the president has not had a smooth ride at home: in December 2004 two parties withdrew from the governing coalition. The larger of the two, the Brazilian Democratic Movement Party, reportedly voted to field their own candidate in the 2006 presidential election, with press articles reporting criticism of the president's progress on social policy issues.

	1990	1995	2001		
Population	**148.0m**	**159.5m**	**172.4**	**180.654** (2004 figure)	
Investment (% of GDP)	**20.2**	**22.3**	**21.2**	**20.3** (2002)	
Trade (% of GDP)	**15.2**	**17.2**	**27.4**	**29.4** (2002)	

	2001	2002	2003	2004	2005 (est)
Current account balance (US$bn)	**23.225**	**-7.628**	**4.016**	**6.458**	**2.068**
Gross domestic product per capita, constant prices (R)	**5767.554**	**5797.726**	**5710.627**	**5870.202**	**6006.607**
Gross domestic product, constant prices (annual % change)	**1.3**	**1.9**	**-0.2**	**4.0**	**3.5**
Inflation (annual % change)	**6.8**	**8.4**	**14.8**	**6.6**	**5.9**

Sources: IMF, World Bank and UN population division

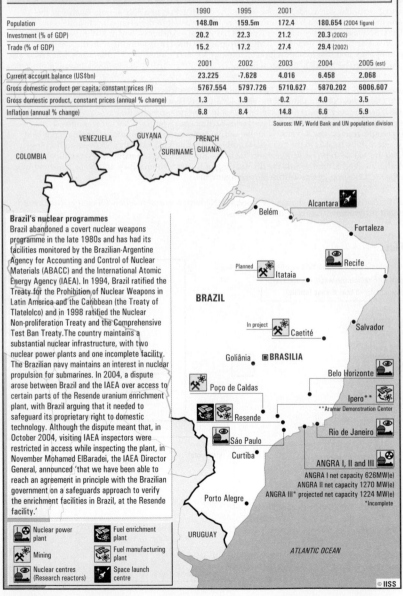

Brazil's nuclear programmes
Brazil abandoned a covert nuclear weapons programme in the late 1980s and has had its facilities monitored by the Brazilian-Argentine Agency for Accounting and Control of Nuclear Materials (ABACC) and the International Atomic Energy Agency (IAEA). In 1994, Brazil ratified the Treaty for the Prohibition of Nuclear Weapons in Latin America and the Caribbean (the Treaty of Tlatelolco) and in 1998 ratified the Nuclear Non-proliferation Treaty and the Comprehensive Test Ban Treaty. The country maintains a substantial nuclear infrastructure, with two nuclear power plants and one incomplete facility. The Brazilian navy maintains an interest in nuclear propulsion for submarines. In 2004, a dispute arose between Brazil and the IAEA over access to certain parts of the Resende uranium enrichment plant, with Brazil arguing that it needed to safeguard its proprietary right to domestic technology. Although the dispute meant that, in October 2004, visiting IAEA inspectors were restricted in access while inspecting the plant, in November Mohamed ElBaradei, the IAEA Director General, announced 'that we have been able to reach an agreement in principle with the Brazilian government on a safeguards approach to verify the enrichment facilities in Brazil, at the Resende facility.'

Nuclear power plant

Mining

Nuclear centres (Research reactors)

Fuel enrichment plant

Fuel manufacturing plant

Space launch centre

VENEZUELA
GUYANA
FRENCH GUIANA
SURINAME
COLOMBIA

Alcantara
Belém
Fortaleza

Planned Itataia
Recife

BRAZIL

In project Caetité
Salvador

Goliânia ▣BRASILIA

Belo Horizonte

Poço de Caldas

Ipero**
**Aramar Demonstration Center

Resende

Rio de Janeiro

São Paulo

Curtiba

ANGRA I, II and III
ANGRA I net capacity 626MW(e)
ANGRA II net capacity 1270 MW(e)
ANGRA III* projected net capacity 1224 MW(e)
*Incomplete

Porto Alegre

URUGUAY

ATLANTIC OCEAN

© IISS

AMERICAS Tough year in the Caribbean

In 2004, a series of tropical storms and hurricanes wreaked havoc across the Caribbean, with Hurricane *Ivan* – which transited the region from 7–14 September – reportedly the most powerful storm in ten years. Hurricane *Ivan* was reported to have killed 70 people. However, Tropical Storm *Jeanne*, which hit Puerto Rico and the US Virgin Islands on 15 September, and which killed an estimated 11 in the Dominican Republic when it struck on 17 September, caused flash flooding in Haiti that killed nearly 1,500. International assistance programmes have been mobilised to respond to each of these emergencies – the impact of which, given the long-term damage to livelihoods, will be felt for some time.

According to DFID, 'Hurricane *Ivan* crossed over northwestern Cuba as a category 5 hurricane on 13 September.' Havana organised the evacuation of some 1.5m people.* Earlier, on 13 August, Cuba was hit by Hurricane *Charley*, which led to flooding in low-lying areas of Habana Province. The state organised the evacuation of over 215,000 people from high risk areas. The IFRC reports that over 70,000 houses and thousands of hectares of crops were damaged

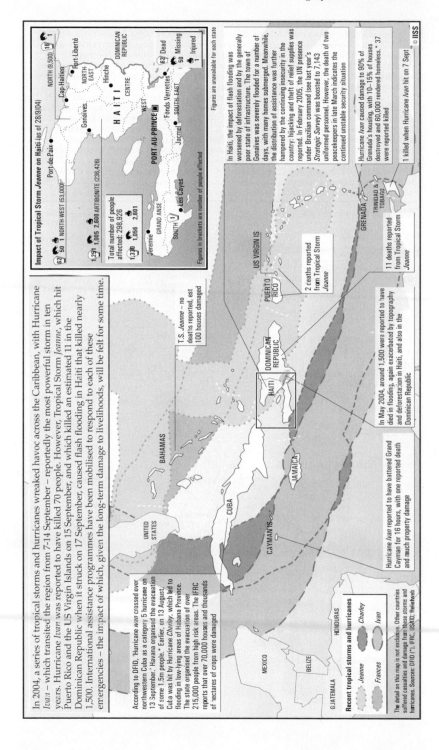

Recent tropical storms and hurricanes

- *Jeanne*
- *Charley*
- *Frances*
- *Ivan*

The detail on this map is not exclusive. Other countries suffered casualties and damage from these storms and hurricanes. Sources: DFID (*), IFRC, USAID; Reliefweb

Hurricane *Ivan* reported to have battered Grand Cayman for 16 hours, with one reported death and much property damage

T.S. *Jeanne* – no deaths reported, est 100 houses damaged

2 deaths reported from Tropical Storm *Jeanne*

In May 2004, around 1,500 were reported to have died in flooding, again exacerbated by topography and deforestation in Haiti, and also in the Dominican Republic

11 deaths reported from Tropical Storm *Jeanne*

Hurricane *Ivan* caused damage to 90% of Grenada's housing, with 10–15% of houses destroyed and 60,000 rendered homeless.* 37 were reported killed

1 killed when Hurricane *Ivan* hit on 7 Sept

In Haiti, the impact of flash flooding was worsened by deforestation and by the generally poor state of infrastructure. The town of Gonaïves was severely flooded for a number of days, with many homes submerged. Meanwhile, the distribution of assistance was further hampered by the continuing insecurity in the country: hijacking and theft of relief supplies was reported. In February 2005, the UN presence under Brazilian command (see last year's *Strategic Survey*) was boosted to 7,143 uniformed personnel. However, the death of two peacekeepers in late March indicates the continued unstable security situation

Impact of Tropical Storm *Jeanne* on Haiti (as at 28/9/04)

NORTH (9,500) 16 1

Dominican Republic

Port-de-Paix

Cap-Haïtien

Fort-Liberté

NORTH EAST

Gonaïves

NORTH WEST

Hinche

1 NORTH-WEST (53,000)

HAITI

CENTRE

WEST

Fonds Verrettes

SOUTH-EAST

PORT-AU-PRINCE

Jacmel

1,005 2,600 ARTIBONITE (236,426)

Total number of people affected: 298,926

Jérémie

1,330 1,056 2,801

1,291

GRAND ANSE

SOUTH 1

Les Cayes

67 Dead

50 Missing

Injured

Figures in brackets are number of people affected

Figures are unavailable for each state

UNITED STATES

BAHAMAS

CUBA

JAMAICA

CAYMAN IS.

HAITI

DOMINICAN REPUBLIC

PUERTO RICO

US VIRGIN IS

TRINIDAD & TOBAGO

GRENADA

MEXICO

BELIZE

GUATEMALA

HONDURAS

© IISS

ASIA Afghanistan: drug problems persist

In recent years, the opium cultivation and production levels in Afghanistan have led to international concern, with some analysts expressing fears that Afghanistan could become a 'narco-state.' The International Narcotics Control Board's 2004 Annual Report noted that Afghanistan's 'widespread drug problem has become a severe threat to this new democracy, as well as the stability and economic recovery of the country as a whole. Illicit opium poppy cultivation continues to increase in Afghanistan, supplying three quarters of the world's heroin…'. Indeed, from 2003–04, opium cultivation increased by 64% according to the UN Office on Drugs and Crime (UNODC) which, in 2004, stated that 'valued at $2.8 billion, the opium economy is now equivalent to about 60% of Afghanistan's 2003 GDP.' However, figures released by UNODC in its March 2005 'Rapid Assessment Survey' allowed for guarded optimism: in a majority of provinces there was a downward trend in opium cultivation. UNODC reported that farmers were refraining from planting because of 'respect for the Government's ban on opium poppy cultivation and fear of eradication. … While farmers in the North were preparing their land for poppy cultivation, they were closely following eradication activities in southern Afghanistan to assess the possible risk'. But the scale of the problem facing Kabul and the international community remains daunting.

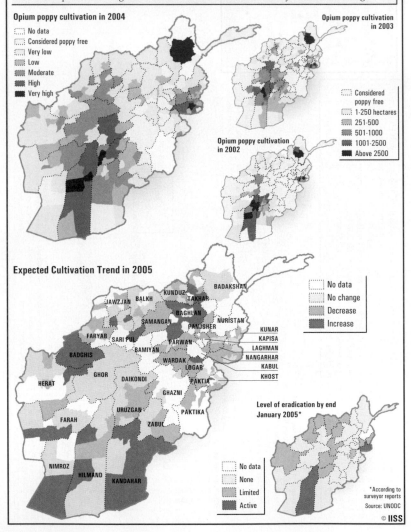

Opium poppy cultivation in 2004

- No data
- Considered poppy free
- Very low
- Low
- Moderate
- High
- Very high

Opium poppy cultivation in 2003

- Considered poppy free
- 1-250 hectares
- 251-500
- 501-1000
- 1001-2500
- Above 2500

Opium poppy cultivation in 2002

Expected Cultivation Trend in 2005

- No data
- No change
- Decrease
- Increase

BADAKHSHAN · KUNDUZ · JAWZJAN · BALKH · TAKHAR · BAGHLAN · SAMANGAN · NURISTAN · PANJSHER · FARYAB · SARI PUL · PARWAN · KUNAR · KAPISA · BAMIYAN · LAGHMAN · BADGHIS · WARDAK · NANGARHAR · LOGAR · KABUL · GHOR · DAIKONDI · KHOST · HERAT · PAKTIA · GHAZNI · URUZGAN · PAKTIKA · FARAH · ZABUL · NIMROZ · HILMAND · KANDAHAR

Level of eradication by end January 2005*

- No data
- None
- Limited
- Active

*According to surveyor reports
Source: UNODC

© IISS

ASIA Afghanistan's first election

Afghanistan's first democratic election, on 9 October 2004, passed relatively peacefully with 8,024,536 valid votes cast, despite threats from Taliban remnants to disrupt the polls. Hamid Karzai, who had led the interim administration, was elected to the presidency with over half of the vote, and in December 2004 announced his first cabinet. However, the legislative elections originally scheduled for May 2005 have been postponed – a March announcement set a date in September 2005. Karzai was reported to have blamed the delay on 'technical matters'. Meanwhile, the 8,000 troops of the International Security Assistance Force, under NATO command, continue to operate in Kabul and certain locations outside the capital, as do US forces engaged on operations in support of *Operation Enduring Freedom.*

Hamid Karzai: Independent
4.44m (55.4%)

Abdul Rashid Dostum: Independent
0.80m (10.0%)

Abdul Latif Pedram:
Hezb-e Congra-e Mili Afghanistan
0.11m (1.4%)

Haji Mohammad Mohaqiq: Independent
0.94m (11.7%)

Syed Ishaq Gilani: Nuhzat-e Hambastagee
Mili Afghanistan
0.08m (1.0%)

Younus Qanooni:
Hezb-e Nuhzat-e Mili Afghanistan
1.31m (16.3%)

Massooda Jalal: Independent
0.09m (1.1%)

Others: 0.25m (3.1%)

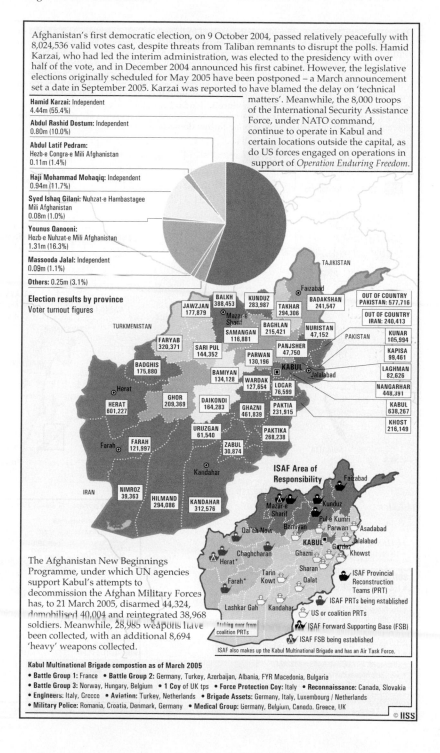

Election results by province
Voter turnout figures

TAJIKISTAN

Faizabad

TURKMENISTAN

BALKH 388,453
KUNDUZ 283,987
BADAKHSHAN 241,547
TAKHAR 294,306

JAWZJAN 177,879
Mazar-e Sharif
BAGHLAN 215,421
NURISTAN 47,152

SAMANGAN 116,881

FARYAB 320,371
SARI PUL 144,352
PANJSHER 47,750
KUNAR 105,994

BADGHIS 175,880
PARWAN 130,196
KAPISA 99,461

BAMIYAN 134,128
KABUL
Jalalabad
LAGHMAN 82,626

Herat
WARDAK 127,654
LOCAR 76,599
NANGARHAR 448,391

HERAT 601,227
GHOR 209,369
DAIKONDI 164,283
GHAZNI 461,839
PAKTIA 231,915
KABUL 638,267

URUZGAN 61,540
PAKTIKA 268,238
KHOST 216,149

Farah
FARAH 121,997
ZABUL 30,874

Kandahar

NIMROZ 39,363

IRAN

HILMAND 294,086
KANDAHAR 312,576

PAKISTAN

OUT OF COUNTRY
PAKISTAN: 577,716

OUT OF COUNTRY
IRAN: 240,413

ISAF Area of Responsibility

Faizabad

Mazar-e Sharif
Kunduz
Pul-e Kumri
Parwan
Asadabad

Qal'eh-Now
Bamiyan
KABUL
Jalalabad

Chaghcharan
Ghazni
Gardez
Khowst

Herat
Tarin Kowt
Sharan

Farah
Qalat

Lashkar Gah
Kandahar

The Afghanistan New Beginnings Programme, under which UN agencies support Kabul's attempts to decommission the Afghan Military Forces has, to 21 March 2005, disarmed 44,324, demobilised 40,004 and reintegrated 38,968 soldiers. Meanwhile, 28,985 weapons have been collected, with an additional 8,694 'heavy' weapons collected.

ISAF Provincial Reconstruction Teams (PRT)

ISAF PRTs being established

US or coalition PRTs

Taking over from coalition PRTs

ISAF Forward Supporting Base (FSB)

ISAF FSB being established

ISAF also makes up the Kabul Multinational Brigade and has an Air Task Force.

Kabul Multinational Brigade compostion as of March 2005
• **Battle Group 1:** France   • **Battle Group 2:** Germany, Turkey, Azerbaijan, Albania, FYR Macedonia, Bulgaria
• **Battle Group 3:** Norway, Hungary, Belgium   • **1 Coy** of UK tps   • **Force Protection Coy:** Italy   • **Reconnaissance:** Canada, Slovakia
• **Engineers:** Italy, Greece   • **Aviation:** Turkey, Netherlands   • **Brigade Assets:** Germany, Italy, Luxembourg / Netherlands
• **Military Police:** Romania, Croatia, Denmark, Germany   • **Medical Group:** Germany, Belgium, Canada, Greece, UK

© IISS

ASIA Asia's tsunami: a disaster unfolds

On 26 December 2004, an earthquake off the coast of Indonesia's Aceh province set off a series of tsunami waves that devastated parts of Southeast Asia (especially Sumatra), Indian Ocean islands, Sri Lanka and southern India and led to deaths as far away as East Africa. An unprecedented response both from donor governments and their civil societies saw a record amount of international assistance pledged. However, a key task for UN agencies and non-governmental organisations (NGOs) operating across the affected area will be to maintain this early momentum into the medium and long-term as rescue efforts transform into reconstruction and rehabilitation. Furthermore, as a complicating factor, it is clear that longstanding security problems in Indonesia's Aceh province and in Sri Lanka have not died down in the wake of the tsunami. A second large earthquake in the region, on 28 March, killed up to 1,000 people on Nias, Simeulue and the Banyak Islands, prompting further domestic and international relief efforts.

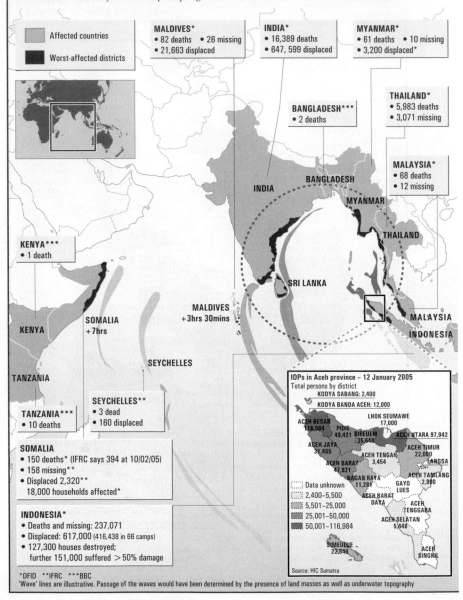

Affected countries

Worst-affected districts

MALDIVES*
- 82 deaths
- 26 missing
- 21,663 displaced

INDIA*
- 16,389 deaths
- 647, 599 displaced

MYANMAR*
- 61 deaths
- 10 missing
- 3,200 displaced*

BANGLADESH***
- 2 deaths

THAILAND*
- 5,983 deaths
- 3,071 missing

MALAYSIA*
- 68 deaths
- 12 missing

INDIA

BANGLADESH

MYANMAR

THAILAND

KENYA***
- 1 death

SRI LANKA

KENYA

SOMALIA
+7hrs

MALDIVES
+3hrs 30mins

MALAYSIA

INDONESIA

SEYCHELLES

TANZANIA

SEYCHELLES**
- 3 dead
- 160 displaced

TANZANIA***
- 10 deaths

SOMALIA
- 150 deaths* (IFRC says 394 at 10/02/05)
- 158 missing**
- Displaced 2,320**
  18,000 households affected*

INDONESIA*
- Deaths and missing: 237,071
- Displaced: 617,000 (416,438 in 66 camps)
- 127,300 houses destroyed;
  further 151,000 suffered >50% damage

*DFID **IFRC ***BBC
'Wave' lines are illustrative. Passage of the waves would have been determined by the presence of land masses as well as underwater topography

IDPs in Aceh province – 12 January 2005
Total persons by district
KODYA SABANG: 2,400
KODYA BANDA ACEH: 12,000
LHOK SEUMAWE 17,000
ACEH BESAR 116,984
PIDIE 49,421
BIREUEM 35,648
ACEH UTARA 97,942
ACEH JAYA 31,465
ACEH TENGAH 3,454
ACEH TIMUR 22,000
LANGSA
ACEH BARAT 47,921
NAGAN RAYA 11,281
GAYO LUES
ACEH TAMIANG 2,800
ACEH BARAT DAYA
ACEH TENGGARA
ACEH SELATAN 5,448

Data unknown
2,400–5,500
5,501–25,000
25,001–50,000
50,001–116,984

SIMEULUE 22,840
ACEH SINGKIL

Source: HIC Sumatra

International financial assistance

On 6 January 2005, a summit in Jakarta organised by the Association of South East Asian Nations (ASEAN), brought together many of the key players from within and outside the region. Aid pledges made at the summit included US$764m from Australia, $680m from Germany, $500m from Japan, $350m from the US, $96m from the UK, $80m from Sweden, $68m from Spain, $66m from France, $66m from Canada, $60m from China and $50m from South Korea. At the summit, 'Kofi Annan called for almost $1bn to be channelled towards UN-led relief programmes [and] more than 90% of this sum was pledged at a subsequent donors' conference on 12 January'. On 9 February, the US announced that President Bush was seeking $950m as part of the supplemental request for tsunami relief efforts. Other countries' pledges were also amended. However, on 18 March, at a meeting of international donors in Manila, the Asian Development Bank warned that there was a significant potential for gaps, overlaps and duplication in recovery efforts.

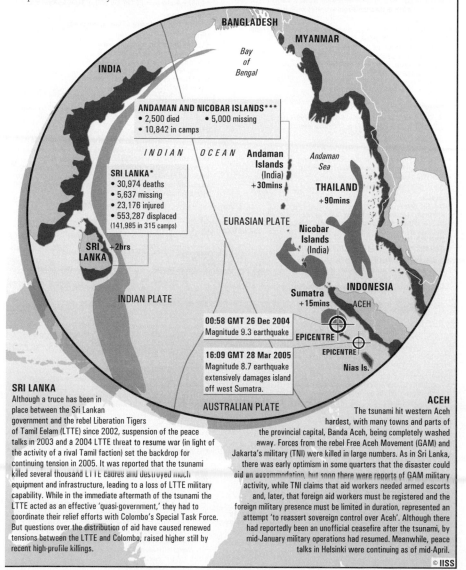

BANGLADESH

MYANMAR

Bay of Bengal

INDIA

ANDAMAN AND NICOBAR ISLANDS***
- 2,500 died
- 5,000 missing
- 10,842 in camps

INDIAN OCEAN Andaman Islands (India) +30mins

Andaman Sea

THAILAND +90mins

SRI LANKA*
- 30,974 deaths
- 5,637 missing
- 23,176 injured
- 553,287 displaced
(141,985 in 315 camps)

EURASIAN PLATE

Nicobar Islands (India)

SRI LANKA +2hrs

INDIAN PLATE

Sumatra +15mins

INDONESIA

ACEH

00:58 GMT 26 Dec 2004
Magnitude 9.3 earthquake

EPICENTRE

16:09 GMT 28 Mar 2005
Magnitude 8.7 earthquake
extensively damages island
off west Sumatra.

EPICENTRE

Nias Is.

AUSTRALIAN PLATE

SRI LANKA

Although a truce has been in place between the Sri Lankan government and the rebel Liberation Tigers of Tamil Eelam (LTTE) since 2002, suspension of the peace talks in 2003 and a 2004 LTTE threat to resume war (in light of the activity of a rival Tamil faction) set the backdrop for continuing tension in 2005. It was reported that the tsunami killed several thousand LTTE cadres and destroyed much equipment and infrastructure, leading to a loss of LTTE military capability. While in the immediate aftermath of the tsunami the LTTE acted as an effective 'quasi-government,' they had to coordinate their relief efforts with Colombo's Special Task Force. But questions over the distribution of aid have caused renewed tensions between the LTTE and Colombo, raised higher still by recent high-profile killings.

ACEH

The tsunami hit western Aceh hardest, with many towns and parts of the provincial capital, Banda Aceh, being completely washed away. Forces from the rebel Free Aceh Movement (GAM) and Jakarta's military (TNI) were killed in large numbers. As in Sri Lanka, there was early optimism in some quarters that the disaster could aid an accommodation, but soon there were reports of GAM military activity, while TNI claims that aid workers needed armed escorts and, later, that foreign aid workers must be registered and the foreign military presence must be limited in duration, represented an attempt 'to reassert sovereign control over Aceh'. Although there had reportedly been an unofficial ceasefire after the tsunami, by mid-January military operations had resumed. Meanwhile, peace talks in Helsinki were continuing as of mid-April.

© IISS

ASIA Asia's tsunami: the international military response

The military dimension

Given the immense scale of devastation seen in parts of the affected areas, the only way of initially moving large quantities of supplies was to use specialist aircraft, helicopters and vehicles. Domestic military capabilities were used, as were those of other regional and extra-regional nations: 'Loosely coordinated military forces' from India, Australia, Singapore and Malaysia, as well as the US – in conjunction with national and international NGOs – … spearheaded the main relief efforts in Aceh, southern Thailand and Sri Lanka'.

Australia and New Zealand: *Operation Sumatra Assist*
At its high point the Australian Defence Forces had over 1,000 personnel deployed in the Banda Aceh region, headquartered in Medan, while New Zealand had around 65 personnel in Jakarta, Medan and Banda Aceh. On 5 January Australia established a logistics hub at Butterworth airbase in Malaysia to increase flexibility, and in light of the stress placed on existing facilities in Indonesia.

Forces included:
• LPD HMAS *Kanimbla* with 2x *Sea King* and 2x army LCM8 landing craft
• 8x C-130 *Hercules* (1 from New Zealand); 4 in-theatre and 4 as air bridge between Darwin and Sumatra
• 150 army engineers and equipment
• Logistics personnel; water purification plant • ATC personnel
• ANZAC field hospital (with New Zealand personnel)
• 4x UH-1 *Iroquois* helo at Banda Aceh
• 1x Boeing 707 in a transport role; 1x Beech 350 *King Air*

Pakistan
Pakistan despatched medical, engineer, relief and reconstruction teams to Sri Lanka and Indonesia.

Forces deployed included:
Sri Lanka:
• 6x C-130 flights • AORH PNS *Moawin*, a supply ship w/ 2x *Sea King* (then to Indonesia) • Naval field hospital
• FFGH PNS *Khaibar*, a guided missile destroyer w/ 1x *Alouette* (then to Indonesia)

Indonesia:
• 7x C-130 flights
• 250-strong team deployed in 1x army field hospital in Lamno (80km SW of Banda Aceh); naval medical facility in Samolanga (75km west of Lhoksemawe) and other locations
• AORH PNS *Moawin*, a supply ship w/ 2x *Sea King*
• FFGH PNS *Khaibar*, a guided missile destroyer w/ 1x *Alouette*

On goodwill visit to Maldives on 26 December 2004.
Assistance mobilised under *Operation Madad*:
• FFGH PNS *Tariq* w/ helo
• AORH PNS *Nasr* (supply ship w/ helo) • 1x C-130 flight

MALDIVES

Japan
Japan's substantial military contribution to the relief effort, involving some 1,000 personnel including medical and transport specialists, constituted the country's largest overseas deployment since the end of World War II. Personnel were deployed to Thailand, Indonesia and Sri Lanka, among other locations.

Overall, forces included:
• 2x DDGHM *Kirishima* and *Takanami*; 1x DDHM *Kurama*
• 2x AOE *Hamana* and *Tokiwa* • 1x LPD *Kunisaki* • 2x LCAC
• Medical units in Banda Aceh • 3x *Chinook* and 2x *Black Hawk* • 1x C-130

Germany
German naval assets were transferred to relief efforts from their regular duties as part of *Operation Enduring Freedom*. In Banda Aceh, German medical units operated with their Australian and US counterparts and in total, Germany deployed around 380 personnel to the region.

Forces included:
• 1x AORH *Berlin* – outfitted as hospital ship with 2x *Sea King* • 1x FFG *Mecklenburg-Vorpommern* • 2x Airbus A-310 transport a/c
• Mobile rescue centre in Banda Aceh

Spain: *Operación Respuesta Solidaria*
Spain despatched around 600 personnel from the army, navy and air force in total to support its operations in the affected areas, stationing the *Galicia* off Aceh.

LPD *Galicia* with 3x Agusta Bell 212, dive teams, 2x landing craft, a field hospital and assorted medical equipment and reconstruction materials.
• 3x C-235 • 2x C-130

Singapore: *Operation Flying Eagle*
The largest-ever overseas operational deployment by Singapore's armed forces saw the headquarters element of the country's rapid deployment division (21DIV) lead Singapore's response.

• 1,057 in Medan (with OC Ops, Cdr 21 Div), Banda Aceh and Meulaboh
North Sumatra:
Ships: • 3x LST *Endurance, Endeavour, Persistence*
Aircraft:
• 6x CH-47D *Chinook* • 2x *Super Puma*
• C-130 *Hercules*/Fokker 50: 76 missions
• 2x fd hosp at Meulaboh and Banda Aceh
• 2 engr teams (heavy equipment)
• 2x ATC coordination teams (Medan, Banda Aceh)
• 1x mobile ATC tower (Banda Aceh)

Phuket, Thailand
• 121, incl 80 Singapore Civil Defence Force and some SAF (2x *Super Puma*).

Malaysia
Helicopters, aircraft and over 400 personnel from the Royal Malaysian Air Force served in relief operations in Medan and Aceh, while the Malaysian government allowed the international assistance operation to use its airbases and airspace and established a relief hub at Subang airbase outside Kuala Lumpur. A field hospital was established, while the Royal Malaysian Navy also delivered a number of relief shipments to Indonesia.

UK: *Operation Garron*
Soon after the tsunami hit, UK government responses – coordinated by the Department for International Development and the Foreign and Commonwealth Office – requested the assistance of UK military assets.

Forces included:
• Liaison and Reconnaissance Teams to Sri Lanka, Indonesia and Thailand • 1x FFGH (HMS *Chatham* + 2x *Lynx*)
• 1x ARH RFA *Diligence* • 1x AGSH HMS *Scott* • 2x C-17
• 1x *Tristar* KC-1 • 2x Bell 212 (from Brunei)
• Medical and engineering personnel

France: *Operation Beryx*
French forces, totalling around 1,300, deployed to various locations including the Maldives, Sri Lanka, Thailand and Indonesia. • CVHG *Jeanne d'Arc* (1x *Alouette*; 2x *Gazelle*; 2x *Puma*)
• DDGH *Georges Leygues* (1x *Alouette*) • DDGH *Dupleix* (w/ *Lynx*) to Maldives • AORHM *La Marne* (w/ *Alouette*) off Meulaboh
• 7x *Puma* based at Sabang • 2x C-160 *Transall* based at Medan
• 1x *Atlantique* 2 at Surat Thani in Thailand
• 1x *Fennec* off Thailand • 1x A-310 also used
• 1x C-135 also used

US: *Operation Unified Assistance*
US assets were deployed from Hawaii, South Korea and Japan, as well as from the US and forces afloat, and included army, navy, air force, marine corps and coast guard personnel. Marines were deployed from III Marine Division, out of Okinawa, while in Sri Lanka, marines from the 9th Marine Expeditionary Support Battalion and sailors from the 7th Seabee Battalion provided engineering support. At 12 January 2005, the US had 15,455 personnel participating in *Operation Unified Assistance*. By the time CSF-536 ceased operations in tsunami-affected countries, on 14 February, US forces had drawn down to 683 personnel.

Aircraft (at 12/01/05)
- 4x C-17 (USTRANSCOM) • 6x C-5 (USTRANSCOM) • 14x C-130 • 2x KC-130
- 5x MC-130 • 6x P-3 • 4x C-2 • 41x fixed-wing (+52x TACAIR ALCSG, +6x AV-88 TACAIR BHRESG) • 51x helos (+4x AH1-W BHRESG)

Ships (at 12/01/05)
- 11x USN • 6x MPS • 5x USNS logistics • 1x USCG cutter • 1x survey ship • 1x HSV

Aircraft (at 14/02/05)
- 1x C-17 (USTRANSCOM) • 2x C-5 (USTRANSCOM)
- 2x KC-130 • 5x fixed-wing • 14x helos

Ships (at 14/02/05)
- 2x USN • 2x USNS logistics • 1x survey ship • 2x HSV
- 1x hospital ship

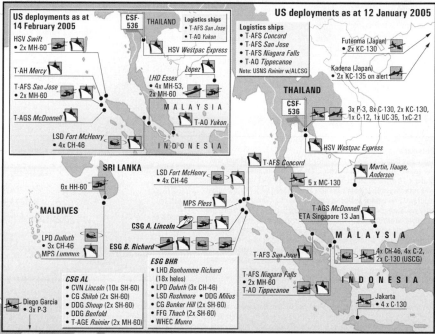

US deployments as at 14 February 2005

CSF-536

THAILAND

Logistics ships
- T-AFS *San Jose*
- T-AO *Yukon*

HSV *Westpac Express*

Lopez

HSV *Swift*
- 2x MH-60

T-AH *Mercy*

T-AFS *San Jose*
- 2x MH-60

T-AGS *McDonnell*

LHD *Essex*
- 4x MH-53, 2x MH-60

M A L A Y S I A

T-AO *Yukon*

LSD *Fort McHenry*
- 4x CH-46

I N D O N E S I A

US deployments as at 12 January 2005

Logistics ships
- T-AFS *Concord*
- T-AFS *San Jose*
- T-AFS *Niagara Falls*
- T-AO *Tippecanoe*
Note: USNS *Rainier* w/ALCSG

Futenma (Japan)
- 2x KC-130

Kadena (Japan)
- 2x KC-135 on alert

THAILAND

CSF-536

3x P-3, 8x C-130, 2x KC-130, 1x C-12, 1x UC-35, 1x C-21

HSV *Westpac Express*

SRI LANKA

LSD *Fort McHenry*
- 4x CH-46

T-AFS *Concord*

Martin, Hauge, Anderson

6x HH-60

MPS *Pless*

5 x MC-130

MALDIVES

CSG *A. Lincoln*

T-AGS *McDonnell*
ETA Singapore 13 Jan

M A L A Y S I A

ESG *B. Richard*

T-AFS *San Jose*

4x CH-46, 4x C-2, 2x C-130 (USCG)

LPD *Dulluth*
- 3x CH-46
MPS *Lummus*

ESG BHR
- LHD *Bonhomme Richard* (18x helos)
- LPD *Duluth* (3x CH-46)
- LSD *Rushmore* • DDG *Milius*
- CG *Bunker Hill* (2x SH-60)
- FFG *Thach* (2x SH-60)
- WHEC *Munro*

T-AFS *Niagara Falls*
- 2x MH-60
T-AO *Tippecanoe*

I N D O N E S I A

Jakarta
- 4 x C-130

CSG AL
- CVN *Lincoln* (10x SH-60)
- CG *Shiloh* (2x SH-60)
- DDG *Shoup* (2x SH-60)
- DDG *Benfold*
- T-AGE *Rainier* (2x MH-60)

Diego Garcia
- 3x P-3

India
Assistance to tsunami-affected areas of the Indian mainland and islands was mobilised under *Operation Sea Waves*, managed through India's Integrated Defence Staff. India declined international military assistance for these operations, judging that it had sufficient domestic resources. Instead, New Delhi offered its military forces in order to assist relief operations in other affected areas, particularly Sri Lanka, the Maldives and Indonesia.

Forces included:
Sri Lanka: *Operation Rainbow*
The Indian army deployed one field hospital and provided medical assistance in 30 relief camps. Army engineers and signals specialists were also employed, as were army and navy infrastructure repair teams, dive teams and recovery teams. The air force and coast guard were also heavily involved in relief efforts. Vessels were either deployed to Galle, Trincomalee or Colombo.

- 5x Mi-17 and Mi-8; 2x Il-76, 1x Do-228 a/c, 1x *Islander* a/c • AORH INS *Aditya* (1x helo, medical and dive teams) • FFH INS *Taragiri* w/ helo
- PSOH CGS *Samar* (w/ helo) • AGSH INS *Sandhayak* (hospital ship) • PSOH INS *Sukanya* • FSGSM Corvette INS *Kirch*, LST INS *Ghorpad* and LCU 33
- AGSH INS *Sutlej* (w/ *Chetak*) • PSOH INS *Sharada* • AGSH INS *Jamuna* (hospital ship w/ *Chetak*) • AGSH INS *Nirdeshak* (w/ helo and divers)
- AGSH INS *Sarvekshak* (hospital ship w/ *Chetak*)

The Maldives (*Operation Castor*)
Two mobile surgical teams, communications assistance and general reconstruction assistance
- Mi-17 helo flights • DDGHM INS *Mysore* • FFH INS *Udaygiri*
- PSOH CGS *Sagar* • PSOH CGS *Vigraha*
Transport aircraft: • Il-76 flights • Coastguard Do-228 • 2x IAF BAe-748

Indonesia (*Operation Gambhir*)
- AGSH INS *Nirupak* (hospital ship w/ *Chetak*) • FSGHM Corvette INS *Khukri*

Assistance was provided by the militaries of other nations, including Denmark, Russia, Norway, Switzerland, South Korea and China.

Flag markings at particular locations are not exclusive; other nations often will have had a presence in the locality.

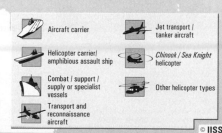

Aircraft carrier	Jet transport / tanker aircraft
Helicopter carrier/ amphibious assault ship	Chinook / Sea Knight helicopter
Combat / support / supply or specialist vessels	Other helicopter types
Transport and reconnaissance aircraft	

© IISS

AFRICA Southern Africa's year of elections

Namibia

On 21 February 2005, Hifikepunye Pohamba took over the presidency of Namibia from Sam Nujoma, who had led the country since independence in 1990. The party to which both men belong, and which Nujoma will possibly lead until at least 2007, the South West Africa People's Organisation (SWAPO), was assessed to have won a sweeping victory in the parliamentary elections, held concurrently with the 15–16 November 2004 presidential poll. Analysts pronounced the elections generally free and fair. However the Electoral Institute of Southern Africa (EISA), for instance, identified areas for improvement. Legal challenges to the results also led to the High Court ordering a recount of some ballots before the final makeup of the National Assembly could be decided.

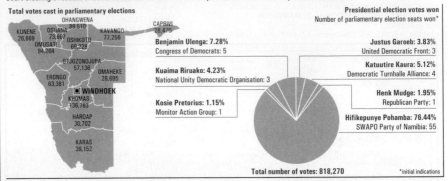

Total votes cast in parliamentary elections

OHANGWENA 89,510
OSHANA 73,667
KUNENE 26,669
OSHIKOTO 68,328
OMUSATI 94,264
KAVANGO 77,256
CAPRIVI 28,470
OTJOZONDJUPA 57,136
ERONGO 63,381
OMAHEKE 28,695
■ WINDHOEK
KHOMAS 136,763
HARDAP 30,702
KARAS 39,152

Benjamin Ulenga: 7.28%
Congress of Democrats: 5

Kuaima Riruako: 4.23%
National Unity Democratic Organisation: 3

Kosie Pretorius: 1.15%
Monitor Action Group: 1

Presidential election votes won
Number of parliamentary election seats won*

Justus Garoeb: 3.83%
United Democratic Front: 3

Katuutire Kaura: 5.12%
Democratic Turnhalle Alliance: 4

Henk Mudge: 1.95%
Republican Party: 1

Hifikepunye Pohamba: 76.44%
SWAPO Party of Namibia: 55

Total number of votes: 818,270   *initial indications

Botswana

The ruling Botswana Democratic Party of President Festus Mogae won the general elections of 30 October 2004 with a substantial majority, giving it 44 out of 57 seats. The high turnout (76.2% of registered voters) was reflective of Botswana's position as the nation with Africa's longest multi-party democracy and there were reports of a vibrant campaign, although some analysts viewed the opposition parties as too fragmented to mount an effective challenge. Botswana's economy is relatively buoyant, but while there are initiatives to assist diversification away from its dependence on diamond mining, the HIV/AIDS epidemic has hit the country hard: one third of its population carries the virus. However, unlike certain other countries, anti-retroviral drugs are readily available to the population. In March 2005, the government started providing anti-retrovirals to the armed forces.

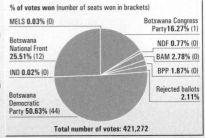

% of votes won (number of seats won in brackets)

MELS 0.03% (0)

Botswana National Front 25.51% (12)

IND 0.02% (0)

Botswana Democratic Party 50.63% (44)

Botswana Congress Party 16.27% (1)

NDF 0.77% (0)

BAM 2.78% (0)

BPP 1.87% (0)

Rejected ballots 2.11%

Total number of votes: 421,272

South Africa

Ten years on from the end of apartheid, the African National Congress (ANC) again won a landslide victory in the nation's third general elections, from 14–15 April 2004. The ANC increased its support across the country, taking 146 regional seats in all, with the second place Democratic Alliance taking 50 seats. The Inkatha Freedom Party, whose vote in Kwa-Zulu Natal was for the first time surpassed by that of the ANC, saw its leader, Mangosuthu Buthelezi, dropped from the Cabinet by Mbeki. Mbeki himself was re-elected to the presidency by the newly-elected MPs in mid-April 2004.

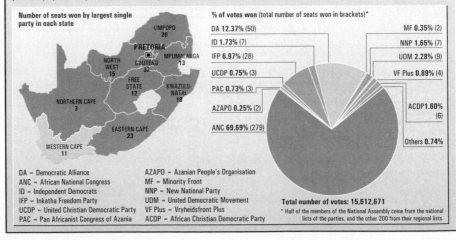

Number of seats won by largest single party in each state

LIMPOPO 20
PRETORIA ■
MPUMALANGA 13
NORTH WEST 15
GAUTENG 32
FREE STATE 12
KWAZULU-NATAL 18
NORTHERN CAPE 3
EASTERN CAPE 23
WESTERN CAPE 11

% of votes won (total number of seats won in brackets)*

DA 12.37% (50)

ID 1.73% (7)

IFP 6.97% (28)

UCDP 0.75% (3)

PAC 0.73% (3)

AZAPO 0.25% (2)

ANC 69.69% (279)

MF 0.35% (2)

NNP 1.65% (7)

UDM 2.28% (9)

VF Plus 0.89% (4)

ACDP 1.60% (6)

Others 0.74%

DA = Democratic Alliance
ANC = African National Congress
ID = Independent Democrats
IFP = Inkatha Freedom Party
UCDP = United Christian Democratic Party
PAC = Pan Africanist Congress of Azania

AZAPO = Azanian People's Organisation
MF = Minority Front
NNP = New National Party
UDM = United Democratic Movement
VF Plus = Vryheidsfront Plus
ACDP = African Christian Democratic Party

Total number of votes: 15,612,671

* Half of the members of the National Assembly come from the national lists of the parties, and the other 200 from their regional lists.

Malawi

With former president Bakili Muluzi still leading Malawi's United Democratic Front (UDF), some analysts asserted that the 20 May 2004 election of former economist Bingu wa Mutharika (UDF) would reinforce Muluzi's influence on the presidency. However, Mutharika's post-election anti-corruption campaign, which impressed the IMF's February 2005 mission to the country, led to a reported rift with the former leader and 'criticism from within the UDF'. In February 2005, the president resigned from the UDF, reportedly saying that he 'no longer [had] support within the party ... because of [his] anti-corruption stance'. It was reported that, on 15 March, Mutharika had registered a new political outfit, called the Democratic Progressive Party and through which, according to IRIN, 'taking into account pledges of support from independent MPs and smaller opposition parties, Mutharika could control 80 of 193 seats in parliament'.

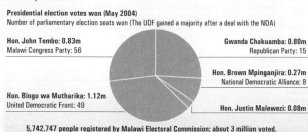

Presidential election votes won (May 2004)
Number of parliamentary election seats won (The UDF gained a majority after a deal with the NDA)

Hon. John Tembo: 0.83m
Malawi Congress Party: 56

Gwanda Chakuamba: 0.80m
Republican Party: 15

Hon. Brown Mpinganjira: 0.27m
National Democratic Alliance: 8

Hon. Bingu wa Mutharika: 1.12m
United Democratic Front: 49

Hon. Justin Malewezi: 0.08m

5,742,747 people registered by Malawi Electoral Commission; about 3 million voted.
(Voting took place in 187 out of 193 constituencies. Independent candidates won 39 seats.)

Zimbabwe

Parliamentary elections took place on 31 March, resulting in the expected Zanu-PF victory. The opposition Movement for Democratic Change (MDC), which had seen substantial numbers of supporters at its pre-election rallies has said that the elections 'cannot be judged free and fair', an opinion echoed by some foreign analysts and organisations; indeed before the election itself, Human Rights Watch said that 'major problems with the registration process, voter education and election monitoring that marred previous elections have not been remedied [and that] the elections are highly unlikely to reflect the free expression of the electorate'. However, observers from the Southern African Development Community were reported to have described the elections as open, transparent and professional. The results mean that President Mugabe now has the required 2/3 majority in parliament needed to change Zimbabwe's constitution.

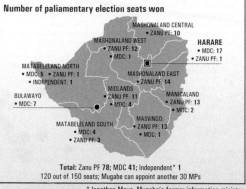

Number of paliamentary election seats won

MASHONALAND CENTRAL
• ZANU PF: 10

MASHONALAND WEST
• ZANU PF: 12
• MDC: 1

HARARE
• MDC: 17
• ZANU PF: 1

MATABELELAND NORTH
• MDC: 5 • ZANU PF: 1
• INDEPENDENT: 1

MASHONALAND EAST
• ZANU PF: 14

MIDLANDS
• ZANU PF: 11
• MDC: 4

BULAWAYO
• MDC: 7

MANICALAND
• ZANU PF: 13
• MDC: 2

MATABELELAND SOUTH
• MDC: 4
• ZANU PF: 3

MASVINGO
• ZANU PF: 13
• MDC: 1

Total: Zanu PF 78; MDC 41; Independent* 1
120 out of 150 seats; Mugabe can appoint another 30 MPs

*Jonathan Moyo, Mugabe's former information minister

Mozambique

The conduct of Mozambique's presidential and legislative elections, held on 1–2 December 2004, was generally viewed in a positive light by outside observers, though there was disappointment at the low turnout (around 36%) in both polls. The opposition Renamo party was reported to have raised doubts over the result. Meanwhile, in February 2005, the US-based Carter Center said that Mozambique's 'National Elections Commission (CNE) has not administered a fair and transparent election in all parts of Mozambique.' Although the centre said that the result was not in doubt, it raised concerns that 'the problems observed by The Carter Center could have had serious consequences in a closer election'. Nonetheless, Frelimo's Armando Guebuza was sworn in as Mozambique's new president on 2 February 2005, replacing Joaquim Chissano, who had occupied the seat since 1986.

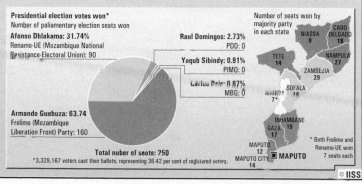

Presidential election votes won*
Number of paliamentary election seats won

Afonso Dhlakama: 31.74%
Renamo-UE (Mozambique National Resistance-Electoral Union): 90

Raul Domingos: 2.73%
PDD: 0

Yaqub Sibindy: 0.91%
PIMO: 0

Carlos Reis: 0.87%
MBG: 0

Armando Guebuza: 63.74
Frelimo (Mozambique Liberation Front) Party: 160

Total nuber of seats: 250
*3,329,167 voters cast their ballots, representing 36.42 per cent of registered voters.

Number of seats won by majority party in each state

NIASSA 9
CABO DELGADO 18
TETE 14
NAMPULA 27
ZAMBEZIA 29
MANICA 7
SOFALA 18
INHAMBANE 15
GAZA 17
MAPUTO 12
MAPUTO CITY ■ MAPUTO 14

* Both Frelimo and Renamo-UE won 7 seats each

© IISS

AFRICA The impact of HIV/AIDS in Southern Africa

HIV/AIDS is continuing to have a devastating impact on southern African countries. Although the UN agency UNAIDS reports that the greatest increases in people living with HIV/AIDS are in Eastern Europe and Central Asia, the worst effects are still felt in sub-Saharan Africa . 'Just under two-thirds (64%) of all people living with HIV are in sub-Saharan Africa, as are more than three quarters (76%) of all women living with HIV' - with the region holding 10% of the world's population. Although adult prevalence might have recently been relatively stable, UNAIDS says that this 'can disguise the worst phases of an epidemic – when roughly equally large numbers of people are being newly infected with HIV and are dying of AIDS'.

Impacting women hardest
More women than men are infected with HIV in sub-Saharan Africa and this statistic is more pronounced among younger women (15–24). A prevalence rate sometimes higher than 30% is seen in Botswana, Lesotho, Namibia and Swaziland. However, prevalence rates also vary within countries: in South Africa, a survey quoted by UNAIDS states that prevalence rates are over '30% in Free State, Mpumalanga and KwaZulu-Natal (reaching 37.5% in the latter) while ranging between 13% and 17.5% in Western Cape, Northern Cape and Limpopo'.

HIV prevalence among pregnant women – a snapshot:

• Swaziland: 39% (2002)   • Zimbabwe: 25% (2003)   • Malawi: 18% (2003)   • Zambia: 16% (2003)

Angola
• Population: 14.78 million
• Life expectancy at birth: 40
• GNI per capita: $1,730
• HIV prevalence: adults 15-49: 3.9%
• Living with HIV: adults 15-49: 220,000
• Adults & children living with HIV: 0-49: 240,000
• Women 15-49 living with HIV: 130,000
• AIDS deaths in 2003: 21,000
• Estimated numbers needing anti-retroviral (ARV) therapy, 2004: 34,500
• Estimated numbers receiving ARV therapy, Dec 2004: 3,500*

Botswana
• Population: 1.79m
• Life expectancy at birth: 40
• GNI per capita: $7,770
• HIV prevalence: adults 15-49: 37.3%
• Living with HIV: adults 15-49: 330,000
• Adults & children living with HIV: 0-49: 350,000
• Women 15-49 living with HIV: 190,000
• AIDS deaths in 2003: 33,000
• Estimated numbers needing ARV therapy, 2004: 75,000
• Estimated numbers receiving ARV therapy, Dec 2004: 39,000*

Lesotho
• Population: 1.8m
• Life expectancy at birth: 36
• GNI per capita: $2,710
• HIV prevalence: adults 15-49: 28.9%
• Living with HIV: adults 15-49: 300,000
• Adults & children living with HIV: 0-49: 320,000
• Women 15-49 living with HIV: 170,000
• AIDS deaths in 2003: 29,000
• Estimated numbers needing ARV therapy, 2004: 56,000
• Estimated numbers receiving ARV therapy, Dec 2004: 3,000*

Madagascar
• Population: 17.9m
• Life expectancy at birth: 56
• GNI per capita: $720
• HIV prevalence: adults 15-49: 1.7%
• Living with HIV: adults 15-49: 130,000
• Adults & children living with HIV: 0-49: 140,000
• Women 15-49 living with HIV: 76,000
• AIDS deaths in 2003: 7,500
• Estimated numbers needing ARV therapy, 2004: 16,000
• Estimated numbers receiving ARV therapy, Dec 2004: not known

Mozambique
• Population: 19.1m
• Life expectancy at birth: 43
• GNI per capita: $210
• HIV prevalence: adults 15-49: 12.2%
• Living with HIV: adults 15-49: 1.2m
• Adults & children living with HIV: 0-49: 1.3m
• Women 15-49 living with HIV: 670,000
• AIDS deaths in 2003: 110,000
• Estimated numbers needing ARV therapy, 2004: 199,000
• Estimated numbers receiving ARV therapy, Dec 2004: 8,000*

Zambia
• Population: 10.9m
• Life expectancy at birth: 39.7
• GNI per capita: $770
• HIV prevalence: adults 15-49: 16.5%
• Living with HIV: adults 15-49: 830,000
• Adults and children living with HIV: 0-49: 920,000
• Women 15-49 living with HIV: 470,000
• AIDS deaths in 2003: 89,000
• Estimated numbers needing ARV therapy, 2004: 149,000
• Estimated numbers receiving ARV therapy, Dec 2004: 22,000*

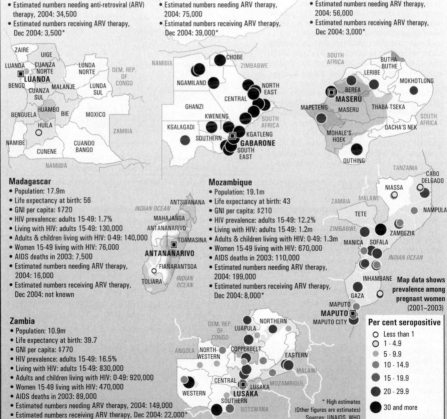

Map data shows prevalence among pregnant women (2001–2003)

Per cent seropositive
○ Less than 1
○ 1 - 4.9
◑ 5 - 9.9
● 10 - 14.9
● 15 - 19.9
● 20 - 29.9
● 30 and more

* High estimates
(Other figures are estimates)
Sources: UNAIDS, WHO

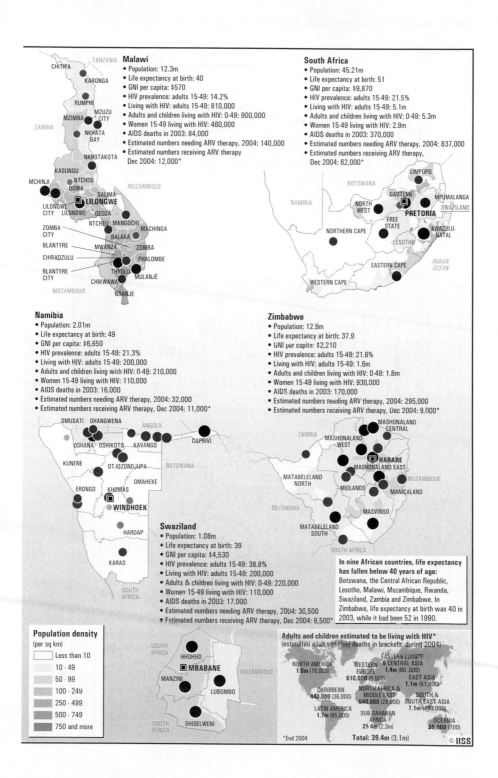

Malawi
- Population: 12.3m
- Life expectancy at birth: 40
- GNI per capita: $570
- HIV prevalence: adults 15-49: 14.2%
- Living with HIV: adults 15-49: 810,000
- Adults and children living with HIV: 0-49: 900,000
- Women 15-49 living with HIV: 460,000
- AIDS deaths in 2003: 84,000
- Estimated numbers needing ARV therapy, 2004: 140,000
- Estimated numbers receiving ARV therapy Dec 2004: 12,000*

South Africa
- Population: 45.21m
- Life expectancy at birth: 51
- GNI per capita: $9,870
- HIV prevalence: adults 15-49: 21.5%
- Living with HIV: adults 15-49: 5.1m
- Adults and children living with HIV: 0-49: 5.3m
- Women 15-49 living with HIV: 2.9m
- AIDS deaths in 2003: 370,000
- Estimated numbers needing ARV therapy, 2004: 837,000
- Estimated numbers receiving ARV therapy, Dec 2004: 62,000*

Namibia
- Population: 2.01m
- Life expectancy at birth: 49
- GNI per capita: $6,650
- HIV prevalence: adults 15-49: 21.3%
- Living with HIV: adults 15-49: 200,000
- Adults and children living with HIV: 0-49: 210,000
- Women 15-49 living with HIV: 110,000
- AIDS deaths in 2003: 16,000
- Estimated numbers needing ARV therapy, 2004: 32,000
- Estimated numbers receiving ARV therapy, Dec 2004: 11,000*

Zimbabwe
- Population: 12.9m
- Life expectancy at birth: 37.9
- GNI per capita: $2,210
- HIV prevalence: adults 15-49: 21.6%
- Living with HIV: adults 15-49: 1.6m
- Adults and children living with HIV: 0-49: 1.8m
- Women 15-49 living with HIV: 930,000
- AIDS deaths in 2003: 170,000
- Estimated numbers needing ARV therapy, 2004: 295,000
- Estimated numbers receiving ARV therapy, Dec 2004: 9,000*

Swaziland
- Population: 1.08m
- Life expectancy at birth: 39
- GNI per capita: $4,530
- HIV prevalence: adults 15-49: 38.8%
- Living with HIV: adults 15-49: 200,000
- Adults & children living with HIV: 0-49: 220,000
- Women 15-49 living with HIV: 110,000
- AIDS deaths in 2003: 17,000
- Estimated numbers needing ARV therapy, 2004: 36,500
- Estimated numbers receiving ARV therapy, Dec 2004: 6,500*

In nine African countries, life expectancy has fallen below 40 years of age: Botswana, the Central African Republic, Lesotho, Malawi, Mozambique, Rwanda, Swaziland, Zambia and Zimbabwe. In Zimbabwe, life expectancy at birth was 40 in 2003, while it had been 52 in 1990.

Population density
(per sq km)
- Less than 10
- 10 - 49
- 50 - 99
- 100 - 249
- 250 - 499
- 500 - 749
- 750 and more

Adults and children estimated to be living with HIV*
(estimated adult and child deaths in brackets, during 2004)

- NORTH AMERICA 1.0m (16,000)
- WESTERN EUROPE 610,000 (6,500)
- EASTERN EUROPE & CENTRAL ASIA 1.4m (60,000)
- EAST ASIA 1.1m (51,000)
- CARIBBEAN 440,000 (36,000)
- NORTH AFRICA & MIDDLE EAST 540,000 (28,000)
- SOUTH & SOUTH-EAST ASIA 7.1m (490,000)
- LATIN AMERICA 1.7m (95,000)
- SUB-SAHARAN AFRICA 25.4m (2.3m)
- OCEANIA 35,000 (700)

*End 2004   Total: 39.4m (3.1m)

© IISS

AFRICA West Africa: positive signs amidst continuing tensions

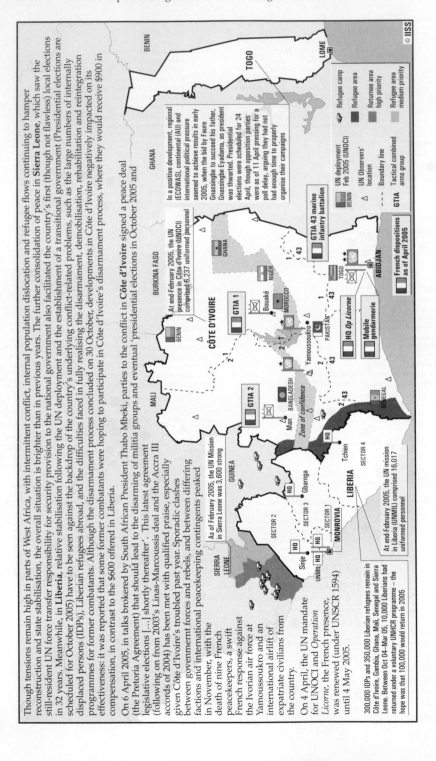

© IISS

Though tensions remain high in parts of West Africa, with intermittent conflict, internal population dislocation and refugee flows continuing to hamper reconstruction and state stabilisation, the overall situation is brighter than in previous years. The further consolidation of peace in **Sierra Leone**, which saw the country's first (though not flawless) local elections in 32 years. Meanwhile, in **Liberia**, relative stabilisation following the UN deployment and the establishment of a transitional government (Presidential elections are scheduled for October 2005) have to be seen against the backdrop of the country's underlying conflict-related problems, such as the large numbers of internally displaced persons (IDPs), Liberian refugees abroad, and the difficulties faced in fully realising the disarmament, demobilisation, rehabilitation and reintegration programmes for former combatants. Although the disarmament process concluded on 30 October, developments in Côte d'Ivoire negatively impacted on its effectiveness: it was reported that some former combatants were hoping to participate in Côte d'Ivoire's disarmament process, where they would receive $900 in compensation, in contrast to the $600 offered in Liberia.

On 6 April 2005, in talks brokered by South African President Thabo Mbeki, parties to the conflict in **Côte d'Ivoire** signed a peace deal (the Pretoria Agreement) that should lead to the disarming of militia groups and eventual 'presidential elections in October 2005 and legislative elections [...] shortly thereafter'. This latest agreement (following on from 2003's Linas-Marcoussis deal and the Accra III accords of 2004) has been met with qualified praise, especially given Côte d'Ivoire's troubled past year. Sporadic clashes between government forces and rebels, and between differing factions and international peacekeeping contingents peaked in November, with the death of nine French peacekeepers, a swift French response against the Ivorian air force at Yamoussoukro and an international airlift of expatriate civilians from the country.

On 4 April, the UN mandate for UNOCI and *Operation Licorne*, the French presence, was renewed (under UNSCR 1594) until 4 May 2005.

300,000 IDPs and 350,000 Liberian refugees remain in Côte d'Ivoire, Gambia, Ghana, Mali, Senegal and Sierra Leone. Between Oct 04–Mar 05, 10,000 Liberians had returned under a voluntary UNHCR programme – the hope was that 100,000 would return in 2005

In a positive development, regional (ECOWAS), continental (AU) and international political pressure seemed to achieve results in early 2005, when the bid by Faure Gnassingbe to succeed his father, Gnassingbe Eyadama, as president was thwarted. Presidential elections were scheduled for 24 April, though opposition parties were as of 11 April pressing for a poll delay, arguing they had not had enough time to properly organise their campaigns

At end-February 2005, the UN presence in Côte d'Ivoire (UNOCI) comprised 6,237 uniformed personnel

As of February 2005, the UN Mission in Sierra Leone was 3,600 strong

At end-February 2005, the UN mission in Liberia (UNMIL) comprised 16,017 uniformed personnel

BENIN

TOGO

LOME

GHANA

BURKINA FASO

CÔTE D'IVOIRE

MALI

GUINEA

SIERRA LEONE

LIBERIA

Bouaké

GTIA 1

MOROCCO

GHANA

NIGER

TOGO

BENIN

PAKISTAN

Yamoussoukro

BANGLADESH

GTIA 2

Man

Zone of confidence

SENEGAL

Tchien

SECTOR 4

Gbarnga

SECTOR 3

SECTOR 1

SECTOR 2

Sinje

MONROVIA

UNMIL

ABIDJAN

HQ *Op Licone*

Mobile gendarmerie

GTIA 43 marine infantry battalion

French dispositions as of April 2005

Refugee camp

Refugee area

Returnee area high priority

Refugee area medium priority

UN deployment Feb 2005 (UNOCI)

UN Observers' location

Boundary line

Tactical combined arms group

GTIA

Middle East / Gulf

American policy remained the central determinant of strategic developments in the Middle East/Persian Gulf region. The US-led armed attempt to remake Iraq as a democracy was intended, in significant part, to change the political status quo in the region so as to make it less conducive to transnational Islamist terrorism. There is no doubt that the Iraq intervention changed the status quo. While there has been abundant scepticism as to whether it has done so for the good, that scepticism abated somewhat in 2004–05. As predicted, the minority Sunni population, which Saddam Hussein had favoured as he repressed the majority Shi'ites, largely boycotted the 30 January 2005 Iraqi elections, and religiously based Shi'ites under the leadership of Grand Ayatollah Ali al-Sistani held sway. But conservative estimates of voter turnout indicated a relatively healthy 58%, and in the election's aftermath Sunni politicians agreed to participate in the drafting of a new Iraqi constitution. In March 2005, the US military estimated that there were 12,000–20,000 hard-core insurgents in Iraq, which represented no change from the previous October. But while insurgency attacks on coalition forces numbered 40–50 per day in March 2005, they had diminished substantially and the Iraqi populace had grown increasingly intolerant of them. In April 2005, several Iraqi Sunni leaders encouraged Sunnis to join the new Iraqi security forces. Shi'ites and Kurds were engaged in dialogue on how to secure the interests of the both in one government, and top positions in the new government had been allocated in an ostensibly equitable manner among the three principal Iraqi groups. US forces were not close to leaving, and the new Iraqi polity was a fair distance from self-sufficiency. But palpable progress had been made.

Palestinian Authority (PA) President Yasser Arafat – deemed a terminally unacceptable partner for peace by both US President George W. Bush and Israeli President Ariel Sharon – died in November 2004, giving way to the more moderate Mahmoud

Abbas (familiarly known as Abu Mazen). Sharon changed his worldview, rejecting the notion of a 'Greater Israel' encompassing all or most of historical Palestine, perhaps in part because Bush's willingness to spend American blood in the region and political capital in remaking the Middle East made him confident in the American commitment to promoting region-wide political reform. More broadly, intensive engagement in the peace process by both the US and the European Union encouraged rapid and positive political movement in early 2005. Sharon proceeded with his plan to end the Israeli presence in Gaza and much of the West Bank. On 17 March 2005, Hamas, Palestinian Islamic Jihad and other Palestinian armed groups agreed to a tentative cease-fire until the end of 2005, and Hamas agreed for the first tim to participate in parliamentary elections, in July 2005. These developments made the prospect of a formal settlement of the Israeli–Palestinian conflict a real possibility.

In turn, Egypt and Jordan – the two Arab countries formally at peace with Israel – appeared to appreciate the need to complement Israeli and Palestinian initiatives towards peace. Egyptian President Hosni Mubarak hosted the first Israeli–Palestinian summit in over four years, which King Abdullah II of Jordan also attended, in Sharm el-Sheikh on 8 February 2005. The meeting produced, in addition to salutary proclamations of good intentions from Sharon and Abu Mazen, the return to Israel of Egyptian and Jordanian ambassadors, who had been withdrawn as the second intifada began in 2000. Egypt also hosted the crucial March meeting of the Palestinian armed factions that culminated in the cease-fire, and firmed up border security to prevent the smuggling of weapons into Gaza. Jordanian Foreign Minister Hani al-Mulki met with Sharon on 6 March in Jerusalem; it was the first time a Jordanian foreign minister had set foot in Israel since 2001. Although Sharon would not allow the Jordanian-trained Badr Brigade of Palestinian soldiers to deploy on the West Bank, he supported Jordan's training PA security forces. The two men also discussed cooperative bilateral projects such as building a canal from the Red Sea to the Dead Sea and the construction of a joint Eilat–Aqaba airport. Saudi Arabia, for its part, in March 2005 reiterated its proposal for the normalisation of relations between Israel and all Arab states upon political agreement between the Israelis and the Palestinians.

Syria continued to be a troublesome state, but one whose strategic options had shrunk significantly since the US intervention in Iraq had deprived it of cheap oil and a ready market for its goods, further still when Arafat's death revived the Israeli–Palestinian peace process and contracted Syria's pretext for provoking Israel through terrorist sponsorship. It had continued to provide political support to Palestinian armed groups and assistance to Hizbullah (which in turn sporadically harassed the Israel Defense Forces and aided Palestinian terrorists), and refused to withdraw its 14,000 troops and pervasive intelligence presence from Lebanon. Syria's suspected involvement in the 14 February 2005 bombing death of former Lebanese Prime Minister Rafik Hariri – who had opposed Syria's continued occupation of Lebanon – may have indicated desperation to hang on to its one remaining strategic asset.

In any case, assuming Damascus was involved – the attack was publicly blamed on an obscure Islamist terrorist group – Damascus overreached. Full American support for democratisation in the region and its military proximity helped condition a popular uprising against Syria in Lebanon on account of Hariri's murder, which in turn prompted pro-Syrian Prime Minister Omar Karami to resign. Even bigger pro-Syrian demonstrations, engineered by the Syria- and Iran-backed Lebanese militant group Hizbullah, followed in Beirut, whereupon Karami was reinstated. But the Syria–Lebanon crisis paid the larger strategic dividend of aligning France with the United States in pressing Syria to withdraw through jointly sponsored UN Security Council Resolution 1559. Key Arab states – including Saudi Arabia and Jordan – also threw their weight behind this effort. In early April 2005, the Syrian government promised UN envoy Terje Roed-Larsen that its military and intelligence assets would be withdrawn from Lebanon by the end of the month. This capitulation helped sustain momentum behind US, French and UN pressure on Syria to disarm Hizbullah. These circumstances appeared favourable to the revival sooner rather than later of the Syrian track of the Middle East peace process – though this time around the Palestinian track clearly took precedence.

Saudi Arabia, relieved of the political burden of US military deployments in-country and awakened to the indigenous jihadist terrorist threat, was slowly undertaking limited political reform. With Israel taking a more conciliatory stance and Iraq at least making a go of the democratic experiment, in February 2005, Mubarak authorised multiparty elections in Egypt. The small Gulf Cooperation Council states (Bahrain, Kuwait Oman, Qatar) as well as Jordan, Morocco and Yemen continued gradual political and reforms and efforts towards greater international economic integration. In particular, the Kuwaiti government renewed efforts (previously frustrated by parliament) to give women the vote in May 2004, Qatar announced country-wide parliamentary elections (scheduled for 2005) in June 2004, and Bahrain became the first Gulf country to legalise political parties and in May 2004 signed a Free Trade Agreement with the United States.

Unsurprisingly, the Gulf state that proved hardest to manage was Iran. As the clerical establishment consolidated power in unduly influenced parliamentary elections in February 2004, and reformists appeared just as intent as conservatives in developing a nuclear capability against the wishes of the United States, Europe and the Arab world, hopes that internal upheaval would push Iraq along a path of international political rehabilitation like the one Libya ultimately took dimmed. Neither coercive American pressure – ultimately backed by a decidedly remote threat of regime-changing US military force – nor European economic incentives appeared to modify Iran's duplicitous behaviour *vis-à-vis* the International Atomic Energy Agency with respect to its uranium-enrichment programme. With the 'good cop, bad cop' routine thus frustrated, both Europe's and the United States' Iran policy seemed adrift by February 2005. In March, however, the United States changed gears and announced its support for the European approach of attempting to dissuade Iran from pursuing a nuclear-weapons capability primarily by way of economic inducements. It was likely to give this approach a chance to succeed until summer 2005, when the June 2005 Iranian elections might furnish changed circumstances that could inform a new policy.

On balance, US policy in 2004–05 appeared fairly effective in emboldening regional actors in the Middle East and Gulf to rally against rogue states and implement gentle political reforms. But the inspirational effect of the Iraq intervention on transnational Islamist terrorism was a residual and highly disturbing problem. For example, in Egypt – where radical Islam has been effectively if brutally suppressed – Islamist terrorist threats seemed to resurge with a bombing at the Al-Azhar mosque, one of Cairo's main tourist areas, on 7 April 2005; four people –an American man, two French nationals, and the bomber – were killed and 17 people injured. A previously unknown group calling itself the Islamic Brigades of Pride in Egypt claimed credit for the attack, saying that it carried out the bombing in retaliation against the United States and other 'colonial powers' for oppressing Muslims in Iraq and the Palestinian territories.

Nevertheless, Saudi Arabia – perhaps the most abundant Arab source of recruits and funding for the transnational jihadist terrorist movement – decisively awoke to the salience of al-Qaeda's indigenous threat to the kingdom, ramping up counter-terrorist operations and cooperation with the United States. While Riyadh raised concerns about thickening bilateral military and economic relationships between the smaller Gulf states and the US, it also recognised the need for greater regional cooperation against terrorism. Thus, on most major foreign-policy fronts, 2005–06 shaped up as a considerably more hopeful year in the region than the previous one had been.

Iraq: Quagmire or Opportunity?

The removal of Saddam Hussein has proved to be the beginning and not the culmination of a long and very uncertain process of state building. Iraq today is a country desperately in need of governing institutions – bureaucratic, military and political. The ultimate success or failure of regime change and the stability of the new Iraqi state will depend upon the speed and efficiency with which these new institutions are built. On the military side, the new Iraqi government will have to build an army, almost from scratch, that is strong enough to impose order on the country as a whole. The magnitude of the task it faces is indicated by the fact that 155,000 US troops failed to impose order during two years of occupation. On the bureaucratic front, the new government also confronts an immense challenge. The Iraqi state erected under 35 years of Ba'athism collapsed in the aftermath of the US Army's seizure of Baghdad on 9 April 2003. The new government of Prime Minister Ibrahim al-Jaafari will have to reconstruct the administrative capacity of the state from the ground up, building institutions that link the society to the hub of decision-making in the fortified Green Zone in Baghdad. Of equal importance for government legitimacy and state–society relations is the creation of political organisations that can capitalise on the unexpectedly successful elections of 30 January 2005.

Law and order

At the heart of any definition of governmental capacity is the state's ability to impose order on its population and to effectively monopolise the use of force across the whole of its territory. The speed with which US and coalition forces removed Saddam Hussein's regime certainly impressed the Iraqi population. However, the central issue that came to haunt the lives of ordinary Iraqis and still dominates Iraq is the US military's inability to impose and guarantee order. This security vacuum is the first and most pressing problem facing the new Iraqi government.

What began in April 2003 as a lawless celebration of the demise of Saddam Hussein's regime grew into three weeks of uncontrolled looting and violence. The growing perception among Iraqis that US troops were not in full control of the situation helped turn criminal violence and looting into an organised and politically motivated insurgency. Ex-members of the security services, Ba'ath Party loyalists and those close to Saddam's family re-grouped as the occupation failed to convert regime change into general order. Taking advantage of the coalition's vulnerability, they began to launch hit-and-run attacks on US troops with increasing frequency and skill. A rising disenchantment with the occupation fuelled the increase in politically motivated violence and served to expand the roster of perpetrators. In an effective application of asymmetric warfare, small bands of highly mobile assailants, making use of local knowledge, inflicted increasing combat fatalities – totalling over 1,160 by early April 2005 – on the American military. As US troops attempted to take a less public role and were redeployed to more secure bases outside urban areas, the insurgents sought more accessible targets, which the nascent institutions and personnel of the new Iraqi state provided. These attacks reached their peak on 28 February 2005 with the bloodiest single attack since regime change. A devastating suicide car bomb assault on an army recruiting centre in Hillah, a town 100km southeast of Baghdad, killed at least 115 people and injured another 132. Between June 2004 and February 2005, an estimated 1,342 Iraqi soldiers and police were murdered in insurgent attacks.

The tactic adopted by a small minority of those perpetrating the violence, radical Sunni jihadists, has an even greater potential to radically destabilise Iraqi society. Prominent Kurdish and Shi'ite figures as well as religious buildings and ceremonies have been targeted by suicide bombers in an attempt to raise sectarian tensions and increase the possibility of civil war. On 21 January 2005, a Shi'ite ceremony in a Baghdad mosque and a wedding party in a village south of the capital were struck, killing 22 – concluding a week in which over 100 Iraqis died in insurgent violence. In February, in the run-up to the Shi'ite festival of Ashura, suicide bombers targeted three different mosques in and around Baghdad, killing over 25 worshippers. An area southwest of Baghdad surrounding the towns of Latifiyah and Iskandariyah on the road to the Shi'ite holy city of Karbala has become the epicentre of sectarian attacks, with Shi'ite pilgrims from Baghdad being frequently murdered.

Iraqi politicians have been keen to blame the use of suicide bombers and the overall rise in sectarian violence more on foreign jihadists than on indigenous insurgents. But they may have overstated their case. There is no question that Arab fighters from neighbouring countries and behind them the organising capacity of al-Qaeda in Iraq have played a role in the insurgency and the suicide bombings that have plagued Baghdad. Mobilised through diffuse and informal networks across the broader Middle East, they appear to have been making their way to Iraq in an uncoordinated fashion. But their numbers appear to be comparatively low, estimated by the US Army to be between 500 and 2,000. The actions of Abu Musab al-Zarqawi, a Jordanian-born Islamist who publicly proclaimed his allegiance to Osama bin Laden in autumn 2004, have been presented as evidence of a sustained al-Qaeda presence in Iraq. American officials have argued that al-Qaeda infiltrated Iraq through its links to the Kurdish Islamist group Ansar al-Islam, which emerged after a split in the Kurdish Islamist movement. After the US-led overthrow of the Taliban in Afghanistan, Ansar's ranks were undoubtedly augmented by al-Qaeda fighters. However, Ansar was a small group with little popular support, and the product of fractious Kurdish politics rather than widespread political mobilisation. It is doubtful that a small Kurdish group with no history of operating outside Iraqi Kurdistan could rapidly reconstitute itself in and around Baghdad and organise a series of very effective car bombs in a matters of months. Moreover, the efficiency of the attacks, their regularity and the speed with which they were organised in the aftermath of Saddam's fall all point to predominantly Iraqi involvement and direction in an initially reactive campaign. Any overarching organisation behind the insurgency therefore is likely to be a hybrid, with remnants of the old Ba'athist regime acting in alliance with indigenous Sunni Islamic radicals and a small number of foreign Sunni fighters, so as to activate Sunni fears of Shi'ite and Kurdish domination and a widespread resentment at foreign occupation.

Another source of violence may be the most worrying and the hardest to deal with. This can be usefully characterised as Iraqi Shi'ite Islamism strongly shaped by the twin ideological influences of radical Islam and nationalism. An early indication of this phenomenon can be seen in the city of Falluja, 35 miles west of Baghdad. Falluja has been known in Iraq as the *medinat al masajid*, or city of mosques, and is renowned for its adherence to conservative Sunni Islam. It also had a reputation, along with its neighbouring city Ramadi, as a place of lawlessness where Saddam Hussein's influence was at its weakest. The revolt that dominated the city was triggered by the killing of 17 demonstrators by US troops in the town in April 2003. This caused a spiral of violence and revenge that destabilised the whole northwest of Iraq. It resulted in the murder of four men working for a private US security contractor in March 2004, a bloody month-long siege by US Marines through April and, finally, an all-out ground and air assault on the city in October. This prompted the majority of the city's population of 300,000 to flee. Much of Falluja itself was destroyed by the fight for its control.

The radical cleric Muqtada al-Sadr has been the political figure who has most formidably rallied the nationalist and radical Islamic trends among Shi'ite sections of the population. Sadr's support originates in the poorest and most disadvantaged sections of the Shi'ite population. As the occupation forces failed to deliver significant improvements to people's lives, Sadr's popularity began to increase. In the run-up to the coalition's handover of power to the interim Iraqi government on 28 June 2004, Sadr's rhetoric and actions became more extreme in an attempt to convince the Coalition Provisional Authority (CPA) that he could not be excluded from the post-occupation political settlement. Sadr deployed his own militia, the Mahdi Army, to increase his power in the large Shi'ite slum of Baghdad, al-Tharwa, now called Sadr City, and across the south of the country. Sadr's upping his rhetorical radicalism while highlighting his military capacity made it strategically difficult for the CPA to ignore him. But it proved ill judged for the coalition to confront his organisation at the same time as US Marines were trying to contain the Falluja uprising. The CPA, by closing down Sadr's newspaper and arresting Sheikh Mustafa al-Yacoubi, one of Sadr's key deputies in Najaf, drew him into open conflict. The resulting revolts in key towns across the south of Iraq – Basra, Amara, Kut, Nassiriya, Najaf, Kufa and Karbala – as well as in Baghdad itself, highlighted two unsettling realities. Firstly, Sadr's organisation had been preparing for just such a confrontation for at least 12 months, rallying the Mahdi Army. Secondly, even with that lead-time, the geographic scale of the southern uprising indicated a 'bandwagoning' effect; other smaller militias and local armed groups used the cover of Sadr's confrontation to launch their own pre-emptive operations against coalition forces. The constituency that Sadr aspires to represent – economically disadvantaged and politically alienated Shi'ites – will not disappear. The widespread casualties resulting from the suppression of the revolt, particularly in Baghdad, have created a wellspring of resentment that is likely to take years to diffuse, which means that Sadr or politicians like him will have continued access to a constituency large enough to fuel instability.

Although the use of indiscriminate violence has alienated the majority of Iraqi public opinion across all sections of society, the carnage it has produced has been a major setback for state-building and stability. Those deploying this form of violence appear to believe that the resulting chaos will de-legitimise the Iraqi government and hasten the departure of US troops, leaving a political and security vacuum that they would be best placed to exploit and eventually fill. For the general Iraqi population, however, it is not political predation but rampant criminal violence that makes their lives so perilous. The US Army estimates that criminality is to blame for 80% of all violence in Iraq. The organised criminal groups predate regime change, having come to prominence in the mid-1990s at the peak of the social and economic suffering caused by sanctions when Saddam Hussein's grip on society was at its weakest. These groups have been revitalised by the lawlessness of present-day Iraq, in which they can capitalise on readily available weapons, the lack of an efficient police force and the United States' highly incomplete intelligence about Iraqi society.

Counter-insurgency

Long-term plans for regaining control over the country have focused on building up the capacity of the indigenous Iraqi security forces. Prior to the handover of sovereign authority in June 2004, the US military planned the creation an army of 25,000 soldiers, in addition to a paramilitary guard of 51,000. However, a force this size would have represented a fifth of the army at Saddam Hussein's disposal. In spite of setting aside $1.8bn for the task, the coalition had trouble raising and training this comparatively modest force. In April 2004, with the Falluja and Sadr revolts, the new security force faced its first major challenge. At this point, the new Iraqi Army consisted of two battalions. Up to half of the First Battalion resigned during training in December 2003, citing low pay and poor conditions. Most of the Second Battalion, when pressed into service alongside US Marines during the siege of Falluja, refused to fight, arguing that they had joined the new army to fight Iraq's enemies and not Iraqis.

To compensate for the slow pace of army recruitment and training, the Iraqi Civil Defence Corps (ICDC) was set up. Much more ad hoc in its recruitment and training, this force was composed of an uneasy amalgamation of former employees of the old security forces, members of the militias formed by political parties and people desperate for paid work. A week before taking power in June 2004, Interim Prime Minister Ayad Allawi announced that the ICDC, renamed the National Guard, would form the Iraqi government's main vehicle for enforcing order. By October 2004, the National Guard had recruited 41,000 troops, 20,000 short of its target. The 36th Battalion of the National Guard has become the main striking force of the Iraqi armed forces, being deployed against the Mahdi Army in Najaf in August and in Falluja in October 2004. Though it did not perform badly, this unit of the guard had been heavily recruited from the Kurdish *Peshmerga* militias of the Kurdish Democratic Party (KDP) and the Patriotic Union of Kurdistan (PUK), and some senior guard commanders were reportedly arrested for collaboration with the insurgents themselves. These facts suggest some of the problems of discipline and loyalty in a force so quickly recruited, trained and deployed.

The brunt of everyday law enforcement has fallen to the Iraqi police force. Relying heavily on personnel from the old force, recruitment and retention have been much more successful, with numbers of enlistees estimated between 73,000 and 92,000. But training and equipment have been slow in arriving. In mid-April 2004, it was estimated that only 13,000 members of the force had received training, and complaints of poor equipment and scarce weaponry have been ongoing. Unsurprisingly, the police in many southern towns and in Falluja, when faced with political violence, either refused to fight or in some cases joined the insurgents. The focus on quantity rather than quality has meant that trainers have had very little time to instil standards of discipline and loyalty into the security force as a whole. Best estimates suggest that it will take up to five years to create anything close to effective an indigenous force able to impose and guarantee order across the country.

During summer 2004, the US Embassy in Baghdad developed a strategy to break the back of the rebellion in the run-up to the elections of January 2005. US forces would bring 20–30 key towns in the northwest back under the control of the coalition and the Iraqi government before the election campaign started. Samarra, a town of 200,000 65 miles north of Baghdad, just below Tikrit, was to be the first town to be seized, with Falluja being the defining moment of the campaign. Things appeared to be going to plan when 5,000 troops took control of Samarra on 1 October 2004. Falluja came under sustained attack and then occupation on 8 November 2004. But the seizure of Falluja did not result in the pacification of rest of northwestern Iraq. The 'dynamic cordon' placed around the city by the US Marines in the middle of October did not prevent large numbers of fighters from leaving Falluja prior to the well-publicised attack. The campaign itself was greeted by an upsurge in violence across the whole of the region, with suicide bombings killing 39 people in recently reoccupied Samarra. In Mosul, Iraq's third-largest city, a revolt resulted in attacks on nine police stations and the desertion of 3,200 of the city's 4,000 police.

The legacy left the Iraqi government by the occupation forces is daunting. The government faces an insurgency estimated to be between 20,000 and 50,000 strong. These fighters are organised in as many as 70 cells, operating largely independently and at best with attenuated coordination. With no coherent centre of gravity and no overall leadership, the insurgency cannot be defeated simply by the application of brute force. The government of Ibrahim Jaafari does not have the capacity to replace US forces with the speed needed to turn the tide of the revolt. The dangerous interregnum after occupation but before the birth of a credible Iraqi army therefore may evolve into the status quo. This development would see the government controlling areas of Baghdad but little else, and the insurgency and the various militias across the country the main sources of coercive power for the vast majority of the population.

Forestalling such a result by filling the security vacuum is the first and most difficult problem any Iraqi government will have to tackle. That it can succeed on a strictly operational basis, using only hard counter-insurgency and counter-terrorism measures, where the collective forces of the world's sole remaining superpower failed, is a daunting expectation. Furthermore, while it may be politically expedient for American and Iraqi politicians to stress the non-Iraqi dimension of the insurgency, strategically an inordinate emphasis on foreign fighters may well undermine attempts to tackle the underlying causes of violence. By expending considerable time and energy blaming foreign jihadists, the more proximate causes of the insurgency's strength – the failure to establish law and order, the insufficient headway in re-building Iraq's infrastructure and the resulting alienation of the population – could become marginalised. Instead of focusing primarily on military solutions and the depredations of foreigner *provocateurs*, the most promising approach may be to develop a coherent political strategy for combating the insurgency. This would involve listening to radical voices within both the Shi'ite and the Sunni communities and ultimately integrating them politically while at the same time demobilising the militias or at the very least limiting their capacity to deploy violence. This will clearly be a difficult task, but the alternative military strategy has to date proved very unsuccessful.

Politics and democracy

US war aims in Iraq were primarily about change, the removal of Saddam Hussein's regime and its replacement with one less prone to violent adventurism, domestic repression and the development of weapons of mass destruction. But once the institutions of government had collapsed, the task facing the occupation became complex and potentially contradictory. The establishment of order, beyond the control of violence, became the primary goal. The building of a new political order would ultimately mean guiding Iraq towards a government that was in broad agreement with US foreign-policy aims. This would entail not only minimising the role of former members of the old regime but also identifying and sidelining other political forces that might interfere with a pro-US agenda. This had to be done in conjunction with the labour-intensive task of building a nationwide system of government. In recognition of regime change, that government had to be legitimate, both internationally and, even more importantly, domestically. Forging such a government would involve, at some stage, not only giving the government back to suitable Iraqis, but back to an Iraqi governing elite that was either popularly elected or at least could mobilise a significant section of Iraqi popular opinion to support its rule.

The transitional law of March 2004 set a clear timetable for progress towards democracy, starting with the national elections held at the end of January 2005. The vote was intended to herald the start of an intense exercise in consultative democracy. A 275-member assembly was to be elected to serve for a year. The assembly's main task, however, is to draft a constitution presently scheduled to be finished by the middle of August 2005. This constitution will be submitted to a referendum no later than October, then used to conduct elections for a fully constitutional government by 15 December. That government will take power by the end of 2005. The hope of the Iraqi government, as well as its allies in Washington and London, was that the bulk of Iraq's estimated 13.9m eligible voters would participate in this series of national votes and in so doing give the Iraqi government the democratic legitimacy and stability it so desperately needed.

The countdown to the January 2005 elections started on 1 November 2004 with voter registration. The next stage in the process was the registration of the candidates and parties who were seeking election. The Transitional Administrative Law set stringent standards of eligibility. Candidates had to have a 'good reputation' and no criminal convictions 'involving moral turpitude', and they could not have been senior members of the Ba'ath Party or the old regime's secret services. Candidates had to sign a declaration certifying that they met these qualifications and to collect 500 signatures in support of their application. The election itself was structured around a single constituency, with candidates needing 30,750 votes to get elected. In addition to organising the election around one national constituency, the candidates and parties seeking election were encouraged to run as part of a nationwide list, with those positioned at the top of the list standing the best chance of getting elected. This was done with the overt aim of cross-communal coalition building but also so that the electoral machinery would not become too complicated.

Early on, the US Embassy in Baghdad favoured what was termed a 'monster coalition' list that would unite all the parties that had dominated the Iraqi Governing Council and who formed the bulk of the interim government's cabinet. The plan was promoted on the basis that it would prevent one party or group dominating the administration, allowing Iraq's first elected government to rule in a pluralistic and consensual manner. But it was widely attacked as being anti-democratic in that it would not give the electorate a choice of parties to vote for, yet again suppressing the growth of indigenous political parties by favouring those who had recently returned from exile. The prospect that the election would be dominated by a US Embassy-inspired coalition ticket was dramatically reduced by the actions of Grand Ayatollah Ali al-Sistani. As the religious head of Iraq's Shi'ite community, Sistani has continually pressed for early elections as the only way to reduce violence, guarantee Iraq's movement to democracy and decrease the influence of the United States in running the country. In mid-October, Sistani's spokesperson announced that the Ayatollah had encouraged the formation of a six-person committee to 'coordinate' the creation of a 'Shi'ite' list, the United Iraqi Alliance (UIA), for the elections. Parties and individuals could join this list if they agreed to vote as a bloc in the new parliament, not to challenge the 'Islamic character' of the Iraqi people and not to back any legislation that ran counter to *sharia* law. Negotiations focused on the proportion of political parties versus independent candidates to be placed on the list and whether the radical cleric Muqtada al-Sadr would join.

Out of a total of 228 candidates on the list, less than half represented the 11 parties in the coalition. The rest were individuals picked by the committee for their standing within society. Nevertheless, the turnout and voting of the Shi'ite community, an estimated 60% of the Iraqi population, was greatly influenced by Sistani's role in creating the UIA and his edict that it was the duty of all Iraqis to participate in the elections. Although the Shi'ite section of society did not vote uniformly or solely on the basis of their religious identity, the grouping of such a large number of parties seeking the Shi'ite vote together on one list had a defining influence on the composition of the parliament formed after 30 January. As the election campaign began in earnest, it became clear that only two other coalitions had the ability to mount a sustained challenge to the UIA. The first was Allawi's Iraqi List and the second was the Kurdish list formed by the two main Kurdish parties, the KDP and the PUK. On election day, 8.5m Iraqis, or some 58% of the whole electorate, voted, defying insurgent groups that launched nine suicide bombings in Baghdad and 260 attacks across the country as a whole. Turnout rose to between 82% and 92% in the Kurdish north and between 61% and 71% in the south of Iraq. The final result gave the UIA 48% of the vote and 140 seats in the 275-member assembly. The Kurdish Alliance won 75 seats and Allawi's list 40. During the first week of April, the assembly selected a president, the veteran Kurdish leader Jalal Talabani, and two deputies, the Shi'ite former finance minister Adel Abd al-Mahdi and the former temporary president Ghazi al-Yawer. The head of the Islamic Dawa Party, Ibrahim Jaafari, a Shi'ite, was elected prime minister by the assembly on 7 April. Hoshyar Zebari, a Kurd, was named foreign minister. An agreement was also reached to name a Sunni Arab as head of the Defence Ministry, and more broadly to accord Sunnis no fewer than six ministries. Jaafari had two weeks to name his cabinet.

A coalition of Sunni mosques across the country, the Association of Muslim Scholars (*Hayat al-Ulama al-Muslimin*), led the campaign for Sunni Muslims to boycott the elections. After the US assault on Falluja it was joined by the Iraqi Islamic Party, whose leader, Mohsen Abdul Hamid, called for the elections to be postponed for six months. By mid-November 2004, 14 other organisations had formed the Iraqi Founding National Assembly (IFNA), an umbrella group for all those refusing to take part in the polls while the country remained occupied by US forces. The boycott campaign appeared to be successful. For example, only 2% voted in Anbar province, an area of northwestern Iraq with a high concentration of Sunni voters. The boycott meant that the Sunni community – as much as a quarter of the whole population – would not be represented in the new assembly. Although some Sunni leaders counselled working with elected Iraqis in drafting the new constitution, the most influential ones did not. On the heels of its exclusionary success, the

IFNA may well evolve into a broad anti-occupation front, acting as the political voice for the various different groups involved in the insurgency.

The fact that 58% of the electorate braved insurgent violence to cast their votes indicates the strength of support for the growth of a democratic Iraq. The UIA was the main victor. However, the large and unwieldy coalition did not win the elections through the construction of an efficient party machine that leafleted, campaigned and got the voters to the ballot box. Instead, success turned on the endorsement of Sistani, which, though welcome, was hardly a systemic and recursive solution to Iraq's political challenges. Moreover, the violent rebellion currently dominating all aspects of Iraqi life springs in part from a sense of marginalisation prevailing in sections of Iraqi society. Thus, notwithstanding the inspirational symbolic success of the January 2005 elections, the Sunni groups' voluntary disenfranchisement may have the effect of intensifying the Sunni people's sense of alienation and the anger they feel towards the new government. The new parliament is now dominated by politicians who explicitly identified themselves as Shi'ites and who mobilised their voters on that basis. Those excluded from this process, voluntarily or not, would be largely from the Sunni communities of the northwest. Having no stake in the constitutional process, the temptation to support the men of violence is probably much greater.

Security still paramount

The military task of defeating the Ba'athist regime was relatively straightforward, but the political task has been complex, unpredictable and costly. With the collapse of Iraq's governing institutions in April 2003, the political mission of reforming the state was transformed into an exercise in state building, which is a three-stage process. Firstly, order must be re-imposed; then the administrative capacity of the government must be rebuilt; and, finally, sustainable economic development must be put in place. Two years after the change in regime, there is little indication that the US military and its indigenous partner, the new Iraqi government, are close even to completing the first stage in this process. There is a security vacuum in Iraq, with the institutions of law and order lacking the strength to guarantee stability in Baghdad, let alone across the country as a whole.

The enthusiasm of a majority of Iraqis for the democratic process – manifested by a relatively high turnout in the January 2005 elections – suggests that the American state-building initiative is at least not a hopeless quagmire. But if there are genuine democratic opportunities in Iraq, the election certainly has not made their realisation automatic. The new government still direly needs both legitimacy and administrative capacity. By delivering 275 elected members to the new assembly, the January vote has given the new government a basis from which to build countrywide legitimacy. Yet this is far from guaranteed. The assembly and its members will be involved in detailed and somewhat obscure negotiations about the new constitution. The danger is that those elected, shut away in the heavily fortified

Green Zone arguing about the legal structures of government, will lose touch with the hopes and expectations of those who elected them. Any resultant post-election political demobilisation of the Iraqi people would increase the disappointment and anomie that came to dominate Iraq in the months after the Ba'athist regime fell.

For the government to build on the success of the elections, it needs to put a great deal of time and effort into creating institutional links with Iraqi society. Doing so would require recreating a nationwide civil service linking the country to the government in Baghdad. Political parties, emboldened by their electoral success, would have to build national party machines, whereby activists in local offices could explain the policies being developed in Baghdad to the people at large. In return, these party machines would feed back to the Green Zone the opinions, demands and hopes of that population. Such a dispensation would create a much-needed bridge between the government and its population. The two parties that dominate the UIA are the Dawa Islamic Party and the Supreme Council for the Islamic Revolution in Iraq. They would appear to be best positioned to establish the party apparatus needed to ensure fluid communications between the elected and the electorate.

Of more immediate importance will be the new government's ability to control the country. By January 2005, US forces had set themselves the target of training several divisions of the Iraqi army, as well as 50 or more battalions of the Iraqi National Guard. The issue, however, is not just a matter of numbers of troops, the quality of their training and the speed of their deployment. To be successful, these new forces will have to become a visible testament to the new state's capacity to control the country. They would incrementally replace the US Army, and would be accepted by the population at large as the efficient and legitimate arm of a new Iraqi state. In April 2005, there was little sign that this was happening at the pace hoped for by the US military. A realistic timetable for such a major and extended exercise in recruitment, training and institution-building would be at least five years. In the meantime, without the amelioration of popular discontent by political means, the absence of law and order will still dominate the everyday lives of Iraq's population. Accordingly, effective diplomatic redress to politically motivated violence is essential. Disarmament, demobilisation and reintegration (DDR) may be UN buzzwords, but they are integral to successful state-building (as seen in recent years, for example, in Sierra Leone). The Iraqi government and the United States would best focus on drawing the political representatives of the insurgency into discussions about trading in their weapons and participating in the democratic process. In 2005–06, the degree to which DDR and related activities complement hard counter-insurgency and counter-terrorism and discussions among the elected elite on the constitutional structure of the Iraq state and polity is likely to be the most salient measure of progress in Iraq.

Iran: Ongoing Crisis

Supreme Leader Ayatollah Ali Khamenei proclaimed the Iranian year 1383, which began in March 2004, as the 'year of accountability'. The opaque character of the theocratic government has been the regime's most salient achievement, in that it has allowed that government to perpetuate itself. Khamenei was referring to the government's responsibility to inform the people on their progress related to 'rendering services to the entire nation, creating science, establishing justice and alleviating poverty and discrimination in society', pledging (but not delivering) a newfound transparency in domestic politics. In fact, ambiguities regarding Iran's relationship with Iraq, its ties to al-Qaeda, the election of the seventh parliament (Majlis) and potential presidential candidates for the 17 June 2005 election, the nuclear programme and the economy have continued to dominate the political scene. In any case, it is highly unlikely that any aspiration of accountability would be extended to Iran's foreign policy. The clerics at the helm of the Iranian state appear to have used confusion and deception with success. The international community, 26 years after the Iranian revolution, continues to be perplexed by Iran's decision-making structure, and hampered by an inability to identify and categorise Iran's most important political players.

Majlis machinations

The aftermath of the parliamentary elections in February 2004 that yielded a conservative victory left little doubt about the conservative clerical reassertion of power. President Mohammed Khatami's 1997 and 2001 election and re-election, along with the victory of reformist candidates of the 2000 parliament, had offered domestic and international constituencies the promise of political change within Iran. But the overwhelming national and international support for the reformist president was threatening to the conservative and hard-line ideologues of the revolution. With the divine authority of the *velayat-e-faqih* sanctioning a conservative reconsolidation, they used the institutions of the Guardian Council and the judiciary to discount parliamentary laws and arrest and detain Khatami allies.

The parliamentary elections of February 2004 were the final battleground for achieving the conservative resurgence. The Guardian Council, with its two-pronged constitutional mandate for approving parliamentary bills and vetting parliamentary candidates, had refused, among many bills, the reformist attempts at liberalising the press. Most importantly, it had also rejected the eligibility of over 3,600 candidates, including 84 members of the incumbent parliament, to run for the February elections. According to the election guidelines, candidates could be barred from running for any number of reasons, ranging from bribery charges to refusing to support the constitution and the notion of the *velayat-e-faqih* and the Supreme Leader. Among the many disqualified candidates was the president's brother, Mohammad Reza Khatami. In the end, the conservatives achieved their end, winning 156 of the 290 seats, thereby inaugurating a new breed of unknown conservative politicians into the seventh Majlis.

Iran's Majlis has been prone to broad-ranging ideological swings from one four-year election cycle to the other. The aftermath of the Iran–Iraq war brought a leftist parliament to power in 1992, while in 1996 the pendulum swung right, returning the conservatives to the helm. The 2004 conservative renaissance, after the 2000 reformist victory, thus followed an established pattern. As most deputies are replaced after each election, it bears stressing that the real power in the Majlis rotates among a handful of top leaders with revolutionary credentials. Commencing work on 27 May 2004, the new parliament promised an end to factional politics. The largest bloc among this year's right-wing winners – *Abadgaran* (developers) of Islamic Iran – represent a last-minute coalition of centre-right candidates allegedly hand-picked by the Supreme Leader's office and endorsed by the Council of Guardians. The overwhelming majority of these deputies are new faces pre-selected from a list of loyalist rank-and-file – some from military, security and intelligence forces – with limited knowledge of domestic or world affairs, and no legislative or administrative experience. These frequently silent delegates follow the guidance and direction of about 25 professional politicians from among the Islamic Republic's 250-member nomenklatura. Significant policy changes thus do not necessarily track the ostensible ideological labels of the new deputies.

Gholam Ali Hadad Adel was predictably elected speaker of the parliament. He is the first non-cleric to hold the post since the revolution. Despite his non-religious credentials, Hadad Adel maintains close familial as well as ideological bonds with the Khamenei, as their children married in 1997. The collaborative relationship with the Guardian Council has allowed the current parliament more success than its predecessor. A working relationship between parliament and Khatami and his cabinet has come harder. In response to the conservative alignment of the Majlis, Khatami withdrew his twin bills to curtail the power of the Guardian Council and to increase the authority of the presidency. While the Majlis in its first parliamentary mandates was forced to approve Khatami's cabinet, Khatami himself had pre-emptively reshuffled his team of ministers to give it greater cohesion in the face of parliamentary adversity. Despite an initial façade of peaceful coexistence, by October 2004 the parliament had begun impeachment proceedings against Khatami's transport minister, Ahmad Khorram.

Accused tangentially of failing to improve Iran's dismal air, rail and road safety record and primarily for awarding a Turkish–Austrian consortium a contract to run the capital's new $500 million Imam Khomeini International Airport, Khorram came into conflict with the elite, loyalist Iranian Revolutionary Guards Corps, which has a coalition of 80 in the Majlis. The Guards shut down the airport just hours after it was officially inaugurated in May 2004, warning that the airport had to remain closed until it no longer jeopardised national security: they claimed that Khorram's approval of Turkey's financial and operational involvement in running a national asset tarnished the republic's Islamic credentials because Turkey had links with Israel. The conservative parliament voted to cut the investment stake of Turkcell – the Turkish cell phone company that won the tender to build a mobile phone network in Iran – from 70% to 49%.

Both affairs exemplify burgeoning political and economic problems. Attracting much needed foreign direct investment (FDI) was one of the main pillars of the government's third and fourth development plans. However, the state-subsidised and nationalised, bloated, nature of the Iranian economy has been a difficult beast to tame. Longstanding fears that FDI will lead to foreign interference in Iranian internal affairs – the ranking historical example being the Anglo–Iranian relation-ship, which spawned a huge and inefficient bureaucracy to sustain the regime's system of patronage – has prevented significant progress in privatisation. Already shaky investor confidence has diminished as a result of these events.

To prevent future crises of this nature, the parliament has inserted itself into the debate on FDI by submitting a bill that affords it veto power over foreign invest-ment deals. Moreover, the legislation is also blocking a portion of the reform plan designed to give exploration rights to foreign oil companies. Without such guaran-tees, Iran will unlikely meet its desired goal of doubling its oil output by 2020 to 8m barrels a day. Currently, oil companies can participate in Iran only under fixed-return arrangements called buybacks. Iran is paying a price for these policies. It has barely found enough investment for the oil industry to stem the long decline in output that began after the 1979 revolution. There have been no major discoveries since the late 1970s, industry sources say. Iran is also losing out to Qatar, which is working the giant natural gas field that the two countries share at a far greater pace than the Iranians. Still, the attraction of Iran's fields, which produce close to 4m barrels a day and have the world's second-largest natural gas reserves, remains. The Sino–Iranian dynamic percolating in the form of commercial and strategic ties has recently yielded a 25-year liquefied natural gas (LNG) contract worth $20billion on top of an exchange of 150,000 daily barrels of crude oil at market prices. Both Royal Dutch/Shell Group and Total are negotiating for massive LNG projects, and Total and BP plc remain interested in an oil field called Bangestan.

A second consequence of the restrictive parliamentary measure is the preven-tion of the sale of state-run banks and of foreign banks' subsidiaries in Tehran. In effect, the Majlis has re-imposed state controls and derailed any progress towards liberalising the economy. The government's pervasive role in the economy also provides numerous opportunities for corruption – from tax assessors' accepting the common gift of gold coins to insiders taking payoffs on big contracts. Nevertheless, in the hope of creating an 'Islamic Japan', the parliament announced an agenda for the parliamentary year that included a 2005–10 development plan that would allocate oil revenues to increase human and physical resources, diminishing prostitution and corruption and addressing the International Atomic Energy Agency (IAEA) additional protocol. It is improbable that these ambitious goals will be realised in an environment of domestic political apathy (born of frustration) and international uncertainty.

Domestic doldrums

The slow conservative resurgence is designed to insulate the Islamic republic from the growing domestic discontent most prominently emerging from the country's youthful majority. The hope of a Tehran Spring in 1999 gave rise to a significant challenge from within as the youth actively demonstrated and rallied for liberalised social, political and economic policies. After observing the conservative backlash through the detention and jailing of fellow students as well as the targeting of Khatami and his cabinet, a deflated population has exited from political participation. While such a political exodus might be ephemeral, it has eased conservative victories in both the municipal and Majlis elections. Voter turnout for both was decidedly low compared to the overwhelming participation in the election of Khatami in 1997 and 2001. This non-participatory attitude works to the benefit of the clerical cadre, who prefer a politically sedentary constituency. Oil prices as high as $50 a barrel have benefited Iran by generating revenue sufficient to support their public and external finances. Although the high oil prices are dynamically little more than an economic band-aid for Iran's chronic and systemic problems, the government has discounted oil-price reductions by depositing excess revenue into a savings fund.

Official and unofficial Iranian economic statistics are inconsistent but on any measure dismal. The official unemployment rate in late 2004 hovered around 13%, and most economists put it at about 20%, with an estimated 3m people listed as jobless and young men most heavily affected. The need to create employment is among the regime's highest priorities. Roughly 800,000 new jobs are required annually, but the government has only succeeded in creating half that number. In August 2004, the International Monetary Fund (IMF) warned that failure to control public spending on subsidies could contribute to reduced growth rates and economic volatility. Reining in subsidies, though, could unleash the wrath of the masses that rely on this government support to finance their salary shortfalls. Indeed, the next president, to be elected in June 2005, will likely have a mandate for economic reform.

Presidential posturing

The resounding conservative Majlis victory, facilitated by the Guardian Council, foreshadows a similar success story in the June 2005 presidential elections. While a conservative victory is predicted and almost guaranteed, what is most interesting about this election is that numerous candidates are contending for the top post. As seven candidates have thus far declared themselves interested and eligible, this election could be Iran's most pluralistic contest to date. As of April 2005, the announced conservative group are Ali Larijani, former head of the state-run television and radio, Ali Akbar Velayati, former foreign minister, Mahmood Ahmadi-Nejad, Tehran's mayor, Mohsen Rezai, Expediency Council secretary, and Ahmad Tavakoli, Tehran parliamentary representative. The two reformist candidates are Hojatoleslam Mehdi Karrubi, the former speaker of the parliament, and Mustafa Moin, former minister of science, research and technology. All these hopefuls are battling to increase their domestic image and profile.

Although each candidate has the backing of a political party, neither the conservative nor reformist bloc is monolithic. The former is distinctly divided between a more pragmatic neo-conservative bloc, where members argue for practical policies designed to foster economic liberalisation, and more traditionalist elements who seek to maintain the ideological vision of the revolution. The neo-conservatives were among the beneficiaries of the Majlis elections and have strong links to the Revolutionary Guard. Together they have worked through the Majlis to reverse any liberalising trends implemented by the previous parliament. Inherently, this group fears that an increased foreign presence in Iran will lead to interference in Iran's internal affairs. Reformists generally demand political liberalisation. However, the most acute divisions within this group are economic, as some advocate Western-style liberalisation while others seek to maintain the socialist model.

In any case, the Guardian Council's vetting process will be instrumental. It was recently reported in the Iranian newspaper *Sharq* that the council does not intend to reject any candidates and hopes to meet the public's desire for a free election. This leniency might be intended to ensure an increase in political participation. Nonetheless, candidates must pass through the vetting process, proving that they are not only eligible to run but also competent to fulfil the position. Many observers believe that the final announcement of the candidate group will include the former president, Ali Akbar Hashemi Rafsanjani. Rafsanjani's foray into the 2005 elections could dramatically alter the outcome. He is recognised as a quintessential pragmatist, and perhaps the only figure who could unite the parties. As one of the most powerful politicians in Iran today, Rafsanjani has successfully reinvented himself throughout the revolution's 26-year tenure. A revolutionary collaborator with Khomeini, Rafsanjani was among the co-founders of the historically powerful Islamic Republican Party. Rafsanjani was elected as the first speaker of the parliament from 1980–89 and was appointed acting commander of the armed forces in the last year of the Iran–Iraq war. He was also among the negotiators of the pragmatic Reagan-era arms-for-hostages deal, which could be a significant indicator of a more pragmatic and cooperative Iranian foreign policy should he come to power.

Elected president in 1990, Rafsanjani's two terms were deemed part of Iran's 'era of reconstruction'. He pursued rapprochement with the West and used his influence to force the release of American hostages in Lebanon. His legacy as president remains coloured by the tense factional politics that arose after the death of Khomeini and the end of the Iran–Iraq war. Rafsanjani's vision for Iran consists of a delicate balance of economic liberalisation and rational calculations to restore Iran's image among the community of nations. Such a balance will be difficult to achieve against the strident opposition of the ideological adherents of the revolution. Still, Rafsanjani's power is extensive. He is currently chairman of the ever-powerful Expediency Council that arbitrates between the Majlis and Guardian Council, as well as deputy chairman of the Assembly of Experts, the elected body that designates the Supreme Leader. In an effort to perpetuate the atmosphere of speculation, as of early March 2005, Rafsanjani had yet to make any definite announcement of his candidacy or policies. Stating that he has a few months remaining before committing to the race, he has intimated that his candidacy depends on the capability and popular support of the other contenders. He has maintained that 'in principle, I am inclined not to participate. My main reason is for the people not to think that the regime is dependent on only a few people.' Rafsanjani is likely to return to the political scene only if he has a popular mandate. Under no circumstances does he want to replicate his embarrassing loss in the parliamentary elections of 2000.

Rafsanjani's entrance into the election landscape could lead to the withdrawal of a number of the already-declared candidates. Ali Akbar Velayati and Mohsen Rezai have said that they will also remove themselves from the race if Rafsanjani joins it. As close associates of Rafsanjani, these two would find satisfaction in his prospective platform. Ali Larijani, Ahmad Tavakoli and Mehdi Karrubi, however, are determined to run regardless of Rafsanjani's decision. Not only are these three factionally opposed to Rafsanjani, but Larijani and Tavakoli, in particular, would be particularly threatened by the consequences of his cultural and economic liberalisation policies and their effect on security and foreign matters.

The outcome of this election could have profound consequences for both economic and foreign-policy decisions. While Rafsanjani's candidacy will not be embraced by the majority population, he might be welcomed in light of his strong hand and tactical negotiation skills in effecting the drastic measures needed to repair Iran's strained economic and foreign relations. With the economy sustained by oil-revenue life-support amid the looming nuclear crisis and antagonism with the United States, many have speculated that perhaps only someone with Rafsanjani's stature could move Iran's status in the world towards a tipping point.

Nuclear nemeses

With uncertainty surrounding Iran's presidential election, a similar air of elusiveness clouds Iran's nuclear strategy. The long-running negotiation process with the IAEA and the European Union Three (EU-3) – France, Germany and the United Kingdom – has been at the top of the agenda of the international community. In light of intelligence failures with regard to Iraq's weapons WMD programme, avoiding similar mistakes while simultaneously ending Iran's nuclear ambitions is paramount.

The shrouded nature of the Iranian regime, of course, has presented many an obstacle to the IAEA and EU. Additionally, the absence of a domestic consensus evident from conflicting messages and rhetorical posturing on the country's nuclear programme continues to obscure the situation. For the Iranians, their pursuit of a nuclear weapons capability is guided by an inherent need for deterrence, as well as national prestige. After their eight-year long war with neighbouring Iraq, in which Iranians were subjected to chemical-weapons attacks, years of economic sanctions and international isolation, Iran's position in the middle of a dangerous strategic neighbourhood in which India, Pakistan and Israel already posses the coveted nuclear weaponry, and most recently, being surrounded by an antagonistic American presence in Afghanistan, Iraq and the Persian Gulf, has only intensified Iranian security concerns.

Iran, of course, maintains that its nuclear programme is strictly for peaceful purposes. Clinging to the argument that its energy resources are wasting assets, Iran has consistently argued that its nuclear programme merely reflects its pursuit of alternative energy sources. Khamenei has even issued a *fatwa* (religious edict) claiming that production of nuclear weapons is against sharia law and is *haram* – i.e., forbidden. Yet other officials have advanced the argument claiming that in light of Israeli, Pakistani and Indian proliferation, Iran should not be denied the same right. On balance, the Iranian position taken by Khatami appears to summarise the regime's true intentions: 'If we feel others are not meeting their promises, under no circumstances would we be committed to continue fulfilling ours.'

Since its agreement with the EU-3 in October 2003 to suspend its enrichment program, the regime has been evasive and has not shown good faith. Iran signed the Additional Protocol in December 2003, promising full cooperation with more intrusive IAEA inspections of Iran's facilities. However, by early 2004 it was evident that Iran had not fully declared its past enrichment research and was continuing efforts to conceal suspected nuclear activities. By summer 2004, the October 2003 arrangement was essentially negated as the IAEA and EU intensified their criticism of Iran while the Iranians reciprocated with equally bold accusations that the EU had failed to fulfil their promises to remove the Iranian dossier from the IAEA agenda. In response to a critical IAEA resolution in June 2004, Iranians announced their intentions to resume manufacturing parts for uranium-enrichment centrifuges and begin producing large quantities of uranium hexafluoride, the gaseous form of uranium used as feed material for centrifuges. At the same time, the Iranians revealed their plans to build a heavy-water research reactor in Arak.

The June 2004 IAEA resolution essentially set a deadline of the end of November 2004 for Iran to restore the suspension of its enrichment programme or face an IAEA resolution referring Iran to the United Nations Security Council. In the complicated political dynamics of the 35-member IAEA Board of Governors, the United States pressed for immediate referral to the Security Council, but Washington was blocked by the EU-3 (joined by Russia and China), who preferred to give Iran more time to correct its safeguards violations and negotiate an agreement to resolve the nuclear issue. In essence, the October 2003 agreement represented a European commitment to oppose referral to the Security Council in exchange for an Iranian commitment to suspend its enrichment programme. As the October 2003 agreement unravelled, however, the EU-3 threatened to join Washington in supporting referral to the Security Council, and Tehran had no confidence that Russia and China would be willing or able to block such a resolution, since the IAEA Board of Governors acts by majority vote.

Faced with this threat of referral to New York, Iran relented. On 15 November 2004, under threat of sanctions, the Iranian government agreed to restore the 'temporary' suspension of its uranium enrichment programme, pending efforts to negotiate a permanent agreement with the EU-3. In skeletal form, the agreement proposed by the EU would affirm Iran's cooperation in (1) halting all efforts to attain a nuclear weapons capability; (2) ratifying the Additional Protocols in the parliament; and (3) negotiating expanded trade and cooperation endeavours with the EU and support for Iran's accession to the World Trade Organisation (WTO). More specifically, the EU proposed to guarantee that Iran would be permitted to pursue a nuclear power fuel supply, civilian nuclear technology and even a light-water research facility if Iran permanently abandoned its efforts to develop a nuclear fuel cycle (that is, uranium enrichment or plutonium separation) capability. ElBaradei has affirmed Iran's suspension of uranium enrichment-activities. However, Iran has made clear that it regards the duration of the suspension as temporary and has warned that it will resume enrichment activities if its talks with the EU-3 do not produce acceptable results. Additionally, in the wake of this new agreement, the exiled Iranian opposition group, the National Council for Resistance in Iran, has attempted to subvert the deal by accusing Iran of continuing a secret uranium-enrichment programme. Thus far, the existence of a covert enrichment programme cannot be demonstrated.

The EU hopes to fashion an agreement with Iran based on the Libyan model. In exchange for normalised relations and a removal of sanctions, Libya has renounced its WMD programmes and has also become a partner in the 'war on terror'. The Bush administration is less confident of the parallel. During the US presidential election countdown, the administration continued its policy of outsourcing the issue to the EU while remaining vocal against Iran – a kind of default 'good cop, bad cop' policy. However, in the aftermath of Bush's victory, the administration began to modify its uncompromising position vis-à-vis Iran . On her February 2005 tour of European capitals, Secretary of State Condoleezza Rice was vociferous in her opposition to Iran's Islamic regime. Castigating the clerical theocracy as an 'outpost of tyranny', Rice consistently reinforced the US stance of non-partic-ipation as well as non-incentivisation. Following President Bush's tour of Europe in March, however, the US decided to support the EU-3 diplomacy by agreeing not to block the initiation of WTO membership talks with Iran and to approve on a case-by-case basis the export of US-made spare parts for civilian aircraft in Iran as part of any nuclear deal with Iran. In large measure, Washington's move was tactical. By agreeing to lend support to European diplomacy, the US intended to shift blame onto Iran for any failure to reach a diplomatic agreement and secure European support for referral to the UN Security Council if the EU-3 talks collapsed. Nonetheless, Washington's tactical manoeuvre crossed an important political threshold and opened the way for Tehran to name a price in terms of American security guarantees and inducements that would be required for Iran to abandon its nuclear fuel cycle programme.

As of April 2005, it was unclear whether Iran would pursue such a gambit. Although the suspension remains in place, there are continuing questions about Iran's past and current nuclear activities. In February 2005, for example, Iran grudgingly relinquished documents to the IAEA indicating that it contemplated purchasing nuclear-bomb-making technology – including technology required for the critical process of casting uranium metal – from the illicit commercial network run by top Pakistani nuclear scientist A. Q. Khan as early as 1987. Iran also began building storage tunnels north of its Isfahan uranium conversion facility without informing the IAEA and refused to allow additional IAEA access to the Parchin military site, where US experts believe Iran may be testing high-explosive nuclear-weapon components. Most importantly, Iran has strongly rejected the EU-3 demand that it permanently end its enrichment programme, claiming that no price is high enough to convince Iran to give up its right to an enrichment programme, which Iran says is essential for energy independence and national pride. Instead, Iran has proposed that it be allowed to continue its enrichment programme under a variety of technical limits, including continuous IAEA monitoring and restrictions on the size of the facility. The EU-3 has rejected these variations because they would still make it possible for Iran to develop a nuclear-weapon breakout capability.

Some optimistic Iran-watchers contend that the clerics are seeking to avoid a contest with the Security Council and the United States, and therefore will eventu-ally accept a long-term moratorium on its enrichment programme in exchange for a face-saving package of inducements. More pessimistic observers have postulated that the talks are part of a duplicitous Iranian plan designed to buy them time while they secretly continue to pursue their nuclear aspirations or until Tehran judges that it is in a strong enough position to walk away from the talks and withstand whatever action the Security Council can muster. Most likely, Tehran will not make this fundamental decision until after its June presidential elections and inaugura-tion of a new government in the autumn puts its domestic house in order.

American antagonism

As Iran's new neighbour in the region – to the north, south and west – the United States is closely monitoring Iran's every move. American interests in both Iraq and Afghanistan are now intertwined with those of Iran. Both countries have a stake in the security and stability of the region and in securing the triumph of their national interests. For the Bush administration, having witnessed groundbreaking elections in Iraq and Afghanistan, the top priority is to ensure that the campaign in the 'war on terror' does not end in vain. The administration has been unrelenting in seeking to transform the tragedy and alarm of 11 September into an opportunity for change in the region. In Washington, Iran is seen as a major barrier to success in this effort. Having tactically diversified its contacts and interests in Iraq and Afghanistan, Iran is strategically positioned to protect its ambitions while subverting those of the United States. The 'Great Satan' may have done Iran a favour by displacing its two most menacing neighbours; however, relations between Iran and the United States have yet to evolve beyond their 26-year pattern of hostile rhetoric and diplomatic spurning.

Substantially the same issues that animated bilateral relations in the 1970s and 1980s continue to colour the respective Iranian and American mindsets. Iran feels threatened by the active American encirclement of the Middle East. The United States not only disapproves of the theocratic nature of the Iranian regime, but also takes issue with Iran's sponsorship of terrorism, pursuit of WMD, and destabilising interference in Israeli–Palestinian affairs. The clerics ultimately seek respect and legitimacy, and favourable resolution on issues of frozen assets and sanctions. The United States wants absolute Iranian renunciation of its WMD programme, full participation in the 'war on terror' and an end to interference in the peace process. To achieve this end, the Bush administration has refused any direct discussion or participation in the ongoing nuclear diplomacy, while agreeing to contribute modest American incentives to support European diplomacy. In addition, said Bush, 'we are a party to the talks or a party to the process as a result of being a member of the IAEA. In other words, we're on the IAEA board with some 30-odd nations. So we've been very much involved with working with the Iranians and the world to achieve a goal that we share with the Europeans and that is for Iran not to develop a nuclear weapon.'

The rhetoric from Washington revolves around the hope of rebuking – and ultimately pressuring – Iran through the legal framework of the Security Council. With a resolution of condemnation, the Bush administration hopes that political isolation and economic sanctions could force Iran to forego its nuclear-weapon options. Ultimately, UN Security Council actions could create the political and legal basis for the United States to emulate the 1981 Osirak reactor bombing in Iraq and try to delay Iran's nuclear programme militarily. Military experts, however, have noted that Iran's dispersal and concealment of its nuclear assets make precision strikes a dubious proposition, and that with the United States over-extended in Iraq and with little allied support, a robust ground campaign could be operationally and diplomatically disastrous. The Islamic government has placed its nuclear facilities in or near urban and highly populated areas and made them difficult to identify. Robust military action would also galvanise anti-American opinion throughout the region, and perhaps the world. If Washington's long-term ambition for Iran were forcing some form of regime change, such an attack could have the perverse consequence of reinforcing the revolutionary anti-American standing of the clerical elite by intensifying Iranian nationalism.

Against this backdrop, an article by Seymour Hersh in *The New Yorker* magazine claimed that the US government was conducting covert operations in Iran. After much speculation on the validity of this claim, confirmation that surveillance drones were being flown over Iran to gather more information on Iran's nuclear-weapon programme as well as to collect information on the country's defence capabilities was released. While the Iranian government has publicly displayed its *Shahab*-3 missile, which has a 1,500-kilometre range, precise details on the country's military resources remain vague. The Bush administration's Iran policy is still under review. Repeatedly, with a preface of hostile rhetoric, Bush himself, Secretary of State Rice and Secretary of Defense Donald Rumsfeld have maintained that while an attack on Iran is not imminent, the option remains available. While prospects of an American attack remain slim in the near term, an Israeli one is also possible if remote. Israel would face the same logistical problems as the United States, needing to hit at least three sites to ensure the destruction of Iran's nuclear-weapon capability – rather than just the one required to take out Iraq's capability in 1981. Further, the strategic ramifications of such a strike would be profound, as Iran would could well respond with its conventional *Shahab*-3 missiles and non-conventionally through Hizbullah or Palestinian armed groups.

Iran has unapologetically supported Hamas, Palestinian Islamic Jihad, and the Popular Front for the Liberation of Palestine–General Command, as well as Hizbullah, with funding, safe haven, training and weapons. Iran chastised the late Palestinian Authority (PA) President Yasser Arafat for his negotiations with the Israelis, but then became a direct player in the Israeli–Palestinian conflict by attempting to transfer arms via the ship *Karine-A* to the PA in December 2001, after the second intifada began. It is worth remembering that this move on Iran's part induced the Bush administration to abandon pre-11 September notions of exploring a rapprochement with Iran in favour of isolating and pressuring Iran as a member of the 'axis of evil'. Neither the conservative clerical establishment nor even the reformist government considers the Palestinian armed groups or Hizbullah terrorists, and both elements believe that Iran – as the world's standard-bearer for political Islam – is justified in underwriting armed opposition (by the 'forces of national liberation') to the state of Israel. Recent developments stemming from the death of

Arafat in December 2004, however, hold out new hope for the substantial amelioration of the Israeli–Palestinian dispute.

Mahmoud Abbas, the new president of the Palestinian Authority, has taken
sufficient action against armed factions to bring Israeli Prime Minister Ariel Sharon
gingerly back into negotiations on the implementation of the 'road map' to a
Palestinian state, and Washington has signalled proactive involvement in peace-
brokering efforts. Such efforts could well bear fruit over the next two or three years.
If they also yield a competent secular Palestinian government that could coercively
control armed factions (Islamist and otherwise) and provide for the population's
welfare, those factions would find it difficult to gain the operational latitude and
political traction needed to maintain terrorist operations at the strategic level.
Without viable terrorist proxies, Iran would have no realistic opportunity to continue
effective sponsorship. Its motivations and justifications for doing so – to wit, the
defence of oppressed fellow Muslims – would also be reduced. Furthermore, Syria
– Hizbullah's landlord in Lebanon and Israel's arch-enemy – has been Iran's partner
in sponsoring terrorism in the Middle East. Damascus's strategic options against
Israel have dwindled with the demise of Saddam Hussein (who provided Syria
with cheap oil and ready markets) and pressure from the United States and France
for it to quit Lebanon, and those options would be further curtailed by substantially
lower tensions between Israel and the Palestinians. By extension, this development
would limit Iran's freedom of action in the Middle East.

In the light of world scrutiny over its nuclear programme, Iran has moderated
its public position with regard to Israel. Iran naturally condemned the murder of
Hamas leader Sheikh Ahmad Yassin in 2004, but since the death of Yasser Arafat
has been remarkably coy and quiet as to the renewal of the peace process. Although
many ideological conservatives in Iran disapprove of such a development, as the
anti-Israel stance is among the principal foreign policy pillars of the revolution, Iran
could continue to temper its vocal opposition to Israel as a realpolitik calculation.
Despite a more moderate tone from Tehran, Israel is most actively threatened by
Iran's nuclear posturing. Israeli Prime Minister Ariel Sharon's government would
actively support destroying or stalling Iran's nuclear programme. Israeli officials
also accuse Hizbullah, acting on behalf of Iran, of seeking to recruit Palestinian
suicide bombers to undermine the peace process.

In the wake of former Lebanese Prime Minister Rafik Hariri's murder on
14 February 2005, Iran has publicly reaffirmed its traditional alliance with the
Ba'athist regime in Syria. Dramatic ideological differences between the two regimes
notwithstanding, Syria was the only regional country that sided with Iran during
its eight-year war against Iraq. Together they have synergistically increased their
leverage in neighbouring Lebanon. Most Lebanese as well as most Western officials
believe that Damascus had a hand in Hariri's murder. Such accusations come at a
time when the UN (through Security Council Resolution 1559), the United States

(by way of the Syrian Accountability Act) and France are trying to force Syria into releasing its political grip on Lebanon and withdrawing its extensive intelligence network there along with its 14,000 troops. With Iran facing a similar barrage of coercive international diplomacy, the February 2005 renewal of the Syrian–Iranian mutual defence pact can be viewed as an act of defiance by both regimes, but perhaps one that is more symbolic than substantive. In March 2005, Damascus agreed to a full withdrawal from Lebanon and began the process. Although Hizbullah itself remains a powerful political and military force in Lebanon, without Syria's overall political control of the country, Iran's freedom to support the group would be significantly curtailed.

Bush's re-election was ironically well received among Iran's clerical elite. Historically, the clerical regime has been more comfortable with Republican administrations. Democrats, while perhaps more moderate on their Iran policy, are considered duplicitous. With memories of Carter and Clinton, the mullahs have not reconciled the offers of goodwill from Clinton-era Secretary of State Madeleine Albright with the more ominous package of economic sanctions. Republicans have a reputation for being candid and direct in intentions and actions. It was during the Reagan administration that, despite a pronounced loathing for the Iranian theocracy, the administration negotiated the arms-for-hostages deal. Moreover, 'axis of evil' rhetoric aside, the clerics prefer the conviction of the current Bush administration over Democrats perceived to be slippery and indecisive. But this attitude turns mainly on the desirability to religious ideologues of a stark foil and few subtle alternatives, for the Bush administration remains inclined to pressure Tehran.

In its report issued in summer 2004, the 9/11 Commission concluded that Iran continues to be a state sponsor of terror, with some tactical contacts with al-Qaeda. Iran, however, is largely Shi'ite and al-Qaeda is dominated by Wahhabi Sunni Muslims, and this schism appears to have precluded any ideological integration or planning-level collaboration. The rise of the Taliban in Afghanistan as a regional strategic rival in 1996, and al-Qaeda's union with the Taliban, sharpened differences between Iran and al-Qaeda further still. But since the liberation of Afghanistan in late 2001, many al-Qaeda members fleeing Afghanistan have been captured in Iran, which has refused to extradite these suspects to the United States but instead returned a number to their country of origin. The Iranians have admitted to a degree of this activity – much of which may have been grounded in mercenary or intelligence-recruitment motivations – while denying as yet unproven allegations of a planning link between Iran based al-Qaeda members and the Riyadh bombing in May 2003. The Iranians may also have considered al-Qaeda members in hand as bargaining chips vis-à-vis the United States with respect to its nuclear programme. But while suspicions of Iran's relationship with al-Qaeda remain no more than that, Iranian and American rhetoric and miscommunication continues to impede any progress on the diplomatic front.

Iraq intricacies

The veiled nature of Iranian policies has been confusing to Washington. Yet Iran's behaviour in Afghanistan and Iraq is scarcely surprising given its geopolitical interests in both countries. Moreover, these interests are not only predicated on current economic and political concerns, but also ancestral and religious ones. Shi'ites constitute a majority in both countries. Iranian and Iraqi Shi'ites share shrines, the two countries have historically engaged in trade and commerce, and, most recently, now-dominant Iraqi Shi'ite groups, such as al-Daawa and the Supreme Council for the Islamic Revolution in Iraq, spent years of exile in Iran. Ayatollah Ali Sistani, the most powerful Shi'ite cleric in Iraq, is of Iranian origin, born in the city of Mashad; in turn, Iran's judiciary chief, Ayatollah Mahmoud Hashemi Shahroudi, was born in Najaf, Iraq.

Nevertheless, the Iraq War has been a mixed blessing for Tehran. Saddam Hussein waged a brutal war against Iran from 1980–88. His ouster removed a deep and painful thorn from Iran's side, and liberated Iranian Shi'ites' religious brethren – the 65% Iraqi Shi'ite majority that Saddam had brutally repressed. Yet Tehran remains uncomfortable with American occupying forces in Afghanistan as well as Iraq, on its eastern and western flanks. Moreover, in Iraq, a new and powerful source of Shi'ite religious authority beyond Tehran's control could arise and test the already vulnerable doctrinal basis – *velayat-e faqih* – of a regime founded on a narrow interpretation of Shi'ite thought. Iraqi Shi'ites' traditional opposition to the mixing of religion and politics has intellectually reinforced Iranian reformists who question the primacy of religiously based political authority in Iran. More broadly, the rise of the very nationalistic Iraqi Arab Shi'ites – made more salient by 30 January 2005 elections that proceeded more smoothly than expected – may challenge Iran's international Shi'ite supremacy. Finally, the prospect of a strong US-backed Iraqi government makes Tehran very nervous, especially if Baghdad were to allow the United States to retain military bases in Iraq.

Iran, then, could have substantial motivation to (1) make sure that Iraqi Shi'ites, while maintaining control of the country in accordance with their majority, do not become so strong or unified a moderate, nationalistic force as to rival Iran, and (2) drive a wedge between the US and Iraqi governments. But Iran does not appear, in general, to have acted on these motivations by unleashing terrorism. According to a former Iranian intelligence officer, the special operations directorate (known as the Quds Force) within the Revolutionary Guard did arrange the infiltration of hundreds of operatives who used charities and journalists in Iraqi cities as cover, and had engineered the assassination of Ayatollah Muhammad Bakr al-Hakim, a moderate and popular Shi'ite cleric, in August 2003. There are considerable doubts about this claim, as other sources indicate that the firebrand cleric Muqtada al-Sadr was solely responsible. Still, a substantial clandestine infrastructure in Iraq supposedly includes 2,700 safe houses in Baghdad alone. In May 2003, a member of Iran's powerful 12-cleric Council of Guardians also exhorted Iraqis to stage suicide attacks against coalition forces, following the Palestinian model. Yet the US command in Baghdad indicated that al-Sadr's militia, which led the Shi'ite uprising against coalition forces in April 2004, was not backed by Iran. As of May 2004, there were only 14 Iranians in coalition custody.

More generally, the degree of international – and especially American – scrutiny that Iran is now under on account of its nuclear and ballistic missile programmes tends to militate against terrorist agitation in Iraq. Iran was the only country other than the United States to extend decisive support to the Iraqi elections in January 2005. Issues of WMD and terrorism have prevented significant Iranian–American cooperation over their mutual interests. Fear that Iraqi Shi'ites hope to replicate the Iranian theocracy skew American calculations. But Ayatollah Sistani has rejected the Iranian model of *vilayat-e-faqih*, or guardianship of the jurisconsult, in favour of a more pluralistic system. As Iran's de facto neighbour in the region, the United States appears well advised to find a more productive means of dealing with the regime in Tehran in order to further its democratic agenda in Iraq.

Less substance, similar form

Support for what most Western officials regard as terrorist organisations – such as Hizbullah and the Palestinian armed factions – is ingrained in Iran's national creed. Article 3 of the Iranian constitution provides that the country's foreign policy must be premised on 'Islamic criteria, fraternal commitment to all Muslims, and unsparing support to the freedom fighters of the world'. In addition, Article 154 proclaims Iran's support for 'the rightful struggle of the oppressed people against their oppressors anywhere in the world'. The current emphasis on asymmetric warfare in Iranian military doctrine may also indicate a continuing inclination to sponsor terrorism. The reformist government's desire for international political legitimacy and a more pragmatic tilt on the part of some members of the clerical establishment have tempered Iranian provocations, and positive developments in the Israeli–Palestinian peace process could shrink Iran's pretexts and opportunities for supporting Palestinian militants and Hizbullah in operations against Israel.

Geopolitical considerations, however, have the potential to induce Tehran to destabilise Iraq through terrorism – though it has not yet attempted to do so. Close and critical international attention to Iran's nuclear and missile programmes cuts against Iranian risk-taking through terrorist sponsorship. But if American threats of military intervention to pre-empt or prevent an Iranian nuclear-weapon capability become more pronounced and credible, this constraining influence could be offset. Iran could then regard US military overstretch in Iraq as a factor inhibiting a major military operation against Iran; one way of taxing the US military in Iraq would be to encourage and support rebellion by Shi'ite factions against the Iraqi government or direct attacks against US forces. But such a course would be a dangerous and improbable one for Iran, as it would risk antagonising rather than discouraging Washington.

Any façade of accountability will not be a prime regime concern in the latter part of 2005, as issues of foreign affairs will preclude any real political or economic change. Although the regime could mitigate popular discontent with economic salves, it is more likely to sensationalise and condemn outside attacks on its record as a proliferator and sponsor of terrorism to preserve national solidarity and its own security. Thus, the upcoming presidential election could impact Iran's responsiveness to the EU and the United States. The Bush administration will most likely await the outcome of the election before formalising an Iran policy. While it is assumed that a conservative monopoly of all of the country's political institutions is inevitable, who the winning candidate will be could still dramatically influence Iran's international trajectory. Rafsanjani's return to popular politics could strike a necessary balance between pragmatic and factional orientations as his more moderate liberalisation plans could assuage both domestic and international constituencies. But the election of a more malleable president could continue to enhance the power of traditional revolutionary ideologues. Such a development could, but need not, move Iran towards a strategic confrontation with the United States. Khatami, the reformist, has promised that 'Iran will turn into a burning hell for aggressors', while Rafsanjani, the more conservative pragmatist, has invited the United States to 'enter through the gates of peace'. Regardless of who becomes president, then, an approach to foreign policy that employs confusion, duplicity and a kind of soft brinkmanship appears likely to continue.

Saudi Arabia's Evolutionary Change

Because the American campaign to transform Iraq into a westward-leaning beacon of democracy was not assured in early 2005, Saudi Arabia adjusted its internal and regional policies, to better reflect perceptions of threat emanating from an increasingly Shi'ite-led Baghdad. Riyadh feared a revival of Shi'ite nationalism in Iraq, backed by Iran, that could potentially inspire (or incite) Saudi Arabia's own marginalised Shi'ite minority to challenge Sunni domination of the country. Faced with such an epoch-making prospect, Saudi leaders adopted time-tested mechanisms to cushion political blows to their carefully constructed and legitimising politico-religious alliance. Riyadh's actions were, by and large, well received by Saudis deeply concerned with a wave of terrorist acts within the kingdom – whether the work of al-Qaeda itself or simply inspired by Osama bin Laden – that jeopardised the relative tranquillity that most enjoyed. Remarkably, support for the Al Saud family reached new heights, as wary citizens approved of Riyadh's strong-fisted – even brutal – counter-terrorism measures. The fact remained that the United States and Saudi Arabia still had to adjust their relationship to defend it against bin Laden's post-11 September ('9/11') designs.

After 11 September, leading American foreign-policy analysts deemed unsustainable the basic compact forged by Franklin D. Roosevelt and Abdulaziz bin Abdulrahman Al Saud on 14 February 1945, which defined US–Saudi ties. The 60-year partnership was forged on the premise that Washington would protect Riyadh's oil resources in exchange for full access at reasonable prices. Although both countries celebrated the compact's 60th anniversary, public opinion in each state was dominated by suspicion of the other, prompting an official American government review of the relationship in early 2005. Such a reassessment notwithstanding, the Bush administration generally sought to justify its association with an autocratic regime, where the lack of democracy was blamed in part for breeding anti-Western (especially anti-American) extremism.

US Ambassador James Oberwetter, a Texan with close ties to the Bush family, acknowledged that both sides were re-examining the relationship in the post-9/11 environment. Reportedly, the newly appointed Oberwetter persuaded former Secretary of State Colin Powell of the value of such a re-examination, after Oberwetter's first meeting with Prince Saud al-Faisal, the foreign minister, who told him openly the relationship was drifting. The foreign minister emphasised that Riyadh was gravely worried about American interpretations of Saudi motives. Beyond political differences over the Arab–Israeli conflict as well as the war in Iraq, he noted the sustained campaign of Saudi demonisation under way in American circles as the primary reason for the putative drift.

Prince Saud had a point. Saudi observers in the US identified the extreme press coverage that purported to expose intrinsic socio-religious flaws as a source of tension between the two countries. Summary journalistic assessments, as well as skewed academic analyses, all concluded that something was terribly wrong in and about Saudi Arabia. One commentator focused on 'hatred' (to decipher how Saudi Arabia apparently sustained global terrorism), while another reached the conclusion that Washington had sold its soul for Saudi crude (in effect, 'sleeping with the devil'). Yet another perceived the ruling Al Saud family's extensive assistance and relief work in several Muslim countries as 'two faces of Islam' with a clear suggestion that Riyadh constituted the deformed and evil side. The respected New York-based Freedom House joined in the debate, accusing the Saudi government of using mosques and cultural centres in the United States to spread intolerance for non-Muslims. Both governments agreed, however, that two fundamental issues were key to US–Saudi relations: terrorism in all its facets, and regional security affairs in the aftermath of the war in Iraq. The latter issue was especially problematic because it pitted several neighbouring Gulf Cooperation Council member states against Saudi Arabia and, even worse, led to a redeployment of significant American military equipment and personnel from the kingdom to Qatar and Kuwait.

Evolving fundamentals of the US–Saudi relationship

On 29 July 2003, the Bush administration refused to declassify a 28-page redacted section of a congressional report about the Saudi government's alleged role in financing the 9/11 hijackings. Prince Saud flew to Washington to ask the president of the United States to release the section in question. He declared that the speculation was 'an outrage to any sense of fairness' and that the secrecy was causing Saudi Arabia to be 'wrongfully and morbidly accused of complicity in the tragic terrorist attacks'. The Saudi diplomat argued that public accusations was 'based on misguided speculation ... born of poorly disguised malicious intent' and that his country was being 'indicted by insinuation' without an ability to reply to 'blank pages'. The congressional report may well have implied Saudi complicity in financing certain individuals or groups, but the equally authoritative National Commission on Terrorist Attacks Upon the United States (the so-called '9/11 Commission') concluded that there was no evidence that the Saudi government had any participation in, or in any way funded, the attacks, or for that matter provided al-Qaeda with financial assistance. Nevertheless, a majority of Americans continued to believe the exact opposite.

It was difficult to ascertain whether Riyadh's strong response after the 12 May 2003 Riyadh bombings, when 35 people, mainly Saudis, were killed, changed American views that the Al Saud were genuinely mobilised to face their foes. The violence continued with another massive bomb on 8 November 2003 that killed 17 expatriate workers, mostly Arabs, and a bomb targeting an Interior Ministry building on 21 April 2004. Six foreign workers were killed on 1 May 2004 in Yanbu, and 22 were gunned down at the Oasis compound in al-Khobar on 29 May. In quick succession, on 8 and 12 June, unidentified gunmen shot two American citizens in Riyadh, followed, on 18 June, with the beheading of Paul Johnson, an American oil engineer taken hostage three days earlier. Authorities fatally wounded Abdulaziz al-Muqrin, al-Qaeda's Saudi leader and one of the most wanted Saudis, and accused him of carrying out that dastardly act. Non-Americans were also targeted throughout the year. On 6 June, a BBC news team was attacked in Riyadh, killing cameraman Simon Cumbers and seriously wounding correspondent Frank Gardner. On 3 August, an Irish citizen was shot dead in his Riyadh office, and on 15 September a Briton was murdered at a Riyadh shopping mall. In Jeddah, Laurent Barbot, a French national working for the electronics firm Thales, was killed on 26 September. Dozens of Indian and Pakistani workers died in various assaults that were swiftly mounted by security forces eager to nab as many terrorists as possible. On 18 October, a top-ranking militant, Abdulmajid bin Muhammad Abdullah al-Manaiah, was among three insurgents killed in a spectacular Riyadh shoot-out. On 6 December 2004, a bomb attack on the US Consulate in Jeddah resulted in the death of five people, all expatriate workers. Credit for most of these attacks was claimed by a group styled 'al-Qaeda in the Arabian Peninsula', suggesting a close link between al-Qaeda's core leadership and tending to confirm bin Laden's re-sharpened focus on his homeland.

The attacks and counter-attacks demonstrated that Riyadh was faced with a multi-pronged challenge, fusing domestic, regional and international crises into a single threat against the Al Saud ruling family. Although Riyadh adopted an iron-fisted policy towards its opponents, outside – especially American – pressure forced the monarchy to address financing and educational dimensions of putative challenges. To that end, Saudi Arabia adopted new fiscal regulations to stem the funding of terrorist organisations and, in an epoch-making initiative, decided to re-educate members of the clergy. Even though a report by the Financial Action Task Force (FATF), an intergovernmental body including the G8 member-states, concluded that the kingdom's laws and regulations satisfied all current needs to combat illegal transfers, additional mechanisms were adopted to limit financial transfers for thousands of Saudis. Various charities were muzzled, severely curtailing their abilities to raise and distribute funds, as collection plates were removed from all public venues. Still, rounding up suspect individuals who engaged in such transactions was quite limited, due to lack of details. Riyadh froze bank accounts or arrested criminals only when specific suspects were identified. This practice, though intended in part to strengthen the Saudis' intelligence networks, was not always satisfactory to Washington, which demanded that something be done about all suspects with as little delay as possible and without close regard to any legal rights.

Success came as American and Saudi authorities clamped down the charity organisations. In 2004, al-Haramain was shut down after evidence was collected regarding branch activities supporting al-Qaeda in Bosnia, Albania, Chechnya and East Africa. Although US officials were ready to share intelligence details with the Saudis, some – especially those at lower working levels at the Treasury Department – were reluctant to extend full cooperation. Although they vindicated Riyadh, the commissioners on the 9/11 panel expressed frustration that Saudi officials allegedly failed to come to grips with the Faustian bargain they allegedly entered into with the religious community. Several concluded that the Al Saud 'ceded whole parts of their government to religious elements' that presumably fomented or at least acquiesced in extremist positions. US wariness notwithstanding, joint operations resulted in the apprehension of several key culprits. Juan C. Zarate, the US Treasury assistant secretary for terrorist financing and financial crimes, in congressional testimony on 30 September 2004 revealed that 'Saudi millionaires Yasin al-Qadi and Wa`el Hamza Julaidan, as well as the terrorist financing facilitator known as Swift Sword' were all arrested and their assets frozen. Together, the two governments identified 13 al-Haramain Islamic Foundation branches that, in turn, were placed under surveillance or completely shut down. Concrete Saudi steps, including enhanced customer identification requirements, Saudi rial-only accounts, restrictions on deposits and withdrawals, prohibitions on cash transactions from charitable accounts and on ATM/credit card links to such accounts and, perhaps most importantly, proscriptions against international transfers from charitable accounts, were all taken in full coop-eration with US Treasury officials. In fact, the Riyadh-based US-Saudi Joint Terrorist Financing Task Force (JTFFT) established a close agent-to-agent working relation-ship that, at least since autumn 2003, has permitted Federal Bureau of Investigation (FBI) and Internal Revenue Service (IRS) investigators unprecedented access to Saudi bank accounts, suspects and witnesses as well as other highly sensitive infor-mation. Given this unparalleled level of cooperation, few Saudi bank records have escaped close US scrutiny between late 2003 and the present – a circumstance that is, in and of itself, unique among Muslim nations.

Indigenous Saudi counter-terrorism efforts

In late 2003, Saudi heir apparent Crown Prince Abdullah bin Abdulaziz Al Saud ordered a sustained crackdown on known Saudi charities to significantly reduce unmonitored donations, a portion of which allegedly lubricated shadowy terrorist organisations. Simultaneously, police units successfully penetrated various Islamist cells, leading Interior Minister Naif bin Abdulaziz Al Saud to publish – on 6 December 2003 – a list of 26 most-wanted terrorist suspects. The counter-terrorism campaign picked up momentum when the Ministry of Education authorised a complete revi-sion of several textbooks, excising egregious or fanatical interpretations of Muslim scriptures. Equally important, and much noticed by observers, were various official commentaries that denounced all acts of terrorism. Shaikh Saud Al-Shiraim, the imam of the Mecca Grand Mosque, declared on 9 July 2004 that the killing and terrorising of innocent victims 'must never be justified but confronted and stopped by all available means'. Earlier, another imam at the Mecca Grand Mosque, Shaikh Abdul Rahman Al-Sudais, cautioned his followers not to heed 'misleading edicts that promote extremism … [because] nobody will approve such horrible crimes'. On 22 April 2004, Shaikh Abdulaziz Al-Shaikh, the grand mufti and chairman of the Council of Senior Religious Scholars, issued his strongest warning yet: 'it is forbidden to cover up for such sinful people [terrorists] and whoever does so, will be their partner in the crime … It is also forbidden to justify the acts of these crimi-nals … You have to be vigilant and have strong will in defending the religion and the Muslim country against these people.'

Riyadh's full-fledged public relations campaign did not abate throughout the year. In early December 2004, Saudi television aired candid interviews with the parents of several jihadists, who insisted that their children had fallen prey to 'a deviant death cult' (i.e., al-Qaeda) and that most were innocent victims. Interior Minister Naif insisted that no mercy could be shown to those that challenged internal stability. He declared that more than 700 arrests were made since 2003, including the June 2004 killing of al-Muqrin, followed a few months later by the slaying of his successor Saleh al-Oufi. To further clarify his long-term intentions, Naif persuaded senior religious figures to accept a systematic re-education within the ranks. An estimated 1,500 clerics were hauled off to rehabilitation camp for reorientation towards greater tolerance, while leading clerics were persuaded to recant earlier pronouncements deemed libellous and erroneous.

Saudi authorities pledged to uproot al-Qaeda's structure in the kingdom at their February 2005 'Counter Terrorism International Conference'. Crown Prince Abdullah called for the creation of an international anti-terrorism centre for quick information sharing but stressed that the war against terrorism could not be won unless the world addressed three other global crimes that fed terrorism: arms smuggling, drug trafficking and money laundering. His call received regional backing, but a new UN-based counter-terrorism body was not the preferred Western – especially not the preferred American – solution.

Stability of US–Saudi relations

While senior Saudi officials recognised that carefully nurtured alliances and measured assumptions were no longer enough to sustain a positive image of Saudi Arabia in the United States, Saudi efforts to win the favour of major Western powers fell short of what Crown Prince Abdullah or Foreign Minister Prince Saud al-Faisal sought to accomplish in 2004. In a remarkably frank address to the Council on Foreign Relations (CFR) in New York, Prince Saud lamented the loss of Saudi–American goodwill, pledging to 'stop the drift towards alienation and suspicion, and return to the mutual understanding and trust that defined our traditionally healthy relationship'. Vowing to restore broken ties, the foreign minister disassociated al-Qaeda's teachings from the Wahabi creed, distinguishing the organisation's primary objective – re-establishing a transnational Islamic caliphate – from Riyadh's own agenda. He reminded all that bin Laden called for the destruction of the Saudi state as currently constituted. More pointedly, Prince Saud provided a primer of Saudi history, from the ruling family's traditional antagonists from the Ikhwan in the 1920s to its modern equivalents. The foreign minister elaborated what a Saudi ultra-conservative was, what he presumably stood for, and how that was different from the vast majority of modern Saudi citizens eager to sign up in full to globalisation.

To buttress his claims, Prince Saud provided evidence of public support for the government in tackling terrorist attacks, illustrating how most Saudis loathed those who spread havoc and, paradoxically, how the religious establishment in the kingdom was 'proving to be the body most qualified to de-legitimise al-Qaeda's claims'. The foreign minister insisted that there was no 'quarrel' between Saudi Arabia and the United States, and called for the two countries 'to join forces … against the uncivilised, the criminal, and the unjust'. According to Robert Jordan, a former US ambassador to Saudi Arabia, 'Americans and Saudis [were now] sitting shoulder-to-shoulder in a secret location viewing intelligence [in] real time'. In fact, contrary to popular discourse, bilateral cooperation in the war on terrorism was closer than generally assumed. According to Ambassador J. Cofer Black, Saudi Arabia was 'a strong ally ... taking unprecedented steps to address an al-Qaeda menace'. Joint intelligence exchanges moved at a steady pace, institutional road-blocks notwithstanding.

The Saudis, then, had their share of grievances against the United States as well as vice-versa. Saudi leaders expressed their displeasure that few Americans were considering Saudi perspectives after a seven-decade friendship, and further lamented that Americans failed to back carefully crafted initiatives to help resolve the Arab–Israeli conflict as well as problems in Iraq. The Saudi perception is that Crown Prince Abdullah expended substantial political capital to gain League of Arab States backing at the 2002 Beirut Summit to accept a final peace settlement in exchange for full Israeli withdrawal to the 1967 borders, only to be dismissed by both Washington and Jerusalem. Likewise, in July 2004, Washington swiftly dismissed a Riyadh proposal for an all-Islamic peacekeeping operation for Iraq. (The Arab League's conditions for its deployment, however, rather unrealistically specified that the force would replace American troops and operate under UN cover. It was also unclear how many Arab countries were willing to make signifi-cant operational commitments.)

Questions about long-term access to Saudi oil were first raised in the mid-1990s but were significantly exaggerated after 2001. Leading American lawmakers preferred to nurture alternative sources, especially from Canada and Venezuela, ostensibly to end import dependence. The canard that Saudis would once again 'blackmail' the United States – as they were perceived to have done in 1973 – resurfaced in American rhetoric from some quarters. Nevertheless, actual imports from Saudi Arabia into the United States began to decline in late 2002, and the trend continued through 2003 and into 2004. In 2003, the United States imported an average of 1,726,000 barrels of oil per day (b/d) from Saudi Arabia, or roughly 15% of its daily imports. A year later, Canada and Mexico surpassed it (with 1.563m and 1.552m b/d) although Saudi Arabia ranked third with 1.449m bpd (or about 12% of daily imports). The average 1.5m b/d sold to the United States represented a significant portion of Saudi daily production, which averaged 8.4m b/d. Still, the US government's International Energy Outlook forecast that Saudi Arabia would produce 22.5m b/d by 2025, of which an undetermined percentage would be allocated for the North American market. Riyadh has generally been willing and ready to meet customer demands. What changed in recent years, however, was the Saudis' eagerness to offer American companies a discount to maintain their principal supplier role. In the past, Aramco, the Saudi state oil concern, considered it a wise business practice to offer various discounts to its preferred American partners, but it abandoned such schemes after 2002 due to increased competition in the highly competitive oil market.

Furthermore, in the 2004 open competition for Saudi gas exploration and development contracts, not a single US company won a contract. This commercial alienation, along with very limited American crude oil imports from Saudi Arabia in 2004, prompted Washington to try harder to maintain its energy alignment with Riyadh for the next few decades. In 2004, the US imported over 10m b/d, more than half its daily consumption. While Riyadh supplied an estimated 15% of total US imports, it was clearly understood by senior Energy Department officials that no other country could replace Saudi Arabia as a reliable source, especially as China, Japan and other Asian economies were poised to increase their own imports from the Gulf. The United Kingdom and Indonesia, once oil exporters, have now shifted into the net importer category, further straining global energy markets. Energy Department analysts forecast stiff competition for access to Saudi crude, a phenomenon that necessitated careful American manoeuvrings. Post-9/11 American suspicions of Muslim and Arab countries and their populations were likely to have strategic implications in rapidly evolving energy markets.

Finally, it is also worth noting that Saudi crude – relatively 'heavy' and hard to refine – has almost always sold at a discount from the West Texas Intermediate (WTI) benchmark prices reported in the media. WTI, a single grade sold on the futures market not available from Saudi Arabia, was not typical of what oil importing companies paid for crude. Therefore, actual import prices for Saudi crude were considerably less than publicised figures. If Saudi Arabia left such technical niceties to expert discussions in the past, the post-9/11 environment required that it present its case far better than ever before. Accordingly, in February 2005, Saudi Arabia announced that it planned to double the number of drilling rigs (to 70) it operated to explore and develop new oil and gas fields to meet growing world demand. Oil Minister Ali Naimi declared that the kingdom intended to lift its production capacity by another 2m b/d to 12.5m b/d by 2010. Naimi did not rule out a 15m b/d level should demand warrant it. To meet such objectives as it shifted strategy, Riyadh supplemented by an additional $500m dollars its exploration and development budget, raising it to $2.7bn per year, even though the kingdom spends a mere 90 cents to find and develop a barrel of oil compared with $6 for Western competitors. These initiatives were heavily publicised to alert world opinion to the kingdom's intrinsic value and, presumably, to enhance awareness that internal stability in the kingdom was a prerequisite to steady access to Saudi crude at reasonable prices and that the complex tensions across Saudi society therefore needed to be taken into account in assessing the kingdom's diplomatic positions.

Political reforms

The Bush administration seemed to take these factors on board: the US–Saudi relationship, despite sensationalistically adverse publicity in the United States, has stabilised since the Iraq intervention in March 2003. Some American observers saw this development as evidence that Washington – for the sake of cheap oil – was essentially turning a blind eye to what went on inside Saudi Arabia's borders, even though radical Islamist activity and attitudes appeared to fuel hatred towards the West and to support global jihadism. This was a misapprehension. Rather, the Bush administration came to recognise that the unique cross-cutting constituencies from which the Al Saud derives legitimacy make the imposition of fast, revolutionary change a dangerously destabilising proposition. The better course is to consolidate counter-terrorism cooperation and gently urge gradual political reform that does not push the envelope of regime security in a way that could actually benefit Islamists. To be sure, the oil-for-security compact remained the foundation of the US–Saudi relationship. But atop that foundation rested the two new pillars of counter-terrorism and internal reforms.

The war in Iraq sent shock waves throughout the Gulf region but especially in Saudi Arabia because of the kingdom's custodianship of the two holy mosques in Mecca and Medina. Riyadh remained exquisitely conscious of its responsibilities to the Muslim world but especially towards its Sunni adherents. Yet the recognition of the need for political reforms dawned after the 1979 Mecca Grand Mosque takeover. The Al Saud realised then that the cocoon ensuring their security was challenged at the very core. Over a short period of time, senior Al Saud officials commissioned studies to identify what ailed the kingdom and how best to address internal grievances. In March 1992, Saudi Arabia promulgated its 'Basic Law of Government' to establish, among other things, a representative consultative council. Although the Majlis al-Shurah experimented with policy debates, consultation and consensus – the two bases for public participation – did not take hold among the ultra-conservative ruling family. Rather, public discourse took on a new dimension – in the form of the petition – which redefined how Saudis accessed authority.

A slew of rather sophisticated supplications, addressed to the monarch and the heir apparent, became both frequent and public. Since early 2003, prominent Saudi reformers, led by Abdullah al-Hamed, argued that the best way to counter the spread of Muslim extremist thoughts was to transform the kingdom into a constitutional monarchy. Al-Hamed, along with Matruk al-Faleh and Ali al-Diminni, as well as with 13 other activists were promptly arrested in March 2004, although only the three named individuals were still in custody in early 2005 awaiting trial. Remarkably, Saudi reformists adopted a highly circumspect approach – bordering on the reverential – towards the ruling family. Although the substance of their demands was nothing short of revolutionary – challenging the ruler's absolute power – Crown Prince Abdullah took them seriously enough to meet with leading petition signatories, and authorised national dialogues as a partial rejoinder. In December 2003, June 2004 and September 2004, national dialogue rounds were held to discuss sensitive and controversial questions about Saudi governance. Saudis from all walks of life debated religious differences, educational concerns, the causes of extremism, gender matters and municipal elections.

The 13–15 June 2004 National Dialogue on Women held in Medina – the city, historically paramount in Islam, that first took in the prophet Muhammad as a political refugee – was a remarkable one in the conservative context of Saudi politics. When the monarch was urged to 'assign a body to study a public-transport system for women to facilitate mobility' most dismissed the exercise for its futility. But although the resulting effort failed to resolve a fundamental question – whether to accord women the right to drive – the mere fact that it was raised at all constituted a liberal advance. In the event, dialogue participants prepared 19 fresh recommendations on ways to improve women's lives in the kingdom. Subsequent to the dialogue, Hanadi Hindi, a Saudi woman who had trained for and been granted a pilot's license in Jordan, signed a contract with Prince Alwaleed bin Talal bin Abdulaziz in January 2005, joining his roster of private pilots and thereby implicitly challenging the country's ultra-conservative clerics.

Dialogue participants also debated divorce laws and the super-sensitive question of child custody. Al Saud leaders purposefully aimed to introduce real reforms in this area of sharia law after one of the kingdom's most popular television personalities, Rania al-Baz, had gained immense public sympathy for her custody travails. Al-Baz had been severely beaten by her husband, and invited photographers into her hospital room to record her injuries. She spoke out against her husband's abusive behaviour in public and filed for dissolution of her marriage, asking for custody of her children. She was granted a quick annulment and, surprisingly, won custody of her children even though under traditional Islamic law a father would be granted custody. Al-Baz also formed a support group to publicise abuse cases in the kingdom. Al Saud reformists were inspired to take some broader action, but understood that the creation of special courts to adjudicate similar cases, along with the establishment of additional women's only courts, would ruffle feathers. The dispensation that the Al Saud arrived at was that all judges would still be religious men in an interim period – by implication, until such time when women magistrates would be trained to assume such burdens. But the Al Saud signalled that they expected establishment figures entrusted with interpreting the law to become 'more aware' of women as human beings.

It remains an open question this dialogue will eventually empower the kingdom's growing female student population – an estimated 55% of all university attendees, whose life expectancy in 2004 was 70 – to assume new civic responsibilities. In 2005, Saudi women still made up only 6% of the workforce. Nevertheless, for the first time in Saudi history, women's rights and other formerly taboo social subjects were aired more or less openly. Even in the Arab and wider Muslim context, Saudi Arabia remains retrograde in the area of women's rights. A fifth of Algeria's Supreme Court judges are women, and a respectable number of judicial posts in North Africa and the Levant are held by women. Women in other Gulf States work as diplomats and ministers, serve in the armed forces and fill various high-level business posts. But women, with the increasing acquiescence of the Al Saud, are starting to empower themselves in the kingdom. Lubna Olayan, who manages a leading private industrial group, spoke – unveiled – at the 2004 Jeddah Economic Forum. Olayan was not the first Saudi to be 'seen' in public – Thoraya Obeid, the UN's family-planning agency head in New York, regularly appeared unveiled on television – but Olayan set a trend. In early 2005, women were regularly broadcasting the news on Al-Ikhbariyyah, Riyadh's round-the-clock satellite network. The Saudi foreign minister revealed in late February 2005 that the foreign ministry was about to hire its first class of women diplomats. These changes constituted real progress, even if their pace were painstakingly slow.

The national dialogues set the tone for additional political changes in Saudi Arabia. Al Saud leaders responded to public demands by accepting the idea of political participation, even if the process was not entirely transparent. Popular electoral processes were introduced at the municipal level. Elections occurred in Riyadh on 10 February 2005, followed by polls in the Eastern Province and several southern provinces in early March, and in the west and north in April. The Riyadh contest produced a healthy voter turnout of 75%. Candidates were permitted to advertise in newspapers and set up their own websites, to solicit votes in person, and to announce policy agendas publicly. Although election campaigns were limited to local issues (traffic congestion, building youth recreation centres, environmental concerns and public services), and half of the 178 municipal posts would eventually be appointed, a significant precedent was established, leading optimistic Saudi commentators to foresee national Majlis al-Shurah elections. That body, though still consultative, was slated to be increased from 120 to 150 members and steadily gained influence in proposing and challenging legislation.

The Al Saud's behaviour in 2004 reflected the conflicting political influences to which it had to cater. It authorised the important national dialogues, yet jailed a group of reformists in March 2004 without addressing any of their grievances. Reformists, rather than dissidents, called for the establishment of a constitutional monarchy that essentially supported Al Saud authority. Whether the balancing act was necessary to maintain public order was debatable, although Riyadh was certainly emboldened by numerous arrests of jihadist elements. In September 2004, the cabinet prohibited all state employees – including academics, who are subject to state regulations – from questioning policies enunciated by the Al Saud. This decree reinforced what appeared increasingly salient: that incremental reforms would be introduced, but only on a carefully laid out timetable of the government's choosing.

The Morocco conference

Saudi sensitivity to foreign pressure was visible in late 2004 when Riyadh expressed its views on the wave of reforms in the Greater Middle East. Foreign Minister Prince Saud dismissed popular American clash-of-civilisation theories, explaining to Colin Powell and other dignitaries gathered in Rabat, Morocco on 11 December that civilisations could not possibly compete since they complemented each other. The foreign minister underscored the fact that there was 'no argument between us either regarding the universality of the values of liberty, equality, and fraternity, or the Jeffersonian democratic ideals or Wilsonian principle of self-determination'. But he argued that their implementation should be advanced by inspiration rather than be 'driven by intimidation, fear or through the barrels of a gun'. Prince Saud acknowledged the need for political and economic changes even as he chided his Western, especially American, interlocutors for being less than fully honest in tackling issues that had lingered for decades – in particular, the Israeli–Palestinian conflict, which he said had fostered 'extremism, terrorism and hatred'. The corollary is that proactive American and European engagement in resolving that conflict – prospects for which are more hopeful in the wake of Arafat's death – are likely to prompt further Saudi co-operation and possibly accelerate political reform.

Regional leadership

The Saudi foreign minister's proclamation in Morocco came a month after a scathing critique that he levelled at fellow Gulf Cooperation Council (GCC) member states at the first International Institute for Strategic Studies (IISS) Gulf Security Conference (the Gulf Dialogue) in Manama, Bahrain. On 5 December 2004, Prince Saud stunned his IISS-invited listeners by declaring that it was 'alarming to see some members of the GCC enter into separate bilateral agreements with international powers, on both the security and economic spheres, as precedence over the need to act collectively'. The allusion was clearly to Bahrain, Kuwait and Qatar's military arrangements with the United States and more specifically to Bahrain's recently concluded Free Trade Agreement with the United States that the Saudi leadership saw as unacceptable. The excoriation was disingenuous given that the military relationships that he criticised essentially replaced the one that Saudi Arabia had enjoyed (to the consternation of bin Laden and his followers) with the United States for almost 15 years, and given that the United States' Afghanistan air campaign was prosecuted from the Al-Kharj facilities, and all civilian traffic at Hail Airport near the Iraqi border was cancelled in March 2003 to permit US Special Forces operations as well as search-and-rescue missions to be carried out without obstruction. But the message was plain and genuine: GCC states should put neighbours ahead of foreign governments to avoid socio-political strife (*fitna*) caused by religious schism on a regional scale.

This message reflected a substantial measure of geopolitical frustration and worry. Regional political reforms were closely tied to what the United States did in Iraq and the Gulf region, and repeated calls for an American withdrawal from Saudi Arabia, uttered in public to regain the Al Saud's battered legitimacy, picked up momentum in 2002 and 2003. Talal bin Abdulaziz, the maverick 'free prince' who was fully rehabilitated some years ago and was a confidant of Crown Prince Abdullah, articulated the view that Saudis would like to see American troops pack their bags. That senior Al Saud officials were willing to risk rupturing one of their core alliances surely reflected intense internal family pressures. Under Abdullah's leadership, the Al Saud muzzled domestic opposition – even issuing public 'lectures' to senior members of the ulama – and intended to establish hegemony among the smaller Arab Gulf States. At GCC gatherings, Abdullah reminded his fellow Arab rulers that the military draw-down of the United States from Saudi Arabia was significant, and that they should not offer convenient replacements lest Saudi Arabia's domestic problems spill over into their sheikhdoms. The Iraq intervention enabled the United States to redeploy its troops from Saudi Arabia to Qatar without appearing to have capitulated to bin Laden, and removed a major source of domestic political strain from the kingdom. But that intervention also led to the establishment of a second Shi'ite power, in addition to Iran, in the Gulf. Thus, Prince Saud's larger plea was for Sunni solidarity.

Indeed, GCC leaders as well as Saudi religious figures perceived the Shi'ite accession to wholesale majority authority in Baghdad following January 2005 parliamentary elections in Iraq with concern. While they all accepted the rise of a pluralistic neighbour, many anticipated problems between a victorious majority and the minority Arab Sunni population, especially if the insurgency were to metamorphose into a civil war. After the fall of Saddam Hussein, Saudi Arabia expanded much effort to support its Sunni Iraqi brethren. The Al Saud, along with all GCC ruling families, worried that potential Iraqi Shi'ite acts of revenge against their erstwhile Sunni oppressors could bleed into the Arabian Peninsula. Progressive Iraqi initiatives, including the drafting of a constitution with a bill of rights, provisions for freedom of press, religion and assembly, and the establishment of a federal state with large autonomous regions, were all unsettling to Saudi officials. Perhaps the most difficult question facing Riyadh was the Iraqi constitutional debate on whether Islam will be 'the' or 'a' source of law in Baghdad. In the latter case, Saudi Arabia might reject Iraq's democratic experiment, rally Muslim states to its theocratic cause and defend its religious rights to proclaim the inviolability of sharia law.

Equally important, given the inbred Wahabi hostility towards Shi'ite Muslims and their political marginalisation and repression within Saudi Arabia, Saudi clerics – and much of the Saudi public – are unlikely to alter their view that Iraqi (and other) Shi'ites are heathens. Instead, the Al Saud could come to perceive Iraqi Shi'ites as forming an axis with Washington that could divide the Muslim world.

The Saudi dilemma

In late 2004, Saudi Arabia claimed that it nearly defeated homegrown Islamist terrorists, but the December 2004 attack on the US Consulate in Jeddah cast some doubt on this proposition. To be sure, Riyadh unleashed its security forces with vengeance after the May 2003 bombings and, over a one-year period, arrested 19 out of 26 most-wanted men. But while the Jeddah deaths were all Saudis or non-US nationals, its bold nature presented a political dilemma for Riyadh. After thousands of arrests, there remained within the kingdom a reservoir of Islamist opponents of the regime that were determined to topple the monarchy.

In mid-February 2003, Osama bin Laden released a statement calling on Muslims to oppose 'allies of the devil' – an exhortation which, at least in the kingdom, reverberated at the highest levels of government. Saudi Arabia was caught on the horns of an acute dilemma: how to remain true to its character without jeopardising its very survival. The kingdom's senior religious cleric, Shaikh Abdulaziz Al Shaikh, called for unity at a time when its 'enemies' were undermining Islamic doctrine itself. This call was made in Mecca at the conclusion of the Hajj in a sermon televised worldwide. Riyadh released a few dissidents and assessed the implications of the Iraq War on the Al Saud. Parallel to its carefully monitored response to the Iraq War – allowing Saudis to vent their frustrations while cooperating with the Anglo-American war effort – Crown Prince Abdullah introduced systematic reforms, prompted the Council of Ulama not to remain idle, and sought to introduce sorely needed discipline within the GCC and the Middle East generally. The kingdom's steps in 2004 and early 2005 continued this political and geopolitical evolution.

Strategic position and domestic politics: more complex, but still stable

As to Saudi Arabia, the critical strategic question in early 2005 was whether negative popular perceptions in the United States, as well as rapidly deteriorating institutional contacts, could so shake the foundations of the strategic relationship between Saudi Arabia and the United States that the new pillars of the relationship – counter-terrorism and political reform – would crumble. The tentative answer appeared to be no. Saudi Arabia's importance as a reliable oil supplier and an irreplaceable swing producer remain paramount in the calculations of both Riyadh and Washington. That said, the effect of US intervention in Iraq has had complex ramifications for the kingdom. One on hand, it has relieved the Al Saud of the political (and indeed, religious) burden of US troops on Saudi soil and thus opened up opportunities for robust counter-terrorist measures and gradual political reform, the latter of which can probably proceed without unduly alienating either conservative or reformist elements. On the other, it has raised the spectre of a competing Shi'ite-ruled Arab state allied with the United States.

The Saudis faced a challenge from the Shi'ites right after the 1979 revolution in Iran, and they were able to repel it with the full backing of the United States. The Saudis have contained radical Wahabi Islamists through tribal politics and payoffs, but simultaneously facing down the Wahabis and Saudi Shi'ites backed by Iran and Iraq would probably be impossible without the thoroughgoing support of the United States. Thus, as US–Iranian relations have become increasingly strained over

Iran's nuclear programme, the Saudis have increased their counter-terrorism cooperation with the United States. The regime has also made it clear to the Americans that its own political security was in danger as internal pressures mounted, and this reality – along with the kingdom's durable importance as the world's largest oil producer – has prompted a quieter brand of US diplomacy with respect to political reform. Paradoxically, this dispensation – in conjunction with heightened popular domestic discomfort with jihadists who target Saudis as well as Westerners – has increased the kingdom's leeway for imposing reforms. Nevertheless, the potential for reform remains modest – limited by, among other things, the outside risk of radicalisation, which the process presumptively seeks to avoid.

Even if Iraqi oil and non-Gulf sources decrease US dependency on Saudi Arabia, Washington appears committed to thwarting any move by Iraqi Shi'ites to establish a theocracy. This attitude is reinforced by Washington's compelling need to serve Iraqi Kurdish and Sunni interests in pluralistic rule and to politically defuse the largely Sunni insurgency in Iraq, as well as the desirability of dampening Iranian threat perceptions of a rival Arab Shi'ite state and thus diminishing Tehran's inclination to move forward with nuclear-weapons and ballistic missile programmes. On balance, therefore, bilateral relations between the United States and Saudi Arabia are likely to remain stable, and the Al Saud's position for the time being appears secure.

Tipping Point in the Middle East

Towards the end of 2004, dramatic events transformed the Israeli–Palestinian struggle in the space of little over a month. The first was the death of Yasser Arafat in Paris on 11 November. He had been transferred to a French military hospital on 29 October after showing symptoms that were consistent with leukaemia, but which were never diagnosed as such. He died in a coma, amid a tempest of intrigue – spread by his wife Suha, among others – to the effect that he had been poisoned to make way for his political rivals. Although these rumours were fuelled for a short while by the inexplicable refusal of the French government to disclose the results of Arafat's autopsy, they soon subsided. The fact was, while the chairman of the Palestine Liberation Organisation (PLO) and president of the Palestinian Authority (PA) was admired, even revered, by many Palestinians, his departure was a relief to his own people. Over the four-year duration of the second intifada, over 3,000 Palestinians and roughly 1,000 Israelis had been killed. There was no desire to inquire deeply into the circumstances of his death; the impulse, rather, was to look to the future. Arafat had been both impetus and impediment to Palestinian independence.

Prelude

In November 2003, Israeli Prime Minister Ariel Sharon mooted the serious possibility of Israel's unilateral withdrawal from Gaza. The Israelis, however, judged that this would require – for political as well as operational reasons – aggressive and, from the Palestinians' standpoint, intrusive counter-terrorism operations since the PA had abjectly failed to halt terrorist violence. Israeli policies included the building of a security barrier (or fence), Israel Defense Forces (IDF) counter-terrorist actions in Gaza in preparation for withdrawal and targeted killings of the leaders of Hamas, the largest of the armed Palestinian militant groups. On 14 March 2004, a Hamas suicide attack in Ashdod port, launched from Gaza, killed 11 and wounded 20. *Operation Continuous Story*, targeting 'top figures from all terror organisations', began on 15 March in Gaza (focusing on Rafah refugee camp, in the area bordering Egypt). Over the course of three weeks, 37 Palestinians were killed and 80 wounded. Some 111 houses were demolished or badly damaged and 25 acres of land bulldozed. The idea was to create a buffer zone, so as to deny terrorists access to the Gaza neighbourhoods to which guns were smuggled from Egypt through underground tunnels, as well as to eliminate Hamas and other terrorist operatives.

During *Continuing Story*, on 22 March 2004, Israeli forces killed Hamas spiritual leader Sheikh Ahmed Yassin. He was replaced by Abd al-Aziz Rantisi. Sharon's plan to withdraw from Gaza was welcomed by US President George W. Bush at a meeting in Washington DC on 14 April. Rantisi, however, was eliminated in a targeted killing on 17 April 2004 in Gaza city. At that point, Israeli–Palestinian violence in Gaza spiked. Another major IDF operation, later named *Operation Rainbow*, began on 13 May. Another 43 Palestinians were killed and another 181 acres bulldozed; 90,000 people lost electric power and water service. *Operation Active Shield*, from 28 June until 5 August 2004, was officially intended to put an end to Hamas's *Qassam* rocket fire into Israel, but also aimed to further widen the buffer zone and suppress resistance pending withdrawal; the IDF killed 22 more Palestinians and cleared 975 more acres. Similarly motivated and designed operations were mounted in September and October.

A number of senior militant figures have been killed or wounded by the IDF since it began its policy of targeted killing. Yassin, however, was a special case. He was half blind and a paraplegic, and his killing elicited vehement popular and official protest from Europe and throughout the Muslim world. Funeral marches in Gaza were a deliberate and impressive show of force by Hamas. According to a poll taken by the Palestinian Center for Research and Cultural Dialogue after his death, 31% of Palestinians in the West Bank and Gaza would have voted for Hamas, compared to only 27% for Fatah. In Israel's counter-terrorism calculus, however, the operational benefits of disrupting the terrorist apparatus at the strategic planning level were judged to outweigh the political cost of momentary Palestinian outrage. That calculus appeared to embody four main considerations.

Firstly, while targeted killings of Hamas leaders may be provocative in the short term, the movement was already maximally radical and could not become appreciably more so. Although Yassin had manifested sporadic flexibility – for instance, theoretically accepting Jews as a client population in an Islamic state comprising mandatory Palestine – Rantisi consistently maintained that peace could take hold only after Jews had left that territory for their countries of origin, and he was bullish on Hamas's strengthening links with Hizbullah and Iran. Secondly, hitting mainly lower-level operatives arguably encouraged the leaders to be bolder by giving them less to fear. Thirdly, Rantisi was widely considered to be the most formidable opponent of the PA (which had imprisoned him for 21 months in the late 1990s). Eliminating him therefore stood to strengthen the PA vis-à-vis Hamas, and eventually to improve scope for the PA's constraining the group politically or by force. Fourthly, and perhaps most importantly, given the disarray in the PA, Hamas's spinning Israeli withdrawal as a victory – in the same way Hizbullah has successfully characterised Israel's May 2000 withdrawal from south Lebanon – potentially opened the door for Hamas's political primacy in Gaza, the disintegration of Fatah there and, consequently, continuing instability. According to a March 2005 Palestine Center for Policy and Survey Research (PCPSR) survey, 75% of Palestinians did in fact consider Israel's planned withdrawal from Gaza as a victory for the Palestinian armed struggle. A tough stance against Hamas prior to withdrawal was intended to counter any impression among the Palestinians that Israel was acting out of weakness, to cripple Hamas operationally so that it could not use Gaza as staging area for attacks in Israel, and to ensure the potency of Israel's military deterrent even after withdrawal.

The evidence suggests that the Israeli assessment was generally correct. Terrorist attacks in the West Bank diminished markedly after Yassin's death – even though Bush's April 2004 statement that territorial negotiations would have to account for 'major Israeli population centres' there and support for the security barrier might have been expected to increase violence. Rantisi's avowed revenge for Yassin's death never came to pass. During his five-week tenure, Hamas carried out only one suicide bombing, killing an Israeli policeman. As of April 2004, Israeli security forces were stopping 80–90% of Palestinian attacks, compared to 50% early in the second intifada. At the same time, the liquidation of the two Hamas leaders apparently shifted Hamas's internal balance of power from the relatively pragmatic Gaza-centred 'inside' leadership that heeded Yassin to the more hardline Damascus-based 'outside' leadership (with which Rantisi sided) under Khaled Mashaal, head of the Political Bureau. Yet Mashaal's behaviour indicated that that the putative hardliners themselves may have felt intimidated by Israel's tough counter-terrorism policy. He resisted anointing Rantisi as Yassin's full-fledged successor, confining his leadership status to Gaza. In addition, he diffidently instructed Hamas-Gaza to keep secret the name of Rantisi's successor, and the group may even have settled for an interim collective leadership, which hinted at a relatively quiescent mood. Hamas retracted an intemperate threat, implied after Rantisi's death, to attack the United States. Yassin's death also deprived Hamas of its most charismatic leader. The targeted killing of Rantisi, then, underscored Israel's unwillingness to acquiesce to Hamas's predominance in Gaza. The bulldozing of Palestinian dwellings reinforced the message. While the tactical aim of the offensive was to preclude the smuggling of weapons from Egypt into Gaza, the strategic aim was to preserve the Israeli deterrent.

American re-engagement

Following Arafat's death, the character of Israeli military operations in the Palestinian territories momentarily changed. On 12 November 2004, the IDF activated *Operation New Leaf–The Day After* – planned the previous year – to bolster security while also ensuring that 'Palestinians' dignity is preserved' during Arafat's funeral in the West Bank town of Ramallah and the three-day period of mourning. The IDF sealed the occupied territories, withdrew from all West Bank population centres, reinforced deployments around Ramallah and en route to Jerusalem, eased West Bank Palestinians' access to Ramallah for the funeral, and allowed PA officers in Ramallah to carry weapons in order to facilitate crowd control. There was virtually no violence during the three-day operation. Politically, Arafat's death was equally salutary. For the Bush administration and Israel, Arafat's demise must have seemed like the seal on the triumph of the president's re-election in November 2004. From Washington's perspective, the United States now had regained some of the room for manoeuvre that it had lost with its repudiation of Arafat and insistence on democratisation as the precondition for Palestinian statehood. Both of these principles had been set forth in Bush's Rose Garden speech of 24 June 2002. Yet the unwillingness of Arafat's Tunis elite to jettison him, especially given their own lack of popularity or stable constituencies, undercut any American hope that Bush's stratagem might work, and the fate of Palestine's initial flirtation with a more genuinely parliamentary form of government – in which security responsibilities, inter alia, were to be devolved to a prime minister and ministerial bureaucracy – was brutally curtailed by Hamas on one side and Arafat on the other.

In that episode, the then prime minister, Mahmoud Abbas – generally known as Abu Mazen – had been attempting publicly to pry his de jure authority over the so-called security services from Arafat's de facto grasp, just as Hamas launched a devastating terrorist attack against a bus in Jerusalem on 19 August. Unable to wrest this control in the midst of the ensuing crisis, Abu Mazen's already threadbare credibility with his Israeli counterpart, Israeli Prime Minister Ariel Sharon, was soon beyond any hope of salvage. In the meantime, Arafat's barely veiled characterisation of his prime minister's quest for authority as the behaviour of an American stooge undermined Abu Mazen's standing among a deeply weary and sceptical Palestinian public. Manipulated and humiliated, he resigned. Thus ended Palestine's experiment with the democratic process that Washington had declared essential to American support for Palestinian statehood.

Arafat's death removed the two barriers to American re-engagement that Washington had stipulated in the Rose Garden speech. The United States could once again deal directly with the Palestinian leadership, while broad Palestinian interest in democratisation would be unshackled from Arafat's 35-year reign of violence-prone authoritarianism. Bush signalled his intention to press for progress in a 12 November 2004 meeting at the White House with British Prime Minister Tony Blair, for whom American intervention in the Israeli–Palestinian conflict was both a moral imperative and a political necessity. In that meeting, Bush stated that 'it is fair to say that I believe we've got a great chance to establish a Palestinian state … and I intend to use the next four years to spend the capital of the United States on such a state'. He went on to commit the United States to the 'roadmap' developed by the Quartet (the United States, Russia, the United Nations and the European Union), and to assert that Palestinian statehood could become a reality in 2009. This timetable evidently captured the administration's safest guess regarding the lead time the Palestinians and Israelis would need to stabilise their respective domestic political arrangements and negotiate a final status accord that would establish an international border, resolve problems related to repatriation of Palestinian refugees, adjudicate rival claims to Jerusalem and determine the future of Jewish settlements in territory to fall under Palestinian jurisdiction.

Replacing Arafat

The immediate effect of these developments on Palestinian politics was galvanising. Abu Mazen, who had served Arafat and the PLO since the mid-1960s, emerged from a brooding part-time exile to run for the chairmanship of Fatah, the biggest party within the PLO, and the presidency. Abu Mazen scored well in November public opinion polls, despite his lack of charisma and his association with the 'old guard' (that is, the Fatah militants exiled from Beirut to Tunis in 1982 after their disastrous involvement in Lebanon's civil war, and subsequently repatriated en masse to Gaza after the signing of the Oslo Accord in 1993). Not only did Abu Mazen garner a 40% approval rating, but his party, Fatah, also did exceptionally well. Fatah's robust ratings, however, owed more to Hamas's declaration that it would boycott the upcoming elections than to any perception that Fatah had miraculously transcended its history of corruption and fecklessness and would henceforth advance Palestinian interests with courage, integrity and intelligence. Suddenly, there simply seemed to be no alternative.

This was not entirely true. Waiting in the wings was Marwan Barghouti, the 45-year old former head of the Tanzim, Fatah's paramilitary outfit. The 'wings' in this case were those of an Israeli prison in Beersheba, where he is serving five consecutive life terms for murders he is alleged to have ordered in the course of the al-Aqsa intifada. Barghouti is the darling of the 'young guard', the Palestinian generation raised under occupation and which came of age during the first intifada, after

1987. They have been the champions of grass-roots democratisation, as they chafed under Old Guard domination and watched Israeli settlement activity continue even as the Old Guard – spectators in Tunis while Barghouti and his peers served time in Israeli jails – did nothing. Indeed, Barghouti himself had served a six-year sentence before being deported in 1987.

On 1 December, Barghouti announced that he would challenge Abu Mazen for the presidency. Despite supporters' cries of 'with our blood and souls, we will redeem you, Marwan', his wife's competent media presence and Barghouti's own popularity among his generation – enhanced by his own media savvy – his candidacy failed to acquire traction. His standing in the polls was respectable, but his 40% approval rating merely matched Abu Mazen's – a curious development, given the low esteem in which the Old Guard has customarily been held by most Palestinians. Moreover, approval ratings are not the same as votes. Discouraged, Barghouti withdrew his candidacy a few days later, only to reassert it and then withdraw for good on 13 December.

Several factors accounted for Barghouti's aborted launch. The opposition of the Fatah party stalwarts was crucial. None saw his leadership as plausible, in large part because it would have perpetuated a situation wherein the Palestinians' elected leader was a pariah to his most vital interlocutors, the president of the United States and prime minister of Israel. Even his prison comrades failed to support him, judging that Abu Mazen was more likely than Barghouti to extricate them from Israeli custody. The Israelis, for their part, made it clear that Barghouti's inauguration as president would not lead to an amnesty or parole arrangement, or, indeed, any change in his confinement conditions. At root, there was a widespread perception that Arafat's death had created opportunities that would be lost through a symbolic gesture of resistance in the form of Barghouti's election. Palestinians wanted a leader who could gain American backing and strike a deal with Israel.

Abu Mazen appeared to fit this bill better. In particular, he had conspicuously avoided catering to the craving for violent catharsis. In a 14 December 2004 interview in Arabic with the London-based *al-Sharq al-Awsat* newspaper, he said he believed in 'a legitimate right of the people to express their rejection of the occupation by popular and social means', but continued 'the use of arms has been damaging and should end'. Abu Mazen had said this at least twice before, privately, to leaders of Palestinian militant groups, and, in English, to Western audiences. This time there could be no misunderstanding or temporisation. The man running for the presidency of Palestine has publicly declared his long-held view that the violent uprising was a catastrophic mistake. Despite the countervailing view of a plurality of Palestinian opinion poll respondents that the intifada had achieved gains in the struggle with Israel, Abu Mazen was elected on 9 January 2005 by an overwhelming margin, winning 65% of the vote. Thereafter, he moved quickly to attempt to rebuild a debilitated PA and Fatah. But because, as a member of the unpopular Old Guard, he lacked a power base of his own, he must rely on local leaders to secure popular support and co-optation strategies – such as incorporating the Fatah-derived al-Aqsa Martyrs' Brigades in to the PA security apparatus.

Sharon's epiphany

The second dramatic development affecting the dynamics of the conflict is the apparent transformation of Sharon. In May 2004, Israel's eventual unilateral withdrawal from Gaza and the erection of the security barrier in the West Bank – both endorsed by the United States – seemed to have the potential to effect a revolutionary change of the status quo in the Israeli–Palestinian conflict. The effective partition was based on an absence of trust that, in Israel's view, had rendered negotiated peace impossible for the moment. But strategically, Israel's moves were implicit acknowledgment that any post-1967 Zionist aspiration to a 'Greater Israel' extending from the Mediterranean Sea to the Jordan River was demographically untenable. On a more tactical level, they were warnings to the Palestinians that restraining terrorism remained the sine qua non of reviving the peace process premised on the 'roadmap' and prospects for the creation of a Palestinian state. In December 2003, Sharon gave the keynote address at a major policy conference held annually in the Tel Aviv suburb of Herzliya. It was there that Sharon first announced his plan for unilateral disengagement from Gaza, using, ironically, the Hebrew equivalent of the term King Hussein applied in 1988 when he declared that Jordan had renounced its legal and administrative claims to the West Bank. His speech was preceded by his statement that Israel does not want 'to rule over millions of Palestinians forever' and that 'Israel, which wants to be a model democracy, cannot sustain the occupation for a length of time'.

This theme, which could well have been authored by Yossi Beilin, the renowned spokesman of Israeli doves, was developed further in the Herzliya speech. Sharon acknowledged that a situation 'where one [nation] rules over another would be a horrible disaster for both peoples'. 'Disengagement', he conceded, 'recognises the demographic reality on the ground specifically, bravely and honestly. Of course it is clear to everyone that we will not be in Gaza in the final agreement. This recognition, that we will not be in Gaza, and that, even now, we have no reason to be there, does not divide the people and is not tearing us apart … disengagement from Gaza is uniting the people'. By invoking the demographic dilemma – namely, that an Israeli state that disenfranchises an entire class of people cannot be a democracy, while an Israel that enfranchises Palestinians will cease to be Jewish – the architect of the settler movement endorsed the central claim of the left and denied the viability of Israeli occupation not just of Gaza, but of the West Bank. The speech was therefore a pivotal moment.

The rhetorical drama was underscored by practical steps Sharon had already taken. He had discarded his right-wing cabinet, sought a unity coalition with the

Labour Party and requested changes in the Basic Law to allow the appointment of Shimon Peres as second deputy prime minister with responsibility for the peace process. Within the Likud Party, Sharon repeatedly engaged in brinkmanship to prod his party toward support for disengagement, a policy regarded by many stalwarts as emotionally unpalatable and politically hazardous. In the legislative and bureaucratic domains, the government took the administrative and legal measures that would be required for disengagement to work, by drafting, for example, a compensation law for evacuees, creating a disengagement administration, and working with NGOs and the Egyptian government to provide humanitarian services and security in Gaza in the wake of Israel's withdrawal. More importantly, Sharon announced that he would proceed in coordination with the Palestinian leadership, rather than unilaterally. On 31 March 2005, facing the risk that the collapse of his budget would force new elections, Sharon pulled together sufficient support in the Knesset to pass the budget. At that stage, the major procedural obstacles to the implementation of his Gaza withdrawal plan were removed.

Challenges and obstacles

There is little doubt that the majority of Israelis desire a peaceful settlement. And Palestinian attitudes have shifted since Arafat's death. According to the March 2005 PCPSR poll, 68% of Palestinians opposed the continuation of armed attacks against Israeli targets from Gaza after the Israeli withdrawal, and 84% wanted a return to negotiations on a comprehensive settlement rather than any interim measure. But there remain obstacles that are not negligible. The most salient challenges, however, consist of distinct minorities.

The armed Palestinian Islamist groups, of which Hamas is the largest and strongest, present the greatest threat to peace. On 16 November, Hamas announced that it would not participate in the 9 January election for the new president of the PA that Abu Mazen ended up winning so handily, condemning the prospective election as 'a continuation of Oslo'. The smaller Palestinian Islamic Jihad took the same stance. Subsequently, however, Abu Mazen and other Arab leaders were able to convince the militant groups to test the non-violent political waters. On 8 February, Abu Mazen announced a de facto truce on the part of Hamas and other armed groups. Except for a suicide bomber that killed five at a Tel Aviv nightclub on 25 February, the truce was relatively effective. In Cairo, on 17 March 2005, 13 Palestinian armed factions – including Hamas – agreed to an informal truce to last, tentatively, through the end of the year. Yet all ten of the cease-fires declared or offered by Hamas between 1993 and 2002 were unequivocally tactical – having emerged when Hamas needed breathing space to regroup following pressure from a superior adversary (either Israel or the PA) – and none lasted longer than a few weeks. Hamas's March 2005 cease-fire too was hedged, characterised merely as a 'current atmosphere of calm in return for an Israeli commitment to stop all forms of aggression against ... the Palestinian people'. Indeed, Hamas has termed the cease-fire not a *hudna*, which in Arabic has a sense of formality and obligation and Islamic principles make difficult to break, but rather a *tahdi'a*, which merely means 'lull'.

Beyond the cease-fire, however, Hamas's statement that it would participate in Palestinian Legislative Council elections, for the first time, in July 2005 was ostensibly among the most hopeful political developments in the Israeli–Palestinian peace process. The statement reversed Hamas's firm stance of refusing to be part of any institutions that emerged from the 1993 Oslo Accords. The genuineness of the group's newfound interest in unarmed politics seemed to be underscored by Hamas's requirement – conceded by Abu Mazen – that half the seats in a given voting district be chosen by proportional representation, which would generally increase the representation of the voters' second choice, as Hamas would tend to be. But caution is required. Political participation was also tactically useful to Hamas in service of the armed struggle. The legitimacy that it would bring might facilitate its removal from official EU and even US lists of proscribed terrorist organisations, easing fundraising efforts, and could relax Western pressure on Syria to have Hamas leaders expelled from Damascus. Most importantly, the truce plus the political foray would provide Hamas with ample cover for rebuilding its terrorist infrastructure, which Israeli operations have virtually levelled. Hamas's formal political goal is the eradication of the Israeli state and the creation of an Islamic state covering all of historical Palestine, which is not realistically attainable by political means (if only marginally more so by force). Thus, Hamas could well simply bide its time by expanding its constituency through a flirtation with non-violent politics (recalling that of Hizbullah or the Provisional Irish Republican Army), waiting for a Palestinian state to materialise, and then reverting to a radical agenda: Islamist victory, maximal re-assertion of the Palestinian right of return and continued armed opposition to Israel's very existence.

Notwithstanding Palestinians' post-Arafat coolness towards political violence, the March PCPSR opinion polls suggested that Hamas would fare well against its secular rivals – the largest being Fatah – which remain riven by corruption and infighting bred by Arafat's divide-and-rule stratagems. Some 67% of Palestinians condemned the Tel Aviv nightclub attack and 75% approved of the militants' cease-fire, and they tended to attribute Hamas's success in December 2004 and January 2005 local elections to its incorruptibility and discipline. Support for Hamas rose from 18% to 25% (though it is substantially lower in the West Bank than in Gaza), while support for Fatah declined from 40% to 36% across the board. But Hamas has other political options, as it has not needed to be peaceful to be popular. Its support has often *increased* when it raised the level of violence. Hamas's social welfare infrastructure, not its capacity to deliver a workable peace with Israel, has been central to its political appeal. Ominous, too, is the fact that to secure the 17 March cease-fire, Israel had to release 500 Palestinian prisoners (of about 7,000 in total) from its jails and schedule 400 more for release. Should Hamas and the others return to violence, they would be able to draw from a deeper talent pool.

There are also militant Israelis who pose dangers to the peace process. The most potent group would be Israeli settlers in the Palestinian territories, whom the Sharon government feels it must placate by retaining a number of Israeli settlements on the West Bank in which about 200,000 Israeli settlers live. Washington, in turn, is hard pressed to chastise Sharon too sharply after he has come so far. In late March 2005, the Israeli government announced that it would add 3,500 housing units to Maaleh Adumim, the largest West Bank settlement. US Secretary of State Condoleezza Rice cast the expansion as 'at odds with American policy', but only a few days later Dan Kurtzer, the US ambassador to Israel, stated that it was unrealistic to expect Isarel to withdraw completely from the West Bank. European Union (EU) Minister for Foreign Affairs Javier Solana noted that the Israeli plan departed from the roadmap, which calls for a freeze to all settlement construction on the West Bank. More direly, senior Palestinian officials said that the Maaleh Adumim expansion would endanger the peace process by rendering the PA's efforts under Abu Mazen – principally, the 17 March truce – to rein in terrorism. Significantly, stopping settlement activity ranks high on West Bank Palestinians' list of negotiating priorities (along with prisoner release, cessation of construction in the separation barrier, and the re-admission of Palestinian labour to Israel).

An unsteady tipping point

In spring 2004, American Middle East expert Henry Siegman lamented that Sharon could not be to the Palestinians what de Gaulle had been to the Algerians. At the time, things did not look promising. Over the course of the ten months following Sharon's speech at Herzliya, neither Israeli military operations in the Palestinian territories nor Palestinian terrorism abated. Only Arafat's death brought about these developments. But while it may still be improbable that Sharon will ever utter the Hebrew equivalent of 'je vous ai compris' to his Palestinian counterpart, in the wake of Arafat's death the comparison does not seem so outlandish. Stark changes have been heralded not only by Arafat's death but also by Sharon's apparent conversion and Bush's commitment to use American influence to achieve a final status accord. The Israeli–Palestinian conflict is very close to a tipping point, a paradigm shift. But it is a highly volatile one. Arafat no longer stands in the way. Instead, whether Israel's implementation of the Gaza withdrawal plan changes the substance and pace of the peace process will depend substantially on the degree to which Hamas and the other armed Palestinian militant groups stand down – either voluntarily, to test their non-violent political power, or due to effective counter-terrorism on the part of the PA. US and European diplomacy will have to support both possible levers of terrorist restraint.

Each side has economic incentives to quell political violence, moderation of which helped the Palestinian economy grow by 6.1% in the first half of 2004 and the Israeli economy by 3.3% (annualised) in the third quarter. But the fundamentals of the terrorism–diplomacy nexus in the Israeli–Palestinian conflict appear to have remained essentially the same. It is imprudent for either the Israelis or the secular Palestinian leadership to assume that Hamas and other religiously motivated terrorist groups are politically amenable to shifting their strategic objective of eliminating the Israeli state. They must somehow discount the possibility that Hamas et al. would use any Palestinian state as a platform for attempting to do so and thereby destabilise the region once again. Accordingly, it would be best if the Palestinian militant groups – especially Hamas – were disarmed for any Palestinian state to be stable. If that task were to fall to outside actors (e.g., a US-led force, as suggested by some in late 2003) or Israelis, the secular Palestinian leadership would be unable to garner the respect of the people and would find governing on a sustainable basis difficult if not impossible. The principal hurdle to be overcome before moving decisively towards a Palestinian state is therefore still re-empowering the secular Palestinian institutions both as welfare providers and as enforcers of security.

At the same time, all parties need to allow for the outside possibility that Hamas is genuinely ready to modify its objectives and settle for a state that falls territorially short of historical Palestine, in which it seeks political legitimacy and primacy. If so, Hamas's involvement in mainstream Palestinian decision-making would tend to harden official Palestinian negotiating positions. This prospect arguably makes it desirable for a degree of moderation in Hamas to be nurtured by some level of inclusion in wider political dialogue. The EU – more sympathetic with Palestinian militants both rhetorically and substantively, as shown by its protracted refusal (finally ended in 2003) to include Hamas's charitable wing on its list of terrorist organisations – would be a more credible contact than the United States.

To be sure, the United States must help forge the final resolution of the Israeli–Palestinian conflict by acting as an energetic and fair honest broker between mainstream Palestinians and the Israelis. A harder line on Israeli settlements in the West Bank is likely to be required. But Hamas and its cohort may well be irreconcilable opponents of the existence of the state of Israel. To make matters worse, Hamas's considerable charitable works – which have shined against PA corruption and administrative ineptitude – have enabled it to sustain a critical level of grassroots political support as well as terrorist financing. The PCPSR poll found that 91% of Palestinians favoured the PA's fundamental reform. Thus, the United States must do much more than midwife a formal agreement and a new state. It needs to help empower (operationally as well as politically) the secular leadership of the PA to challenge and disarm Hamas and other militant groups, provide for the Palestinian people and thus make the PA a viable substitute for Hamas, and establish a monopoly on the use of force. But the climate for all diplomacy – Israeli and Palestinian, American and European – will be most centrally determined by the unfolding of the Israeli withdrawal from Gaza.

Africa

Though Africa continued to be somewhat off the beaten strategic path, it also has gradually drawn more attention from the rest of the world. The reasons were both bad and good. On the negative side, the Sudanese government's brutal campaign of ethnic cleansing, pitting the favoured Arabs against black Africans in the country's Darfur region, revealed a harsh and wilful government still resistant to international pressure. Autocratic Zimbabwean President Robert Mugabe, having run his once quite prosperous country into the ground with confiscatory land policies and corruption, engineered his party's victory in March 2005 parliamentary elections through intimidation and coercion while disapproving major powers and timid African ones – most conspicuously and typically, South Africa – looked on with hands essentially folded. The government and rebels in Côte d'Ivoire proved unable to reconcile, necessitating the ongoing presence of reluctant foreign peacekeeping troops. Christian–Muslim violence in northern Nigeria escalated, increasing the likelihood that Nigeria would emerge as a major jihadist hub or at least a rich source of terrorist recruits. Much of the continent remained plagued by poverty and AIDS – though Botswana, where mineral wealth and comparative economic competence have yielded a high per-capita GDP and distribution of anti-retroviral drugs have helped to contain the AIDS problem, was arguably a bright spot.

Further hopeful developments included the ambitious but resource-poor African Union's political assertiveness, which at least kept the international community focused on the Darfur calamity and provisionally prompted a peaceful transition from old-style dictatorship to democracy in Togo. (The AU's competence and authority, however, stood to be further challenged if Togo's ruling family attempted to rig planned elections, which remained a distinct possibility.) The peace process in Sierra Leone slowly entrenched stability through demobilisation, 'truth and reconciliation', legislative

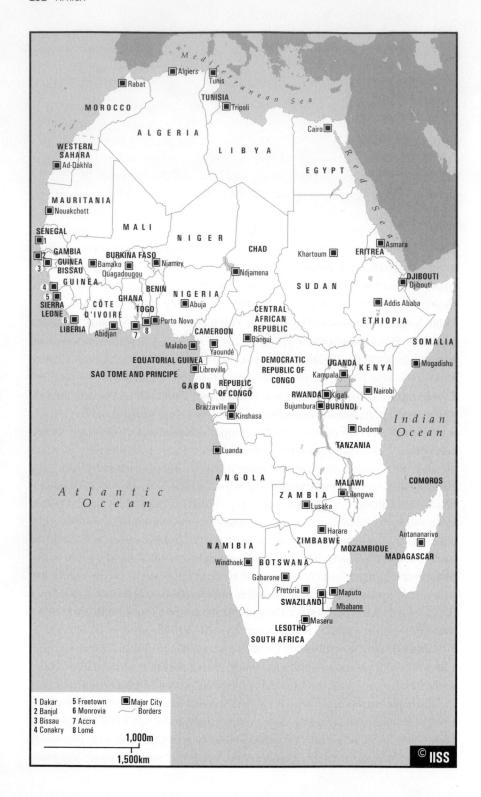

Mediterranean Sea

Algiers ■

Tunis ■

Rabat ■

TUNISIA

Tripoli ■

MOROCCO

ALGERIA

Cairo ■

LIBYA

EGYPT

Red Sea

**WESTERN
SAHARA**

Ad-Dakhla ■

MAURITANIA

Nouakchott ■

MALI

NIGER

Khartoum ■

Asmara ■

ERITREA

SENEGAL
■ 1

GAMBIA
■ 2
GUINEA
3 ■ **BISSAU**

4 ■

5 ■
**SIERRA
LEONE**

6 ■
LIBERIA

BURKINA FASO

Bamako ■ Niamey ■

Ouagadougou ■

GUINEA

GHANA

**CÔTE
D'IVOIRE**

TOGO

Abidjan ■

BENIN

NIGERIA

Abuja ■

Porto Novo ■
7 8

Ndjamena ■

CHAD

SUDAN

**CENTRAL
AFRICAN
REPUBLIC**

DJIBOUTI
Djibouti ■

Addis Ababa ■

ETHIOPIA

SOMALIA

Malabo ■

CAMEROON

Yaoundé ■

Bangui ■

EQUATORIAL GUINEA
Libreville ■

SAO TOME AND PRINCIPE

GABON

**DEMOCRATIC
REPUBLIC OF
CONGO**

UGANDA

Kampala ■

KENYA

Mogadishu ■

**REPUBLIC
OF CONGO**

Brazzaville ■

Kinshasa ■

RWANDA Kigali ■

Bujumbura ■ **BURUNDI**

Nairobi ■

*Indian
Ocean*

Dodoma ■

Luanda ■

TANZANIA

*Atlantic
Ocean*

ANGOLA

MALAWI

Lilongwe ■

COMOROS

ZAMBIA

Lusaka ■

Harare ■

Antananarivo ■

NAMIBIA

Windhoek ■

ZIMBABWE

BOTSWANA

MOZAMBIQUE

MADAGASCAR

Gabarone ■

Pretoria ■

Maputo ■

SWAZILAND

Mbabane

Maseru ■

LESOTHO

SOUTH AFRICA

1 Dakar	5 Freetown	■ Major City
2 Banjul	6 Monrovia	Borders
3 Bissau	7 Accra	
4 Conakry	8 Lomé	

1,000m

1,500km

© **IISS**

reform and democratic elections. Through the brokering efforts of the United States, the UK and Norway, a power- and oil-revenue-sharing peace agreement ending the long civil war between the Islamic Sudanese government and the non-Muslim southern Sudanese was finally reached in January 2005. Largely clean national elections were held in Botswana (October 2004), Malawi (May 2004), Mozambique (December 2004), Namibia (November 2004) and South Africa (April 2004) – further indication that multiparty democracy was not just taking hold but strengthening its grip.

Still other aspects of the African scene were ambiguous. Institutional and political debility afflicted regional organisations other than the African Union (AU) and the Economic Community of West African States; in particular, the Southern African Development Community appeared notably futile and, in blessing Zimbabwe's tainted elections, craven. The political rehabilitation of the Democratic Republic of the Congo proceeded in fits and starts, inhibited by pockets of conflict between non-state groups and the residual geopolitical preoccupations of Rwanda and Uganda, former enemies of the Kinshasa government. Oil production increased, as did GDPs, as the United States and other major powers sought to diversify supply sources in light of instability in the Middle East (and Nigeria) and Venezuela's political unreliability. West Africa's production was expected to double by 2010. Yet insecurity in the Gulf of Guinea – where there is more piracy than anywhere else in the world – has necessitated US maritime assistance to West Africa's meagre navies and coast guards. Even with the world's largest UN peacekeeping operation securing the country, Liberian factions only managed to limp towards a consolidated peace.

In the security arena, the fairly auspicious advent of the AU, the G8 initiative to enhance African regional and sub-regional peacekeeping capabilities by 2010 through train-and-equip programmes, and efforts of the UN Department of Peacekeeping Operations to ramp up its capabilities in light of the new and larger missions, augur better days ahead. So does the prospective strengthening of existing bilateral assistance programmes, including the United States' African Contingency Operations Training and Assistance Programme and France's Reinforcement of African Peacekeeping Capacities initiative, which features pre-positioned battalions and equipment in Djibouti, Gabon and Senegal. In April 2004, the EU also established the €250m Africa Peace Facility to support African-run peacekeeping initiatives in Africa and strengthen of the capacity of the AU and its sub-regional components to design, plan and implement peace operations. Yet even these generous avenues of outside help probably are not sufficient to offset the need for more substantial hands-on contributions from developed countries – the most telling example being France's undertaking as the predominant and indispensable leader of the UN peacekeeping operation in Côte d'Ivoire.

In the non-military sphere, the New Partnership for African Development (NEPAD) seemed to epitomise Africa's longstanding and current dilemmas. The poverty-eradication and good-governance mechanism has been spearheaded by South African President Thabo Mbeki and Nigerian President Olusegun Obasanjo, and as such represents a noble effort by ranking African powers to take the lead in addressing the region's profound economic and political problems. NEPAD added enrolees to its peer-review mechanism and launched the African Peace and Security Council in 2004, but it also drew criticism from Senegalese Foreign Minister Cheikh Tidiane Gadio for having too much 'vision' and not enough 'implementation'. As of October 2004, fewer than half of 52 facilitation projects, only six of 18 capacity-building projects, and a mere seven of 36 investment programmes were at any stage of implementation – a factor that discourages donor nations from contributing to the initiative. Mbeki, in response, identified the cruel 'catch-22' of the African politico-economic condition. 'The lack of capacity at regional levels', he noted, 'is such that even when we have mobilised the necessary resources, we are held back by the fact that we cannot translate some of the good and visionary ideas into concrete, implementable programmes'. In other words, Africa requires resources to develop capacity, but needs capacity to exploit resources. There is no doubt that, prompted by major powers' post-11 September strategic preoccupations, African nations are taking greater responsibility for themselves. But NEPAD is also premised on the fact that they cannot do without substantial outside resources both up front and on the back end of any initiative.

Sudan: Africa's New Test Case

Sudan in 2004–05 became the locus of remarkably intense international attention and activity which has brought into play a host of international mechanisms – from the UN Security Council, the International Criminal Court (ICC), the African Union (AU) and its Peace and Security Council, and the regionally based Intergovernmental Authority on Development. Sudan's travails have also drawn in a range of key coun-tries – the United States, members of the European Union (EU), Libya, Egypt, Nigeria – all seeking a lasting solution to Sudan's chronic instability and the enduring anguish of the Sudanese people. Despite this unprecedented breadth of international effort, the situation remains dangerous and profoundly unstable.

International engagement
There has been, to be sure, one major salutary development. The government of Sudan and its principal military adversary of more than 20 years, the Sudan People's Liberation Movement (SPLM), signed a comprehensive peace agreement, known as the Naivasha Comprehensive Peace Agreement (named for the Kenyan town in which the bulk of government-SPLM negotiations took place), on 9 January 2005, putting an end to one of Africa's bloodiest and longest-running civil wars.

The agreement was endorsed by the UN Security Council, which then authorised 10,700 UN troops to monitor and enforce the peace. A donors' conference in Oslo in early April was likely to deliver billions of dollars in post-conflict reconstruction assistance. But as the north–south peace process moved laboriously to a negotiated settlement, the conflict in Sudan's western region of Darfur provoked a new round of international censure. The UN Security Council authorised a UN Commission of Inquiry into the conflict, which in turn recommended a referral to the ICC and compiled a sealed list of 51 potential indictees. The United States – surprisingly, given its general opposition to the ICC – acquiesced to the ICC referral. Sudan had become the central focus of a global movement to end impunity and bring to justice those responsible for war crimes and genocide.

The African Union assumed a lead role in the peace operation in Darfur in 2004, authorising 3,200 observers and troops to monitor a frequently violated ceasefire. This unprecedented undertaking for the AU has starkly underlined the enormous disparity between AU aspirations and capacities, particularly in confronting a crisis of the scale and complexity of Darfur. Under the chairmanship of Nigerian President Olusegun Obasanjo, the AU also assumed the lead in Abuja-based political negotiations on Darfur, but failed, through early April 2005, to generate any meaningful results. Libya has stepped forward with help on both the humanitarian and diplomatic front in Darfur, and will likely continue to play an active role in the run-up to the AU summit in July 2005, originally to be hosted in Khartoum and now moved to Tripoli.

Whether these multiple international initiatives brought greater stability or predictability is highly uncertain. In principle, the Naivasha agreement lays the basis for a transformation of the Sudanese state, an opening of political space for Sudan's many aggrieved and marginalised populations, and a potential way forward for a political settlement in Darfur. In practice, prolonged and intractable conflict in Darfur will stoke political rifts within Khartoum, divide the international community, make implementation of the north–south agreement a secondary priority for the government of Sudan and encourage other groups excluded from the Naivasha process to take up arms to redress their grievances. External investments in diplomacy, adequate pressures and guarantees, and robust security arrangements, including capable and well-equipped peacekeepers, may help temporarily stave off a worst-case scenario of disintegration and collapse. But the Naivasha peace process and the crisis in Darfur have thrown into relief the limitations as well as the possibilities of international cooperative efforts, diplomacy, humanitarian assistance, peacekeeping and moral exhortation. In 2005–06, international resolve and the ability of outside parties to balance competing priorities will be sorely tested.

Already there is a deepening tension between those constituencies that demand that individuals responsible for the egregious abuses in Darfur be tried and punished and those that see implementation of the peace accord as a top priority. With the

Security Council's referral of Darfur suspects to the ICC, Sudanese President Umar al-Bashir is now required not only to relinquish substantial power and resources to the south, but also to turn senior members of his inner circle over to an international court whose legitimacy his government does not recognise. These mounting pressures on Khartoum, already riven by personal and political antagonisms, are likely to destabilise an already fragile centre and embolden its opponents, both north and south, to delay a political settlement or stall on previous commitments. The question for the international community becomes: how hard can Khartoum be pressed before it fragments, and at what point does the government become simply incapable of implementing commitments or reform? As egregious as the Sudanese government's abuses have been, it is possible that a power vacuum at this juncture could undermine any progress made to date and re-ignite or prolong conflict.

As internal and international pressures mount on Khartoum, the government will be prone to react in ever more defensive and regressive ways. Among the most immediate will be those surrounding implementation of the Naivasha agreement and the calculations of both the government and SPLM leader John Garang in setting the pace and sequence of meeting their respective commitments. There is a serious risk of stall and drift, and an urgent need to quickly demonstrate the viability and legitimacy of the agreement, to win the confidence and continued commitment both of Sudan's citizens and the international community. In Darfur, there is a strong risk of continued escalation, stoked by external forces, a mounting humanitarian toll and a failure of political negotiations. In the east and elsewhere, there remains the challenge of ensuring that other marginalised groups have an adequate stake in the evolving political framework and are not driven by continued exclusion to escalate armed confrontations. Also key is striking an appropriate balance between opening political space within Khartoum by holding individuals to account, versus ensuring adequate cohesion and leadership at the centre to effect the transition.

Long slog to Naivasha

The January 2005 signing of the Naivasha agreement was the final step in more than two years of arduous and detailed negotiations between the government of Sudan and the SPLM and its armed wing, the Sudanese People's Liberation Army. These negotiations occurred under the auspices of the East African regional body, the Inter-Governmental Authority on Development (IGAD), supported by a troika of the United States, the United Kingdom and Norway, ably mediated by Kenyan General Lazaro Sumbeiywo. The final agreement, which incorporates 12 previously signed agreements and protocols, provides for a national government, with representation from both sides of the north–south conflict, and a separate government of southern Sudan. Current Sudanese President Umar al-Bashir will stay on as head of state, and SPLM leader John Garang will serve as first vice-president as well as head of the southern government. The National Assembly will comprise specific percentages of the ruling National Congress Party (NCP), the SPLM, and other northern and southern political forces, with elections slated for the third year after signing. Revenues from southern oil fields will be evenly divided between Khartoum and the southern government. With global oil prices at $55 per barrel, this will mean a massive inflow of funds (approximately $1bn in the first year) to the new southern government, which as yet has little in the way of financial infrastructure or administrative capacity.

On the security front, the agreement calls for an internationally monitored ceasefire with UN peacekeepers (of which the UN authorised 10,700 in March 2005). The north and south will maintain separate armed forces, with integrated units of 21,000 soldiers (half SPLM, half government) to be deployed to sensitive areas, including the still-disputed regions of Abyei, Nuba Mountains and Southern Blue Nile. Both north and south will maintain separate currencies, and *sharia* law will remain applicable to Muslims in the north. The status of *sharia* in the capital Khartoum will be determined by an elected assembly. The most immediate task will be to draft and adopt an interim national constitution, due ten weeks after the signing. In April 2005, this process is already encountering difficulties and is behind schedule.

Despite the highly detailed character of the agreement (the English version is over 200 pages), two critical factors, both intrinsic to the negotiation process itself, will present significant implementation challenges. Firstly, central to the agreement is the stipulation that after a six-year interim period, southern Sudan, in partnership with the government, will organise an internationally monitored referendum, in which the people of south Sudan will vote either to confirm the unity of Sudan or to secede. This provision – a major concession on the part of the government – was agreed early in the process, in the Machakos Protocol of 20 July 2002. It served two primary purposes. Firstly, it enshrined as the sine qua non of the negotiations and any eventual agreement the principle of self-determination for the south, and allayed southern fears that it would be pushed into an unfavourable political settlement or one which the government would fail to implement fully. Secondly, it provided an incentive to the government of Sudan to strike a deal that would make unity attractive to the south, and thus, at least in the initial six-year post-conflict phase, to make every effort to redress southern grievances. The drawback of this provision is that it will make it more difficult for the Sudanese to build a common long-term strategic vision of Sudan, and introduces an element of uncertainty and impermanence into implementation and long-term reconstruction planning that is apt to stoke suspicion and distrust between the parties and lead to further stalling. This ambiguity is cause for particular concern in the security sector, where an agreed strategy and timeframe for demobilisation, demilitarisation and reintegration of militia groups will be crucial.

The second difficulty is that, although Naivasha has been termed a north–south agreement, it is in fact deal between an authoritarian, exclusivist regime and an authoritarian, exclusivist military movement, neither of which has shown much inclination or ability to represent or serve their purported constituencies. The legitimacy of the agreement as a national framework is therefore very much in question. In the north, even within the government, hardliners and security hawks are deeply distrustful of the accord and are to be increasingly resistant as power- and wealth-sharing reduce political slots available to the NCP faithful and revenue allocations to the central government. Even more contentious will be selling the accord to other northern interests. The umbrella opposition group National Democratic Alliance (NDA) has announced a boycott of the constitutional review commission, claiming inadequate representation in that forum, and has expressed dissatisfaction with the 14% stake in government allocated to northern opposition groups. The percentage of political posts allocated may eventually set NDA members in competition with themselves and other northern groups. If or when, for example, the government of Sudan cuts successive deals with the Darfurian rebel groups or the Beja Congress in eastern Sudan, pressures will mount to increase their representation in the national government, creating greater strain within Khartoum, the NDA, or both. It is unclear whether the NCP or the SPLM would be willing to renegotiate the already agreed upon allocations.

Southern Sudan will face challenges of its own. Even SPLM Deputy Chair Salva Kiir has expressed concern that the Naivasha agreement was not vetted by any representative institution in the SPLM or southern Sudan. Other southerners, both inside and outside of the SPLM, fear the excessive centralised power will personally accrue to SPLM Commander John Garang, who in his long tenure as head of the movement has shown little proclivity to democratise or establish even rudimentary political or administrative structures. There is a pressing need for an intra-South dialogue with meaningful outreach to Nuer tribal groups, many of who fought in pro-government militias during the war against the Dinka-dominated SPLM. Alliances within the south have generally been borne of political–military expedience. With military conflict now ended, calculations will change, and competition will mount for the vast resources that will likely flow from both oil revenues and from the international community into post-conflict reconstruction.

These potentially destabilising uncertainties and the difficult task of implementation that lies ahead should not detract from the historic step forward that the Naivasha agreement represents or the achievement of the negotiating parties, the mediators and the concerted efforts of the international community. The role of the United States, which brought to the table the leverage that previous mediation efforts had lacked, was critical in moving negotiations forward, impelled by three factors: powerful domestic US constituencies who viewed the conflict as an attack by an Islamist regime against the Christian populations of the southern Sudan; perceived shifts in Khartoum itself, including a newfound eagerness to end its international isolation, and the sidelining in 1999 of Bashir's mentor and rival,

Islamist theoretician Hassan al-Turabi; and an apparent willingness on the part of Khartoum to cooperate more fully on global counter-terrorism, a shift which preceded the attacks of 11 September, but became all the more important to US policymakers thereafter.

Those international and regional actors who pushed hardest for a process of negotiation did not presume that ending the north–south conflict, although a major achievement and desirable goal in itself, would be a panacea for Sudan's multiple ills. But a decision was made early on to give a political settlement to that war – which had killed over two million, displaced over four million, and which had devastated southern Sudanese society through brutal attacks and aerial bombardments of relief sites and civilian populations – top priority. If that conflict continued to rage, there could be no progress anywhere in Sudan on human rights, political participation, economic decay and regional destabilisation. The strategy of engaging the two principal combatants, the SPLM and the government, in negotiations, was controversial when first proposed at the end of the Clinton administration, especially among the vocal and activist Sudan constituency in the United States, made up primarily of conservative evangelical Christians who considered negotiations with the Sudanese government anathema. This constituency saw fundamental regime change in Khartoum as the only way forward, but short of major international (primarily American) military investment or intervention, offered few viable strategies for getting there.

The Bush administration, which received strong electoral support from a conservative Christian base, adopted an approach that, while not entirely impartial, was nonetheless more pragmatic than ideological and more in line with the approaches of other key interested governments – namely Norway, Kenya and the UK. The revitalised IGAD process that resulted in 2002 was based on a strict prioritisation of issues, the first being a negotiated settlement between the two chief protagonists and a sidelining of players, both external and internal, who might slow or impede that goal. This approach was ultimately successful in pushing the two sides to a settlement and in bringing Sudan one step closer to political transformation. But it also had serious costs, the most profound of which materialised in Darfur.

Deterioration in Darfur

Khartoum's massively disproportionate response to an initially localised insurrection, the rebel leadership's lack of political acumen and cohesion, and an international community divided on how best to proceed and wary of derailing the Naivasha process have all impeded a solution to the crisis in Darfur. The conflict there arose from a complex interplay of local and national dynamics. Long neglected by the government in Khartoum, the region is profoundly underdeveloped, with little if any health, education or security infrastructure. Drought and ecological decline over the course of 30 years have exacerbated competition for fertile land, pasture for livestock and access to water and other resources. Territorial conflict between Chad and Libya (Darfur was used as a staging ground by both countries, and local people were co-opted as fighters) left the region awash with arms, and in the absence of any viable official police presence, vigilantism became the norm. Political manipulation by Khartoum and the pan-Arab aspirations of Libyan leader Muammar Gadhafi in the 1980s and 1990s gave rise to a new perception of ethnic affinities along 'Arab' versus 'African' lines.

The current crisis was set in motion in February 2003, when the Darfur Liberation Front (which soon thereafter renamed itself the Sudan Liberation Front, or SLA) launched a series of attacks on local police stations, destroying government property and looting arms. Attacks escalated in March and April with more ambitious raids on Kutum, Tine and El Fashir, which destroyed several Sudanese military aircraft and killed over 100 government troops. The SLA's declared agenda, spurred by the southern rhetoric of a 'New Sudan' and the success that the SPLA was then having in winning concessions from the government, was to win greater political representation in Khartoum and to end Darfur's political and economic margin-alisation. The SLA was soon joined by the Justice and Equality Movement (JEM), whose leadership was linked to sidelined Islamist ideologue Hassan al-Turabi and his followers. The JEM, too, seeks to end Darfur's marginalisation, but its goals are tied more closely to a national Islamist agenda and regime change. Both groups have members in eastern Sudan and in Eritrea, which is deeply hostile to the government in Khartoum.

The government was clearly caught off-balance by the attacks. With attention focused on the Naivasha process and a minimal security presence in Darfur, Khartoum resorted to its time-tested strategy of using the paramilitary Popular Defence Force (PDF) and local ethnic militias to restore order. In this instance, it turned principally to members of the northern camel-herding Rizeigat, a generally poor, landless sub-group, which had long-standing scores of its own to settle with the Fur and Zagahwa, from whom the SLA and JEM draw their membership. These militias are known as the Janjaweed. With government support (and in some cases air cover) and a free reign, the Janjaweed unleashed a violent campaign of pillage and rape, driving civilians from their homes, and leaving a swath of charred, empty villages in their wake. Khartoum initially denied links to the Janjaweed and dismissed the fighting as a localised, internal affair, but overwhelming evidence points to strategic, logistical and planning direction. What is less clear is how effectively the government controlled these militias, and whether, even if willing, it would be capable of reigning them in.

There are signs that Khartoum itself was split on the appropriateness of the response. An initial calculation may have been that the Darfur flare-up could be quickly snuffed out before drawing international attention or setting a precedent for other groups who felt excluded from the Naivasha process. Hardliners may have viewed the insurgency as a fundamental threat to the NCP and encouraged a campaign of terror and ethnic cleansing against civilian populations. Whether it was miscalculation or deliberate strategy is to a degree irrelevant. As the UN International Commission of Inquiry on Darfur concluded in January 2005: 'Although the [Sudanese] Government may have intended to kill rebels and destroy villages for counterinsurgency purposes, it was foreseeable, especially considering the history of conflicts between the tribes and record of criminality of the Janjaweed, that giving them authorization, or encouragement, to attack their long-term enemies, and creating a climate of total impunity, would lead to the perpetration of serious crimes. The Government of Sudan willingly took that risk.'

Whatever its initial intent, the government of Sudan showed little inclination to pursue a political solution to the escalating crisis. A cease-fire negotiated in September 2003 by the Chadian government (which now enjoyed fairly warm relations with Khartoum) was short lived, and it soon became clear that Chad had neither the leverage nor the impartiality to lead mediation efforts. Despite growing media attention and mounting allegations of genocide, in much of 2003–04 the international community was divided on how best to proceed. The US State Department was reluctant to push Khartoum too hard, since the Naivasha process was moving forward, albeit slowly. The shadow of Iraq also limited Washington's capacity to move the Security Council towards favouring sanctions and military intervention in Sudan. US Democrats successfully upped the political stakes, introducing Darfur as an issue in the presidential campaign, accusing the administration of complacency in the face of genocide, a label that Bush and Secretary of State Colin Powell (as well as European allies) initially resisted. Powell eventually did issue an official US declaration in September 2004 that genocide was occurring, but while it appeased certain constituencies, it did not generate a new strategy for ending the crisis. The UN Security Council was hamstrung, with China, Russia, Algeria and Pakistan opposed, for economic and ideological reasons, to punitive measures against Khartoum. Sudan is a major source of oil for China and a lucrative arms market for Russia. A UN resolution passed in July 2004, calling on the Sudanese government to rein in the Janjaweed or suffer unspecified consequences, was largely ineffective. The Arab League showed little inclination to get involved.

Absent viable alternatives, the international community pinned its hopes on the AU, which had offered to provide a monitoring force and to mediate peace talks in Abuja. This was a great deal to expect from the relatively new organisation, which had yet to cut its teeth on a situation anywhere near as complex and massive in scale as the Darfur crisis. AU troops on the ground have reportedly been energetic, disciplined and outspoken. But their numbers (as of April 2005, approximately 2,200 of an eventual 3,200 members in an area the size of France) and logistical and managerial capacity is simply not up to the task. The AU mandate – limited to monitoring and reporting on the frequently violated cease-fire and to intervention only if attacks occur in their immediate vicinity – can do little to ameliorate the overall security situation, which has deteriorated into a cycle of raids, roadblocks and retaliation against civilians by all sides of the conflict.

The AU was initially loath to be seen as an appendage of Western interests and was slow in asking for the assistance it needed to quickly deploy to Darfur. Coordination with the donor community has since improved, but the lack of lift and logistical support and sustained high-level financing remain major blockages. The AU deployment was originally envisioned as a year-long, stop-gap remedy, eventually to be subsumed into a UN peacekeeping mission, although there was no explicit strategy or planning toward this end or that of facilitating direct UN support for the AU operation. The AU was also reluctant to request NATO support, even as discussion in early 2005 tilted towards doubling AU deployments to over 6,000. AU-led mediation efforts in Abuja have been slow, bogged down in mutual recriminations and refusal from either side to compromise. The SLA and JEM have demonstrated little strategic vision, and there are serious disconnects between those rebel leaders negotiating in Abuja and their military counterparts on the ground. The rebel groups may see the UN rebuke of Khartoum and the vote on the ICC as an opportunity to stake out a more favourable bargaining position. The government calculation may be that it can continue to use Naivasha to stave off any threat of genuine sanction. All sides appear to be operating with little refer-ence to the plight or interests of the civilian populations in Darfur, where violence and humanitarian hardship continue unabated. Another round of talks was slated for late April 2005, but unless the AU is able to ramp up its leverage with the parties, with international help, the exercise is unlikely to bear fruit any time soon. Unexpected support, however, has come from Libya, which has agreed to open a new truck route and guarantee safe passage through Libya of food aid and other humanitarian supplies to Darfur and to refugee camps in eastern Chad. Gadhafi also hosted an informal meeting of Darfurian leaders in Tripoli, and although these talks were not formally linked to the Abuja process, some observers saw them as an opportunity for Darfur's leadership to articulate and debate local issues without the immediate pressure of staking out fixed negotiating positions.

The UN Security Council's referral of Sudan to the ICC adds a major new dimen-sion of uncertainty. Washington's abstention was a surprise to many, although the choices available to it were equally awkward. A vote against the referral would have let Khartoum off the hook, and opened up Washington to accusations from US domestic constituencies of inaction in the face of genocide and charges of hypocrisy and unilateralism from European allies. The final calculation appeared to be that Sudan was too important to be sacrificed to US antipathy to the court, and that the referral would put Khartoum's transgressions fully in the spotlight. Based on the experience of tribunals in Rwanda, Yugoslavia and Sierra Leone, the ICC deliberations on Sudan may eventually change the configuration of power in Khartoum, building pressure for a change of senior personnel. This could very likely contribute to greater instability and uncertainty – thousands of protesters demonstrated against the referral shortly after the Security Council announcement was made public in Khartoum. The government saw a serious coup attempt in 2004, and the risk of a military coup, Islamist revanchism, or simply a political meltdown into rivalries and chaos cannot be discounted.

Rumblings in the east

Eastern Sudan, yet another deeply impoverished and marginalised region, has all the makings of a destabilising crisis as well. Clashes in Port Sudan in late January between members of the Beja ethnic group and Sudanese police left an estimated 14–29 people dead and hundreds reportedly arrested. Eastern Sudan is home to over a million Darfurians who have migrated over the last decade in search of work, and the Eritrea-based Beja Congress recently issued a joint declaration with the SLA, vowing to 'continue their struggle together to end marginalisation, poverty, ignorance and backwardness'. The Beja Congress has also joined forces with another eastern rebel group, the Free Lions, to form the coalition Eastern Front, and both groups boycotted talks held in Cairo in January 2005 between Khartoum and the NDA, claiming that the forum failed to address the problems of eastern Sudan. The Beja will not be the only group to recognise that traction with Khartoum requires international leverage, and that armed resistance, no matter how fruitless or devastating in the short run, offers the best chance to draw the attention required. But whether Khartoum will learn to pre-empt such resistance through co-optation and liberalisation is uncertain. The advent of the SPLM into a new government of national unity will be an opportunity for new alliances to emerge, but the SPLM's long-term calculations are at this point very unclear. Eritrea, which has ties both in Darfur and in the East, will have a pivotal role in settling or aggravating cross-border disruption in eastern Sudan. The international community will need to make every effort either to move Asmara to play a constructive, collaborative role in political negotiations or to quickly short-circuit its ability to cause further cross-border disruption.

Challenge and hope

Not since apartheid's final decade in South Africa has a country in Africa drawn the kind of global attention and diplomatic investment that Sudan has received in 2002–05. But any sustained and fundamental transformation is likely to take a very long time and will test the resolve and staying power of the international community for years. There will be no single, defining moment when stability, prosperity and political openness seem assured, and there is every likelihood of major setbacks, crises and disappointments. The Naivasha agreement was a hopeful step, but it is now clear that the country has entered a new phase of uncertainty and fragility, with multiple vectors of instability threatening the hard-won gains of the last three years.

For the near future, indications are good that key players in the international community will keep Sudan on the agenda. The US acquiescence to the ICC referral is a strong indication that Washington, on Sudan at least, is prepared to maintain a pragmatic approach that will align it more closely with the UN and European allies. Secretary of State Condoleezza Rice's selection of Deputy Secretary Robert Zoellick to oversee the Sudan portfolio is another strong signal of high-level US commitment, and the US Agency for International Development is gearing up to become a major player in Sudan's post-conflict reconstruction. The AU sees in Sudan an opportunity to establish the credibility of its Peace and Security Council, demonstrate that intra-African solutions are effective, and secure more resources and a greater voice in managing African conflicts. Obasanjo and Gadhafi both have personal stakes in establishing their roles as continental leaders and mediators, and are likely to remain diplomatically engaged. Their challenge will be to draw other key African states – Chad, Eritrea, Uganda and Egypt – into a constructive and multilateral partnership. Sudan will remain high on the UN Security Council's agenda for 2005 as strategic and ideological debates over a way forward continue to play themselves out in that forum. Security concerns, particularly for the people of Darfur, but also in consolidation of the north–south peace, will remain a paramount. UN Secretary-General Kofi Annan's Special Envoy Jan Pronk has established himself as an outspoken, proactive force on Sudan. Proponents of the ICC will endeavour to prove the effectiveness of that mechanism. And the troika of states most invested in the Naivasha process will undoubtedly seek to preserve the achievements made possible by three years of arduous work and enormous investment there.

The highly demanding multilateral challenge will be to harness passion, ideology, humanitarian impulse and self-interest within a pragmatic, concerted approach that will best serve the interests of the Sudanese people. The United States, the EU, the UN Security Council, the AU and regional African leaders will be hard-pressed to better integrate their efforts – both in peace operations and diplomacy. They will have to engage at a higher level to move forward negotiations on Darfur, address the regional forces that stoke the crisis (especially those emanating from Chad and Eritrea) and to create elementary security on the ground through enlarged peace operations in Darfur and in other flashpoint areas of Sudan. For example, while implementation of the Naivasha agreement will itself need careful management and monitoring, two parallel and vastly uneven peace operations in Sudan make little sense. The glaring disparity between the UN deployment of 10,700 in support of Naivasha and the AU force in Darfur (even when it reaches full capacity) will have to be remedied. Otherwise, elementary security in Darfur will remain painfully elusive. But at the centre of any solution for Sudan will be the efforts of Sudanese people themselves. Ultimately, the question for Sudan will be whether the country's leadership and citizens, either out of sheer exhaustion or self-interest, can forge a common vision of a participatory, inclusive and diverse society, and muster the political energy to effect a fundamental political transformation. If not, Sudan will remain a diplomatic annoyance and international welfare case, with resonances of Liberia and Somalia. If, with the aid of outside actors, the Sudanese people can make the transformation, Sudan could become a powerful example of Africa's progress.

Congo's Political Break-out Year?

2005 is slated to be the year of independent Congo's first multiparty elections in 40 years. The transition leading up to the national elections has followed some significant steps towards the reconstitution of a state – previously named Zaire – that had been systematically eviscerated for more than three decades by its long-serving autocratic president, Mobutu Sese Seko. If elections take place as scheduled and are recognised as a legitimising act by the military and political forces seeking to seize on the vacuum resulting from the state's collapse, the decade-long wars of the Zairean succession will be finally brought to an end.

The first war, which began in October 1996 and gave the *coup de grâce* to the moribund regime of the ailing dictator, ended eight months later when Laurent Kabila and his Alliance of Democratic Forces for the Liberation of Congo (AFDL), supported by Rwanda, Uganda and Angola, completed their march across the country and took the capital Kinshasa on 17 May 1997. Mobutu died of prostate cancer in exile several months later. But Kabila's allies turned against him (or he against them) over the following year and the second war, which began on 2 August 1998, saw the eastern provinces of the renamed Democratic Republic of the Congo (DRC) fall to the Congolese Rally for Democracy (RCD), again supported by Rwanda and Uganda but not Angola. Kabila was assassinated on 16 January 2001. The second war soon came to a stalemate, however, as neighbouring (and distant) countries lined up behind one side or the other, while at the same time they sought to take advantage of the vacuum of power for their own purposes.

It was the year-long effort of nearly two dozen attempts by Congo's neighbours to mediate an end to the War that started the schedule toward elections. The Lusaka Agreement of 10 July 1999 was brokered by South Africa for the states of the Southern African Development Community (SADC), three of whom (Angola, Namibia and Zimbabwe) were allies of the Kinshasa regime. The Agreement called for a cease-fire in place and a sharing of power among the various Congolese parties, as rebels and government were counted as equals. However, the Agreement had been negotiated among sovereign states and it took another three months to bring the rebel movements into the Agreement to begin an Inter-Congolese Dialogue

(ICD). Joseph Kabila's succession to the presidency after his father's assassination introduced a new sense of cooperation and active politicking to the Lusaka process. The parties met in the in Sun City in February 2001 under South African mediation to further negotiate the power-sharing details of the agreement, but negotiations broke down, as the government of Kabila manoeuvred to move from equality to *primes inter pares* status. It then shifted from internal to inter-state negotiations, and signed peace agreements with Rwanda and Uganda on 30 July and 6 September 2002, respectively, providing for the withdrawal of their troops from Congo.

Preparing the ground for elections

Elections and the reestablishment of the institutions of not just government but the state by mid-2005 were the goal of a power-sharing agreement reached in Pretoria on 16 December 2002, again under the mediation of South African President Thabo Mbeki. The first step was the promulgation of a provisional constitution on 2 April 2003, drafted by a UN team of Swiss jurists and based on the Pretoria Agreement and previous Congolese constitutions. The second was the installation of a transitional government on 30 June 2003 on the formula of 1+4 – that is, with Kabila as interim president with vice-presidents drawn from the four major opposition sectors: former foreign minister Abdoulaye Yerodia Ndombasi for Kabila's People's Party for Reconstruction and Development (PPRD), former businessman and former Mobutu supporter Jean-Pierre Bemba for the Movement for the Liberation of Congo (MLC), lawyer Azarias Ruberwa for the RCD-Goma, and former international civil servant and former RCD leader Arthur Zahidi Ngoma for the non-violent opposition. The strongest force of the non-violent opposition, the Union for Democracy and Social Progress (UDPS) led by Etienne Tshisekedi, however, remained outside the process, as he still considered himself rightful prime minister from the epoch of the Sovereign National Conference over a decade earlier. Although the formula is based on political accommodation among enemies rather than on governing effectiveness among collaborators, each of the vice-presidents is charged with a governing sector as well as representing a political tendency – Bemba with economy and finances, Ruberwa with defence and security, and Yerodia and Zahidi with other sectors. Under the vice-presidents is a government of some 50 ministers and deputy ministers. In rough parallel, a 500-person transitional parliament was selected from representatives of the government, the rebel groups and militias, the non-violent opposition, and civil society.

The installation of the government began the clock ticking with an eye towards elections within two years. The government lacked authority, notably in proportion to the distance from the capital, and has been marked more by competition among the five political leaders than by cooperation among five super-ministers. Vice-President Ruberwa suspended the participation of the RCD in the transition government on 23 August 2004 until he was brought back into the government ten days later through Mbeki's mediation. Five major pieces of legislation were needed for the process to move ahead: a nationality law, an amnesty law, a statute providing for military organisation, one providing for decentralisation (that is, provincial organisation) and electoral provisions. The first, which restores Congolese nationality to the Kinyarwanda-speaking populations of the east, was passed by the transitional parliament on 25 September 2004 but remains to be applied. The others have been before parliament since autumn 2003, and as of March 2004 were still awaiting resolution. The amnesty law is particularly delicate, since the culture of impunity as a key to participation in the government clashes with the culture of accountability that the parties seek to install for the future. The government in March 2004 authorised the International Criminal Court (ICC) to investigate human-rights abuses in Congo, but only those occurring after the Court's inauguration date on 1 July 2002; the ICFC Chief Prosecutor announced on 23 June 2004 that it would begin work, focusing on Ituri.

Military organisation has also proceeded slowly. The task is to integrate a small number of the over 350,000 combatants in the wars of the Zairean succession into a unified national 150,000-man Armed Forces of the Democratic Republic of Congo (FARDC) and national police, including the Rapid Intervention Police and the roughly 4,000-man Special Presidential Security Group (GSSP), and to subject the rest to a process of disarmament, demobilisation and reintegration (DDR). According to UN Security Council Resolution 1565 of 1 October 2004, the first was the key to the second: a new FARDC would be the agent of disarmament. One critical aspect of the military reorganisation problem is the weakness of the new army – numbering only about 60,000 in April 2005 – which to be effective has to assert its unified military authority over the disparate and hostile antecedents of its troops. Integration has occurred only at the upper officers' level, not among the rank-and-file. If a rebel group agrees to disarm, it joins the DDR process; if not, it must be disarmed forcibly. Kinshasa has made no budgetary provision for DDR and no move in the direction of forcible disarmament, although by early 2005 it declared itself ready to do so. Disarmament, principally of the FDLR, remains an RCD-Goma precondition for progress toward elections. The FARDC has attempted to take on rebel armies in the east and was able to reassert government control of Bukavu in June 2004, but it has proven too weak to forcibly disarm rebel groups, and too shaky to assert discipline over its own soldiers' looting, raping and pillaging, or simply deserting.

The alternative to voluntary or forcible disarmament is cooperation, but another aspect of the FARDC's weakness has been its reliance on cooperation with some of the very rebel groups it is supposed to bring under its control. This was a microcosm of the central dynamic problem of the government itself. Lacking the ability to assert its sovereignty over the whole country, the government often has had to make local alliances with groups that contest its sovereignty; instead of strengthening its national authority, it has become a captive of local conflicts rather than controlling them. Since neighbouring states – notably Rwanda and Uganda – also employed the same strategy through alliances with local rebel groups, they have locked local conflict into international confrontation, while making the international relations subordinate to local disputes.

The fourth key issue is the establishment of a politico-administrative structure for the country, embodying a mixture of centralised and decentralised power. Since the Mobutu regime was characterised by extreme centralised neglect and kleptocracy, and the wars of the Zairean succession have been marked by assertions of local control in the absence effective centralised authority, decentralisation remains important as a means of bringing the state to the people and recognising particular local needs. Governors of the ten provinces and commanders of the ten military regions are appointed by Kinshasa but determined substantially by local political allegiances. Thus, Kinshasa has employed two contradictory strategies in its civil and military appointments, seeking to buy into local realities while at the same time sending loyalists to assert local control. It has opposed power-sharing at the regional/local level ('vertical power-sharing', akin to federalism), hoping to use 'horizontal' or centralised power-sharing at the national level as a way of constraining leaders of political groups within a national government.

Finally, the technical preparations for the election have remained wanting. As of March 2005, 40,000 polling places were needed, manned by some 80,000 police and 200,000 polling officials, none of which were ready. On all five fronts, the process of preparing for elections was behind schedule, but the most important was the absence of a unified administration and security across the country. Frequently, the shortcomings on several fronts have amplified one another, as could be seen in a number of incidents in the second war that shook the country in 2004.

Geopolitics and petty politics

In 2004–05, broad areas of control throughout the country broke down into factional holdings and mobile alliances, setting the stage for at best slow progress on the key issues. The parties, large and small, subsequently sought political assurances of their role, before the elections, because they were not sure the elections will confirm their power and viability. But if they do not get that assurance, they would probably consider it in their interests to hinder the process and continue to manoeuvre to maximise their power. As the International Crisis Group has put it: 'spoilers – Congolese and non-Congolese alike – who have nothing to gain from a successful transition concluded by free and fair elections regularly manipulate the acute ethnic and political tensions … to contest some of its key components such as the territorial reunification of the country, the transfer of tax revenues to Kinshasa, the DDR process and the creation of a national army under a unified command'. The basic groups in Congo are Kabila's regime centred on Kinshasa in the west, with the PPRD, formed in March 2002, as its political organisation; the RCD in the Kivus, with Rwandan support; and the MLC in Orientale and Equateur provinces in the north, with Ugandan support. It is in the East – Kivus and Orientale – that the sharpest confrontation over the key issues occurs, as shown by crises in 2004.

The government's aim has been to extend its political control through twin strategies. However, despite the military cease-fire included in the Lusaka and Pretoria agreements, Kabila has also used the FARDC and police against the militias of other government partners – in particular, redeploying thousands of soldiers to the east April–June 2004 and also utilising local groups in its military operations. Like the others, the government camp is split between those 'soft-liners' close to the president and supporting his political manoeuvring and those hardliners left over from his father's government who fear the transition process will threaten their formerly predominant position. Two overnight coups in 2004, on 27–28 March and 10–11 June, were suspected to be associated with the latter group. Correctly suspected or not, several important hardliners were fired in the aftermath of the second attempt. These included Army Chief of Staff General Liwanga Mata-Nyamuniobo; the head of the presidential military household (set up by associates of Laurent Kabila after his assassination); the presidential security advisor (replaced by 'soft-liner' Guillaume Samba Kaputo); and Minister of the Presidency Augustin Katumba Mwanke, as well as Security Minister Mwenze Kongolo and Plan and Reconstruction Minister Denis Kalume, first suspended in 2003. The result was a more cohesive presidential team, and one that was tactically flexible. In July, the PPRD, a relatively new organisation, filled its top positions in preparation for the elections. Former Communications Minister and government spokesman Vital Kamerha was chosen to head the party, and a mobilisation and organisation apparatus was established.

The RCD split into a number of factions, the largest being RCD-Goma, headed by Ruberwa, with its approximately 30,000-man National Congolese Army (ANC). RCD-Goma has turned out to be the main opponent of Kinshasa, favouring vertical power-sharing and ambivalent about, and only tentatively committed to, the transition process to elections. In early 2005, it was in control of South Kivu and the southern parts of North Kivu, with Rwandan support, although not especially popular with the population it purports to represent. Further, its governance has not been particularly beneficial to the region in terms of either security or of the distribution of its revenues gained from taxes on border trade and mining of coltan and diamonds, estimated at $1 million a month. RCD-ML (Liberation Movement), with about 3,000 men in the Congolese Peoples Army (APC), who held sway in northern North Kivu (Beni and Lubero Districts) with Ugandan support, and the smaller RCD-N (National), are of minor importance, although they hold a few ministries. RCD-ML is friendly to Kinshasa but does not want to hand over its taxes and mineral revenues to the central government.

In the Congolese context, RCD-Goma itself has been riven by an internal dispute between those who see their future within the transitional government and process ('Kivutiens') and those who feel that process threatens their positions acquired through the first and second war ('Banyarwanda'). Over the course of 2004, this rift and the loss of Bukavu in South Kivi weakened the RCD-Goma and Ruberwa as a result, leading to his ten-day withdrawal from the government in late August to assert his importance. The MLC has become a more coherent, disciplined organisation, operating across northern Congo with a 20,000-man army, with Ugandan support.

The remaining factions are smaller, localised in their base in the East and often quite fluid in their alliances. Reflecting a process seen elsewhere – for instance, in Liberia and Sudan – these smaller groups broke up and returned to violence to demand a share of the power for the benefit of their leaders. In the Ituri district, the eastern part of Orientale Province, the herding Hema people, related to the Kirwanda-speaking populations of the area, have long been locked in the local version of a worldwide historic conflict, between pastoral and farming peoples, against the landed Lendu. The Hema are represented by the Union of Congolese Patriots (UPC) of Thomas Lubanga, following a disagreement with a RCD-ML leader in 2002 in Sun City, and is the only regional group to be recognised as a political party involved in the transition government. Soon after, UPC lost its Ugandan support and turned to Rwanda and RCD-Goma as allies. Fighting in Bunia in mid-2003 followed, leading to the French-led European intervention known as *Operation Artemis*. Personal politics and the alliance shifts produced a new Hema organisation, the Party for the Unity and the Safeguard of the Integrity of Congo (PUSIC) led by Chief Khawa, with a militia of roughly 2,000 and support from Uganda, controlling the Irumu area in southeast Ituri next to North Kivu. The party of the Lendu (and other farming groups) is the Front for National Integration (FNI), led by Floribert Ndjabu, with forces estimated at 27,000 in the Djugu area in eastern Ituri, where has drawn its economic support from control of the Mongbwalu gold mine, and in Bunia.

In 2004, the Hema–Lendu conflict has been tempered, to be replaced by internal splits and fights among and within the movements (as well as attacks on competing groups outside the growing Hema–Lendu cooperation, such as the local Nande businessmen). The UPC chief of staff, Floribert Kisembo, broke away with some 500 members as UPC-K, leaving the UPC-L with forces estimated anywhere from 3,000 to 15,000, most of whom are child soldiers. The two UPCs as well as the FNI fight over control of Bunia. In Djugu, the FNI is contested by the Patriotic Forces of Resistance in Ituri (FPRI) with 5,000–9,000 men. Other armed groups with territorial control are the Peoples Armed Forces of Congo (FAPC) of Jerome Kakwavu who split from the UPC, taking with him around 6,000 men, controlling Aru and Mahagi areas in northeast Ituri district. The FAPC is closely supported by Uganda and allied with the Peoples Force for Democracy in Congo (FPDC), which has only 300 men. Thus, Uganda has protected its sphere of influence, the core of which is the MLC, through alliances across ethnic lines with the UPC-K, RCD-ML, PUSIC, and FAPC in Ituri district, isolating the UPC-L from the other Rwandan-supported area of the RCD-Goma in the Kivus.

However, all of these groups, large and small, in northeast Congo (the Ituri district of Orientale Province that aspires to provincial status) have been united by a desire to overcome their isolation from the transition process. At the same time, they have divided over the way to do it – the choice being either to force their way into the process or to stymie it. The Transitional Government invited the Ituri groups to a meeting in Kinshasa on 10–14 May 2004 to bring peace and security, as well as government control, to the region and to clear the way for elections. The result was an Act of Engagement, in which the government agreed to study the seven groups' demands in return for a pledge of disarmament, local peace and national unity – all preconditions for an electoral process. But the participants split into two groups – the UPC-L and FNI (the new Hema–Lendu alliance, which Rwanda appears to support) that demanded a number of high-level positions in the national and regional governments ('vertical power-sharing'), and the rest with more limited demands, including recognition as political parties and revenue-sharing from Kinshasa. Even if the top leaders are satisfied, lieutenants in the militias tend to be harder-liners looking for positions are more inclined to return to violence (as they then did, in July). Despite the assurances in the Act of Engagement, Kinshasa made it plain that government ministries and provincial positions would not be redistributed. Since the current transitional process was the result of regional groups' efforts to buy into central government through the use of violence, smaller groups have taken up the lesson on their own accounts and, with nothing to lose in the face of central government neglect and neighbours' encouragement, take up arms to force their own way in as well, or if not, to destroy the integration process that threatens to destroy them.

Two other groups fall outside the category of political parties but very much in the centre of conflict and insecurity in eastern Congo. One is the Mai-Mai, actually a congeries of local groups seeking to defend themselves against the impingement of various other groups on the local population. The Mai-Mai (a term referring to water, either as a magical protection against bullets or as what protective magic turns bullets into) has made alliances according to opportunity to ward off external disruptions. Other local defence forces in the region include Banyamulenge elements (Congolese Tutsi) who contest the right of such groups as the RCD-Goma to speak for them. Such local groups, especially in the Kivus, including Banyamulenge, have come together to counteract the Rwandan-backed dominance of RCD-Goma and the growing Hema–Lendu cooperation.

The final group is the prime remaining external source of much of the conflict, the Democratic Forces for the Liberation of Rwanda (FDLR), a force of some

8,000–10,000 (Rwanda claims 15,000–18,000) composed of remnants of the 140,000 former Rwandan forces of the Hutu government of Juvenal Habyarimana, the ex-FAR (Armed Forces of Rwanda) and *interahamwe*, who fled their country when the current government of Paul Kagame took over after the genocide of 1994, augmented by new recruits. Many of the original group were killed by the Rwandan Army in Congo during the first war (1996–97), and many others have been repatriated to Rwanda and still others resettled in Congo, but some 10,000 were incorporated in 1998 into the Congolese army, where they have remained. The remaining FDLR, established in 2000, is a mixture of old Rwandans from the genocide a decade ago and younger elements, unemployed and embittered. Weak and exhausted, and no longer able to accomplish their aim of overthrowing the Kagame government, they have nevertheless remained quite capable of making raids on Rwanda and of terrorising the population of the Kivus. The FDLR has continued to be politically and militarily useful for Kinshasa, although they have not received supplies from the Congolese government since 2002, and have often allied with the Mai-Mai. They are still a prime stumbling block of the Lusaka and Pretoria agreements, which called for their disarmament, and therefore provide an unfortunate excuse to Rwanda for its interference in east Congolese affairs. Many of the *génocidaires* have joined the voluntary disarmament programme, but those who remain in the FDLR now require forcible disarmament, which is beyond the capabilities of the FARDC and the willingness of the UN Military Observer Group in Congo (MONUC).

Ituri and Bakuvu

This setting was the background to local outbreaks of violence in eastern Orientale and the Kivus that underscored the fragility of the transition process toward elections. While similar circumstances for insecurity have also been developing in Kasai and Katanga, in Kivu alone – RCD-Goma territory according to the Pretoria Agreement – the death toll has been estimated by the International Rescue Committee at 90 times greater than that along the cease-fire line between government and rebel territories. In Ituri, the Luanda Agreement of 30 September 2002 providing for the withdrawal of Uganda forces from Congo caused a reversal of alliances and the splintering of factions, as noted, and the replacement of Uganda by Rwanda as the chief supporter of the remaining UPC-L. It also created the 177-member Ituri Pacification Commission (IPC) and in turn (in April 2003) the Ituri Interim Administration (IIA) and the Ituri Disarmament and Community Reinsertion (DCR) Program. However, before the latter could take place, the Ugandan withdrawal created a vacuum in and around Bunia that all groups, including the government, and their allies rushed in to fill. It took the international community to elbow its way in and fill the vacuum on its own, through *Operation Artemis*, the European Union (essentially, French) Interim Emergency Multilateral Force (IEMF) in July 2003 and then MONUC's Ituri Brigade (composed of Bangladeshi, Pakistani and Nepalese troops), which saw considerable action in early 2005, killing 50 in early March. Politico-military groups and their alliances continued to disintegrate and realign, despite the attempt through the May 2004 Act of Engagement to establish some sort of order within the region and in its relations with Kinshasa. In July, fighting broke out again, between the FNI and the FAPC, amid reports of intra-FAPC fighting and shifts of support to the FNI from Uganda or some Ugandan elements.

Since there has been no effective control by MONUC, Kinshasa's FARCD or either of the interested neighbours, the situation has become characteristically unstable as groups and factions vie for marginal advantage. The appointment in mid-2004 of new judges for the court system and of a District Commissioner for Ituri (Petronille Vaweka) with local ties and PPRD membership and Lendu and Hema deputies were important steps, but their effectiveness depends on the re-establishment of security. Without military support from MONUC or Kinshasa, the district is likely to continue to be unstable and vulnerable to competing attempts for control by the neighbouring states and for factional manoeuvres for advantage by local would-be leaders and followers.

Another more serious crisis in 2004 occurred in Bukavu in February and then May–June, with ramifications that typify the problems of the East. In the beginning of February fighting broke out between Kinshasa's newly appointed FARDC commander of the 10th military region (South Kivu), General Prosper Nyabiolwa, and the RCD-Goma governor of South Kivu, Xavier Chiribanya, over the attribution of the province and a weapons stockpile. The government suspended Chiribanya (who had previously been condemned to death for participation in Laurent Kabila's assassination), who accepted his suspension under pressure from MONUC. Fighting resumed at the end of the month between the forces of Nyabiolwa and those of his former ANC deputy, Colonel Jules Mutebusi, over the arrest of a former ANC and now FARDC officer, Major Joseph Kasongo, who was then freed under pressure from ONUC and returned to Bukavu in a MONUC plane to Kinshasa's embarrassment. Nyabiolwa was then recalled, as was Mutebusi, who refused to return to Kinshasa for fear of his safety. Bukavu remained divided between two ostensibly FARDC officers and their forces – symbolic of the problems of military reunification and transitional government cooperation.

The dispute over the control of South Kivu province, entangled in personal politics, resurged in late May 2004, when an adjunct of Mutebusi was arrested by the FARDC under the new military region commander General Félix Mbuza Mabe. Immediately aided by troops from the VIII military region of North Kivu under ANC General Laurent Nkunda, Mutebusi took Bukavu (the provincial capital) and Kamanyola. Besieged by 10,000 new FARDC forces rushed to the region, the ANC rebels held the two cities for one and three weeks, respectively, in early June, causing several hundred casualties and 30,000 Kinyarwanda-speaking refugees who fled to Rwanda and Burundi; the rebels withdrew under threat of an EU intervention, Mutebusi's forces to disarmament by the FARDC and Nkunda's forces back to North Kivu. MONUC sat out the fighting, evacuating some civilians but not intervening in the fighting.

A spillover effect of the conflict in the east occurred on 13 August, when 130 of the Banyamulenge refugees from Bukavu who had fled to Gatumba in Burundi were massacred. While the original suspect was the extremist Burundian Hutu group, the New Liberation Forces (FNL), responsibility for the massacre seems to point instead to Congolese forces, including Mai-Mai, FDLR, Congolese Hutus, and even forces associated with General Mabe. The attack was one of the reasons for the RCD-Goma's ten-day withdrawal from the government. Clashes between the Mai-Mai and the ANC have continued

The government contest with the RCD-Goma in Bukavu, followed by the Gutamba massacre, exacerbated Rwanda's sense of grievance with the transition government, leading to direct threats from Kigali to return to Congolese territory and clean out the FDLR at the end of the year. While no members of the Rwandan Peoples Army (RPA) have been officially identified in Congo, Rwandan support for its allies continued as did fighting in the Kivus at the turn of the year, impeding the electoral transition process.

The Great Lakes conflict and the international community

With the local conflicts nourished by the external parties and the external conflicts tied to the local rivalries and animosities, the international community has sought ways to break into the chicken-and-egg riddle of the wars of the Zairean succession. An effective government, with a strong military arm and a coherent national policy, would seem to be the sine qua non of taming the local conflicts, but the government is tied to its local allies and their disputes and the local conflicts are fed and watered by Uganda and Rwanda, their geopolitical rivalry and their dispute with Congo. The 2002 agreements between the two neighbours and Congo have produced the withdrawal of the bulk or perhaps all of the two armies, but for that reason their contacts with their local allies have become all the more important and their material and political support remains necessary.

One formal step was undertaken at the end of 2004. A proposal had been long on the table, notably from France, to hold an International Conference on the Great Lakes Region, and Ibrahima Fall, Special Representative for the UN Secretary-General (SRSG) for the Great Lakes was working for a meeting to be held in June 2004. In the end, it took until 20 November to bring together 14 heads of state from the region (Congo, Rwanda, Burundi, Uganda, Tanzania, Kenya, among others) in Dar es-Salaam to sign a declaration on the region as 'space of lasting peace and security'. Kabila and Kagame were again brought together a week later by the presidents of Nigeria and France and the Belgian prime minister during the Francophone Summit in Ouagadougou, Burkina Faso. But in between the two meetings, Kagame had announced his intention to dispose of the NDLR on Congolese territory, and the following month he reinforced his threat.

Kabila and Kagame were summoned to Abuja by African Union (AU) and Nigerian President Olesegun Obasanjo on 25 June after the Bukavu conflict, where they reaffirmed the Pretoria principles and agreed to a joint verification mechanism, but it will take more than one meeting to bridge the interest gap between the two. At its Libreville summit, the AU endorsed the need for forcible DDR and pledged military assistance to carry it out, specifically against the FDLR. But the ASU has not been able to gather enough forces even to carry out it prior engagement in Darfur, Sudan, and is unlikely to be disarming Congo in the near future.

With Resolution 1565 on 1 October 2004, the UN Security Council responded to the previous inadequacy of MONUC in size and mandate by authorising an increase to 16,700 troops (two-thirds of the Secretary-General's request of 23,900) but still with restrained rules of engagement. The two previous resolutions – 1279 of 30 November 1999, and 1493 of 28 June 2003 – had set the figure at 5,537 and 10,800 troops, respectively. While MONUC was mandated to directly engage to impose a cease-fire in Ituri, as of March 2005 it still had not established a presence in the Kivus.

Now and then

Progress towards elections has been slowed by problems of security and preparedness. In April 2005, the chances of meeting the 30 June 2005 deadline seemed minimal at best. Several possibilities remained open. Kabila could issue a one-time extension of the deadline for six months, as permitted in the Pretoria Agreement. Even that would require some fancy political footwork. He could hold an indirect vote, calling on appointed officials, both from Kinshasa and from the other power-sharing partners or even local groups, to vote in the name of the people; this option would scarcely pass any democratic or legitimising test. He could rush to an election without a census, simply holding a voter registration drive among the country's 60 million people; such a move is possible, although still technically and politically difficult, since a full census to update the last one 20 years ago is not absolutely necessary for the establishment of a voter list. He could hold elections where possible, in some or much of the country but not in the east. This, however, would validate RCD-Goma's claims of government ineffectuality in the east and weaken the validity of the results as representative of the whole country. Or he could default, with the loss of international legitimacy and the corresponding accreditation of Rwanda's claims and spoiler groups' manoeuvring.

In addition to preparations for the elections themselves, the matter of security is the key to their occurrence. DDR, in turn, is the key to security, particularly with regard to the FDLR. There have been indications of serious cooperation by Kinshasa in this effort, but this activity further depends on the UN Security

Council's authorisation of a larger MONUC with rules of engagement that allow a direct and visible role. At the beginning of 2005, MONUC was still low and slow, hampered by a desire to remain neutral no matter who is in conflict, with neither a search nor a preventive mandate, and a Chapter VI attitude that 'we are not here to make war or peace but only to hold a peace that the parties have agreed to'. Its mandate comes up for renewal in March 2005, when these problems need robust attention.

The International Committee in Support of the Transition – composed of the ambassadors to Congo from the US, the United Kingdom, France, Germany, Japan, Belgium, Canada, the EU, and South Africa, Angola, Gabon, Zambia and the AU, plus MONUC – has grown slowly into an active oversight role with respect to the transition process and its players and sought to provide greater coordination among its members. But for the Kinshasa government to move decisively towards competence and viability, the Committee needs to establish greater coordination with the policies of the international financial institutions, whose lending should perhaps be tied to progress by the recipients – notably the Congolese, Rwandan and Ugandan governments – in implementing the Lusaka and Pretoria Agreements. Following the wars of the Zairean succession, Congo remained less a stable state than a multi-layered process of local, regional and national machinations and international community actions, with each layer dependent on but also controlling the others.

It will be difficult to break the various vicious cycles that preclude political stability from the bottom up. Ideally, international actors – treating sovereignty as responsibility – would act to stop them from the top down. But the US, and to a lesser extent the United Kingdom, are militarily and diplomatically overburdened elsewhere, and their post-11 September strategic interests in sub-Saharan Africa, though keen, are focused on terrorism – the one security threat that Congo does not acutely pose. The French have extended themselves in Congo, but are not likely to go much farther given worsening problems and potentially deepening commitments in Côte d'Ivoire. The fledgling AU is preoccupied with Darfur and has not yet proven itself as a regional player. International responsibility therefore still redounds to the UN, which itself remains taxed by heavy obligations in West Africa and elsewhere. If 2005 is to be a political break-out year for Congo, it seems that it will have to be the Congolese, the Rwandans and the Ugandans that step up to the plate themselves. While the past record makes this prospect lamentably unlikely, it's worth remembering that the Ugandans' strategic repositioning in 2002 and Kinshasa's compromises have afforded major advances over the past three years. With marginally more international supervision and support, welcome progress, if not outright rebirth, could materialise.

Roiling West Africa

West Africa continued to be sub-Saharan Africa's region of pervasive conflict. Relatively speaking, there was quite a bit to be happy about in 2004–05. Peace was further consolidated in Sierra Leone, and African Union (AU) pressure appeared to condition a peaceful transition to democratic government in Togo following the death of its autocratic president, Gnassingbe Eyadema, in February 2005. But although United Nations and major-power involvement in Liberia and Côte d'Ivoire indicated that the region had not been strategically overlooked, the barriers to fully fledged peace in those two countries – especially Côte d'Ivoire – remained considerable. Intensifying ethnic and religious tensions in Nigeria also raised a notable red flag.

Instability in Côte d'Ivoire

The situation in Côte d'Ivoire continued to deteriorate in 2004, and the country remained physically and militarily divided. The parties to the conflict did not honour the peace agreements and accords, and diplomatic attempts to 'normalise' the situation were consistently frustrated. The high level of distrust between the government and the warring parties made the situation immensely complex and delicate. There was also some regional concern that the conflict could have a contagion effect, thus destabilising neighbouring countries. Official and rebel figures seemed at times to be exaggerated, and it is difficult to assess which are accurate. Nevertheless, that the conflict in Côte d'Ivoire caused 300 deaths during 2004 is a reasonable estimate. In addition, the UN High Commissioner for Refugees (UNHCR) estimates that in 2003, some 50,000 Ivorian refugees fled their country, mainly to Liberia, Guinea and Mali. Since then, perhaps 15,000 have returned. As of April 2005, about 500,000 Ivorians were internally displaced.

2004 started optimistically, as rebel ministers attended their first cabinet meeting on 6 January since their withdrawal from government on 23 September 2003. After France intervened militarily under *Operation Unicorn* in late 2002, the January 2003 French-brokered Linas–Marcoussis Accord had halted the fighting between the government of President Laurent Gbagbo and rebels controlling most of northern Côte d'Ivoire, and created a government of national reconciliation. However, Guillaume Soro, rebel leader of the so-called New Forces, soon made it known that he emphatically opposed President Laurent Gbagbo's plan to hold a referendum on three of the major law reforms provided for in the Accord. Although parliament had approved a constitutional change on the criteria for presidential candidates on 20 December 2003, Gbagbo insisted on holding a referendum on Article 35 of the constitution – the clause that defines the eligibility of presidential candidates. Rebels suspected that Gbagbo was using the referendum to prolong his stay in power by rigging the vote. On 27 February 2004, the United Nations (UN) Security Council unanimously passed Resolution 1528, which called for the deployment of the UN Operation in Côte d'Ivoire

(ONUCI) at a strength of 6,240 military personnel and 350 police officers. ONUCI deployed on 4 April, with an initial 12-month mandate. Its responsibilities include observing the cease-fire, assisting with disarmament and reintegration of ex-fighters, dealing with confiscated weaponry and helping to prepare for the presidential election scheduled for 2005. As of 31 December 2004, ONUCI comprised 6,215 uniformed personnel (of which 4,000 were French), including 5,846 regular troops, 154 military observers and 215 civilian police. In addition, there were 252 international civilian support personnel and 155 local staff on the ground.

Hope for Côte d'Ivoire's swift rehabilitation was severely dented on 25 March 2004, when hundreds of Ivorians, led by the main opposition groups, attempted to stage a march in Abidjan to protest against Gbagbo and his party, the Front Populaire Ivoirien (FPI). Protesters were attacked by what was described as a combination of Ivorian security forces and militia members, and the rebels suspended their participation in the coalition government. On 17 May, UNHCR published a report on the 25 March violence, and concluded that the police, the army and their paramilitary allies had killed at least 120 people, 'disappeared' 20 and injured another 274 during the two days of violence. The inquiry also found that individuals from northern Côte d'Ivoire and immigrants from Burkina Faso, Mali and Niger were targeted. Gbagbo categorically rejected the report, citing instead the official death toll of 37. Nonetheless, the UN announced that it was planning further investigations on human-rights abuses since the beginning of the civil war in September 2002. Meanwhile, the security situation remained volatile on both sides of the cease-fire line. On the night of 6 June 2004, unidentified armed men attacked the village of Gohitafla from the north. The Force Armées Nationales de Côte d'Ivoire (FANCI, the National Armed Forces of Côte d'Ivoire) and French forces intervened; in the subsequent clashes, 15 rebels and five FANCI soldiers were killed.

On 8 June, FANCI dispatched Mi-24 helicopter gunships to bomb the convoy of rebel commander Cherif Ousmane in Kounahiri, killing at least 12 people. The attacks severely strained the peace process and prompted the New Forces to reinforce their military presence north of the 'line of confidence' separating rebel and government forces and, notionally, territory. The helicopter attack also triggered violent protests in Abidjan by pro-government *jeunes patriotes* – Young Patriots – who accused both FANCI and the French forces of failing to protect civilians. The protesters burned tires and threw rocks in front of the French embassy and later threatened the local population, damaging their cars and property. The attacks, which targeted mainly French citizens, were also directed at the French forces, Westerners generally and UN staff.

In July 2004, West African leaders and the UN Secretary-General Kofi Annan met in Accra, Ghana for the Accra Summit, which provided a detailed framework for peace. A number of regional and international organisations were actively engaged in the Ivorian peace process. The AU, the Economic Community of West African

States (ECOWAS), the New Partnership for Africa's Development (NEPAD) and the UN were all involved in providing assistance and mediation. Expressing their concern over the situation, several countries also sought to provide assistance, most notably Algeria, France, Nigeria, Senegal, South Africa and the United States. The agreement that emerged, known as the Accra III accords, required the government to legislate legal and political reforms by 31 August, and scheduled the launch of a country-wide disarmament programme for 15 October. The New Force rebels subsequently lifted the curfew imposed upon Korhogo (the site of June clashes) and resumed its participation in the transitional government, leading to the reconvening of parliamentary sessions.

The Accra III accords temporarily restrained both the government and the rebels. In late September, however, the security situation again deteriorated after the government failed to pass legislation providing for the political and legal reforms required by the accords, thus leaving unresolved contentious issues such as Côte d'Ivoire's nationality code and the eligibility and rights of the four million foreign migrants originating from other West African nations (mainly Burkina Faso, Guinea and Mali). Fuelled by rumours of an impending coup, tensions and distrust between the warring factions increased frustration over the presence of the foreign peacekeepers. On 21 September, the pro-Gbagbo Young Patriots gave the French peacekeepers an ultimatum to withdraw from the demilitarised zone separating the government-held south from the rebel-held north. Three days later, stirred by rumours of a plot to assassinate Gbagbo, the government deployed FANCI troops throughout Abidjan, the capital, setting up roadblocks and identity checks, and conducting tank and helicopter patrols.

October and November 2004 witnessed serious escalation. Because the government had reneged on promises of political and legal reform by 31 August, the New Forces ignored a 15 October deadline for disarmament. As tensions between the warring factions increased, frustration grew over the presence of foreign peacekeepers. Both President Gbagbo's supporters and the New Forces openly re-armed. On 26 October, two trucks apparently travelling from Abidjan were found to contain weapons intended for pro-government supporters in infiltrated rebel territories. The New Forces claimed that the government and rival faction leader Ibrahim Coulibaly were behind the weapons transfer. On 28 October, the New Forces declared a state of emergency, withdrew ministers from the transitional government, imposed a curfew in the rebel-controlled north, and threatened a resumption of hostilities. On 4 November, the Ivorian Armed Forces launched *Sukhoi-25* airstrikes on the rebel stronghold in Bouaké. Nine French soldiers deployed to the central rebel area were killed by Ivorian aircraft fire on 6 November. French President Jacques Chirac responded by ordering the destruction of all Ivorian planes involved in the ceasefire violations. The French peacekeepers put four Ivorian *Sukoi*-25 planes and three helicopters out of commission.

Amid persistent rumours of a coup, foreigners – mostly French and some British citizens – were evacuated. On 5–7 November, hundreds of demonstrators descended massively into the streets of Abidjan and other cities. The Young Patriots led efforts to disrupt French movements at the international airport and were met with warning shots from French helicopters. The International Committee of the Red Cross documented that 410 people sustained injuries during the weekend's demonstrations. French troops were believed to have killed more than 20 people. *Radio Television Ivorienne* (RTI) broadcasted that France was planning to abduct Gbagbo, prompting further demonstrations by the 'patriots' and other pro-Gbagbo supporters. UN staff were temporarily transferred to Ghana, but returned to the country by the end of the month to resume humanitarian work. The UN Security Council subsequently issued various warnings, and adopted an arms embargo on 16 November through Resolution 1572, though subsequent attempts were apparently made to obtain arms from Libya and Egypt. More broadly, the New Forces refused to implement Accra III's disarmament, demobilisation and reintegration programme, accusing the government of violating agreements and procuring arms. The process is intended to disarm an estimated 30,000 combatants, including 25,000 rebel troops.

On 3 December, South African President Thabo Mbeki, acting on behalf of the AU, arrived in the country to meet with the government and rebels in order to revive the peace process. The White House, for its part, excluded Côte d'Ivoire from the list of countries eligible for assistance under the African Growth and Opportunity Act (AGOA). UN Security Council sanctions were postponed, however. On 15 December, Mbeki unveiled a four-point proposal for peace, citing the need to commence DDR and to review Article 35, which he hoped would break the impasse and pave the way for October 2005 elections. By early 2005, ONUCI had made marginal progress in the security sphere, joining with the Ivorian armed forces in 24-hour patrols in Abidjan. On 7 April 2005, following Mbeki's mediation efforts, the government and the rebel factions agreed to end hostilities, start disarmament and plan new elections, signing a new accord in Pretoria. But political progress, having stalled in 2004, will be difficult to regain. In the meantime, for the peacekeeping effort to contain the security situation, the French will need to maintain their substantial commitment of troops. On 4 April 2005, ONUCI's mandate expired. The Security Council unanimously extended it a month to prevent a 'complete breakdown' in security, in contemplation of a further extension to April 2006.

Slow advance in Liberia

Since the exile of former President Charles Taylor in August 2003, the subsequent establishment of a transitional government, and the deployment of the United Nations Mission in Liberia (UNMIL) peacekeeping operation, the situation in Liberia has markedly improved. While Monrovia remains troubled by rioting and an increase in criminal activity, violence has been episodic and conflict-related fatalities relatively low. The country still, of course, has serious conflict-related problems. UNHCR estimates that 350,000 Liberian refugees are still living in neighbouring Côte d'Ivoire, Gambia, Ghana, Mali, Senegal and Sierra Leone, and that 300,000 displaced persons remain in Liberia. Over the course of 2004, UNMIL increased in strength to a total of 15,788 uniformed personnel, including 14,501 troops, 189 military observers and 1,098 civilian police. By June, UNMIL had deployed to 13 of Liberia's 15 counties. Senegalese peacekeepers reached Maryland county near the Ivorian border on 22 June, paving the way for new disarmament, demobilisation, rehabilitation and reintegration (DDRR) cantonments in Zwedru and Tappita.

Liberia's disarmament process concluded on 30 October. During the period, three new cantonment sites were opened in Ganta (Nimba county), Voinjama (Lofa county) and Harper (Maryland county), respectively targeting former soldiers of Charles Taylor's army, rebel fighters from Liberians United for Reconciliation and Democracy (LURD) and those from the Movement for Democracy in Liberia (MODEL). By 30 October, the disarmament process had, since its resumption in April 2004, registered approximately 95,000 combatants from the warring factions. The UN provided each disarming combatant with $300 in compensation. In all, 27,000 small arms were recovered, along with 6.84 million bullets and 29,830 rounds of heavy ammunition (for mortars and rocket-propelled grenades). The total number of registered combatants is almost three times the original estimate of 38,000, and about 50,000 had been disarmed and demobilised since the process began in December 2003. However, although the possession and use of weapons was prohibited as of 31 October by both UNMIL and the Liberian transitional government, the total quantity of recovered weapons was alarmingly low. The disarmament process in Liberia was negatively affected by developments in neighbouring Côte d'Ivoire. Some former MODEL combatants at the Harper disarmament site were apparently disrupting the process, as they hoped to participate in Côte d'Ivoire's disarmament process instead, where they would receive $900 in compensation rather than the $300 provided in Liberia.

On 5 May 2004, however, as part of the DDRR process Liberia's transitional government and UNMIL launched a campaign to recruit and train 3,500 police officers to form the Liberian National Police (LNP). The project will be supervised by the 1,100-strong UN international civilian police force in Liberia. On 13 July, the Liberian transitional government officially established the LNP. The force is expected to recruit and train 1,800–1,900 police officers before the presidential and parliamentary elections in October 2005. A number of foreign government contributed funds to finance the DDRR process. On 25 March, the US announced that it had earmarked about $50m to assist former Liberian combatants and communities. The money will mainly be spent within the framework of the newly created 'community infrastructure programme' run by the US contractor Development Alternatives Incorporated. On 26 April, Japan announced a $3.64m emergency grant for the disarmament and reintegration of Liberian child soldiers. Despite these resources, the DDRR process was far from unproblematic. On 17 May, an argument about the payment of a resettlement grant to ex-combatants, for example, culminated in riots in Monrovia by forces loyal to the former Liberian president Charles Taylor, which left at least one person dead.

Some $520m for post-conflict assistance was pledged during the February 2004 donor conference. As of October, however, only $244m had been received. The shortfall hindered reconstruction initiatives across the board, ranging from humanitarian aid to the reintegration of former combatants to the rehabilitation of the nation's infrastructure. Donors have attributed their reticence to the Liberian government's corruption and are reluctant to provide further funds in the absence of fiscal responsibility. The UN Security Council, for its part, in September identified corruption and the general fragility of the peace as two main reasons for not lifting its sanctions on Liberia's diamond, timber and arms trade. On 28 October, the World Bank, the International Monetary Fund (IMF) and the Liberian government agreed to correctional measures intended to instate fiscal transparency; nevertheless, the Security Council passed Resolution 1579 on 21 December, extending sanctions for another 12 months, subject to review in May 2005.

Friction within political parties (most of which are former armed factions) also produced sub-critical insecurity in 2004. In May, a row erupted between members of LURD's political branch over the composition of the Finance Ministry. One group, led by Edward Farley, LURD's executive committee spokesman, threatened to disrupt the DDRR process unless Finance Minister Luseni Kamara was ousted and replaced by Finance Cabinet Director Soko Sackor. Ultimately, Kamara maintained his post, as another LURD faction, including 36 senior military officers, opposed the reshuffle and threatened to respond with a 'military showdown'. In December 2004, the Armed Forces of Liberia protested and vandalised property, as they accused the transitional government of not paying their arrears, which UNMIL then swiftly arranged to be paid. On 30 December, militants led by Joseph Power Zackor, a general under the Taylor regime, attacked a police station after police tried to arrest his group for extorting money from road passengers. But the signing of the Electoral Reform Bill on 17 December – which the US feared the transitional government would delay on the pretext of taking a census first – held out prospects for a fully participatory election in October 2005 that might bring greater political stability. Under the new law, a simple majority will determine the outcome of presidential, senatorial and mayoral elections. A more complex system will be introduced for the House of Representatives. Each of Liberia's 15 counties will have two of the 64 House seats, with the remaining 34 redistributed to counties according to the size of their population, which will be determined by voter registration.

Throughout the year, the Special Court for Sierra Leone attempted to try Charles Taylor, whom the Sierra Leonean government has accused of holding 'the greatest responsibility' for the Sierra Leonean civil war and who has been indicted on 18 charges relating to war crimes. Following his indictment on 4 June 2003, pressure had been mounting both nationally and internationally to bring Taylor before the Court. On 12 March 2004, the UN Security Council unanimously adopted Resolution 1532, by which a travel ban was imposed on Taylor, his family and other associates, and relevant property and bank accounts were frozen. Taylor's lawyers filed a petition with the Liberian Supreme Court on 16 March claiming that the Court lacked jurisdiction to search the defendant's properties in Liberia. Taylor's defence team also argued that as a serving head of state at the time of the alleged crimes and indictment, Taylor would remain immune from prosecution – an argument finally rejected by the Appeals Chamber on 31 May. But Nigeria continues to harbour the former leader and refuses to hand him over without a formal request from the transitional Liberian government. Liberian Interim President Gyude Bryant has appeared reluctant to request such extradition, fearing that Taylor's presence in-country would fuel instability. On 7 July 2004, the Liberian parliament decided against issuing an extradition request, in spite of pressure by human-rights organisations and the UN.

Sierra Leone: an improbable bright spot

The security situation in Sierra Leone remained calm throughout most of 2004. President Ahmad Tejan Kabbah officially dissolved the National Committee for Disarmament, Demobilisation and Reintegration on 4 February 2004, after 72,490 fighters had been disarmed and 71,043 demobilised, including 6,845 child soldiers. A total of 56,700 former combatants had registered for reintegration over five years. This left a shortfall of 8,945 known fighters who had supposedly opted for 'self-reintegration', perhaps to avoid the stigma that official reintegration might have created. By the end of 2004, the United Nations Mission in Sierra Leone (UNAMSIL) had been downsized to 4,274 uniformed personnel from a peak of around 17,500 in 2002. In light of the wider regional security situation, its mandate was extended until June 2005. But UNAMSIL has transferred the responsibility of providing security in Sierra Leone itself to the national government. To facilitate this objective, UNAMSIL worked closely with Sierra Leone's security committees and conducted several joint exercises with the police and the army to improve the local capacity of the security sector. A joint tactical exercise, code-named *Exercise Hammer Strike*, was conducted on 5–15 January 2004, involving the UNAMSIL Sector East Quick Reaction Force and troops from the Republic of Sierra Leone Armed Forces (RSLAF). In early August, the government ratified a National Security and Central Intelligence Act, which would bolster the government's capacity to provide security. In mid-August, the UK pledged £4.5m in technical assistance for the RSLAF. The actual transfer of responsibility was completed in two stages, each marked by a ceremonial celebration: the eastern province was handed over on 10 August 2004, and the western region, including the capital Freetown, on 24 September. The responsibility for the security of Freetown was transferred on a two-month trial basis. The trial proved successful and the security responsibility of the government became permanent.

The Special Court for Sierra Leone officially opened in Freetown on 10 March 2004. The Court faced immediate complications, as General Issa Sesay, the former interim leader of the rebel Revolutionary United Front (RUF), filed a motion to have the Court's president, Justice Geoffrey Robertson of the United Kingdom, removed from office. Sesay's defence team accused Robertson of bias against the rebel group, whom he had accused of crimes against humanity in a previously published book. The Appeals Chamber of the Court ruled that Justice Robertson would hear cases involving the African Forces Revolutionary Council (AFRC) and the Civil Defence Militia (including the tribal militia known as Kamajors) but be disqualified from all cases involving the RUF, particular those dealing with senior members of the rebel group. The trial of three members of the Civil Defence Force (CDF) started on 4 June. Former Interior Minister and CDF National Coordinator Sam Hinga Norman, CDF National Director of War Moinina Fofana and CDF High Priest Alieu Kondewa appeared in court to face charges of killing, raping and terrorising thousands of people, recruiting child soldiers and committing acts of cannibalism as described by the Chief Prosecutor of the UN-sanctioned Special Court, David M. Crane, during the opening proceedings. Norman's trial was repeatedly adjourned, as he asked to conduct his own defence, a request rejected by the Court on 8 June. The Special Court also formally charged Sesay, RUF internal security chief Augustine Gbao, and RUF battlefield commander Morris Kallon with 18 war crimes each. In an emotive opening statement, Crane claimed that the three men standing trial were among those with the greatest responsibility for the Sierra Leonean civil war and that their prosecution would be an act of justice.

During a high-level ceremony at the UN headquarters in New York on 28 October, Sierra Leone's Truth and Reconciliation Commission (TRC) published its final report, which contained recommendations on how to reconcile individuals, communities and the nation in the hope of preventing future conflict. The 1,500-page report includes a 3,000-page annex of 7,000 testimonies documenting the 1991–2002 conflict in its entirety – from the causes of war, to its impact on women and children and other abuses, to the role of natural resources in the conflict. The TRC was founded in 2000 as part of the Lomé Peace Agreement, and has since worked alongside the Special Court. The recommendations of the TRC are legally binding.

Sierra Leone made progress in the political realm as well as the security and judicial spheres. On 22 May, Sierra Leone held its first local elections in 32 years, giving the 2.27m registered Sierra Leonean voters the opportunity to elect their representatives in more than 390 regional and municipal districts. Out of the 17 registered parties in the country, only two participated in the election: the ruling Sierra Leone People's Party (SLPP) and the main opposition group and former sole party, the All Peoples Congress (APC). Also, and for the first time since democracy was reintroduced in 1996, 370 independent candidates were allowed to participate. Lack of funding prevented the Revolutionary United Front Party (RUFP), a party established from RUF remnants, from fielding candidates. In total, 1,560 candidates competed for 390 electoral wards. No violent incidents were reported during the elections. The process was, however, heavily criticised by opposition members who, from the early stages, denounced gross interference by tribal 'chiefs' favouring the ruling SLPP. Whether these accusations were accurate or not, the elections were at times highly eccentric. In six of 310 districts, voting was postponed until 5 June, when candidates complained that their names had been printed next to the wrong party symbol. There were also a high number of seats predetermined in unopposed single-candidate contests. Some 83 local government positions were thus declared even before the elections took place; 77 of these seats went to members of the SLPP and six to the APC.

Though varying greatly between 11% and 100%, voter turnout was generally low, with a national average of below 40%. The results of the elections came as a surprise for the SLPP, which had secured 70% of the votes in the 2002 general elections and had expected a landslide victory. The SLPP lost its majority in Freetown, which fell to the APC, 20 seats to four. A second key APC victory occurred in the northern town of Makeni. The shift was perceived by observers as an indictment of Kabbah's inability to improve living conditions in the country. Nevertheless, the ruling party managed to keep a firm grip in its traditional strongholds in the eastern and southern parts of Sierra Leone, winning large majorities. The EU financed the elections at a cost of $8m, despite Brussels' earlier decision to withhold money due to the lack of transparency in the disbursement of funds during the 2002 elections.

No conflict-related fatalities in Sierra Leone were reported in 2004. Political stability and the tentative restoration of state authority permitted a further 30,000 Sierra Leonean refugees to return to their country in 2004. By the end of July 2004, about 280,000 Sierra Leoneans had returned home, about 180,000 with UNHCR help. Despite these positive developments, diplomats fear that Sierra Leone may eventually slide back into chaos if a strong government, backed by a reliable police force and military, is not developed. The Sierra Leonean government is often accused of high-level corruption by its citizenry, and has been warned by the World Bank and bilateral donors as well as the TRC to improve fiscal transparency. Sierra Leone has also held the lowest ranking on the Human Development Index for seven straight years. Deplorable road conditions constrain further repatriation and reintegration operations, as does lack of employment for people returning. Thus, meeting in Goree Island, Senegal, on 20 February 2004, the heads of all UN peacekeeping missions in West Africa stated that a rapid withdrawal of UN forces from Sierra Leone could pose a threat to other peace operations in the region, and stressed the need for a carefully designed exit strategy. They also warned of rising tensions in Guinea, which borders three of the five countries that are undergoing transitions to peace. On 31 March 2004, the UN Security Council voted to extend the peacekeeping mission in Sierra Leone by six months until June 2005. The Security Council agreed to maintain a small force of 3,250 peacekeepers in the country, but this force was slated to be scaled down in the first half of 2005.

Nigeria's Christian–Muslim problems

Religious tensions between northern Muslims and Christians in Nigeria rose in 2004–05. Nigeria is the most populous state in Africa, and has sub-Saharan Africa's highest Muslim population, which constitute roughly half of its 130m people. Conflict brewed in Plateau state throughout the first half of 2004, and was pacified only when Nigerian President Olusegun Obasanjo deployed security forces and initiated a peace agreement. The National Commission for Refugees says that some 800,000 people have been displaced as a result of communal and religious clashes over the past four years. The ongoing dispute between the central and state governments over Nigeria's polio vaccination campaign is indicative of the level of ethnic and religious mistrust in the country. On 24 February 2004, Niger became the fourth state to boycott the government's vaccination drive, claiming that it was part of a Western plot to reduce the Muslim population by spreading infertility and the human immunodeficiency virus (HIV). Although an independent study on a random sample of the polio vaccine showed no traces of anti-fertility or HIV agents, two northern states, Bauchi and Zamfara, retained their boycott into April 2005.

In January 2004, authorities in Plateau state banned a radical Muslim group, the Council of Ulamma, or the Muslim Council of Elders, which they claimed was preaching religious hatred and intolerance. Previously, the Council – an authoritative religious body with considerable influence in the Muslim community – had published a newspaper advertisement accusing the state authorities of anti-Muslim bias. These allegations were the likely result of a security-force raid on 31 December 2003 in Jos, the capital of Yobe state, in targeting a suspected base of an extremist Muslim sect, al-Sunna Wal Jamma. In the 1980s, both the Council of Ulamma and al-Sunna Wal Jamma were suspected of inciting outbreaks of religious violence in northern Nigeria, in response to which the Nigerian Army was called in. Al-Sunna Wal Jamma is composed mainly of middle- and upper-class university and polytechnic students and aims to establish strict Islamic rule in Nigeria. Though the organisation does not seem to enjoy popular support among the majority of Nigerian Muslims, the group has demonstrated an ability to create broader tension between Christians and Muslims in the northern states. After remaining quiescent for years, in 2003–04 the group gained significant support. In January and February 2004, al-Sunna Wal Jamma launched several guerrilla attacks in Yobe state. The militants hid in camps near the border with Niger, crossing into Niger when pursued by Nigerian government troops.

The government has launched an investigation to ascertain the sect's sources of weaponry and funding and whether it has foreign connections. In February 2004, a Sudanese man was arrested on suspicion of channelling funds from the Middle East to al-Sunna Wal Jamma. Also, the head of the Almundata Al-Islam Foundation, Muhiddin Abdullahi, was detained in Kano state and accused of financing the sect. According to intelligence sources, the leader of the group is Mohammed Yusuf, who is believed to have escaped to Saudi Arabia. On 21 September 2004, approximately 20 armed al-Sunna wal Jamma members (locally known as the Taliban) attacked two police stations in Bama and Gworza in northeastern Borno state, killing four police officers and two civilians and injuring many more. The group is also believed to be behind several abductions in the region. According to the police commissioner, these attacks were intended to avenge the death of al-Sunna wal Jamma comrades in the December 2003 security-forces operation in Yobe. On 24 September, the Nigerian security forces responded by raiding the sect's hide-out in the Gworza hills, near the Cameroon border, killing 27 sect members and arresting a significant leader, Abubakar Aliyu Abubakar. Two police officers were killed in the raid, bringing the total number of police deaths to six. The sect retaliated on 8 October, targeting a police patrol and causing an undisclosed number of casualties.

Throughout early 2004, Plateau state experienced a cycle of ethnic and religious violence. The sectarian violence took place amid declining public confidence in Nigeria's multiparty political system, poverty and the increasing radicalisation of the Muslim north. In February, Muslim militants launched an attack on a church in Yelwa. According to the state authorities, at least 48 people were killed in the violence. Nigerian security sources believe that the attackers were hired mercenaries from Chad and Niger. On 24 April, clashes erupted between Christian Tarok fighters and their Muslim Fulani rivals at Bakin Chiyawa in the Shendam district. By 27 April, at least 20 people had died in intense fighting in which both sides used guns, bows and arrows, and machetes. On 2 May, the Tarok militiamen slaughtered hundreds of Muslims in Yelwa. The victims were shot with automatic rifles, hacked to death with machetes and burned alive in their homes. The attack was apparently retaliation for the February church attack, and prompted further violence between the two groups. Police had withdrawn from the area and did not return until after the killings. Yelwa community members felt betrayed by the police and local government. When the security forces and police did return, however, they launched a large-scale zero-tolerance operation to counter planned militant attacks, dismantling all illegal roadblocks with orders to shoot anyone suspected of causing trouble. The local authorities also announced measures to stop the recurring violence, including a dusk-to-dawn curfew in Yelwa.

Despite these efforts, attacks by Christian militias continued, killing as many as 600 people in Yelwa in the first week of May alone. On 18 May, armed Muslims launched a reprisal attack on five Christian villages near Yelwa, killing 20 people.

The violence spread to other northern states. On 10 May, religious violence in which 30 people were killed erupted in Kano state. Mobs of youths armed with clubs, machetes and jerry-cans of petrol roamed the streets attacking suspected Christians. The next day, an estimated 30,000 Kano residents, mostly Christians, fled their homes and took refuge at military and police barracks. On 12 November, the *Vanguard* newspaper reported that buildings were being burnt to the ground by angry mobs in the Eastern State of Anambra; up to 27 people were killed. Reports also emerged that ethnic and religious confrontations were occurring in Ora-Igbomina, Osun state. A government report on the violence in Kano, issued on 21 December 2004, concluded that 84 people had been killed in the attacks. The report also recommended that the state-security arrangements be reviewed.

On 18 May, following repeated accusations of not tackling the violence, Obasanjo declared a state of emergency in Plateau state. He also dissolved the Plateau state legislature and dismissed the elected governor Joshua Dariye, replacing him with Chris Alli, a retired army major general, as interim administrator for the next six months. On 21 May, Alli offered cash payments for the surrender of weapons by rival Muslim and Christian militia groups in the state. The amnesty lasted until 7 June, after which the possession of weapons was considered 'a conscious preparation for violence, bloodshed and murder' and therefore a crime. Alli offered 200,000 naira ($1,515) for automatic weapons or for information leading to the recovery of weapon caches, and 25,000 naira ($189) for each locally made rifle. On 16 July, Obasanjo and Alli unveiled a proposed peace process, including timelines for a preliminary voluntary-disarmament period, and the later launch of *Operation Cordon and Search*, a military campaign to recover illicitly held weapons. Other than the arrest of 15 suspected militiamen on 1 September 2004, which led to the recovery of an undisclosed quantity of arms and ammunition, these measures yielded few operational successes. Nevertheless, the situation in Plateau gradually stabilised. Obasanjo's plan also envisaged that, barring further violence, emergency rule would terminate by November. Obasanjo and Alli called upon all citizens, Muslim and Christian alike, to respect and assist in implementing a peace process. Large quantities of illegal weapons, however, are believed to remain in the hands of local militias. Alli's tenure ceased on 17 November, when power was transferred back to Joshua Dariye.

A September 2004 government report by the Committee of Rehabilitation and Reconciliation of Internally Displaced People (IDPs) estimated that 53,787 people had died, around 280,000 people had been displaced, and approximately 25,000 houses had been destroyed as a result of violence in Plateau state between September 2001 and May 2004. The report's parameters and guidelines may have led to a degree of overstatement, but the situation clearly borders on dire. On 16 September, the government's five-person delegation of elders, led by the Dean of the Social Science Faculty at the University of Jos, made an appeal to 25,000 IDPs in

Plateau state to return home. The delegation assured the IDPs that the government had resolved the crisis in the state. The following month, Obasanjo encouraged the National Assembly to create a reconciliation commission for Plateau. The commission was tasked with conducting investigations and hearings to establish a complete picture of the causes, nature, motives and extent of human-rights violations committed in Plateau between June 2000 and May 2004. The commission also investigated the possible role of Plateau state policies in causing and perpetuating the violence. Finally, the commission was tasked with defining the conditions in which an amnesty or policy of forgiveness would be appropriate and how best to consolidate a lasting peace.

Overall, Abuja has not been completely inattentive to some of the more superficial causes of unrest in Nigeria. The government boosted its efforts against militia violence, including a campaign against small-arms proliferation and disarmament where appropriate. Serious efforts were undertaken to curb the use of illegal arms. For instance, the Inspector General of Police, Alhaji Mustafa Balogun, reported in April 2004 that the Task Force on the Recovery of Firearms and Ammunition had seized 110 high-calibre weapons, 92 other small arms and large amounts of ammunition in the course of two weeks. Arrest operations had resulted in 89 arrests, and the deaths of 35 suspects and seven Task Force personnel. But many officers were accused of indiscriminately using force and causing civilian casualties. On 24 and 29 June, Nigerian police searching for weapons in the Plateau state fired at a crowd deemed threatening, killing several villagers. Human Rights Watch claimed that in Kano, Nigerian police had used excessive force and may have committed unlawful killings. Thus, zealous enforcement ran the risk of alienating its targets' wider community.

Ways forward

The fledgling AU has demonstrated its determination to be more effective than its largely feckless predecessor, the Organisation of African Unity. ECOWAS has responded to West Africa's acute security demands by becoming most capable and responsible security organisation in Africa. In West Africa, both proved their bona fides on the diplomatic front in February 2005, after Togo's strongman president, Gnassingbe Eyadema – perhaps the last African 'big man' – died at age 69. The Togolese army immediately installed Eyadema's son Faure Gnassingbe as president. He promised elections within 60 days, but this did not stifle local and regional protests over what appeared to be dynastic, as opposed to democratic, succession. The AU and ECOWAS quickly threatened sanctions and urged national governments to do the same. Faure thereupon stepped down in favour of the (elected) speaker of parliament, who would serve pending elections. Although Faure may attempt to rig the elections, a relatively smooth, non-violent democratic transition in a country that has not seen true democracy may also be possible. In any case, the AU and ECOWAS appear determined to remain seized of the matter.

It was, at least tentatively, a fine moment for the two groups, but they have found success harder to come by where boots on the ground are required, as in Sudan, Liberia and Côte d'Ivoire. What the AU and ECOWAS lack are not good intentions but sufficient resources. There are currently four UN peacekeeping missions underway in West Africa. The UN's biggest mission worldwide is in Liberia (15,000 troops), and there are smaller ones in Côte d'Ivoire, Sierra Leona and, on the sub-region's northern periphery, Western Sahara. The UN Department of Peacekeeping Operations has made it clear that African contributions are crucial complements to UN efforts – indeed, the AU spearheaded the eventual UN mission in Burundi, ECOWAS the one in Liberia – and the AU has urged the creation of regional brigades to respond to emergencies. On this score, West African governments – particularly Nigeria – have probably been the most responsible in Africa. Further, in June 2004, West African defence ministers composing the ECOWAS Defence and Security Commission pledged to create a 6,500-strong quick-reaction force, with 1,500 troops making up the leading element (dubbed the ECOWAS Task Force), another 3,500 troops constituting a back-up brigade and a reserve contingent of 1,500 available if required. The Task Force is to be deployable within 30 days, the brigade within 90 days and self-sustaining for another 90 days. Regional logistics depots already up and running in Mali and Sierra Leone would be at the force's disposal.

But these resources are not enough to fill West Africa's pressing needs. Trained, professional armies – the UK's in Sierra Leone, France's in Côte d'Ivoire – have proven necessary to sustain and consolidate peacekeeping efforts initially undertaken by ECOWAS. This reality reinforces the view that large-scale assistance, beyond train-and-equip help, will be required to enable ECOWAS – and, *a fortiori*, the other sub-regional African groups – to approach self-sufficiency in establishing and maintaining regional security and stability. And West Africa's particular challenges run deeper still. Nigeria's Christian–Muslim problem may be the most underrated potential source of jihadists in the world. While the US has recognised a prospective strategic terrorist threat to oil-producing states and assets in the Gulf of Guinea, it has so far responded mainly by helping to strengthen maritime security with out-of-area US European Command naval patrols. It may be diplomatically awkward for Washington and other major capitals to insinuate themselves into the internal security policy of an 'anchor state' like Nigeria. But if Abuja does not get a better handle on indigenous religious tensions, it may behove outside powers to do just that.

Zimbabwe: Mugabe's Impunity

The stalemate between the ruling Zimbabwean African National Union–Patriotic Front (Zanu–PF) party and its main opposition, the Movement for Democratic Change (MDC), has brought the country to a standstill. Struggling under the burden of unchecked economic hardship since the start of the crisis, the Zimbabwean people are exhibiting a deepening exhaustion with a political process that has brought them only violence and broken promises. If the 31 March 2005 parliamentary election had in fact been conducted properly, the MDC might have won, or at the very least denied Zanu–PF the two-thirds majority needed to change the constitution. However, the government was determined to avoid this divisive outcome and put in place an array of formal and informal impediments to opposition success. The willingness of southern African leaders to support the government of President Robert Mugabe irrespective of these violations of democratic practice, despite their recent commitments aimed at enhancing open elections, seems to signify that the politics of African solidarity will substantially maintain the grim status quo in Zimbabwe.

Tentative economic reform

The Zimbabwean economy, already severely damaged by four years of politically inspired actions aimed at dislodging the white commercial farming sector and disrupting the rise of a black opposition party, continued its downward slide. The country's GDP growth remained negative, slipping by 11% in 2002, 8.2% in 2003 and 2.5% in 2004, earning the country the woeful status of the world's fastest-shrinking economy. Inflation ran at the astounding rate of over 600% in January 2004, while it was estimated that two out of three Zimbabweans were unemployed. Illegal immigration to neighbouring South Africa, Botswana and even Mozambique has been a response to economic collapse, with foreign remittances often serving as a lifeline for family still back in the country. Dwindling incomes and scarce food supplies, coupled to the collapse of social services, have contributed to placing five million Zimbabweans on the brink of starvation.

The contraction of key exports like agriculture, tourism, manufacturing and, to a lesser extent, mining was behind much of Zimbabwe's poor performance. In the absence of vital agricultural and financial inputs, as well as provisions for training or extension services, the wholesale expropriation of commercial farming property through the 'fast-track' land reform has been an unmitigated disaster. The drift back to urban areas by putative 'war veterans', leaving in their wake unplanted fields and ruined infrastructure, represents the dysfunctional communalisation of a once-productive sector of the economy. Even those farms that found their way into the hands of the Zanu–PF elite and are maintaining a semblance of normal commercial practice are suffering from the dilatory effects of inflation, transport costs, difficulties with credit and the limits imposed by deteriorating infrastructure.

Adding to the dire circumstances of ordinary Zimbabweans is the spectacle of HIV/AIDS, which has cut a swathe across society in the last decade. With a third of the population said to be infected by the disease and health services barely functional due to the economic crisis, there is little hope of arresting the march of AIDS through the ranks of the young and productive. Life expectancy in Zimbabwe, once amongst the highest in sub-Saharan Africa, has fallen to 32 years, and it is reported that a Zimbabwean child dies every 15 minutes from AIDS. The government's response to date has been one of neglect, coupled to its ever-present instinct for corruption revealed in the imposition of an 'AIDS tax' on all salaries that supposedly went into a national fund to combat the disease, but public aid has yet to materialise. This critical situation has been further compounded by limited access to donor funds owing to the hostile attitude taken by Harare towards foreign NGOs.

It is true that by the end of 2004 some of the key economic indicators suggested that the Zimbabwean economy was no longer in free-fall, partially a result of a host of stringent measures introduced by the government under its new Reserve Bank governor, Gideon Gono. For example, Gono has taken aim at the black market and corruption by putting together a foreign currency auction system that seeks to channel foreign investment directly through the Reserve Bank (rather than into the accounts of top officials). He has used monetary policy to bring down inflation to its April 2005 average of under 150%, and rewarded businesses that use good practices with concessional (30%) loans. He has also – at some political risk – suggested that beneficiaries of the land-reform programme be bound by performance contracts that establish production targets of particular crops. Under Gono, the country's fractious relations with the International Monetary Fund (IMF) have improved as Zimbabwe has resumed repayment of its outstanding debt – albeit with what are essentially token disbursements of $50 million at this stage. One result of his policies can be seen in the area of foreign currency inflows, which – though minuscule by the standards of the heyday of 4% GDP growth in the 1980s – have gone up from $300m in 2003 to $1.7bn in 2004.

The overall aim of what has been dubbed an 'internal structural adjustment programme' is to stabilise the economy and mend fences with the international community such that Zimbabwe is no longer subject to official and de facto restrictions or boycotts. Ironically, the same callous disregard that the Mugabe regime has displayed towards human suffering in the heat of the political crisis has served the regime well as it has forced through some painful corrective steps on a population already traumatised by severe economic dislocation and violence. Indeed, the hope in Harare may be that international financial authorities, which approve of fiscal discipline and Zimbabwe's conformity to neo-liberal tenets, will be tempted to pave the way for Mugabe's international rehabilitation. At this stage, however, there is no evidence that Zimbabwe's economic fundamentals have altered sufficiently to do anything more than slow down the process of decay.

While relatively successful to date, there are indications that Gono's efforts to resuscitate the Zimbabwean economy and, in particular, rid it of the most egregious corrupt practices, is already running into conflict with established Zanu–PF interests. For example, rumours, which he hotly denies, that Gono is planning to invite back white commercial farmers in order to raise agricultural productivity and curry favour with the international community, indicate little political confidence in fiscal and market-oriented reforms. Ultimately, Gono's standing within the government is subject, like that of his fallen predecessor Simba Makoni, to the whims of Mugabe. Outside investors remain sensitive to Zimbabwe's volatile economic environment. A measure of this could be seen in the tepid international response to the Trans-Limpopo Spatial Initiative, which seeks to emulate the success of the Maputo Development Corridor to the south. With opposition party control over many municipalities, Harare has been unable to convince South African and other foreign investors to furnish the financial capital needed to get it off the ground. Violence and systematic fraud in the parliamentary election only served to remind outside investors of the country's economic instability.

Mugabe's political resilience

The land issue, once so critical to shaping the crisis, has finally moved off centre stage. This is in part due to the official government position in Harare, which declared in late 2003 that 'fast-track' land reform had achieved its redistributive objectives. (In a bitter irony, displaced white commercial farmers now working in Zambia have managed to increase that country's tobacco harvest from 14,300 tonnes in 2003 to 52,000 tonnes in 2004, figures that are expected to contribute to a rise in Zambia's exports of $83m, representing over three times the earnings accrued the previous year.) The removal of land from the public eye, nonetheless, is problematic for the regime in a number of ways. The emotive power that land reform brought to previous election campaigns is no longer available, and without it the government will have to face a population whose perspective on domestic politics has been formed mainly by the negative impact of government policies on their daily lives. The parliamentary elections should have been an opportunity for the citizenry to press for amelioration of these dire conditions, if not outright change. With the focus now squarely on the economic crisis and the attendant political fallout, the government's task of winning domestic support has become all the more difficult. However, despite these new circumstances – for reasons explained below – the political situation in the country is unlikely to change as a result of the election.

Mugabe himself – president since independence in 1980 and leader of Zanu–PF – remains at the heart of Zimbabwe's ongoing crisis. His remarkable ability not only to weather the treacherous politics of severe economic decline, but also to profit politically from it, is testament to his acute political instincts and diabolical management of the crisis. A student of revolution, Mugabe exploited the land issue to retain power and isolate the opposition movement, and is now in the process of blaming others in the Zanu–PF inner circle for its excesses. Mugabe, who is 81, has shown signs of flagging health but has lost none of his desire to control the country. The emphasis on acquiring a two-thirds majority in the elections reflects a revival of the plan to create a formal exit from the day-to-day tribulations of power that would still afford him an important voice in government affairs. Ironically, the tentative details of the arrangement – a ceremonial presidency, enhanced powers for the prime minister and a new legislative chamber manned by senior appointees with the capacity to block legislative action – harkens back to the very changes proposed in the defeated constitutional referendum of February 2000 that inspired the political dimensions of the contemporary crisis in the first place.

The paralysis of Zanu–PF in failing to adopt a post-Mugabe position exposes the predatory character of the party elite, which is unable to make out a morally defined case in opposition to the president. This was best illustrated in the sudden demotion of Jonathan Moyo, once the high-profile minister of information and architect of regime's vitriolic campaign against the MDC and the West at the height of the land-reform campaign. Opportunistic and ambitious, the former academic took up his post in government without an established power base within Zanu–PF. As the latest phase of manoeuvring for coveted senior posts within the party got underway before the Zanu–PF party congress, Moyo actively sought to build a constituency that would enable him to both lessen his reliance on Mugabe and prepare the ground for a future contest for the presidency. Moyo, Zanu–PF parliamentary speaker Emmerson Mnangagwa and five other provincial party chairs were spectacularly unsuccessful in their bid to wrest the party from Mugabe. Moyo was ousted from government and characterised as 'enemy number one' by his former patron. In the March 2005 election Moyo, running as an independent, won the rural Tsholotso constituency, while Mnangagwa is currently under arrest and suspended from party activity.

The sidelining of Mnangagwa, once one of Mugabe's closest confidants and still occupying a high position with Zanu–PF, spells an end to the forlorn hope of the South African government that a putative 'moderate' faction within the party would ease the president out. This dispensation was the aim of a maladroit attempt by South Africa to collaborate with Mnangagwa and MDC leader Morgan Tsvangirai in 2002. The forced confession of a South African spy suggests that it retains a hold on the official imagination in Pretoria. Mnangagwa has demonstrated a remarkable ability to survive periodic purges within the party, and he is reported to be amongst the richest men in the country, with his own links to the Zimbabwean military nurtured during its intervention in the Democratic Republic of the Congo and before that through his involvement in the suppression in Matabeleland. The fate of other Zanu–PF pretenders to the throne or those who have fallen out with the president has not been as benign. Former Finance Minister Chris Kuruneri and provincial party chairs Phillip Chiyangwa and James Makamba were detained without trial for over a year.

With the party unreliable, riven by internal divisions and rocked by scandal, Mugabe's dependence on the twinning of his own Shona clique, the Zezuru, with that of the country's security forces has become the bedrock of his residual claim to power. Never far from the surface of Zimbabwean politics, tribal affiliation is a source of growing discontent amongst the larger Karanga group that made up the bulk of the Zanu–PF leadership during the liberation war and early independence period. With his two deputies, the commanders of the army and the air force, and the commissioner of the police all Zezuru, Mugabe has taken no chances in his efforts to hold on to power. Costly arms purchases, such as $200m on fighter jets from China, at a time when the country is effectively bankrupt, are manifestly linked to Mugabe's need to keep key figures within the military happy. Pre-election boosts to the wages of military and security service personnel also reflect this strategy, as did the heavy military presence during the 2002 presidential elections.

While the governing party is turning more fractious, the weakness of the MDC is becoming increasingly evident. Divisions within the trade-union movement, a critical base for the opposition party and Tsvangirai's home, have erupted into a public debate questioning the costs to members of the lengthy and open confrontation with the government. A sense of alienation experienced by some of the contributing organisations in civil society from the trade-union base of the MDC is another source of unhappiness within certain circles of the movement. The ability of the government to undermine the ability of the MDC's elected representatives – for example, Elias Mudzuri, the mayor of Harare – to carry out their basic functions has had a discouraging (and undoubtedly intended) effect on supporters of change. Others were thrown in prison, like MP Roy Bennett, who allegedly shoved a government minister. More generally, the combined impact of systematic persecution by security forces and Zanu–PF youth militias (known locally as the 'Green Bombers'), coupled with court actions, imprisonment and media restrictions, all coming against the backdrop of unremitting economic hardship, has contributed to a general weariness within the MDC and its constituents. The passage in early 2005 of the bill designed to curtail external funding for Zimbabwe's human-rights groups and intended to include other civil-society organisations – key bastions of anti-Mugabe support – has had the dual effect of threatening the regime's most vocal opponents with closure and underscoring their reliance on outside support.

With the state structures of persecution already in place, apart from selective instances of intimidation and violence against opposition party MPs and their supporters, the build-up to the election has proved relatively quiet when compared to years past. Disenfranchisement of 3.5m Zimbabweans living abroad (who are presumed to be anti-Mugabe if not MDC supporters) and tampering with voter rolls have been part of the government's overall strategy to stave off electoral defeat.

So too are the selective extension of food aid to recognised Zanu–PF supporters, salary increases to key public servants, primarily in the security services, and the denial of public assistance to MDC strongholds. While Zanu–PF has dominated the official media, has shut down virtually all independent sources and has a government-sponsored war chest of Z$3.38bn to finance its campaign, the MDC too has benefited from the Political Parties Finance Act and received Z$3.12bn. However, it must pay exorbitant fees for air-time in the state-controlled media while the government is given ample free publicity.

That being said, the generally dispirited campaign run by Zanu–PF prior to the 2005 elections is arguably related to the loss of Moyo's propaganda talents, as well as the absence of the land issue with which to motivate its traditional constituencies. Zanu–PF claims of uncovering MDC 'hit men' trained in South Africa was widely seen as an election ploy aimed at the South African government and drew little interest domestically. The MDC's urban base delivered seats in all the major municipal areas, as well as some in Manicaland and even possibly a few seats in Mashonaland West. However, with the credibility of the MDC having slipped among 'swing' voters and weariness having set in, there was widespread apathy about the elections and a relatively low turnout. While Zanu–PF's traditional grip over the crucial rural constituencies showed signs of weakness, there also appeared to be less confidence amongst ordinary Zimbabweans that the MDC offered a viable and electable alternative. In any case, election monitors, allegedly ejected from their posts, were scarce in the rural Zanu–PF strongholds and the party did well in those areas. The MDC outperformed Zanu–PF in urban centres, where the monitors were more abundant. Election monitors could not verify either the number of ballots printed or the accuracy of voter lists, which Zanu–PF was believed to have filled with the names of dead or non-resident Zimbabweans. One out of ten voters was turned away from polling stations. Of 120 contested seats, Zanu–PF won 78, the MDC 41 and an independent candidate one. This result reflected a loss of 16 seats for the MDC. With an additional 30 appointed seats constitutionally accorded to Mugabe, Zanu–PF now enjoyed more than a two-thirds majority – more than enough to change the constitution to ensure Mugabe's continued political power even if he were to exit electoral politics, by allowing him to handpick a successor before the 2008 presidential elections.

Regional influences

The spectacle of renewed confrontation with the international community has galvanised Southern African Development Community (SADC) action. At an SADC heads-of-government meeting in Mauritius in August 2004, the leaders agreed to a new protocol for elections which set out specific criteria for their management and provided the organisation with regionally approved benchmarks on democratic practice. While some observers had hoped that this marked a renewed and deeper commitment to conducting elections across the region in conformity with international standards, it appears that the agreement in Mauritius was as likely to serve as a minimalist position for Southern African governments seeking regional acceptance of electoral results.

The Zimbabwean government reaction has been, predictably, to employ means that break with the spirit (if not the letter) of the Mauritius Protocol. It proposed the controversial bill limiting foreign funding to human-rights organisations only a few days after the agreement was signed. The refusal of Harare to allow the SADC parliamentary observer group to monitor the elections was clearly based on their negative findings in covering the 2002 presidential elections. The same goes for its unwillingness to invite the widely respected regional non-governmental organisation, the Electoral Institute for Southern Africa, to observe the elections. The SADC observer mission, staffed by appointees who did not appear committed to substance of election monitoring, had declared the 2002 poll to be valid. Its commendation of Armando Guebuza in Mozambique's recent presidential and parliamentary elections, despite the findings of international electoral observers of systematic and obvious fraud by the governing Frelimo Party, presaged the SADC's acquiescence to the 2005 Zimbabwean elections.

Within the SADC, South Africa remains the most important player on the Zimbabwe issue. During an official visit to the country last year, US President George W. Bush declared that his South African counter-part, Thabo Mbeki, was America's 'point man' on Zimbabwe. Mbeki's pursuit of 'quiet diplomacy', though widely discredited internationally, sadly remains the lodestar for southern African action. Yet the very premise of this form of constructive engagement – that South Africa's close economic ties to its neighbour preclude public confrontation with Mugabe because that would ultimately damage its own interests – has in fact done exactly that. With the collapse of the Zimbabwean economy and thousands of destitute Zimbabweans crossing the border into South Africa, trade relations have deteriorated, investments in Zimbabwe have been hurt or lost outright through expropriation and South Africa's own international image has suffered.

South Africa's apparent ambivalence towards events and political parties in Zimbabwe was highlighted by the capture of a South African intelligence agent in early 2005. The affair involving the South African, who revealed after being tortured by the Zimbabwean Central Intelligence Organisation that his contacts within the Zanu–PF elite included Mnangagwa, provoked sharp exchanges between Harare and Pretoria. More broadly, it underscored the ambiguity that informs the South African government's approach and, concurrently, the deep suspicion of South African intentions held by the Zanu–PF elite. None of this, however, apparently deterred Mbeki from stating publicly, in advance of the elections, his belief that the poll would be 'free and fair'. South African Minister of Labour Membathisi Mdladlana, who heads South Africa's own observer mission, echoed this position upon arrival in Zimbabwe more than a week before elections. In response, an angry MDC severed all contact with the various official South African delegations except that of the African National Congress (ANC), whose observers had sought to distance themselves from Mdladlana's comments. The deputy of the South African observer mission, Ngoako Ramatlhodi, went further in meeting with the MDC against the specific orders of Mdladlana. In spite of this reconciliation with the opposition party, the South African government officially declared, without substantiation, that Zimbabwe was within its rights to ban the SADC parliamentary observer mission.

In contrast to Mbeki's public utterances and commitment to constructive engagement, the ANC coalition partners, Congress of South African Trade Unions (Cosatu) and the South African Communist Party (SACP), have become more vocally critical of Mugabe's government. In the case of the former, Cosatu delegates visited Zimbabwe in October 2004 and January 2005 to hold talks with their trade union counterparts (who, of course, are linked closely to the MDC) and were summarily thrown out by angry government officials. Cosatu leader Zwelinzima Vavi vowed to return to the country (though subsequently ANC intervention convinced him to drop planned discussions with Zimbabwean human-rights groups) and to organise boycotts and protests at the Zimbabwean embassy and the Beit Bridge border post. Cosatu has also called for a postponement of the elections, echoing MDC concerns about faulty voters' rolls, severe restrictions on political rallies, human-rights violations and other obstructions. The SACP has tried to engage, through its own youth groups, the Zanu–PF youth brigades and cajole them away from violent electoral politics (though, at the same time, it has sought to emulate Zanu–PF in calling for an immediate resolution of South Africa's own land question).

South Africa's role in supporting Mugabe's regime remains one of the most exasperating dimensions of the crisis in Zimbabwe. Mbeki's timid approach may be based on the ANC's abiding fear of a trade-union-based opposition party (the contours of which are already in place) emerging in South Africa, coupled with the increasingly dubious belief that a negotiated settlement is possible with Mugabe. An unexpected legacy of the South African position will be popular Zimbabwean disbelief and suspicion of the sincerity of the ANC-led government and SADC.

While the virtual elimination of the white-settler factor from Zimbabwean politics has cleared the way for a public reassessment of Mugabe's rule by southern African leaders, it is a mark of the power of the 'anti-imperial' discourse that Mugabe has invoked throughout the crisis that no regional government seems willing to openly challenge him. The formative experience of colonialism and the struggle against it are still the defining ideological contours for independent African states and societies across the region – even those that are themselves are no longer led by liberation-era figures. The rapturous reception that Mugabe receives from African audiences outside of Zimbabwe is an indication of the enduring appeal of these antecedents, even if Mugabe himself stands for practices that run counter to the notions of reconciliation and respect for democracy inherent in, for example, the South African experience. The fact that the land issue has been placed on the public agenda of Namibia and South Africa – which have their own legacies of disparity between the white commercial farming sector and black subsistence producers – against the wishes of their governing parties demonstrates the power of Mugabe's rhetoric. Even Botswana, with its established reputation for good governance and transparent business practices, has found it expedient to tone down its criticism of events in Zimbabwe.

Of equal concern is the manner in which the AU is addressing the Zimbabwean issue. Upon learning that the AU's Commission on Human and Peoples' Rights was about to publish a report critical of Zimbabwe's human-rights record, Stan Mudenge, Zimbabwe's foreign minister, issued strenuous objections to the procedures used by the organisation. With the active collusion of Southern African governments, Mudenge was able to get the report withdrawn on a technicality and it has since disappeared from public sight. The tragedy is that, by catering to Harare, the AU has failed one of its first major tests on human rights, coming close to the conduct of its notoriously ineffectual predecessor, the Organisation for African Unity. The South Africa-led New Economic Partnership for Africa's Development (NEPAD), predicated upon establishing standards of good economic and political governance across the continent, is likely to suffer a blow – however indirect – to its credibility as well, due to Zimbabwe.

The international community: rhetoric and inaction

Throughout Zimbabwe's political and economic crisis, the EU and the UK in particular have led the way in criticising the Mugabe regime and imposing penalties in the form of targeted sanctions on Zanu–PF elites. The UK first proposed the framework for gradual and equitable land reform, and Mugabe's sponsorship of the lawless appropriation of land owned by white farmers also harmed large numbers of black workers on those farms who depended on them for their livelihoods. Thus, British civil society has remained resolutely opposed to the regime and was partially successful in winning a boycott by key players of the England cricket tour to Zimbabwe in 2004. But the failure of these measures to produce 'regime change' in Harare has resulted in a reassessment of the European role. While the Scandinavians, Dutch and British remain actively opposed to Mugabe (while seeking nonetheless to continue forms of development assistance through their respective NGOs), the French and others within the EU have demonstrated a willingness to come to some form of accommodation with the Zimbabwean government.

The lack of European unity on Zimbabwe has led to an assertion of American leadership, most vividly seen in the decision to include Zimbabwe amongst a list of outlaw governments ripe for 'regime change'. Washington's sharp criticism of Zanu–PF contrasts with its professed support for South Africa's role as the regional leader managing the Zimbabwe issue. With Britain in the midst of promoting African interests at the G-8 summit through the African Commission, it is clearly politic for London to stay away from this volatile issue, which would jeopardise Blair's African credentials. The Bush administration's outspoken language on Zimbabwe has already drawn criticism from Mbeki himself. How long increasingly divergent US and South African positions can be maintained without harming bilateral relations remains to be seen.

The Commonwealth, which suspended Zimbabwe in 2002 and, against Mbeki's virulent opposition, extended that status at the Abuja conference in December 2003, is likely to remain a platform for the issue as long as other African states from outside the region hold firm. Zimbabwe's withdrawal from the Commonwealth, though satisfying for the Zanu–PF party leadership, does not mean that the issue itself will not be the subject of discussion (as apartheid South Africa discovered). Nigeria's unease with the South African government's increasingly forthright claim to continental leadership may factor into its willingness to take a harder stance on Zimbabwe as a way of demonstrating its own leadership credentials to the West.

Finally, although Mugabe has publicly called for a new axis of support from China against the 'Anglo-American conspiracy', his hopes may be misplaced in the long term. Beijing is increasingly aware of the costs of associating with pariah regimes in Africa (most recently, Sudan), has complained privately about Mugabe's erratic conduct and, like Libya before it, is experiencing the problems of dealing with a predatory regime. The Zimbabwe government, for its part, has tried to court Asian states through, for example, the promotion of Chinese-language studies in the country and the launching of twice-weekly flights to Singapore. China's growing investment in Zimbabwe contrasts with the quiet withdrawal of some key Malaysian interests in the region – though Mahathir Mohammed's close personal relationship with Mugabe is likely to ensure continued diplomatic support for the regime.

No easy way out

The land question, which was a legitimate source of discontent for many rural people, has lost all saliency in contemporary Zimbabwe. In its place is an acknowledgement that 'fast track' reforms not only contributed to the country's downward spiral but, through piecemeal perversion by the judiciary and legal system, have undermined the constitutional basis of democratic politics in Zimbabwe. At the same time, the possibility of widespread civil violence – which earlier in the decade seemed genuine – has receded. Despite some scattered calls for Zimbabweans to take to the streets to oust Mugabe, the MDC and its supporters appeared to have little stomach for anything beyond short-lived non-violent protest. In the aftermath of the March 2005 elections, the challenge for the government and opposition is to find sufficient common ground to lay the foundation for the future. It is true that negotiated settlements and governments of national unity have not been a serious feature of the political landscape of Zimbabwe since the collapse of dialogue between the government and the opposition in June 2002. However, as Zimbabweans face the fallout of the elections, they may have to ask themselves if the road to peace is not best secured through some form of shared governance at least as a transitional device. Given the mutual animosity between the two sides, however, perhaps this can only be contemplated once Mugabe steps down. The question remains how that result can be achieved. There appear to be no clear answers.

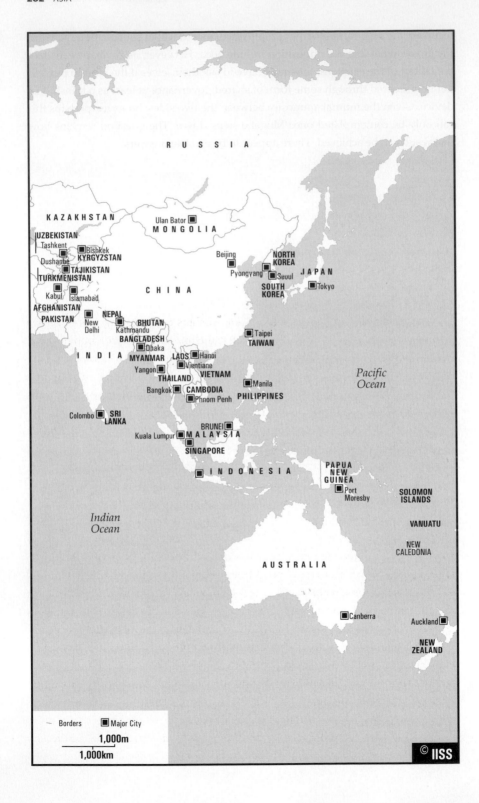

RUSSIA

KAZAKHSTAN

Ulan Bator ■
MONGOLIA

UZBEKISTAN
Tashkent ■ Bishkek
Dushanbe ■ KYRGYZSTAN
TAJIKISTAN
TURKMENISTAN

Beijing ■

NORTH
KOREA
Pyongyang ■ Seuul
SOUTH
KOREA

JAPAN

Tokyo ■

Kabul ■ Islamabad
AFGHANISTAN
PAKISTAN New
Delhi

CHINA

NEPAL ■
BHUTAN
Kathmandu
BANGLADESH
■ Dhaka

Taipei ■
TAIWAN

INDIA

MYANMAR LAOS ■ Hanoi
■ Vientiane
Yangon ■ VIETNAM
THAILAND

Pacific
Ocean

Bangkok ■ CAMBODIA
■ Phnom Penh

Manila ■

PHILIPPINES

Colombo ■ SRI
LANKA

BRUNEI ■
Kuala Lumpur ■ MALAYSIA
SINGAPORE

INDONESIA

PAPUA
NEW
GUINEA
■ Port
Moresby

SOLOMON
ISLANDS

Indian
Ocean

VANUATU

NEW
CALEDONIA

AUSTRALIA

■ Canberra

Auckland ■

NEW
ZEALAND

~ Borders   ■ Major City

1,000m

1,000km

© IISS

Asia

Continuing trends in Asia in 2004–05 showed signs of producing more decisive change. China's relative quiescence under the pressure of profound internal political and economic adjustments gave way to a more outward-looking foreign policy. This development had foreboding aspects, such as a defence build-up and a more threatening posture on any attempt by Taiwan to secede, and more encouraging ones, such as its central role in the Six-Party Talks on North Korea's nuclear programme. That said, the talks did not bear fruit, with Pyongyang insisting on bilateral attention from the United States and simultaneous concessions, and Washington requiring North Korea to make concessions before furnishing any rewards. South Korea appeared to assume a de facto harder line against the North, though it did not abandon residual hope about the capacity of a more open and conciliatory policy to tame Pyongyang. As regional threats from North Korea remained salient, the risks of a US–China confrontation over Taiwan appeared to increase incrementally, and the global spectre of transnational terrorism remained salient, Japan continued to move away from the institutionalised pacifism that had characterised its foreign policy since the Second World War – supporting US efforts in Iraq, continuing involvement in American missile-defence development in Asia, and broadly carrying forward a more extroverted defence and security policy.

On the subcontinent, against substantial domestic distractions and pressures, India and Pakistan tried to maintain momentum towards the amelioration of bilateral relations through negotiations on Kashmir and other traditionally disruptive issues. While arms purchases from the United States by both countries reflected their respective compulsions to hedge against the peace initiative begun in early 2004, their leaders appeared determined to stay engaged. India, in particular, showed its resolve to become an important regional player by extending wide-ranging assistance following the massive tsunami in Southeast Asia (which radiated outward for hundreds of miles) in December 2004. The momentary regional solidarity that the tsunami generated, however, belied myriad security problems in Southeast Asia – from separatism and Islamist extremism in Indonesia and the Philippines to rising Muslim radicalism in southern Thailand to the threat of piracy and maritime terrorism in the Malacca Strait. While national governments generally showed political stability and strengthened their counter-terrorism postures, and regional cooperation improved in some areas (such as maritime security), the Association of South East Asian Nations continued to be a disappointing forum for multilateral security cooperation.

In Sri Lanka, the tsunami had an exacerbating effect on the conflict between the government and the secessionist Liberation Tigers of Tamil Eelam (LTTE); a cease-fire has been in effect since February 2002 but political negotiations have been stalled over differences between the government's and the LTTE's preferred agendas. The LTTE complained that the government was not channelling sufficient international aid into areas of their de facto control, which the government denied. Divisions within the rebel movement also threatened the stability of the cease-fire, as an LTTE leader and five other rebels were killed in an ambush on 8 February 2005 while returning from discussions about post-tsunami relief and recovery. A Tamil breakaway group was suspected, and the government condemned the killings.

In Central Asia, there were strains of both stability and instability. Afghanistan appeared to be shaping up as a qualifiedly successful state-building venture, as Hamid Karzai was easily re-elected president in December 2004 and major humanitarian crises did not arise. Drug trafficking there remained an acute and growing problem, however. Moreover, in the wider region, the unsteadiness of longstanding authoritarian regimes was symbolised by a coup in Kyrgyzstan in March 2005. Regimes elsewhere were more secure, but it became clear that Central Asia could no longer be regarded as a coherent geopolitical entity. Actual and potential challenges to regional security – primarily in the form of resource conflict, drug trafficking and radical Islamism – thus will become even more difficult to manage. The prospect of these threats being evaluated and acted upon in any comprehensive fashion by the states involved during the course of 2005 is very slim. This reality of local inattention reinforced the short-term need for continued deep major-power involvement in the region, the security fulcrum of which remains Afghanistan.

The United States was still Asia's ranking power, but it was being tested – especially by the North Korea crisis and, more subtly and gradually, by a rising China. Yet Pyongyang's roguish behaviour had the effect of strengthening Japan's, South Korea's and China's relationships with the United States. Furthermore, the United States sought to reinforce Indonesia's tentatively cooperative spirit by reviving military-to-military contacts suspended for several years over human-rights concerns. US security relationships (both military and law-enforcement) with the Philippines,

Thailand and Singapore deepened, as the former two were named US 'major non-NATO allies' and the latter otherwise recognised as an indispensable partner. An evolving American policy of qualified engagement with Myanmar stood to improve the US image in the region, which has generally suffered over its Middle East policy. The United States managed to maintain a delicate balance in its relationships with Pakistan – an essential counter-terrorism partner, also newly anointed a 'major non-NATO ally' – and India. Washington's efforts in Afghanistan remained centred on counter-terrorism, but Europe's complementary state-building role and gradually increasing American focus on state-building tasks (including counter-narcotics) were salutary. While political and economic competition between the United States and China for primary influence in Southeast Asia remained a looming engine of strategic change, the détente between the two countries deferred serious disruption. But indeed deferral, more than arrival, seemed the watchword for strategic developments in Asia.

Continuing Crisis on the Korean Peninsula

2004 was a turbulent year for the Korean Peninsula, a region that remains one of Asia's most troublesome. At the centre of current crisis is uncertainty about the future direction of North Korea and, particularly, about the nuclear-weapon programme that restarted in 2002. In spite of Beijing's efforts, diplomacy intended to resolve this problem through the Six-Party Talks has made little progress. Adding to the difficulty, relations between North Korea and its neighbours – South Korea and Japan – have been on a roller-coaster ride, seeming to make important gains during the first six months of the year, then plummeting to new lows. Hovering over this critical nuclear proliferation problem has been continued tension in America's 50-year alliance with South Korea, although 2004 was certainly not as difficult as the first three years after President George W. Bush's election in 2000.

The US vs North Korea

North Korea's effort to build nuclear weapons remains the most daunting security issue facing the region. The crisis erupted in 2002 with the collapse of the 1994 US–North Korea Agreed Framework, designed to freeze and then dismantle Pyongyang's programme, after the United States claimed to have discovered an undisclosed effort to produce highly enriched uranium. Initial concerns that the renewed confrontation between Washington and Pyongyang could lead to military conflict gave way to the Six-Party Talks attended by the United States, North Korea, South Korea, Russia, Japan and China. Three rounds of discussions have been held since 2003. Unfortunately, the talks have made almost no progress. At the last round, in June 2004, the United States put on the table a new proposal outlining a long and complicated process of denuclearisation of North Korea that included provisions for the following:

- An undertaking – after North Korea unilaterally declares its nuclear-weapon activities, including any effort to enrich uranium – whereby the parties will enter into a provisional multilateral security arrangement with Pyongyang, begin a study to determine North Korea's energy requirements and begin discussion of steps necessary to lift remaining American sanctions against the North.
- An agreement on implementation providing for disabling, dismantling and eliminating all of the North's programmes followed by the provision of heavy fuel oil by non-US parties.
- A three-month preparatory period during which implementation would begin.
- A commitment to provide North Korea, once dismantling was complete, with 'lasting benefits' based on the energy requirements survey, and to discuss lifting sanctions.
- After dismantling, a 'wholly transformed relationship' with the United States that will call for addressing other concerns, including human-rights problems, the elimination of chemical and biological weapons, and 'a less provocative conventional force disposition'.

The June proposal, while an important step forward because it provided a clear roadmap for solving the nuclear issue, still differed significantly from North Korea's negotiating position. The most important difference was that it asked North Korea to take important steps in eliminating its nuclear programme up front while reserving American incentives for the end of the process. Since the crisis broke out in 2002, the Bush administration had come to embrace the 'Libya model' as its preferred solution. Patterned after the agreement reached with Libyan dictator Muammar Gadhafi in December 2003 to eliminate his weapons of mass destruction (WMD), that model meant that North Korea would have to do away with its nuclear-weapon programme first; only then would the United States provide the incentives Pyongyang was seeking. The model also held out the possibility that Washington would eventually accept the regime of Kim Jong Il, as it had the government in Libya, if he agreed to the American position.

Pyongyang has expressed disdain for Gadhafi and the Libyan model. Granted, other participants in the Six-Party Talks have already agreed to provide North Korea with heavy fuel oil early on in any agreement to help meet its energy needs. But Pyongyang wants to see, from the outset, a tangible sign of America's seriousness in trying to improve political relations, in accepting the North Korean regime and in implementing a negotiated settlement. The US insistence that it will only provide benefits to the North after Pyongyang has completed dismantling adds to North Korea's fear that the US approach will not ensure the survival of Kim Jong Il's regime. This fear has given rise to Pyongyang's other demand that steps taken by both sides should be 'simultaneous' so it has greater assurance that, as implementation proceeds, the United States will meet its part of the bargain.

Moreover, the American position makes it quite clear that North Korea's effort to enrich uranium must be explicitly included from the very beginning in any process of elimination. Pyongyang still vehemently denies that it has such a programme. Privately, however, North Korean Foreign Ministry officials have hinted that they might be able to discuss this matter under the right circumstances – namely, in bilateral talks with the United States and if Washington reconsiders its negotiating position. Whether those hints mean Pyongyang has such a programme remains unclear. Focusing on the first stage of an agreement, Pyongyang would freeze its plutonium-production programme. That means shutting down its operating reactor and reprocessing plant at Yongbyon under international inspection. The North has also suggested that, depending on what the United States is willing to do in return, it might permit the inspections necessary to determine how much plutonium has been reprocessed from the 8,000 spent fuel rods removed from storage and International Atomic Energy Agency (IAEA) inspection in 2002. This plutonium, and any other spent fuel rods, could be placed under international control. Pyongyang has suggested a number of steps the United States might take in return, including the resumption of oil shipments.

Under other circumstances, Pyongyang might have seen the Bush administration's June proposal as a predictable opening negotiating position. Indeed, in the initial discussions leading up the Agreed Framework, the two sides often made proposals that required the other to go first for very little in return. But the atmosphere of distrust between Washington and Pyongyang built up during the first four years of the Bush administration coloured the North's negative reaction to the proposal. Moreover, at some point shortly after the June session, Pyongyang appeared to make a strategic decision to wait until after November 2004 in hopes that the Bush administration would be replaced by a more flexible Kerry team. In the meantime, with the collapse of the Agreed Framework, Pyongyang has been slowly building up its ability to produce nuclear weapons. A key step was taken in 2003, when North Korea removed the 8,000 spent fuel rods under IAEA supervision from their previous location and claimed to have reprocessed them to produce weapons-grade plutonium, although it is unclear whether Pyongyang used the huge plant at its Yongbyon facility designed for that purpose.

In January 2004, a team of Americans led by Siegfried Hecker, a former head of the Los Alamos National Laboratory, visited North Korea and the Yongbyon facility. Aside from meeting with senior Foreign Ministry officials in charge of the Six-Party Talks, the visiting Americans were given an extensive briefing on the state of North Korea's nuclear programme and a tour of Yongbyon. The Americans were shown the North's operating 5MW reactor and its reprocessing facility as well as the sites of two larger reactors under construction in 1994 and subsequently frozen by the Agreed Framework. The North Koreans told the Americans that they were re-evaluating whether to renew construction of these two reactors which, if completed, could produce significant amounts of plutonium.

Most significantly, the American team was shown what the North Koreans claimed was plutonium metal. Whether that metal was fabricated from the spent fuel rods removed from IAEA supervision in 2003 or from an earlier batch the United States suspected was removed from North Korea's operating reactor remains unclear. But the demonstration, if real, may have shown for the first time that North Korea had the technical skill necessary to build a nuclear weapon – to wit, the ability to form the explosive core of such a weapon. In spite of Pyongyang's decades-old effort to build nuclear weapons, doubts still remain that the North could design a bomb, although the Central Intelligence Agency told the US Congress in 2003 that the North had 'validated the designs' without explosive testing. If that were true, Pyongyang could have enough material to build about seven bombs. Moreover, if North Korea continues to operate its nuclear reactor and unloads another batch of spent fuel rods in the next few years, there may be enough additional material for another five or six weapons.

In addition, there is the continuing concern about North Korea's secret effort to produce what may be highly enriched uranium (HEU), another type of fissile material that could be used to build a bomb. The first signs of that programme appeared during the second term of the Clinton administration when American intelligence picked up hints of cooperation between North Korea and A.Q. Khan, the father of Pakistan's nuclear bomb. The administration had planned to pursue the matter with the North Koreans, in addition to pressing Pakistan, perhaps even raising the issue during a presidential visit to Pyongyang that never happened. In retrospect, cooperation between Khan's smuggling network and Pyongyang seems to have accelerated during 2001, after the Bush administration took office. When Washington confronted the North Koreans, they denied the existence of such a programme. The United States then cut off heavy fuel oil deliveries to Pyongyang, and insisted that the North dismantle its programme. The 1994 agreement subsequently collapsed.

Controversy continues to swirl around the accuracy of American information and the programme's full extent in 2004. Sceptics – including non-governmental experts as well as China and South Korea – asserted that the North Korean effort was much less advanced than the United States claimed. Washington does not appear to have a 'smoking gun'. Nevertheless, there is strong evidence of a long history of collaboration between Pyongyang and Khan. Moreover, as a result of the demise of Libya's nuclear programme and disclosures about Khan's assistance to Iran, it is clear that his smuggling network was able to provide extensive material help to its clients.

These factors reinforce suspicions that North Korea's effort is just as likely to be more advanced as less advanced than available information indicates.

In any case, Pyongyang has been careful in revealing the full extent of its efforts. Understanding the delicate situation, Pyongyang knows that it must slowly unveil its programme to get other countries used to the idea that it might possess nuclear weapons and to avoid military action by the United States. At the time of the Hecker visit, North Korean officials claim that they possessed a 'nuclear deterrent' was met with scepticism by the American delegation since they did not demonstrate an ability to design and build a device or to mount it on a delivery vehicle. If the North Koreans had demonstrated such a capability, however, the region might have been plunged into a more serious crisis – a fact they fully understood. At the beginning of 2005, however, Pyongyang did make a public statement to the effect that it had nuclear weapons, though it was not accompanied by any concrete demonstration.

With the continued diplomatic stalemate and North Korea's slow-motion nuclear build-up, the prognosis for resolving the crisis remains uncertain. While much will depend on the two key players—the United States and North Korea – neither seems willing to change their current approach. The second Bush administration's national-security decision-makers, who are essentially the same as the first term, seem disinclined to modify the American approach. Further, the departure of Colin Powell as secretary of state and his replacement by former national security advisor Condoleezza Rice removes from the administration a key advocate of engagement with North Korea. The upshot is likely to be a continuation of the Six-Party Talks rather than the separate bilateral meetings requested by the North Koreans. The priority will therefore be to convince Pyongyang that it should accept the 'Libyan model'.

North Korea, for its part, seems to feel no rush to compromise on its demand that Washington must be an integral part of any solution from the beginning. From Pyongyang's perspective, time is on its side. Its efforts to prevent the other participants in the Six-Party Talks from forming a united front that might take harsh action, such as securing UN sanctions, against the North have so far been successful. China and Russia, both members of the Security Council, remain unconvinced that Washington has made a serious effort to peacefully resolve the crisis. Moreover, there do not seem to be any significant internal economic pressures driving the North towards compromise. In spite of some difficulties encountered in implementing economic reforms begun in July 2002, and the continuing spectre of food shortages, the North appears confident it can weather the storm. That may be in part because of assistance provided by China and South Korea. Overall, hopes remain alive in Pyongyang that it can have a nuclear-weapon arsenal and at the same time escape international isolation.

China's stake

China is caught in the middle of this problem by virtue of its improving relationship with the Bush administration and remaining ties to Pyongyang. Accordingly,

Beijing has tried to play a bridging role in the Six-Party Talks. Substantial Chinese interests are at stake. Concerned about stability on its northeastern border and the prospect of the spread of nuclear weapons to other countries, particularly Japan, as a result of the North's programme, Beijing views Pyongyang's nuclear effort as destabilising. However, China is also concerned that, if pushed too hard through tough measures such as the economic sanctions that many in Washington advocate, North Korea might collapse, triggering problems just as catastrophic as a nuclear-armed Pyongyang. These include an uncontrollable flow of refugees into China, political instability on the peninsula, an enormous burden of economic reconstruc-tion and reunification that would severely handicap South Korea, and the danger that Seoul could inherit the North's WMD or that those weapons might find their way into the wrong hands.

Threading this policy needle has been difficult. Privately, China is probably more in tune with Pyongyang's proposals, favouring step-by-step denuclearisation based on simultaneous concessions by both sides. But publicly, it has been noticeably restrained in criticising the United States. Particularly noteworthy has been China's effort to step up contacts with North Korea's senior leaders, including a surprise visit by Kim Jong Il to Beijing in April 2004. In sessions with Chinese President Hu Jintao and other top leaders, Kim reaffirmed his strong interest in the Six-Party Talks and indicated that settlement of the nuclear issue was a high priority. The visit took place only a week after US Vice-President Dick Cheney stopped in Beijing, symbolising China's central role in trying to resolve the nuclear crisis. But high-level diplomacy seemed to run out of gas when a visit by senior party leader Li Changchun to Pyongyang in September 2004 failed to draw the North back to the negotiating table.

Japan and North Korea

North Korea's relationship with Japan, increasingly dominated by Tokyo's concerns over its citizens abducted by Pyongyang over two decades earlier, also took a serious nosedive in 2004. In May, Japanese Prime Minister Junichiro Koizumi visited Pyongyang for the second time in two years to try to jump-start normalisa-tion talks between the two countries and to make progress on the issue of Japanese nationals abducted by the North Koreans. As a result, five children of abductees who had already been repatriated to Japan were allowed to travel abroad and the North agreed to investigate ten other disputed cases. In return, Japan committed to providing 250,000 tonnes of food aid to North Korea through the World Food Programme – its first disbursement since 2001 – and $10m of medical supplies. Then, in the autumn, US Army defector Charles Jenkins was reunited with his Japanese wife and family, who had earlier returned to Japan, removing another source of bilateral agitation. But prospects for progress were dashed by the end of the year. As part of an agreement reached by diplomats of the two countries, North Korea returned two sets of remains that it claimed were abductees who had died. However, DNA testing showed that the remains were not those of kidnapped Japanese nationals but rather that the bones belonged to a number of other people. In response, Japanese public opinion shifted sharply towards supporting a harder line towards Pyongyang, including economic sanctions by Tokyo.

Koizumi resisted pressure to take quick action but appeared increasingly isolated, as both major parties prepared legislation that included the potential use of economic sanctions. Other more gradual options were also under consideration, including new laws that would amount to maritime sanctions by requiring all ships visiting Japan to carry insurance against oil spills and liabilities. Since the North's ships do not have that costly coverage, they would be prevented from entering Japanese ports. The North Korean reaction to these developments was unsurprising, with the Foreign Ministry blasting any move towards sanctions as tantamount to 'a declaration of war'. Working-level talks between Japanese and North Korean diplomats have attempted to work out differences on the abduction issue but have made little progress.

South Korea's ambivalent behaviour

Other developments in countries participating in the Six-Party Talks seemed only to complicate matters further. In autumn 2004, under pressure from the IAEA, South Korea admitted that it had secretly enriched uranium in 1979–81, separated small quantities of plutonium in 1982, experimented with uranium enrichment in 2000 and manufactured depleted uranium munitions in the mid-1980s. None of these activities in and of themselves represented a serious effort by South Korea to obtain nuclear-weapon materials, although they did expose poor government regulation of the scientific community. However, since President Park Chung Hee had an active programme to develop nuclear weapons during the 1970s – a programme that was ended only after intense pressure from the United States – the revelations triggered a new wave of international concern in spite of Seoul's longstanding adherence to the Nuclear Non-Proliferation Treaty. While the South has cooperated with the IAEA in clearing up the matter, North Korea tried to exploit the issue, saying it wanted to discuss the South's experiments before agreeing to further Six-Party Talks on its own programme. Still, the revelations' negative spillover into relations between the two Koreas and the Six-Party Talks seems to have been minimal, overshadowed by more fundamental problems between Washington and Pyongyang.

Under these trying circumstances, it has proven difficult for the two Koreas to keep their relationship on an even keel. South Korea has attempted to pursue a more conciliatory policy towards the North than has its close ally, the United States. While the growth of inter-Korean meetings, reunions of separated families and trade has been quite impressive since the June 2000 summit, this has not insulated inter-Korean relationships from severe fluctuations. Using a soccer analogy, one expert commented that 2004 was a 'game of two halves'. Until mid-year, it appeared the

South's conciliatory approach was producing important results. The first-ever general-level inter-Korean military talks were held at Mount Kumgang in May 2004. The first session, focusing on a maritime agenda in view of periodic clashes in the Yellow Sea during crab season, produced agreement on a number of confidence-building measures, including regular naval contacts via a military hotline. Subsequently, however, the North failed for the most part to pick up the phone, answering only three of Seoul's 14 daily calls. The two also agreed to end the loudspeaker propaganda war that has waged in the Demilitarised Zone (DMZ) for decades.

Beginning in July 2004, however, North–South relations precipitously declined. Part of the reason may have been Seoul's continuing ban on South Koreans heading north to mourn the death of Kim Il Sung, a man whose life was dedicated to destroying the South Korean regime. Following the tenth anniversary of his death in July 2004, a number of key North–South meetings were cancelled. A mass airlift of almost 450 North Korean refugees to the South from Vietnam in late July prompted a furious reaction from Pyongyang; it struck a particularly sensitive nerve given its scale and the increasing focus in Washington on North Korean human-rights violations. A third reason for the worsening of bilateral relations may have been internal political developments in North Korea. In addition to a shake-up in the leadership – one of Kim Jong Il's periodic purges to keep his subordinate on their toes – significant changes were made in the top leaders handling North–South relations.

Still, Pyongyang seems to have exercised sufficient care not to jeopardise economic relations. Work on the Kaesong Industrial Zone, created just north of the DMZ to house South Korean firms, continued. Particularly significant was the beginning of a daily shuttle-bus service to the zone from Seoul in September. This development, accompanied by agreement the same month between Hyundai Asan and Pyongyang that tourists could drive their own cars to the Mount Kumgang tourist area in the North via the eastern Donghae trans-DMZ corridor, signalled that this barrier, once impenetrable, was becoming increasingly porous.

The testy US–South Korea alliance

The uncertain situation on the peninsula has been further aggravated by stresses in the US alliance with South Korea, which has been a cornerstone of American strategic policy in Northeast Asia for over 50 years. A number of fissures in the bilateral relationship have threatened to undermine the alliance. Differences between the two countries have focused on how to address the problem of North Korea, perceived American unilateralism in its international policies and the growing anti-American sentiment that has crystallised over the US troop presence in South Korea. In 2004, the alliance seemed to achieve some equilibrium, but the potential for difficulties remain. Polls showed that most South Koreans still support the status quo, with the majority of South Koreans still having warm feelings for the United States. But concerns about the aggressiveness of US foreign policy and particularly its tougher approach to North Korea remained, and became more pronounced after Bush was re-elected in November 2004.

After the election, in a speech in Los Angeles, South Korean President Roh Moo Hyun, noting that the Korean people had not yet recovered from the trauma of the Korean War, warned that taking a new hard line on North Korea could have 'grave consequences'. He emphasised that a peaceful resolution to the crisis 'will be the single most important factor in strengthening our friendship'. Roh added that South Korea could not cooperate with anyone supporting 'regime change' in Pyongyang, the neo-conservative's preferred approach to dealing with North Korea. While the South Korean opposition party criticised his remarks, Roh continued his campaign during sessions at the ASEAN Plus Three Summit meetings with the Chinese and Japanese leaders, and during a tour of Europe. The remarks evidently had some resonance inside the Bush administration, since in early December, Stephen Hadley, the newly appointed national security advisor, told visiting South Korean legislators that US policy sought the 'transformation' of North Korea rather than 'regime change'. It is unclear, however, whether this remark reflected a genuine substantive or merely cosmetic change in US policy.

Another objective of Roh's highly visible public comments was to re-emphasise South Korea's 'leading role' in the Six-Party Talks. Privately, South Korea has not seen eye-to-eye with what it believes has been the Bush administration's inflexible approach at the talks. But Seoul has played a careful game, trying to avoid any overt criticism of Washington's stance while seeking to nudge the Bush administration in a more conciliatory direction. For example, in the aftermath of the June 2004 American proposal, while the South Koreans understood the American proposal fell short of what might be required to jump-start negotiations, they claimed some of the credit for coaxing the administration to put a new position on the table.

South Korean Deputy Foreign Minister Lee Soo Hyuck outlined his country's more forthcoming position at the same session. Firstly, the South Koreans called for a North Korean pledge up front to dismantle all nuclear-weapon-related programmes and to begin dismantling almost immediately; they did not, however, call on the North to acknowledge or reveal suspected uranium-enrichment activities. Secondly, unlike the opening American position that would essentially ban any nuclear activities in the North, Seoul left the door open for the provision of nuclear energy to North Korea since the light-water nuclear reactor project, to be provided under the currently suspended Agreed Framework, has been largely financed by the South. Thirdly, South Korea favoured providing Pyongyang with immediate benefits, including the provision of heavy fuel oil, at the beginning of the dismantling process. Finally, Seoul's proposal would step up progress towards political and economic normalisation between the North, on the one hand, and the United States and Japan in the context of dismantling the nuclear programme, and not condition normalisation on the solution of other outstanding issues, as in the American proposal.

On the broader alliance front, Washington and Seoul appeared to weather the storm created by America's plans to alter its long-standing military relationship with the South. The United States shocked Seoul in May 2004, first with its decision to withdraw the 2nd Brigade of the 2nd Infantry Division, some 3,600 troops, from the DMZ and to send them to Iraq. Then, a few weeks later, the United States indicated that the transfer was part of an overall shift of 12,500 troops from South Korea as part of the global realignment of American military forces, to be completed by 2005. The decision seemed to come as a surprise to the South Korean government. The United States claimed it had briefed Seoul on this possibility a few months earlier at a meeting of the Future of the Alliance Talks, but many South Koreans suspected that the movement of US troops back from the DMZ was an effort to punish Seoul for the perceived rise of anti-American sentiment. Few seemed to recall that American troop reductions had taken place in the past – for example, in 1971, as part of the Nixon doctrine that called for the defence of Asia by Asians – and that debates about reduction had arisen during previous administrations.

In any case, the United States subsequently modified its stance. Seoul's assertion that higher numbers of US troops were still needed to deter North Korea stuck a sympathetic chord in Washington, as did South Korea's point that it would need more time to ramp up its forces to become less dependent on the United States. While Seoul has increased its defence budget to modernise its weapons, Roh has begun to promote the concept of 'cooperative self-reliant defence'. This effort, along with expanding the comprehensive alliance relationship with the United States, formed the basis of a new defence policy drawn up by the South Korean National Security Council. In May, the government announced that preparations had begun for US troop reductions, while South Korea's self-defence capabilities were to be increased and the US–Korea alliance was to remain intact. In October, a new agreement was reached stating that the United States would withdraw only 5,000 troops by the end of 2004, including the 3,600 already deployed in Iraq, and pull out the remainder by 2008. Agreement was also reached on relocating the headquarters of the UN Command and the Combined Forces Command from the centre of Seoul to another city, removing a steady irritant in the bilateral relationship. Still on the agenda was a South Korean request to reduce the amount it pays to help maintain US forces on the peninsula, currently about $623m.

Reinforcing the impression that the military component of the alliance was still fairly healthy, Seoul dispatched 3,000 combat troops and military engineers to Iraq in support of the American effort. The government had already sent 670 troops in mid-2003 despite strong opposition from its domestic supporters. While the National Assembly voted in favour of the new move in February 2004, it was delayed as the government searched for a location relatively safe from insurgent activities. But public opposition mounted as the news broke of American abuse of Iraqi prisoners and, by late April, it appeared a majority of National Assemblymen thought the decision should be reconsidered. A few months later, however, the controversy ended as the ruling party resolved internal disagreements and decided to uphold the February vote. The deployment was completed by the end of 2004.

Escaping the diplomatic vacuum

Perhaps the most striking feature of the situation on the Korean Peninsula in 2004 was the continued lack of a clear and decisive American vision for its future and for that of Northeast Asia. The crux of that problem remains the issue of whither North Korea. For reasons both operational (in particular, Seoul's position within range of massive North Korean artillery) and diplomatic (lack of support from other Asian powers) the Bush administration has been unable to pursue what is probably its preferred approach, seeking the end of the dictatorship in Pyongyang. Yet Washington, for understandable reasons, cannot bring itself to negotiate directly and bilaterally with the North Korean regime, since that would confer legitimacy on Pyongyang. As a result, the United States' default position is to wait for the North to make a serious mistake that will firmly unite the other participants in the Six-Party Talks in support of the tough measures the Bush administration so fervently desires. In the meantime, it appears that Washington is effectively acquiescing to the slow build-up of a nuclear arsenal by a country that not only has been an enemy for five decades but which also poses a severe threat to Japan, the linchpin of the United States' strategic position in Asia. On top of that, Washington may be underrating the corrosive effect that its policy is having on a long-standing alliance with South Korea that remains useful, if not strategically vital.

The steps Washington needs to take to correct this problem are fairly clear. With a diplomatic vacuum now prevailing, the American approach towards North Korea has neither carrots nor sticks. Any effective policy in dealing with Pyongyang will need both. The key to fixing this problem will be adjusting the US position in the Six-Party Talks in preparation for serious negotiations with Pyongyang. Those negotiations may have to be viewed not as a means of reaching a diplomatic solution to the current crisis, but more importantly as an indispensable tool for preparing the ground for tougher measures – should they become necessary – by winning the hearts and minds of the other participants. If the North rejects reasonable proposals, that will put Washington in a much stronger position to pursue other measures outside of the Six-Party Talks.

In service of this objective, the United States would need to articulate a forward-looking vision for the future that would galvanise support for its efforts in the region, particularly in South Korea. Denuclearisation of the Korean Peninsula would only be one element of such a plan. Others might include the elimination of long range ballistic missiles from the peninsula; political and economic normalisation of relations between North Korea and South Korea, other neighbours and the United States itself; and a wholesale improvement in the human-rights situation in

North Korea. Hard-liners in Washington would inevitably reiterate the argument that the United States and its partners tried and failed to project and realise such a vision in the late 1990s and earlier this decade, and that North Korea should not on principle be allowed to sell the same goods twice. That is a rhetorically compelling line, but one that has only perpetuated Pyongyang's impunity. Washington need not submit to bilateral talks. But, in April 2005, a more flexible US approach within the six-party context seems the only way forward.

China: Growing Power, Troubled Diplomacy

In 2004–05, China's standing as a consequential power whose interests and actions bear on the pressing strategic issues of the day became more vividly – and, arguably more starkly – apparent. China's transformation, underway for two-and-a-half decades, has been one in which a formerly local power of second rank, labouring under an anachronistic political system, a faltering economy and a parochial geostrategic mindset, has emerged as a regional power with global presence and preoccupations. China cannot yet be considered a truly global power. Daunting problems at home exert the primary pull on the attention of China's leadership and are a drain on the country's stretched resources. Though increasing, China's conventional military power cannot yet be projected to any great effect beyond its own vicinity. While China's economic magnetism is compelling, the country lacks the kind of political appeal that would rally others to it en masse, or create the affinities on which broader and more durable strategic relationships could be built. While China has not yet arrived as a global power, however, that prospect seems at least to be coming into closer focus.

Three indications emerged in 2004–05. Firstly, China's continuing investment and export boom, demanding increasing inflows of raw materials and other inputs, became a decisive influence on world energy markets and commodity prices. China's importance to the other three centres of global economic power, and therefore the importance of Chinese foreign economic policy, also became clearer. International economists noted China's role in helping to support the dollar and finance the US current account and fiscal deficits through purchases of US Treasury bills. This, and the disinflationary impact of cheap Chinese exports to the United States, it was argued, was crucial in allowing the Federal Reserve to maintain the loose monetary policy on which America's domestic economic buoyancy depended. Signs of an upswing in Japan after years of stagnation were also attributed to strengthened trade with China, while the volume of China's bilateral trade with the European Union (EU) eclipsed for the first time its bilateral trade with the US and Japan.

Secondly, China's diplomatic activity increased outside Asia (where Beijing nevertheless kept up an impressive tempo, hosting the inaugural meeting of the ASEAN Regional Forum Security Policy Conference in November 2004). Its outreach was especially evident in Africa, Latin America and the Middle East. Much of this was stimulated by the pursuit of greater energy security, but typically sought to invest new or revivified relationships with some strategic and political content.

Thirdly, China emerged as the subject of a noisy and bitter disagreement within the transatlantic alliance, weakening attempts to achieve a rapprochement between Europe and America after the exhausting arguments over the invasion of Iraq. The debate, stimulated by the determination of some European countries to lift the arms embargo imposed on China by the EU after the Tiananmen Square massacre of in 1989, revealed a conspicuous lack of consensus regarding China's current role in international affairs, the form that it was likely to take in future and the means that Europe and America ought to employ in their dealings with China to ensure that their long-term interests were safeguarded as well as understood. The United States and the EU each at various points accused the other of cynicism or naiveté in its view of China; both sides thought China an important enough matter to row about.

The complexity as well as the extent of China's international interactions has been laid bare. In many ways, 2004–05 was not a good one for Chinese diplomacy. China's efforts to achieve greater security of supply in commodities and energy, and to serve narrowly drawn short-term national security interests, have led it into controversial relationships with countries such as Sudan, Iran and North Korea. Having established a reputation in Asia in recent years for its diplomatic deftness, China last year showed that it had not lost the capacity for missteps and stumbles, especially in areas that touched on nationalist sentiment and outstanding territorial disputes. Its sharp rebuke of Singapore over the visit to Taiwan in July 2004 of then prime minister-designate Lee Hsien Loong, as well as a heated argument with South Korea over the historical status of the ancient Goguryeo kingdom, compromised China's careful efforts to reassure its neighbours about the implications of its rise.

Some of Beijing's major relationships also took a turn for the worse. Antipathy between China and Japan was compounded by a series of Chinese naval incursions into the seas around Japan throughout 2004. It was further fuelled by Tokyo's increasing willingness to criticise China's military modernisation publicly and to proclaim, in a joint statement with the United States on 19 February 2005, that China's dispute with Taiwan affected Japan's security. At the same time, the exceptionally warm weave of Sino-American diplomacy of the last three years began to look a little threadbare over Washington's incandescent objections to the lifting of the EU arms embargo, reflecting grave American apprehensions about China's record on human rights, its proliferation practices, its military modernisation and its ultimate intentions towards Taiwan. The frustrating drift in the Six-Party Talks over North Korea's nuclear programme also eroded some of the prestige that had previously accrued to Beijing as the convenor and principal mediator of the talks, while China's arbitrary intervention to remove the leadership of Hong Kong proved controversial in the territory and abroad.

Politics at home

China's domestic political scene in 2004–05 was generally less troublesome than its foreign policy. In September 2004, Jiang Zemin formally relinquished the chairmanship of the Communist Party's Central Military Commission (CMC), or high command. The chairmanship of the identical CMC that is maintained, largely for presentational reasons, in the structure of the Chinese state was also handed over at the March 2005 annual meeting of the parliamentary National People's Congress. With these moves, the three most senior positions in China – general secretary of the Communist Party, president of the state, and head of the military – were combined in the person of Hu Jintao.

The precise sequence – and more especially the timing – of these events had not been widely anticipated. Most observers had interpreted Jiang Zemin's retention of his military post for almost two years after stepping down from all other formal responsibilities in November 2002 as indicative of a dogged wish to continue to decisively influence government, even after submitting to a rejuvenating generational change of China's leadership. Matters of policymaking were seen through the prism of a Hu–Jiang power struggle, though it never came fully into public view. Concerns were raised in some quarters – reportedly including the military – in China that this configuration of divided power was straining loyalties and undermining the clarity and implementation of policy. In other areas, the assumed tussles were seen as contributing to an unwelcome hardening of policy lines, including towards Taiwan, as apparently posturing leaders competed to advertise their credentials on matters of national security and sovereignty.

A number of explanations for Jiang's retirement have been advanced. One gives credence to the notion of a power struggle, but argues that Jiang had belatedly come to understand that his prestige and power would be better preserved if he put himself above formal office and the day-to-day fray and assumed the mantle of *éminence grise*. His interventions might be more effective and less resented for being selective. Another theory holds that Jiang tried but failed to cling to power, and that his resignation and the failure to have his chief lieutenant, Vice-President Zeng Qinghong, appointed a vice-chairman of the CMC marked a significant political triumph for Hu over both his loitering predecessor and the man widely thought to be his principal rival. Yet another account proposes that Jiang had intended all along to step down after a decent interval, thereby ritualistically emulating and seeking to equate himself with former paramount leader Deng Xiaoping, a man of rather greater authority who took this approach in the early 1990s. Whatever the correct interpretation, Jiang's retirement probably marks the beginning of a period of political consolidation for Hu in the two years leading up to the next Communist Party Congress in 2007, at which he is expected to be confirmed for a second term. Until then, he will not be able to effect significant changes in the composition of key decision-making bodies he inherited from Jiang. Hu seems likely, and indeed instinctively inclined, to adopt a consensual style of leadership, in which he quietly and gradually puts his stamp on government. The success of that effort will not be clear until the outcome of the 2007 congress, but his political authority should be much enhanced by then.

Although Hu has sought to cast himself as a man of the people and of those who have yet to benefit from China's development, and not as the representative of the eastern and southern coastal elites, and while he has shown enthusiasm for some institutional and procedural transparency in government, his revealed political instincts are, on balance, conservative. He and his colleagues will continue to prefer the pursuit of bureaucratic competence, the re-centralisation of administrative powers and the development of better policy tools over political liberalisation. Reinforcing this attitude is the lesson of the frustrated attempt in 2004 to dampen an economy suffering from excessive over-investment and signs of macroeconomic imbalance with administrative orders, which were applied too indiscriminately or simply circumvented by businesses or ignored by local authorities. The instinctive conservatism of the leadership was also displayed in its nervous reaction to the death, in January 2005, of the octogenarian Zhao Ziyang, the former reformist Communist Party general secretary under house arrest since 1989. He had appeared in Tiananmen Square on the eve of the declaration of martial law and violent crackdown on the pro-democracy movement, commiserating with students and urging them to disperse rather than face what he only implied was coming. China's leadership, who tightly controlled media coverage of Zhao's demise and the circumstances of his funeral, evidently feared that his death could trigger sympathetic demonstrations and calls for a reassessment of the Party's verdict that the crushing of the pro-democracy movement was correct in all respects. The Party will probably have cautiously interpreted the failure of such protests to materialise as confirmation of its view that political passions can be subdued and memories expunged by continuing economic advances.

Similarly anxious authoritarianism infused China's approach to Hong Kong in 2004–05. The resignation on 12 March 2005 of Tung Chee-hwa as Hong Kong chief executive, ostensibly on health grounds, and his instant appointment as one of several vice-chairmen of China's comparatively obscure Chinese People's Political Consultative Conference, appeared to be, in reality, outright dismissal by Beijing. Tung, Beijing's preferred choice upon the transfer of Hong Kong's sovereignty from the United Kingdom to China in July 1997, had struggled to make a success of his administration, strained as it was by deep economic malaise and by reversals such as the outbreak of Severe Acute Respiratory Syndrome (SARS). However, it was his dutiful championing of an item of heavy-handed legislation favoured by Beijing to counter acts of 'sedition' in Hong Kong that provoked the most intense local public hostility. In July 2003, half-a-million people took to the streets to protest the legislation and other aspects of policy. Many of them were critical of Beijing and called for acceleration in the pace of democratisation in the territory. China's leaders appeared to lose faith in Tung over his failure to anticipate and manage the public mood. China's initial response was to take steps to improve trade between China and the Special Administrative Region, offering Hong Kong economic relief. These measures had some soothing effect on public opinion. But Beijing nevertheless seems to have concluded that stability required Tung's departure before the end of his second term in 2007.

Tung's resignation has not emerged as a notable matter of regret for the people of Hong Kong, and the acting chief executive – the British-trained civil servant Donald Tsang – is widely regarded as a sound administrator. However, the episode has been seized on by pro-democracy and anti-China lobbies that worry about the implications of Tung's effective dismissal for the putatively high degree of autonomy promised Hong Kong under the principle of 'one country, two systems'. They have also taken issue with Beijing's stated wish that the next chief executive, to be selected in July 2005 by an 800-member body that is largely sympathetic to Beijing, and who is likely to be Donald Tsang, should serve for only the two remaining years of what would have been Tung's term, rather than for a full five-year term as provided for by Hong Kong's Basic Law. China's stance probably reflects the calculation that a two-year term by Tsang would exert a welcome settling effect on the territory, while allowing Beijing to gauge his performance without investing too much political capital in him. But there are limits to the freedom with which China can direct events. Systematic overt intervention in Hong Kong's affairs would carry political costs, in terms of demands for faster democratic reform toward fuller direct suffrage. It would also stoke Taiwanese scepticism towards proffered 'one country, two systems' formulas. Insofar as the legislative and executive branches of the US government continue to take a keen interest in upholding Hong Kong's guaranteed prerogatives, diplomatic costs would also be incurred. On current indications, however, China seems ready to bear at least some of those costs.

Dealing with America

The relationship between China and the United States underwent a subtle but definite change over the last year. Diplomacy was carried out at a brisk pace and at a senior level. Vice-President Dick Cheney visited Beijing for consultations in April 2004. He and President George W. Bush met Chinese Foreign Minister Li Zhaoxing in Houston, Texas, in June. Then-secretary of state Colin Powell held discussions with Li at the ASEAN Regional Forum's ministerial summit in July and made a trip to China in October, and the two men spoke regularly by telephone. In November,

Presidents Bush and Hu met at the Asia–Pacific Economic Cooperation (APEC) summit in Santiago, Chile. Condoleezza Rice made two trips to China, the first as national security advisor in July 2004 and the second as the new US secretary of state in March 2005. Contacts between military leaderships were also kept up: in July 2004 Admiral Thomas Fargo, then the commander of US Pacific Command, visited China, while General Liang Guanglie, the chief of the General Staff of the People's Liberation Army, made a trip to Washington DC in October.

Over the last three years, however, the relationship between China and the United States has been held in a particular pattern that no longer seems as secure as before. Following the worrying tensions produced by the April 2001 collision of US and Chinese military aircraft over the South China Sea, but more especially after the events of 11 September 2001, Beijing and Washington made a determined effort to downplay their differences and concentrate on common interests and their useful-ness to each other. The United States wished to focus on counter-terrorism, and China, subject to certain caveats and limitations, wanted to present itself as a partner in that campaign. As the United States became embroiled in interventions in Afghanistan and then Iraq, the logic of avoiding arguments with China, and of mobilising China in efforts to deal with other energy-absorbing contingencies such as North Korea's nuclear activities, became compelling. China hoped that America's desire to cement bilateral ties, and its wish to avoid a distracting crisis in the Taiwan Strait, would lead the Bush administration to set aside its initial policy of robust support for Taiwan in favour of one that explicitly restrained pro-independence forces on the island. It had been heartened in this last regard by the public admonition of Taiwan President Chen Shui-bian that Bush issued in December 2003 from the White House, in the presence of a beaming Chinese Premier Wen Jiabao.

With these considerations in mind, Beijing, in thinking about the implications of the November 2004 US presidential election, tilted towards preferring a second Bush term. To be sure, China's mainstream foreign-policy community felt that Democratic presidential candidate John Kerry would have jettisoned the most controversial and muscular elements of US foreign policy under Bush – the preven-tive use of military force and the circumvention, in the last resort, of the United Nations – and adopted a traditional form of diplomacy with which China was more comfortable. He might, they reasoned, also take a more flexible approach to North Korea than the Bush administration seemed prepared to. Yet Beijing did not relish the prospect of tutoring another American president on the subtle semantic intricacies of the cross-strait dispute and the 'one China' policy. Moreover, a Kerry administration would, they felt, be more vulnerable than Bush's to pressure from conservative Congressmen who looked frostily on China and warmly on Taiwan, and Kerry's comparative closeness to the US labour movement might require him to take a more protectionist view of trade between the United States and China, where America was recording ever more staggering deficits.

Some of Beijing's lingering apprehensions (and hedging instincts) with respect to the Bush administration were captured in an editorial by the distinguished former Chinese foreign minister Qian Qichen, published on the eve of the US presidential election in the *China Daily* newspaper. Entitled 'US Strategy to be Blamed', the article fulminated, in terms which serving Chinese officials avoided, against the Iraq intervention and the doctrine of pre-emption upon which it was based, forecasting that this would prove a costly and counterproductive strategic folly that had already inflicted lasting damage on America's relationships. For those Chinese strategists who take the most conspiratorial view of America's long-term intentions towards China – seeing an ambition to contain and encircle China and to keep it divided from Taiwan – these observations were both true and comforting. The troubled occupation of Iraq had laid bare America's diplomatic and military overstretch, just as the build-up to the intervention had been accompanied by a decline in its international normative and political appeal. This seemed to open up the possibility of geostrategic realignments from which China might opportunistically benefit; Europe was seen as a particularly attractive target. Chinese strategists who had worried about the release of unrestrained American power in ways ultimately detrimental to China's interests now began, instead, to conceive of an America that had bitten off more in Iraq than it could comfortably chew, was diplomatically on the back foot and would have to make policy compromises to ingratiate itself with its remaining partners.

What neither the mainstream nor the fringe of the Chinese strategic community could have anticipated were unsettling (to them) developments in the tone as well as the fortunes of US foreign policy in the months following Bush's re-election. Far from articulating more modest and limited foreign policy goals, Bush in his January 2005 inauguration speech and State of the Union address spoke in epic, grandiloquent terms about America's ambition – and mission – to spread freedom and democracy throughout the world. He plainly conceived of US foreign policy not as having entered a phase of cautious consolidation, but as being expansive and ready to capitalise on the strategic investments made during his first term. The largely unexpected success of the Iraqi general elections in January 2005 provided the Bush administration with rare vindication. Adopting an uncomplicated narrative, it saw developments in Iraq as part of a larger evolving trend which it had either helped bring about or to which it offered crucial support. In the Middle East, this trend included demonstrations against the Syrian occupation of Lebanon, resulting in a pledge by Damascus to withdraw by the end of April; in Egypt and Saudi Arabia it featured the tentative extension of democracy and competitive politics. Further afield, the trend included the successful anti-authoritarian uprisings between 2003 and 2005 in Georgia, Ukraine and Kyrgyzstan. Within this scheme, the Bush administration also worked with some success to repair relations with EU members and, following the death of Palestinian President Yasser Arafat in November 2004, re-engaged in the Israeli–Palestinian peace process. It also proved able to modify its diplomacy towards Iran, lending greater support to European initiatives to negotiate a permanent cessation of Tehran's nuclear activities and for the first time offering inducements of its own. At issue for Beijing was the extent to which Washington would now feel freer to revert to the more forward and critical approach to China that had been a prominent feature of the early months of Bush's first term.

Rogue relations?

Irritants in the Sino-American relationship in 2004–05 arose out of Beijing's capacity and willingness to impede American diplomatic initiatives towards governments that Washington considers potentially dangerous or unsavoury. In the case of Iran's nuclear activities, there was growing frustration in Washington at Beijing's vocal opposition to any referral of the matter to the UN Security Council. Beijing argued at length that Iran was cooperating satisfactorily with the International Atomic Energy Agency (IAEA) and that any resort to the Security Council would be unnecessarily provocative. Beijing set out this position during a meeting in Tehran in November 2004 between Chinese Foreign Minister Li Zhaoxing and Iranian President Mohammad Khatami. It was not a view held exclusively by China. Throughout 2004, an extensive international debate took place on the most effective tactical approach to take towards Iran, and the European countries leading the diplomatic effort regarded referral to the Security Council as an option of last resort that gave them negotiating leverage. Others feared that the United States' intention was to accumulate a catalogue of Security Council resolutions against Iran that would provide, as in the case of Iraq, a legal basis and occasion for coercive action.

From Washington's perspective, however, China's stance was motivated by narrower national interests that had little to do with crafting the most effective non-proliferation policy. Indeed, since taking office in 2001, the Bush administration had in dozens of instances imposed sanctions on Chinese entities and state-linked conglomerates for alleged proliferation practices, including transfers of missile-related and other sensitive technologies to Iran. China's attitude was seen through the prism of its mounting concerns about energy security. After Saudi Arabia, Iran is the largest supplier of oil to China, accounting for almost 14% of China's 2003 imports. Iranian officials have talked of their desire to see China replace Japan as their largest export market. In October 2004, Beijing and Tehran concluded a memorandum of understanding under which Iran would sell $70bn of crude oil and liquefied natural gas to China over the next 25–30 years. The agreement provided for the involvement of China's state energy companies in the exploration and development of Iran's Yadavaran oil field. Many of these agreements, Washington reasoned, might be complicated or jeopardised, were the Security Council eventually to impose sanctions on Iran or if the United States confronted Iran more forcefully over its nuclear ambitions.

Similar motives were attributed to China in its diplomatic response to the atrocities unfolding in the Darfur region of Sudan, which the United States early on described as a form of genocide perpetrated by Arab militias against black Africans. China is the principal foreign investor in Sudan's oil industry, and the country's leading trading partner. It is also alleged to be Sudan's most important source of arms and ammunition, which have been used by the Khartoum government against southern rebels. With its partner Pakistan, Beijing in July 2004 abstained from Security Council Resolution 1556, which called on Khartoum to disarm the militias, and it repeatedly threatened to veto any resolution that imposed sanctions on the Sudanese government for its failure to take effective action. In September 2004, China decided to abstain on much-redrafted Resolution 1564, which threatens sanctions but, contrary to American wishes, does not automatically impose them. As of April 2005, Beijing had not weakened its resistance to sanctions.

Thus, Washington sensed an emerging pattern in which Beijing was willing to forgive the errant behaviour of states that China considered of importance to its national security interests. There appeared to be growing concern in policy circles that the principle was being applied to North Korea's nuclear activities as well. In the initial stages of the Six-Party Talks – which include North and South Korea, Japan, China, the United States and Russia – Washington undoubtedly welcomed Beijing's activism in convening and sustaining the discussions. Partly as a matter of choice, because of its unwillingness to deal bilaterally with Pyongyang, and partly as a matter of necessity, in view of its preoccupation with Iraq and terrorism and of the paralysing policy debates inside the Bush administration about how to handle North Korea, Washington conceded the initiative to Beijing. An implicit American critique of Beijing's position, however, soon developed. In this view, China prioritised the stability of the North Korean regime over countering proliferation risks; seemed to regard the Six-Party Talks as a process worth sustaining for its own sake rather than as a mechanism for achieving North Korea's disarmament; was too timid using leverage over Pyongyang; and did not take seriously enough the implications of Pyongyang's desire to clandestinely develop a uranium-enrichment strand to its nuclear programme. The counter-critique was that the United States minimised North Korea's security concerns, some of which China saw as legitimate, and that US insistence on complete and verifiable disarmament prior to receipt of rewards by Pyongyang was fanciful.

By the June 2004 round of Six-Party talks, Washington had recalibrated its position somewhat. In its new proposal, North Korea would be required to declare its intention to disarm, and within three months impose a freeze on its nuclear programmes, including its clandestine uranium-enrichment programme. It would prepare a detailed inventory of all nuclear materials and infrastructure. In return, Seoul would resume shipments of heavy fuel oil. Following a period of three months, North Korea would begin to dismantle its nuclear infrastructure under international monitoring and allow the removal from the country of sensitive materials. Once this began, the United States and others would offer a provisional multilateral security guarantee, to be finalised on completion of the disarmament process. Talks would also begin on energy assistance and removing North Korea from the US State Department's list of state sponsors of terrorism, a move that could unlock funding from multilateral development banks. The other four parties to the talks broadly welcomed this new degree of flexibility as at least moving in the right direction, and the United States looked to China in particular to extract a serious response from North Korea. But Pyongyang settled into a mode of procrastination, seemingly struggling to devise a reply that rejected the proposal – which it thought insufficiently generous – but without the appearance of undue intransigence.

Chinese–North Korean bilateral exchanges continued. On 12 September 2004, Li Changchun, a member of the Chinese Communist Party's Politburo Standing Committee, travelled to Pyongyang to meet North Korean leader Kim Jong Il. On 18–20 October, Kim Yong Nam, North Korea's second most senior leader, travelled to Beijing. As the November 2004 US presidential election approached, though, Pyongyang demonstrated no particular desire to return to the Six-Party Talks table, preferring to await the outcome of the poll in the barely concealed hope that a Kerry administration might adopt a less demanding negotiating position. While publicly urging a resumption of talks at the earliest possible opportunity, Beijing probably understood, and as a practical matter had some sympathy, with North Korea's reasoning. But Pyongyang's elusiveness continued well beyond the inauguration of the new Bush administration and the appointment of key foreign policy officials. In early February 2005, Michael Green, senior director for Asian Affairs at the US National Security Council, was therefore dispatched to Beijing to convey a personal letter from Bush to Hu Jintao that reportedly highlighted the urgency of a resumption of talks and detailed US intelligence assessments of North Korea's nuclear programme. A few days later, on 10 February 2005, Pyongyang proclaimed that it possessed nuclear weapons and declared the 'indefinite suspension' of its participation in the Six-Party Talks, citing the 'hostile policy' of the United States and lashing out at Japan. During a 21 February meeting in Pyongyang with Wang Jiarui, Hu's personal envoy, Kim Jong Il blandly indicated that an 'indefinite suspension' was not the same thing as a permanent withdrawal, and that Pyongyang would consider re-engaging if what he called 'mature conditions' could be established and if the United States showed 'trustworthy sincerity'. This was also the line developed by North Korean Prime Minister Pak Pong Ju during a visit to Beijing on 24–27 March. Pak's trip had been immediately preceded by the visit of US Secretary of State Condoleezza Rice, who underlined Washington's commitment to the Six-Party Talks but also its growing frustration with Pyongyang. Options other than the current diplomatic approach might have to be contemplated, she suggested.

In US assessments, North Korea probably has at least three immediate goals: to continue to advance its nuclear capabilities; to allow itself to be enticed by Chinese largesse to eventually return to the Six-Party Talks; and, most importantly, to ensure that any such return occurs on the understanding that the June 2004 proposal put forward by Washington is not a point of departure for negotiations – that is, that the slate has been wiped clean. This being so, Washington will try to persuade Beijing that meaningful discussions, rather than diplomatic ritual, can only result if China, as the only country with effective influence over North Korea, is willing to pressure and cajole rather than to entice and reward. Even measures that stopped short of a referral of the matter to the UN Security Council – a step that China, as in the case of Iran, has stoutly opposed – would, Washington felt, introduce a positive new dynamic into the diplomacy. Yet, as of early April 2005, Beijing had given no sign that it subscribed to this reasoning or that its patience with North Korea had in any sense approached exhaustion; the value of preserving the stability of its dysfunctional and potentially chaotic neighbour still trumped the longer-term costs of a Japan that was expanding its regional security role on the pretext of the North Korean threat, and a United States that for ostensibly the same reason was entrenching its military position in Asia. Ultimately, the degree of coordination which Beijing and Washington are able to achieve on the question of North Korea will depend on how the overall tone and substance of their relationship. The signs are less promising in this regard than they have been.

Military modernisation and the EU arms embargo

Between April 2004 and April 2005, the pace, extent and implications of China's military modernisation became the subject of acute international interest and the focus of an unresolved argument among the United States, the EU and other Asian powers. Significant advances were noted in China's efforts in several areas in 2004. The first of these concerned the Central Military Commission, which in addition to coming under the chairmanship of Hu Jintao in September 2004 was expanded to include, for the first time, not only the head of the ground forces but also the heads of the People's Liberation Army Air Force (PLAAF), the People's Liberation Army Navy (PLAN) and the 2nd Artillery, or strategic rocket forces. The initiative was probably motivated by the recognition that the kinds of contingencies China may face in the future – including, above all, any conflict over Taiwan – will require it to possess the capability to mount sophisticated joint operations involving all or most services. An expanded high command provides a venue in which a more rounded and integrated defence modernisation policy can be developed, and will aid in the clarification of priorities and the allocation of resources.

Specific aspects of Chinese military doctrine and policy priorities were also clarified over the last year. In its latest Defence White Paper – issued in December 2004 and considered a fuller document than those that have gone before it – particular emphasis was devoted to a 'Revolution in Military Affairs with Chinese characteristics' as the guiding principle of defence reform, allied to a stress on what was called the 'informationalization' of the armed forces, by which is meant the integration of information technology into all areas of China's defence reforms. The Defence White Paper also indicated that China was giving priority to the modernisation of its strategic rocket forces, air force and navy. Indeed, particular activity has been noted in recent years in the development of a submarine capability that would strengthen China's hand in imposing a blockade on Taiwan and deterring or countering a naval intervention by the United States over the island. China has begun to take delivery of eight *Kilo*-class submarines from Russia to add to the four already in its fleet. The first of the new Type-094 ballistic missile submarines was reportedly launched in 2004, following the earlier launch of two Type-093 nuclear-fuelled attack submarines. In June 2004 the first of a new *Yuan* diesel submarine class was launched, while production of the *Song* diesel submarine was also stepped up last year. As far as the PLAAF is concerned, a $1bn deal was reportedly reached between China and Russia for the supply of 24 Su-30 multi-role fighter aircraft.

Among the defence policy trends cited by the Pentagon in its 'Annual Report to Congress on the Military Power of the People's Liberation Army', released in July 2004, particular attention was drawn to China's efforts to enhance its own defence industrial base; develop better joint logistical systems and mount joint exercises, including with some foreign militaries; develop military space capabilities, including reconnaissance and communications, that can be used to counter the space-based assets of other militaries; boost its command, control, communications and computer intelligence reconnaissance and surveillance (C⁴ISR) capabilities; and enhance its arsenal of short- and medium-range ballistic missiles and land-attack cruise missiles. More generally, the Pentagon asserted that China had drawn a number of tactical lessons from *Operation Iraqi Freedom* that it might seek to apply in any conflict with Taiwan.

Meanwhile, the resources of the Chinese armed forces continued to grow. During the annual session of the National People's Congress in early March 2005, China announced a 12.6% increase in its official defence budget, to $29.9bn. As on previous occasions, Chinese officials stressed that much of the increase in the budget would be absorbed by salary costs and welfare outlays. But the budget was again organised so that it did not take account of funds set aside for foreign procurements of military technology. The size of the foreign procurement budget is not known, but is likely to be substantial. This is a matter of necessity as much as choice: although China's defence industrial base has in recent years been subjected to significant bureaucratic and structural reforms designed to enhance innovation and efficiency, it is not yet in a position to meet China's defence needs. As a result, China has come to rely on Russia for heavy and modern items of defence technology such as fighter aircraft, surface vessels and submarines. It has also looked to Israel for supplementary and specific technologies, including battle tanks, military transport aircraft and especially airborne warning and control systems (AWACS). US pressure has, however, tended to limit transfers from Israel to China. In 2000, the Clinton administration forced the cancellation of a deal to transfer the *Phalcon* AWACS and subsequently tried to ensure that there would be no further sales of or upgrades to *Harpy* unmanned aerial vehicles. Following representations from the Bush administration, Israeli Minister of Defence Shaul Mofaz in March 2005 convened a meeting of the heads of Israel's defence companies to warn them against making any contact with Chinese entities without explicit prior written approval.

Although problems can sometimes arise in trying to integrate and marry many differing types of defence technology acquired from a wide range of sources, Beijing in practice has a significant incentive to diversify its sources of supply. Accordingly, it has for many years pressed for the lifting of the arms embargo imposed by the EU following the 1989 suppression of the Chinese pro-democracy movement. Chinese diplomats have railed against the pariah status that the embargo implies, seeing it as inconsistent with China's proclaimed standing a responsible member of the international community, unwarranted and intolerable as an interference in its domestic political affairs, and unjustifiable in view of the new 'maturity' in the strategic partnership it is trying to build with the EU. Yet military considerations are hardly absent from China's calculations. The lifting of the embargo and the improved access to European defence technologies that it might provide – or could be presented by China as providing – would probably give Beijing increased leverage in its negotiations with existing defence suppliers. China has on occasion grumbled about Russia's tendency to withhold some items of defence technology that Moscow has been willing to supply to others, especially India. The lifting of the embargo might, in Beijing's view, usefully prompt Russia to adopt a more forthcoming stance and encourage Israel to defy American pressure to limit its defence sales.

Beijing seems to have no expectation that the lifting of the EU arms embargo would result in transfers of major platforms and heavy items of lethal defence technology, since European public opinion and American and Asian objections would not easily permit this. Instead, China would look to Europe for certain items of defence technology, much of it having dual-use applications, that would enhance the effectiveness of platforms sourced from elsewhere, better integrate China's military capabilities and overcome information-technology deficiencies in a range of areas. Most defence experts assume that priorities for China would include better jet aircraft propulsion and naval propulsion systems; improvements, through information-technology inputs, to the security and reliability of military command-and-control systems; more effective aircraft and naval weapons guidance and fire-control systems; and upgraded communications and surveillance capabilities to provide China with a more accurate and comprehensive picture of the 'battle space' in which its forces operated.

The EU embargo, which has no legal force and has been regulated by a code of conduct consisting of several loose operative criteria, has not prevented defence transfers from Europe to China. According to press reports, defence-related transfers, carried out under special licenses, amounted to $416m in 2003. A report compiled by the private US-based International Assessment and Strategy Center in early 2005 provided some insight into the forms and scope of European–Chinese defence transfers in recent years. It highlighted the application of sophisticated turbofan engine technology, supplied to the Xian Aircraft Corporation by Rolls-Royce in the UK, in the development of China's JH-7A fighter-bomber for the navy and air force; the use of technology and design information supplied by Eurocopter and Agusta of Italy in the production of transport and attack helicopters, where Chinese indigenous capabilities have traditionally been weak; the use of German diesel engines in the *Song* attack submarine and French diesel engines in China's Type 054 stealthy frigate; Italian sales and co-production of trucks that are to be fitted with anti-tank weapons; and British transfers to China of dual-use micro-satellite technology that, it was argued, could be used for military surveillance and communication purposes as well as in efforts to guide attacks on the satellites of other states.

Movement towards lifting the EU arms embargo began in late 2003, as French President Jacques Chirac, and subsequently German Chancellor Gerhard Schröder, strongly advocated its repeal. Momentum gathered throughout 2004. In public remarks, French and German officials advanced the argument that the embargo was an impediment to the kind of constructive relationship Europe wished to build with China, that it served to exclude rather than to integrate China into the international system, and that substantial improvements to human rights – usually expressed in terms of social and economic freedoms, rather than political liberties – had been made in China since 1989. While accepting that the issue of how best to engage China is a legitimate matter of debate, critics of the French position attributed narrower motives to Paris. By leading calls to lift the embargo, it was argued, France stood to ingratiate itself to China irrespective of whether its efforts succeeded, which could prove useful in other commercial contexts. In fact, public French reasoning on this issue only became more opaque, as initial efforts to downplay the practical military significance of lifting of the embargo gave way to a seemingly disingenuous analysis set out in early 2005. French Defence Minister Michelle Alliot-Marie now claimed that increased access to European defence technology would have the effect of slowing China's indigenous defence-industrial reforms and give Europe the means by which to regulate the pace and scope of China's military build-up.

This argument was not widely accepted, least of all in the United States, where efforts to resist the lifting of the embargo only got into full swing in the latter part of 2004 and early 2005. Quiet representations from US diplomats and briefings in Europe from US intelligence officials were followed by angry protests from

Congress, led by senior figures such as Senator Richard Lugar, chairman of the Senate Foreign Relations Committee, and Senator Joseph Biden, the committee's ranking Democrat. Wide sections of Congress began to voice support for measures that would restrict transfers of sensitive American technologies to Europe in the event that the embargo was repealed, fearing that these might be passed on to China's military. Visiting Europe in February 2005, Bush stressed his 'deep concern' about the measure Europe was contemplating, while during a visit to Asia in late March Secretary of State Condoleezza Rice reminded Europe in barbed terms that Asia's security was being upheld by America, and that Europe was little more than a free-rider on the regional burdens which the United States had assumed. There was remarkable bipartisan unanimity on the issue in the United States, where arguments focused on three themes: human-rights abuses in China were still too extensive to merit the 'reward' of a repeal; the political signal sent by a repeal would harden Beijing's stance towards Taiwan, where the risk of conflict was already high; and, regardless of European reassurances, lifting the ban would increase the prospect that the United States might, in the event of a conflict over Taiwan, find itself on the receiving end of defence technology supplied to China by NATO allies. On 5 April 2005, Deputy Secretary of State Robert Zoellick raised the stakes of European action, stating at a Brussels press conference that transatlantic relations would be seriously undermined if 'European equipment helped kill American men and women in conflict'.

The intramural EU diplomacy on this issue has been fraught. Although a lifting of the embargo could be vetoed by any of the EU's 25 members, those countries sceptical about the wisdom of lifting the ban – both on the question's own terms, and as a matter affecting transatlantic relations – were reluctant to be singled out as sources of resistance, fearing diplomatic retribution from China. The vehemence with which France and Germany had set out their position meant that a prospective decision to lift the embargo had been telegraphed to China in the strongest terms. This made it difficult for other countries, such as Britain, to dial the EU back to a middle position, in which any lifting of the embargo would be contingent on a reinforcement of the code of conduct governing arms transfers to all countries and some sense of reciprocity from China, including on human rights. By the end of 2004, notwithstanding the apparent hand-wringing within the EU, the decision to proceed with the repeal had for all intents and purposes been made. Broadly, France called for the least restrictive terms and the greatest haste, while Britain, Poland and the Scandinavian countries argued for more restrictive terms and flexibility on timing. On 17 December 2004, the European Council stated that it would 'continue to work towards the lifting of the arms embargo' and it invited the Luxembourg presidency of the EU in the first half of 2005 to 'finalize the well-advanced work in order to allow for a decision'. It also stressed, however, that the lifting of the embargo should not result in a qualitative or quantitative increase in arms transfers, highlighted the importance of a revised code of conduct that paid special regard to human rights, regional security and the security of allied and friendly states, and called for a 'tool box' of measures to be put into place following any lifting of the embargo.

On this basis, the UK tried to reassure the United States that, as politically regrettable as the lifting of the embargo was, an opportunity had now been created to put something better into place. The case made was that the embargo established in 1989 amounted to no more than a political statement. It covers only lethal platforms and end-use items, and does not pay full regard to dual-use technology. Moreover, because of an arms exemption laid down in the Treaty to Establish the European Community, the embargo could not be legally binding. The code of conduct is not legally binding either, but it is intended to set down guidelines, as well as to try to coordinate national export-control policy instruments that are legally binding. The code of conduct establishes criteria against which export licenses should be approved or denied: the impact on human rights; the impact on regional peace and security; the interests of friendly and allied states; and risk of diversion of sensitive technology. EU officials have indicated that some of these criteria, like that on human rights, will be reinforced, and that work is under way to take account of 'intangible technology transfers', such as knowledge transfers, and scope for reverse engineering. Critics of the code of conduct claim its criteria are far too vague and subjective to be effective and meaningful, while the dual-use nature of the technology Beijing was likely to seek would magnify ambiguities and thus the risk of increased transfers. The 'tool box' being developed by the EU would require notification by EU states every three months of export licenses approved. A review of exports carried out over the last five years would be conducted, as would a review of denials over the last three years. On the basis of the findings of these surveys, there would in principle be scope to recalibrate export controls. However, because the 'tool box' would only provide for retrospective notification, it would have less meaning as an export-control measure than an arrangement in which prior notification was required. Meanwhile, as of early April 2005, a debate regarding how long the 'tool box' should remain in force had reportedly still to be resolved.

By early April 2005, the received wisdom that the embargo would be lifted under the Luxembourg presidency was challenged by the strength of American opposition, resistance from some national parliaments of Europe, and the slow pace of diplomacy in the EU. The matter was also complicated by China, which used the annual session of its National People's Congress to codify in law its option to use 'non-peaceful' means in dealing with Taiwan, rather than to ratify the UN Covenant on Civil and Political Rights (a step that would have been more effective in dampening sceptical opinion in the EU). It seemed plausible that, if the matter of the embargo slipped into the British presidency of the EU in the second half of 2005, a deferral into 2006 might be expected. The calculations of the government of British Prime Minister Tony Blair, who is likely to be re-elected on 5 May, went beyond a wish not to have to preside over a decision staunchly opposed by Washington. It also reflected a sense that the British presidency provided a rare opportunity to advertise the positive elements of the EU to the British public and to advance the British agenda for Europe ahead of the uphill struggle Blair faced in ensuring a 'yes' vote in the planned referendum on the European constitutional treaty. A transatlantic argument over China would provide a costly distraction.

Taiwanese travails

Predictably, Taiwan proved a vocal opponent of the lifting of the EU arms embargo, arguing that it would further disrupt an already volatile cross-strait situation and materially threaten the island's security. Not having anticipated the surprising re-election in March 2004 of President Chen Shui-bian, China struggled initially to respond to the prospect of having to face, for the next four years, a Taiwanese leader who seemed intent on asserting the separate identity of the island and whom Beijing therefore could not treat as valid negotiating partner. But in the days leading up to Chen's inauguration address on 20 May 2004, Beijing evidently decided that it needed to send a strong political signal to Chen, as well as to the United States, highlighting the 'red lines' it had drawn on many previous occasions. During a visit to London on 11 May, Chinese Premier Wen Jiabao broadly indicated that Beijing was giving thought to a 'Unification Law' that would give legal backing to its claims over Taiwan and lawful authority to act in pursuit of them. On 17 May, China's Taiwan Affairs Office issued a statement which began by spelling out the scope for cross-strait dialogue, military confidence-building measures, and commercial and transport links – provided Taiwan first accept the 'one China' principle – but ended by warning the authorities in Taipei against a 'dangerous lurch towards independence', through which they might invite 'their own destruction by playing with fire'.

American pressure, combined with the domestic political implications of a slender and contested margin of victory in the presidential election, worked to produce a mild inauguration address compared to Chen's campaign rhetoric. Chen stated, inter alia, that planned constitutional reforms would not touch on the issue of sovereignty or be approved by a referendum; they would only seek to resolve bureaucratic anomalies and inefficiencies, and be adopted through existing parliamentary mechanisms. Beijing received the assurances sceptically. In the months that followed, attention focused mainly on respective military exercises being carried out by Chinese and Taiwanese forces, and on the efforts of the Taiwanese government to steer defence spending bills through the legislature. Chen, however, subsequently used his National Day speech on 10 October to speculate about the possibility of resuming dialogue with China through the use of a constructively ambiguous formula, last used for talks held in Hong Kong in 1992. The suggestion was rebuffed by China, which restated its position that the acceptance of the 'one China' principle by Taipei was the precondition for talks – a concession that, from Chen's perspective, would leave little to negotiate about except the terms of submission.

Three factors arose in the last quarter of 2004 to further poison cross-strait relations. The first was the re-emergence of diplomatic competition between Taiwan and China. On 3 November, Taiwan announced the establishment of diplomatic relations with Vanuatu, only for the South Pacific state to switch recognition back to Beijing on 14 December following a change of government. China's success continued in January 2005, when it induced the Caribbean island state of Grenada to recognise Beijing. The second factor was Beijing's decision to push ahead with the drafting of the unification law. The third development was the onset of campaigning for elections to Taiwan's Legislative Yuan, or parliament. Beijing (and most outside observers) expected Chen Shui-bian's Democratic Progressive Party (DPP) to capitalise on its presidential election victory, capturing a convincing majority in the legislature, especially given that Chen had begun to drop the moderation and restraint concerning Taiwan's status, identity and constitution he had reluctantly exhibited in the first months of his second term. The concern harboured by Beijing, and to some extent by Washington, was that significant gains in the legislature for the DPP and its smaller and more radical associate, the Taiwan Solidarity Union, would embolden Chen and further enfeeble the opposition Kuomintang (KMT) and People's First Party (PFP), which both favoured better relations with China. Against this backdrop, the result of the 11 December elections provided a significant measure of relief. The DPP managed only to gain two seats, holding 89 in total, while its TSU ally lost one, taking the combined share to 101 out of 225; the KMT saw its share rise from 68 to 79, while its partner, the PFP, saw the number of its seats drop from 46 to 34. DPP officials, and a number of outside observers, were reluctant to attribute the failure to make more substantial gains entirely to a rejection by the electorate of the party's identity-based campaign platform. But the practical implications of the outcome were clear: the absence of a parliamentary majority will act as a decisive constraint on the legislative ambitions of the Chen administration, while the opposition KMT has been buoyed by a success that has interrupted a catalogue of setbacks.

The altered political dynamic in Taiwan, welcomed though it was, created dilemmas for Beijing in view of its decision to draft what by now was being termed an 'anti-secession law'. The need for a political statement of such force had ebbed after the Legislative Yuan elections. Progress had in the meantime also been achieved in agreeing to air links between China and Taiwan for the duration of the Lunar New Year celebrations. Yet the wheels had been set in motion, and a definite political and presentational risk was perceived in halting a process that was now well advanced. Although little is known about the precise gestation of the law, it seems plausible that Beijing will have tweaked and recalibrated it in response to developments in

Taiwan, so that the text presented at the National People's Congress on 14 March will have been less sharp than originally conceived. Its ten Articles, the eighth of which asserts the right to use force against Taiwan in the event of secession or the complete exhaustion of diplomacy to prevent it, contain familiar demands and warnings. Yet they do not incorporate provisions that tie Beijing's hands: the circumstances for the use of force are set out in general terms, and no timelines for reunification are elaborated. Some analysts have also perceived a very tentative overture in the reference contained in Article 7 to the possibility of holding negotiations with Taipei 'on an equal footing' and 'in steps and phases and with flexible and varied modalities'. Be that as it may, the reaction in Taiwan was predictably brusque, featuring mass demonstrations to protest the law and threats to counter with an 'anti-unification law'. Chen had been given an issue to seize on and an opportunity to recapture the political initiative at home.

A return to diplomatic feistiness?

Washington tersely dismissed China's anti-secession law as unhelpful and unnecessary. While it probably conceived of the Taiwanese response in the same light, it is China that the US sees as primarily responsible for injecting this significant complication into the cross-strait dispute. The Bush administration may in consequence look more wearily on Beijing's oft-repeated demand that Washington should do more to restrain Taipei, contributing to a deterioration in bilateral relations already threatened by policy disagreements in other areas. American perceptions of China as a potential military threat to the United States, and an intruder into the transatlantic alliance, would be magnified by a lifting of the EU arms embargo. It might also make Washington more sensitive to the appearance of diplomatic competition in other regions, and more prone to respond on tougher terms. Recent Chinese flirtations with a virulently anti-American Venezuelan regime as an oil supplier will do little to lessen the irritation of the United States in this regard. From an American point of view, acquiescence to Washington's preferred harder tactics on North Korea could redeem Beijing, but that is very unlikely to materialise. The result of the visit to Pyongyang of Chinese President Hu Jintao, expected in the first half of the year, will be of heavy significance. For now, the outcome of these factors seems likely to be a denouement – though perhaps a reasonably controlled one – to the period of quiet Sino-American relations that ensued from 11 September. It was perhaps with all these dangers and problems in mind that Washington in April 2005 signalled the initiation of an unprecedented regular 'global dialogue' with China, to be led on the American side by Deputy Secretary of State Robert Zoellick.

India and Pakistan: Cautious Engagement

As India and Pakistan cautiously engage diplomatically, there are concerns over their ability to sustain the fragile peace process. Encouraged by an improved bilateral security environment – a cease-fire on the border that has lasted over 16 months and the resumption of a bus service between the Indian and Pakistani parts of divided Kashmir – officials have held the most wide-ranging and comprehensive dialogue in decades. But with differences looming large on a number of key issues, including the Kashmir dispute, the momentum could be lost. Leaders in both countries face grave distractions.

In Pakistan, there is rising violence by Islamist extremist and sectarian groups, increasing strife in Baluchistan and the possibility of ethnic or Islamist repercussions arising from the controversial counter-terrorism military operations (with some US collaboration) in the tribal areas of South Waziristan near the Pakistan–Afghanistan border. To be sure, Pakistan's economy is picking up after years of sclerosis, there have been some notable successes against al-Qaeda, and Pakistan–US relations are on an upswing. However, the fragile stability of the regime – based as it is on a single individual, President Pervez Musharraf – is even more salient than these developments.

India is also unsteady, if for different reasons. Following the surprise general election victory of the Congress-led coalition in May 2004, the political transition was extended and confused. The coalition – formed by nearly 15 centre-left parties in a pre-election alliance – had to immediately ensure additional support in parliament to enable a claim to government. This was compounded by Congress Chief Sonia Gandhi's decision to decline the premiership. Following the swearing in of a widely respected Sikh economic reformer and technocrat, 71-year old Manmohan Singh, as the fourteenth prime minister on 22 May 2004, the formation of government was delayed further by a struggle among the ruling parties for ministerial portfolios. With a slim majority in parliament, the ruling United Progressive Alliance (UPA)'s quest for political calm remains fraught.

Robust dialogue

Immediately after the Indian elections, there was anxiety in the international community – and in Pakistan – as to whether the new Indian government would continue the diplomatic engagement with Islamabad that former prime minister Atal Bihari Vajpayee had initiated and support the peace process. Although the Congress Party election manifesto advocated dialogue with Pakistan on the Kashmir dispute, the party's foreign and security policy document, published in April 2004, criticised the National Democratic Alliance (NDA) government for having 'agreed to discuss the territorial status of Jammu and Kashmir with Pakistan' – an allusion to the significant Vajpayee–Musharraf 6 January 2004 joint press statement.

By focusing on agreements and confidence-building measures with Pakistan 'up to 1996', the document also failed to acknowledge important bilateral developments – including official 'talks on talks' in February 2004. This was compounded by new Foreign Minister Natwar Singh's statements that the 1972 Simla Agreement was the 'bedrock' of relations with Pakistan and the Sino-Indian model the basis for the India–Pakistan peace process. Nevertheless, the government made it clear that relations with Pakistan will be its top priority. Both Prime Minister Singh and UPA chairperson Sonia Gandhi publicly indicated a desire to support the peace process and dialogue with Pakistan, as did Natwar Singh on several occasions. The Indian government began to demonstrate publicly its commitment to the existing peace process agenda. The first set of formal bilateral talks – after a three-year hiatus – began on 19–20 June 2004, on nuclear confidence-building measures (CBMs).

The bilateral diplomatic engagement since June 2004 has occurred at four levels. High-level contacts took place between Natwar Singh and his Pakistani counterpart, Foreign Minister Khurshid Mahmud Kasuri, in June 2004. They met on six other occasions through April 2005. Manmohan Singh and Musharraf met for the first time in September 2004 in New York, and again in Delhi in April 2005, on the sidelines of the last one-day cricket match between the two countries in the 2004–05 test series. The two prime ministers also met in Delhi in November 2004, and back-channel meetings between the two chiefs of the national security establishments have taken place. While these contacts create an atmosphere of progress, they can also generate irrational expectations, as in the case of the disastrous Vajpayee–Musharraf summit in Agra in July 2001.

The most politically meaty category of talks – known as 'composite dialogue' – involves a set of eight disputes and issues, including 'peace and security, Jammu and Kashmir, the Tulbul navigation project/Wular barrage, friendly exchanges, Siachen, Sir Creek, terrorism and drug trafficking, and economic and commercial cooperation'. The process began in December 2004. Talks on six of these subjects in April–June 2005 are to be followed by a meeting of foreign secretaries in July–August 2005 – and subsequently, foreign ministers – to review overall progress. The first meetings in six years on the Kashmir dispute have taken place, though the pace of dialogue continues to be slow, with only two scheduled meetings on each subject a year.

The third and fourth categories are technical and expert-level dialogue and CBMs, respectively. In the former, the range of subjects under discussion has risen dramatically. They include nuclear and conventional CBMs, Srinagar–Muzaffarabad and Amritsar–Lahore bus services, a rail link between Munnabao and Khakhrapar, the Baglihar power project, and meetings between narcotics control authorities, between paramilitary and coast guard forces, and of the joint study group on trade and economic cooperation. There have been some positive developments in the expert-level talks on narcotics control in light of the huge increase in opium production in Afghanistan in 2004. The first meeting of narcotics officials in seven years took place in June 2004. Both countries agreed to share intelligence and adopt a coordinated strategy to prevent drug trafficking and smuggling across their borders. A Memorandum of Understanding on this subject is expected to be finalised.

Although in early April 2005 a formal expert-level group on energy security had yet to be constituted, there was considerable shared optimism on this issue, premised on the possibility of a $3–4.2bn, 2,600km natural gas pipeline from Iran to India via Pakistan that would build mutual economic – and related political – interdependencies. Discussions between petroleum ministers on availability of and access to energy resources in the region were scheduled to take place in 2005, perhaps in coordination with a senior Iranian representative. Key issues, such as a discounted price and transmission and transit charges, need to be examined. In his visit to Delhi in November 2004, Prime Minister Shaukat Aziz made a case for this pipeline as a 'stand-alone issue'. However, Delhi implicitly linked it to Pakistan's granting India Most Favoured Nation status, which Aziz subsequently made clear was itself tied to a solution on Kashmir. However, following an abrupt change in policy emphasising the promotion of bilateral economic linkages, Natwar Singh in February 2005 agreed to look more openly at constructing a pipeline through Pakistan, subject to concerns over security and assured supplies. While such a pipeline is in the interests of both countries, it is still years away. One problem is the source of supply: US Secretary of State Condoleezza Rice clearly indicated, on her maiden visits to India and Pakistan in March 2005, that Washington would frown on Iran – the apparent frontrunner – as that source. Yet other sources of supply – including Central Asia – would be problematic, as pipelines would have to pass through Afghanistan.

The most significant bilateral progress so far has been in CBMs. Over a hundred CBMs have been proposed by the two sides – in September 2004, India alone suggested 72 – focusing on enhancing people-to-people contacts and economic and commercial cooperation. Moreover, CBM discussions have moved from political one-upmanship to more substantive attempts at building mutual trust. For example, following the mutual acknowledgement that nuclear capabilities 'constitute a factor for stability' in June 2004, the two sides agreed to establish a permanent hotline between the foreign secretaries to reduce nuclear risks, and to conclude an agreement with technical parameters on the pre-notification of missile flight tests. Although there has been no operational progress on either of these issues to date, the two foreign ministers in February 2005 promised to finalise the latter agreement by July 2005. A number of differences remain – e.g., on whether to incorporate cruise missiles or not, the appropriate distance of launch sites from the border (50 or 100km), and the notification of missile trajectories. Although in practice both countries unilaterally provide prior information of missile tests, this ad hoc arrangement has given rise to confusion, misunderstandings and allegations of violations in the past. In January, 2005 they exchanged their lists of nuclear installations and facilities, in conformity with their 1988 agreement.

CBM discussions relating to Kashmir have also borne fruit. The cease-fire – unilaterally initiated by Pakistan in November 2003 and reciprocated by India – has continued to hold, notwithstanding minor allegations of violations by small-arms and mortar fire by both sides in January and February 2005. Not since 1989 has a cease-fire on Kashmir lasted so long. The resumption of an inter-Kashmiri bus service between Srinagar and Muzzafarabad in April 2005– announced during Natwar Singh's visit to Islamabad in February 2005 after being suspended for nearly 60 years – boosts the peace process, reunites divided families and encourages linkages between Indian-administered and Pakistani-administered Kashmir. Both countries have shown considerable flexibility in these negotiations, backing down from previously rigid positions. India finally agreed that only entry permits – not passports – would be required for travel across the Line of Control (LoC), having previously insisted on passports implicitly to support the characterisation of the LoC as an international border. Pakistan, in turn, dropped its demands that such travel be UN supervised and limited to Kashmiris, now allowing Indian and Pakistani nationals as well. Concerns by the Indian opposition Bharatiya Janata Party (BJP) over infiltration by bus-borne militants have been deferred. While most Kashmiri leaders have welcomed this cross-border transportation link, hardline separatist leader Syed Ali Shah Geelani has criticised it as sidelining the resolution of the Kashmir dispute. A few militant groups have threatened to attack the bus.

The joint statement between Singh and Musharraf on 18 April 2005, in Delhi on CBMs focusses on additional inter-Kashmiri routes and initiation of cross-LoC trade. More broadly, an unprecedented number of people-to-people visits between the two countries have occurred, including journalists, politicians, pilgrims, business people and cricket fans. In early 2005 approximately, 8,000–10,000 special visas were being granted every month by both countries, even though individual tourist visas had yet to be granted by either side. In March–April 2005, the Pakistani cricket team played its first full tour in India in six years; in October 2004, the first visit of a group of Pakistani journalists to Indian-administered Kashmir took place, followed a month later by a reciprocal visit of Indian journalists to Pakistani-administered Kashmir and the Northern Areas. Other CBMs implemented included the release of fishermen and civilian and defence personnel in each other's jails, relaxation of visa rules, and facilitation of visits to religious shrines.

Calmer Kashmir

With the continuing cease-fire on the LoC, security on the ground in Indian-administered Kashmir has improved. Although violence in Indian-administered Kashmir has continued, only about 750 civilians were killed in 2004, compared to nearly 1,000 in 2003. These attacks, largely carried out with rockets, grenades and mines, targeted mainly security forces personnel and politicians. Cross-border infiltration has also substantially diminished – and not only in the forbidding winter months as has been typical. In late 2004, General N.C. Vij, then Indian army chief, indicated that the number of militants in Indian-administered Kashmir had decreased by 50% to under 1,000. In December 2004, Indian Home Minister Shivraj Patil informed the Lok Sabha (the lower house of parliament), that infiltration had decreased by 60%. This reduction is a result of the near-completion of the fence on the Indian side of the LoC (running for nearly 600km of the 740km LoC), the deployment of sensors, more effective patrolling by the security forces and Musharraf's hardened stand on jihadist groups, as well as the cease-fire itself.

The general elections in Indian-administered Kashmir were held relatively peacefully in April–May 2004, as were the municipal elections in January–February 2005. Consequently, on the eve of his first visit to Indian-administered Kashmir as prime minister in November 2004, Manmohan Singh announced a reduction in the deployment of troops in the winter. Pakistan welcomed the move as 'a step in the right direction'. On 17 November, the first column of Indian troops moved out from Anantnag district. Within days, approximately 10,000–30,000 troops were redeployed outside Indian-administered Kashmir, even though this still represented only a minor proportion of the estimated 250,000 Indian army troops in the state. According to the new Indian army chief, General J.J. Singh, further reductions will await an assessment of the security environment carried out in summer 2005. There has reportedly been no progress in the dismantlement of militant infrastructure in Pakistani-administered Kashmir, a long-standing demand from Delhi – implicitly agreed to by Musharraf in January 2004 – and a number of militants are reportedly poised to infiltrate from militant 'camps' in Pakistani-administered Kashmir into Indian-administered Kashmir. Thus, the Indian army still planned to raise six battalions of the Rashtriya Rifles – established in 1990 specifically for counter-terrorism – from Indian-administered Kashmir, with an eye towards expanding this unit to 12 battalions.

The first two rounds of foreign-secretary-level talks on Kashmir – in June and December 2004 – made no progress. In view of differing priorities and considerations – and little hope of tangible progress in the immediate or short term – both countries agreed simply to continue the dialogue to find a peaceful negotiated 'final' settlement. At the first summit meeting between Manmohan Singh and Musharraf in New York on 24 September 2004, both agreed to explore possible options for a 'peaceful, negotiated settlement', interestingly keeping the word 'final' as well as any allegation of cross-border terrorism out of the joint statement. On 25 October, Musharraf boldly suggested that a solution to the Kashmir dispute acceptable to Pakistan, India and the Kashmiris would need to proceed in three stages. Firstly, both countries would have to identify appropriate regions on both sides of the LoC. Secondly, they would have to demilitarise them. And, thirdly, their status would have to be changed through independence, joint control or a UN mandate. He added that Pakistan's traditional demand for a referendum was impractical, while

India's bid to make the LoC a permanent border was unacceptable. At the same time, he did not elaborate on what he identified as the 'seven regions' of Kashmir – two in Pakistan and five in India (based on an ethnic and 'geographical' basis), nor on their exact future status. While this announcement was clarified as an attempt at initiating internal debate – as opposed to a proposal to India – it drew immediate criticism from influential sections of the Pakistani and Kashmiri communities, which were displeased, respectively, with the dilution of Pakistan's demand for a plebiscite and with the absence of prior consultation.

India's immediate reaction was to snub Pakistan for seeking publicity on the issue, rather than taking it up in the 'composite dialogue', and to describe Musharraf's announcement as 'off the cuff' remarks. A detailed rejection of his remarks came from Manmohan Singh in Srinagar on 17 November, when he stated that India would not accept any proposal for redrawing the international border or further division. The following day, he expressed his belief that 'purposeful and meaningful negotiations' were possible within limits – although he did not elaborate further – and that a 'second partition' of the country was not feasible. Musharraf then emphasised that the LoC was part of the Kashmir problem and not a solution. India's subsequent nine-point strategy for Kashmir – unveiled by Patil at the end of November 2004, focused on initiating dialogue with all groups in Indian-administered Kashmir (especially those who shunned violence), promoting Indians' interaction with Pakistanis, opening the Jammu–Sialkot, Uri–Muzaffarbad and Kargil–Skardu roads, accelerating economic development, and avoiding human-rights violation by security forces.

Musharraf's bold overtures to India – especially his dilution of Islamabad's traditional demand for a plebiscite in Kashmir, reiterated on 25 October – have pitted extremist Islamist and jihadist groups against him. These groups have already been targeted by his crackdown on their activities following the assassination attempts against him in December 2003. There is broad public support in Pakistan for the peace process with India, but not at any cost. Musharraf is keen to be able to pressure India to grant concessions in negotiations over Kashmir, failing which, as he has often stated, one of his options is to limit any meaningful CBMs in the future.

Water disputes

Sharp differences have recently emerged over the flow of water in Kashmir, leading Pakistan to seek World Bank mediation on this issue in January 2005. With water growing scarcer in Pakistan, Islamabad is worried that India may use water to gain political leverage by threatening to block or disrupt flows to the agricultural lands of Punjab, Pakistan's heartland. This fear is accentuated by India's plans to build additional dams on these rivers to meet the electric demands of a power-deficient region. At issue are three major Indian projects: the Tulbul navigation project/ Wular barrage on the Jhelum river; the Baglihar hydroelectric power project on the Chenab river; and the proposed construction of the Kishenganga Dam on the Neelum river. The bilateral dispute pivots on differing legal and technical interpretations of the Indus Water Treaty (IWT). The IWT – signed by India and Pakistan on 19 September 1960 and brokered by the World Bank – sets up a legal regime for determining the rights and obligations of both parties on the use of waters in the Indus basin. India has been largely allocated the use of the three 'eastern' rivers – Beas, Ravi and Sutlej – and Pakistan the use the three 'western' rivers – Chenab, Indus and Jhelum. Both countries have also been given access to each other's rivers for domestic and agricultural use, generation of hydroelectric power (through 'run-of-the-river' plants), and non-consumptive use (including navigation). All these rivers flow from the Himalayan mountain ranges of Indian-administered Kashimir into Pakistani-administered Kashmir, and Pakistan's Punjab and Sindh.

The dispute over India's construction of the Tulbul navigation/Wular barrage at the mouth of the Wular Lake – suspended after three years of construction in 1987 – involves whether it is aimed at storing water, which would obstruct the water flow to Pakistan, or maintaining a better water level during the dry season. In a clear indication that there is little scope for agreement at the moment, there was no mention of this aspect of the 'composite dialogue' in the foreign ministers' joint statement in September 2004. The dispute about the Baglihar power project – under construction since the 1990s, with completion expected in 2008 – turns on its design, size and water-storage capacity. Following talks in June 2004, Delhi provided data on the water flow of the Chenab river in December, prior to another round of discussions in January 2005. Shortly thereafter, Islamabad announced that it had sought World Bank arbitration on the dispute. Delhi perceived this as unjustified, and urged the World Bank to refrain from appointing a neutral expert to resolve the dispute. If Delhi suspends work on the dam – as it has done on the Tulbul navigation project – Islamabad could agree to withdraw its request to the World Bank. Although the World Bank can arbitrate after bilateral discussions, it is reluctant to do so, as it is not a guarantor of the treaty and does not possess any implementation mechanisms or powers.

Pakistan is also concerned about the proposed 330MW Kishanganga hydroelectric dam planned for the Neelum river in the Gurez valley, although no construction activity had taken place as of April 2005. India's aim is to inundate the Gurez valley and create a large reservoir from which a channel and a 27km tunnel will be dug south through the north Kashimir mountain range to redirect the Neelum river waters to the Wular lake at the site of the Tulbul navigation project. Delhi contests Islamabad's objections that the 77m height of the dam and the diversion of the Neelum river to Wular lake violates the IWT, and denies that it would reduce water flows to Pakistan (allegedly by a third). Islamabad is concerned that this could reduce the power generation capacity of its own proposed 970MW Neelum–Jhelum hydroelectric power plant in Pakistani-administered Kashmir.

Differences over other elements of the 'composite dialogue', including Sir Creek and the Siachen glacier, have continued. The Sir Creek dispute involves differences over defining the land boundary in the creek (a 38km-long estuary in the Rann of Kutch marshes) on the Gujarat–Sindh border, potentially rich in oil and gas deposits, and differences over demarcating the maritime boundary. Six rounds of talks have yielded no progress. In August 1999, India shot down a Pakistani plane in this area, increasing sensitivities over this dispute. In January 2005, the two sides conducted a joint survey of the boundary pillars in the horizontal segment in the Sir Creek area, but no breakthrough in negotiations is expected. The strategic value of the Siachen glacier is unclear, but it is a matter of national honour to each country and therefore a source of subsidiary armed conflict. The two countries discussed ways of disengaging and redeploying troops from the glacier in August 2004, in the absence of any negotiated political dispensation. In March 2005, Foreign Minister Kasuri's suggestion that a withdrawal of troops take place on the basis of a near-agreement between the two sides in 1992 got a stiff response from Delhi, which is keen that negotiations are kept within the 'composite dialogue'.

Musharraf's rule

In a widely expected development, Musharraf extended his tenure as army chief beyond 31 December 2004 – the date by which he had earlier pledged to step down from this position. In an address to the nation on 30 December, he declared that he would stay on as army chief until 2007 – as the 17th amendment to the constitution, passed in 2003, permitted – on the ground that any change in internal or external policies at this stage could be extremely dangerous for Pakistan. On earlier occasions, he had emphasised that the current security environment – the fight against terrorism and the peace process with India – required 'unity of command' that only he could provide.

In June 2004, Prime Minister Zafarullah Jamali was forced to resign, reportedly for opposing Musharraf's desire to continue as army chief. Following the interim appointment of Pakistan Muslim League-Q chief, Chaudhry Shujaat Hussain, as prime minister, Musharraf's close associate – and finance minister – Shaukat Aziz was appointed prime minister at the end of August 2004, after his election to the National Assembly. This was followed by far-reaching changes in key corps commanders and senior appointments in October to strengthen Musharraf's military position. Two of Musharraf's trusted aides – Inter-services Intelligence (ISI) directorate chief Lieutenant-General Ehsan ul-Haq and Karachi corps commander Lieutenant-General Ehsan Salim Hayat were promoted to four-star rank and appointed as chairman of the Joint Chiefs of Staff Committee and army vice-chief respectively. Relatively junior officers were appointed as corps commanders, succeeding a half-dozen senior three-star army officers – though the process occurred in an orderly fashion, without public dissent. In October–November 2004, the National Assembly and Senate – amid noisy protests – passed the bill enabling Musharraf to hold both his political and his military post beyond December 2004.

A series of protest rallies against Musharraf's retention of his military status organised by the Muttahida Majlis-e-Amal (MMA) – the largest opposition party in the National Assembly, a coalition comprising six smaller Islamic parties – and joined by the secular opposition failed to generate much enthusiasm. Such events evidence strain in Musharraf's relationship with the MMA, which has governed the troubled North-West Frontier Province (NWFP) since the October 2002 elections and which Musharraf had courted. This strain could provide an opportunity for the secular opposition political parties to foster a better relationship with Musharraf. Tentative steps towards reconciliation have begun with the Pakistan Muslim League (PML-N) led by former prime minister Nawaz Sharif (in enforced exile in Saudi Arabia) and the Pakistan People's Party (PPP) led by Benazir Bhutto (in self-imposed exile in the United Arab Emirates and the United Kingdom). In early February 2005, the two former prime ministers met in Saudi Arabia and signed a three-point agreement to promote democracy in Pakistan. This agreement called for the restoration of democracy in Pakistan, an independent election commission and respect for a popular mandate. Although Musharraf is broadly perceived as anti-democratic, he is ultimately in favour of an 'enlightened' democracy for Pakistan whereby strong central leadership – presumptively Musharraf himself – could ensure political stability.

Meanwhile, Musharraf is hopeful that a better economic performance will help ease social and political tensions and firm up his regime security. Pakistan's real GDP is slated to grow by 6.6% in 2005. The government is aiming at a robust – and not implausible – 7–8% annual growth rate within the next three years. In December 2004, Pakistan pointedly declined a $262 million tranche offered under the IMF 'poverty reduction and growth facility' programme. The decision was intended both as a signal to investors of the economy's improving prospects, and as a domestic political message underlining Pakistan's reduced need for handouts.

Countering extremism in Pakistan

Addressing the nation on Pakistan's National Day on 23 March 2005, Musharraf pointed out that the main threats Pakistan faced were terrorism, religious extremism and sectarianism, adding that the country did not face any external threat. Although he has attempted to deal strongly with sectarian and ethnic extremism in Pakistan, 2004–05 witnessed an increase in extremist attacks and bomb blasts, after an initial reduction in the previous two years. Attempts at administering madrassas (religious schools that often act as incubators of Islamic fundamentalism) continued to encounter difficulties. The number of attacks and assassination attempts against high-level military and government officials rose.

Furthermore, violence between armed militant Sunni and Shi'ite groups did not abate. Extremist Sunni groups such as the Sipah-e-Sahaba and its armed wing,

Lashkar-e-Jhangvi, along with the Shia Tehrik-e-Jafria and its armed wing, Sipah-e-Muhammed, have been the most active in instigating sectarian violence. Backed by funding from the Gulf and popular support, these groups have carried out numerous bomb and other attacks in Pakistan. Sunni extremist groups have also attacked other minorities, particularly Christians. The May 2004 suicide bombing by Sunni militants at the Shi'ite Hyderi mosque in Karachi – killing at least 15 people and injuring more than 200 – prompted the assassination of Sunni cleric Mufti Nizamuddin Shamzai on 30 May in Karachi. Sectarian violence in Karachi increased sharply over the next month, as over 70 people were killed. On 7 October, a car bomb killed more than 40 and injured more than 100 people outside a Sunni mosque in Multan. Two days later, Mufti Mohammed Jamil, a leading Sunni cleric, was shot dead in Karachi. In January 2005, more than 10 people were killed in sectarian violence in Gilgit in the Northern Areas, and in late March 2005 more than 30 people were killed and over 15 injured in a bomb blast at a Shi'ite shrine in Fatehpur, 300km from Quetta.

Extremist militant groups sympathetic to al-Qaeda and the renegade tribal leaders of the NWFP are also involved in attacks against high-level army officials, partly in an attempt to destabilise the government. The most significant attack was in June 2004, on the then-corps commander of Karachi, Lieutenant-General Ehsan Salim Hayat. He narrowly escaped, but 11 people, including seven army personnel, were killed. It was the first terrorist attack on a corps commander, and angered the military. Occurring almost simultaneously with the intensified anti-terrorist military operation in South Waziristan, one of the leaders of the tribal militants, Nek Mohammad, who was suspected of masterminding the attack on Hayat, was killed soon afterwards. On 30 July 2004, a suicide bomb attack was carried out against Pakistan's prime-minister-designate Shaukat Aziz near Fateh Jang in Punjab. The attack narrowly missed Aziz, but killed nine others. Pakistani authorities suspect that extremist Islamic groups linked to al-Qaeda were behind that attack, as well as the December 2003 attacks on Musharraf, for which junior army and air force personnel have been arrested. Musharraf himself has accused al-Qaeda of masterminding these attacks. Al-Qaeda's second-in-command, Ayman al-Zawahri, has issued statements against Musharraf, calling his policies and actions anti-Islamic and urging Islamic groups in Pakistan to eliminate him or overthrow his regime.

These developments notwithstanding, Musharraf has achieved some major breakthroughs in anti-terrorist operations in the cities of Karachi and Lahore, leading to the arrest or killing of some 600 suspected al-Qaeda militants. In July 2004, Pakistani authorities arrested Mohammad Naeem Noor Khan, a suspected al-Qaeda computer and communications expert, in Lahore. Soon thereafter, Ahmed Khalfan Ghailani, a suspected al-Qaeda operative involved in attacks on the US embassies in Kenya and Tanzania in 1998, was arrested. On 26 September 2004, the Pakistani security forces killed Amjad Farooqi – a suspected al-Qaeda operative wanted in connection with the two assassination attempts against Musharraf. Pakistan's military operations in the loosely controlled tribal areas of Wana in South Waziristan, which began in March 2004, have continued. Some 75,000 Pakistani troops are deployed there. About 250 have lost their lives, while some 350 militants – including more than 100 foreigners – are believed to have been killed. In mid-2004, Pakistan reportedly began to use aircraft and helicopter gunships against militants in the mountain ranges of South Waziristan to limit its own casualties. In London in December 2004, Musharraf claimed that the back of al-Qaeda had been broken in Pakistan by smashing its command-and-control centres and logistics bases.

Terrorism is not Musharraf's only security problem. Since early 2005 a conflict has been simmering in the province of Baluchistan, as Baluch nationalists have again taken up arms against rule by Islamabad. Their resentment is based on domination by the Punjabis, marginalisation of their tribes (which account for only 5% of the total population) and uneven distribution of wealth – which is potentially considerable, as there are rich oil, gas and mineral deposits covering 44% of the total area of the country. These antagonisms have been compounded by the establishment of three new cantonments in the province and the launch of two federally sanctioned projects: the Gwadar seaport, recently completed with Chinese financial and technical assistance, and the Saindak copper mining project. An estimated 6,000 troops are in the province. Although Musharraf would like a negotiated solution to restore law and order, in early 2005 the situation appeared to be worsening and additional troops seemed necessary. On four earlier occasions – in 1948, 1958–59, 1962–63 and 1973–77 – insurgency in the province was suppressed by the army.

The main group of Baluch nationalists, the Baluchistan Liberation Army (BLA), has reportedly unified the four main Baluch tribes. Since January 2005, the BLA has intensified its attacks against army bases, police stations and rail, power and communications infrastructure. In January–February 2005, 15 people were killed in several days of fighting in and around the economically and strategically important Sui gas fields, which produce nearly half of Pakistan's current demand. The resultant disruption led to a temporary shortage of gas supplies. In March 2005, more than 300 soldiers from the Frontier Corps were encircled by heavily armed tribesmen in the town of Dera Bagti. More than 45 people, including eight soldiers, were killed in the clashes that followed. In May 2004, three Chinese engineers working on the Gwadar project were killed in a car-bomb attack, reportedly carried out by Baluch tribesmen.

The Indian government's challenges

The shock defeat of the national NDA government in India in May 2004 appears to have been due to a number of factors. These included a strong anti-incumbency vote against the government, the disillusionment of rural voters and ill-timed advertising campaigns of a 'Shining India' trumpeting liberal economic reform. Other key determinants were unfavourable pre-electoral political alliances with regional parties like the Telegu Desam Party (TDP) in Andhra Pradesh and the All-India Ana Dravida Munnetra Kazagham (AIADMK) in Tamilnadu – the latter not winning a single seat in the Lok Sabha. By contrast, the Congress Party's pre-electoral allies – such as the Rashtriya Janata Dal (RJD) in Bihar and the Dravida Munnetra Kazhagam (DMK) in Tamilnadu – were successful vote getters. Of an electorate of 670m, an estimated 58% voted in the 14th Lok Sabha elections over a three-week period.

Like its NDA predecessor, the Congress-led UPA is a minority coalition government formed by 18 centre-left parties. Although the Congress is the largest party with 145 seats – seven more than the Hindu-nationalist BJP, which leads the NDA – its pre-electoral alliance, with a total of 222 seats, fell short of the 272 seats required to constitute a majority in the 543-member Lok Sabha. It is only with the support of the four leftist and communist parties – the Communist Party of India (Marxist), Communist Party of India, Revolutionary Socialist Party and the Forward Bloc, which together hold 59 seats – that the UPA possesses a slim majority of nine seats. Support from other parties opposed to the BJP, but not formally part of the UPA, such as the Samajwadi Party or the Bharatiya Samaj Party, cannot be relied upon.

Initial problems surfaced over the Congress-dominated cabinet. Laloo Prasad Yadav, the maverick leader of the RJD – the second largest party in the UPA, with 21 seats – was reportedly dissatisfied with the cabinet portfolio allocated to him. Seven ministers of the southern regional party, the DMK – with the third-largest number of MPs in the UPA – refused to serve their first day in office until a redistribution of portfolios had been promised. The dispute was resolved on 25 May with the re-allocation of two out of three requested additional portfolios. Although the government's quest for stability – and the completion of its five-year rule – was bolstered by its win in the provincial assembly elections in Maharashtra in October 2004, recent losses and subsequent political shenanigans in the assembly elections in Bihar and Jharkhand indicate how complicated and fraught with uncertainty Indian politics can be. A prime example of their complexity is the contradiction that can exist between the centre and state levels. Congress' opposition at the state-level in Bihar is the RJD, but it is an alliance partner in the centre, which resulted in a seat-sharing formula that was conducive to the defeat of the Congress Party in Bihar. Congress' unilateral announcement of seat-sharing only with the Jharkhand Mukti Morcha in Jharkhand – without discussions with the RJD – also worked against Congress at the centre. A major challenge for the government – and especially UPA chief Sonia Gandhi – will be to ensure that the UPA retains majority support in the Lok Sabha for the full five-year term.

In trying to fulfil this overarching objective, Congress may succumb to the disproportionate influence wielded by the smaller parties on government policy – especially on economic issues. The perceived impact of the leftist parties on economic reforms already resulted, on 17 May 2004, in the largest stock-market drop recorded on a single day in Mumbai. To forestall further declines, Congress has given the key economic and infrastructure portfolios – finance, commerce and industry, power, and petroleum and natural gas – to its own party stalwarts. The UPA's Common Minimum Programme (CMP) – a broad platform on policies and programmes acceptable to all coalition partners and leftist party supporters – attempts to blend social priorities with policies aimed at sustaining higher rates of growth. Key issues such as second-generation labour reforms will have to wait.

Although India's growth rate in 2004–05 remained high, at just under 7%, it declined from 8.5% the previous year. In 2004, India's foreign exchange reserves rose by over $30bn to $131bn in January 2005. Manmohan Singh, however, is keen to speed up reforms to push economic growth to 7–8% annually. This requires an acceleration in the rate of growth of agricultural production to 4% and industrial production to 10–12%. Finance Minister Palaniappan Chidambaran struck a fine balance in the 2005–06 budget, at once furthering economic reforms and advancing the social mandate of the CMP. Manmohan Singh also unveiled a seven-point economic agenda to spur investment, agriculture and rural development. In March 2005, Congress' economic approach appeared to have generated investor confidence. The Sensex (30-stock index) was reaching record highs, above the symbolic 6,900 level.

Congress is also keen to put its stamp on foreign and security policy, as it perceives itself as heir to the 'Nehruvian' worldview – a strong legacy of independent India's first Congress prime minister, Jawaharlal Nehru. Not surprisingly, then, the Congress document on security, foreign and defence policy issued in April 2004 advocates giving 'the policy of non-alignment a new direction'. India's relations with China – which are inherently significant given that the two countries together hold a third of the world's population – appear to be the most promising. The Congress Party has taken credit for having done much in the past to facilitate the breakthrough in Sino-Indian relations. Its achievements include then-prime minister Rajiv Gandhi's December 1988 visit to Beijing, that of his successor Narasimha Rao in November 1996, and the signing of a major accord to reduce tensions along the disputed Sino-Indian border.

At the end of March 2004, the 15th Joint Working Group (JWG) on the India–China boundary issue took place, to deal with the vexed 3,500km border dispute. While India claims 43,000km^2 of Chinese-controlled northern Kashmir, China claims 90,000km^2 of eastern India. The fifth round of border talks between Indian and Chinese special representatives – initiated in 2003 – took place in April 2005. In January 2004, India and China held their first-ever 'strategic dialogue' to broaden the scope of the bilateral relationship. The previous month, India's army chief visited China for the first time in a decade.

The visit of Chinese Premier Wen Jiabao to India in April 2005 boosted this relationship. There was agreement on a three-stage process to tackle the border dispute – of which the first was the signing of an 11-point agreement on 'political guiding principles'. Along with movement on military CBMs alond the LoC, China explic- itly recognised Sikkim as part of India, and in a quid pro quo, India recognised the Tibet Autonomous Region as part of China.

Bilateral trade with China has improved substantially – $13.6bn in 2004, compared to $3bn in 2000. This is planned to increase to $20bn in 2008, nearly equal to current India–US trade. This still accounts for only 1% of China's total foreign trade and only 9% of India's. Propelled by robust economic growth, large populations and expanding military capabilities, both countries loom as 'new major global powers' in the next decade, according to a US National Intelligence Council assessment in 2004. While they are keen to cooperate on a wide range of political, economic, and science and technology issues, they are also aware of their potential as competi- tors – increasingly in terms of access to energy supplies from Central Asia and the Persian Gulf and maritime interests in Southeast Asia and the Indian Ocean.

Military developments on the subcontinent

In a significant development, the Bush administration in March 2005 authorised the sale of F-16 *Fighting Falcon* fighter aircraft to Pakistan, which had been barred by the US Congress from receiving them for 15 years in view of Pakistan's then-clandes- tine nuclear weapons programme. This sale is largely a response to Pakistan's role as a key ally in the 'war on terror'. Its timing led to reasonable speculation that it was also in exchange for Islamabad's cooperation in providing centrifuge compo- nents for inspection by the International Atomic Energy Agency, or in preparation for enhanced US military activity in Pakistan against its western neighbour Iran, or even to continue the F-16 production line in Texas. Islamabad welcomed this decision, which Musharraf publicly indicated would enhance Pakistan's 'strategic capability'. Although Islamabad may initially buy two dozen aircraft, there are no limits imposed on the number, or on the upgraded variants, of aircraft to be acquired. Funds for purchase of the aircraft could come from the annual US tranche of $600m – equally divided between military and economic assistance – flowing out of the $3bn package announced in 2003. In November 2004, Washington also proposed a $1.2bn arms package to Pakistan, including eight P-3C *Orion* maritime surveillance aircraft, anti-tank missiles and *Phalanx* rapid-fire guns.

In an attempt to counter the expected criticism and rhetoric from India – which naturally views the resumption of US–Pakistan arms sales with deep unease, and is especially concerned about the capability that modified F-16s would have of carrying a nuclear payload – the Bush administration simultaneously announced it would allow US firms to bid for India's order for 125 multi-role combat aircraft. This would include the choice of upgraded F-16 and F/A-18 *Hornet* aircraft. It also emphasised that this would not affect the regional balance of power, and would enhance cooperation in the bilateral 'Next Steps in Strategic Partnership', on a quartet of issues – civilian nuclear and space programmes, high-technology trade, and dialogue on missile defence. While the latter announcement muted criticism from Manmohan Singh, who merely noted his 'great disappointment' over the deal with Pakistan, Defence Minister Pranab Mukherjee was less circumspect. He strongly criticised the US government for clearing the F-16 sale and raised concerns over its impact on the fledgling composite dialogue with Pakistan and an arms race with Pakistan. Mukherjee had raised similar concerns at his first meeting with US Secretary of Defense Donald Rumsfeld in Delhi in early December 2004, when he refused to send Indian troops to Iraq. At the same time, however, India remains keen on an agreement with the US to secure the purchase of submarine rescue vehicles and eight to ten P3C *Orion* maritime surveillance aircraft, which will constitute the second major arms deal between the two countries in recent years.

Following Natwar Singh's declaration in parliament in December 2004 that India–US talks on missile defence were limited to 'technical briefings and presentations on missile defence' – and that India had not given any commitment on its participation in missile defence – a US team gave a presentation on the *Patriot* anti-missile system in Delhi in February 2005. This visit – and speculative media reports of a proposed sale of the missiles – brought a strong reaction from Pakistan, which raised concerns over its impact on the peace process. Pakistan's official spokesman noted that such a deal would erode deterrence, engender a 'crisis mode' in bilateral relations, begin an arms race and induce 'higher risk-taking'. In an uncharacteristically forthright fashion, China commented that it hoped India would 'act to benefit peace and stability of Asia, especially South Asia'. Although both India and Pakistan raised similar concerns over the impact of US arms sales to the region, it is unlikely that the peace process will be affected or that an arms race will take place. Indian ballistic missile defence developments are at an early stage, with the government yet to think through the financial costs, effectiveness and strategic impact of such a programme.

More broadly, however, the harsh and reactive Indian rhetoric on the sale of F-16s to Pakistan points up an inconsistency its own strategic identity. India sees itself as a great power worthy of an influential role over an extended region comparable to that of China, and thus deserving of a US policy that treats it as a key strategic player unto itself rather than merely as part of the 'hyphenated' tandem of India-Pakistan. Its handling of the tsunami disaster was consistent with this self-image. India was the third worst-hit country in the tsunami disaster, with over 16,000 dead or missing and almost 650,000 internally displaced, and large swathes of destruction on its Andaman and Nicobar islands in the Bay of Bengal. The Indian Air Force base at Car Nicobar was ravaged by the tsunami (restored to operational status four months later) and the coast guard station at Campbell Bay was badly damaged. The construction site of India's 500MW prototype fast-breeder reactor project was inundated. Despite these immense national troubles, India dispatched naval forces to provide relief assistance both to its own islands and those of neighbouring states.

Indian naval ships were the first to reach Sri Lanka and the Maldives with medical and other relief supplies, and provided support to Indonesia. India's international relief mission involved over 20,000 military personnel and 32 warships (including three coast guard vessels), its largest peacetime relief effort. India coordinated with the United States, Australia and Japan. India also refused to accept relief assistance from international agencies or nations (though it has accepted foreign aid for long-term rehabilitation and reconstruction efforts from the UN and international NGOs). Against such noble behaviour, though, India's reflexive and pointed criticism of US–Pakistan bilateral relations only serves to reinforce Washington's tendency to 'hyphenate'.

Also encouraging 'hyphenation' is the ongoing nuclear confrontation between India and Pakistan. On that front, in a surprising development in March 2005, Pakistan officially confirmed what had been widely suspected: that it had been a source of nuclear technology for Iran. Pakistani Minister for Information and Broadcasting Sheikh Rashid Ahmad publicly admitted for the first time that A.Q. Khan – the disgraced Pakistani nuclear scientist who admitted running an illicit network for nuclear technology – had provided centrifuge components to Iran, albeit in an individual capacity. Musharraf later that month announced that he would send components of discarded Pakistani centrifuges to the IAEA to aid its investigations into Iran's suspected nuclear weapons programme. Foreign Minister Kasuri reiterated that Pakistan would not allow the IAEA to carry out on-site inspections of its nuclear facilities. In an attempt to enhance control over nuclear exports, Pakistan in June 2004 tabled a new export control bill in the National Assembly, involving nuclear and biological weapons and missiles capable of delivering such weapons, which was passed in September. The newly established security component of the Strategic Plans Division of the Nuclear Command Authority has some 10,000 personnel responsible for the security of nuclear and related facilities and installations.

While Pakistan engaged in the highest number of ballistic missile tests in the past year, India focused on new modes of tests of its own missiles. Pakistan's robust testing programme between April 2004 and April 2005 – involving seven ballistic missile tests – constituted nearly a third of its total tests carried out from February 1989. The second test of its medium-range *Shaheen* 2 (*Hatf* 5) missile – with an estimated 2,000–2,500km range and a payload of 1,000kg – took place on 19 March 2005. Significantly, there were three tests of the medium-range *Ghauri* 1 (*Hatf* 5) missile, allegedly acquired from North Korea, with a range of 1,300km and a 1,000kg payload.

Meanwhile, India conducted two tests of its medium-range *Agni* 1 and *Agni* 2 missiles, the latter from a mobile launcher at its test-launch site at Wheeler Island, off the eastern coast of Orissa. The *Agni* has an estimated range of 2,000km and payload of 1,000kg. In addition, India tested the naval version of its short-range ballistic missile, *Dhanush*, for the first time from an artificial underwater platform at its test range at Chandipur-on-sea, also off the eastern Orissa coast. In August

2004, the Indian government reportedly decided to raise two *Agni* missile groups in 2005 as well as two new *Prithvi* groups. These units will be introduced into service with the army instead of the air force, although all strategic forces will continue to be managed by the air force's strategic forces command. India also carried out three tests of its supersonic *BrahMos* cruise missile – jointly developed with Russia – including the first test of the land version of the missile on 21 December 2004, raising to nine the number of cruise missile tests conducted. In late 2004, it was reported that the *BrahMos* could be converted to carry a nuclear warhead, which appeared to indicate that it could be the interim missile of choice for the Indian Navy to obtain a nuclear role.

Differing – but not irreconcilable – perspectives

As complicated and multifaceted as India's and Pakistan's positions in the world are, there is little doubt that solving the Kashmir dispute would ease considerably the challenges that their governments face and allow their mutual obsession to fade. As the official dialogue between India and Pakistan neared a year since its initiation, it was clear that key differences between the two countries – not only over intractable issues such as Kashmir, but also concerning the pace and tempo of the peace process itself – would present considerable challenges. Delhi is keen to promote CBMs – especially people-to-people interactions – in order to build mutual trust to facilitate meaningful and comprehensive engagement. Islamabad is not opposed to CBMs – and indeed initiated a number of important ones – but does not see them as a priority. Instead, the Pakistani government wants to focus on resolving the 'core' dispute of Kashmir, after which it presumes that mutual trust would automatically arise. Both Delhi and Islamabad also play 'linkage politics' at times and places of their own choosing. Delhi has made it abundantly clear that unless militant infrastructure across the LoC in Pakistani-administered Kashmir is dismantled and cross-border infiltration ended, there can be no substantive progress on the dialogue on Kashmir. At the same time, Islamabad has often stated that unless there is progress on Kashmir, there can be no meaningful 'second generation' CBMs or advances on other issues of the dialogue. As to the resolution of the Kashmir dispute itself, there are also clear differences between the two countries relating to whether it is a 'core' issue, the level of representation of Kashmir, the role of the Kashmiris in the dialogue, the possibility of mediation or facilitation by outside powers, and the nature of the resolution.

Both the Indian approach and the Pakistani one are problematic. While it is unlikely that the building of mutual trust per se will lead to a resolution of the Kashmir dispute, it is also unlikely that a Kashmir resolution will realistically take place in the immediate or short term. Islamabad is also not confident that a UPA government – with its slim majority in parliament – will be able to implement any major resolution on Kashmir if it were to materialise. In this light, the key to sustaining bilateral diplomatic engagement will be to ensure that the peace process is a credible one, and that 'deliverables' take place 'on the ground' on Kashmir-based disputes. This can be accomplished in a number of ways. The two sides can further broaden cross-LoC transportation and trade linkages, promote inter-Kashmiri dialogue and economic cooperation, and consolidate the existing unilateral ceasefire on the borders through a public joint statement by the two foreign ministers on its continuation (without prejudice to its final status). The withdrawal of additional army troups from Indian-administed Kashmir could take place, along with the dismantling of militant infrastructure in Pakistani-administered Kashmir, which could open up room for both sides' gradually reducing heavy artillery close to the LoC. Both countries need to build greater economic linkages and networks, especially in the area of energy security, and promote nuclear CBMs. The fledgling dialogue also needs to be institutionalised, with a formal acceptance of all four different tracks along with the creation of a detailed 'road map' for the future. Finally, expectations must be carefully managed. Realistically, the parties should acknowledge that feasible deliverables on Kashmir-based disputes are intended to build confidence that will generate a resolution of the Kashmir dispute in the medium term – a hybrid approach that to an extent harmonises India's focus on CBMs and Pakistan's focus on the Kashmir dispute itself. Otherwise, the momentum of the positive movement in India–Pakistan relations will be lost.

More generally, Pakistan's long-term viability will turn on whether Musharraf can move beyond merely keeping the lid on security problems towards transforming Pakistan into an extroverted, regionally engaged state. He has often stated that his vision for Pakistan is one in which the country emerges as a progressive, dynamic and enlightened Islamic state, playing an effective role in the region and internationally. Servicing this long-term vision, the perception of his continuing centrality to the campaign against international terrorism, and fear of what the alternative to Musharraf might be, will ensure continued Western patience with his governance and support for his government – both of which would facilitate an open-minded approach to Kashmir. But if Pakistan's domestic security becomes still more tenuous, Musharraf's pursuit of a rapprochement with India on Kashmir and other issues will become even more of a political liability. Should Islamists become able to target Musharraf's corps commanders – and potentially Musharraf himself – more successfully, he could feel compelled to drop the rapprochement effort. Terrorist attacks on Musharraf and army officers would also be likely to make the army itself and any successor to Musharraf disinclined to continue Musharraf's policies — particularly those involving India and Kashmir. India's starkest challenges are more inward looking. Congress will have to carry forward economic reform while managing coalition partners and maintaining majority support in parliament if the Indian government is to have the political room to move forward on Kashmir and unshackle India's huge potential as a regional actor.

Afghanistan and the New Central Asian Security Complex

Although continued progress in the reconstruction of Afghanistan in the year to April 2005 has steadily transformed the country's political and security environment, it has, at the same time, unmasked a range of further complex challenges hitherto regarded as of secondary importance. The most significant of these are the urgent need to balance the representation of different ethnic groups in government and the continued expansion of opium production and trafficking across Afghanistan, with the concomitant risk of narco-mafia networks becoming embedded in the still only partially crafted political system. The drug trade also has an important regional dynamic. It is arguable that, for the first time since the era of the Anglo-Russian 'Great Game', Afghanistan is open, and pivotal to both the Central Asian and the South Asian security complexes. While this process of regional integration affords significant opportunities to link markets and facilitate the transit of natural resources, narcotics trafficking and its associated violence also has the potential to disrupt and distort the social and economic fabric of both regions.

At the same time, there are signs that the former Soviet republics of Central Asia are experiencing the backlash of fundamental political change in the more westerly republics of the former Soviet Union, most notably Ukraine and Georgia. After a decade and a half of conflict and turmoil in Afghanistan, and political stagnation in most of Central Asia, the region may therefore emerge in 2005 as a new vortex for cross-regional currents of rapid political, economic and social upheaval.

The security situation in Afghanistan

In 2004, the work of the Combined Forces Command Afghanistan (CFCA) continued to focus on remnants of the Taliban and al-Qaeda in remote southern and eastern areas bordering Pakistan. The Taliban proved incapable of mounting a sustained offensive in summer 2004 and was confined to conducting 'pinprick' attacks on soft targets such as schools, foreign aid workers and local election officials. The attempted assassination on 20 January 2005 of General Abdul Rashid Dostum, the Uzbek militia commander from Mazar-e Sharif, indicates that isolated, and potentially damaging, operations can still be organised, but the disregard shown by ordinary Afghans to Taliban threats to kill voters participating in the October 2004 presidential election also signifies that the movement is a force of diminishing political salience in Afghanistan. The cooperation provided by Pakistani Special Forces in tracking fugitive Taliban in the Federally Administered Tribal Area (FATA) of Waziristan has been sporadic, largely conditioned by sensitivity to local tribal rule and pre-existing Pakistani Inter-Services Intelligence linkages to leading Taliban figures. The remaining active Taliban fighters in the field appear to be boxed in remote mountainous areas, detached from their natural constituency of support, and thus unable either to exercise ideological leverage or to compete with the material incentives offered by the Afghan government and international donors.

The United States is likely to continue to lead CFCA for the foreseeable future. Senator John McCain of Arizona, deputy chairman of the Senate Armed Services Committee, argued in late 2004 for permanent US military bases to be established in Afghanistan, an option that Afghan Defence Minister General Rahim Wardak did not reject. However, given that US Secretary of Defense Donald Rumsfeld offered command of coalition operations in Afghanistan to NATO in October 2004 – a proposal declined by France and Germany – the prospect of a permanent US presence is far from certain. Assuming there is no resurgence of Taliban violence in summer 2005, and the parliamentary elections rescheduled for 18 September 2005 are successfully held, the number of coalition troops in-country is likely to decline from its April 2005 level of 18,000 by the end of the year.

The second major domestic security problem faced by the Afghan government is continued internecine feuding between militia leaders. Progress was made on several fronts during 2004. The number of flashpoints between factions diminished as rival militia leaders from the Northern Alliance increasingly exercised greater restraint, became party to the electoral process and, just as importantly, accepted Hamid Karzai's victory in the presidential election without resorting to violence. Ismail Khan was the one key regional player not willing to engage meaningfully with Kabul, and he was neatly manoeuvred out of his fiefdom in September 2004, after a dispute with a rival warlord gave Karzai the pretext to insert 1,500 troops from the Afghan National Army (ANA) into Khan's stronghold in Herat. Khan initially rejected Karzai's consolation offer to be the minister for mines, but later accepted the post of minister for energy in the first post-election cabinet formed in December 2004.

The policy of strategic co-option of militia leaders was further in evidence with the appointment of General Dostum as chief of staff to the commander of the Armed Forces in March 2005. Initial concerns that this move reflected the weakness of Karzai's position appeared to be misplaced. Dostum scored a respectable 10% in the presidential election, and clearly enjoys solid support among the compact and important minority of Uzbeks in the northwest of the country. Finding a role for Dostum in the military–security hierarchy served to give Uzbeks a short-term presence in government structures prior to the delayed parliamentary elections in September, yet simultaneously barred Dostum himself from standing in the election. Moreover, the integration of Dostum's militia more firmly in to the Disarmament, Demobilisation and Reintegration (DDR) process, and the ambit of the ANA retraining procedures, could neutralise a crucial source of power hitherto independent of central government control.

The DDR programme, operated under UN auspices as part of the Afghanistan New Beginnings Project (ANBP), forms a core component of the combined domestic and international security initiatives designed to demilitarise Afghan society, expand security provision and increase the capacity and competence of domestic institutions. The greatest area of success on disarmament in 2004 was in the cantonment of heavy weaponry. To be sure, this materiel is viewed as increasingly redundant in the changed domestic security climate and indicates that militia commanders increasingly prefer smaller and more flexible forces at their disposal. Nevertheless, the volume of munitions now under the control of the coalition and ISAF forces is impressive, boosted by 8,000 tonnes of explosives recovered from a citadel in Herat after the removal of Ismail Khan.

The main provision of the DDR framework sought the demobilisation and reintegration of up to 100,000 irregular officers and soldiers. This initial estimate of mobilised militia personnel was arrived at somewhat arbitrarily, and the UN Assistance Mission in Afghanistan (UNAMA) subsequently revised this figure downwards to 45,000 in April 2004. The ANBP reported in February 2005 that nearly 38,000 soldiers had been demobilised, and over 33,000 had gone through the reintegration process, which involves a one-off food package, a small daily stipend and assistance with retraining, employment or obtaining a credit line for establishing small farming or craft businesses. The apparent success of the DDR programme, though, can be misleading. Firstly, Afghan militias tend to be mobilised seasonally, and therefore the number of standing troops tends to be small in any event. The proliferation of small arms in Afghanistan allows inactive soldiers to be quickly remobilised if required by a local commander. Secondly, the actual process of DDR has been geographically uneven. At the time of the overthrow of the Taliban, the various militias were grouped together as the Afghan Military Forces (AMF) – notionally, but not actually, under central government control. In southern Afghanistan, some AMF formations continue to assist coalition forces in tracking down Taliban holdouts, and others are used by private contractors to guard road construction projects, such as the $250m US Agency for International Development-funded Kabul–Kandahar highway. There are credible reports that some of the latter groups are either involved in, or turn a blind eye to, large-scale smuggling of drugs from the north to the Pakistani and Iranian borders. Meanwhile, in northern Afghanistan, notably Panjshir province, there has been resistance to demobilisation by Tajiks, who contend that the Northern Alliance did the bulk of the groundwork in defeating the Taliban and yet have enjoyed few political fruits of victory. Militia groups have thus now been categorised into high- and low-threat groups by Regional Verification Committees, with local self-defence militias accorded a lower priority than those capable of projecting force sufficient to destabilise the political environment. This profiling may accelerate the process of disarmament, but the incompatibility of coalition use of AMF forces with the fundamental aims of the DDR process will have to addressed during 2005 for progress to be sustained.

Implementing programmes designed to improve human security hinges on effective working partnerships between international Provincial Reconstruction Teams (PRTs) and agencies and institutions of the Afghan government. PRTs were originally established by coalition forces in early 2003. ISAF, the UN's 8,300-strong peacekeeping force under NATO command, has assumed control of a number of existing PRTs including, in July 2004, the much lauded Mazar-e Sharif team, which was reinforced by a detachment of 280 Scandinavian troops. ISAF subsequently established two further PRTs under Spanish and Lithuanian command in western Afghanistan in late 2004. PRTs have become increasingly multifunctional, providing basic security, directing civil reconstruction projects, brokering ceasefires between rival factions, assisting with the organisation of election security and overseeing aspects of the DDR process. However, further expansion of PRTs is heavily contingent upon the political weight behind the ISAF mission as a whole. The UN unanimously approved NATO's command of ISAF for a further year in October 2004, and is likely to do so again in October 2005, but within NATO itself there is reluctance among member countries to provide personnel and equipment for some of the more difficult provinces, exemplified by NATO's failure to agree the terms of Phase 2 of ISAF in December 2004.

Some of NATO's larger members have made key commitments outside the PRT framework. France is closely involved with the US Army in training the ANA which, by February 2005, had 21,200 soldiers, and was expected to meet its target of 70,000 ahead of schedule in December 2006. The French government also formed a partnership with the UN Development Programme (UNDP) and the Afghan Civil Service Commission in February 2005 to establish the Support to the Establishment of the Afghan Legislature (SEAL) project, which will use the expertise of the French Civil Service to provide the bureaucratic support for the Afghan Parliament due to be elected in September 2005. Germany has won international praise for its work in training a new national police force, numbering 33,000 by March 2005, and likely to expand to 62,000 within two years. With UK forces heavily engaged in counter-narcotics work, the onus will be on middle-sized NATO members such as Spain, Italy, Poland and Turkey to pull their weight if ISAF is to roll out more PRTs across Afghanistan in 2005. The fact that Spain insisted on taking command of the Baghdis PRT on the quiet Afghan–Turkmen border, leaving Lithuania to form the PRT in the much more complex and volatile Ghor region, does not augur particularly well for further expansion.

The political outlook in Afghanistan

Notwithstanding the eternally gloomy prognoses that tend to emerge from many non-governmental organisations (NGOs) and sections of the media, significant movement was made in the construction of both a durable national political infrastructure and political society in Afghanistan during 2004. The carefully sequenced introduction of new institutions since the Bonn conference of December 2001 was vindicated by the largely peaceful presidential elections conducted on 9 October 2004. The presidential election date had been delayed in order to allow further time to register voters and, although there were reports of over-registration and of lower female voter participation in some of the conservative Pashtun regions, the overall turnout of almost 80% (40% of whom were women), out of a registered electorate of 11.5 million, was highly encouraging. The Taliban's failed attempt to disrupt the poll, together with the orderly conduct of voting on the day, indicated that most Afghans were keen to reject extreme Islamism and to embrace the new political order.

Karzai comfortably won the poll with 55% of the vote, which was unsurprising given his national profile and moderate stance, the more or less open support given him by donor states, and the divisive histories of the leading opposition candidates. Yunus Qanuni, the principal Tajik candidate, was second with 16%, but significantly failed to carry the Badakhshan region of Tajiks. This was partly because Panjshiri Tajiks were perceived to be somewhat self-serving, but was also due to Karzai's shrewd choice of Ahmad Zia Massoud, brother of the iconic Ahmad Shah Massoud, the military commander of the Northern Alliance assassinated by al-Qaeda on 10 September 2001, as his vice-presidential running mate. The popular vote split to some degree along ethnic lines, but major candidates in all democratic elections have their heartland bases of support, so this voting pattern need not presage a fracturing of the national polity. Initially, it was envisaged that parliamentary elections would be held simultaneously with the presidential elections. However, an array of technical problems led to numerous slippages in the timetable for the parliamentary elections until, in late March 2005, a date of 18 September 2005 was finally set.

There were risks in postponing the parliamentary elections. By September 2005, Karzai will have governed by presidential decree for nearly a year with no multi-ethnic institutional balance to executive rule, a significant period during which discontent among various 'excluded' groups – Tajiks in particular – has already begun to surface. This tendency may be exacerbated further if ongoing dialogue between the government and moderate Taliban elements leads to a national amnesty for all except 50–100 top Taliban commanders. Repeated changes to the electoral cycle also damage Karzai's legitimacy and give the impression of rule by diktat. In late March 2005, for example, there were serious protests in Balkh province over Karzai's refusal to remove Balkh Governor Ata Mohammed Nur over the latter's alleged complicity in killings in the Kaldar district town of Hayratan, on the Uzbek–Afghan border. On the other hand, there is a strong case for extending further time to the UN–Afghan Joint Electoral Management Body (JMEB) to fix the electoral boundaries, allow more voters to register, make progress with DDR to allow the election to take place in a demilitarised environment, enable political parties to formulate their manifestos and, lastly, to complete the construction of the new parliament building, which is to be funded principally by the Indian government.

The National Assembly will consist of the *Wolesi Jirga*, the directly elected lower house, and the *Meshrano Jirga*, or House of Elders, which will be two-thirds elected from the regions and one-third appointed by the government. The Law on Political Parties approved in September 2003 requires party membership to be at least 700, with the stipulation that no party can retain a militia. A further Law on Elections signed in May 2004 allows candidates to stand either on a party footing or as independents. There have been complaints that the JMEB is not sufficiently independent of the presidency and that the power granted to the Supreme Court to refuse party registration is open to abuse. Both charges have substance. The Supreme Court in particular is dominated by allegedly corrupt clerics who have limited knowledge of technical, secular issues and whose decisions to ban women singers on television and disbar one candidate who questioned the practice of polygamy were so out of step with Afghan society that they were simply ignored.

Counter-narcotics policy

The issue of opium production gained in priority on both the domestic and the international agenda in Afghanistan during 2004. This was partly a function of the settling of the country's hard security profile, which has allowed formerly second-order issues to attain greater prominence, and partly due to a significant expansion in opium production. The UN Office on Drugs and Crime (UNODC) estimated that 4,200 tonnes of opium were produced in Afghanistan during 2004, an increase of 600 tonnes on 2003 and constituting 87% of global production. According to UNODC, the trade now accounts for up to 60% of Afghanistan's annual GDP, and is worth $3bn to the domestic economy (and ultimately $40bn on the Western European market).

The clear danger is that the profits yielded by drug production and trafficking are sufficiently large for the leading players to seek to protect their market share through the infiltration or corruption of political and legal institutions. Once embedded, these networks are then extremely difficult to extirpate. This reality, allied to evidence of linkages between drug trafficking and terrorism, informs US counter-narcotics policy in Afghanistan. Although the UK was nominated by the G-8 as the lead nation in combating the drug trade in Afghanistan, US eradication initiatives set the agenda in 2004, with their emphasis on 'fast and furious' destruction of crops to rebalance the deterrence threshold to the point where the higher returns from poppy production were not sufficiently attractive to producers. This robust approach, conditioned by US experiences in Colombia, has proved to be highly controversial, alienating farmers as far apart as Helmand and Badakhshan provinces, and causing 30 NGOs to sign a joint letter to US Secretary of State Condoleezza Rice in January 2005 requesting that emphasis be placed on tracking mid-level traffickers and promoting alternative livelihoods, rather than on straightforward eradication. Disturbing reports also surfaced in November 2004 and February 2005 of the aerial spraying of poppy fields with herbicide in Helmand province, although US officials have strenuously denied that they were responsible. These reports, in conjunction with substantiated reports of the systematic abuse of detainees by coalition forces in Afghan detention camps, caused the United States in

2004 to squander much of the goodwill it earned through the removal of the Taliban in 2001. Yet the greater emphasis of UK counter-narcotics initiatives on 'winning hearts and minds' through the payment of compensation, buying up opium crops and funding alternative livelihoods in partnership with provincial governors has also proven to be problematic, with reports of some governors diverting funds, or using resources simply to eliminate rival production networks.

The Afghan government remains hopeful that the formation of a national Counter-Narcotics Department (CND) in September 2004, created to coordinate the activities of enforcement bodies and provide a unified chain of command down to regional level, will lend greater coherence to the national counter-narcotics strategy. The principal task during 2005 will be to establish, and then advise farmers of, comprehensive alternative livelihood arrangements, while making clear that imme-diate eradication will take place if further poppy harvests are grown. The fusion and close sequencing of both the robust and discreet approaches offers the best oppor-tunity of reducing the yield at source. The Afghan CND has signalled its intention to focus primarily on the destruction of laboratories and disruption of trafficking networks, plainly aware that payments to small poppy farmers are fuelling rapid and much-needed recovery in the rural sector of the economy. Opium production is likely to increase slightly, or level off, in 2005 as the market becomes saturated and enforcement and eradication measures kick in. The Pentagon's request for $257m in emergency funding for counter-narcotics work – a fourfold increase on the budget for 2004–05 – indicates not only the much higher priority afforded crop destruction and interdiction, but also the increased integration of coalition military forces, chiefly through intelligence and logistics, in crop eradication programmes. However, as the Afghan government has acknowledged in its National Drug Control Strategy for 2004, there must also be a significant role for prevention, education and rehabilita-tion, particularly in relation to the growing number of domestic heroin users, many of whom are refugees returning from camps in Pakistan.

Prospects for Afghanistan's recovery

Afghanistan still remains at, or close to, the bottom of world league tables for literacy, infant mortality and public health. The UNDP's *Human Development Report 2004* painted a grim picture of a chronically insecure state, with dismal levels of access to essentials such as safe drinking water. However, the problems of poverty are now displacing the earlier problems of conflict, and this in itself provides an opportunity to find and implement solutions. There is tangible willingness among Afghans to move the country away from violence and back to peaceful productive work. In that sense, the UNDP report appears dated and overly pessimistic.

It is too early to definitively trace the trajectory of socio-economic reconstruction in Afghanistan, but the signs are increasingly positive. Underpinned by a wide-spread desire for social order, practical measures such as the mass vaccination of children and accelerated mine clearance saved thousands of lives in 2004. More than 40% of schoolchildren in the school year 2004–05 are girls. Roads are under construction, electrical power lines are being laid across the border from the Central Asian Republics (CARs), and political momentum is finally gathering behind the projected Trans-Afghan gas pipeline, which will supply domestic users and provide important transit revenues and local employment. A relatively free media is also flourishing in Kabul. The domestic picture in Afghanistan can therefore be characterised as one of emerging complexity – the positive trends of economic growth and relative political stability still remain contingent on the accommodation of powerful regional and ethnic interests. Karzai will need both to play his own hand well, and to maintain the support and interest of the international community, if his goals for reconstruction and development are to be met in 2005.

The Central Asian scene

The normally quiescent former Soviet CARs experienced unusual levels of political tension in the year to April 2005. The principal reason for this was the increasing disconnectedness between society and political elites. Each of the Central Asian presidents has now been in power for well over a decade, and some for nearer two, leading the latter to believe that they can operate with impunity in a fashion reminiscent of the Soviet era. How this social discontent will find its voice is as yet unclear. In Kazakhstan and Kyrgyzstan, with their nomadic heritage and more open, secular and multi-ethnic societies, the language of resistance is likely to take the form of democracy or nationalism. In Uzbekistan and Tajikistan, a strain of Islamist protest – though not necessarily violent – could emerge. Turkmenistan remains an isolated enigma with a flattened civil society and no coherent alternative political voice to speak of. Parliamentary elections were held in all of the CARs in the year to March 2005 but, given that political power resides almost exclusively within the executive, the impact of most of the elections on government policy was negligible.

In Kazakhstan, the poll in September 2004 was heavily managed by President Nursultan Nazarbayev's entourage to ensure that his Otan ('Fatherland') Party emerged as the victor. Asar ('All Together'), the new political party set up by Nazarbayev's ambitious daughter Dariga, was kept in check and did not score as well as predicted. The relationship between father and daughter is interesting, and Dariga's stance in relation to the presidency over the next year will reveal the extent to which she is emerging as an independent political figure or will remain reliant on her father's patronage and indulgence.

The mainstream political opposition in Kazakhstan, the most stable and prosperous CAR, has been sufficiently invigorated by the 'Orange Revolution' in Ukraine to make President Nursultan Nazarbayev think carefully about his political strategy for re-election in October 2006. He may calculate that the 'mini-wave' of post-Soviet democratisation in 2003 and 2004 will run aground well before the scheduled presidential poll, and therefore adhere to the existing election timetable. Alternatively, he may decide either to hold a referendum to prolong his rule (a tactic he has used previously), or call a snap election, in late 2005 or early 2006, to prevent the increasingly vocal and articulate middle-class opposition in Almaty from gathering momentum. As a pre-emptive strike, the reformist political party Democratic Choice of Kazakhstan, which is bankrolled by young, educated entrepreneurs, was outlawed in December 2004. Nazarbayev faces the same problem as other ex-communist, post-Soviet presidents in that his core support comes from deferential, elderly or rural voters away from the major urban centres. In cosmopolitan and increasingly prosperous Almaty, Nazarbayev is viewed less of a bulwark of stability than as a political dinosaur and a corrupt obstacle to change. However, in contrast to other CAR leaders, Nazarbayev can rely on the support of a large constituency of ethnic Slavs who value his association with the Soviet period and respect both his experience and scrupulous emphasis on the maintenance of inter-ethnic harmony.

The Orange Revolution in Ukraine was not born of economic dislocation or decline, but rather of diminished trust in the political elite, accentuated by the disastrously heavy-handed attempt by Russian President Vladimir Putin to influence the outcome of the election. Similarly, the booming economy in Kazakhstan will not necessarily insulate Nazarbayev from the winds of change. There are, however, key structural differences between Ukraine and Kazakhstan – the higher proportion of Russian regime loyalists in Kazakhstan, the lack of a charismatic alternative figurehead with a clear reform programme, the inherently limited appeal of strident Kazakh nationalism, and the absence of a 'smoking gun', like the Georgi Gongadze tapes in Ukraine, around which a sentiment for change could crystallise.

The situation in Kyrgyzstan is, thus far, atypical. The 'Tulip Revolution' that ousted President Askar Akayev appears to have resulted in a recycling rather than a turnover of political elites. Kurmanbek Bakiyev, Felix Kulov and Rosa Otunbayeva, the leading figures in the 'Coordinating Council', all served Akayev in government for many years, during which period evidence of corruption, electoral manipulation and harassment of opposition politicians was accumulating. The eruption in Kyrgyzstan has both long- and short-term causes. Akayev was widely perceived as a nepotistic and remote palace ruler, a view enhanced by the extremely profitable fuel supply contracts Akayev family members enjoyed with US forces stationed at Kant airbase, near Bishkek. Attempts to legally disbar certain candidates from standing in the February–March 2005 elections, allied to clumsy and ineffective efforts to manipulate the media, intimidate anti-government parties and, finally, alter the first-round election results, created a groundswell of opposition to the regime. Paradoxically, the killing of six protestors by police during a demonstration in March 2002 in southern Kyrgyzstan may also have indirectly caused the collapse of Akayev's government. Following that incident, which left this small and usually peaceful country somewhat traumatised, the use of force in 2005 was ruled out by the government. This left law-enforcement agencies with very few options to restore order, and enabled protestors to seize government buildings in the southern cities of Osh and Jalalabad on 18 March 2005. Once the state had abdicated its monopoly on the use of violence, there was little to prevent protest from spreading to Bishkek, where eventually the government fell on 24 March 2005. Akayev's silence in the intervening week was probably crucial to his demise, and his early exit from the country confirmed that he was neither feared nor respected, a fatal deficit in Central Asia.

The provisional government, formed after wrangling between the previous and new parliaments, is unlikely to deviate substantially in policy from its predecessor. Both Russian and US military bases are likely to stay, and economic policy will remain geared to further transition to the market. The major change is likely to be in the constitution of the elite. A broader-based government, with more representatives from the Osh region, is likely to emerge from the parliamentary and presidential elections scheduled for 10 July 2005. Akayev's signal failure to distribute the appointments and fruits of office more widely ultimately cost him the support of influential social and economic elites. This tendency is likely to be corrected in the short term but, given Kyrgyzstan's multi-ethnic character, it will also be vital to bring ethnic Uzbeks, Russians and Germans into political institutions at a high level to ensure lasting political stability. The police and army declined to come to Akayev's defence. The opposition movement's leader, former prime minister Kurmanbek Bakiyev, was appointed interim president. Within four days, order had been substantially restored. Both Russia and the United States indicated that they would recognise and work with the new administration. Putin offered Akayev asylum.

In Uzbekistan, a new bicameral legislature was established in 2004, with the first elections to each chamber being held in December 2004 and January 2005. These were largely a non-event, contested only by officially registered pro-government parties, who rubber-stamp government policy. President Islam Karimov is firmly of the view that opening even the slightest aperture to reformers is likely to bring the whole edifice of establishment power crashing down. The manner of Akayev's political defenestration is highly unlikely to have modified that perspective. Discontent at the arbitrary and corrupt governance endemic in Uzbekistan has therefore been left to simmer just below the surface, with only the occasional eruption. Internal opposition to the Karimov regime is diverse and inchoate. In April and July 2004, there were shoot-outs and suicide bombings in Tashkent and Bukhara, aimed initially at police and local officials and then, in an entirely new departure, at the US and Israeli Embassies in Tashkent. The ruthless surveillance and clampdown by the Uzbek government on those Muslims unwilling to adhere to the form of Islam officially sanctioned and promoted by the state has created a generation of young, motivated Islamist radicals. Opposition to restrictive new laws on small traders caused more flashpoints, with riots in Kokand and the Ferghana Valley in November and December 2004. The laws are widely seen to be benefit officials with business interests in larger enterprises, and have made life extremely difficult for small shuttle traders importing cheap goods from China. There is also growing impatience with the very slow pace of privatisation among members of the small urban (often foreign-educated) technocrat class, who have found few openings in either business or government bureaucracies for their skills. Profiles of the April 2004 suicide bombers indicate that elements of the frustrated middle classes form the core of underground Islamist sects such as Hizb-ut Tahrir and Jamiyat. Although there is no evidence that President Karimov's grip on power is weakening, unless there is some relaxation of control of the levers of economic, if not political, power sporadic, and potentially violent, expressions of dissent are likely to recur in Uzbekistan during 2005.

The situations in the more remote and less populous CARs of Turkmenistan and Tajikistan are less combustible. Parliamentary elections in Turkmenistan held on 19 December 2004 signified very little, as all the candidates were hand picked by the regime and stood on virtually identical manifestos. The relatively low turnout indicated a general level of apathy and cynicism with the electoral process. Policy is subject to the personal whims of President Saparmurat Niyazov, so the most important political players are arguably 'gatekeepers', like Prosecutor-General Kurbanbibi Atajanova, who control the flow of information that reaches Niyazov. Although foreign journalists tend to focus on the comical aspects of Niyazov's personality cult, this aspect of the regime was greatly toned down during 2004: there are far fewer portraits and statues of Niyazov in evidence around Ashgabat. Instead, Niyazov's book *Ruhnama* now dominates political discourse and is compulsorily taught in schools and universities to the detriment of academic subjects. The content of *Ruhnama* is not in itself objectionable – it consists of a rather idiosyncratic reading of the history of the Turkmen people, together with homilies on the conduct of one's personal life. But a generation of schoolchildren and students are becoming increasingly ill equipped to function in the global economy once Niyazov leaves the political stage and the country starts to re-engage with the outside world.

Tajikistan's parliamentary elections, held on 28 February 2005, also failed to meet international standards of freedom and fairness. President Imomali Rahmonov's People's Democratic Party won 80% of the vote on a turnout of over 88% – statistics recalling the Soviet era. In contrast with their Kyrgyz neighbours, Tajiks have very little appetite for public protest against Rahmonov's regime less that a decade after their devastating civil war. Disaffection with government corruption is widespread in regions such as Badakhshan and Kurgan-Tyube, but the ruling Kulabi elite, headed by Rahmonov, has a firm hold on the institutions of power, with the only – slight – prospect of political upheaval in 2005 stemming from intra-elite business conflicts.

New geopolitics

In the half-generation that has passed since the dissolution of the Soviet Union, the CARs have developed their own identities and forged new and diverse relationships with key regional and international partners, yet there are both tangible and less visible legacies and interests that bind the region together. The relationship with Russia is the principal common tie. Given that the revolutions in Georgia and Ukraine may have rendered the Commonwealth of Independent States politically moribund, and thus presented Russia with the arduous and time-consuming task of establishing new Eurasian political and security relationships, in the meantime Russia is likely to look increasingly to Central Asia to consolidate its geostrategic position. Indeed, the positive reappraisal of Russia's role in Central Asia that began in 2003 was furthered in 2004 with the development of joint energy projects, the signing of a strategic partnership declaration between Russia and Uzbekistan in June 2004 and the realisation that, at times of civil unrest or political crisis, Russia will instinctively and unhesitatingly back the incumbent elites against opposition forces. If the nascent contours of a vaguely defined Eurasian space – essentially comprising Russia, Belarus and the CARs – could be traced in 2004, so also could deeper and more profound linkages between Central and South Asia, driven by hydroelectric and hydrocarbon projects, the development of transport infrastructure and educational exchanges. Iran is likely to remain diplomatically (and, to some extent, economically) isolated during 2005. Thus, both Pakistan and India are aware that China's highly focused energy security strategy, manifested in a heightened commercial profile in the Caspian basin, requires both South Asian neighbours to engage with Central Asia more substantively – particularly as the gradual emergence of civil peace in Afghanistan has opened transit and pipeline routes for overland trade.

Accordingly, Central Asia can no longer be regarded as a compact geopolitical entity. During 2004, the contours of two larger security complexes – broadly, the central former Soviet space and South Central Asia, both of which encompass the CARs – could be discerned. Each region has sub-complexes – notably the Caspian Sea, the Pamir/Ferghana Valley knot and the volatile Afghan–Pakistani border regions – which present actual and potential challenges to regional security, primarily in the form of resource conflict, drug trafficking and radical Islamism. The prospect of these threats being evaluated and acted upon in any comprehensive fashion by the states involved during the course of 2005 is very slim. Such attention may become imperative in the medium term. But the reality of local inattention reinforced the short-term need for continued deep major-power involvement in the region, the security fulcrum of which remains Afghanistan.

Fragile Stability and Resolve in Southeast Asia

In the four Southeast Asian states where there were national elections during 2004 and early 2005, the popular vote favoured strong leadership and programmatic agendas over charisma, as well as secularism when there was an Islamist alternative. In Malaysia, the March 2004 general election saw the ruling Barisan Nasional (BN) coalition, dominated by the United Malays National Organisation (UMNO), re-elected in a landslide victory, bringing it 198 out of 219 parliamentary seats, its greatest ever majority. Crucially, the number of parliamentary seats held by PAS (Partai se-Islam Malaysia, the Malaysian Islamic Party), which had become the largest opposition force in parliament following the previous general election in 1999, fell from 27 to seven. While the election result resoundingly affirmed the popularity of new Prime Minister Abdullah Ahmad Badawi, who had succeeded Dr Mahathir Mohamad in November 2003, the redrawing of electoral boundaries, the use of the Internal Security Act against opposition politicians, the government's highlighting of apparent links between PAS and terrorist suspects, and the intolerant image projected by PAS all contributed to the BN's overwhelming victory.

In the Philippines' national election in May 2004, incumbent President Gloria Macapagal-Arroyo was re-elected, narrowly defeating her leading challenger, Fernando Poe Junior, a well-known movie star. The charismatic Poe was endorsed by a three-party opposition coalition as well as a clique of 50 retired senior military officers and had great appeal for poorer Filipinos. However, his political inexperience, the advantages accruing to Arroyo as incumbent, the business elite's strong backing for her and the lustre added to her campaign by her vice-presidential candidate, former TV news show host Noli De Castro, were all factors that contributed to the outcome. Poe and his supporters contested the election result. The film star's death in December initially sparked fears on the government's part that its opponents, including military officers and former president Joseph Estrada, might exploit the funeral to incite a revolt aimed at installing a junta with Poe's wife, Susan Roces, as figurehead president. These concerns soon subsided.

Prime Minister Thaksin Shinawatra's Thai Rak Thai (TRT) party won a landslide victory with 70% of the popular vote and more than three-quarters of the parliamentary seats in Thailand's February 2005 national election, enabling it to form the first single-party government in the country's history. Although Thailand had suffered significant problems – notably a major upsurge in separatist violence in the three Muslim-dominated southernmost provinces since January 2003 – during the four years since the previous election, the TRT benefited electorally from the country's strong economic performance. Thaksin's decisive handling of relief efforts following the impact of the December 2004 tsunami on the tourist resort of Phuket (where at least 8,000 people were killed) also played to the government's advantage. However, the TRT fared poorly in the Muslim south, where it failed to secure any seats.

Indonesia: a new president and ongoing security concerns

By contrast, the second round of Indonesia's first-ever direct presidential election in September 2004 brought significant change when retired three-star general Susilo Bambang Yudhoyono unseated the incumbent president, Megawati Sukarnoputri. The disappointing performance of Megawati's PDI-P (Indonesian Democratic Party for Struggle) in the April legislative elections, and then of Megawati herself in the presidential election, reflected widespread popular frustration with the government's failure to improve living standards. While Susilo campaigned on a mildly reformist platform, ideology played no significant part in the presidential election; both he and Megawati presented essentially conservative secular-nationalist outlooks. On paper, Susilo's electoral coalition was considerably less impressive than Megawati's, but his campaign mobilised a supporting network of retired military officers and NGOs, mitigating his lack of formal party machinery. More importantly, Susilo attracted overwhelming backing from supporters of the Golkar Party, which had emerged as winner of the earlier legislative elections. Susilo won 61% of the vote against Megawati's 39%. The near-absence of campaign violence represented a triumph for Indonesia's young democracy and Susilo's election highlighted the electorate's increasing sophistication. Moreover, the demonstration of political secularism by most Indonesian voters silenced those who had predicted Indonesia's imminent caving-in to radical Islamism. In December, Susilo's vice-president, Jusuf Kalla, was elected chairman of Golkar, the largest parliamentary party, which he then withdrew from the opposition Nationhood Coalition. At least in the short term, this development dramatically strengthened President Susilo's government, which had previously lacked a firm parliamentary power-base. However, by the beginning of 2005 tensions between Susilo and Jusuf were becoming apparent.

Though Susilo's victory in Indonesia – by far Southeast Asia's largest, most populous and by many measures most important state – was undoubtedly significant, there was a danger of exaggerated expectations. Susilo's record as a senior minister in Megawati's government was not altogether impressive, and critics pointed to his indecisiveness in dealing with security problems, precisely the area where he could have been expected to act authoritatively. Ultimately, the need to satisfy diverse interests may hamper Susilo's policy implementation as much as it did Megawati's. Nevertheless, there were some positive signs. At the beginning of March 2005, Susilo's government decided to reduce fuel-price subsidies substantially, a measure which was politically risky but necessary in order to tackle a crippling budget deficit. But despite a military reshuffle in February in which the reputedly moderate Lieutenant-General Djoko Santoso replace the hardline General Ryamizard Ryacudu (whose tough internal security policies had sometimes seemed counter-productive) as army chief of staff, it was still not clear that Jakarta's capacity for handling the serious security challenges that it faced would be substantially increased under the new administration.

The Indonesian government's main security focus remained its counter-insurgency campaign in Aceh, where Megawati's administration had allowed the Indonesian armed forces, Tentara Nasional Indonesia (TNI), to launch a major military offensive during 2003. This was the largest TNI operation since the invasion of East Timor in 1975. Though a state of 'civil emergency' replaced martial law in Aceh in May 2004, it was far from clear that the military operation had succeeded in crushing separatist sentiment, and the government emphasised that troop levels would not necessarily be reduced. The TNI claimed that almost 2,000 Acehnese separatists had been killed, another 2,000 had been arrested and 1,300 had surrendered during the year of martial law. However, it seemed likely that most of these 'rebels' were actually just Acehnese civilians caught up in the conflict. Military operations – and widespread human-rights abuses perpetrated not only by government forces but also the insurgent Acehnese Freedom Movement, or Gerakan Aceh Merdeka (GAM) – continued. A suspiciously high turnout of 94% in the April legislative elections – from which locally based parties were banned, as they are throughout Indonesia – led to allegations that the authorities had compelled Acehnese voters to participate. After his election, Susilo expressed his determination to resolve the conflict, and spoke in vague terms of the need for a new agenda in Aceh relating to religion, social issues and the economy. But his record as the coordinating minister for politics and security who approved the 2003 offensive had hardly marked him out as a conciliator in Aceh, and in November he renewed the province's civil emergency status for a further six months. The prospect of renewed peace talks between Jakarta and GAM (which continued to insist that full independence should be on the agenda) seemed remote.

At the end of the year, the tsunami produced by the earthquake off the coast of Aceh killed almost quarter of a million people on the west coast of the province, including hundreds of military and police personnel, and made more than 600,000 people homeless. With the provincial governor already arrested on corruption charges and the provincial capital, Banda Aceh, largely destroyed, the local administration effectively collapsed. Compounding the disaster was the national government's paralysis in the face of the scale of the devastation. According to Coordinating Minister for People's Welfare Alwi Shihab, the administration was in a state of 'panic' for the first 48 hours. Though Jakarta allowed foreign journalists into the province, exposing it to the international media for the first time since May 2003, Jakarta was initially apparently reluctant to allow international aid agencies to enter. GAM declared a cease-fire and government security forces focused on relief efforts, but within days there were reports of renewed armed activities by GAM, and the TNI claimed that aid workers needed military escorts. Like the subsequent insistence that foreign relief personnel must be registered and that other states' military presence must be finite, this represented an attempt by Jakarta and the TNI to reassert sovereign control over Aceh, which had seemed to be slipping as foreign NGOs, journalists and troops flooded into the province. Simultaneously, the TNI was evidently continuing its counter-insurgency campaign. Army Chief of Staff Ryamizard claimed on 20 January that the TNI had killed more than 120 rebels over the previous two weeks. Though Jakarta outlined plans for rebuilding Aceh, and tentative peace talks were held in Helsinki in late January, there was no sign of any softening in either side's political position: the rebels continued to demand independence, while Jakarta still offered the Acehnese nothing more than 'special autonomy'.

At the Indonesian archipelago's other geographical extreme, the Papuan Freedom Organisation, or Organisasi Papua Merdeka (OPM), continued its struggle. Though the OPM's military operations were necessarily considerably more dispersed and less intensive than GAM's and took second place to political activism, the pro-independence campaign necessitated the deployment of additional troops to Papua during the legislative and presidential elections. Abuses by the security forces continued, particularly in the highlands, where a major military operation began in September. As in the case of Aceh, the 'special autonomy' status assigned to Papua in 2001 fails to meet local aspirations for self-determination. However, though many Papuans were prepared to accept special autonomy as a step towards independence, a 2003 presidential decree – apparently intended by Megawati's administration as a divide-and-rule measure – splitting the territory into three provinces frustrated efforts to set up a Papuan People's Assembly. Though Susilo in principle supported the notion of dialogue as a route to solving the Papuan problem, there were no indications that he would preside over any startling initiatives.

Low-level communal clashes erupted again in some parts of Indonesia where there had been serious ethnic conflict earlier in the decade. In Maluku in April 2004 there was a resurgence of Christian–Muslim fighting, resulting in 40 deaths. The clashes prompted Jakarta to deploy additional troops and police and provided a pretext to arrest and prosecute leading figures in the Maluku Sovereignty Front (Front Kedaulatan Maluku), a mainly Christian separatist movement. There was also sporadic violence in Central Sulawesi. However, these incidents did not indicate a return to the conditions that had prevailed in 2000–01, when it had seemed possible that religious conflict could lead eastern Indonesia into Yugoslavia-style civil war and disintegration.

Chaos in the southern Philippines

In the southern Philippines, there were grounds for optimism that negotiations between the Manila government and the Moro Islamic Liberation Front (MILF), suspended since 2001, might soon resume and bring the prospect of an end to the latter's armed rebellion. Though a key issue – the extent of the Moro people's 'ancestral domain' – remained unresolved, and Muslim clan conflicts, together with the continuing presence in MILF-controlled territory of Jemaah Islamiah (JI) and Abu Sayyaf Group (ASG) terrorists, continued to threaten the cease-fire, both the Manila government and the Muslim insurgents made concessions intended to build confidence. In February 2004, the two sides agreed to resume Malaysian-brokered peace talks. March saw an initial visit to Mindanao by a Malaysian Army Advance Survey Team, a precursor to the International Monitoring Team (IMT) intended to supervise the cease-fire once formal talks commence. In July, the MILF agreed to cooperate with government forces against a JI contingent as well as kidnapping gangs which had found sanctuary in rebel-controlled areas. Other confidence-building measures included the government's dropping of criminal charges against MILF personnel over bombings in Davao City in 2003. MILF allegations of cease-fire violations by the government after the Philippine Air Force struck supposed JI and ASG terrorist targets inside rebel-controlled territory in mid-November delayed the resumption of negotiations. Nevertheless, the IMT – comprising 50 Malaysian and ten Bruneian military observers commanded by a Malaysian major-general – deployed in October; in December a small number of Libyans joined the team. Moreover, by late 2004 it seemed that the MILF was softening its demand for an independent state in favour of a federal solution allowing substantial Moro autonomy. While there was a further serious cease-fire violation in mid-January, when 60–100 MILF guerrillas attacked an army outpost in southern Mindanao's Maguindanao Province, peace talks were scheduled to re-commence in Malaysia in April 2005.

Meanwhile, the armed wing of the Communist Party of the Philippines (CPP), the 12,000-strong New People's Army (NPA), appeared to be expanding its geographical reach. Peace negotiations between Manila and the CPP stalled after exploratory talks in Oslo in February and March 2004. At issue was not only the Arroyo government's failure to lobby for the removal of the CPP/NPA from the United States' and European Union's lists of terrorist organisations (which the communists had set as a precondition for further talks), but also what the communists referred to as the 'Hacienda Luisita massacre', in which police breaking up a violent demonstration at former president Corazon Aquino's estate in mid-November 2004 killed 14 demonstrators. For its part, Manila pointed to the NPA's killing of ten Armed Forces of the Philippines (AFP) troops engaged in flood relief, also in November, as evidence of the communists' ill will. In December, CPP leaders claimed that the NPA had attained a 'critical mass' and called on its members to intensify their efforts to overthrow Arroyo's government. While this appeared to be a far-fetched objective, notwithstanding the Philippines' economic and political fragility, it reinforced the AFP view of the CPP/NPA as the country's most serious internal security threat.

Thailand's southern turmoil

Violence in Thailand's three Muslim-dominated southernmost provinces, which had revived in January 2004 when four soldiers were killed during a raid on an army base in which 380 weapons were stolen, continued to escalate. On 28 April, hundreds of Muslim youths attacked police stations, village defence posts and district offices throughout the south. Government security forces, apparently forewarned, reacted fiercely and killed 108 of the attackers, including many who had sought refuge in a mosque. As 2004 continued, there were frequent lethal attacks, apparently by Muslim militants, on police officers, government officials, schoolteachers and even Buddhist monks and ordinary civilians, as well as arson attacks on government schools. In late October, after troops killed nine protestors in the town of Tak Bai, almost 80 other demonstrators (out of hundreds arrested) died from being 'stacked like bricks' in army trucks. In all, the southern Thai conflict led to almost 600 deaths during 2004. Despite Thaksin's claim at the end of the year that four 'ringleaders' behind the violence had been arrested, lethal bomb attacks and shootings continued in early 2005. In mid-February, a car bomb was used for the first time in southern Thailand, killing six people in the border town of Sungei Golok.

Given that armed activity mounted by the Pattani United Liberation Organisation and other separatist groups had apparently withered a decade previously, the scale of the violence in Thailand's south during 2004 surprised and perplexed the authorities in Bangkok. Though Thailand's government initially blamed 'bandits' for the renewed violence, it was soon apparent that it reflected a new wave of separatist activism rooted in socio-economic and political grievance and orchestrated by new politico-military organisations, notably the Pattani Islamic Warriors' Movement – or Gerakan Mujahideen Islam Pattani (GMIP). It also seemed possible that media coverage of the Palestinian intifada and Iraqi resistance to the US-led occupation of Iraq may have inspired Thai Muslim youths to support this new rebellion against Bangkok's rule. While there was consensus in Bangkok that more responsive governance and the delivery of effective economic and social development were vital if separatist sentiment was to be undermined, achieving an appropriate balance between a development-oriented hearts-and-minds strategy on the one hand, and tough responses by the security forces on the other, has proven difficult for Thaksin's government. During 2004, perhaps as little as 15% of development aid allocated by Bangkok to the south was delivered to the region, the bulk being absorbed by the bureaucracy. Bangkok's often heavy-handed policies – seen at their worst in the 28 April and Tak Bai incidents but also in Thaksin's quickly rescinded threat to cut development funding for 350 'red zone' villages assessed as sympathetic to militants – risked expanding local support for the nascent insurgency. It could also provoke sympathy for the revolt from Muslims elsewhere in Southeast Asia, and possibly stimulate links between local rebels and JI's pan-regional terrorist network, which has used southern Thailand as a sanctuary since 2001. Yet there were signs of a more sophisticated approach in February 2005, when Bangkok appointed former prime minister Anand Panyarachun to head a National Reconciliation Commission comprising members of parliament, officials, police and military officers, and members of the southern Muslim community.

Terrorism and counter-terrorism

JI, the largest regional terrorist network aligned with al-Qaeda outside the Middle East, remained a key security challenge for several Southeast Asian states. The Indonesian authorities continued to make counter-terrorism a priority, and by March 2004 had convicted more than 30 people (including three who were sentenced to death) for their involvement in the October 2002 Bali bombings. Evidence that cleric Abu Bakar Bashir, chairman of the Indonesian Mujahidin Council – or Majelis Mujahidin Indonesia (MMI) – was JI's 'emir' mounted in early 2004, and in April he was immediately re-arrested (probably at least in part as the result of pressure from Washington and Canberra) under the 2003 anti-terrorism law, on release from serving a prison sentence for immigration offences. Abu Bakar's trial on terrorism charges, most importantly his alleged role in the Bali bombings and the 2003 attack on the Marriott Hotel in Jakarta, commenced in late October; in early March 2005 he was sentenced to 30 months in prison for conspiracy. The sentence drew criticism from both Abu Bakar's supporters and from those – particularly the US and Australian governments – who thought a much longer jail term would have been appropriate. Important JI figures, including the bomb-makers Azahari bin Husin and Noordin Mohammad Top, remained at large and the terrorist group's continuing potency was displayed graphically in October when a suicide van bomber struck outside Australia's Jakarta embassy, killing nine and injuring 180. Under Susilo's administration, a new dimension to the heightened security precautions was the nationwide deployment of multi-agency intelligence teams to provincial police headquarters. Susilo also appointed a well-regarded retired general, Syamsir Siregar, to head the national intelligence agency and lead Indonesia's counter-terrorism efforts.

In the Philippines, concern focused on JI's use of sanctuaries in areas controlled by factions of the MILF. In February 2004, at least 15 new JI members reportedly graduated from a training camp within the MILF stronghold of Camp Abu Bakar. During the following month, the Philippine authorities dispatched intelligence officers to interrogate JI members detained in Indonesia and Malaysia over their links with the MILF. In May, the security forces' *Operation Brown Batik* uncovered JI's 'money trail' in the Philippines and led to the capture of its national financial officer, Jordan Mamso Abdullah; in December three alleged JI 'bomb experts' carrying funds to finance attacks in Manila and the south were arrested in the southern city of Zamboanga. While the MILF denied it cooperated with JI, it conceded that renegade commanders might be engaged in such collaboration.

Worryingly for Manila, there was growing evidence that the beleaguered and reportedly factionalised ASG, hitherto oriented towards hostage-taking for ransom and relatively small-scale bombings, was turning to large-scale terrorism and was cooperating not only with other Philippine militant factions but also with JI. In February, the ASG claimed responsibility for a major incident: the explosion and fire that killed 116 people on board SuperFerry 14 close to Manila. A month later,

Arroyo alleged that the arrest of four ASG members and the seizure of explosives had prevented a 'Madrid-level attack' on Manila. In July the AFP asserted that its operations had reduced the ASG to less than 60 armed personnel, divided among several splinter groups. However, AFP claims in November that an airstrike had 'almost certainly' killed the ASG's leader, Khadafi Janjalani, while he was meeting JI operatives, proved to be over-optimistic. A similar airstrike in late January was also claimed to have targeted Janjalani and his JI associates, but despite killing as many as 40 insurgents it apparently failed to eliminate the ASG chief. By early 2005, it was evident that the ASG had also linked up with a breakaway faction of the Moro National Liberation Front (MNLF), which had entered into a peace settlement with Manila in 1996. In early February, MNLF renegades who still supported their deposed chairman, Nur Misuari, backed by ASG personnel, attacked an AFP convoy on the island of Jolo, provoking a major 'punitive action' by government forces. The offensive, which included airstrikes, displaced more than 50,000 civilians but succeeded in subduing the rebellion.

Under extreme pressure in the south, in mid-February the ASG – apparently in an attempt to punish Manila or as a diversionary tactic – staged three bomb attacks which left 13 dead in Manila's financial district and the southern cities of General Santos and Davao. Three ASG suspects arrested in connection with the bombings in early March revealed that further attacks were planned. In mid-March, ASG prisoners attempted to break out of their high-security prison in Manila, but after a 24-hour stand-off 28 prisoners, including three senior ASG figures awaiting trial for kidnapping foreigners in 2000–01, were killed when security forces intervened. In the wake of the prison incident, ASG operations chief Jainal Antel Sali ('Abu Solaiman') threatened to 'bring the war to Manila'. The elevated threat from terrorism in early 2005 led Manila to revive an earlier proposal for an Anti-Terrorism Act intended to combat terrorist financing while giving broader powers to the security forces.

Within Southeast Asia, counter-terrorism cooperation remained patchy, and based essentially on bilateral rather than region-wide intelligence links. Nevertheless, in February 2004, delegates from 25 Asia-Pacific nations convened for the Bali Regional Ministerial Meeting on Counter-Terrorism, organised jointly by Australia and Indonesia. Most importantly, the two convening countries announced the impending establishment of the Jakarta Centre for Law Enforcement Cooperation (JCLEC). Intended to be operational by the end of 2004 in both regional capacity-building and operational roles, JCLEC is led by a senior Indonesian police officer and largely funded by Australia at a cost of almost $30m (AU$38m) over five years. The new centre's operational remit distinguished it from the existing US-financed Southeast Asian Regional Centre for Counter-Terrorism in Kuala Lumpur and the International Law Enforcement Academy in Bangkok, both restricted to training and research roles.

Maritime security

During 2004, the security of shipping against potential terrorist threats as well as piracy in Southeast Asian ports and waters, particularly in the Malacca and Singapore Straits, emerged as a key concern for states inside and outside the region. There was no clear evidence of connections between maritime criminals and terrorists in the region. Nevertheless, against a background of rising piracy in the straits and warnings by Lloyds' List and Singapore ministers in late 2003 over the possibility of terrorists using hijacked vessels as floating bombs to attack ports or maritime chokepoints, in March 2004 Admiral Thomas B. Fargo, commander-in-chief of US Pacific Command, revealed that the Pentagon was formulating a Regional Maritime Security Initiative (RMSI). According to Fargo, RMSI would involve not only closer intelligence-sharing with Southeast Asian states, but also deployment of US Marines and special operations forces on high-speed vessels to interdict maritime threats. Though Singapore supported RMSI, Indonesia and Malaysia asserted that security in the Straits was the responsibility of littoral states and that the introduction of foreign forces might provoke terrorism.

However, the third Asia Security Conference (Shangri-La Dialogue), organised by the International Institute for Strategic Studies in Singapore in early June, facilitated convergence between the positions of the interested parties. In the aftermath of the Shangri-La Dialogue, the ministerial meeting of the Five Power Defence Arrangements (FPDA) – involving Australia, Malaysia, New Zealand, Singapore and the United Kingdom – agreed that the scope of the grouping's already maritime-focused military exercises should be widened to include maritime counter-terrorism. Soon afterwards, Indonesia proposed trilateral coordinated naval patrols in the Malacca Strait, involving its own forces and those of Malaysia and Singapore. The first such patrol commenced in late July. Moreover, in late June, Admiral Fargo visited Malaysia, and the two sides were reported to have 'mended fences', with the United States emphasising its respect for littoral states' sovereignty and Malaysia welcoming Washington's offer of practical assistance in support of its efforts to combat piracy and to pre-empt maritime terrorism. With its under-funded navy and marine police, poor economic conditions, and inadequate law enforcement, Indonesia, though, crucially remained a weak component of the tentatively emerging regional maritime security architecture. A resurgence of piracy in the Malacca Strait in March 2005, following a lull since the beginning of the year (probably induced by the presence of large numbers of foreign naval vessels engaged in post-tsunami disaster relief in Aceh), highlighted the need for closer regional collaboration on the issue.

Extra-regional powers and Southeast Asian security

The debate over Southeast Asian maritime security highlighted the extent to which the region's security has increasingly been of interest to extra-regional powers.

The most obvious development has been Washington's view of Southeast Asia as the 'second front' in the global campaign against terrorism. However, as reactions within Southeast Asia to the RMSI proposal demonstrated, the Bush administration's focus on counter-terrorism has accentuated divergences amongst Association of South East Asian Nations (ASEAN) members with respect to their security links with the United States.

Washington's security relations with the Philippines, Singapore and Thailand have intensified. During 2003, both Manila and Bangkok were accorded 'major non-NATO ally' status and granted substantial security assistance packages, while Singapore announced that it would be negotiating a Framework Agreement on security cooperation with Washington. In 2004, the United States' security and defence cooperation with all three states was far-reaching. Bilateral military exercises with the Philippines included Balikatan 2004 in February, involving 2,500 US troops (mainly marines) in Central Luzon. Meanwhile, under *Operation Enduring Freedom–Philippines*, US forces closely supported AFP efforts to destroy the ASG. In Thailand, the annual exercise *Cobra Gold*, most recently held in May 2004, remained by far Southeast Asia's largest war-game; over the years it has evolved from a bilateral US–Thailand affair into multilateral manoeuvres also involving small contingents from Singapore, the Philippines and Mongolia, with observers from 11 other countries. In 2004, a counter-terrorism element was injected into *Cobra Gold* for the first time. Thai and US special operations forces also intensified their joint training. US defence and security cooperation with Singapore remained the closest and most far-reaching in Southeast Asia, reflecting Washington's view that – semantics aside – the city-state was now effectively an ally. All three states provided access to military airfields and, in Singapore's case, Changi Naval Base, facilitating the movement of US forces between their US and Pacific bases during the wars in Iraq and Afghanistan. The Philippines, Singapore and Thailand all contributed token forces to the US-led coalition occupying Iraq. The Philippine contingent's premature withdrawal after a Filipino worker was kidnapped in Iraq in July caused temporary irritation in Washington but did not damage the overall bilateral relationship, which remained crucial to US regional objectives in the context of the worldwide campaign against terrorism.

Indonesia and Malaysia have both, to a degree, cooperated with the United States in the counter-terrorism effort. While both Washington and Jakarta would like to see US military aid to Indonesia restored, continued US concern over the TNI's human rights abuses and its role in the 2002 Timika incident in Papua (in which two Americans were killed) continued to prevent defence cooperation beyond the limited provision of training in the United States under the International Military Education and Training Scheme. Nevertheless, since 2002 Washington has actively supported Jakarta's counter-terrorism measures, notably by helping to upgrade Indonesia's police force, and has evidently been heartened by Susilo's election and his emphasis on counter-terrorism. Similarly, in Malaysia's case, Washington quietly welcomed Badawi's accession after the tensions in US–Malaysia relations under Mahathir, and gave due credit for Malaysia's counter-terrorism efforts. Nevertheless, it was clear that the determined US emphasis on counter-terrorism has strained US relations with Indonesia and Malaysia. In both cases, there has been a growing Islamic basis in addition to the established nationalist rationale for resenting the United States' regional role, as the governments of the two states have needed to avoid alienating domestic Muslim constituencies by cooperating too closely or too obviously with Washington.

The US security role in Southeast Asia has become more powerful than at any time since the Cold War, if defined in 'hard' military terms. Indeed, as a result of the Pentagon's Global Posture Review, announced in September 2004, its military profile in the region is likely to increase, with more use being made of facilities in Southeast Asia. At the same time, the United States remains Southeast Asia's most important trading partner. However, during 2004 there was a growing sense throughout the region that US influence was nevertheless declining, partly as a result of Washington's counter-terrorism focus. In November 2004, an Asia Foundation report suggested that a more coordinated US strategy for Southeast Asia would involve greater use of 'soft power', for example, through annual US–ASEAN summit meetings, a US–ASEAN free trade agreement and a major initiative to engage Southeast Asian Muslims. There were already signs of more nuanced approaches in US policy in the region – for example, Washington's announcement in September that it would provide $157m to improve basic education provision in Indonesia as part of a $468m aid package over five years. Moreover, at the end of 2004, all indications were that Washington would seize the opportunity provided by the regional tsunami disaster to display its soft power in terms of leading and funding relief and reconstruction efforts.

While the United States faced challenges in maintaining its regional influence, China continued its drive to become an important strategic player in Southeast Asia. Since the late 1990s, Beijing's more sophisticated diplomacy (epitomised by its New Security Policy and new-found enthusiasm for multilateralism), geostrategic patience (marked by its less assertive policy in relation to territorial claims in the Spratleys) and growing economic leverage have substantially allayed Southeast Asian governments' reservations over China's emerging regional role. In November 2004, agreements on trade and dispute settlement signed at the ASEAN–China summit boosted the institutionalisation of economic relations that first found expression in the 2002 Framework Agreement on Economic Cooperation, which established the target of an ASEAN–China Free Trade Area by 2010. Tightening economic relations between China and Southeast Asia have been accompanied by a tentative security entente, encapsulated in the ASEAN–China Strategic Partnership for Peace and Security, agreed in October 2003 and followed by a detailed 'Plan of Action' in

November 2004. China's intensifying engagement with ASEAN during 2004 was just part of Beijing's broader strategy of multilateralism in Asia as a whole, apparently aimed at leveraging its growing economic and diplomatic clout to heighten the legitimacy of its regional security role while minimising that of the United States. As well as promoting the ASEAN+3 initiative (which is likely to be transformed into the more grandly titled East Asia Summit in 2005), China has become increasingly enthusiastic with regard to the ASEAN Regional Forum (ARF), taking the lead in establishing the ARF's Security Policy Conference for senior defence officials, which convened for the first time in Beijing in November 2004.

ASEAN members are not simply acquiescing in China's 'peaceful rise', but are rather continuing to hedge their bets, primarily by accepting the need for the United States to maintain a central role in regional security. In effect, the continuing US security interest, including a substantial military presence in the vicinity of Southeast Asia, relieves Southeast Asian governments of the need for immediate concern over China's increasing security-related activity. At the same time, Southeast Asian states have continued to benefit from the détente between Washington and Beijing that began after 11 September and which has, for the time being, deferred the threat of overt competition between them for influence. As long as relations between Washington and Beijing remain on an even keel, Southeast Asian governments – which are keen to enjoy positive relations with both China and the US – will be spared pressure to choose between taking one side or the other. A key concern for ASEAN members maintaining close security and defence ties with the United States, though, is the potential for Sino-US confrontation over Taiwan, which could force hard choices on Southeast Asian governments.

Compared with the United States' pre-eminence and China's efforts to play a more important part in the region's political and security affairs, the roles played by what might be called the 'second-tier' extra-regional powers – Japan, Australia and India – were relatively limited. Since the end of the Cold War, there has been considerable debate in Japan over the widely perceived need to become a more assertive 'normal power'. There is every prospect that Japan's emerging capacity for power projection will be integrated into its alliance with the United States and there is little chance of Tokyo becoming an autonomous military actor. Nevertheless, Japan – concerned over the security of its energy supplies – has since the late 1990s suggested joint 'Ocean Peacekeeping' (OPK) patrols to Southeast Asian governments as a way to combat piracy. Despite Southeast Asian governments' previously ambiguous responses, the speech presented on behalf of Japan Defense Agency Director-General Shigeru Ishiba at the Shangri-La Dialogue in June 2004 reiterated the OPK idea. During January 2005, more than 1,000 Japanese Self-Defense Force personnel participated in post-tsunami relief operations in Indonesia, and in March Tokyo announced that Japan would participate (albeit on a small scale) in the May 2005 *Cobra Gold* exercise in Thailand. This will be the first time that Japanese land forces have taken part in a multinational exercise.

Australia, alarmed over what it perceived to be a growing threat to its interests from Islamic terrorism, heightened its security cooperation with several Southeast Asian states. For example, beyond its close counter-terrorism collaboration with Indonesia, Canberra also staged a joint military exercise with Singapore in November 2004, focusing on developing responses to potential terrorist use of chemical, biological or radiological weapons and, as part of efforts to expand the Philippines' counter-terrorism capacity, in July deployed special forces to train AFP elements. This increasing assertiveness was not always welcomed in the region, and the Indonesian and Malaysian governments maintained their traditional suspicion regarding Canberra's motives. This was particularly clear in December 2004, when Australia drew the ire of Jakarta and Kuala Lumpur by announcing a planned 'maritime identification zone' aimed at pre-empting maritime terrorist threats up to 1,000 nautical miles from the homeland.

While the gradually increasing security roles of Japan and Australia have not been entirely welcome in the region, India's growing role – which may in a small way provide an additional hedge against China's growing assertiveness – has proved less controversial. As in the cases of China and Japan, India's security role in Southeast Asia has grown in tandem with efforts to bolster economic relations. During 2004, India's military links with Singapore intensified in the wake of a bilateral Defence Cooperation Agreement signed in October 2003, and in September 2004 the two sides agreed to hold their first naval exercise in the South China Sea in 2005. Indian discussions with Malaysia on enhanced maritime security cooperation in September pointed to the likelihood that New Delhi would soon resume its naval patrols in the Malacca Strait. In the meantime, India continued its series of joint patrols with Indonesia, and in October 2004 signed a memorandum with Myanmar on security cooperation, which was soon followed by coordinated bilateral military operations against Manipur and Naga rebels operating on the two countries' borders.

ASEAN security cooperation

A plethora of bilateral arrangements, mainly covering intelligence exchange, military training and joint exercises, remained the most prevalent form of security cooperation between Southeast Asian states. However, the intensity and quality of this cooperation varied widely across the region. For example, while bilateral defence links were particularly strong between Singapore and Thailand (which in November 2004 intensified bilateral defence relations with a memorandum of understanding covering air force training), they were virtually non-existent between long-time ASEAN members and Cambodia, Laos, Myanmar and Vietnam.

Meanwhile, stymied by intra-Southeast Asian rivalry, mistrust and suspicion, multilateral security cooperation under the auspices of ASEAN remained largely potential rather than actual. Since the late 1990s, the diversity and seriousness of the threats confronting Southeast Asia had provoked considerable debate over the

ASEAN's security role. At ASEAN's annual summit in 2003, Indonesia initiated moves to establish an ASEAN Security Community (ASC) as part of a project to construct a broader ASEAN Community also including economic and social communities by 2020. The nature of the ASC was spelled out in more detail in the Vientiane Action Programme (VAP), issued at the ASEAN summit in November 2004, which listed five 'strategic thrusts' aimed at achieving results by 2010: political development (including the promotion of human rights and the prevention of corruption); the shaping and sharing of norms (notably efforts to adopt a regional code of conduct in the South China Sea, and various counter-terrorism measures); conflict prevention (including establishment of an ASEAN Arms Register and the promotion of maritime security cooperation); conflict resolution and post-conflict peacebuilding.

While the ASC might facilitate cooperation against terrorism and other transnational threats in the long-term, it seemed unlikely to boost Southeast Asian states' collective ability to defuse more conventional threats, whether domestic or interstate in nature. The continued insistence on non-interference, though understandable, seemed likely to impede robust conflict resolution. The VAP spoke rather unconvincingly of 'regional arrangements for the maintenance of peace and stability' being established through 'national peacekeeping centres' and of building on 'existing modes of peaceful settlement of disputes' as the main conflict resolution 'innovations' under the ASC. There was no specific mention of how the existing ASEAN High Council might be transformed into an effective judicial mechanism.

ASEAN's apparent irrelevance to worsening internal security problems in Thailand's south, to Myanmar's continuing domestic political drama (which in October 2004 saw the relatively pragmatic prime minister and chief of military intelligence, Khin Nyunt, ousted), or to the eruption of tension between Indonesia and Malaysia over conflicting maritime claims in the Sulawesi Sea in early 2005, despite the acute interest and concern of neighbouring states in each case, highlighted the group's shortcomings in the security sphere. Moreover, at the end of the year, despite the nationally driven efforts of Singapore and, on a smaller scale, Malaysia to help their stricken neighbours, the tsunami-induced humanitarian crisis produced no significant immediate response from ASEAN as an institution, despite the huge amount of discussion in the region of 'human security' issues over the previous decade. It was not until the US proposed a consortium led by itself, Japan, India and Australia to coordinate relief efforts that Singapore took the initiative in Southeast Asia and called for an ASEAN-organised emergency summit to discuss the crisis.

Stability vs insecurity

By early 2005, there were good grounds for assuming that, following national elections, the domestic politics of Indonesia, Malaysia, Thailand and perhaps even the Philippines would stabilise for the next several years. In the cases of Indonesia

and the Philippines, which both remained fragile states, the accession of governments with clear democratic mandates could provide firmer bases for ameliorating
economic weakness and mitigating serious security problems. Nevertheless,
Indonesia, the Philippines and Thailand faced serious internal security problems. In
Indonesia, the problems of Aceh remained acute. Though the prospects for ending
the MILF rebellion in the southern Philippines seemed fairly good, the relatively
small but criminalised ASG posed a persistent challenge to Manila's authority,
particularly as it struck alliances with other Muslim-based groups. It seemed quite
possible that dissident MILF elements might continue their struggle, possibly in
alliance with the ASG, despite any settlement between Manila and the mainstream
MILF. Meanwhile, the CPP/NPA appeared to be gaining strength and a negotiated
settlement was not in prospect. In southern Thailand, the government and security forces appeared to have little clear idea of how to manage resurgent separatist
violence, sometimes responding in a counter-productive fashion. Governments in
the region continued to grapple with the problem of JI, which retained the capacity
to mount terrorist bombings, and appeared to have found sanctuary in Mindanao
as well as in Indonesia. A potential link-up between southern Thai separatists and JI
was a worrying possibility, as was the possibility of collaboration between maritime
criminals and terrorists in the straits.

Despite the ASC proposal, ASEAN seemed unlikely to develop quickly as a
vehicle that could help its members to manage the diverse security problems they
faced more effectively. In the absence of effective multilateral security cooperation
within the sub-region, Southeast Asian governments' security cooperation policies
have increasingly seemed to parallel the fashion for economic bilateralism within
ASEAN and between ASEAN members and extra-regional partners (particularly
the United States). This was seen most clearly in Singapore's bilateral security
networking, but every other Southeast Asian government pursued similar arrangements to a greater or lesser degree. The continuing strong US security interest in
Southeast Asia has allowed ASEAN governments to view China's rising power and
assertiveness with greater equanimity than might otherwise have been the case,
while the post-11 September détente between Washington and Beijing has spared
Southeast Asian governments the need to choose between warm relations with one
or other of the two main extra-regional powers. At the same time, the growing
interest of Australia, India and Japan in Southeast Asian security has provided
ASEAN governments with additional hedging options. On balance, in 2005 in
Southeast Asia stability seemed likely to trump insecurity – if not easily – while
bilateralism would as usual prevail comfortably over multilateralism.

Japan's Diplomatic, Economic and Political Vitality

Japan's boldness in supporting American state-building efforts in Iraq enshrines a steady increase in Japanese defence and security policy activism that has been in train since the late 1990s, underpinned strikingly in December 2004 with the publication of the country's new National Defense Program Outline (NDPO), the first effort since 1995 to provide a detailed exposition of the country's strategic challenges and doctrinal and planning priorities for the medium-term future. Japanese Prime Minister Junichiro Koizumi's unambiguous support for the United States-led initiative in Iraq in part reflects the close personal affinity between the Koizumi and the US President George W. Bush. It also reflects Tokyo's calculation that cooperation with the United States globally helps to advance its regional interests, most notably vis-à-vis North Korea in the context of both the Six-Party Talks on nuclear weapons and the politically sensitive issue of unaccounted-for Japanese citizens abducted by North Korea in the 1970s and 1980s.

Japan in Iraq

Koizumi has demonstrated an unwavering commitment to the US-led presence in Iraq. In June 2004, in anticipation of the planned handover of formal administrative control to the Iraqi authorities, Koizumi announced at the G-8 summit at Sea Island, Georgia, that Japan would maintain its presence of about 500 Self-Defense Force (SDF) personnel in the Samawah region of southern Iraq. The announcement generated critical press and opposition party commentary in Japan for a number of reasons. Koizumi was attacked for making a major policy commitment on the delicate question of overseas troop deployments without first securing the support of the Japanese Diet. Use of the SDF beyond Japan's borders has long been a touchy issue in Japan, both because of the constitutional restriction on the use of Japan's military for anything other than purely defensive military operations (as defined by Article 9 of the Constitution), and in light of longstanding legal conventions that have prevented the country from exercising its UN-based right to participate in collective security initiatives. Koizumi made clear that no new legislation would be required to extend the SDF mission in Iraq, thereby conveniently side-stepping the need for parliamentary approval or a setpiece debate on the issue. Ensuring that Japan's forces could continue to operate in the region in the context of the new multinational initiative was achieved thanks to the semantic (disingenuous in the eyes of some critics) sleight-of-hand on the part of the Japanese Cabinet Legislation Bureau, which argued that Japan's post-handover role in Iraq should be characterised as 'cooperation' (*kyoroku*) with rather than 'participation' (*sanka*) in the UN-sanctioned multinational initiative.

Japan's policy towards Iraq has also reflected a genuine belief on the part of the Liberal Democratic Party (LDP)-led coalition government that Japan's own distinctive historical and cultural traditions provide it with lessons and experiences that make it uniquely qualified to advise on the practical challenges of establishing a new government in Iraq as well as promoting stability in the wider Middle East. Post-war Japanese leaders, consistent with the country's view of itself as facing in two directions – both towards the West and Asia – have long-stressed the country's ability to play a mediating role in post-conflict situations. This, coupled with the live historical memory of Japan's post-Second World War experience of recovery and reform under the US-led occupation of 1945–52, has encouraged some in Tokyo to stress Japan's ability to provide constructive advice on how to develop positive relations with a Middle East that remains culturally unfamiliar to many in the secular West. The clearest expression of this thinking has been the Japan Arab Dialogue Forum, launched by Tokyo in September 2003 and designed to promote economic and political reform in the region, as well as a three-year educational initiative announced by Japan in June 2004 to provide schools and teaching for more than 100,000 individuals as part of a wider G-8-sponsored Greater Middle East Initiative. In private conversations with Bush, Koizumi reportedly has been keen to emphasise the importance of respecting the distinctive cultural traditions and autonomy of states in the region while avoiding any suggestion that new reforms are being imposed on Arab countries.

Continuing security realism

Throughout 2004 and early 2005, there was considerable evidence of the Japanese government's willingness to promote policy reforms and initiatives intended to enhance Japan's security in the face of potential challenges both at home and abroad. In mid-April 2004, following the kidnapping of three Japanese civilians in Iraq, the Koizumi government adopted an uncompromising position of no concessions in the face of demands by the kidnappers that Japan withdraw its SDF forces from Iraq. This position appeared to be vindicated by the release of all of the hostages unharmed four days after their capture. The government's tough stance was particularly striking in light of adverse public opinion in Japan, with some polls in spring 2004 reporting slim majorities opposed to the Japanese presence in Iraq. Interestingly, despite this ambivalence towards Japan's Iraq policy, Japanese public opinion responded positively to Tokyo's hardline position, with as many as 74% in one *Asahi Shimbun* poll supporting the government's decision not to concede to the hostage-takers' demands. This support in part reflected widespread feeling in Japan that the Japanese hostages were themselves partially responsible for their situation, having ignored an earlier government advisory not to travel to Iraq.

In general, it was striking in 2004 how public opinion adapted to the human costs associated with the Japanese presence in Iraq. Past overseas deployments of Japanese peacekeeping forces have typically been associated with acute public sensitivity to Japanese casualties, and there was speculation following the deployment of Japanese contingents to the region in early 2004 that the Koizumi government would be politically vulnerable to that risk. Such fears do not appear to have been realised. While the Democratic Party of Japan (DPJ), the main opposition party, has questioned the constitutional and legal basis for the continuing SDF presence in Iraq, the deaths of two Japanese journalists in May, the beheading of a Japanese hostage in October and a rocket attack on the SDF Samawah encampment in October did not result in an unambiguous call for an immediate Japanese withdrawal. Practical questions remain over how best to protect Japan's peacekeepers, who are in Iraq to provide logistical and reconstruction support and strictly prohibited from using their weapons for purposes other than self-defence. Consequently, the SDF contingent has relied on protection from Dutch forces, and from May 2005 is to be protected by Australian troops responsible for the security of Samawah. This somewhat anomalous situation, in which troops are protecting other troops, has led some critics in Japan to argue for a more flexible, permissive standard for weapons use by Japan's military forces.

Japan has also more rigorously addressed the challenges of homeland security. In May 2004, the government launched a series of raids on ten locations throughout Japan in pursuit of alleged al-Qaeda operatives linked to Lionel Dumont, a suspected French terrorist. On 14 June, the government, in close cooperation with the DPJ, enacted a comprehensive package of seven key pieces of legislation intended to provide a comprehensive new legal framework for dealing with emergencies in and around Japan, building on legislation first passed in 2003. The new legislation covers a variety of issues, including the role and responsibilities of local governments in managing civilian evacuation and rescue procedures, guidelines for the airing of national public announcements via the country's media, and cooperation between Japanese and US military forces regulating the use of private land and provision by the SDF of weapons and ammunition to American troops.

The clearest and most far-ranging indication of the government's willingness to give serious thought to security issues was the official release of the NDPO. It set out the country's ten-year strategic vision, along with the related five-year Military Defense Build-up Plan (MDBP), covering the period 2005–09. Such reassessments are relatively infrequent (the last two outlines were released in 1976 and 1995), and are viewed as responses to fundamental shifts in the international and regional security challenges facing Japan, which now arise from North Korea and China and from non-state sources such as transnational terrorist groups. Central to the new doctrine detailed in the NDPO is a clear stress on the importance of flexibility and a more adaptive and rapidly responsive force structure. Achieving this goal will involve cuts in existing forces: a 30% reduction in the Ground Self-Defense Forces (GSDF) tanks and heavy artillery; retirement of three of the Maritime Self-Defense Forces (MSDF) ships; and a slimmed-down Air Self Defense Force (ASDF) of 260 combat aircraft. In part, the build-down in forces reflects the perennial bureaucratic conflict between a fiscally conservative Ministry of Finance and the Japan Defense Agency (JDA). For the second year in a row, in 2005, overall defence spending will fall by 1% of the total budget. However, the rethinking of Japan's security policy is far more than a cost-cutting exercise, and involves ambitious new initiatives, including the establishment of a central rapid-reaction force to deal with terrorist attacks and national emergencies, as well as recognition that the peacekeeping functions of the SDF should in future be viewed as on a par with the traditional role of preserving the nation's territorial integrity.

This fundamental shift also reflects a sea change in public attitudes towards defence policy and especially new thinking among Japan's politicians. To an extent, this change has been informed by specific enquiries, such as that conducted by the Prime Minister's Council on Security and Defence Capabilities (chaired by Hiroshi Araki), which in October 2004 issue a report arguing in favour of closer US–Japan defence cooperation and of new legislation governing the deployment of SDF overseas. Much of the shift in attitudes can also be linked to the steadily evolving public debate in favour of constitutional change. There now exists a broad consensus behind a possible reworking of Article 9 – which prohibits the use of Japanese forces except strictly in self-defence – and an explicit lifting of the ban on participation in collective security initiatives. The communities favouring such changes remain relatively fluid and span the political spectrum, within both the LDP and the opposition DPJ. With two key parliamentary committees due to issue their final reports on constitutional reform in May 2005 and with the government committed to publish draft legislation on constitutional reform by November 2005, to coincide with the 50th anniversary of the founding of the LDP, 2005–06 is likely to a critical period for linking new strategic thinking with the wider political reform process.

To be sure, the challenges faced by the government are considerable. Within the governing coalition, the numerically dominant LDP has had to share power with its smaller, but pivotally important, junior partner, the New Komei Party. Komei has moved away from a broadly pacifist stance towards accepting the need for a more flexible security policy. By early 2005, for example, the party appeared to have accepted long-standing pressure in some quarters within the LDP to upgrade the status of the JDA from a government agency to a fully fledged ministry – a key symbolic and practical change. Less flexibly, however, Komei remains opposed to strong political pressure within the LDP and the JDA, reinforced by Keidanren (the Japan Business Federation), in favour of a full lifting of the longstanding ban on Japanese arms exports. In place since 1967, the arms export ban has become a symbol of the non-offensive defence posture of Japan and the country's commitment and reassurance to its neighbours to avoid a return to the disastrous militarist policies of the 1930s. In the wake of a critically important agreement between Washington and Tokyo in 2003 to collaborate in the joint development of a comprehensive missile defence programme, Komei has accepted the need to relax the arms export ban to facilitate bilateral technical cooperation in producing interceptor components for the new missile defence programme. However, the party has resisted a blanket lifting of the arms export ban. Critics counter that by failing to remove the arms export ban in the new NDPO, Japan has been unnecessarily hamstrung in a number of key security areas – prevented, for example, from collaborating with the United States and other Western powers in the development of the new F-35 Joint Strike Fighter, or in selling mothballed Japanese destroyers to Southeast Asian countries anxious to bolster their preparedness for regional maritime security challenges.

Nevertheless, on balance, the domestic environment on security has shifted sufficiently to allow for active consideration of significant new security initiatives, to be promoted in 2005–06, including:

- Discussion in January 2005 of the need to introduce a new legal framework to govern the despatch of the SDF overseas in peacekeeping operations, together with a relaxation of the existing set of five principles limiting the use of the SDF outside Japan.
- An LDP–DPJ agreement in January 2005 on plans to establish a Joint Information Council and Joint Information Headquarters to improve coordination between government security and disaster specialists and to allow rapid decision-making by the prime minister.
- New cabinet-approved legislation, submitted in February 2005, allowing the prime minister to give advance authorisation to the head of the JDA to order a missile interception to repel a ballistic missile attack against Japan.

Japan's revitalised UN diplomacy

In tandem with Tokyo's high profile security activism, in September 2004 the Koizumi government launched a renewed diplomatic initiative to win a permanent seat for Japan on the UN Security Council. Press reports suggested that the initial impetus for this measure came from within the Gaimusho (Japan's Ministry of Foreign Affairs), and that Koizumi may initially have been sceptical about the merits of such a campaign. However, by 21 September, following his speech to the UN General Assembly, it was clear that Koizumi was fully behind the new campaign. The Japanese government has aligned itself with Germany, India and Brazil in pushing an earlier proposal, dating from 1997, to increase the number of permanent Security Council members by five, while adding a four non-permanent members. A second proposal, backed by then Australian foreign minister Gareth Evans, envisages the addition of seven or eight quasi-permanent members elected for four- to five-year terms, with the prospect of re-election to ensure continuity, but no veto rights to the new members.

Tokyo has been able to take heart from UN Secretary-General Kofi Annan's commitment to reform, and also from evidence of a growing number of General Assembly members in favour of Security Council expansion. Japan has also been taking active steps to highlight the strength of its own claim for recognition, underlined by its substantial financial commitment to the UN as the second largest contributor after the

United States. Similarly, Japan has sought to highlight its internationalism by hosting the third Iraq donors' conference in October 2004, considering an SDF mission to Sudan, and swiftly committing troops and materiel to the December 2004 tsunami crisis in Southeast Asia. Yet Japan's bid faces obstacles from a number of directions, most acutely from countries such as Italy, Mexico, Pakistan and South Korea, which remain opposed to the 1997 initiative and which, in the case of South Korea, are loath to certify the heightened political and diplomatic status that a permanent seat on the Security Council would entail. Equally troubling to Japan is the ambivalence of the United States. While senior US officials, including Bush, have made clear that they support Japan's bid, the Bush administration has yet to develop a clear policy position on UN reform. In fact, senior Japanese officials have reason to worry that general skepticism, if not outright hostility, towards the UN within the White House, symbolised by the nomination of John Bolton (an outspoken critic of the UN) to the post of US ambassador to the UN, indicates that Washington would ultimately block expansion of the UN under any formula. If this were the case, Japan's effort to make the case for membership would probably fail.

US–Japan security dialogue

Overall relations between Washington and Tokyo, however, have remained broadly positive and constructive. 2004 marked the 150th anniversary of the signing of the Treaty of Kanagawa – the first formal treaty between the two countries – and the mood music from officials on both sides of the Pacific was harmonious, with outgoing US ambassador to Japan Howard Baker characterising the bilateral relationship in February 2005 as the 'best it has ever been' in the course of his three-and-a-half year tenure in Japan. Confidence in the strength of the relationship has been underlined by the willingness of US defence officials to push for a major reassessment of the bilateral security partnership. In the context of Washington's Global Posture Review, which envisages, over the next ten years, a 10,000-man reduction in the existing 42,000-troop US military deployment in Japan, the United States has been eager to persuade the Koizumi government to enter into detailed discussions on how best to restructure US–Japanese military cooperation, including revamping the size and location of US military bases in Japan, to ensure a more flexible and responsive security alliance. US proposals include:

- relocating the headquarters of the 1st US Army from Washington State to Camp Zama in Kanagawa Prefecture;
- transferring the command functions of the 5th Air Force from Yokota Air Base in Tokyo to the 13th Air Force in Guam;
- transferring US naval units at Atsugi Air Base in Kanagawa to Iwakuni Air Base in Yamaguchi; and
- moving a number of US Marine Corps units in Okinawa Prefecture to other locations in Japan.

The main purposes of these proposals are to enhance the flexibility of US forces in the Far East, to bolster America's ability to assist in the defence of Japan and South Korea, and to underline in US strategic thinking the importance of Japan as the key forward position in meeting the security challenges associated with the arc of instability extending from the Middle East, via Taiwan, as far as North Korea.

US plans for restructuring its forces in Japan have been on the table since the end of 2003 and American negotiators during 2004 expressed some irritation at what appeared to be an unwillingness or reluctance on the part of their Japanese counterparts to respond in detail to the US proposal. In part, Tokyo's hesitation reflected political realities at home. Base restructuring is likely to lead to local opposition from those communities slated to receive new detachments of American forces, and in the run-up to the Upper House elections of July 2004, the Koizumi government was anxious to avoid highlighting these issues. Beyond such local sensitivities, the Japanese government has also been worried that force restructuring might signal a reduction in the deterrent function of US forces in Japan, and has also been concerned that the more flexible use of American forces would qualify the terms of Article VI of the US–Japan Mutual Security Treaty, which restricts the role of US troops in Japan to dealing with security challenges in the Far East.

Public statements by American officials appear to have alleviated some of these concerns, and since September 2004, partly due to the direct intervention of Koizumi, Japan has signalled its intention to enter into substantive discussions with US policy planners on bilateral defence cooperation. Press reports in January 2005 indicated that Washington and Tokyo had agreed to issue by summer 2005 a new US–Japan Joint Declaration on Security, updating an earlier declaration from 1996. In turn, this will usher in the revision of the 1997 US–Japan Defense Cooperation Guidelines, addressing a range of bilateral issues including logistical cooperation between US and Japanese forces, guarding American and Japanese military facilities in Japan, and common strategic objectives. Further confirmation of progress in such discussions emerged following the 'two-plus-two' meeting of US and Japanese foreign and defence officials on 19 February 2005, when the two governments indicated their agreement on the need to jointly address regional security challenges associated with North Korea and China. Strikingly, the official declaration from this meeting underlined the importance of a 'peaceful resolution of issues on the Taiwan Strait' – the first time since the late 1960s that Japan has indicated unambiguously and publicly its support for the US position of opposing any military action by mainland China against Taiwan. Not surprisingly, the declaration prompted an angry reaction from the Chinese government, which sees such statements as an unwarranted threat to Chinese sovereignty and remains deeply suspicious of growing security cooperation between Japan and the United States.

Bilateral security cooperation, while very important, should not obscure occasional points of tensions and divergence between Washington and Tokyo as well as administrative changes that may prompt a subtle shift of emphasis on Japan matters in the new Bush White House. To some Japanese observers, a second Bush administration will invariably entail a partial retreat from the high point of alliance cooperation associated with the first Bush administration – largely due to a change of key players. The departure from the new administration of Secretary of State Colin Powell and his deputy Richard Armitage removes from the decision-making frame two officials viewed in Japan as especially knowledgeable and sensitive to Japanese concerns. Other Japan/Asia hands, such as Michael Green at the National Security Council and Richard Lawless, deputy undersecretary of defense for Asia-Pacific affairs, remain in place. But their influence may be offset by others, like Deputy Secretary of State Robert Zoellick, who is viewed by some Japanese officials, on the basis of his earlier role as US Trade Representative, as something of a hardliner on Japan-related issues. The appointment of Thomas Schieffer as Howard Baker's replacement as ambassador to Japan is a departure from past convention given his limited exposure to Japan-related issues, although Schieffer's close personal ties to Bush may ensure that Japanese concerns remain well represented in the White House.

Okinawa has continued to prove a source of bilateral irritation following a US helicopter crash in August 2004 that sparked large local public protests and criticism of US safety measures as well as apparent delays on the part of the United States in agreeing to suspend further helicopter flights to allow such safety concerns to be addressed. Similarly, limited progress in finalising plans for the relocation within Okinawa of the US Futenma Marine Air Station from Ginowan to Nago have highlighted the continuing sensitivity of basing issues and the intricate practical aspects involved in lowering the US military profile on the island. The unresolved case of Charles Jenkins, a former American serviceman who had allegedly deserted to North Korea during the Korean War and who subsequently married Hitomi Soga, one of the Japanese abductees, further complicated relations with the United States. Washington's refusal to provide a guarantee that Jenkins would not be court-martialled for desertion were he to return to Japan to be reunited with Soga prevented Jenkins and his daughters from accompanying Koizumi and the remaining family members of the former abductees back to Japan on 22 May. In July, following a reunion of the Jenkins family in Jakarta, Jenkins was allowed to travel to Japan, where he was hospitalised and eventually handed over to the US military authorities. On 2 November, Jenkins was found guilty of desertion, sentenced to 30 days' confinement and dishonourably discharged from the US Army.

Finally, delays in resolving a long-standing bilateral dispute over unfettered access for US beef into the Japanese market have threatened to rekindle bilateral trade tensions. Japanese consumers and the country's Food Security Commission remain concerned at the risks of US beef contaminated by mad cow disease, while Washington has been critical of what it sees as unnecessarily long bureaucratic delays in addressing such safety concerns – so much so that Condoleezza Rice, in her first visit to Japan as secretary of state in March 2005, publicly and forcefully urged Japan to find a quick solution to the problem. Notwithstanding such public statements, the overall relationship remains very positive and such economic disagreements are a far cry from the heated bilateral trade disputes of the 1980s. Rice's visit to Japan both symbolically and substantively underlined the strategic and political importance of Japan to US East Asian policy. That importance is likely to increase rather than diminish over time.

Regional tensions

While relations between Tokyo and Washington have been broadly positive, the same cannot be said of relations between Japan and some of its closest neighbours. Japan's relations with North Korea have been dogged by two persistent issues: the international standoff reflected in the stalled Six-Party Talks over Pyongyang's nuclear-weapon programme; and continuing tensions over the fate and status of Japanese abductees taken to North Korea in the 1970s and 1980s. On the first issue, the Koizumi administration's negotiating leverage has been relatively limited, given the need to adopt a position that meets the expectations and policy preferences of the other players in the process, most keenly those of South Korea and the United States. However, Koizumi's one-day visit to Pyongyang on 22 May 2004 (his second since his earlier North Korea visit in September 2002) appeared to open up a number of promising avenues. North Korea agreed to the release of all but three of the family relatives of the original five Japanese abductees who had been allowed to return to Japan following the original 2002 summit meeting. Japan, in return, offered the North a modest package of emergency food and medical assistance and held out the prospect of further assistance and the avoidance of economic sanctions should North Korea comply with the terms of the Japan–North Korea Joint Declaration of September 2002. Importantly, both countries agreed to enter into a regular dialogue, while Kim Jong Il appeared to accept that a nuclear freeze would be a viable first step towards the eventual elimination of the North's nuclear-weapon capability. In turn, the summit established the basis for a series of ministerial meetings over the course of 2004, culminating in November in Pyongyang with the provision by North Korean authorities of detailed information relating to the fate of additional Japanese abductees and unaccounted-for family members.

Despite these promising developments, the Koizumi government quickly encountered a number of problems. To begin with, the prime minister's risky visit to the North, while moderately boosting his public standing in the short term, had nowhere near the political value that his September 2002 visit had generated. Koizumi was sharply and publicly attacked by abductee family members in Japan for failing to do enough to press the North Koreans. North Korea–Japan relations experienced a sharp deterioration in December 2004 with the revelation in Japan that human bone remains presented by the North Koreans to the Japanese as evidence of the death of Megumi Yokota, one of the unresolved abductee cases, were most probably not genuine. Sophisticated DNA testing in Japan appeared to indicate that the remains belonged to two other, unrelated individuals. This in turn provoked a public outcry in Japan, with conservative politicians in particular denouncing Pyongyang for duplicity and calling for the imposition of sanctions against North Korea. The North Koreans, for their part, broke off direct telephone communication with Japan and accused the Koizumi government of acting in bad faith and of intentionally engineering an incident designed to lead to a breakdown in bilateral relations. The Koizumi government sought to resist calls for sanctions, conscious that the any direct measures risked further provoking the North Korea (Pyongyang having publicly threatened to treat any imposition of economic sanctions as an act of war), and that sanctions would almost certainly derail any prospect of a reactivation of the Six-Party Talks process. Nonetheless, mounting public criticism forced Tokyo in March 2005 to implement the terms of the Marine Oil Pollution Compensation Guarantee Law, banning ships of 100 tons or more lacking insurance against damage associated with oil spills from docking at Japanese ports. Since the majority of North Korean ships do not have this insurance, the measure represented an indirect means of closing off trade that generates each year officially some ¥27.3bn-worth of revenue for the North Korea – a 'stealth sanction', in effect. As expected, this provoked a swift response from the North and demands by Pyongyang that Japan be barred from further rounds of the Six-Party Talks.

As the 40th anniversary of the normalisation of relations between Japan and South Korea, 2005 should have been an auspicious year for bilateral ties between Seoul and Tokyo. Against the backdrop of a generally close personal relationship between Koizumi and South Korean President Roh Moo Hyun, talk of a possible visit to South Korea by the Japanese Crown Prince and Princess, and a wider atmosphere of deepening cultural ties between the two countries (fuelled by a popular soap-opera driven 'hanryu boom' in Japan), the relationship appeared headed in a very positive direction. However, in February 2005 the announcement by Shimane prefecture in southern Japan that 22 February would be designated 'Takeshima Day' – a reference to contested island territory approximately midway between Japan and the South Korea – sparked a major diplomatic row, fuelled by strong emotional reactions in both countries and an apparently deep-seated perception gap between the two governments.

For South Korea, Takeshima – or Tokto, as it is known in Korean – is unambiguously Korean territory. Japan formally assumed control over the territory in 1905, the beginning of Japan's de facto political control over the Korean Peninsula. Any attempt to assert continuing Japanese rights over the territory is not only seen by Koreans as historically illegitimate and illegal but is also viewed as symptomatic of Japan's unwillingness to acknowledge and atone for its past colonial and wartime excesses. High-profile public statements by Roh vigorously rebutting the Japanese claim generated puzzlement in official quarters in Japan, prompting speculation that Roh was attempting to boost his domestic political standing by exploiting an emotional issue that unites Koreans across the political spectrum. In South Korea, by contrast, there was similar surprise and concern at Japanese government actions, with many observers arguing that the Shimane declaration was tacitly supported if not encouraged by a Koizumi administration anxious to line up support among conservative nationalists in Japan easily galvanised by such territorial issues. Both sides' impressions probably represent an exaggeration. Roh's outspokenness on the territorial issue is consistent with his public remarks on other sensitive foreign policy issues (such as policy towards North Korea) and reflected his general commitment to open government and a frank discussion of controversial historical issues. Koizumi, for his part, has sought to calm emotions since the outbreak of the controversy. Moreover, Japan's foreign ministry officials, who genuinely lacked administrative authority to block a local government from acting independently on such a matter, claim to have sought to dissuade Shimane prefecture from making the original controversial announcement. Whatever the truth of the matter, the issue remains a continuing source of friction overshadowing progress and dialogue in other areas.

Territorial issues also have been a major source of tension between Japan and China. Following the arrest and deportation by the Japanese authorities of a group of Chinese activists who had landed on Japan's Senkaku islands (known and claimed by China as the Daiyoutai) in March 2004, the Security Committee of Japan's House of Representatives unanimously passed a resolution reinforcing Japan's claim over the islands – the first time such a resolution has been passed since 1995. Beijing, to signal its displeasure, in March postponed a planned conference with Japan on maritime research and cancelled a ceremony acknowledging Japanese yen loans to China. Similar tensions have emerged due to repeated interventions into Japanese territorial waters of what the Chinese claim are ocean-research vessels, unresolved disputes over access to valuable natural gas reserves in the East China Sea, and the sighting in early November 2004 of a Chinese nuclear submarine in Japan's territorial waters. Despite strong pressure by the Japanese business community to avoid such tensions in the face of rapidly growing interdependence between the Chinese and Japanese economies (China has now eclipsed the United States as Japan's most important trading partner), bilateral relations have further deteriorated in the face of popular Chinese hostility towards Japan (fuelled by a very active Internet-driven grassroots campaign), and official Chinese complaints over recently released Japanese history textbooks which, in Chinese eyes, present distorted and inaccurate interpretations of Japan's wartime behaviour in China. In Japan, cross-party parliamentary support for a tougher response to Chinese actions is pushing the government to adopt a more forceful rhetorical position towards

Beijing, reinforced either by a number of symbolically important actions, including: a joint Japanese–US official statement in February 2005 in favour of a peaceful resolution of the Taiwan issue; the Koizumi government's announcement in March 2005 that all yen loans to China will end by the start of the 2008 Beijing Olympics; and Japan's objection to the European Union's possible lifting of its ban on arms exports to China. Koizumi has not made an official summit visit to China since October 2001. Deepening discord strengthen the argument in favour such a meeting.

Heightened political competition at home

Two key factors coloured domestic political developments during 2004–05. The first was Koizumi's remarkable political longevity. By the end of April 2005, he will have been in office for four years – a tenure that surpasses that of all his predecessors from the 1990s. The second factor was the emergence of a genuinely competitive and dynamic two-party system, such that it is now possible to imagine a scenario in which the opposition DPJ might replace the Liberal Democrats as the governing party.

Koizumi's long tenure as prime minister is explained in no small measure by the absence of any obvious rivals within the LDP having the influence and stature to replace him as party leader in the immediate future. Koizumi's strength has been bolstered by the decline of the once-dominant Hashimoto faction within the LDP, in part because of structural changes to the electoral system dating from the early 1990s. More recently, the revelation that the faction's leader and former prime minister, Ryutaro Hashimoto, had been the illegal recipient of a ¥100m donation from the Japan Medical Association, raising the prospect of a criminal indictment (which ultimately did not occur) and prompting in turn Hashimoto's resignation as faction leader in July, further reinforced the image of a faction in slow but irreversible decline.

Koizumi benefited from signs of improving economic conditions at home. During the first quarter of 2004, the Japanese economy boasted an annualised growth rate of 6.1%, outpacing the United States (4.4%) and the European average (less than 2%). In his June 2004 meeting with Bush, Koizumi was able to emphasise the underlying improvement in economic fundamentals, highlighting a decline in nonperforming loans, a fall in unemployment, rising stock prices and a growth revival fuelled by increasing consumption and investment rather than the country's traditional reliance on an export-led recovery. Nearly a year later, in late March 2005, this essentially bullish view of the economy appeared to have been sustained. Real GDP growth for 2004 stood at 2.7%, driven by a recovery in personal consumption and revived interest in capital investment, which was fuelled by corporate expectations of an end to deflation. The only distant cloud on the horizon appeared to be some concern over the health of overseas economies and the likely impact of this on Japan's export earnings. In the United States, a rapidly expanding budget deficit has generated worries about the sustainability of US government spending plans, while in China, now Japan's largest trading partner, eventual cyclical downturns in capital investment and consumption are likely to dampen Japanese export growth. Despite such concerns, Bank of Japan Governor Toshihiko Fukui adopted a very positive tone in late March, pointing to modest but sustained economic recovery at home.

Much of Koizumi's success as LDP leader and prime minister has been rooted in his ability to present himself as a vigorous promoter of radical political and economic reform, challenging a deeply conservative and interest group-dominated party. Koizumi's image as someone willing and able to take on the party machine, and as a leader committed to reform with 'no sacred cows' to protect, has been qualified by the reluctance of his party. In the run-up to the July 2004 elections to the Upper House of the Diet, there were delays to and a weakening of measures proposed by Japan's Fair-Trade Commission to strengthen the country's anti-monopoly legislation. Similarly, plans to enhance the revenue-raising and spending independence of local government (as part of a 'triple reform' package) have been dented in part by Ministry of Finance resistance to the undermining of its policymaking authority. Perhaps most importantly, on the key issue of postal privatisation – the reform initiative with which Koizumi is most closely identified – old-guard opposition from within the LDP has hampered rapid progress. Technological issues may hold up the planned April 2007 privatisation of the mail, savings and life insurance elements of Japan's postal service. Furthermore, resistance from within the LDP delayed the government's submission to the Japanese parliament of its legislative draft for postal privatisation.

In the face of domestic political difficulties, Japan's leaders have often turned to foreign policy as a means of securing policy successes that will boost their standing in the eyes of the electorate back home. Koizumi is no exception. Yet, even here, as demonstrated by the limited bounce Koizumi enjoyed from his May 2004 visit to Pyongyang, he has not been able to make much political mileage. This basic problem has been exacerbated by the growing strength of the DPJ, which has been able to capitalise on the electoral boost it received following its relatively strong performance in the Lower House elections of November 2003. The high-profile salience of the issue of pensions reform during the first half of 2004 then provided an opportunity for the party to stress its policy differences with the government. While the LDP advocated a relatively unpopular package of rising premiums and reduced benefits, the DPJ proposal embodied, in the eyes of some, a more fundamental and strategic rethink of existing policy, guaranteeing a minimum pension benefit level to all employees via a rise in Japan's consumption tax. The unpopularity of the government's pension package was reinforced by the revelation of a major scandal involving non-payment of past pension premiums by large numbers of politicians, including senior members of the government. The LDP was able to insulate itself from some of the political fallout of this controversy following the resignation of then chief cabinet secretary Yasuo Fukuda in May 2004. Subsequently, the DPJ was put on the back foot following revelations that many of its Diet representatives were also guilty of non-payment of premiums, and DPJ party leader Naoto Kan was forced to resign after it became clear that, despite his vociferous criticism of the government on this issue, he too had failed to make past payments.

Kan's resignation opened the door to an important leadership change within the DPJ. Initially, Ichiro Ozawa, former leader of the Liberal Party and a powerful figure in opposition politics, took over as DPJ leader in May 2004. However, he stepped down very quickly when it became clear that he was also guilty of non-payment of premiums. His successor, Katsuya Okada, has had a rejuvenating impact on party fortunes, helping to offset the disappointment of three unexpected by-election defeats for the DPJ in late April 2004. Okada has a number of important advantages as party leader. Only 50 when he assumed the leadership, he can credibly present himself as a new generational alternative to Koizumi and many (although not all) of Koizumi's potential successors within the LDP. Harvard educated, a former Ministry of International Trade and Industry bureaucrat, and a member of the Diet elected five times, Okada can claim a considerable amount of policy experience and expertise. Moreover, despite not having an especially strong factional base within the party, his image as a pragmatic, consensus politician has been very helpful in allowing him to create unity and common purpose within a heterogeneous party that has often suffered from personal and policy-related internal divisions. Confirmation of the rising fortunes of the party came dramatically on 11 July 2004 with an Upper House election in which the DPJ, by 50 to 49, narrowly won more seats than the LDP – the first defeat for the government in an Upper House contest since 1989. As only one half of the 242 seats of the Upper House are contested every three years, this result was not sufficient to unseat the government, which retained a majority of 139 seats together with the smaller coalition party, New Komei. Nevertheless, symbolically and practically it represented a setback for the LDP, particularly since the DPJ is popular among a growing and increasingly influential pool of floating voters and had performed well in both urban and rural areas, including constituencies often regarded as traditional LDP electoral strongholds.

New constraints

Japan's foreign and security policies in 2004–05 have been characterised by strong continuities from the previous year, focused on a continuing commitment to maintaining a visible presence in assisting with the post-conflict situation in Iraq, vocal and high-profile cooperation with the United States, (both in the Middle East and East Asia), and serious but politically risky efforts to improve bilateral relations with the North Korea. In addition to these ongoing policies, there have been new initiatives – most prominently, a determined effort to make the case for a permanent Japanese presence on the UN Security Council, difficult bilateral disagreements with China and South Korea over territorial issues, and the perennial and seemingly intractable question of Japan's view of its twentieth-century history and its responsibility for wartime excesses. Gradual economic recovery at home has given Koizumi some breathing space and flexibility in addressing both foreign and domestic policy concerns. However, in the face of resistance from conservative forces within his own party opposed to further administrative reform and economic deregulation, a rejuvenated and energetic opposition party, and the widespread recognition that party rules prevent the him from remaining in office longer than September 2006, there are real doubts about how much Koizumi will be able to achieve in 2005–06. Nevertheless, in the sphere of foreign and security policy, given the evolved severity of global threats, the shift from introversion to extroversion that he has overseen appears durable.

Prospectives

The principal feature of international relations in 2003–04 was the transatlantic split over Iraq and the nature and style of American foreign policy. The November 2004 US presidential election gave US President George W. Bush a second term, which in turn prompted some soul-searching in Washington about how to more effectively enlist allied help in implementing the 'Bush doctrine' and in Europe about how to better influence its implementation. The primary features of world affairs in 2004–05, then, are the inclination of the United States to present Europe with an acceptable foreign policy and Europe's willingness to approach the United States in a pragmatic and conciliatory fashion rather than a dogmatic and unyielding one. To be sure, as of March 2005 the number of nations participating in Iraq's political reconstruction had declined to 24 from 36 a year earlier, and Europeans had not shown greater enthusiasm for relieving any of the United States' state-building burden in Iraq. But these realities merely signified a consensus that the United States must bear the bulk of operational responsibility for what it started – not that Europe wished it to be humbled in doing so. Somewhat surprisingly, then, the disruptions of the greatest amplitude in the near term are likely to occur along some axis other than the transatlantic.

Transatlantic accommodation

There are three principal components of the new transatlantic accommodation. Firstly, the United States – having experienced a degree of alienation over Iraq – has understood that even the lone superpower cannot accomplish whatever it wants to do unilaterally, and has become as willing to work with allies as the Bush administration's ideological traffic will bear. In her January 2005 Senate confirmation hearings, incoming US Secretary of State Condoleezza Rice reinforced the impression that the prevailing view in the Bush administration was that the time for diplomacy had arrived. Secondly, European governments have accepted that they must deal with the world as it is rather than as they wish it to be, and that the real world unavoidably includes rogue regimes for which the threat of force, and an American government ideologically committed to an idealistic and ambitious foreign policy inclined to use that threat (selectively) to advance democracy and individual liberty throughout the world, are an indispensable means of influence.

The third component of the post-Iraq transatlantic convergence was a kind of strategic serendipity. Fortuitous developments in key strategic areas have allowed both sides to turn a page without losing face, as it were, and address fresh challenges in unison. Perhaps the most important of these events was the death of Palestinian leader Yasser Arafat in November 2004, which permitted the United States and Israel to re-engage robustly with the Palestinians – as European capitals had pushed them to do – without abandoning the principle of not dealing with terrorists. A second development was Syria's recalcitrance in maintaining its military and intelligence presence in Lebanon and apparently orchestrating the assassination of anti-Syrian former Lebanese prime minister Rafik Hariri in February 2005. Syria's conduct was sufficiently reckless that the United States and France, the most ardent European critic of US policy, co-sponsored UN Security Council Resolution 1595 demanding that Syria quit Lebanon. This facilitated Damascus's capitulation and it agreed to withdraw by 30 April 2005.

Arafat's demise and Syria's folly have helped the United States and Europe to come together on Middle East policy. But the breadth and depth of transatlantic harmony and collaboration will be stiffly tested on other fronts. If the EU, as it has been inclined to do since 2003, lifts its longstanding arms embargo against China in 2005, transatlantic relations will become severely strained. How to deal with a rising China could then become a source of transatlantic crisis potentially as toxic as how to manage Saddam Hussein's threat to Middle East/Gulf security. One interesting idea for lowering the risks of such an eventuality was raised by the United Kingdom in early 2005. The UK has proposed that a regular strategic dialogue be instituted between European governments and the United States on Asia–Pacific issues. While initially intended as a means of delaying the lifting of the EU arms embargo and therefore a transatlantic confrontation, such a dialogue would in essence be an ongoing policy discussion on the West's relations with China. That would tend to run counter to the hegemonic instincts of the United States, which has long been the dominant Western power in Asia, but also to the interests of some European governments in maintaining foreign policies that in Asia are focused on trade rather than wider strategic considerations. But the imbroglio over the embargo itself has already inaugurated a de facto transatlantic strategic dialogue on China. Taking the opportunity to expand the substantive scope of transatlantic consensus may be worth the compromises that each side would have to make.

The severest immediate challenge to the US–Europe relationship will arise over Iran. The transatlantic 'good cop, bad cop' approach to diplomacy with Iran has involved tacit cooperation as much as deliberate collaboration between Europe and the United States. Broadly speaking, the United States now appears willing to devote greater energy to multilateral diplomatic solutions to proliferation problems, while European capitals recognise the need for more 'American-style' threats to stem the nuclear ambitions of certain states – in particular, Iran – while presenting positive incentives (such as security guarantees) for compliance with non-proliferation norms. In spring 2005, the United States acknowledged that a more integrated programme of threats and inducements was required to manage Iran's nuclear-weapon intentions, as Washington deferred to the so-called 'EU-3' – France, Germany and the United Kingdom – to come up with a package of inducements and demands that would halt Iran's bid for a nuclear-weapon capability. American deference to Europe on Iran is likely to end around September 2005, when, it is hoped, Iran can deliver a deal, after Tehran has had time to sort out new political alignments after Iran's June elections.

As to whether collaborative diplomacy will work, the critical question will be whether the effective definition of Iran's 'cessation' of nuclear-weapon activity forged by the EU-3 and the Iranian government will satisfy Washington. A transatlantic crisis could come at the end of 2005, if the EU cuts a deal with Iran that involves an unsatisfactory definition. For example, the EU-3 might only be able to deliver a multi-year moratorium with IAEA verification to ensure enrichment could not take place. In these circumstances, Iran would have very strong diplomatic cover for resisting US pressure to make any more concessions. In so resisting, Tehran would drive a wedge between Europe and the United States. The disastrous Iraq debate might then be replicated. Europe might argue that while Iran could conceivably retain a nuclear breakout capability, it would not dare follow through on building a bomb with international inspectors on the ground and the threat of sanctions hanging over it; the United States would counter that the risk was not one that the world could afford to take and that a sanctions policy needed to be implemented immediately. The EU-3 will need to take this dismal possibility on board in pursuing a diplomatic solution with Iran, bearing in mind that pre-emption and prevention have merely been muted rather than discarded as United States strategic options.

China's re-awakening

While it was clear in spring 2005 that transatlantic relations were entering a new pragmatic phase, leaders outside of Europe were less certain about whether they could comfortably adjust to Bush for four more years. The Bush administration also had questions about whether it could work smoothly with other leaders. Perhaps the most emphatic question arose over China. Ostensibly, China's rise continued in its post-11 September quiet mode, constrained by major internal economic and political adjustments and a qualified common interest with the US (and Europe) in keeping North Korea in line. Yet persistent rumblings of Taiwanese independence and Japan's increasingly extroverted defence policy, as well as India's increasing involvement in East Asia, also became salient destabilising influences. Beijing accelerated military modernisation plans, including the purchase or construction of submarines, surface ships, fighter aircraft and short-range missiles conspicuously useful for a blockade or invasion of Taiwan. In turn, pre-11 September notions about the malign intent of a rising China – prevalent when US–China relations reached their post-Cold War nadir over the collision of a US spy plane and a Chinese fighter in April 2001 – began to resurface in Washington.

Japan has shifted its policy to allow its military forces to participate in 'out-of-area' operations, and has sent troops to Iraq. US and Japanese officials are considering enhancement of command and control centres in Japan and cooperation on theatre missile defence. Moreover, in 2004 Tokyo officially characterised China as a 'threat', while the United States and Japan in February 2005 jointly identified security in the Taiwan Strait as a 'common strategic objective'. The United States now unequivocally favours a permanent UN Security Council seat for Japan, and appears keen on forging an enhanced maritime alliance with Japan. At the same time, Sino-Japanese relations are tense. Nationalism generally is on the rise in both countries. Tokyo is worried that China will back (if not encourage) North Korean provocations against Japan and block oil lanes should it move militarily on Taiwan. Beijing, for its part, is nervous about the closer and more ambitious US alignment with Japan that appears to be in the offing, and perceives Rice as a more hawkish figure than her predecessor, Colin Powell. South Korea has weighed in with concerns of its own, saying that it does not want to have to choose between China and the United States on Taiwan and other contentious regional issues.

In this light, the United States will have to exercise special care not to erode the post-11 September stability of US–China relations. Particularly as China passed a law in early 2005 authorising the use of force to prevent Taiwan's secession, measured American diplomacy may not be easily arrived at. The United States will have to strike a balance between acknowledging that China's political and economic evolution has rendered unification a realistic possibility and recognising Taiwan's longstanding defiance of mainland communism and its political grievances and fears. This balance may call for more than simply reiterating the United States' 'one China' policy with respect to the Taiwan issue and periodically admonishing the Taiwanese government to turn down the volume on the rhetoric of independence. Some in the United States may feel compelled to remove some of the 'strategic ambiguity' surrounding any obligation it may or may not fulfil to defend Taiwan against a Chinese attack.

Strategic challenges elsewhere

In the wake of the United States' occupation of Iraq, security in the Middle East/Persian Gulf region remains tenuous and in flux. Possibly the most salient overarching issue for regional security is how Iran and Saudi Arabia will deal – inevitably in very different ways – with an Iraq whose Shi'ite majority is politically pre-eminent. Iran has keen interests, difficult to balance, in both supporting the national political primacy of its Shi'ite brethren in Iraq and ensuring that they do not become so internationally prominent as to threaten Iran's putative status as the leader of Shi'ite Islam. Riyadh's priority is also nuanced: to ensure that the rise of Iraqi Shi'ites does not embolden Saudi Arabia's Shi'ite minority to challenge the Sunni-dominated status quo while also supporting the US-led state-building effort in Iraq so as to preserve the health of the US–Saudi special relationship. Washington sees the virtue of stability in both sets of interests, which would be served by careful American stewardship of Iraq's national development. But the United States' supervisory role should be as far 'over the horizon' as possible to tamp down Muslim suspicions of American neo-colonialism, which have already helped fuel the Iraqi insurgency and had arisen among Arab leaders in connection with the original version of the 'Greater Middle East Initiative' revealed in early 2004.

Better prospects for resolution of the Israeli–Palestinian conflict – stemming from Arafat's death, the subsequent empowerment of secular Palestinian moderates and Israeli Prime Minister Ariel Sharon's marshalling the support of the Knesset for his plan to withdraw from Gaza – also augurs well for greater regional stability. But hopes turn critically on the Gaza withdrawal plan. The best gauge of the potential for peace will be the degree to which its implementation by the Israelis changes the substance and pace of the peace process. That, in turn, will depend substantially on the degree to which Hamas and the other armed Palestinian militant groups stand down – either voluntarily, to test their non-violent political power, or due to effective counter-terrorism on the part of the Palestinian Authority. US and European diplomacy will have to support both possible levers of terrorist restraint.

Sub-Saharan Africa is still in dire shape, needing sustained peacekeeping contingents in at least four locales: Liberia, the Democratic Republic of the Congo, Côte d'Ivoire and Sierra Leone. With the exception of the Economic Community of West African States (ECOWAS), regional security groupings have not performed well in Africa. Their efforts have been generally hindered by a political standard of non-interference. The advent of the African Union (AU), the G-8 initiative to enhance African regional and sub-regional peacekeeping capabilities by 2010 through train-and-equip programmes, and efforts of the UN Department of Peacekeeping Operations to ramp up its capabilities in light of the new and larger missions augur better days ahead. So does the prospective strengthening of existing bilateral assistance programmes, notably those of the United States and France. But the efficacy of these programmes – some of which focus more on counter-terrorism than peacekeeping – is likely to be limited due to the wholesale dearth of 'force enablers' – especially strategic and tactical lift capabilities – available to African military forces. The potential need for humanitarian intervention in Sudan, Nigeria's rising Christian–Muslim violence, and the disastrous ripple effect that Côte d'Ivoire's collapse could have in geopolitical as well as security terms suggest that whether European militaries should contemplate 'out of area' missions in Africa as a part of their standing remit will and should remain a live issue.

In its back yard, the United States is facing new, if nascent, challenges. A left-leaning Brazil and, to a lesser extent, Argentina have sharply questioned the United States' traditionally preferred neo-liberal political–economic orthodoxy for Latin America. The pragmatism of Brazilian President da Silva ('Lula'), however, has provided the United States with some breathing room, and perhaps allowed it to continue to focus hemispheric concern narrowly on trade issues, on Colombia's narcotics and insurgency ills, and on Venezuela as a potential rogue state. Colombia's counter-narcotics and counter-insurgency efforts are at least containing the Revolutionary Armed Forces of Colombia (FARC), and Venezuelan President Hugo Chávez's options are limited, notwithstanding his dislike and distrust of Washington. But increasing political instability in Bolivia, Ecuador and Chile means that the United States may have to revisit its policies with respect to the Andes' 'southern crescent'. There is a risk that one, two or all three of these countries could step into any narco-trafficking breach left by a partially pacified Colombia. The United States may need to work harder to re-engage these countries in order to influence economic reform and reconciliation between elites and deprived classes (especially, in Bolivia and Ecuador, indigenous peoples) sufficiently to ensure political stability and sustainable government commitments to security and anti-drug policies. Possible tools include more robust trade benefits and preferences, but deeper political as well as economic engagement appears required for substantial effect.

US grand strategy during Bush's second term

An American grand strategy that carefully harmonises military, diplomatic and political means with strategic ends has not yet fully crystallised, but in late 2004 and 2005 there were signs that it was at least materialising. Certainly Bush struck a decisive chord in setting forth a freedom and liberty agenda in his inaugural and State of the Union addresses in January 2005. It became clear that, like it or not, the Bush administration's reaction to 11 September was remaking US foreign policy in a revolutionary way – comparable in degree to Franklin Delano Roosevelt's response to Pearl Harbor. Certainly the administration has absorbed the lesson that the capability of securing the nation against most states is not necessarily effective against non-state terrorists using asymmetric techniques of warfare, or against rogue states, which may be less susceptible to deterrence. Washington's most substantial post-11 September strategic adjustment has been to enunciate the need for preventive as well as pre-emptive action against terrorists or their state sponsors. *Preventive* measures against inchoate threats, argued the Bush team, may be necessary to protect American and allied interests because imminent threats subject to *pre-emptive* measures will not always be detectable in time to take effective action. Senator John Kerry, Bush's opponent in the 2004 presidential election, conceded that he would not forsake either option. Thus, despite the discredited WMD justification for the preventive Iraq war, and deeper strategic arguments for the war that remain questionable, pre-emption and prevention appear to be firmly planted first principles of a new US grand strategy.

Reserving the right to take preventive action is arguably within the boundaries of international law – the right to self-defence being meaningless if a state is not allowed time to act. But from an outside perspective, the assertion of that right involves a breach of sovereignty and appears to violate a right that is equally sacrosanct in international law – non-interference. Thus, the United States proceeded in Iraq without the specific consent of the United Nations. Arguably, of course, Iraq may have been in breach of a cease-fire arrangement, and that breach might have removed the obligation of others to respect the cease-fire. Also, perhaps the structure of the UN Security Council was obsolete, and not reflective of international consensus. But beyond legal and political arguments, for the world's superpower both to claim a right of pre-emption and to appear to possess the exclusive ability to exercise it seemed unduly hegemonic, and an invitation to be held in check by a balancing community of nations. Before the Iraq intervention and during its early stages, Washington assumed that its good intentions and a universally held esteem for the liberal institutions that it would promote in Iraq would offset these legal and geopolitical problems. This proved dramatically incorrect, as the Iraq people, large segments of the international community, and some parts of the American public have been dissatisfied and sometimes alarmed by both American strategy and American tactics with respect to Iraq. And even the lone superpower requires allies and partners to do what it wants. Indeed, discord over Iraq and its portents has affected the capacity of the United States to execute its broader foreign policy – in particular, to convince the bulk of Islam not irreconcilably opposed to the United States that Washington seeks an amicable relationship with Muslim countries and populations. To present a palatable grand strategy, then, the United States must legitimise its manner of projecting hard power – in particular, pre-emption qua prevention – through the application of soft power.

To accomplish this, the United States must demonstrate to other important governments that its military action will redound to their interests. The United States accomplished this essentially diplomatic task during the Second World War, the Cold War and in virtually all post-Cold War conflicts through Afghanistan in 2001. Although American power was unrivalled in the West for the last half of the twentieth century, it generally (though not always) recognised the need for genuine consultation with its allies and partners on matters of strategic moment and conducted its diplomacy accordingly. US leaders also have usually recognised the virtues of measured and precise language, which was among the key elements of successful nuclear deterrence. And America – at least since the Second World War – has been good at articulating a strategic vision. The Truman doctrine, Kennedy's soaring rhetoric and Reagan's phrasemaking all set a decisive tone and a fairly clear path.

During Bush's first term, his administration did not appear inclined towards collegiality, especially with respect to Iraq. The national trauma of 11 September gave him some leeway to behave without the input of most allies and partners, but the unexpected absence of a terrorist attack on the United States over the subsequent three-and-a-half years has made that devastating event a less and less persuasive carte blanche. Nor was his language particularly measured or precise. Statements like 'bring 'em on' in reference to Iraq and jihadist insurgents were provocative, while the mantra of *engaging the terrorists overseas so they won't attack us at home* glossed over the issue of how effective the policy was. Furthermore, the overt championing of US global hegemony in the 2002 National Security Strategy document – while hardly revolutionary in substance – was discomfiting in its stridency. Finally, George W. Bush, like his father, has found it difficult to project a coherent vision.

The Bush doctrine – marrying pre-emption and the spread of freedom and liberal democracy in order to marginalise terrorism and rogue regimes – is intuitively powerful, but it required both further articulation and more thorough integration into the architecture of US foreign policy. As recently as 1999, as Governor Bush campaigned for the presidency, Condoleezza Rice, with her well-known quip in *Foreign Affairs* that the 82nd Airborne Division should not be escorting children to kindergarten, implicitly derided state-building and the ground-level construction of liberal democracies as inappropriate for a power of the United States' rank. In 2005, state-building was integral to the Bush doctrine, and being undertaken at great cost in Iraq. For most of the Iraq effort, the United States has had to ad lib, since its foreign-policy establishment was not geared for state-building. Culture lagged both ideology and policy. At least at the outset of the intervention, the United States was neither psychologically nor practically equipped to do the job. As Bush's second term began, National Security Advisor Stephen Hadley appointed Elliot Abrams deputy national security advisor for global democracy strategy. But this could only constitute the beginning of the massive culture shift that needs to take place in the US foreign-policy establishment for the Bush doctrine to be effective.

While the United States has not taken off the table pre-emptive or preventive military action against North Korea and Iran, in order to preserve as strong a deterrent as possible, it has also made it clear that diplomacy is preferred over the military option. Bush's language has also been more tempered, as noted in a February 2005 *Wall Street Journal* article on his tour of Europe. While hegemony remains implicit in US policy – which is nothing new – the importance of allies and partners is receiving far more emphasis from the White House. And the Bush doctrine is gaining clarity. American persistence and resolve in Iraq, focus on Iran's nuclear programme, pressure on Syria and re-engagement in the Israeli–Palestinian conflict have driven home the strategic reality that the United States will not be driven from the Middle East by bin Ladenism. Saudi Arabia's support for US policies (e.g., pushing Syria's withdrawal from Lebanon), increased counter-terrorism cooperation and efforts at political reform, as well as robust US military and economic relationships with the small Gulf states, reinforce the point. But if the Iraq intervention has led to greater respect for US power by respectable Middle Eastern governments, it has also led to greater disdain for US institutions and leadership among Muslim populations (and therefore improved recruitment for al-Qaeda and its affiliates) as well as rogue regimes (and therefore made them more inclined to counter US power with nuclear capabilities).

Accordingly, perhaps the Bush administration's first task during his second term should be to carefully assess what perverse effects the Iraq (and Afghanistan) interventions have had, and determine how best to minimise such effects in the future. Among the new emphases that ought to emerge is a re-invigoration of multilateral non-proliferation efforts, including an overhaul of the Nuclear Non-Proliferation Treaty. UN sanctions after the First Gulf War, for instance, now appear to have inhibited Saddam Hussein's efforts to reconstitute WMD. Cooperative efforts in other areas – Cooperative Threat Reduction, the Proliferation Security Initiative and the Six-Party Talks on North Korea's nuclear activities – have shown promise. Significantly, each has been led by the United States, indicating a somewhat healthier multilateral vocation in Washington than is often presumed. But to inspire international confidence in that vocation, the United States needs to explain how far it is (and indeed, is not) willing to go along the path of multilateralism.

The US administration's second endeavour might be to get a better sense of how to implement its world democratisation programme, especially in the broader Middle East. Democratisation is taking hold in Afghanistan and, less firmly, in Iraq itself, as it has in, for example, Indonesia and Turkey. Thus, as John Lewis Gaddis observed in *Foreign Affairs*, it seems wrong to conclude that Islam and democracy are inherently incompatible. Bush's chief instinct – that promoting democracy will ultimately outflank terrorism – appears correct. The sobering reality of the Iraq war and its aftermath, however, has been that the mere assertion of US power through 'shock and awe' followed by an offer to help facilitate a democratic transition through armed state-building does not automatically produce a happy, Western-oriented, politically compliant population. As intended, the United States has already changed the political status quo in the Middle East by way of the Iraq war, but only in terms of geopolitical and power calculations. Outside Iraq, US policy has not, in any clear way, made democratisation in the wider region much easier. The smaller Gulf Cooperation Council states have a gently reformist cast, but that predated the Iraq intervention. While Saudi Arabia has made tentative moves towards political reform, the delicate balance of the Kingdom's domestic politics suggest that reform on the national level may be difficult to manage. Reformists in Iran have not been able to translate democratically based popularity into power, and Western governments tend to rate a true democracy in Pakistan at this stage a prohibitive strategic risk, being far more comfortable with President Pervez Musharraf's secular authoritarianism.

Both the United States and Europe have recognised, of course, that there is no 'one size fits all' prescription for democracy, and that each state prompted by the West must reform at its own pace. The corollary is that, to the extent that great powers are to facilitate democratic transitions, they must customise their policies. Yet there needs to be policy space for those countries that are indeed inspired by the examples of American and European democracy – Georgia and Ukraine may be two – to move swiftly, as well as, conversely, those whose particular domestic, local or regional circumstances – perhaps Kyrgyzstan and probably Lebanon – have been primarily responsible for their democratic impulses. It is not enough for Washington or Brussels to extol the 'Rose Revolution' and the 'Orange Revolution' as exemplars; they also have to figure out just why they occurred and how to help the respective populations consolidate them through the extension of benefits from the larger community of democratic nations.

Washington, then, needs to think harder about both how to democratically reform particular countries and how to ensure that their relationships with the United States (and other major powers) yield durable rewards that are apt to entrench reforms once they are made. Doing so will advance US grand strategy in several ways. Firstly, it will make it easier to form a picture of a remade world order – to craft a compelling vision of the outcome of US strategy. Secondly, linking democratic reforms with national interests will begin to close the gap between the goals of US grand strategy and facts on the ground. Finally, it will go farther than the United States has thus far towards convincing Muslims that however powerful the United States may be, its intentions vis-à-vis the Muslim world are benign and the fruits of its policies palpable. While the latter will promote the immediate end of discouraging anti-Americanism and terrorism, it will also serve the long-term objective of allowing Islam and the West to coexist harmoniously.

Back to basics

If avoiding the clash between Islam and the West that bin Ladenism contemplates is the ultimate objective of any sensible post-11 September grand strategy, a subsidiary requirement is that the West remain unified and intact. Accordingly, sustainably smooth transatlantic relations are still a priority. Prospects for attaining them are better in 2005 than they were in 2003, but success is by no means certain. In 2003, Europe and the United States appeared to have the genuinely different worldviews ascribed to them by Robert Kagan and Robert Cooper, and brought their differences to a head over Iraq. In 2005, after a reality check for each side, their worldviews seemed closer. Yet major philosophical differences are still there, and it is hard to be confident that pragmatic cooperation between Europe and the United States on Iran will promote a more intimate merger of European and American interests or even perspectives. Closer collaboration could also magnify those differences and render the two sides even more mutually repelled. The schism of 2003 at least made common transatlantic interests stand out in bold relief. In 2005, Europe and the United States are intensely focused on a single common interest: persuading Iran not to pursue a nuclear-weapon capability. So far, coordination has increased rather than decreased. The salient risk is that one side or the other will decide that collaboration has reached the point of diminishing returns and go its own way. Were that to happen in the case of Iran, Europe and the United States could find themselves back in 2003. Both sides would do well to remember that the only major strategic player that benefited from the transatlantic rift that occurred over Iraq was al-Qaeda.